D0079080

Present Value Models
and
Investment Analysis

Present Value Models
and
Investment Analysis

LINDON J. ROBISON

Michigan State University

PETER J. BARRY

University of Illinois, Urbana-Champaign

The Academic Page
Northport, Alabama

Library of Congress Cataloguing in Publication Date
Robison, Lindon J. and Barry, Peter J.
    Present Value Models and Investment Analysis

    Includes bibliographical references and index.
    1.   Present Value
    2.   Investment Analysis
    3.   Financial Management
    4.   Benefit-Cost Analysis
96-84188

All rights reserved

Publisher: Linda K. Carroll
Interior Design: Linda K. Carroll
Cover Design: William Nicholas

©1996 Lindon J. Robison and Peter J. Barry

All rights reserved. No part of this book may be
reproduced, in any form or by any means,
without permission in writing from the publisher.

Printed in the United States of America
10   9   8   7   6   5   4   3   2   1

ISBN 0-945704-00-3

The
Academic
Page

4000 Mitt Lary Road
Northport, Alabama 35475

Table of Contents

Preface

Present values and the time value of money are pervasive concepts in economic and financial analysis. Present values are of interest in virtually every case involving multi-year payments and long-lived investments. Effective use of present value (*PV*) tools is needed to enhance long-term decision making, measure financial performance, value tangible and intangible durables, determine investment utilization strategies, account for risks, and understand liquidity relationships over time. Most textbooks and professional literature that treat *PV* models are targeted to specific types of applications, such as financial management, resource economics, real estate appraisal, engineering, and so on. A comprehensive treatment of the foundations of *PV* analysis and its many areas of application is lacking.

This book is intended to provide such a comprehensive focus. It introduces the concepts of *PV* analysis, shows how *PV* models are constructed, and develops a wide range of applications. Included among these applications are investment and liquidity analysis, taxation, rate-of-return measures, bid and sell prices, risk considerations, loan analysis, land transactions, farm management, natural resource use, enterprise budgeting, leasing, public project analysis, and the valuation of research. More advanced applications are reflected in chapters on replacement principles, design and selection of durables, risk modeling, and dynamic optimization.

A major feature of the book is the consistent use of geometric series modeling to summarize relationships between key economic and financial variables. A widely used algebraic expression is the present value of an annuity, calculated in most finance textbooks and programmed on most business calculators. The geometric series concept together with consistent treatment of cash flows, timing, homogenous measures, investment lives, and total costs and returns ensures accurate and effective application of the *PV* models.

The book is intended for advanced undergraduates, graduate students, and professionals in the U.S. and other countries who have introductory experience with *PV* concepts, economic theory, and finance. The reader should also be able to manipulate algebraic expressions and be able to differentiate simple functions. The book is designed as a stand-alone course in *PV* models and investment analysis. Many chapters, however, can be read independently or used as supplemental readings for other courses. To facilitate the book's use in classroom instruction, extensive review questions and application questions are located at the end of each chapter. Instructors and other readers may request and receive from the publisher a set of answers to these questions.

As the book developed, we benefited greatly from the review comments and suggestions provided by a large number of students and colleagues. Some former Michigan State University graduate students who made helpful contributions include William G. Burghardt (deceased), Mark Cochran, Larry Lev, Mark Krause, Young Chan Choe, Robert King, Beverly Fleisher, Pamateba Diendere, Steven Koenig, Brian Paterson, Kyosti Pietola, Marcelo Siles, Ross Love, Thomas Espel, David Trechter, Tiffany Phagan, Brian Radke, Kent Gwilliams, Jaako Kangasniemi, Hugo Ramos, and Randy Lewis. Other colleagues who reviewed specific chapters include John Brake, Allen Featherstone, Glenn Pederson, Steven Hanson, David Leatham, Steven Koenig, Ted Graham-Tomasi, Vernon Eidman, Karen Klonsky, Arne Hallam, Wesley Musser, and Greg Perry. Knut Walstedt and Berth-Arne Bengtsson of the Swedish University of Agricultural Sciences also provided valuable discussion and review contributions. Steven Hanson, a Michigan State University colleague, provided valuable suggestions that improved several chapters.

Several other colleagues at Michigan State University served as authors or co-authors of specific chapters. James Oehmke authored Chapter 20 on the Valuation of Research. Eric Crawford wrote Chapter 19 on Project Analysis. Robert Myers and Steven Hanson wrote Chapter 23 on Advanced Risk and Present Value Analysis. And, Robert Myers co-authored Chapter 24 on Dynamic Optimization. Mark Krause, now at North Dakota State University, wrote Chapter 15 on Farm Management Applications. We thank them for their important contributions.

Debbie Greer and Diana and Jason Shukis helped prepare early drafts of some chapters. Jeanette Barbour has carried the lion's share of the book's preparation in a dedicated, careful, and highly able fashion. Finally, we appreciate the assistance of Linda Carroll who has been so helpful in making the publication of this book possible.

Lindon J. Robison
Peter J. Barry

Part 1

Introduction to Present Value Models

Chapter 1

Introduction to Present Value Models and Investment Decisions

Key words: borrowing, cash flows, consumption decision, durables, endurables, expendables, final product suppliers, financial intermediaries, financial markets, geometric series, government, households, information markets, insurance, interest, investment analysis, lending, present value, proprietary firm, risk, service extraction rates, source and use of funds, taxes, time-dated cash flow.

Introduction

Present value *(PV)* models are important tools for capital budgeting, investment analysis, and other types of financial analysis. An investment is defined as an outlay of cash in exchange for expected future cash returns. Thus, any analysis of a firm's activities (involving the time-dated exchange of dollars can be evaluated in an investment analysis framework.) By converting future cash flows to their present cash equivalent, *PV* models provide decision-makers with information needed to make investment decisions. The cash flows in *PV* models are assumed to result from profit-maximizing decisions made in each time period that determine: (1) the optimal rate of service that can be extracted from durables (multiple-use investments) and endurables (indestructible investments); and (2) the use of expendables (single-use investments). Thus, single-period profit-maximizing models and *PV* models are related to each other in important ways.

The extensive and diverse applications of both *PV* models and profit-function analysis are well established in the literature. However, they are rarely presented together as complementary theories, despite the fact that both are needed to solve resource allocation problems in an optimal way. The goal of this book is to conceptualize and illustrate a broad set of applications of *PV* models. In the process, the link between timeless (static) profit functions and *PV* models will be explicitly established.

The most frequent application of *PV* models has been to evaluate and rank alternative investment choices. In this use, analysts sum the discounted cash flows associated with different investments and then compare the resulting present values. Investment budgets and financial plans are then formulated. This use of *PV* models is important. Chapter 6 of this book will explicitly address investment ranking. Yet, ranking investments is only one of many possible applications for *PV* models.

Economic theories in a dynamic setting can also be developed using present value models. To achieve this end, *PV* models are expressed algebraically to describe important economic relationships involving time and future expectations. Algebraic models can frequently be summarized into compact notation using geometric summations. These models help explain capital gains, effective tax rates, liquidity problems, replacement recommendations, maximum-bid and minimum-sell prices for durables, and other such phenomena.

Finally, this book explains how *PV* models can be applied in various economic subdisciplines, (including) farm management problems, privately- and publicly-owned natural resources, evaluation of benefits from research, project analysis, and the relationship of *PV* models to other dynamic models.

Historical Background

(One of the first applications of *PV* concepts was by Stevin in 1582 when he proposed using interest tables for selecting loans.) Jones and Smith claimed that one of the earliest applications of *PV* models to nonfinancial capital budgeting decisions was by Wellington, an American civil engineer. His 1887 book, *The Economic Theory of the Location of Railways*, dealt with the problem of whether or not a railway line should be constructed. He employed *PV* models to solve the problem. In 1907, Fisher, an American economist, referred to *PV* models in his important book, *The Rate of Interest*. *PV* models were also a part of Fisher's 1930 book, *The Theory of Interest*, a revised version of his earlier work.

In the same year that Fisher's landmark work was published, Grant, an engineering professor at Stanford University, published his classic textbook, *Principles of Engineering Economy*. In his book, Grant discussed the principles of present worth, the rate of return, and the equivalent annual cost methods for making capital budgeting decisions. These methods continue to underlie contemporary capital budgeting decisions. Articles by Boulding and by Samuelson in 1935 and 1937 issues of the *Quarterly Journal of Economics* were pioneering pieces on the role of the internal rate of return and the net present value criteria in capital theory and investment analysis. However, widespread study and application of these methods did not begin until the 1950's.

Two important books provided the intellectual background for capital budgeting applications of *PV* models. One was Friederich and Vera Lutz's 1951 book entitled *The Theory of Investment of the Firm*. The second was Dean's 1951 book entitled *Capital Budgeting* which contributed much of the original work on capital budgeting. These works served as building blocks for subsequent theoretical and managerial developments in finance.

In 1955, Lorie and Savage pointed out the problem of multiple internal rates of return. Their article was followed by a host of other articles analyzing the relationship between the internal rate of return and the net present value approaches to capital budgeting. Especially noteworthy was Hirshleifer's 1958 article that clarified the theoretical base of the present value and internal rate-of-return criteria.

Hirshleifer's 1970 book, *Investment, Interest, and Capital*, is still an industry standard. It extended Fisher's important work with the goal of presenting capital theory as a generalization of economic theory and extending it into the domain of time. The neglect of traditional economics concepts in *PV* models had often led students to overlook the interdependence of profit-maximizing resource use with decisions to invest or disinvest in particular investment. In his introduction, Hirshleifer wrote:

> Economists are only rarely called upon to employ the theory of demand or of cost or of production to assist a government or business administrator or a national planner. But the questions of criteria for efficient investments and optimum financial budgeting are of such urgent practical interest that a whole literature possessing only tenuous connection with "mainstream" economic theory has grown up in response. In fact, it would be more correct to say that three whole subliteratures have grown up; the first in the area of business economics (the problem of "capital budgeting"); the second in the sphere of government expenditure decisions, especially, but not exclusively, in relation to public resource investments ("cost-benefit analysis"); and the third in the crucial but ill-understood topic of national development ("growth strategies").

Later, analysis of *PV* models by Johnson and Quance, Edwards, and others came to be called investment/disinvestment analysis. This language calls attention to the fact that every investment has a corresponding disinvestment, and *PV* models are designed to consider both decisions. Hirschleifer and Perrin identified the investment under consideration as the challenger and the investment considered for disinvestment as the defender. This language is consistent with the focus of investment/disinvestment analysis and is also adopted here.

Investment versus Consumption Decisions

One might begin investment analysis by recognizing consumption as the firm's or individual's goal. Yet, the utility of consumption is often ignored. That is, investment and disinvestment activities are considered independent of the investor's consumption desires. Fisher showed that if perfect capital markets exist, investment activities of the firm are indeed independent of the investor's consumption preferences. Under this approach, investments are undertaken until the present value of the investor's capital stock is maximized. Then, given this optimal level of investment, a utility-maximizing allocation of consumption over time is achieved through borrowing or lending in the financial market. Perfect capital markets allow borrowing or lending at the same interest rate. Under such conditions, opportunities to trade current and future income at the market rate of interest allow investors to measure their exchange activities in terms of the present values. Maximizing the present value of exchanges through investments provides the greatest consumption opportunities, and borrowing or lending permits an allocation of this present value over time to maximize intertemporal consumption preferences. The result is a (theoretical) separation of optimal investment and consumption/financing decisions.

Because this book focuses on the firm or investors in the firm, and not on the consumer, investment and disinvestment decisions are analyzed independent of intertemporal consumption preferences, even when markets are not perfect and transactions costs exist. Thus, investment decisions analyzed in the context of their present values are assumed to provide useful decision information regardless of the investor's time preferences.

Exchanges and Cash Flow Summaries

A firm experiences exchanges with several other types of entities that influence the characteristics of cash flows, and thus the firm's present value. Examples include exchanges involving input and product markets, financial intermediaries, government, and information.

Exchanges involving the sale of products and services to other firms comprise the firm's marketing activities (Figure 1.1). Time is critical in the firm's marketing

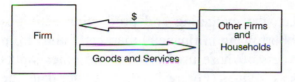

Figure 1.1

Exchanges Between the Firm and Purchasers of the Goods and Services a Firm Produces

decisions for several reasons. Exchanges of the firm's products and services may occur over time. Consequently, the firm may be required to manage inventories of products for sale by comparing the value of dollars received at different points of time with the costs of holding inventories. In this evaluation, the firm will be influenced by interest rates on borrowing to finance storage costs and by interest rates on lending 'opportunities reflecting reinvestment of the proceeds of the product sales.

Another important exchange involves the trade of money for resources used in production. In this exchange, the firm gives up dollars, and in return, receives the resources needed to produce a saleable product. Resources must then be transformed into other saleable products that require time and energy (see Figure 1.2). Production functions describe this transformation for various input/output relationships. These types of transformations are "internal to the firm"; they comprise the subject matter of production economics.

The supply of physical products or human resources may come from various sources. For example, nature supplies rain and sunshine for crop production, workers supply labor, while fertilizer and seed are purchased from other firms. Assembling and coordinating these activities is a major activity.

Time is also important in production activities. Not all intermediate products purchased by the firm are used up in a single period. For example, a tractor, land, and other durable assets supply services for many periods into the future. The combination of investment and production decisions requires the firm to choose an optimal rate of extracting services from the durable assets over time.

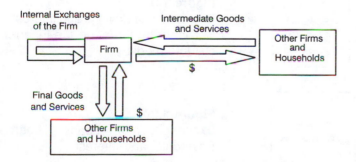

Figure 1.2

Internal Exchanges of the Firm Involving the Conversion of Human, Natural, and Mechanical Inputs to a Final Good

The differences in timing between the marketing and production activities create the possibilities for lending or borrowing in financial markets. Funds from the firm's accumulated income in excess of those used to purchase other inputs are loaned to financial intermediaries as savings (Figure 1.3a). At a later date, the firm receives back its savings, plus an interest payment from the financial intermediary. Time is central to the exchanges with financial intermediaries. Because dollars are both received and given in the exchange, no formal product transformation occurs. Rather, the other difference between what is given and received is the timing of the transactions. Time preferences and the aggregate effects of other factors affecting the supply and demand for funds determine the interest rates on saving and borrowing.

Another important factor in the firm's exchange process is the government. The government creates money to simplify transactions and accounting. The government also provides a mechanism (regulations) to enforce contracts and to prevent cheating and misrepresentation of the products exchanged. It provides defense, education, and transportation services in lieu of citizens having to purchase these services from commercial sources. It even serves as a financial intermediary in the case of various credit and retirement programs. To finance these and other activities, the government either collects taxes or borrows in the financial market, with later repayment from tax revenues. This exchange activity is described in Figure 1.4.

Alternatively, the firm may borrow funds from the financial intermediary and repay the loan plus interest at a later date (Figure 1.3b).

The government usually collects taxes when a firm experiences taxable income. Postponing or altering the timing of the firm's cash flows can often alter its payments to the government. Thus, the exchanges between the firm and financial intermediaries are often altered by anticipated tax obligations. Also altered by

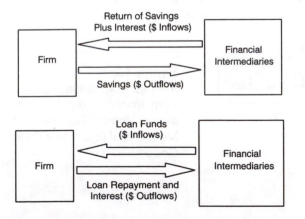

Figure 1.3a
Exchanges of Savings and Interest Between the Firm and the Financial Intermediary

Figure 1.3b
Exchanges of Loans, Loan Payments, and Interest

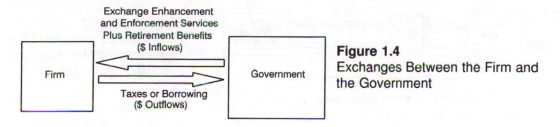

Figure 1.4
Exchanges Between the Firm and the Government

anticipated financial exchanges with the government are the purchases of intermediate and household goods and the sale of products, since both activities may affect tax obligations.

Firms also obtain information from a variety of sources. Information improves the firm's ability to make other profitable exchanges, including exchanges with suppliers of intermediate and final products and services, financial intermediaries, households, and the government. Information markets facilitate the exchange of information and fill gaps or deficiencies in the stock of information available for decision-making. Moreover, the information needed to decide an issue with certainty may not exist. Deficiencies in a firm's information base may lead to uncertainty, i.e., not knowing or having information about the outcome of an investment decision creates uncertainty.

Firm-Level Investment Decisions

Taken together, the activities and exchanges described above generate unique intertemporal patterns of cash flow associated with an investment. However, the comparison of one cash flow pattern with another requires comparable units of measurement. Thus, the cash flow patterns must be measured in dollars at a consistent date. The date chosen usually is the present time period.

Any analysis of the firm's activities that involves the time-dated exchange of dollars is called investment analysis. Several types of investment analyses can occur, involving both financial and non-financial assets. The investment activities involving the firm and financial intermediaries are frequently analyzed. Borrowing and saving activities have already been described. However, financial investments can be further differentiated by type of savings instrument: bonds, stocks, certificates of deposits, and time and demand deposits.

As will be shown in later chapters, investment analysis involving financial and non-financial firms can be treated using the same tools. The unification of approaches occurs because all investment analyses involve time-dated cash flows.

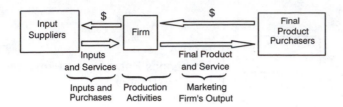

Figure 1.5

Cash Flow Exchanges of the Firm Including Marketing and Production Activities

The unifying tool is conversion of the time-dated cash flows to a common time period when decisions are made, in this case to the present period. Thus, the unifying investment tool converts time-dated cash flows to their equivalent value in the present period.

Investment analyses must consider the firm's production, marketing, and investment activities, because the combination of these activities underlies the generation of net cash flows in each period of the firm's planning horizon. Taken together, the investment, marketing, and production activities of the firm can be summarized by cash flows, beginning with an outflow of cash for durable assets and ending with cash inflows from the sale of products. The cash flows represented by the exchanges in Figure 1.5 are typically described in a firm's cash flow statement and projected in its pro forma cash flow statement.

The firm's exchanges between intermediate and final product buyers lead to a cash flow summary that is similar to the one used to characterize the firm's exchanges with financial intermediaries. In both cases, the firm receives cash from loans or from the sale of products and pays out cash as principal plus interest on borrowed money or funds to purchase intermediate products. In both cases, the cash inflows and outflows occur over time and are not necessarily of the same amount.

Exchange opportunities with other firms create opportunity costs as investment decisions are made. In many cases, a particular investment might involve the firm in a multitude of exchanges. For example, the purchase of durable goods, whose service life extends to several periods, often involves financial intermediaries. Nonetheless, all of these activities can be summarized by net cash flows for the firm in each period.

Cash Flow Patterns and Investment Analysis

As stated earlier, capital investments are typically described by initial expenditures or cash outflows, followed by revenues or cash inflows. In contrast, loans first experience cash inflows to the borrower and then cash outflows representing repayments of principal plus interest payments. Some projects involve both loans and real asset purchases. The point is that cash flows are the important data in *PV* analytic (Bodenhorn). Moreover, regardless of the cash flow pattern, the analytic tool is the *PV* model. Thus, loan analysis and investment analysis involving financial and real investments, respectively, are each handled using the *PV* model.

The pattern and timing of cash flows are especially important. Liquidity and tax obligations are determined by the cash flow patterns. Capital gains (losses) on durable assets are determined by the timing of cash flows. Some investments have cash returns that occur early in the investor's planning horizon, while other investments generate most of their cash returns in later years. These characteristics interact with discount rates to determine the present values of cash flow series.

Durables

Most applications of *PV* models involve investment/disinvestment in, and financing of, durables. Durables have the potential to supply services for multiple time periods, and they retain their identity throughout the multiple period production process. In contrast, expendables are immediately used up in a production process—they either supply services, such as fuel used in energy transfers, or they become a physical part of the transformed output, as in the case of seeds and feedstuffs.

Durables have two types of service capacities. One type is the capacity to supply services in a given time period, its periodic supply capacity. The second is the durable's lifetime capacity or the level of service it could provide over its remaining life under ideal conditions. These two types of service capacity are related. In general, service capacity depends upon a durable's age, accumulation of services already extracted, and design characteristics. Durables may be financial or nonfinancial, and they may be depreciable or endurable.

The capacity of depreciable durables to supply services generally declines over time and with use. All depreciable durables lose lifetime capacity and many durables lose periodic capacity as well. But some durables such as a light bulb suffer only losses in lifetime capacity. The capacity decline may occur as a shorter lifetime, as in the case of a light bulb, or it may occur as a declining level of productivity as time passes and use accumulates. In some cases, the period of decline may be preceded in some cases by increasing productivity, as a machine is "broken in," as human agents learn how to operate a durable, or as breeding livestock reach maturity.

Some durables, called endurables, can maintain their service capacity in perpetuity. Examples of endurables may include poems, musical compositions, great paintings and books, and legal documents that suffer negligible decay through time and use.

Other important characteristics of durables include whether a durable is divisible or indivisible in acquisition and use, the ease with which service provision can be started or stopped (contrast turning on or off a light bulb versus cow/calf production), and whether a durable's design is fixed or variable. Most applications of *PV* models occur under the assumption that a durable's design is fixed. However, design characteristics may be an important part of the analysis. For example, the profitability of acquiring a new building may depend upon its location, size, and surface configuration as well as on the generation of cash flows from enterprises contained in the building. The design of financing programs (amount, type, price, repayment patterns) is another example.

These characteristics of durables will play important roles in the various specifications of *PV* models in the chapters to follow. As will be shown, the selection of modeling approaches depends significantly on the time pattern of the cash flow services, which itself is largely determined by the pattern of service capacities of the underlying durables.

Mathematical Forms of PV Models

Often, particular patterns of cash flows can be conveniently summarized into compact models using algebraic symbols. An algebraic model of the cash flow relationships can provide important analytical insights about various applications of present value concepts.

Present value analysis can be simplified if the time pattern of a cash flow is expressed as a geometric series. That is, if the terms of the series are geometrically related to each other, they can be conveniently summarized and analyzed. Fortunately, the process by which time-dated cash flows are converted to present values often produces a geometric structure, or at least a structure that can be converted to a geometric series by appropriate transformations.

In the following chapters, cash flow series will repeatedly be described using geometric series. However, one should not assume that the focus of geometric series limits the generality of the cash flow series. Many series that at first do not appear geometrically related can be solved as though they were.

Organization of the Book

In Part I of this book, this Chapter and Chapter 2 introduce the study of present value models and describe some common present value models used in investment analysis. Part II of this book builds the tools necessary to analyze practical investment problems and to answer relevant economic questions. Chapter 3 identifies the role of opportunity cost in present value models. Chapter 4 discusses a set of key principles to follow when constructing present value models. Following these principles will yield consistent results and will facilitate the communication between builders and users of present value models. Chapter 5 shows how present value models with varying patterns of cash flows can be reduced to a geometric series for easier analysis. Then to conclude Part II, procedures for ranking investments using present value models are described in Chapter 6.

Part III shows how present value models can address many important and relevant economic questions. Present value models are particularly useful in demonstrating important liquidity relationships among cash flows, inflation, and capital gains. These topics are covered in Chapter 7. Chapter 8 demonstrates how to calculate effective tax rates for various investments based on time patterns of cash flows and capital gains. Chapter 9 compares and interprets economic versus accounting rates of return. Chapter 10 shows how individual demand for durables leads to market equilibrium prices for durables—described as a present value model. Finally, Chapter 11 discusses how risk concepts are incorporated into present value models.

In Part IV, the present value tools and economic relationships are applied to several investment problems. Included are applications to loan analysis (Chapter 12), investments in financial assets (Chapter 13), land purchases and sales (Chapter 14), farm management (Chapter 15), privately-owned natural resources (Chapter 16), enterprise budgeting (Chapter 17), leasing (Chapter 18), project analysis (Chapter 19), and valuation of research (Chapter 20). In each of these chapters, examples are described to enhance the understanding of the concepts and applications.

In Part V, more complicated *PV* models are introduced and solved. These models often employ optimizing techniques of calculus or programming algorithms. The *PV* models studied include: durable disposal, rotation, and replacement problems (Chapter 21); design of depreciable assets (Chapter 22); advanced risk and present value analysis (Chapter 23); and dynamic optimization (Chapter 24).

Review Questions

1. Explain and defend the statement:

    Efforts to find the profit-maximizing level of variable inputs must precede efforts to rank investment choices based on the net present values of future cash flows.

2. Is it possible to study investment analysis independent of consumption analysis? What assumptions are required to allow such a separation?

3. Describe the exchanges that may occur within a firm, between a firm and the government, between a firm and financial intermediaries, and between a firm and the household that owns it.

4. Why is the expression "investment/disinvestment" analysis more characteristic of the study of durable analysis than "capital budgeting"?

5. Define "investment analysis" as used in this Chapter.

6. Explain why the same amount of time-dated net cash flows received in different patterns over time may be valued differently by the firm.

7. Define the terms: durables, expendables, and endurables.

8. Distinguish between a durable's lifetime capacity and its periodic supply capacity.

9. Describe how a durable's ability to supply services may change over time.

10. Explain how present value models used to analyze investments in physical objects such as buildings and machines are similar to present value models used to analyze financial investments such as stocks, bonds, and loans.

11. Describe how time-dated cash flows in present value models summarize the marketing, production, and financial activities associated with a particular investment.

Application Questions

1. Describe the circumstances under which the investment activities of the firm and the consumption goals of the household may conflict. How does the availability of financial intermediaries reduce this source of conflict?

2. Explain why some of the earliest applications of *PV* models occurred in loan analysis.

3. The solution to static profit functions requires one to find the optimal level of a variable input. On the other hand, present value models are most often employed to rank alternative investments. Are these two problems related?

Are different solution techniques required to maximize static profit functions and rank investments? If so, how do the solution techniques differ?

4. In a single equation present value model, how are the firm's production and marketing activities represented? Contrast an "internal to the firm" exchange with exchanges between firms.

5. The focus in investment analysis is on durables. Usually, the question is to rank a finite set of alternative durables according to investment criteria to be described in Chapter 2. Suppose, however, that an infinite set of investment alternatives were available (e.g., you were free to design the durable such as selecting the dimensions of a building. The number of buildings that could be designed each with different dimensions is very large. How would the solution technique used to solve this design problem differ from the usual *PV* problem of ranking a finite set of investment possibilities)?

References

Bodenhorn, D. "A Cash Flow Concept of Profit." *Journal of Finance* 19(1964):16-31.

Boulding, K. "The Theory of a Single Investment." *Quarterly Journal of Economics* 100(1935):475-94.

Dean, J. *Capital Budgeting*. New York: Columbia University Press, 1951.

Edwards, C. "Resource Fixity and Farm Organization." *Journal of Farm Economics* 41(1959):747-59.

Fisher, I. *The Theory of Interest*. New York: The Macmillan Company, 1930. (Revision of *The Rate of Interest*. New York: Macmillan, 1907.)

Grant, E.L. *Principles of Engineering Economy*. New York: Ronald Press, 1930.

Hirshleifer, J. *Investment, Interest, and Capital*. Englewood Cliffs, NJ: Prentice-Hall, 1970.

———. "On the Optimal Theory of Investment." *Journal of Political Economy* 66(1958):329-52.

Johnson, G.L. and C.L. Quance. *The Overproduction Trap*. Baltimore, MD: The Johns Hopkins University Press, 1972.

Jones, T.W. and J.D. Smith. "An Historical Perspective of Net Present Value and Equivalent Annual Cost." *Accounting Historians Journal* (1982):103-10.

Lorie, J.H. and L.J. Savage. "Three Problems in Rationing Capital." *Journal of Business* 28(1955):229-39.

Lutz, F. and V. Lutz. *The Theory of Investment of the Firm*. Princeton, NJ: Princeton University Press, 1951.

Perrin, R.K. "Asset Replacement Principles." *American Journal of Agricultural Economics* 54(1972):60-67.

Samuelson, P.A. "Some Aspects of the Pure Theory of Capital." *Quarterly Journal of Economics* 51(1937):469-96.

Stevin, L. *Tafalen von Interest.* Antwerp: Christoffel Plantijn, 1582.

Wellington, A.M. *The Economic Theory of the Location of Railways*, 2nd edition. New York: John Wiley and Sons, 1887.

Chapter 2

Present Value Models:
Types and Uses

Key words: benefit/cost (BC) model, break-even model, discount rate, equity funds, expendable, internal rate of return (IRR) model, maximum-bid model, minimum-sell model, net present value (*NPV*) model, present value (*PV*) model.

Introduction

A present value (*PV*) model is a mathematical relationship that depicts the value of discounted future cash flows in the current period. *PV* models are primarily used to evaluate investment decisions and the effects of the timing of cash flows and opportunity costs on these decisions.

An essential element of any *PV* model is the discount rate. The discount rate is the price at which a dollar of cash flow is exchanged between time periods. In some models, the discount rate also represents the rate earned on reinvested cash flows. If the market for time-dated cash flows is perfect, then all market participants will trade cash flows between time periods at the same price. Then, the discount or market rate is an opportunity cost of capital for the firm. The firm sacrifices income at the discount rate when it consumes. It earns income at the discount rate when it postpones consumption and invests.

Another element of *PV* models is the time-dated cash flows. These cash flows in each period of the firm's planning horizon are described by the function: $R_t(V_0, p, m, f, G)$. In this function, V_0 is defined as the cost of the investment, and $p, m, f,$ and G are defined as production, marketing, financial, and tax management decisions and activities of the firm, respectively. Together, these decisions and activities determine the cash flow in the tth period of the investment's life.

The future cash flows are converted to their present values by discounting future values at rate r. The result is the net present value NPV of future cash flows. The economically relevant number of periods to evaluate an investment is n. In an n period model, the relationship between the NPV and discounted future cash flows can be expressed as:

$$NPV = -V_0 + \frac{R_1(V_0, p, m, f, G)}{(1+r)} + \frac{R_2(V_0, p, m, f, G)}{(1+r)^2}$$

$$+ \ldots + \frac{R_n(V_0, p, m, f, G)}{(1+r)^n}. \tag{2.1}$$

With a single-equation PV model, one can solve for at most one unknown. Usually, NPV is the unknown, but this need not always be the case. The components of the model that are assumed to be known and unknown determine the type of PV model. Some typical PV models include: NPV models, IRR models, and maximum-bid and minimum-sell models. Other models include break-even models and benefit-cost (BC) models. Each of these is discussed in turn.

Net Present Value Models

The single-equation NPV model assumes all elements of the PV model in equation (2.1) are known except NPV; thus, the investment, production, marketing, tax, and financial decisions are known and the discount rate is given. Equation (2.2) is written as the solution to a NPV problem by suppressing all the variables in equation (2.1) except NPV. Thus, the NPV variable is found by solving equation (2.2):

$$NPV = -V_0 + \frac{R_1}{(1+r)} + \ldots + \frac{R_n}{(1+r)^n}. \tag{2.2}$$

Implicit in the NPV model is the assumption that cash flows can be reinvested to earn rate r. Thus, equation (2.2) could be written as:

$$NPV = \frac{-V_0(1+r)^n + R_1(1+r)^{n-1} + \ldots + R_n}{(1+r)^n},$$

yielding the same value for *NPV*. Another interpretation of the above *NPV* expression is that the initial investment along with the compounded interest costs and the income earned along with its compounded interest costs received in the nth period must be paid. This interpretation of *NPV*, however, requires that the interest rate used to discount the values in period n equals the rates of return available from reinvesting cash flows.

NPV models provide decision-makers with a criterion for selecting investments. If *NPV* in equation (2.2) is positive, then the *PV* of the firm's equity will increase by the amount of *NPV* if the investment is undertaken. A positive *NPV* implies that the firm has discovered an investment that earns a rate of return in excess of the investment's opportunity cost of capital, r. If *NPV* is negative, then the *PV* of the firm's equity will decrease by making the investment.

To illustrate, assume a two-period investment problem with a discount rate of 10 percent. Define the cash flows associated with the investment as V_0 and R_1 equal to $100 and $145, respectively. The *NPV* model is written as:

$$NPV = -\$100 + \frac{\$145}{1.10} = \$31.82. \tag{2.3}$$

The positive *NPV* signifies a profitable investment that will increase the *PV* of the investor's wealth by $31.82 given the discount rate of 10 percent.

Usually the relationship between *NPV* and the discount rate, r, in equation (2.2) is inverse, as described in Figure 2.1. As the discount rate increases, the *NPV* of the cash flows decreases. However, this relationship depends on a pattern of cash flows in which an initial negative outlay is followed by positive cash flows in later periods.

Now suppose the cash flows are initially positive and then negative. This pattern occurs when loans are evaluated from a borrower's rather than a lender's perspective. For example, let $V_0=\$100$, $R_1=-\$110$, and r equal .10. Then, *NPV* equals:

$$NPV = \$100 - \frac{\$110}{1.10} = 0.$$

Notice that *NPV* now increases rather than decreases as r increases. The relationship is described in Figure 2.2.

Almost any polynomial relationship between *NPV* and r can result if cash flow patterns frequently reverse signs. Cash flows that reverse signs in an *NPV* model do not generally invalidate the *NPV* model as a tool for selecting among

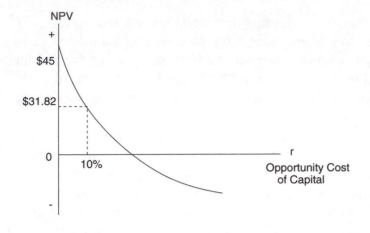

Figure 2.1
A Usual Relationship Between the Cost of Capital and *NPV*

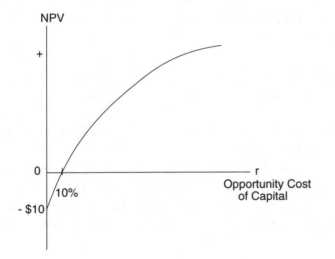

Figure 2.2
The Relationship Between *NPV* and the Discount Rate r when Initial Cash Flow is Positive and Later Cash Flows are Negative

alternative investments. However, cash flows do create problems in the *IRR* model discussed next.

Internal Rate-of-Return Model

In an *IRR* model, *NPV* is equal to zero, and the discount rate, *r*, is unknown and must be discovered. In such a model, the discount rate is the *IRR*. The *IRR* model is particularly useful to the firm wishing to: (1) calculate the rate of return on a new investment opportunity, or (2) calculate the rate of return on an investment to be liquidated. For example, consider the purchase of a new machine whose funding requires the sale of an old machine plus borrowing. The discount rate used to find the *NPV* of the new investment could be the *IRR* of the investment to be liquidated.

Equation (2.4) represents an *IRR* model. Since *NPV* is zero:

$$NPV = -V_0 + \frac{R_1}{(1+r)} + \dots + \frac{R_n}{(1+r)^n} = 0. \qquad (2.4)$$

Equation (2.4) is identical to equation (2.2) except that *NPV* is replaced with zero. With all the variables known except *r*, equation (2.4) can now be solved for *r*. To illustrate the solution to equation (2.4), the *IRR* model is solved with data assumed for V_0, R_1, and R_2 of $100, $145, and -$15, respectively. The model is formulated as:

$$NPV = -\$100 + \frac{\$145}{1+r} - \frac{\$15}{(1+r)^2} = 0. \qquad (2.5)$$

Notice that the cash flow series contains two changes in sign—from negative to positive and then back to negative. The equality that solves for *r* in this example is:

$$\$100 = \frac{\$145}{(1+r)} - \frac{\$15}{(1+r)^2}. \qquad (2.6)$$

Equation (2.6) is a quadratic expression in *r*. To see this, multiply (2.6) by $(1+r)^2$ and collect like terms:

$$r^2 + .55r - .30 = 0. \qquad (2.7)$$

A quadratic expression in *r* can have at most two roots, or values for *r* that satisfy the equation. Whether or not this example produces two, one, or no value for *r* that satisfies the equation depends on how many values of *r* produce an *NPV* of zero. In this case, the values of *r* that satisfy equation (2.7) result in *NPV*=0 and are *r*=0.338 and *r*=-0.888. The value of *r* that minimizes *NPV* is -0.79. To show this, equation (2.7) results for different values of *r* are graphed in Figure 2.3. Because negative opportunity costs are not reasonable, the *IRR* for this example is assumed to be 33.8 percent and not -0.888.[1]

While equation (2.5) produced one negative and one positive root, other quadratic expressions could have produced two positive roots or two negative

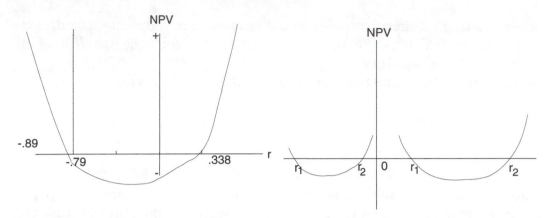

Figure 2.3

A Graph of Equation (2.5)

Figure 2.4

Hypothetical *NPV* and *r* Relationship

roots. These two cases are illustrated in Figure 2.4. In some cases, no root for *r* exists that sets *NPV* to zero. Of course, a three-period *PV* model is cubic in *r*, a four-period *PV* model is a fourth degree polynomial in *r*, and so on. In general, one additional solution for *r* may exist for every sign change in the cash flow series.

Implicit in the *IRR* model of equation (2.4) is the assumption that funds are reinvested at the *IRR* rate. This relationship is seen by writing equation (2.4) as:

$$V_0 = \frac{R_1(1+r)^{n-1} + R_2(1+r)^{n-2} + \ldots + R_n}{(1+r)^n}.\qquad (2.8)$$

On the other hand, if reinvestment rates are known and not equal to the *IRR*, say equal to $r_1, r_2, \ldots, r_{n-1}$, a single *IRR* rate value can be found equal to:

$$r = \left(\frac{R_1(1+r_1)^{n-1} + R_2(1+r_2)^{n-2} + \ldots + R_n}{V_0} \right)^{1/n} - 1,\qquad (2.9)$$

and is illustrated in Example 2.1.

Maximum-Bid and Minimum-Sell Models

The next class of models employs a different criterion. The maximum-bid and minimum-sell models assume *r* is known and *NPV* equals zero; the models then solve for V_0. The variable V_0 generally represents the purchase price of an investment in a maximum-bid price model or the sale price in a minimum-sell price model. In a maximum-bid price model, solving for V_0 indicates how much the buyer can bid for the investment and still earn a rate of return equal to *r*.

Or, from the seller's perspective, V_0 represents a return to the seller given in exchange for the cash flow stream generated by the investment. Solving for V_0 then indicates the minimum price a seller can accept in exchange for the cash flow stream generated by the investment and still earn rate r. In each of these models, the seller is assumed to reinvest V_0 and earn rate of return, r.

The maximum-bid and minimum-sell models are represented by equation (2.10), derived from equation (2.4) under the assumption that *NPV* is zero. Again, r and all other variables are known indicating they are assumed to be known:

$$V_0 = \frac{R_1}{(1+r)} + \ldots + \frac{R_n}{(1+r)^n}. \tag{2.10}$$

The solution to a maximum-bid or minimum-sell model is illustrated using data employed in equation (2.5). In the example below, however, r is set equal to 10 percent, and V_0 is unknown. The solution to this problem is found by solving the equation:

$$V_0 = \frac{\$145}{1.10} - \frac{\$15}{(1.10)^2} = \$119.42. \tag{2.11}$$

The interpretation of this example follows. If a decision-maker invested $119.42 to get $145 after one year and then had to pay out $15 after two years, his rate of return would equal 10 percent. Or, if the decision-maker's cost of

---

Example 2.1: Assuming a Reinvestment Rate

Consider the *IRR* model in equation (2.5); however, add the assumption that funds earned in period one can be reinvested for one period at the rate of 10 percent. Then, the model becomes:

$$\$100 = \frac{\$145\,(1.10) - \$15}{(1+r)^2}.$$

When equation (2.5) was solved, two values of r were obtained. Now, however, when a reinvestment rate is assumed, there is only one solution for r:

$$r = \left(\frac{\$145\,(1.10) - \$15}{\$100}\right)^{1/2} - 1 = 20.2\%.$$

capital were 10 percent and $119.42 were paid, this investment would leave the decision-maker no better nor worse off than under his or her existing investment strategy.

Alternatively, if this model were a minimum-sell model, a seller who received a price of $119.42 for his investment and who could invest the sale proceeds at a rate of return equal to 10 percent, would break even; that is, the investor would be no better nor worse off financially as a result of the sale.

The maximum-bid and minimum-sell prices were the same in this example. This condition will not generally be true. When transactions costs or taxes are different for buyers and sellers, or, when cash flow expectations or discount rates of the buyer and seller differ for the same investment, maximum-bid and minimum-sell prices will also be different.

Break-Even Models

A less important *PV* model is the break-even model. In the break-even model, *NPV* is set equal to zero, and V_0 and r are known. However, the production levels or periodic cash flows are unknown. Suppose the production decision determined some level of output x. The break-even model finds x such that *NPV* is equal to zero. Thus, it finds the x value that solves:

$$V_0 = \frac{R_1[p(x),m(x)]}{(1+r)} + \ldots + \frac{R_n[p(x),m(x)]}{(1+r)^n}. \tag{2.12}$$

Such a model is useful when the output produced is beyond the control of the decision-maker and the objective is to determine the least acceptable level of output that will permit the firm to survive. Break-even models could, however, also be calculated for a break-even tax level or financial activity for which *NPV* is zero.

Benefit/Cost Models

The fundamental types of *PV* models have now been discussed. However, some variants of these models require mentioning because of their popularity. One such variant is a "benefit/cost" model that finds a benefit/cost ratio.

A benefit/cost ratio is found as follows. Let V_0 represent the cost or initial investment outlay and let $R_1, \ldots, R_n$ represent the returns from the investment. The benefit/cost ratio, *BC*, is equal to:

$$BC = \frac{\left[\dfrac{R_1}{(1+r)} + \ldots + \dfrac{R_n}{(1+r)^n} \right]}{V_0}. \tag{2.13}$$

In this case, the *BC* ratio is the *PV* of the cash flows divided by the initial investment outlay.

For example, the *BC* ratio in the example described in equation (2.8) with $V_0 = \$100$ is:

$$BC = \frac{\left[\dfrac{\$145}{1.10} - \dfrac{\$15}{(1.10)^2} \right]}{\$100} = \frac{119.42}{100} = 1.194. \tag{2.14}$$

A *BC* ratio greater than one indicates the investment earns a positive *NPV*; a *BC* ratio less than one indicates the investment earns a negative *NPV*. The main advantage of the *BC* ratio is to indicate a percentage return earned by the investment; in this case, the rate of return is 19.4 percent. However, this percentage is different than the *IRR*. One way to interpret the *BC* ratio and the *IRR* is to say that the *IRR* is the rate, r, that produces a *BC* ratio of one.

One weakness of the *BC* model is the arbitrary separation between benefits and costs. In the example just completed, only the initial cash outlay of $100 was treated as a cost. But the $15 lost in the second period could also be a cost. If this alternative grouping of benefits and costs were used, the *BC* ratio would be:

$$BC = \frac{\dfrac{\$145}{1.10}}{\$100 + \dfrac{\$15}{(1.10)^2}} = 1.173.$$

Thus, the ratio would change from 1.194 to 1.173 by regrouping costs and benefits. A second weakness of *BC* ratios is that they do not reflect size differences of investments. They would not, for example, distinguish between a one dollar investment that earns a 15 percent return from a one million dollar investment that earns the same rate of return. Despite these weaknesses, *BC* ratios are widely used (Gittinger).

The Payback and Average Rate-of-Return Models ——————

The payback criterion solves for the period in which the summation of the undiscounted cash flows from the present to the future just equals the initial investment. Consider the cash flows described in Table 2.1. According to the payback criterion, project *A* is preferred since it recovers the initial investment of $1,000 in two periods. However, project *A* has large negative values in periods 4 and 5. Ignoring relevant cash flows and failing to account for the opportunity cost of capital by not discounting cash flows are shortcomings of the payback model. Moreover, even if the payback model is applied with discounted cash flows, future cash flows beyond the payback period are still ignored. Nevertheless, the payback model is popular with some business people, because of its ease of measurement and interpretation.

The average rate-of-return (*ARR*) model determines a rate of return by dividing the average, annual after-tax profits by the initial cash outlay. For example, investment *B* in Table 2.1 generates total profits of $2,300 over the five-year period, yielding an average profit of $460 per year. Thus, investment *B*'s *ARR* is 46 percent = 460/1,000. The other *ARR*s are *A*=12 percent, *C*=45 percent, and *D*=42 percent. The major problem with the *ARR* is that it fails to account for the timing of returns and the time value of money. Moreover, it generally uses accounting profits rather than cash flows in its evaluation.

Table 2.1	Cash Flows of Four Investments Whose Accumulated Cash Flows Equal the Investment Amount of $1,000 in Different Time Periods			
Year	A	B	C	D
	Cash Flows			
0	-$1,000	-$1,000	-$1,000	-$1,000
1	$100	0	$100	$200
2	$900	0	$200	$300
3	$100	$300	$300	$500
4	-$100	$700	$400	$500
5	-$400	$1,300	$1,250	$600
Total	$600	$2,300	$2,250	$2,100
Average/Year	$120	$460	$450	$420
Average Rate of Return	12%	46%	45%	42%

Which Model Is Best?

Because investment analysis is ultimately concerned with choosing between alternative investments, does the *IRR* or *NPV* give the better answer? Many pages of print have been devoted to the choice of the most appropriate *PV* model with the general consensus favoring the *NPV* model (e.g., see Schall and Haley).

The main benefit of the *NPV* model is that it solves for the increment to current wealth generated by the project. Since present wealth is an important variable, solving for it is reason enough to recommend this model. But critics of capital budgeting have not been satisfied with such a simple defense. Usually, they point out that *NPV* and *IRR* models can produce conflicting investment signals, because the *NPV* (implicitly) assumes that the cash flows are reinvested at the firm's discount rate while the *IRR* assumes that the cash flows are reinvested to earn the *IRR*. The requirements for consistency between *IRR* and *NPV* models will be discussed in Chapters 4 and 6. Many supposed differences between *PV* models are resolved when the models are developed consistently.

More Complicated Models

Single-equation *PV* models can be used to solve for a single variable. *NPV*, maximum-bid and minimum-sell, and *IRR* models each assume that production, marketing, financing, and tax management decisions affecting the cash flows of an investment are already known. Thus, investment decisions cannot be made independent of these other decisions.

Realistically, however, investment, production, marketing, financing, and tax management decisions are made simultaneously. For example, one could not evaluate a machine without knowing the optimal use of the machine. Solving these decisions simultaneously leads to more complicated *PV* models.

Additional equations are required when more than one variable must be found. These other equations are generally found by maximizing the *PV* model for the variable in question. A *PV* model in which net cash flows depend on the size of the investment V_0 is written as:

$$NPV = -V_0 + \frac{R_1(V_0)}{(1+r)} + \dots + \frac{R_n(V_0)}{(1+r)^n}. \tag{2.15}$$

Then, equation (2.15) is maximized with respect to V_0. The first-order condition for V_0 is equation (2.16):

$$\frac{dNPV}{dV_0} = \frac{\partial}{\partial V_0}\left[-V_0 + \frac{R_1(V_0)}{(1+r)} + \dots + \frac{R_n(V_0)}{(1+r)^n}\right] = 0. \qquad (2.16)$$

Let the value of V_0 that solves (2.16) be V_0^*, the optimal value of V_0. The *NPV* model now consists of the two equations, (2.15) and (2.16), and can be solved for two variables, *NPV* and V_0^*.

Equations (2.15) and (2.16) can be interpreted using standard economic logic. Assume that V_0 is a continuously-divisible choice variable. Equation (2.16) finds V_0^* such that marginal returns equal marginal costs for an additional unit of V_0. However, this optimal solution for V_0, V_0^*, does not guarantee that the *NPV* of the investment will be positive or that the investment's rate of return will exceed the required rate of return, r. To compare the return of the investment to the required rate of return requires that equation (2.15) be solved using the optimal value of V_0, V_0^*.

The solution technique that maximizes *NPV* with respect to V_0 assumes continuously divisible investment opportunities and a perfect financial market with a constant r. Most finance and capital budgeting texts, on the other hand, assume finite (few) investment opportunities. Then, the investment with the largest *NPV* is selected.

In equations (2.15) and (2.16), we solved for V_0^* using (2.16). Then we substituted V_0^* into (2.15), and found *NPV*. We could have, of course, set *NPV* equal to 0, solved for a given V_0 and found r (an *IRR* model). Or, we could have assumed r, set *NPV* to zero, and solved for V_0^b, a maximum-bid price, (or solved for V_0^s, a minimum-sell price). The choice of the model depends on the needs of the analyst. The structure of the problem allows a solution to any of the problems described thus far.

Another example of a more complicated model is the replacement model to be discussed in Chapter 21. In this model, the optimal economic life of the investment, n, is unknown along with the *NPV* of the investment. The solution to the problem requires two equations. The first equation is the usual *NPV* equation. Finding the second equation requires the application of the calculus or the differentiation of the *NPV* equation with respect to the last period the durable is owned or operated, n. To be able to differentiate *NPV* with respect to the time to disposal, n must be a continuous variable. This in turn requires that the *NPV* model be expressed as a continuous-time model, and instead of summing discrete periodic cash flows, we employ the calculus technique of integration.[3] The two equations, the *NPV* equation and the first-order equation obtained by differentiating *NPV* with respect to n, are expressed below:

Example 2.2: The Optimal Investment Level in an *NPV* Model

A firm is considering an investment that produces a stream of returns dependent on the level of the investment V_0. This investment/income relationship is: $R(V_0) = V_0 - .001V_0^2$ and is expected to last for two periods. Then, after the second period, the investment's service potential is zero and it is scrapped for zero salvage value. The firm wants to know whether it should invest (is *NPV* > 0), and if so, what is the optimal level of V_0? The firm assumes its discount rate is 10 percent.

The problem is solved by maximizing the expression:

$$\max_{V_0} NPV = -V_0 + \frac{V_0 - .001\ V_0^2}{(1.10)} + \frac{V_0 - .001\ V_0^2}{(1.10)^2}.$$

The optimal V_0, V_0^*, is found by maximizing *NPV* with respect to V_0 and equals:

$$\frac{dNPV}{dV_0} = -1 + (1 - .002\ V_0^*)\left[\frac{1}{(1.10)} + \frac{1}{(1.10)^2}\right] = 0.$$

Since:

$$\frac{d^2NPV}{dV_0^2} = -.002\left[\frac{1}{(1.10)} + \frac{1}{(1.10)^2}\right] < 0,$$

the second-order conditions are satisfied as well. To solve for the optimal level of investment, set the first-order condition equal to zero, and solve for V_0^*:

$$-1 + (1 - .002\ V_0^*)\left[\frac{1}{1.10} + \frac{1}{(1.10)^2}\right] = 0,$$

After some manipulation, the optimal level of investment is found:

$$V_0^* = \$211.90.$$

This result implies that the per period cash flows are:

$$R_1 = R_2 = \$211.90 - .001(\$211.90)^2 \approx \$167.$$

The investment question is answered by substituting the optimal values for V_0^*, R_1, and R_2 into the equation to be maximized:

$$NPV = -\$211.90 + \frac{\$167}{(1.10)} + \frac{\$167}{(1.10)^2} = \$77.93.$$

Because the *NPV* is positive, the investment should be made.[2]

$$NPV = -V_0 + \int_0^n R(t)e^{-rt}\,dt, \qquad\qquad (2.17)$$

and:

$$\frac{dNPV}{dn} = R(n) = 0. \qquad\qquad (2.18)$$

Summary

Several types of *PV* models have been described in this chapter. Each model solves for a different unknown. Each is useful depending on the purpose of the analysis. If the comparison is between an existing and a proposed investment, *NPV* or *BC* models are popular. Chapter 3 explains how the discount rate for *NPV* models represents the *IRR* of the investment to be liquidated to fund the new investment. Thus, both *IRR* and *NPV* measures are required to rank investment choices.

If, on the other hand, the need is to establish a "sell" or "buy" price for an investment, a model with *NPV* or *IRR* as the unknowns may not be appropriate. Minimum-sell and maximum-bid price models are used for these problems.

Finally, as the problem becomes more specific (and difficult), more complex *PV* models are required. These models require more modeling information and additional, more complex equations to find the additional variable(s) than were required for a simple *PV* model. Thus, many different *PV* models are designed to aid in finding solutions to different types of problems.

Endnotes

1. For the quadratic expression:

$$V_0 = \frac{R_1}{(1+r)} + \frac{R_2}{(1+r)^2},$$

the condition for positive roots for *r* can be found using the quadratic formula. Rearranging:

$$(1+r)^2\,V_0 - R_1(1+r) - R_2 = 0,$$

and substituting into the quadratic formula yields:

$$(1+r_1), (1+r_2) = \frac{R_1 \pm \sqrt{R_1^2 + 4V_0 R_2}}{2V_0}.$$

Real roots require that the expression in the square root expression $R_1^2 + 4R_0 V_0$ be positive. Assuming that the conditions for real roots are satisfied, the signs of the two roots in the quadratic *IRR* model described above depend on the signs of:

$$\frac{R_1 + \sqrt{R_1^2 + 4V_0 R_2}}{2V_0} \quad \text{and} \quad \frac{R_1 - \sqrt{R_1^2 + 4V_0 R_2}}{2V_0}.$$

More complicated expressions determine the signs of higher order polynomials.

2. In more complicated problems, Kuhn-Tucker conditions can be used. In essence, these conditions suggest that if *NPV* is decreasing in V_0, the solution requires setting $V_0 = 0$.

3. To express *NPV* as a continuous-time problem requires a continuous-time discount factor $e^{-rt} \approx (1+r)^{-n}$ which will be described in detail in Chapter 21.

Review Questions

1. List the elements of all *PV* models.

2. One of the most important elements of a *PV* model is the time-dated net cash flows. What factors and decisions related to the investment determine the periodic net cash flow?

3. Define the variable *NPV*. What must be known in the *PV* model to allow the analyst to solve for the *NPV* variable?

4. Define the variable *IRR*. What must be known in the *PV* model to allow the analyst to solve for the *IRR* variable?

5. Compare the reinvestment rate assumptions for the *NPV* and *IRR* models. How might these different reinvestment rate assumptions under certain conditions lead to conflicting Investment decisions?

6. Describe the conditions under which the relationship between *NPV* and the discount rate is direct (i.e., they increase or decrease in the same direction) or inverse (when one increases the other decreases).

7. Under what conditions would a decision-maker be interested in knowing an investment's maximum-bid price or minimum-sell price? break-even level of production? or benefit/cost ratios?

8.   The payback and average rate-of-return models are popular among practical business people who need easy-to-calculate investment rules. Describe the main differences between the payback and average rate-of-return models relative to *NPV* models.

9.   More complicated *PV* models solve for more than one unknown, and therefore require more than one equation to find the unknown variables. An example of a more complicated *PV* model is the replacement model that requires the solution for the variables *NPV* and *n*. Where does the second equation needed to find *n* come from?

Application Questions

1.   Calculate the *NPV* of a *PV* model with time-dated cash flows equal to: R_t=$50 for *t*=1,...,5, where the initial purchase price is V_0=$200 and the opportunity cost of capital equals 9 percent. Also, calculate the maximum-bid price and the break-even level of income. Finally, calculate the investment's *IRR* assuming a reinvestment rate of 5 percent.

2.   Describe examples of investment problems where the appropriate model is: a minimum-sell model, a replacement model, a benefit/cost model, an *NPV* model, and an *IRR* model. Does it matter which model is used?

3.   Explain how production, marketing, and financial activities for a particular investment are treated in both a single-equation *PV* model and more complicated *PV* models.

4.   Evaluate the following statements. State whether you agree or disagree and defend your answer.

   (a) The relationship between the discount rate and the *NPV* in an *NPV* model is always inverse. That is, the higher the discount rate the lower the *NPV*.

   (b) A replacement model is a more complicated *PV* model. In contrast to the single-equation *NPV* model where the variable *NPV* is the only unknown, the replacement model has two unknown variables: *NPV* and the durable's optimal life. After the optimal replacement or salvage is found, there is no new information to be gained by solving for the second variable—that is, for the *NPV*.

   (c) An investment with a two-year payback period with neither salvage value nor cash flows after year two has an *IRR* of zero.

   (d) In a *PV* model where the cash flow stream was initially negative followed by positive cash flows, the following two conditions hold:
   – one can solve for a unique *IRR*; and
   – *NPV* decreases with increases in the discount rate.

(e) The reinvestment rate always equals the discount rate unless otherwise stated.

References

Bierman, H., Jr. and S. Smidt. *The Capital Budgeting Decision*, 4th edition. New York: Macmillan Publishing Company, 1975.

Brealey, R. and S.C. Myers. *Principles of Corporate Finance*. New York: McGraw-Hill Book Company, 1981.

Dorfman, R. "The Meaning of Internal Rates of Return." *Journal of Finance* 46(1981):1011-21.

Gittinger, J.P. *Economic Analysis of Agricultural Projects*. Baltimore: Johns Hopkins University Press, 1982.

Levy, H. and M. Sarnat. *Capital Investment and Financial Decisions*, 3rd edition. United Kingdom: Prentice-Hall, International, LTD, 1986.

Schall, L.D. and C.W. Haley. *Introduction to Financial Management*, 3rd edition. New York: McGraw-Hill, 1983.

Sharpe, W.F. *Investments*, 2nd edition. Englewood Cliffs, NJ: Prentice-Hall, Inc., 1981.

Stevenson, R.A. and E.H. Jennings. *Fundamentals of Investments*, 2nd edition. St. Paul, MN: West Publishing Company, 1981.

Part 2

Constructing Present Value Models

Chapter 3

Present Value Models and Opportunity Costs

Key words: challengers, defenders, reinvestment rates, imperfect capital markets, perfect capital markets, returns to assets, returns to equity.

Introduction

A cost is the amount of money, or money equivalent, paid or charged for a good or service. It represents the direct cost of what is given up to obtain something desired or to avoid something disliked. Costs include various components. For example, one might consider the cost of attending a movie to be the price of the ticket plus the transportation cost to and from the theater. This, in fact, may be a good description of the cost of attending the movie, if the movie-goer had no other plans.

Suppose, however, that the movie was playing at the same time that dinner was served where the movie-goer ate his or her meals. Attending the movie means giving up the meal. Now the cost of the movie includes not only the price of the ticket plus transportation costs, but also the value of the skipped meal. The cost of the ticket, transportation costs, and the value of the skipped meal together represent the **opportunity cost** of attending the movie.

If we consider only the prices paid for goods and services as costs, the opportunity cost may be underestimated. This chapter clarifies the differences between opportunity costs and prices of goods and services and shows how opportunity costs are used in present value (PV) models.

Opportunity Costs in Perfect Capital Markets ————————————

The capital (or financial) market is where people trade today's dollars for future dollars, and vice versa. The value of today's dollars are not the same as the value of future dollars. Otherwise, there would be no purpose in trading them. In a perfect capital market, dollars trade between adjacent time periods at the market rate of interest r. For a perfect capital market to exist, the following conditions are required: no barriers to entry; no participant can influence the price; transactions are costless to complete; relevant information about the market is widely and freely available; products and services are homogenous; no distorting taxes exist; and investment possibilities are continuously divisible. All trades in perfect capital markets are made at the market interest rate. Thus the firm's opportunity cost of capital, regardless of the size and economic life of investments, is equal to r.

In a perfect capital market, the firm undertakes productive investments as long as the marginal internal rate of return exceeds the market interest rate or until the net present value (*NPV*) of the firm is maximized. These equilibrium conditions for the firm result from applying the Fisher/Hirshleifer approach to intertemporal choice. This approach is summarized next.

Intertemporal Choice Theory ————————————————————

Optimal investment, financing, and consumption decisions take account of an investor's initial wealth, productive investment opportunities, a perfect financial market, and an intertemporal utility function with dated consumption levels serving as the objects of utility. Equilibrium conditions for the investor reflect equality among the marginal internal rate of return on productive investments, the market interest rate, and the investor's marginal rate of utility substitution between consumption in any two periods.

The procedure for finding optimal investment, financing, and consumption levels can be illustrated graphically. Consider Figure 3.1 in which the two axes represent consumption opportunities at time $t=0$ (present) and time $t=1$ (future). As shown in Figure 3.1, the investor begins at time $t=0$ with wealth OW_0 which may be consumed or invested. Wealth OW_0 can be invested in: (1) a set of productive investments ordered according to diminishing returns along line W_0W_1; and (2) a financial investment (lending) with a rate of return r along line M_0M_1 or W_0M_{1f}. Initially, the return on the productive investments exceeds return r. So, the firm first makes productive investments by moving along curve W_0W_1 instead of line W_0M_{1f}. Moreover, the profitability of the productive investments relative

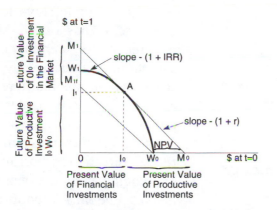

Figure 3.1 The Optimal Investment Decision

to the financial investments can be compared at each level of investment. This comparison is between the marginal internal rate of return (i.e., the slope $-(1+IRR)$ of W_0W_1) of the productive investments and the market interest rate (i.e., the slope of the financial market line $-(1+r)$). The future value of a current dollar invested in productive investments is equal to the (negative) slope of the productive investment curve. The future value of a current dollar invested in the financial market is equal to the (negative) slope of the financial market line.

Beginning at W_0, the optimal level of productive investments is eventually reached at point A, where the marginal *IRR* on productive investments is equal to the market interest rate, r. The optimal level of productive investment, $I_0W_0=OW_0-OI_0$, grows to OI_1 at $t=1$. The optimal level of financial investment, OI_0, grows to I_1M_1 at $t=1$. This combination of productive and financial investments has a present value of OM_0 or a future value of OM_1. The firm's *NPV* for the combination of productive and financial investments described by point A equals the discounted value of future returns less the initial investment equal to:

$$NPV = -OW_0 + \frac{OI_1 + I_1M_1}{1+r} = W_0M_0.$$

The optimal level of investment (A) is consistent with two decision rules used in investment analysis. One rule is to accept all productive investments that add to the investor's *NPV*. The second rule is to undertake all investments whose *IRR* exceeds the market interest rate. In the single-period case considered here, the *NPV* and *IRR* investment rules lead to the same investment decisions.

The investment decision that maximizes *NPV* is determined solely by the rates of return on productive investments relative to the market interest rate. Now consider the investor's desire to consume quantities of goods C_0 now and to consume future goods C_1. The investor's utility function, $U(C_0,C_1)$, and indifference curves have no influence on the optimal investment under these perfect market conditions. However, the utility function does determine the financing policies (lending or borrowing) that yield a utility-maximizing combination of present and future consumption for the investor, given the optimal level of investment.

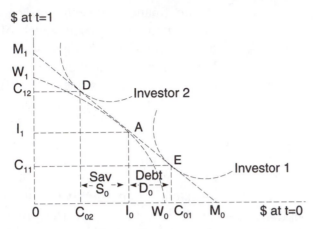

Figure 3.2   Optimal Investment and Financing Decisions for Investors I and II

For example, Investor 1 in Figure 3.2 has a strong time preference for current consumption, as indicated by the steepness of his indifference curves. He will undertake productive investments to point A, and then move in the reverse direction by borrowing D_0, moving along the financial market line M_0M_1 until tangency is achieved at E with the highest attainable indifference curve. In contrast, Investor 2, who has a weaker time preference, will invest to point A and then save S_0 additional funds moving along the financial market line M_0M_1 until tangency with her indifference curves occurs at D.

To show the allocations in greater detail, consider again the case of Investor 1 in Figure 3.2. The preferred consumption choice for Investor 1 (C_{01}, C_{11}) is indicated by point E. To reach E, the investor allocates part (I_0W_0) of initial wealth to productive investments, leaving OI_0 of initial wealth for consumption. The optimal consumption plan is then attained by borrowing amount I_0C_{01}, so that present consumption equals OC_{01}. The amount of the loan plus interest—$C_{11}I_1$= $I_0C_{01}(1+r)$—is then repaid from the returns of the productive investment at time point $t=1$, leaving the desired consumption level OC_{11} at time point $t=1$. Thus, the utility-maximizing consumption levels at point E are OC_{01} at $t=0$ and OC_{11} at $t=1$.

The preferred consumption choice (C_{02}, C_{12}) for Investor 2 is indicated by point D. To reach D, the investor allocates part (I_0W_0) of her initial wealth to productive investments, then saves $C_{02}I_0$, so that present consumption equals OC_{02}. The amount saved plus interest, $I_1C_{12}=C_{02}I_0(1+r)$, increases future consumption possibilities to OC_{12}. Thus, the utility-maximizing consumption levels at D are OC_{02} at $t=0$ and OC_{12} at $t=1$.

Both investors have the same present values of investment decisions, but different utility-maximizing financing decisions. For both investors, at optimal points D and E in Figure 3.2, the slopes of the financial market line, the productive investments line, and the indifference curves are equal. Thus, equality occurs among the investor's marginal rates of utility substitution between present and future consumption, the market interest rate, and the marginal investment return.

The financial markets provide the important service of allowing a redistribution of consumption opportunities over time through lending or borrowing, for a given level of present wealth. In the process, the optimal investment decision is separate from the optimal financing decision. And the market interest rate r represents the opportunity cost for the productive investments under the perfect financial market condition stipulated here.

Imperfect Capital Markets: Challengers and Defenders

A perfect capital market allows unlimited borrowing or lending at a constant interest rate r. However, perfect capital markets are a fiction, although markets for some financial investments are considered highly efficient. Rates of return on savings rarely equal the rate paid to borrow funds. Moreover, rates of return on investments typically depend on the size and economic lifetime of the investments. Hence, in the real world, investors face imperfect capital markets.

The terms *challengers* and *defenders* are now introduced to help describe opportunity costs in *PV* models in imperfect capital markets. A challenger is defined as an investment being considered for adoption. A defender is the investment that must be sacrificed to adopt the challenger (Perrin).

Defenders may include investments that must be liquidated, investments that must be foregone, or credit reserves (unused borrowing capacity) that could be exchanged for debt funds. Thus, an interest rate on a loan can serve as the *IRR* on a defender only if the credit reserve used up has no value. In imperfect markets, however, the *IRR* of the defender, r, and the market rates of interest may not be equal.

In a later chapter, we will discuss the consistency conditions that must be met to compare challengers and defenders. For now, it is important to recognize that for liquidated defenders to fund challengers, they must be of the same amount and be committed for the same time period. Let this amount be V_0^d . Thus, if a defender earns R_1^d one period later, its *IRR* can be found by solving for r in the following expression:

$$V_0^d = \frac{R_1^d}{(1+r)},\tag{3.1}$$

and:

$$r = \frac{R_1^d}{V_0^d} - 1.\tag{3.2}$$

Notice that, in this one-period model, no reinvestment possibilities for R_1^d are considered.

If the challenging investment is adopted, the rate of return, r, must be sacrificed. Thus, r is called the opportunity cost of capital; the rate of return sacrificed to obtain capital V_0^d for one period. The one-period opportunity cost of capital, or the opportunity cost of investing in the challenger, measured in dollars, is rV_0^d, the opportunity cost of capital r times the acquisition cost of the investment V_0^d.

To reflect the opportunity cost of capital in the evaluation of the challenger, the opportunity cost rV_0^d is subtracted from the challenger's earnings along with the acquisition cost of the challenger. Then, *NPV* equals:

$$NPV = \frac{R_1^c - (1+r)\, V_0^d}{(1+r)} = -V_0^d + \frac{R_1^c}{(1+r)}. \qquad (3.3)$$

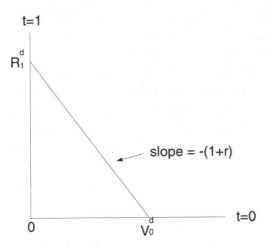

Figure 3.3a   Calculating the IRR on a Defender

The comparison between a defender and a challenger can be illustrated graphically. In Figure 3.3a, a defending investment of OV_0^d earns OR_1^d one period later. One plus the *IRR* on this investment, $(1+r)$, is the negative slope of the straight line that connects points R_1^d and V_0^d.

Now suppose that instead of investing V_0^d in the defending investment, V_0^d is invested in a challenging investment that returns $R_1^c > R_1^d$ after one period (Figure 3.3b). The present value of OR_1^c equals OA and is found by discounting OR_1^c by one plus the opportunity cost of capital, $(1+r)$. The opportunity cost of capital for this problem is the rate of return sacrificed by not investing in the defender (r). The *NPV* of the challenger is the present value of OR_1^c less V_0^d:

$$NPV = -O\,V_0^d + \frac{OR_1^c}{(1+r)} = V_0^d A.$$

Graphically, the *NPV* of the challenger is V_0^dA in Figure 3.3b where the negative slopes of the solid lines are $-(1+r)$. The dashed line $R_1^c V_0^d$ is the challenger's *IRR*, which in this case, exceeds the defender's *IRR*.

    To summarize, a challenger is an investment being considered for adoption. A defender is the investment sacrificed to invest in the challenger. The defender's *IRR* is the rate of return sacrificed or given up to invest in the challenger. The defender's *IRR* is called the opportunity cost of capital and it may depend on the size of investment and remaining economic life of the defender.

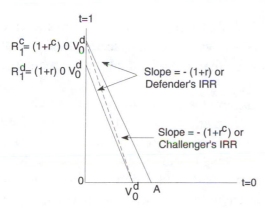

Figure 3.3b   Calculating the Challenger's *NPV* Using the Defender's *IRR*

Definition: The opportunity cost of capital is the *IRR* of the defender sacrificed to invest in the challenging investment.

Reinvestment Rate Assumption

    Calculating a defender's *IRR* may be difficult for two reasons. First, consider a general *IRR* model in which the r equates the *NPV* of the investment to zero. The model is written as:

$$NPV = -V_0^d + \sum_{t=1}^{n} \frac{R_t^d}{(1+r)^t} = 0. \tag{3.4}$$

    As discussed in Chapter 2, the *IRR* model in (3.4) suffers a technical difficulty in that it is a polynomial equation of the nth degree. Consequently, the solution to (3.4) may have multiple roots (*IRR* values) that satisfy the equation depending on the number of sign changes in the cash flow series. Some series of cash flows may have more than one *IRR* that satisfy equation (3.4) and, in some cases, the *IRRs* may be negative or nonexistent. Interpretation of the *IRR* is difficult in these cases.

    A second difficulty pointed out earlier is associated with the well known, but often underemphasized, reinvestment rate assumption of equation (3.4); namely, that the cash flows received each period can be reinvested at the calculated *IRR* for that investment. This relationship can easily be seen by multiplying each cash flow in equation (3.4) by (1+r) raised to the appropriate power:

$$V_0^d = \frac{\sum_{t=1}^{n} R_t^d (1+r)^{n-t}}{(1+r)^n}.$$
(3.5)

The point of equations (3.4) and (3.5) is that reinvesting cash flows at rate r to the nth period does not change the present values of the series; the present value is still V_0^d. The implicit assumption is that the discount rate equals the reinvestment rate.

The usual formulation of *PV* models assumes a reinvestment rate equal to a defender's *IRR*. But in less than perfect capital markets, rates of return depend on the length, size, and other characteristics of the investment. Thus, periodic cash flows generated by the investment may not always be reinvested at the defender's *IRR* calculated over n periods. When reinvestment rates r^r are not equal to the discount rate (i.e., $r^r \neq r$), the *IRR* associated with a cash flow is changed by reinvesting the flow. Thus, we write the new *IRR* model as:

$$V_0^d = \frac{\sum_{t=1}^{n} R_t^d (1+r^r)^{n-t}}{(1+r)^n} = 0.$$
(3.6)

Clearly, the *IRR* in equation (3.5), may be different than r, the *IRR* in equation (3.6). This difference is created by assuming cash flows are reinvested at rate r^r until the end of the planning horizon.

There is a benefit that results from introducing reinvestment rates in equation (3.6). It is that a unique value for r can be found in equation (3.6) equal to:

$$r = \left[\frac{\sum_{t=1}^{n} R_t^d (1+r^r)^{n-t}}{V_0^d} \right]^{1/n} - 1.$$
(3.7)

The above approach is essentially the modified internal rate of return (*MIRR*) proposed by McDaniel, McCarty, and Jessell and adopted in texts by Brigham and Gapenski and others. McDaniel et al. showed that the *MIRR* approach resolves technical *IRR* problems associated with sign changes and inconsistent rankings with *NPV*, except when alternative investments differ in size. A difficulty with the

MIRR approach is that it does not provide a method for determining the reinvestment rate, without which the unique *MIRR* cannot always be found.

Reinvestment Rates and Imperfect Markets

NPV models like equation (3.4) imply that cash flows R_t are withdrawn from the project at time t. Thus, the amount of the funds invested is reduced in each period of positive cash flow. Thus, any rate-of-return calculation such as would be made in an *IRR* model determines a return on an investment amount that is changing over the life of the investment.

On the other hand, *PV* models like equation (3.6) describe investments in which no funds are withdrawn from the project until the end of the project's economic life. Thus, the rate of return is calculated on the original investment amount V_0.

If the reinvestment rate is the same as the discount rate, reinvesting cash flows does not change the overall rate of return or *IRR*. But, if the reinvestment rate is not equal to the discount rate, then reinvesting cash flows changes the *IRR* of the investment. Example 3.1 illustrates how the defender's *IRR* changes when the reinvestment rate $r' \neq r$.

Example 3.1: Finding the Defender's *IRR*

Iwana Knoe has an opportunity to invest \$5,000 in return for a series of payments $R_1^c,...,R_n^c$. In order to evaluate this investment opportunity, she needs to calculate the *IRR* of a defending investment which if liquidated yields $V_0^d = \$5,000$, but requires the sacrifice of five payments $(R_1^d, R_2^d,...,R_5^d)$, each equal to \$1,200. The *IRR* assuming the \$1,200 payments are reinvested at the defender's *IRR* is 6.4 percent. But Iwana believes that each of the payments can be reinvested at the rate of 6 percent. Using equation (3.7), she calculates:

$$r = \left[\frac{\sum_{t=1}^{5} \$1,200\,(1.06)^{5-t}}{\$5,000} \right]^{1/5} - 1 = .0623$$

= 6.23 percent.

Thus, with $r' = 6.0$ percent, the *IRR* is reduced from 6.4 percent to 6.23 percent.

When the rate of return on investments depends on the amount invested or the length of time invested, maintaining comparable investment sizes and economic lives is required to compare challengers and defenders. One simple way to achieve this consistency is to maintain investment sizes by explicitly stating reinvestment rate assumptions.

Alternative Assumptions About Reinvestment Rates

Consider some common (implicit) assumptions made about reinvestment rates. For simplicity the assumptions are illustrated with two-period *PV* models although the assumptions can be applied more generally.

Case 1: Independent Reinvestment Rate

This assumption is illustrated with the two-period *PV* model:

$$V_0^d = \frac{R_1^d}{(1+r)} + \frac{R_2^d}{(1+r)^2} = \frac{R_1^d(1+r) + R_2^d}{(1+r)^2}.$$

The quadratic formula allows us to find *r* equal to:

$$r = \frac{R_1^d \pm \left[(R_1^d)^2 + 4V_0^d R_2^d\right]^{\frac{1}{2}}}{2V_0^d} - 1. \tag{3.8}$$

In the above model, the assumption is made that the reinvestment rate of R_1^d is the same as the discount rate—reflecting a perfect market. Thus, the reinvestment rate is independent of size, timing, or other variables. This assumption is frequently used for deducing analytic results and is adopted throughout the text in part because of its analytic simplicity.

Case 2: Time and Size-Dependent Reinvestment Rates

In a less than perfect capital market, the rate of return may be expected to depend on at least the size and length of time of the investment. For example, reinvesting R_1^d for one period may earn $r(R_1^d, 1)$. Then, the *IRR* for a two-period model can be solved for in the expression:

$$V_0^d = \frac{R_1^d[1 + r(R_1^d, 1)] + R_2^d}{(1+r)^2},$$

and:

$$r = \left[\frac{R_1^d\,[1 + r\,(R_1^d, 1)] + R_2^d}{V_0^d} \right]^{1/2} - 1.$$ (3.9)

Case 3: Time Dependent Reinvestment Rates

A generalized *PV* model allows the discount rate to vary between time periods. In such models, V_0^d is expressed as:

$$V_0^d = \frac{R_1^d}{(1+r_1)} + \frac{R_2^d}{(1+r_1)(1+r_2)} = \frac{R_1^d(1+r_2) + R_2^d}{(1+r_1)(1+r_2)} = \frac{R_1^d(1+r_2) + R_2^d}{(1+r)^2}.$$

In the model above, the time dependent reinvestment rate for period one funds is r_2. Solving for r_2, we find:

$$r_2 = \left[\frac{R_2^d}{V_0^d(1+r_1) - R_1^d} \right] - 1.$$ (3.10a)

It is important to note that r_2 calculated above is the *IRR* earned on the investment in the second period. It would not be used as the *IRR* of the defender. The *IRR* for the model with time dependent reinvestment rates equals:

$$r = \left[\frac{R_1^d(1+r_2) + R_2^d}{V_0^d} \right]^{\frac{1}{2}} - 1.$$ (3.10b)

In Example 3.2, we illustrate how different reinvestment rate assumptions affect *IRR* calculations.

Return to Assets (*RTA*) versus
Return to Equity (*RTE*)

So far, the notions of opportunity cost of capital and reinvestment rates have been introduced without specifying whose capital. Is it equity capital, debt capital, or a combination of debt and equity capital? Or does it matter? Two schools of thought have emerged relative to this question. One approach focuses on the

Example 3.2: Internal Rate-of-Return Calculations

A challenging two-period investment whose purchase price (V_0) is $1,000 is considered for adoption by the firm. The defender will return $65 in year one ($R_1^d$) and $1,100 in year two ($R_2^d$).

Now suppose that the usual assumption was made that a perfect market exists and that all funds earned the *IRR* rate of return. Then, the *IRR* is found by solving for r using equation (3.8):

$$r = \frac{\$65 \pm [(\$65)^2 + (4)(\$1,000)(\$1,100)]^{\frac{1}{2}}}{(2)(\$1,000)} - 1 = 8.18 \text{ and } 1.63 \text{ percent.}$$

The *IRR* equal to 8.18 percent is selected because it appears more realistic.

Next, suppose R_1^d can be reinvested for one year at $r(\$65,1)=5$ percent. To find r, the *IRR* for a two-period investment, we use equation (3.9):

$$r = \left[\frac{\$65(1.05) + \$1100}{\$1000} \right]^{\frac{1}{2}} - 1 = 8.09 \text{ percent.}$$

Finally, suppose the goal is to calculate r_2 assuming $r_1 = .05$. In this case, the assumption is that the discount rates vary between time periods. Then, we use equation (3.10a) and find that the marginal *IRR* equals:

$$r_2 = \left[\frac{\$1100}{\$1000(1.05) - \$65} \right] - 1 = 11.68 \text{ percent.}$$

To interpret these results, if the $65 could be reinvested to earn the internal rate of return (8.18 percent) for one period (yielding $70.32), then the internal rate of return of a $1,000 investment yielding $1,170.32 at the end of the second period would be 8.18 percent. If, however, the reinvestment rate is less than 8.18 percent, and in fact is equal to 5 percent, then it is logical to expect a lower internal rate of return—in this case 8.09 percent.

> ### Example 3.2, Cont'd.: Internal Rate-of-Return Calculations
>
> The marginal *IRR* r_2 of 11.68 percent exceeds both *IRR* calculations of 8.09 percent and 8.18 percent. This is because the rate of return in the first period, 5 percent, was below the compound or *IRR* rate.

returns associated with the total assets invested regardless of whether they are financed by debt or equity. Thus, the firm's opportunity cost is measured by a weighted average of opportunity costs of equity and debt. Another school of thought focuses on returns to equity. That is, cash flows are measured net of any principal and interest payments on debt, and the opportunity cost of equity capital serves as the discount rate. The difference between the two approaches is important because most firms rely on a combination of debt and equity to fund assets. Reduced to its essence, the issue is whether periodic funds generated by the asset earn at the weighted average cost of capital or at the average rate of return earned on equity.

Returns to Assets *(RTA)*

Many financial texts argue that the opportunity cost of capital is a function of the ratio of initial debt, D_0, to initial equity, E_0, or D_0/E_0. High ratios of debt to equity are assumed to require higher opportunity costs. Thus, the relationship between the opportunity cost and the ratio of debt to equity (D_0/E_0) is direct. Namely, as one increases the amount of debt relative to equity to fund a project requiring V_0, the opportunity cost expressed as a function of the ratio (D_0/E_0), $r(D_0/E_0)$, increases. Stated another way, the assumption is that regardless of the size of the project, the opportunity cost $r(D_0/E_0)$ is an increasing function of the ratio D_0/E_0.

To illustrate the *RTA* approach and its implicit assumptions, consider a single-period asset consisting of cash outflow V_0 at the beginning of the period financed by debt D_0 and equity funds E_0 and cash inflow R_1 at the end of the period. The *IRR* in this case is found by solving for $r(D_0/E_0)$ in the expression:

$$V_0 = \frac{R_1^d}{[1+r(D_0/E_0)]},$$

and:

$$r(D_0/E_0) = \frac{R_1^d}{V_0} - 1.$$

Then, a challenging asset that earns R_1^c is evaluated by the expression:

$$NPV^A = -V_0 + \frac{R_1^c}{[1+r(D_0/E_0)]} = \frac{R_1^c - [1+r(D_0/E_0)]\,V_0}{[1+r(D_0/E_0)]}, \qquad (3.11)$$

and assumes V_0 can be reinvested at rate $r(D_0/E_0)$. The appropriateness of this assumption depends on the opportunity cost of capital being a function of the ratio D_0/E_0 which is assumed constant.

The *RTA* approach is widely used in corporate finance where well-developed markets exist for trading and pricing of both debt and equity capital. Thus, the *RTA* approach is likely appropriate for large firms that have a stable relationship between debt and equity.

Returns to Equity (*RTE*)

An alternative to the *RTA* approach assumes that marginal debt and equity opportunity costs depend on the debt and equity levels, rather than on the debt-to-equity ratio. Define the marginal opportunity cost of debt to be $r(D_0)$, a function of debt D_0, and define the marginal opportunity cost of equity capital to be $r(E_0)$, a function of equity E_0. Then, define average opportunity costs of debt to be $\bar{r}(D_0)$ and equity to be $\bar{r}(E_0)$. Figure 3.4 indicates the average and marginal cost curves associated with different levels of debt D_0 and equity E_0. Economic theory suggests that to minimize the cost of funds for use in financing, equality is required between the marginal opportunity costs associated with the use of debt and equity capital. Thus, in Figure 3.4, $r(D_0)=r(E_0)$. The average costs of debt D_0 and equity E_0 associated with the equilibrium condition $r(D_0)=r(E_0)$ are $\bar{r}(D_0)$ and $\bar{r}(E_0)$, respectively. Notice that as shown in Figure 3.4, $\bar{r}(D_0)$ and $\bar{r}(E_0)$ need not be equal.

However, the discount rate used in *PV* models is not a measure of the marginal cost of funding the project; rather, it is the average cost. Although an optimal combination of debt and equity is based on the equality of marginal opportunity costs, the average costs associated with using E_0 and D_0 are, respectively, $\bar{r}(E_0)$ and $\bar{r}(D_0)$. Let the weighted cost of capital be:

$$\bar{r}(E_0 + D_0).$$

$$\bar{r}(E_0)\left(\frac{E_0}{V_0}\right) + \bar{r}(D_0)\left(\frac{D_0}{V_0}\right), \quad (3.12)$$

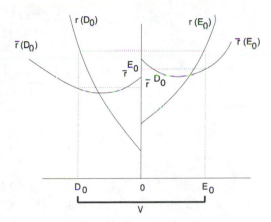

where V_0 equals $E_0 + D_0$.

Suppose a level of funds equal to V_0 is required to finance a particular challenger. Moreover, assume that the least cost combination of debt and equity is shown by D_0 and E_0, respectively. As shown in Figure 3.4, the marginal opportunity costs of these two sources of funds are equal at these levels. That is, the cost of raising the last dollar of funds for financing the challenger is the same regardless of whether it is

Figure 3.4 Equilibrium Conditions that Determine the Optimal Combination of Debt and Equity Funds to Provide Investment Funds $V_0 = E_0 + D_0$

debt or equity. Meanwhile, the average opportunity costs of using debt and equity funds may be different and depend on the size of the investment (V_0).

To illustrate the *RTE* approach, consider a single-period investment consisting of a single outflow V_0 at the beginning of the period financed by equity E_0 and debt D_0, and a single inflow R_1 at the end of the period. The *IRR* in this case is found by solving for $\bar{r}(E_0)$ in the expression:

$$E_0 = \frac{R_1^d - D_0[(1 + \bar{r}(D_0))]}{[1 + \bar{r}(E_0)]}, \quad (3.12)$$

and:

$$\bar{r}(E_0) = \frac{R_1^d - D_0[1 + \bar{r}(D_0)]}{E_0} - 1. \quad (3.13)$$

Then, a challenging investment that earns R_1^c and assumes a reinvestment rate of $\bar{r}(E_0)$ is evaluated by the expression:

$$NPV^E = -E_0 + \frac{R_1^c - D_0[1 + \bar{r}(D_0)]}{[1 + \bar{r}(E_0)]}$$

$$= \frac{R_1^c - D_0[1 + \bar{r}(D_0)] - E_0[1 + \bar{r}(E_0)]}{[1 + \bar{r}(E_0)]} \qquad (3.14)$$

$$= \frac{R_1^c - V_0[1 + \bar{r}(E_0 + D_0)]}{[1 + \bar{r}(E_0)]}.$$

Suppose $\bar{r}(E_0 + D_0) = \bar{r}(D_0/E_0)$ so that end-of-period wealth is the same in (3.11) and (3.14). Then, because $\bar{r}(E_0)$ does not generally equal $r(D_0/E_0)$, NPV^A in equation (3.11) cannot generally equal NPV^E in equation (3.14), even though $\bar{r}(D_0/E_0)$ and $\bar{r}(D_0 + E_0)$ in equations (3.11) and (3.14), respectively, are equal. Example 3.3 illustrates the different results that may result from the *RTE* and *RTA* approaches.

The two valuation models produce different results because they assume a different opportunity cost or rate of reinvestment for the end-of-period profit. The *RTA* approach values the end-of-period profit as though its value today could be invested to earn $r(D_0/E_0)$ during the period. The *RTE* approach values the end-of-period profit as though its value today could be invested to earn $\bar{r}(E_0)$ during the period. The reinvestment rate that actually describes the reinvestment opportunities of the firm determines which, if either, model is correct. A second difference is associated with assuming the investment amount equals $V_0 = (D_0 + E_0)$ in calculating returns to assets versus an investment of E_0 when calculating returns to equity.

In the remainder of this book, we frequently assume that the reinvestment rate is the discount rate. This assumption, frequently employed in *PV* models, is a useful approximation. It also permits the development of some analytic results that could not be as easily derived under more complicated reinvestment rate assumptions. Nonetheless, analysts should be aware of the many alternative reinvestment rate assumptions and adopt appropriate ones for the analysis.

Opportunity Costs and Next Best Investments

A frequently stated *PV* model maxim is to use the *IRR* of the next best investment opportunity as the discount rate for the challenger. It is important to understand how to apply this advice.

Consider two mutually-exclusive investments *A* and *B*. Also assume that regardless of which investment is adopted—a third investment *C* will be liquidated to finance the new investment. Clearly, investment *C*, an existing investment

Example 3.3: Weighted Capital Costs and *RTE* versus *RTA*

A firm is facing an investment opportunity requiring $2,000 on which $1,000 is to be raised from equity funds (E_0) at an average cost of 13 percent and $1,000 is to be raised from debt funds (D_0) at an average cost of 7 percent. Assume $r(D_0/E_0)=10$ percent. Also assume that the weighted cost of capital for the $2,000 investment is:

$$\bar{r}(D_0+E_0) = \frac{\bar{r}(E_0)E_0 + \bar{r}(D_0)D_0}{E_0 + D_0} = \frac{(.13)(\$1,000) + (.07)(\$1,000)}{\$2,000}$$

$$= 10 \text{ percent.}$$

Assume that this project returns $2,210 at the end of the investment period. Then:

$$-V_0[1+r(D_0+E_0)] + R_1 = -\$2,000\ (1.10) + \$2,210 = \$10.$$

The conflict between the *RTE* and *RTA* approaches occurs if this investment is valued in present dollars. Using the *RTA* approach, the discount rate of $r(D_0/E_0) = 10$ percent is used and:

$$NPV^A = \frac{\$10}{1.10} = \$9.09.$$

On the other hand, if the *RTE* approach is used, a discount rate of $\bar{r}(E_0)$ equal to 13 percent is used and:

$$NPV^E = \frac{\$10}{1.13} = \$8.85.$$

While the present value remains positive using either approach, the difference in NPV^E and NPV^A may be significant.

already held by the firm, is not the defender. Instead, *B* is the defender appropriate for evaluating *A*.

Next consider another investment scenario. As before, assume the firm is considering investing in one of two mutually-exclusive investments, *A* and *B*. Assume the firm will finance the investment in *A* and *B* by liquidating one of two existing investments or credit reserves, C and D. The question is: What is the defender and what is the challenger? The firm now faces two separate investment problems. One is to find the least cost source of funding and the other is to find the investment earning the greatest rate of return.

First consider the investment problem involving the least cost source of financing. To find the least cost source of funding, one of the financing sources is denoted the challenger; the other is the defender. So the *IRR*s of the sources of funding C and D are found and compared. In this case, the smallest *IRR* (since it is a cost) is preferred.

Finally, consider a third investment problem. This problem requires an investment owned by the firm, a defender, to be liquidated if a new investment, a challenger, is to be acquired. To compare the defender and challenger, the *IRR* of the defender is calculated as though the investment were newly made or remained in place. In this way, the opportunity cost of the defender is calculated based on the rate of return the firm would lose if the defender were liquidated to acquire the challenger.

The three investment choices are now illustrated.

An Application: Multiple Investment Opportunities and Sources of Financing

Suppose the firm of Igotta Choose **must** decide between two mutually-exclusive one-period investments. Each project requires the same investment amount and returns one period later are R_1^A and R_1^B for investment projects A and B, respectively. The cash flows and *IRR*s are reported in Table 3.1.

It is important to note that the source of funds for financing A and B is not stated. Thus, the rate of return is measured relative to the amount invested—namely, V_0. The choice between A and B is made based on a comparison of r^A versus r^B, or based on the *NPV*s:

$$NPV^A = -V_0 + \frac{R_1^A}{(1+r^B)},$$

versus:

$$NPV^B = -V_0 + \frac{R_1^B}{(1+r^A)},$$

where r^B is the discount rate for A and r^A is the discount rate for B. Suppose $r^A > r^B$ so that A is preferred to B as a new investment.

Table 3.1 Choosing between Mutually-Exclusive Investments

Invest-ments	Cash Flow at $t=0$	Cash Flow at $t=1$	IRR
A	$-V_0$	R_1^A	$r^A = R_1^A / V_0 - 1$
B	$-V_0$	R_1^B	$r^B = R_1^B / V_0 - 1$

Table 3.2 Choosing between Mutually-Exclusive Sources of Funds

Source of Funds	Cash at $t=0$	Cash Flow at $t=1$	IRR
C	V_0	$-R_1^C$	$r^C = R_1^C / V_0 - 1$
D	V_0	$-R_1^D$	$r^D = R_1^D / V_0 - 1$

Next, suppose the firm recognizes two sources of funds for investing in either project A or project B. Denote these sources as C and D and let their one period returns be R_1^C and R_1^D, respectively. The cash flows associated with the liquidation of C or D are described in Table 3.2.

Suppose also that $r^C < r^D$ so that C is preferred to D as a source of funds. (Since r^C and r^D are recognized as costs, the smaller one, r^C, is preferred.) Thus, the firm decides to liquidate C to fund A if the resulting investment adds to its *NPV*. To determine if investing in A and liquidating C increases its *NPV* the firm calculates:

$$NPV = -V_0 + \frac{R_1^A}{(1+r^C)}.$$

If *NPV* > 0, then A is adopted and C liquidated.

Identifying defenders is an important task of applied investment analysis that has many practical implications. The importance of correctly identifying the opportunity cost is illustrated using a recent problem facing the Farm Credit System, the nation's largest agricultural lender. Example 3.4 typifies the problems faced by private firms; namely, to identify the correct discount rate to use.

Investment, Production Relationships, and Opportunity Cost

In this section, we consider the relationship between a firm's investment and production decisions, giving emphasis to the appropriate specification of opportunity costs. In principle, the distinction between investment and production

Example 3.4: The Importance of Correctly Calculating the Opportunity Cost of Capital

The Farm Credit Banks (*FCBs*) are an important federally-supported source of funds for agriculture. In 1987, the quality of their loan portfolios had declined. As a result, the Agricultural Credit Act of 1987 mandated that the *FCBs* and the Farmer's Home Administration (*FmHA*) restructure (renegotiate) loan terms of delinquent borrowers if loan losses were less than the cost of foreclosure. Deciding whether foreclosure or restructuring is less costly for the *FCBs* requires a comparison of their *NPV*s of the cash flows received under the two alternatives. The present value, of course, depends on the discount rate. The question is: What is the appropriate discount rate for the Farm Credit Banks (*FCBs*)?

At the time of the analysis, the *FCBs* had delinquent loans that carried a 12.5 percent interest rate. Its credit-worthy customers were paying 10 percent interest. Its marginal cost of acquiring loan funds was 8.5 percent, but its average cost of loanable funds was 10.5 percent. The question faced by the *FCBs* was: Which of the above is the appropriate discount rate?

The answer can be found by asking the question: What is the challenger for the funds invested in the delinquent loan? Or stated another way: What will the funds generated by the liquidated asset be used for?

In the example, the new loan rate had changed so that a discount rate of 12.5 percent on new loans was no longer appropriate. One might consider using the current interest rate of 10 percent (ignoring the issue of service charges, etc.). But with declining loan volume, funds were not directed toward making new loans. Thus, the appropriate discount rate should be tied to the cost of the bonds that would be retired. So the question was: Should 8.5 percent, the marginal cost, or 10.5, the average cost of outstanding bonds, be used?

To pay off existing bonds would require a repurchase in the secondary bond market at rates that reflect the current marginal cost of borrowing. Given this outcome, a discount rate based upon the expected marginal cost of borrowing funds seemed appropriate and was recommended (Lins and Robison).[2]

decisions is based primarily on the timing of transactions. Investments are usually represented by an initial outlay of capital expenditures followed by cash returns in subsequent time periods. Production decisions are usually represented in a timeless or static context in which no time interval is specified between costs and returns. In practice, of course, most production decisions do involve time intervals between costs and returns. The interval may be very short in the case of assembly lines in factories, or it may cover several months in the case of agricultural production. Thus, production decisions may also involve time value of money considerations, similar to time discounting in longer time investment situations.

To begin, consider finding the marginal opportunity cost of the last unit of an input x in a production process. The standard timeless production problem can be expressed as:

$$\pi = pf(x;s) - p_x x - F, \tag{3.15}$$

where π is profit from the production activity; p is the price of the output produced; $f(x;s)$ is the production function defined over x for a fixed level of durable services s where $f'>0$; $f''<0$; and p_x is the price of the input x, and other fixed cash costs such as insurance and taxes are represented by the constant F. The profit-maximizing level of x in equation (3.15) is found by solving the following first-order condition:

$$pf'(x;s) - p_x = 0$$
$$\text{or} \tag{3.16}$$
$$pf'(x;s) = p_x.$$

The firm maximizes profit by setting the marginal value product of the input, $pf'(x;s)$, equal to the marginal factor cost of the input, p_x. In this case, the input price, p_x, is also the opportunity cost, or what the firm gives up to earn the marginal value product, $pf'(x;s)$.

In the production problem described above, the investment decision involves the last unit of x, where p_x is sacrificed and $pf'(x;s)$ is earned. The equivalent of an *NPV* expression would be the difference: $pf'(x;s)-p_x$, and if the difference is positive, the investment should be made.

When the firm operates without constraints in its use of x, its opportunity cost associated with the use of x is the price of the input p_x. Its only sacrifice is the money paid to purchase x. Thus, the acquisition price p_x is also the opportunity cost of acquiring x. A modification to the problem yields a result in which the opportunity cost is not equal to the purchase price of the input. The changes that create a new marginal opportunity cost are an alternative investment that earns a rate of return r and a budget constraint B.

Assume the firm described above has an alternative to producing $f(x;s)$. This alternative investment I earns a rate of return r. The firm's new profit function is:

$$\pi = pf(x;s) - p_x x - F + rI, \qquad (3.17)$$

subject to the budget constraint $B = I + p_x x + F$ and $I, x \geq 0$. Timeless production theory assumes that the input x is instantaneously transformed into output $f(x;s)$. Returns on investments, however, are usually paid per unit of time. Nonetheless, for this example, imagine an investment that provides an immediate return. To find the optimal x, first solve the budget constraint for I and then substitute the result into equation (3.17). Instantaneous profits are now expressed as:

$$\pi = pf(x;s) - p_x x + r(B - p_x x - F). \qquad (3.18)$$

The optimal allocation of x, x^*, to the production process is found by solving the first-order condition:

$$pf'(x;s) - p_x(1+r) = 0$$
$$\text{or} \qquad (3.19)$$
$$pf'(x;s) = p_x(1+r).$$

Again, the investment decision is concerned with the last unit of x purchased. Moreover, the decision to purchase the last unit depends on the difference between the challenger's marginal return $pf'(x;s)$ and the marginal opportunity cost of the defender $p_x(1+r)$.

The input will be allocated up to the point where the marginal value product, $pf'(x;s)$, is equal to the marginal opportunity cost, $p_x(1+r)$. The marginal opportunity cost is different from the earlier case because the firm not only gives up the purchase price p_x when using the input, but also the return it could have earned from investing in I. Thus, the opportunity cost for the last unit of x is no longer the price of the input p_x, but is $p_x(1+r)=p_x+rp_x$. The first part of the opportunity cost, p_x, is the amount invested. The second part, rp_x, is the foregone return from purchasing x rather than leaving the money invested and earning at the rate of r percent.

Valuing the Durable

Having determined optimal variable input allocations of x, x^*, we now consider a related investment decision. This decision asks: Is investing in the durable that provides services s worthwhile? Recognizing that the durable is capable of providing services for many periods in the future, we let R_1, R_2, etc., represent the net cash flows attributed to the durable after subtracting out variable and fixed cash costs in each time period. Then, we subtract out the durable's present cost of V_0 and add the present value of its salvage values after n periods of providing services. The result is:

$$NPV = -V_0 + \frac{pf(x_1^*;s_1) - (1+r)(p_x x_2 + F)}{(1+r)}$$

$$+ \frac{pf(x_2^*;s_2) - (1+r)(p_x x_3^* + F)}{(1+r)^2} \qquad (3.20)$$

$$+ \ldots + \frac{pf(x_n^*,s_n) - (1+r)(p_x s_n^* + F)}{(1+r)^n} + \frac{V_n}{(1+r)^n}$$

$$= -V_0 + \frac{R_1^*}{(1+r)} + \frac{R_2^*}{(1+r)^2} + \ldots + \frac{R_n^*}{(1+r)^2},$$

where r is the *IRR* of a defender that must be sacrificed to fund the project.

To summarize, *NPV* represents the net present value of returns from the durable. It is found by summing the net cash flows in each period that result from producing and selling a product and paying for the cost of variable inputs and other fixed costs–not including the cost of the durable's services. The variable R_t represents net cash earned by the investment at age t. V_0 represents the durable's acquisition price, and V_n represents its salvage value n periods later. The economic life or the planning horizon for the durable is represented by the variable n. Only when *NPV*>0 should the investment be made.

Another kind of sacrifice (and opportunity cost) may occur when the firm is considering several new investments, but has a fixed amount of investable funds. In this scenario, the opportunity cost is the rate of return sacrificed by not investing in the alternative investments. Example 3.5 illustrates this type of choice.

Opportunity Costs for Lumpy Investments

PV models often deal with discrete or lumpy decisions such as to invest in project *A* versus project *B*. In this case, the opportunity cost is calculated for an entire project rather than for the last unit of input purchased. Example 3.6 illustrates the point.

Example 3.5: Alternative Production Processes

Suppose the firm can invest in two production processes, $q_1 = f(x_1)$ and $q_2 = g(x_2)$. Assume that q_1 and q_2 are both sold at a constant price p. Also assume the two processes employ a fixed quantity of the input x in amounts x_1 and x_2, respectively. Then, profit from the combined production is:

$$\pi = p\left[(f(x_1) + g(x_2))\right] - p_x x - F, \tag{3.21}$$

subject to the constraint that $x = x_1 + x_2$.

To introduce the constraint into the problem, x_2 is replaced with $(x - x_1)$. Profits π can be written as:

$$\pi = p\left[f(x_1) + g(x - x_1)\right] - p_x x - F. \tag{3.22}$$

Now consider the opportunity cost of investing in more units of x_1 holding x constant. Differentiating π with respect to x_1 yields:

$$\frac{d\pi}{dx_1} = \frac{\partial f}{\partial x_1} - \frac{\partial g}{\partial x_1} = 0. \tag{3.23}$$

Now $\partial g / \partial x_1$ is the marginal opportunity cost of increasing x_1, because no additional purchases of x were made. Units produced in investment g were sacrificed. So, the reduced production in investment $g(x_2)$ is the marginal opportunity cost of production in investment $f(x_1)$.

Summary

The discount rate in *PV* models represents a rate of return earned by a defender, and sacrificed to acquire a challenger. Choosing the appropriate discount rate is perhaps the most difficult task of investment analysis. The choice essentially involves the identification of challengers and defenders and opportunity costs associated with defenders.

The relevant costs in economic models have always been opportunity costs. These costs reflect what is given up when an alternative is chosen. This chapter has examined how the calculation of opportunity costs is influenced by time. Of course, the calculation associated with any particular investment depends critically

Example 3.6: Average Opportunity Costs

Suppose a firm faces the decision to invest V_0^f in a durable that results in profits:

$$\pi^f = pf(x_f; s_f) - p_x x_f - V_0^f,$$

where s_f are services from the durable and x_f are variable inputs. Alternatively, the firm can invest V_0^g in a one-period durable that results in profits:

$$\pi^g = pg(x_g; s_g) - p_x x_g - V_0^g,$$

where s_g are services from the durable and x_g are variable inputs. For consistency, assume $V_0^f + p_x x_f + F = V_0^g + p_x x_g + F = B$ or that each project requires the same level of investment B. The average returns from each project "f" and "g" are calculated as:

$$\frac{\pi^f}{B} = r^f,$$

and:

$$\frac{\pi^g}{B} = r^g.$$

Calculated in this way, r^f and r^g are the average rates of return on projects "f" and "g," respectively. The decision is to invest in project f if $r^f > r^g$ and to invest in project g if $r^g > r^f$. In this timeless example, π^f and π^g are analogous to *NPV*s and the average rates of return r^f and r^g are analogous to *IRR*s in multiperiod investment problems.

on whether the resource is being liquidated to invest in an alternative or whether the resource is to be acquired. In addition, this chapter has pointed out that opportunity costs change whenever the effective constraints on the investment opportunity set are changed. All of these questions will require additional attention in later chapters.

Endnotes

1. There may be cases where the costs of the financing source cannot be compared independent of the returns on the investment. In such cases, all

combinations of financing and investing must be calculated and compared to find the best combination.

2.   See the comment by Rao and Pederson and the reply by Lins and Robison.

Review Questions

1.   Explain the difference between the price of an input versus an input's opportunity cost. When are they the same?

2.   Opportunity costs in production models are expressed as dollar values while opportunity costs in present value models are expressed as rates of return; namely, the discount rate. Could they both be expressed as rates or dollar values? If so, explain how you would make the calculations.

3.   Define investment challengers and defenders. How are they used to find opportunity costs?

4.   How is the opportunity cost of capital found in perfect and imperfect capital markets? If the capital market is imperfect, can different individuals earn different rates of return even on the same investment? Defend your answer.

5.   For an *n* period internal rate-of-return model, how many opportunity costs of capital are possible? Explain why.

6.   Suppose that the rate of return on an investment is a function of its size (or term). How does this condition affect the construction of *NPV* and *IRR* models that implicitly assume that the reinvestment rate is the discount rate for the *NPV* model and the *IRR* in the *IRR* model?

7.   Explain the difference between the Return to Assets (*RTA*) model and the Return to Equity (*RTE*) model.

8.   In the *RTE* model, the cost of financing is subtracted from the net cash flow, and the discount rate reflects the opportunity cost of the investor's equity capital. What guideline would you follow to decide whether to subtract the cost of financing from the net cash flow or to include the cost of debt in the discount rate?

9.   Under what assumptions is the weighted cost of capital the appropriate opportunity cost of capital?

10.   How does requiring a specific investment or source of funds alter the selection of the challenger and defender, where the latter is used to determine the opportunity cost of capital?

Application Questions

1. Describe the opportunity costs of enrolling in a course in present value methods. Under what conditions would it equal the tuition and other incidental costs associated with taking a university course?

2. To understand opportunity costs in a timeless model, (a) calculate the opportunity cost of capital for the last unit of x purchased in an investment whose timeless profit function is described below:

    $$\pi_0 = pf(x) - p_x x + r(B - p_x x) = \$10\,(x - .01x^2) - \$2x + .05\,(\$100 - \$2x),$$

    where $p = \$10$ is the output price, x is the variable input, $p_x = \$2$ is the price of the variable input, $r = .05$ is the opportunity cost of capital, and investment $I = B - p_x x$ where $B = \$100$ is the firm's capital budget.

    (b) Next, express the opportunity cost on the last unit of x purchased as a percentage of the total cost and calculate the average rate of return for all x's purchased.

    (c) When should the average and marginal rates of return be used to evaluate investments?

3. Give examples of challengers and defenders using investment decisions you've made. Explain how you distinguished between challengers and defenders.

4. Calculate *IRRs* for the two-period models when (a) the reinvestment rate equals the *IRR*; (b) the reinvestment rate is size and length-of-time dependent; and (c) the reinvestment rate is time dependent. In your calculation assume $r_1 = .08$, $r(\$50, 1) = .06$, $R_1 = \$50$, $R_2 = \$65$, and $V_0 = \$100$.

5. Suppose that reinvestment rates are a function of size only. Under this assumption, which model, the return to asset *(RTA)*, the return to equity *(RTE)*, or some other model, would you recommend? Defend your answer.

6. The goal of investment analysis may be described as finding the highest return challenger and the cost-minimizing source of financing. Under what conditions is such a two-step procedure appropriate?

7. If only one investment is possible, you would use the *IRR* of the least cost defender as the discount rate. If several challengers were available, the discount rate is the *IRR* of the next best challenger, even though the funds for investing in the challenger come from the least-cost defender. Do you agree or disagree? Please defend your answer.

8. Under what conditions is the interest rate in the capital market the appropriate discount rate to use in *PV* models?

9.   Suppose you are committed to an investment of amount V_0. The investment can be funded by liquidating one of two existing investments, each of which when liquidated yields the same amount of funds, but whose *IRR*s, r^A and r^B, are different.

    a.   Under these circumstances, which one of the two investments is the defender and which one is the challenger? Defend your answer.

    b.   Suppose $r^A < r^B$. Which discount rate, r^A or r^B, should be used to evaluate the *NPV* of the new (already committed to) investment? Defend your answer.

    c.   Now consider a modification of the above problem. Assume there are two *mutually-exclusive* investments under consideration. Their *IRR*s, r^C and r^D, are both greater than either r^A or r^B. For the two investment problems, investing in one of two new investment opportunities or disinvesting in one of two existing investments, identify defenders and challengers.

    d.   Considering your response to the questions in (b) and (c), please evaluate the following statement:

        "The appropriate discount rate is often described as the rate of return on the next best investment opportunity. On the other hand, when considering an investment with financing available from two possible defenders, the *NPV*-maximizing solution would be to minimize the cost of financing the defender by using funds associated with the least profitable of the defenders."

10.   Please evaluate the following statement:
You are asked to evaluate an investment in your firm that will require additional labor. Since you have decided to meet this labor demand by shifting labor from other projects, you do not charge labor costs to the new project since no additional labor costs above those already experienced are incurred.

11.   Contrast the difference between the opportunity cost of capital calculated for a seller of an investment versus the opportunity cost of capital for a buyer of the investment. How would each be calculated? (Assume transactions costs are zero.)

References

Ang, J.S. "Weighted Average vs. True Cost of Capital." *Financial Management* 2(1973):56-60.

Barry, P.J., P.N. Ellinger, J.A. Hopkin, and C.B. Baker. *Financial Management in Agriculture*, 5th edition. Danville, IL: The Interstate Publishers, Inc., 1995.

Brealey, R. and S.C. Myers. *Principles of Corporate Finance*. New York: McGraw-Hill, 1981.

Brigham, E.F. and L.C. Gapenski. *Intermediate Financial Management*, 2nd edition. New York: The Dryden Press, 1987.

Fisher, I. *The Theory of Interest*. New York: The Macmillan Company, 1930.

Fiske, J.R. "A Comparative Analysis of the Return to Equity and Weighted Average Cost of Capital Approaches to Capital Budgeting." *Agricultural Finance Review* 46(1986):48-57.

Hirshleifer, J. *Investment, Interest and Capital*. Englewood Cliffs, NJ: Prentice-Hall, Inc., 1970.

Lins, D.A. and L.J. Robison. "Calculating Loan Losses: Restructuring vs. Foreclosure." *Agricultural Finance Review* 49(1989):57-63.

————. "Calculations of Loan Losses: Restructuring versus Foreclosure: A Reply." *Agricultural Finance Review* 50(1990):129-30.

Marty, R. "The Composite Internal Rate of Return." *Forest Science* 16(1970):276-79.

McDaniel, W.R., D.E. McCarty, and K.A. Jessell. "Discounted Cash Flow with Explicit Reinvestment Rate: Tutorial and Extension." *The Financial Review* 23(1988):369-85.

Perrin, R.K., "Asset Replacement Principles." *American Journal of Agricultural Economics* 52(1972):60-67.

Rao, A. and G. Pederson. "Calculation of Loan Losses: Restructuring versus Foreclosure: A Comment." *Agricultural Finance Review* 50(1990):126-28.

Strung, J. "The Internal Rate of Return and the Reinvestment Presumptions." *The Appraisal Journal* (Jan. 1976):23-33.

Chapter 4

Consistency in Present Value Models

Key words: capital gains, the cash flow principle, certainty equivalent, the consistency in timing principle, depreciating durable, geometric means, the homogenous measures principle, inflation rate, the life of the investment principle, nominal discount rate, perpetuity, portfolios, real discount rate, the total costs and returns principle.

Introduction

In Chapter 3, opportunity costs in present value (PV) models were described and illustrated. The sacrifice of a defending investment was used as the opportunity cost for investing in challenging investments. Opportunity costs were shown to play the same role in both PV and static production models. In this chapter, principles that apply to the construction of PV models will be considered. Adhering to these principles will ensure that PV models will be constructed in a consistent manner.

This chapter presents six principles that ensure consistency in the construction of PV models: (1) the cash flow principle; (2) the consistency in timing principle; (3) the homogenous measures principle; (4) the life of the investment principle; (5) the total costs and returns principle; and (6) the geometric mean principle.

Cash Flow Principle

Cash Flow Principle: Summarize economic activities related to the investment using cash flow measures.

To introduce the first principle for constructing *PV* models, consider the static (instantaneous) production process described by the production economics model:

$$\pi = pf(x;s) - p_x x - F, \tag{4.1}$$

where π is instantaneous profits, p is the output price, p_x is the input price, x is an expendable input, s is a fixed level of durable services, $f(x;s)$ is the level of output, and F is a cost (fixed) that is unrelated to the level of output. Profits in equation (4.1) are measured in dollars. Physical units of inputs x and outputs $f(x;s)$ are converted to their cash equivalent by multiplying them by their prices. By converting the physical units of inputs and outputs to their cash equivalent, the production process can be summarized by its net cash outcome.

The difference between the static production model in equation (4.1) and production processes that underlie *PV* models is that, in the latter case, the production process is not instantaneous. However, the need to summarize the intertemporal production processes by a net cash flow is the same. Thus, production, marketing, financial, and all other activities associated with an investment in a particular time period are summarized by a net cash flow. Bierman and Smidt, and Bodenhorn suggested the cash flow principle. With few exceptions, those who work with *PV* models have followed their recommendation. So, the first principle to be followed is to enter only cash flows in the numerations of *PV* models.

Consistency in Timing Principle

Consistency in Timing Principle: Record cash flows in the dollar units of the time period in which they occurred.

An important difference between *PV* models and the static production model in equation (4.1) is that the cash flows represented in equation (4.1) occur at the same time. Thus, there is no inconsistency in the measures of cash inflows and cash outflows. This consistency is not true in *PV* models where cash inflows and outflows typically occur over several time periods.

Just as differences in physical units make comparisons difficult, differences in the timing of cash flows hamper comparisons as well. The time-dated cash flows are not measured in consistent units and are, therefore, not comparable. To achieve comparability, these future cash flows are converted to their present value by discounting them by the exchange price between present and future dollars. The discounting procedure converts all future cash flows to their equivalent cash flow measured in the current period.

To illustrate this latter point, assume that in equation (4.1), the input x was purchased at the beginning of the period and production occurred at the end of the period. If r is the exchange rate between beginning and end-of-period dollars, then the production process could be described in end-of-period dollars or profits, π_1:

$$\pi_1 = pf(x;s) - (1+r)(p_x x + F). \qquad (4.2)$$

Alternatively, the process could be summarized as present value dollars, π_0, by dividing the end-of-period returns by $(1+r)$. This process is represented in equation (4.3):

$$\pi_0 = \frac{pf(x;s)}{(1+r)} - (p_x x + F). \qquad (4.3)$$

Because decisions about the future are made in the present time, the π_0 measure is usually preferred. Because cash flows occurring at different time periods are valued differently, *PV* models must agree on how to record the timing of cash flows. The most difficult application of the consistency in timing principle involves the purchase of durable investments, whose services occur over time. For example, one may ask: When should the cash flow associated with the purchase of capital goods be entered in the *PV* model? When purchased? At some fixed or estimated depreciation rate? Or as repayments on a loan to finance the purchase? The same question arises on the revenue side: When should capital gains be counted as income? When the investment is sold? Or according to some fixed schedule? Further questions concern the valuation of inventories. When should changes in their value be entered in the *PV* model?

These and other questions can cause disagreements among accountants, business analysts, and economists. If these questions are not answered consistently, the construction of *PV* models will cause confusion and inconsistency.

To resolve these questions, the consistency in timing principle requires that cash returns and cash costs enter the *PV* model in the period they are received by the firm. The timing principle is important because the date a cash cost is incurred or a cash return is received alters the value of an investment. Moreover, the time at which a cash flow occurs represents a clearly defined event.

In contrast, when an investment's market value changes, it is likely the result of changes in the expectation of future net cash flows. Consequently, the time to reflect the cash flow changes is when they are experienced. To reflect them when the investment's value changes and also when the cash flows occur would be double counting. There may be, however, cash flows that occur because of changes in investment values that should be reflected. For example, if the increased value leads to increased loans and additional investments, these are summarized by the resulting cash flows. If the investment is sold, the realized value is credited as a cash flow at that time. When an investment is sold, expected changes in future cash flows are forfeited. Counting the cash flow at the time the investment is sold and not counting future cash flows avoids double counting the effect of future cash flows.

Homogenous Measures Principle

Homogenous Measures Principle: Comparisons between challengers and defenders must be made using the same units of measure.

The homogenous measures principle requires that the investment under analysis (the challenger) and the rate of return on the alternative to which it is compared (the defender) are measured in homogenous units. At least six factors in *PV* models must be considered in determining homogenous units: (1) taxes; (2) risks associated with costs and returns; (3) inflation (i.e., nominal versus real values); (4) liquidity, or nearness to cash of the returns and costs; (5) the term of the investment; and (6) the size of the investment. If, for example, the cash flows for a prospective investment are measured in after-tax nominal values with no risk over *n* years with an initial investment of V_0 dollars, then the defender whose *IRR* is used as the discount rate should be measured in similar units. That is, the cash flows of the defender should be specified in after-tax, nominal, and risk-free terms, and the size and term of the defender should resemble those of the challenger.

The importance of the homogenous measures principle is reflected in several other chapters of this book. Maintaining homogenous size and term measures is discussed in Chapter 6. Adjustments for inflation and liquidity to maintain homogenous measures are discussed in Chapter 7. Homogenous adjustments for taxes and risk are considered in Chapters 8 and 11, respectively. Examples 4.1 and 4.2 illustrate the importance of maintaining homogeneity of size and investment term when comparing defenders and challengers.

Next, consider how the homogenous size principle is applied when the firm is facing an investment possibility that, if acquired, will be financed by borrowing. It is usually the case that, when a loan is used to help finance an investment, the cash flows generated by the loan are considered part of the challenger's cash flows. Moreover, homogenous measures of size between defending and challenging

Example 4.1: Maintaining Homogeneity of Term

Tera Van Winkle must choose between two investments of different lives. Both investments initially require $100. Investment A returns $110 one period later. Investment B returns $122 two periods later. Which is preferred? Without knowing about the homogenous measures principle, Ms. Winkle might have calculated the *IRR* of investment A, r^A, as:

$$0 = -\$100 + \frac{\$110}{(1+r^A)},$$

and:

$$r^A = \frac{110}{100} - 1 = 10 \text{ percent.}$$

Then (before studying *PV* models), Ms. Winkle might have calculated the *IRR* of investment B, r^B, as:

$$0 = -\$100 + \frac{\$122}{(1+r^B)^2},$$

and:

$$r^B = \left(\frac{122}{100}\right)^{\frac{1}{2}} - 1 = 10.45 \text{ percent.}$$

But, Tera is too smart to have made such a comparison. Tera recognizes that r^A and r^B are measured over different lengths of time and must be homogenized. So, Tera determines that investment A's returns of $110 can be reinvested at 9 percent. Thus, A's *IRR* can be calculated for the same period of time as B's:

$$0 = -\$100 + \frac{\$110(1.09)}{(1+r^A)^2},$$

and:

$$r^A = \left(\frac{110(1.09)}{100}\right)^{\frac{1}{2}} - 1 = 9.5 \text{ percent} < r^B.$$

Thus, Tera invests in B.

Example 4.2: Maintaining Homogeneity of Size

Mutt N. Jeff is comparing two investments. One provides a return of 15 percent on an investment *A* of $100. Another investment, *B*, returns 12 percent on $1,000. Assume these two investments are mutually exclusive. Which investment should Mr. Jeff choose? Clearly, a 15 percent return is preferred to a 12 percent return. But Mr. Jeff cannot correctly decide which investment is preferred based on rate-of-return comparisons because the amounts invested are not equal. To make the investment comparisons, Jeff notes that he can invest $1,000 in *A* or *B* and answer the question: What will the additional $900 invested in *A* earn? Suppose it earns 10 percent. The rate of return on investment *A* is:

$$\frac{(.10)(\$900) + (.15)(\$100)}{\$1,000} = 10.5 \text{ percent},$$

which is less than the 12 percent return available from investment *B*; therefore, investment *B* is preferred.

investments financed in part by loans are maintained by requiring equal amounts of equity funds. The approach followed in this book includes the cash flow of the loan with returns earned by the challenging investment.

A possible problem of homogenous measures exists, however, when the defender and the challenger require the same equity but different amounts of loan funds. Under this condition the two investments are of unequal size and the question is: Has the principle of homogenous measures been violated?

If the firm has unlimited borrowing capacity or credit, then the opportunity cost of using up an unconstrained reserve is zero and the only cost of borrowing is the interest cost. In this case the homogenous size principle is not violated by allowing the amount of the loans to be different as long as the equity required is the same. However, if the firm's credit reserve is limited and its liquidity value increases as the firm's credit reserve is reduced, then borrowing creates a cost to the firm equal to its interest cost plus a liquidity premium. In this case differential amounts of loans violate the homogenous measures principle unless the differential opportunity costs of different sizes of loans are included in the analysis of the loan. To account for this differential effect created by borrowing different amounts, the cost of borrowings should include a liquidity premium (see Example 4.3). The

Example 4.3: Calculating *NPV*s with Different Loan Amounts

Houses Rus is a large housing construction company. It is considering the construction of a large executive style home on a wooded lot. The cost of the lot plus the cost of construction would equal $350,000.00. Alternatively, Houses Rus could build two middle-income homes on the same lot at a cost of $150,000.00 each. Houses Rus expects to sell the executive style home immediately after construction is completed for $406,000.00. Alternatively, it could sell the two middle-income homes immediately after construction for $344,250.00.

Regardless of which option Houses Rus selects, it intends to invest $50,000.00 of its equity and borrow the rest. The interest cost of borrowing is 11 percent. Houses Rus calculates the liquidity value of its credit reserve to be 1 percent for the first $100,000.00 borrowed, 2 percent for any amount borrowed between $100,000.00 and $200,000.00, and 3 percent for any amount borrowed between $200,000.00 and $300,000.00.

If Houses Rus builds the large executive style home, it will be required to borrow $300,000.00. The interest cost for the construction period for such a loan is:

$$\$100,000(0.12) + \$100,000(0.13) + \$100,000(0.14) = \$39,000.00.$$

If Houses Rus builds the two middle-income homes, it will borrow $250,000.00 at an interest cost for the construction period of:

$$\$100,000(.12) + \$100,000.00(.13) + \$50,000.00(.14) = \$32,000.$$

To rank the two investments Houses Rus calculates their respective *IRR*s. The *IRR* of the executive style home can be found by solving r in the equation:

$$0 = -\$50,000 + \frac{\$406,000 - \$39,000 - \$300,000}{1+r},$$

and:

$$r = \frac{\$67,000}{\$50,000} - 1 = 34 \text{ percent}.$$

Example 4.3, Cont'd.: Calculating *NPV*s with Different Loan Amounts

The *NPV* for the two middle-income houses is calculated to be:

$$NPV = -\$50,000 + \frac{\$344,250 - \$32,000 - \$250,000}{(1.34)} = -\$3,544.78.$$

Based on the *PV* model results, Houses Rus goes ahead with plans to build the executive style house.

liquidity premium for the most part captures the effect of borrowing differential amounts while preserving the homogenous measures principle.

Finally, consider the extreme case where there is only one investment that, if acquired, must be financed 100 percent. In this case the defender is the loan and the appropriate *IRR* of the defender is the interest rate plus a liquidity premium.

Life of the Investment Principle

Life of the Investment Principle: Investments must be constructed with a term equal to the economic life of the investment.

The fourth principle for evaluating *PV* models considers the proper length of time for measuring an investment's cash returns and costs. The economic life of an investment is the number of periods in which the investment generates nonzero cash flows. To see why the length of the time period matters, consider an investment with a potentially infinite economic life, such as land, in which a constant return of R is earned in each time period. If r is the appropriate discount rate, then the present value of this infinite stream of earnings is:

$$V_0 = \frac{R}{(1+r)} + \frac{R}{(1+r)^2} + \ldots = \frac{R}{r}. \tag{4.4}$$

Now suppose the decision maker intends to hold the investment for a finite number of periods, n, after which it will be exchanged for its cash equivalent. The acquisition value, V_0, can now be related to r, R, n, and the sale price, V_n, as:

$$V_0 = \frac{R}{(1+r)} + \dots + \frac{R}{(1+r)^n} + \frac{V_n}{(1+r)^n}. \tag{4.5}$$

But how does one determine a value for the investment at age n, V_n? In some cases, such as the price of a bond or by prior agreement, the investment's future price is known. When the future price is not known, it should be set equal to the present value of all projected income to be received after period n, discounted back to period n.[1] So the value for V_n can be written as:

$$V_n = \frac{R}{(1+r)} + \frac{R}{(1+r)^2} + \dots \tag{4.6}$$

But if equation (4.6) were substituted for V_n in equation (4.5), the result would be the original model in equation (4.4), and the number of periods in the model would be equal to the economic life of the investment. Thus, unless the salvage value is predetermined, PV models must be constructed with a term equal to the economic life of the investment.

For decision-making purposes, in period zero, an economically-relevant length of planning horizon (given the level of the discount rate) is long enough that the investment can take on any terminal value without significantly affecting its present value. That is, if the discount rate is sufficiently high and the terminal value occurs far enough in the future, then the present values of changes in the terminal value are essentially zero—and such changes can be ignored for decision-making purposes. The economically-relevant length of the planning horizon is especially important in evaluating long-term public projects and is further considered in Chapters 6 and 21.

Sometimes an investment's future value, V_n, is assumed to equal the present value, V_0. This results in the expression:

$$V_0 = \frac{R}{(1+r)} + \dots + \frac{R}{(1+r)^n} + \frac{V_0}{(1+r)^n} = \frac{R}{r}, \tag{4.7}$$

as obtained earlier. In this special case, V_0 is equal to V_n only if R is a constant income series. Another way of explaining this result is that the earnings expected by the future owner are the same as those expected by the existing owner. Substituting V_0 for V_n, however, would not generally be acceptable, especially when transactions costs are paid or when the income or cost series follows an irregular pattern.

The "Life of the Investment" principle eliminates the need to reassess the value of the investment in future time periods. It correctly links the *PV* of the investment to the investment's expected returns and costs. In some cases, however, an assessment of an investment's value at regular future intervals may be required. If, for example, annual property tax payments depend on the land's value in the previous period, the land's value must be assessed each period.

An evaluation should maintain consistency with the stream of future returns received after the reevaluation date. To illustrate, consider the case where initial cash returns R_0 are inflating at an inflation rate i and property tax must be paid each period on the investment's current market value. The infinite series that equates the investment's future returns back to the present can be written as:

$$V_0 = \frac{(1+i)\,R_0}{(1+r^*)(1+i)} + \frac{(1+i)^2\,R_0}{[(1+r^*)(1+i)]^2} + \ldots = \frac{R_0}{r^*}, \tag{4.8}$$

where r^* is the real rate or the inflation adjusted discount rate. Since the $(1+i)$ terms in the numerator and the discount factor cancel out, the result is the familiar constant value model. So, in the current period, inflation does not change the investment's market value.

Now suppose the value of the investment is being determined j periods later. The model would then be:

$$V_j = \frac{(1+i)^{j+1}R_0}{(1+r^*)(1+i)} + \frac{(1+i)^{j+2}R_0}{[(1+r^*)(1+i)]^2} + \ldots = \frac{(1+i)^j R_0}{r^*}. \tag{4.9}$$

Then, substituting V_0 for R_0/r^*, the expression for V_j can be written as:

$$V_j = V_0(1+i)^j. \tag{4.10}$$

Thus, the market value in future periods equals its initial value, inflated by the factor $(1+i)^j$.

A similar result would occur for an investment with returns that depreciate over time. For example, consider a durable whose returns declined at the rate of d percent per period.[2] Then, the durable's initial value is:

$$V_0 = \frac{R_0(1-d)}{(1+r)} + \frac{R_0(1-d)^2}{(1+r)^2} + \ldots = \frac{R_0(1-d)}{(r+d)}, \tag{4.11}$$

and *j* periods later, the investment's value at age *t+j* can be written as:

$$V_j = V_0(1-d)^j. \tag{4.12}$$

In this case, the current value of the investment has depreciated. In Chapter 8, we will show how depreciation is used as a tax shield.

It is not clear how the pattern of change in investment values would be altered by periodic payments such as receipt of capital gains, sales commissions, and other transactions costs associated with investment sales. Thus, consistency between the reevaluation of the investment and the return streams only applies to one ownership period. Each transfer of the investment would create a new base value for reevaluating the investment over time. Every time an investment is traded and sales commissions and capital gains taxes are paid, the investment's taxable basis should be adjusted.

The life of the investment principle is in reality an application of "rational expectations." Rather than assuming that expectations of prices are formed adaptively from past experiences, the rational expectations are based on expectations of future events which are, of course, the relevant factors determining a future investment's worth (e.g., Muth).

The important point here is that *PV* models require that attention be given to the cash flows over the economic life of the investment. Even if the investment is traded before its economic life is exhausted, expectations about its cash flows after the sale must be explored to determine its sale price.

Total Costs and Returns Principle —————————————————

Total Costs and Returns Principle: The total costs and returns principle states that all cash costs and returns linked to the ownership or control of a durable should be included when determining its present value.

Consider how the total costs and returns principle is applied in several practical problems. Whenever low interest loans or preferential tax treatments are tied to the ownership of a durable, these concessions will influence the value of the durable, along with the other cash flows generated by the durable. In real estate, while tax assessors and other interested parties prefer to determine a durable's value independent of its financing arrangements, for others, the maximum bid (minimum sell) price is influenced by the financing arrangements. Other considerations, as well as financial instruments tied to the ownership of the investment, affect *PV* models. Sometimes an investment such as land has more than one source of return. Mineral deposits, potential recreational use, and urbanization pressures may create expected returns over and above those associated with agricultural use. Pollution standards may impose costs in addition to those normally experienced. All the costs and returns just described that influence the value of the durable should be included in the *PV* model:

In some cases, land purchased for recreational use does not generate an explicit cash return for its owners. In this case, the expenditures on recreation at other sites are avoided because of land ownership. The saved cash expense could be counted as revenue. In this way, all of the revenues and costs of the project are still counted even though the recreational services of the project are not sold. Thus, the land's value is at least worth the foregone value of the recreational services at another site, and probably more; otherwise, the investment would not have occurred.

This view is consistent with the "project analysis" view of *PV* models. That is, investments with interdependent effects (such as financial arrangements and capital gains taxes) should be considered together as a project (Schall and Haley).

Geometric Mean Principle

Geometric Mean Principle: The proper index for representing the opportunity cost of the defender is its *IRR* or the geometric mean of the defender's earnings.

The geometric mean is a measure associated with products. The geometric mean of a product of *n* numbers is that number which, if multiplied by itself *n* times, equals the original product. For example, geometric mean of the product $(1+r_1)(1+r_2)...(1+r_n)$ equals:

$$[(1+r_1)(1+r_2)...(1+r_n)] = (1+r)^n. \tag{4.13}$$

One plus the defender's *IRR* is equal to the geometric mean of the defender's cash flows. The geometric mean of the defender's cash flows or one plus the defender's *IRR* is also the proper measure to discount the challenger's cash flows in an *NPV* model.

The geometric mean of the defender's cash flows is the proper index of the defender's economic value for the following reasons. First, an investment of V_0

that earns at the geometric mean $(1+r)$ for n periods will equal $V_0(1+r)^n$ or V_n. By investing V_0 at the largest possible geometric mean $(1+r)$, V_n is maximized.

A second reason why the geometric mean is the preferred index of the defender's economic value is that the time required to earn a specific amount, say $\hat{V}$, is minimized by investing an amount V_0 at the largest possible geometric mean. For example, in the equation, $\hat{V} = V_0(1+r)^n$, as $r>0$ increases, n, the time required for V_0 to increase to $\hat{V}$ is decreased.

Next, consider some important characteristics of geometric means. Suppose a fund V_0 is reinvested for n periods at rates $r_i = r + \alpha_i$, $i = 1,2,...n$ so that the value of the fund n periods later equals:

$$V_n = V_0(1 + r + \alpha_1)(1 + r + \alpha_2)...(1 + r + \alpha_n).$$

The question is: What values of $\alpha_1,...,\alpha_n$ subject to the constraint that $\alpha_1 + \alpha_2 + ... + \alpha_n = \beta$ maximize the geometric mean of the products $(1+r+\alpha_1)(1+r+\alpha_2)...(1+r+\alpha_n)$? The answer is: $\alpha_1 = \alpha_2 = ... = \alpha_n = \beta/n$ maximize the geometric means. This result is illustrated in Example 4.4.

Important decisions involve the allocation of the firm's resources to its "portfolio" or collections of investments. Suppose the firm has an amount V_0/n invested in n independent investments that earn $(1+\bar{r}+\alpha_i)$ where $i = 1, 2,..., n$. If the funds are invested for m periods, what values of $\alpha_i > 0$ subject to $\alpha_1 + \alpha_2 + ... + \alpha_n = \beta$ maximize the geometric mean of the firm's investment portfolio? The relationship is described mathematically as:

$$V_0(1+r)^m = [(1+\bar{r}+\alpha_1)^m + (1+\bar{r}+\alpha_2)^m + ... + (1+\bar{r}+\alpha_n)^m](V_0/n).$$

The values of α_i that maximize $(1+r)$ or the geometric mean of the portfolio are $\alpha_j = \beta$ and $\alpha_i = 0$ for $i = 1, 2,..., j-1, j+1,..., n$. Example 4.5 illustrates the investment problem just described.

Summary

Comparing and contrasting objects is an important step in describing and learning about the world around us. *PV* models are constructed with a specific comparison in mind: the comparison between a defending and a challenging investment.

In ordinary life, we take steps to avoid making irrelevant comparisons. For example, comparing the running speed of a chicken and the take-off speed of a Boeing 747 airplane is not likely to yield interesting data about the length of a

Example 4.4: Geometric and Arithmetic Mean Comparison

The Savings and Blown Association (SBA) of Sagebrush, Texas is choosing between two 12-year investment alternatives. One of the investments earns a constant rate of return of 12 percent in each period. The alternative investment earns 6 percent for six years and 18 percent for six years. The one dollar in the first investment at the end of 12 years equals:

$$\$1(1.12)^{12} = \$3.90.$$

Thus, for each dollar (SBA) invests, it receives \$3.90 at the end of 12 years and the geometric mean is 12 percent. The alternative investment does less well:

$$\$1(1.06)^6 (1.18)^6 = \$3.83,$$

returning only \$3.83 per dollar invested. The geometric mean for this investment equals 11.84 percent.

A third alternative has an even greater dispersion; earning 3 percent for six years and 21 percent for six years. After 12 years, it returns per dollar:

$$\$1(1.03)^6 (1.21)^6 = \$3.75.$$

The geometric mean for this investment is 11.64 percent.

runway needed for take-off of either the chicken or the plane. Or, comparing the average height of the Los Angeles Lakers basketball team and the sixth-grade girls basketball team at Kinawa Middle School will not likely help predict the Lakers' win/loss record.

In a similar way, we must take care in the construction of *PV* models so that the comparison between challengers and defenders can be used to determine correct investment decisions. To this end, six construction principles were introduced. These include: (1) the cash flow principle; (2) the consistency in timing principle; (3) the homogenous measures principle; (4) the life of the investment principle; (5) the total costs and returns principle; and (6) the geometric mean principle. The remainder of this book will employ these principles and concepts, and demonstrate their application in the construction and analysis of *PV* models.

Example 4.5: Portfolios and Geometric Means

Folio Port has two branch stores in which he has invested an equal amount of funds. By focusing equal attention on both stores he will earn at the geometric rate of 1.12 at both stores. After 12 years, on every dollar invested, Folio will earn $3.90.

On the other hand, if Folio spends more of his time managing store one, the geometric mean return at store one will increase 6 percentage points to 1.18 and will drop by 6 percentage points to 1.06 at store two where he would spend less time. By differentiating his time between stores, after 12 years Folio will earn on every dollar invested the sum:

$$\$.5(1.18)^{12} + \$.5(1.06)^{12} = \$3.64 + \$1.01 = \$4.65,$$

or $.75 more per dollar than he would if he had allocated his time equally to his two stores. Furthermore, the geometric means of this differentiated effort equals 13.7 percent, an increase of 1.7 percent in the geometric mean over the previous investment.

Endnotes

1. It may be that neither salvage value nor future cash flows are known. In which case the model should be constructed using the best estimates of future cash flows so that the implied salvage value is consistent with assumptions about future earnings.

2. To show that R_t declines at the rate d, calculate:

$$\frac{R_t - R_t(1-d)}{R_t} = d.$$

Review Questions

1. Explain how p, p_x, and r convert physical measures at different points in time to a consistent unit of measure in equations (4.2) and (4.3). What are the consistent units of measure in equations (4.2) and (4.3)?

2. Defend the consistency of timing principle. If one were to convert cash flows to their equivalent value in future periods by compounding them at the

discount rate, does the compounding violate the consistency in timing principle? If not, please explain why not.

3. Describe the homogenous measures required to compare challengers and defenders using *PV* models. Suggest how investment rankings might be altered if homogenous measures are not used.

4. Describe how the homogenous measures principle could help you decide whether or not the discount rate should be adjusted for taxes.

5. What principle for constructing *PV* models is violated with the payback model? (See Chapter 2 for a discussion of the payback model.)

6. Indicate whether you agree or disagree with the following statement and defend your answer:

> Because capital gains are not a cash return until liquidated,
> capital gains should not be included in *PV* models until the
> period they are expected to be liquidated.

7. Explain why the evaluation of the contributions of individual durables may be difficult to find for projects in which the services of many durables contribute to the product. How does the total costs and returns method suggest the evaluation be conducted?

8. Explain how *PV* models use geometric means to compare defending and challenging investments.

Application Questions

1. Defend the violation of the homogeneity of timing principle when the time-dated cash flows are converted to their equivalent worth (by discounting or compounding) and then entering them in the *PV* model in periods other than those in which they occurred.

2. Boxers and wrestlers are matched by weights; that is, they are only required to face opponents of nearly equal weight. University athletic teams are divided into conferences based on the size of the student body, reflecting similar talent pools from which teams are selected. How are efforts in athletics to provide comparisons between nearly equal competitors analogous to the application of the homogenous measures principle in the construction of *PV* models? (Hint: You might approach the question by stating the difficulty of determining which wrestler is best in a match in which one wrestler weighs much more than his opponent.)

3. For some investment project that utilizes the services of several durables, what guidelines can be provided for valuing the durables contributing to the project? Can they be valued individually or must they be valued collectively?

4. Suppose the contribution of a particular input (say land, labor, or management), is valued residually even though its usefulness is clearly dependent on the contributions of other durables. How does this approach violate the total returns and costs approach?

5. An investor must calculate *NPV* for a particular investment. To finance the investment, the firm must borrow at an interest rate of 12 percent. Moreover, the firm faces no effective credit limits. The net cash flow in real dollars associated with the investment will be $400 for each of the next 10 years. At the end of the 10th year, the firm intends to sell the investment and the owner will invest the sale proceeds in an investment alternative that will yield $50 per year in nominal dollars for 10 years. At age 20 years, the durable disintegrates into an invisible humus with no salvage value or disposal costs.

    If the general rate of inflation that is included in the borrowing rate is 6 percent and ignoring taxes, please do the following: build the *NPV* model to analyze the investment described above. At each step of the construction process, indicate which of the six *PV* construction principles is being applied.

6. Discuss which of the six consistency principles identified in this chapter helps resolve the model-building problems identified below:

    (a) A particular investment will be funded by liquidating a firm's tax-free securities. The challenging investment creates a significant tax shield. What is the appropriate discount rate to use in evaluating the project?

    (b) A firm is considering investing in an off-site sewage disposal unit. While the treatment plant offers no direct benefit to the firm, it will likely promote the good will to allow the firm to expand its livestock enterprise from which the firm could expect to earn an additional $50,000 per year in net cash flows over a 10-year period. Should the expected net cash flows be included in the evaluation of the sewage treatment plant or in evaluating the livestock addition? Or is there another investment analysis that should be followed?

    (c) A firm is constructing a building that will be used intensively for eight years and then will be abandoned. There is no anticipated buyer for the abandoned building. What is an appropriate defender to compare with this investment?

7. Suppose you must evaluate an investment in land that has an intrinsic value independent of the cash flows it generates. Such an intrinsic value might be tied to pride of ownership, recreational value, etc. Should the intrinsic value be included in the investment's *PV* equation? If so, how should it be calculated? What consistency principle would help answer this question?

8. Suppose you have a safe investment that requires a six-year commitment and earns $r^s=12$ percent. An alternative investment earns with equal probability 6

percent or 18 percent per year. The annual returns are independent over the course of the six-year commitment. Calculate its expected return of r^y. Finally, a third investment alternative requires you to allocate investment funds between two joint investments, one which earns 6 percent and the second 18 percent for six years. Calculate its rate of return r^d. Please rank these investment choices.

9.   A one-period investment that earns R_1 requires $1,000 of equity and $5,000 of debt at an interest rate of 10 percent. Alternatively, the investment can be financed (for tax purposes) by a land contract offered by the seller. If the latter option is accepted, the price of the investment increases to $6,200 but the loan of $5,200 required for the purchase will be offered by the seller at a reduced interest rate of 6.5 percent. Which loan plan is preferred? What must you assume about the credit reserve to solve this problem?

References

Aplin, R.D., G.L. Casler, and C.P. Francis. *Capital Investment Analysis: Using Discounted Cash Flows*, 3rd edition. Columbus, OH: Grid Publishers, 1984.

Aukes, R. "Double Counting Agricultural Income." *Canadian Journal of Agricultural Economics* 35(1987):463-79.

Barry, P.J. "Double Counting Agricultural Income: A Comment." *Canadian Journal of Agricultural Economics* 36(1988):353-56.

Barry, P.J., P.N. Ellinger, J.A. Hopkin, and C.B. Baker. *Financial Management in Agriculture*, 5th edition. Danville, IL: The Interstate Publishers, Inc., 1995.

Bierman, H., Jr. and S. Smidt. *The Capital Budgeting Decision*, 4th edition. New York: Macmillan Publishing Company, Inc., 1975.

Bodenhorn, D. "A Cash Flow Concept of Profit." *Journal of Finance* 19(1964):16-31.

Klemme, R.M. and R.A. Schoney. "Economic Analysis of Land Bid Prices Using Profitability and Cash Flow Considerations in Finite Planning Horizons." *North Central Journal of Agricultural Economics* 6(1984):117-27.

Lee, T.A. *Income and Value Measurement*, 2nd edition. Baltimore: University Park Press, 1980.

Muth, J.F. "Rational Expectations and the Theory of Price Movement." *Econometrica* (July 1961):315-35.

Robison, L.J. and W.G. Burghardt. *Five Principles for Building Present Value Models and Their Application to Maximum (Minimum) Bid (Sell) Price Models for Land*. Michigan Agricultural Experiment Station Journal Article No. 11051, November 1983.

Schall, L.D. and C.W. Haley. *Introduction to Financial Management*, 3rd edition. New York: McGraw-Hill Book Company, 1983.

Van Horne, J.C. *Fundamentals of Financial Management*, 4th edition. Englewood Cliffs, NJ: Prentice-Hall, Inc., 1980.

Chapter 5

Geometric Series and Present Value Models

Key words: convex decay pattern, geometric decay series, geometric factor, geometric growth series, geometric series, idleness models, light bulb model, linear cash flow pattern, quadratic income patterns, series with repeatable cycles, uniform series.

Introduction

Present value (PV) models can be described numerically for specific investment problems. In these cases, a specific investment is represented and numerically evaluated. In other applications of present value models, the problem may be less specific. For example, one might ask: "How will the present value of farmland change if the income tax rate is raised?" In this case, the focus is on farmland in general, not on the valuation of a specific tract of land. The answer must be more general than a specific number. It involves the qualitative relationships between changes in asset values and changes in the income tax rate.

Algebraic expressions for PV models can be used to summarize relationships between variables. Comparative static analysis can then be performed, leading to testable hypotheses. Projections of future asset values, estimates of present value, and responses of asset values to changes in key variables are easier to estimate using simplified algebraic expressions of the model. Also, qualitative relationships can be more easily checked than numbers not related to each other in a systematic way.

Algebraic expressions of present value models also help to check the consistency of model construction. Errors in logic are more easily found in an analytic form than in a numeric form. Algebraic present value models may be used when the data are inadequate. Finally, algebraic expressions of *PV* models may lead to simplified "rules of thumb." An example is the capitalization formula, where net cash return divided by the real interest rate is used to estimate land values.

This chapter shows how to obtain simplified algebraic expressions for several present value models whose cash flows are related to each other in systematic ways. Examples are constant, geometric, linear, cyclical, and convex decay cash flow patterns. Later chapters will use algebraic expressions of these *PV* models to answer general questions involving relationships among variables. A widely used algebraic expression is the present value of an annuity, calculated in most finance textbooks and programmed on most business calculators.

Geometric Shapes of Earnings Series

The present value models derived in this chapter represent specific assumptions about the earnings of an asset over time. Nine specific series are evaluated: (1) a uniform series; (2) a geometric growth series; (3) a geometric decay series; (4) a linear growth series; (5) a linear decay series; (6) a convex decay series; (7) combined growth and decay series; (8) a repeatable cycle series; and (9) an alternating activity and idleness series. The time paths of earnings for cases 1 through 6 are shown in Figure 5.1. The time paths for cases 7, 8 and 9 are shown in Figures 5.2, 5.3, and 5.4, respectively.

The Geometric Series and Its Sum

Compact algebraic relationships between present and future cash flows can be easily obtained if the terms in the cash flows series are geometrically related. Fortunately, in a wide variety of present value models, the relationships among cash flows over time can be described as geometric series.

In this chapter, we show how to sum geometric series in discrete time period models and demonstrate conditions under which the sum can be used for analytic purposes. The present value tools are then applied to selected problems.

A series of the form:

$$V_0 = Rb + Rb^2 + Rb^3 + \ldots + Rb^n, \tag{5.1}$$

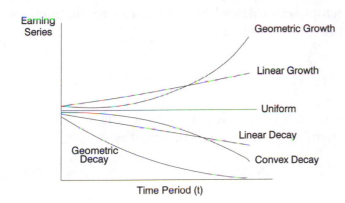

Figure 5.1
Alternative Specifications of
an Asset's Earnings Series

is called a geometric series where V_0 is the sum of the geometric series. In a geometric series, some factor multiplied by the tth term produces the $(t+1)^{st}$ term. In this case, the term b is called the geometric factor of the series described in equation (5.1). The term R is a constant. A geometric series has a well-defined sum under either of two conditions. The first condition is satisfied when the series is of finite length and each term in the series is of finite size. The second condition is satisfied when each term of the series is of finite size and the sum of the series approaches a limit.

If a series approaches a well-defined sum as additional terms in the series are added, the series is said to converge. This condition implies that, for geometric series defined over long time periods, the present values of future terms are approaching zero. Thus, the condition implies the restriction: $-1<b<1$. The case of b less than or equal to -1 is ruled out, since the sum would oscillate between increasingly positive and negative values without converging. The case of b equal to or greater than 1 is also ruled out because the sum of (5.1) does not converge when b equals 1, and when n is large.

Uniform or Constant Series

A specific example of a geometric series is the uniform series. Consider a uniform or constant cash flow, R, received from an investment for n periods and discounted at r percent. The relationship is expressed as:

$$V_0 = \frac{R}{(1+r)} + \frac{R}{(1+r)^2} + \dots + \frac{R}{(1+r)^n}. \tag{5.2}$$

The geometric factor, b, in equation (5.2) is $1/(1+r)$, and since we normally assume $r>0$, then $0<b<1$, and the series converges.

The uniform or constant return series described in (5.2) can be summed by multiplying both sides of (5.2) by $(1+r)$ to obtain:

$$V_0(1+r) = R + \frac{R}{(1+r)} + \dots + \frac{R}{(1+r)^{n-1}}. \tag{5.3}$$

Next, equation (5.2) is subtracted from (5.3). All but the first term on the right-hand side of (5.3) and the last term of (5.2) cancel. The result is:

$$V_0(1+r) - V_0 = R - R(1+r)^{-n}. \tag{5.4}$$

Further manipulation yields:

$$V_0 = \frac{R[1-(1+r)^{-n}]}{r}. \tag{5.5}$$

If n becomes large and $r>0$, then (5.5) reduces to:

$$\lim_{n \to \infty} V_0 = \frac{R}{r}. \tag{5.6}$$

The present value models in (5.5) and (5.6) are widely used in financial analysis. They are equivalent, yet simplified expressions of equation (5.2), and they were derived under the assumption of a uniform series of returns (or costs) that is finite in the case of (5.5) and infinite (or perpetual) in the case of (5.6).

Since the series described by (5.2) and (5.5) will be utilized often, it is assigned the simplified notation:

$$V_0 = \frac{R[1-(1+r)^{-n}]}{r} = R\,US_0(r, n), \tag{5.7}$$

where $US_0(r,n)$ represents the conversion factor for a uniform series of returns, R, given the discount rate, r, and the number of periods, n.

To facilitate the calculation of $US_0(r,n)$, alternative values r and n are tabled in most financial and capital budgeting texts. Tabled values for $US_0(r,n)$ appear in Appendix 1 at the end of this text. The sums in Appendix 1 correspond to equation (5.5) with R set equal to one. Popular business calculators can also be used to automatically compute $US_0(r,n)$ once the user specifies r and n, and sets R equal to one.

To help understand problems that require $US_0(r,n)$ values, a small excerpt from Appendix 1 is shown below. In this text, interest rates are expressed as decimals. In Table 5.1 and in Appendix 1, they are expressed as percentages. The other notation of interest is to recognize r as an annual rate. To convert to a part-of-a-year interest rate, r is divided by m to obtain r/m. Thus, a monthly annuity would be expressed as $US_0(r/12,12n)$, and in general $US_0(r/m,mn)$.

First, turn to Appendix 1 and locate the excerpt displayed in Table 5.1. Note that as the interest rate per period increases, the discounted present value of the sum decreases. For example, a series of 13 payments of $1 discounted first at 9 percent and then at 10 percent has its present value decreased from $7.4869 to $7.1034 in Table 5.1. On the other hand, increasing the number of payments from 13 to 14 and holding the interest rate constant at 11 percent raises the present value from $6.7499 to $6.9819.

An important use of Appendix 1 involves solutions to problems requiring the unknown term (n) or finding an unknown interest rate (r). For example, if you were told that $US_0(r,14)$ equalled 7.3667, then by scanning the row with n equal to term 14, you could determine what column corresponded to the value of 7.3667. An interest rate of 10 percent corresponds to the column value of 7.3667.

On the other hand, suppose that $US_0(.11,n)$ were equal to 7.1909. First, locate 7.1909 in the column labeled 11 percent in Appendix 1. Then, scan the

Table 5.1 Present Value of a Uniform Series of Payments, $US_0(r,n)$

n	. . .	9.00%	10.00%	11.00%	. . .
. . .					
13		7.4869	7.1034	6.7499	
14		7.7862	7.3667	6.9819	
15		8.0607	7.6061	7.1909	
. . .					

Source: Appendix 1.

values for n corresponding to an r value of 11 percent and a value of $US_0(.11,n)$ corresponding to 7.1909. In this case, the n value would be 15. These calculations can, of course, be performed with even greater accuracy using handheld business calculators; however, the principle is the same. This background helps in solving a wide variety of PV problems such as the one illustrated in Example 5.1.

Example 5.1: Present Value of a Uniform Series

Lot O. Luck won a lottery ticket that pays six annual payments of $1,500 each. Assuming Lot's opportunity cost of capital is 10 percent, what is the present value of his inheritance? Letting NPV represent the net present value of his inheritance, Lot writes:

$$NPV = \frac{\$1,500}{(1.10)} + \frac{\$1,500}{(1.10)^2} + \frac{\$1,500}{(1.10)^3} + \frac{\$1,500}{(1.10)^4} + \frac{\$1,500}{(1.10)^5} + \frac{\$1,500}{(1.10)^6}$$

$$= \$1,363.64 + \$1,239.67 + \$1,126.97 + \$1,024.52 + \$931.38 + \$846.71$$

$$= \$6,532.89.$$

A simpler approach, however, would be to identify the geometric factor and the constant of the series and substitute them into the formula $US_0(r,n)$. The constant R is $1,500, r is 10 percent, and n is 6. Then, referring to Appendix 1, $US_0(.10,6)$ is found to equal 4.3553. Substituting these values for R and $US_0(r,n)$ into (5.7), we find:

$$V_0 = R\,US_0(r,n) = (\$1,500)(4.3553) = \$6,532.89.$$

Next, suppose Lot is to receive 12 payments instead of six. Will the present value of his inheritance double? Again, using the formula:

$$V_0 = R\,US_0(r,n) = \$1,500\ US_0(.10,12) = (\$1,500)(6.8137) = \$10,220.54.$$

Doubling the number of years does not double the NPV of Lot's inheritance because the longer Lot waits for payments, the less value they are to him at present.

Generalizing the Uniform Series Model

The general availability of tabled values and calculators to compute $US_0(r,n)$ makes it convenient to use the same tools for computing values for other geometric series besides that of the special form of (5.2). To express the geometric series $Rb+Rb^2+...+Rb^n$ in the $US_0(r,n)$ notation, we must first find the relationship between the geometric factor, b, in (5.1) and the geometric factor, $1/(1+r)$, in equation (5.2).

The relationship between b and r can be found by solving for r in the expression:

$$\frac{1}{(1+r)} = b,$$

which equals:

$$r = \frac{(1-b)}{b}. \tag{5.8}$$

Replacing r with $(1-b)/b$ allows us to write the sum of the geometric series described by (5.1) in $US_0(r,n)$ notation. Thus:

$$Rb + Rb^2 + ... + Rb^n = R\,US_0\left[\frac{(1-b)}{b}, n\right]. \tag{5.9}$$

Moreover, for an infinite geometric series, we replace r with $(1-b)/b$ to obtain:

$$Rb + Rb^2 + ... = \frac{Rb}{(1-b)}. \tag{5.10}$$

The solution to any geometric series can be written as (5.9) when n is finite or (5.10) when n is very large. Only the geometric factor, b, and the constant, R, in the series must be identified.

Example 5.2 illustrates a problem with a series of payments that begin in the present period.

Geometric Growth and Decay Series

Now consider the sum of a geometric series in which the income pattern is not constant, but is subject to a systematic rate of change. Specifically, the income is expected to grow or decline at constant rates, g and d, respectively.

Example 5.2: Present Value of a Lease with Constant Payments

Lucy owns and manages Lug'em and Leave'em, a freight business. She asks: What is the present cost of leasing a trailer for $2,500 a month for 12 months with the first payment due when the lease is signed? She calculates her opportunity cost of capital at the annual percentage rate of 12 percent or 1 percent per month. Then, V_0 equals:

$$V_0 = \$2,500 + \frac{\$2,500}{(1.01)} + \frac{\$2,500}{(1.01)^2} + \ldots + \frac{\$2,500}{(1.01)^{11}}$$

$$= \$2,500 + \$2,500 \ US_0 \ (.01,11)$$

$$= \$28,419.07,$$

where the constant term, R, in the series equals $2,500, n equals 11, and r is 1 percent.

Suppose, for example, that the durable's return at age t is represented by R_t where variable t distinguishes between cash flows at different ages of the durable. If the series grows at a constant rate g, then it would satisfy the expression:

$$\frac{R_{t+1} - R_t}{R_t} = g > 0, \tag{5.11}$$

or, if it declines at constant rate d, then it would satisfy:

$$\frac{R_{t+1} - R_t}{R_t} = -d < 0. \tag{5.12}$$

These restrictions are satisfied by the geometric growth series in which $R_t = R_0(1+g)^t$ and for the geometric decay series $R_t = R_0(1-d)^t$. This model can be used to describe the net present value of a savings account in which R_0 is invested in the beginning and is withdrawn along with accumulated interest in period t. If r is the discount rate and g is the rate of interest accumulation, V_0 is written as:

$$V_0 = -R_0 + \frac{R_0(1+g)^t}{(1+r)^t}. \tag{5.13}$$

In a more general geometric growth model, R_0 might increase in each period at the rate of g percent. This model might represent enterprises such as orchards which improve over some life with age or common stock of a company projecting dividend growth over time. Whatever the reason for expecting the return series to increase, the geometric growth series is represented as:

$$V_0 = \frac{R_0(1+g)}{(1+r)} + \frac{R_0(1+g)^2}{(1+r)^2} + \dots + \frac{R_0(1+g)^n}{(1+r)^n}. \tag{5.14}$$

The geometric factor b in this equation is $(1+g)/(1+r)$. The solution to equation (5.14) requires a solution for:

$$\frac{(1-b)}{b} = \frac{\left[1 - \frac{(1+g)}{(1+r)}\right]}{\left[\frac{(1+g)}{(1+r)}\right]} = \frac{(r-g)}{(1+g)}. \tag{5.15}$$

Now, the solution to equation (5.14) can be written as:

$$V_0 = R_0 \, US_0 \left[\frac{(r-g)}{(1+g)}, n\right]. \tag{5.16}$$

The requirement for convergence is that:

$$-1 < b = \frac{(1+g)}{(1+r)} < 1,$$

and $g<r$.

Assuming this condition is met, the limit of V_0 is written as:

$$\lim_{n \to \infty} V_0 = \frac{R_0 b}{(1-b)} = \frac{R_0(1+g)}{r-g}. \tag{5.17}$$

Having illustrated a geometric growth model with a constant rate of growth, we now illustrate the solution for a geometric decay model with a constant rate of decay. A geometric decay model with a constant rate of decline is expressed as:

$$V_0 = \frac{R_0(1-d)}{1+r} + \frac{R_0(1-d)^2}{(1+r)^2} + \dots \frac{R_0(1-d)^n}{(1+r)^n}. \tag{5.18}$$

Example 5.3: Present Value of a Geometric Growth Series

Sunshine Shades and Hats is a major distributor of sunglasses. Last year, the Company paid a dividend of $3 a share. Shareholders expect this dividend to grow steadily at 6 percent per year for the next six years. At the end of the six-year period, *SSH* stock is expected to sell for $50 a share.

If the required rate of return on *SSH* stock is 12 percent, what should be the market price of *SSH* stock? If V_0 is the market price of *SSH* stock, then:

$$V_0 = \frac{\$3\,(1.06)}{(1.12)} + \frac{\$3(1.06)^2}{(1.12)^2} + \dots + \frac{\$3(1.06)^6}{(1.12)^6} + \frac{\$50}{(1.12)^6}$$

$$= V_0^a + V_0^b,$$

where:

$$V_0^a = \frac{\$3(1.06)}{(1.12)} + \dots + \frac{\$3(1.06)^6}{(1.12)^6},$$

and:

$$V_0^b = \frac{\$50}{(1.12)^6}.$$

Since dividends are growing at 6 percent, the present value of the dividends can be expressed (see equation (5.16)) as:

$$V_0^a = RUS_0\left[\frac{r-g}{1+g}, n\right],$$

where:

$$\frac{(r-g)}{(1+g)} = \frac{0.12-0.06}{1.06} = 5.66 \text{ percent.}$$

Then, since $n=6$ years and $R_0=\$3$:

$$V_0^a = \$3\ US_0(.0566,6) = (\$3)(4.9703) = \$14.91.$$

The discounted value of the future sale price of the stock equals:

$$V_0^b = \frac{\$50}{(1.12)^6} = \$25.33,$$

and the value of *SSH* stock, V_0 is: $V_0 = V_0^a + V_0^b = \$14.91 + \$25.33 = \$40.24.$

Following the same procedure used to solve for V_0 in equation (5.14), the solution to equation (5.18) can be written as:

$$V_0 = R_0 \, US_0 \left[\frac{r+d}{1-d}, n \right], \tag{5.19}$$

for a finite series over n periods, or as:

$$V_0 = \frac{R_0(1-d)}{r+d}, \tag{5.20}$$

when the number of periods approaches infinity.

Example 5.4: Present Value of a Geometric Decay Series

Continuing Example 5.3, now assume that the dividend is expected to decline at 6 percent per year, while the values of all other variables remain the same. Now, the present market value of *SSH* stock would be:

$$V_0 = \frac{\$3(0.94)}{1.12} + \frac{\$3(0.94)^2}{(1.12)^2} + \ldots + \frac{\$3(0.94)^6}{(1.12)^6} + \frac{\$50}{(1.12)^6}.$$

Since the dividends are declining at 6 percent per period, the present value of the dividends can be expressed (see 5.19) as:

$$V_0^a = R_0 \, US_0 \left[\frac{r+d}{1-d}, n \right],$$

where:

$$\frac{r+d}{1-d} = \frac{0.12+0.06}{0.94} = 19.15 \text{ percent.}$$

Then, since $n=6$ years and $R_0=\$3$:

$$V_0^a = \$3 \, US_0(.19,6) = (\$3)(3.3969) = \$10.19.$$

Since the discounted value of the future sale price of the stock is still $V_0^b = \$25.33$, the present value of *SSH* stock is: $V_0 = V_0^a + V_0^b = \$10.19 + \$25.33 = \$35.52.$

Example 5.5: Comparison of Geometric Decay and Growth Series

Consider two tracts of farmland each of which rented last period for $100 per acre. Assume the rental rate is expected to grow by 3 percent per year in one case and decline by 3 percent per year in the other case. Assume the discount rate, r, is 10 percent, and that the land will be held for an infinite time period (n is very large).

Using (5.17), the present land value for the increasing rent case is:

$$V_0 = \frac{R_0(1+g)}{r-g} = \frac{\$100(1.03)}{0.10-0.03} = \$1,471.43 \text{ per acre,}$$

and, using (5.20), the present land value for the decreasing rent case is:

$$V_0 = \frac{R_0(1-d)}{r+d} = \frac{\$100(0.97)}{0.10+0.03} = \$746.15 \text{ per acre.}$$

Linear Cash Flow Patterns

All cash flow patterns of interest do not fit the uniform, geometric growth, or geometric decline patterns. The cash flow patterns may be represented by polynomials which are linear, quadratic, cubic, or of even higher order. The summation of polynomials is based on finding geometric series in each polynomial by appropriate transformations and substitutions. The appropriate transformation depends on the order of the polynomial represented by the cash flow series. In this section, a present value model is solved in which the cash flow pattern increases or decreases linearly. An example of a linear decline would be a straight-line depreciation policy. A higher-order polynomial can be solved using similar techniques, but its solution is beyond the scope of this text.

If the cash flow is increasing or decreasing linearly over time, then it can be easily shown that the first difference of the series is a uniform return series. The uniform return series discounted by rate r is a geometric series as shown earlier. Thus, the solution to solving for the sum of a linear cash flow series is to convert the expression to a sum of first differences.

To begin, assume that the cash flow in the tth period is of the form:

$$R_t = R_0 + \alpha t,$$

for $t = 1, 2, ..., n$ and where the signs of R_0 and α are unrestricted. Thus, the series can be described as linearly increasing ($\alpha > 0$) or decreasing ($\alpha < 0$). The feature of the linear series which makes it easy to sum is the following: $R_t - R_{t-1} = \alpha$, a constant and that for $\alpha > 0$:

$$\frac{R_t - R_{t-1}}{R_{t-1}} = \frac{\alpha}{R_{t-1}} > 0,$$

and:

$$\lim_{t \to \infty} \frac{\alpha}{R_{t-1}} = 0.$$

Therefore, we can write the sum of a linear series as V_0 where:

$$
\begin{aligned}
V_0 &= \frac{R_1}{(1+r)} + \frac{R_2}{(1+r)^2} + ... + \frac{R_n}{(1+r)^n} \\
&= \left[\frac{R_0}{(1+r)} + ... + \frac{R_0}{(1+r)^n} \right] + \left[\frac{\alpha}{(1+r)} + ... + \frac{n\alpha}{(1+r)^n} \right] \\
&= V_0^a + V_0^b,
\end{aligned}
\tag{5.21}
$$

where V_0^a and V_0^b are the first and second bracketed expressions in (5.21), respectively. The series V_0^a is recognized as a uniform series whose sum is $R_0 US_0(r,n)$. The second series, V_0^b, can be summed by multiplying V_0^b by $(1+r)$ and by subtracting V_0^b. The result is:

$$
\begin{aligned}
(1+r) V_0^b - V_0^b = r V_0^b &= \alpha + \frac{2\alpha}{(1+r)} + ... + \frac{n\alpha}{(1+r)^{n-1}} - \left[\frac{\alpha}{(1+r)} + ... + \frac{n\alpha}{(1+r)^n} \right] \\
&= \alpha + \frac{\alpha}{(1+r)} + ... + \frac{\alpha}{(1+r)^{n-1}} - \frac{n\alpha}{(1+r)^n} \\
&= (1+r)\alpha \, US_0(r,n) - \frac{n\alpha}{(1+r)^n}.
\end{aligned}
\tag{5.22}
$$

We solve for V_0^b in (5.22) by dividing the right-hand side of (5.22) by r so that:

$$V_0^b = \frac{(1+r)}{r} \alpha \, US_0(r,n) - \frac{n\alpha}{r(1+r)^n}. \tag{5.23}$$

Finally, we substitute $(R_0US_0(r,n)$ for V_0^a in equation (5.21)) and the right-hand side of (5.23) for V_0^b. The result is:

$$V_0 = R_0 US_0(r,n) + \frac{(1+r)}{r}\alpha US_0(r,n) - \frac{n\alpha}{r(1+r)^n}. \qquad (5.24)$$

If n is very large, then the series converges to:

$$V_0 = \frac{R_0}{r} + \frac{(1+r)\alpha}{r^2}. \qquad (5.25)$$

The most frequently encountered form of equation (5.24) is the straight-line decay model in which, for example, the income pattern of a durable is expected to decline (i.e., depreciate) at a constant until its income-generating capacity is used up (see Example 5.6).

Elasticity Measure and Present Value Models

Elasticity measures are important tools for investors. They can be used to measure how an investment's present worth may be affected by changes in the opportunity cost of capital. The specific elasticity measures calculated next measure the percentage change in V_0 in response to a 1 percent change in $(1+r)$.

Fortunately, we can obtain elasticity measures of V_0 and $(1+r)$ using the geometric summation tools already developed. The calculation provides a useful application of the linear cash flow model (Martin, Cox, and McMinn). Assuming a constant discount rate, the elasticity of V_0 with respect to $(1+r)$ is written as:

$$E_{V_0,1+r} = \left(\frac{dV_0}{V_0}\right) \Big/ \left(\frac{d(1+r)}{1+r}\right) = \frac{dV_0}{d(1+r)}\frac{1+r}{V_0}. \qquad (5.26)$$

This measure is the approximate percentage change in V_0 in response to an increase in r of one percent.

Consider the uniform series described in equation (5.2). Its derivative with respect to $(1+r)$ is:

Example 5.6: Tax Depreciation and Linear Cash Flows

VerRae Taxing has an investment valued at $12,000. Tax laws allow VerRae to depreciate this investment over five years according to the sum of the years' digits beginning in the first period of service. According to this tax depreciation method, the tax years over which depreciation is claimed, 1+2+3+4+5=15, are summed. Then, the percentage of the asset's value allowed to be depreciated each year equals 5/15, 4/15, ..., 1/15, respectively. Clearly, this depreciation schedule is linear. If VerRae's discount rate is 15 percent, the present value of her tax shield can be calculated using equation (5.21). Define T as VerRae's marginal tax rate, and V_0 as the durable's purchase price. Then VerRae writes the present value of her tax shield, a linear sum, as:

$$PV(Shield) = \frac{TV_0(5/15)}{(1+r)} + \frac{TV_0(4/15)}{(1+r)^2} + \ldots + \frac{TV_0(1/15)}{(1+r)^5}$$

$$= \left[\frac{TV_0(6/15)}{(1+r)} + \ldots + \frac{TV_0(6/15)}{(1+r)^5} \right]$$

$$- \left[\frac{TV_0(1/15)}{(1+r)} + \frac{TV_0(2/15)}{(1+r)^2} \ldots + \frac{TV_0(5/15)}{(1+r)^5} \right].$$

In this linear series, VerRae recognizes: $\alpha = -TV_0/15$, $R_0 = TV_0(6/15)$, and $r = 0.15$. Using equation (5.24) and making necessary substitutions, she writes:

$$PV(Shield) = \frac{TV_0 6\, US_0(0.15,5)}{15} - \frac{(1.15)\, TV_0\, US_0(0.15,5)}{(0.15)(15)} + \frac{5\, TV_0}{(0.15)(15)(1.15)^5}$$

$$= TV_0 \left[\frac{US_0(0.15,5)}{15} \left[6 - \frac{1.15}{0.15} \right] + \frac{5}{(15)(0.15)(1.15)^5} \right]$$

$$= TV_0\, [0.732].$$

If $T=0.23$ and $V_0=1,000$, then *PV(Shield)* equals $168.36.

$$\frac{dV_0}{d(1+r)} = -\frac{R}{(1+r)^2} - \frac{2R}{(1+r)^3} - \ldots - \frac{nR}{(1+r)^{n+1}}$$

$$= -\frac{1}{(1+r)}\left[\frac{R}{(1+r)} + \frac{2R}{(1+r)^2} + \ldots + \frac{nR}{(1+r)^n}\right].$$

Then, multiplying $dV_0/d(1+r)$ by $(1+r)/V_0$, the elasticity measure, $E_{V_0,1+r}$, is found equal to:

$$E_{V_0,1+r} = \frac{dV_0}{d(1+r)}\frac{(1+r)}{V_0} = \frac{-\left[\dfrac{R}{(1+r)} + \dfrac{2R}{(1+r)^2} + \ldots + \dfrac{nR}{(1+r)^n}\right]}{V_0} = \frac{-V_0^a}{V_0}, \qquad (5.27)$$

where:

$$V_0^a = \frac{R}{(1+r)} + \frac{2R}{(1+r)^2} + \ldots + \frac{nR}{(1+r)^n}.$$

Since V_0^a is a linear series, it can be summed using the tools alread developed and equals the last two terms of equation (5.24) with R replaced by α and R_0 set equal to zero:

$$V_0^a = \frac{(1+r)}{r} RUS_0(r,n) - \frac{nR}{r(1+r)^n}$$

$$= \frac{(1+r)}{r} V_0 - \frac{nR}{r(1+r)^n}. \qquad (5.28)$$

Substituting V_0^a for in (5.27) the right-hand side of (5.28), an expression for $E_{V_0,1+r}$ is obtained equal to:

$$E_{V_0,1+r} = \frac{-\left[\dfrac{(1+r)V_0}{r} - \dfrac{nR}{r(1+r)^n}\right]}{V_0} = -\frac{(1+r)}{r} + \frac{nR}{r(1+r)^n V_0}.$$

Since $V_0 = R\left[1 - \dfrac{1}{(1+r)^n}\right]/r$, $E_{V_0,1+r}$ simplifies to:

$$E_{V_0,1+r} = -\frac{(1+r)}{r} + \frac{n}{(1+r)^n - 1}. \qquad (5.29)$$

Moreover, in the limit as n becomes large, the elasticity measure simplifies to:

$$\lim_{n \to \infty} E_{V_0, 1+r} = -\frac{(1+r)}{r}. \tag{5.30}$$

Finally, it is important to note that elasticities are measured at particular values of r. Therefore, elasticity measures are only appropriate for small changes in $(1+r)$.

Generalizing the Elasticity Formula

Having found the elasticity measure for the uniform series, it is a small step to generalize it for other geometric series. To do so, we follow the procedures used earlier to sum geometric series. They include:

1. Identify the geometric factor b in the series;
2. Solve for $(1-b)/b$; and
3. Replace r in (5.29) or (5.30) with $(1-b)/b$.

Example 5.7: Elasticity for an Infinite Constant Return Series

Suppose we wish to calculate $E_{V_0, 1+r}$ for the infinite series:

$$V_0 = \frac{R}{(1+r)} + \frac{R}{(1+r)^2} + \ldots$$

Clearly, in such a series $b = 1/(1+r)$ and $V_0 = R/r$. Therefore, substituting for b and V_0 in (5.31), we obtain:

$$\lim_{n \to \infty} E_{V_0, 1+r} = -\frac{(1+r)}{r}.$$

If, for example, an investment generates a perpetual uniform earnings series and the discount rate is $r = .10$, or 10 percent, then the elasticity of an asset's value for a percentage change in the term $1+r$ is:

$$E_{V_0, 1+r} = -\frac{1+r}{r} = \frac{1.10}{.10} = -11.0 \text{ percent.}$$

Replacing r in equation (5.29) with $(1-b)/b$ results in the generalized elasticity expression:

$$E_{V_0, 1 + \frac{1-b}{b}} = -\frac{1}{1-b} + \frac{n}{(1/b)^n - 1}. \tag{5.31}$$

Furthermore, in the limit, equation (5.30) equals:

$$\lim_{n \to \infty} E_{V_0, 1 + \frac{1-b}{b}} = -\frac{1}{1-b}. \tag{5.32}$$

An important observation is that the elasticity in the generalized series is calculated as a percentage change in V_0 in response to a percent change in $(1+(1-b)/b)$ or $(1/b)$. In the uniform series, $b = 1/(1+r)$, and in the geometric growth series, $b = (1+g)/(1+r)$. Examples 5.7, 5.8, and 5.9 illustrate the calculation of elasticity measures.

Example 5.8: Elasticity for an Infinite Geometric Growth Model

Next, suppose that $b = (1+g)/(1+r)$ so that V_0 can be written as:

$$V_0 = \frac{R(1+g)}{(1+r)} + \frac{R(1+g)^2}{(1+r)^2} + \ldots = \frac{R(1+g)}{(r-g)}.$$

Then, substituting for b in (5.30), we find:

$$\lim_{n \to \infty} E_{V_0, 1 + \left(\frac{r-g}{1+g}\right)} = \frac{-1}{1 - \left(\frac{1+g}{1+r}\right)} = -\left(\frac{1+r}{r-g}\right).$$

If, for example, the discount rate r is 0.10, or 10 percent, and the growth rate of earnings g is 0.03, or 3 percent per year, then the elasticity of the asset's value for a 1 percent change in the term $1+r$ is:

$$E_{V_0, 1+r} = -\frac{1+r}{r-g} = \frac{1.10}{0.10 - 0.03} = 15.71 \text{ percent.}$$

Convex Decay Series

The next return series examined is convex decay. Convex decay patterns can be used to describe net cash flows of finite-lived investments including animals and machines. These investments often experience an increasing rate of decline in their service capacity toward the end of their economic lives. While returns each period decline by a constant percent in the geometric decay pattern and by a constant absolute amount in the straight-line pattern, the convex decay pattern is more complex. Mathematically, it can be expressed as:

$$R_t = R_0 \left[1 - (1-d)^{n-t+1} \right],$$

for $t=1,2,...,n$ where d is a decay parameter. Graphically, R_t is described in Figure 5.1.

The convex decay pattern where d is a decay parameter, is written as:

$$V_0 = \frac{R_0 \left[1 - (1-d)^n \right]}{(1+r)} + \frac{R_0 \left[1 - (1-d)^{n-1} \right]}{(1+r)^2} + ... + \frac{R_0 \left[1 - (1-d) \right]}{(1+r)^n}. \tag{5.33}$$

The convex decay series is not itself a geometric series, but is the difference between two geometric series. So, this series can be conveniently solved by separating the convex decay pattern into two geometric series, V_0^a and V_0^b, which after factoring are both uniform series, finite horizon models:

$$V_0^a = \frac{R_0}{(1+r)} + ... + \frac{R_0}{(1+r)^n} = R_0 \, US_0(r,n),$$

$$V_0^b = \frac{R_0(1-d)^n}{(1+r)} + ... + \frac{R_0(1-d)}{(1+r)^n}$$

$$= R_0(1-d)^{n+1} \left[\frac{1}{(1+r)(1-d)} + \frac{1}{(1+r)^2(1-d)^2} + ... + \frac{1}{(1+r)^n(1-d)^n} \right].$$

In the second series, the constant $R_0(1-d)^{n+1}$ multiplies a geometric series. Thus, V_0^b can be written as:

$$V_0^b = \left[R_0(1-d)^{n+1} \right] US_0(r-d-rd, n). \tag{5.34}$$

Example 5.9: Elasticity for a Finite Geometric Growth Model

Finally, assume that n is finite and $b = (1+g)/(1+r)$. Then, substituting for b, $(1+g)/(1+r)$, in (5.31), the result is:

$$E_{V_0, 1 + \frac{r-g}{1+g}} = -\left(\frac{1+r}{r-g}\right) + \frac{n}{\left(\frac{1+r}{1+g}\right)^n - 1}.$$

Continuing the numerical illustration in Example 5.8, if $r=.10$, $g=.03$, and $n=10$ years, then the elasticity of the asset's value for a one unit change in $(1+r)/(1+g)$ is:

$$E_{V_0, 1 + \frac{r-g}{1+g}} = -\frac{1.10}{0.10-0.03} + \frac{10}{\left(\frac{1.10}{1.03}\right)^{10} - 1}$$

$$= -15.17 + 10.76$$

$$= -4.96 \text{ percent}.$$

Finally, if $g=0$, (i.e., $b=1/(1+r)$) and n is finite, then:

$$E_{V_0, 1 + \frac{r-g}{1+g}} = \frac{-(1+r)}{r} + \frac{n}{(1+r)^n}$$

$$= -\frac{1.10}{0.10} + \frac{10}{(1.10)^{10} - 1}$$

$$= -11 + 6.27 = -4.73 \text{ percent}.$$

The present value sum of the convex decay is expressed as the difference between V_0^a and V_0^b or:

$$V_0 = V_0^a - V_0^b = R_0 \{ US_0(r, n) - (1-d)^{n+1} \ US_0(r-d-rd, n) \}. \tag{5.35}$$

In the special case that d equals 1, $V_0^b = 0$ and $V_0 = V_0^a$. If $d=0$, then $V_0^b = V_0^a$ and $V_0 = 0$.

The parameter d is a percentage with a different interpretation than that obtained in the geometric decay model. It is a shape parameter that alters the bending of the convex decay pattern. As d increases, the convex decay becomes less in the early years and greater in the later years (see Example 5.10).

Combined Growth and Decay Series

The combined growth and decay series generalizes the convex decay model by allowing the return patterns to both increase and decrease. Like the convex decay series, the model describes a wide variety of mechanical, physical, and biological assets, and allows for inflation effects as well. Animal health reaches a peak and then declines slowly until the later periods of its productive life. Then, the animal's health, as well as the value of the services it produces, declines rapidly. This series would also be represented by continuous cropped land and buildings. The rate of gain in growing livestock, forests, and fisheries is also characterized by rapid gains early on followed by diminishing gains per unit of inputs. Thus, the combined growth and decay series is encountered in a wide variety of practical investment problems.

A graph of the combined growth and decay series is shown in Figure 5.2.

The combined growth and decay model has five parameters: a growth parameter g, a decay parameter d, an opportunity cost parameter (discount rate)

Example 5.10: Present Value of a Convex Decay Series

Here and Now (H&N), a small business that delivers overnight mail, expects its income to deteriorate over time because of the increases in use of electronic mail services. Last year, H&N earned a return on its operations of $300,000. H&N expects its income stream for the next four years to follow a convex decay pattern with $d=.06$. The required rate of return for H&N's investors is 12 percent. H&N's CEO, Mr. Ugotta B. Kidding, wants to know the present value of H&N's operations.

Using equation (5.35) where R_0 equals $300,000, n equals 4, d equals 6 percent, and r equals 12 percent, V_0 equals:

$$V_0 = \$300,000 \left\{ US_0(0.12,4) - (1-0.06)^5 \, US_0(0.12-0.06-0.0072,4) \right\}$$

$$= \$300,000 \, \{3.0373 - (0.734)(3.5230)\}$$

$$= \$135,423.62.$$

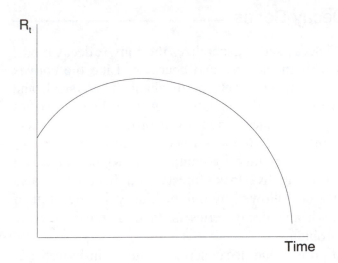

Figure 5.2
Combined Growth and Decay Series

r, a lifetime parameter n, and a constant R_0. The present value expression for the combined growth and decay series is not itself a geometric series; rather, it is the difference between two geometric series.

A mathematical expression for the combined growth and decay model is:

$$V_0 = \frac{R_0(1+g)\left[1-(1-d)^n\right]}{(1+r)} + \ldots + \frac{R(1+g)^n[1-(1-d)]}{(1+r)^n} = V_0^a - V_0^b. \qquad (5.36)$$

V_0^a, the growth series, can be written as:

$$V_0^a = \frac{R_0(1+g)}{(1+r)} + \ldots + \frac{R(1+g)^n}{(1+r)^n} = R_0\, US_0\left(\frac{r-g}{1+g}, n\right).$$

The decay series, V_0^b, can be written as:

$$V_0^b = \frac{R_0(1+g)(1-d)^n}{(1+r)} + \frac{R_0(1+g)^2(1-d)^{n-1}}{(1+r)^2} + \ldots \frac{R_0(1+g)^n(1-d)}{(1+r)^n}$$

$$= R_0(1-d)^{n+1}\left[\frac{(1+g)}{(1-d)(1+r)} + \frac{(1+g)^2}{(1-d)^2(1+r)^2} + \ldots + \frac{(1+g)^n}{(1-d)^n(1+r)^n}\right] \qquad (5.37)$$

$$= R_0(1-d)^{n+1}\, US_0\left(\frac{r-d-rd-g}{1+g}, n\right).$$

Finally, the present value of the combined growth and decay model can be written as:

Example 5.11: Growth and Decay Income Series

The Green Bay Jets are a professional football team. Their talent scout, George Isa Pearl, notes that over the careers of professional football players, their performance first increases and then decreases—a pattern described by the growth and decay model. Letting the present value of the athlete's performance be V_0, he calculates the present worth of an athlete's performance using equation (5.38).

Letting R_0=\$1,000, g=0.10, r=0.15, d=0.08, and n=10, V_0 is calculated to be:

$$V_0 = \$1,000\left[US_0\left(\frac{0.15-0.10}{1.10},10\right) - (1-0.08)^{11}\, US_0\left(\frac{0.15-0.08-0.012-0.10}{1.10},10\right)\right]$$

$$= \$1000\left[7.8951 - (0.40)\,12.4652\right] = \$2,909.01.$$

The income pattern associated with this series is:

$$R_t = (1+g)^t\, R_0\left[1 - (1-d)^{n-t+1}\right] = (1.10)^t (1,000)(1-0.92^{10-t+1}),$$

whose values are graphed below.

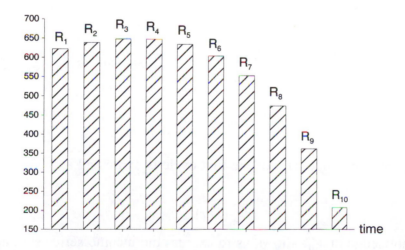

$$V_0 = V_0^a - V_0^b = R_0 \left[US_0 \left(\frac{r-g}{1+g}, n \right) - (1-d)^{n+1} \ US_0 \left(\frac{r-d-rd-g}{1+g}, n \right) \right]. \qquad (5.38)$$

It is of interest to note the following about (5.38). First, for $d=1$, (5.38) reduces to the constant geometric growth rate pattern whose sum is $R_0 US_0(r-g/1+g, n)$. Second, if $g=0$, then (5.38) reduces to the convex decay model whose sum is expressed in equation (5.35). If $d=1$ and $g=0$, then the series reduces to the uniform series. Finally, if $g<0$ and $d=1$, the series reduces to the constant decay rate model.

Repeatable Cycle Series

The earnings series described thus far are characterized by non-repeated patterns. Other series exhibit repeating patterns. Certain types of rotations may produce a repeatable cycle of returns for land. Biological growth cycles may create other series that cannot be solved with a geometric solution rule. As a result, not all series can be summarized using the tools described. In one case, however, repeatable cycle series can be summarized. To illustrate, consider the return series illustrated in Figure 5.3.

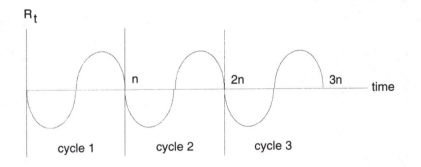

Figure 5.3
Repeatable Cycle
Series

The present value sum of the first cycle is expressed as:

$$V_0^a = \sum_{t=1}^{n} \frac{R_t}{(1+r)^t}. \qquad (5.39)$$

Having knowledge of V_0^a allows us to express the income series sum as:

$$V_0 = V_0^a + \frac{V_0^a}{(1+r)^n} + \frac{V_0^a}{(1+r)^{2n}} + \dots + \frac{V_0^a}{(1+r)^{mn}}. \qquad (5.40)$$

To solve, the constant $V_0^a (1+r)^n$ is factored out leaving the series:

$$V_0 = V_0^a (1+r)^n \left[\frac{1}{(1+r)^n} + \frac{1}{(1+r)^{2n}} + \dots + \frac{1}{(1+r)^{mn+n}} \right].$$ (5.41)

But, equation (5.41) is a recognizable geometric series where:

$$b = \frac{1}{(1+r)^n} \quad \text{and} \quad \frac{1-b}{b} = (1+r)^n - 1.$$

Then, V_0 can be written as:

$$V_0 = V_0^a (1+r)^n \ US_0 \left[(1+r)^n - 1, m+1 \right].$$ (5.42)

Other expressions could be developed for irregular durables whose annualized averages follow other decay patterns. The tools would be applied as if the series demonstrated returns from a single durable.

Idleness Models

Idleness during some portion of the year is a characteristic of many durables. Farm equipment is used intensively during planting and harvest time. During the remainder of the year, the equipment use is far below its potential. Some types of cropland lie fallow (idle) for a year to restore fertility. For most people, the human body requires an idleness period for body repairs and maintenance which usually lasts about eight hours during each 24-hour cycle. Most other durables have similar characteristics. Cars require tune-ups, and factories operate on cycles that conform to human service cycles—more in the day than at night. One example of an idleness problem is described in Figure 5.4. The solid rectangle represents returns in the active periods.

The present value models developed above can be generalized to include the idleness cycles. Consider the solution to a geometric series in which every other period is idle. Returns during the active period are represented by R and the discount rate is r percent. Let the alternating idleness series be expressed as V_0 which is written as:

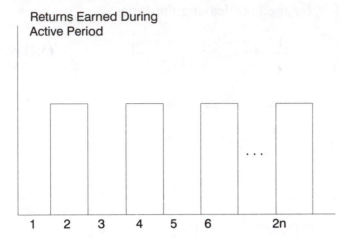

Returns Earned During
Active Period

1   2   3   4   5   6   2n

Figure 5.4
A Graphic Representation of
Alternating Periods of Activity
and Idleness

$$V_0 = 0 + \frac{R}{(1+r)^2} + 0 + \frac{R}{(1+r)^4} + 0 + \ldots + \frac{R}{(1+r)^{2n}}$$

$$= 0 + \frac{R}{(1+2r+r^2)} + 0 + \frac{R}{(1+2r+r^2)^2} + 0 + \ldots \frac{R}{(1+2r+r^2)^n}.$$

Recognizing this last expression as a geometric series whose geometric factor b is equal to $1/(1+2r+r^2)$, the sum of the idleness series is written as:

$$V_0 = R\,US_0\,[2r+r^2, n], \tag{5.43}$$

since $(1-b)/b$ equals $[(1+r)^2-1]$ or $2r+r^2$ and where n is the number of nonzero terms summed.

When n is very large, then the limit of V_0 can be written as:

$$\lim_{n \to \infty} V_0 = \frac{R}{2r+r^2}. \tag{5.44}$$

Example 5.12: Present Value of a Series with Idle Periods

Mr. Apl Saus produces apple cider at his mill during the last six months of each year. The other six months the mill remains idle. He gets a constant return of $6,000 during the six months of operation. The required rate of return for the investment is 12 percent or 6 percent per six months.

On January 1st, the owner wants to know the present value of the next eight years of operations. Using equation (5.43) and letting $n=8$, $r=6$ percent, $R_0 = \$6,000$, and $2r+r^2 = 0.1236$, we calculate:

$$V_0 = R\,US_0\left[2r+r^2, n\right]$$

$$= \$6,000\ US_0\left[0.1236, 8\right] = (6,000)(4.9058) = \$29,434.65.$$

More General Rules

This chapter has demonstrated that many present value models can be reduced to simplified algebraic expressions by summing geometric series. There are some return patterns, however, that cannot be represented as geometric series even after transformations are performed. One such series allows the discount rate to vary over time. But even these more general series can be summed to equal a simplified algebraic expression.

To demonstrate, let V_0 equal:

$$V_0 = \frac{R_1}{(1+r_1)} + \frac{R_2}{(1+r_1)(1+r_2)} + \cdots$$

$$= \frac{R_1}{(1+r_1)} + \frac{1}{(1+r_1)}\left[\frac{R_2}{(1+r_2)} + \frac{R_3}{(1+r_2)(1+r_3)} + \cdots\right].$$

(5.45)

In this model, neither the relationship between cash flows nor the life of the asset are specified. If time were advanced by one period, the new sum, V_1, could be written as:

$$V_1 = \frac{R_2}{(1+r_2)} + \frac{R_3}{(1+r_2)(1+r_3)} + \cdots,$$

(5.46)

which equals the bracketed expression in equation (5.45). Substituting for the bracketed expression, V_1, and solving yields:

$$V_1 = (1+r_1) \, V_0 - R_1. \tag{5.47}$$

The importance of this equation is that V_0, V_1, . . ., can be calculated even though the complete series for R_t is not known; nevertheless, its influence can be measured. To illustrate, consider a series, R_t, that is observed and a series, R_t^u, that is unobserved. The sum, V_0, can be written as:

$$V_0 = \left\{ \frac{R_1}{(1+r_1)} + \dots \right\} + \left\{ \frac{R_1^u}{(1+r_1)} + \dots \right\}$$

$$= \frac{R_1}{(1+r_1)} + \frac{1}{(1+r_1)} \left[\frac{R_2}{(1+r_2)} + \frac{R_3}{(1+r_2)(1+r_3)} + \dots \right] \tag{5.48}$$

$$+ \frac{R_1^u}{(1+r_1)} + \frac{1}{(1+r_1)} \left[\frac{R_2^u}{(1+r_2)} + \frac{R_3^u}{(1+r_2)(1+r_3)} + \dots \right].$$

If the time were advanced one period, the new sum, V_1, could be written as:

$$V_1 = \left[\frac{R_2}{(1+r_2)} + \frac{R_3}{(1+r_2)(1+r_3)} + \dots \right] + \left[\frac{R_2^u}{(1+r_2)} + \frac{R_3^u}{(1+r_2)(1+r_3)} + \dots \right],$$

which can be substituted into (5.48) to obtain:

$$V_1 = (1+r_1) \, V_0 - R_1 - R_1^u. \tag{5.49}$$

From equation (5.47) or (5.49), depending on which equation describes the market, the most fundamental of market equilibrium expressions is derived. Solving for r_1, from (5.49) we obtain:

$$r_1 = \frac{V_1 - V_0}{V_0} + \frac{R_1}{V_0} + \frac{R_1^u}{V_0}. \tag{5.50}$$

As indicated above, the *IRR* or economic rate of return on an asset is equal to the percent return earned as capital gains, plus the percent of returns received in cash, and plus other unobserved returns (such as pride in ownership). The return is expressed as a percentage of the durable's beginning value.

Summary

This chapter has focused on the development of algebraic expressions for a variety of present value problems with geometrically-related cash flows. The "geometrically-related" requirement is not unduly restrictive because many series can be converted to geometric series with appropriate transformations, even if they are not originally of the form described in equation (5.1).

Using a geometric sum, complicated intertemporal relationships can be expressed in simple ways. With these tools in place, present value models can be easily applied to a wide variety of practical problems. A summary of the formulas that will be used throughout the text is provided in Table 5.2.

Review Questions

1. Explain why more general questions involving time-dated cash flows may require algebraic rather than numeric solutions.

2. What procedure is used to algebraically solve a present value model where letters represent possible values?

3. List several ways algebraic solutions of present value models can be used. How can numeric summaries of a present value model be used? Compare the kinds of problems best answered by algebraic and numeric solutions of present value models.

4. List an investment whose associated net cash flows exemplify each of the cash flow patterns described in Figure 5.1.

5. What geometric factor is present in most (if not all) discrete present value models?

6. Identify the geometric factor, the constant, and the sum for the two series described below:

$$(a) \ V_0 = \frac{\$50}{1.05} + \frac{\$50}{(1.05)^2} + \ldots + \frac{\$50}{(1.05)^{10}}$$

$$(b) \ V_0 = \frac{\$50}{(1+r)} + \frac{\$50}{(1+r)^2} + \ldots + \frac{R}{(1+r)^n}$$

Table 5.2 Summary of Geometric Series and Their Sums

Type of Case Flow	Sum When n Is Finite	Sum When n is Infinite
1. Uniform or constant R	$RUS_0(r,n)$	$\dfrac{R}{r}$
2. Geometric decay of R_0 at rate d	$R_0 US_0\left(\dfrac{r+d}{1-d}, n\right)$	$\dfrac{R_0(1-d)}{(r+d)}$
3. Geometric growth of R_0 at rate g	$R_0 US_0\left(\dfrac{r-g}{1+g}, n\right)$	$\dfrac{R_0(1+g)}{(r-g)}$
4. Linear growth (decay) where $R_t=R_0+t\alpha$	$R_0 US_0(r,n) + \dfrac{(1+r)}{r}\alpha US_0(r,n) - \dfrac{n\alpha}{r(1+r)^n}$	$\dfrac{R_0}{r} + \dfrac{(1+r)\alpha}{r^2}$
5. Convex decay of R_0 by the factor $(1-d)$	$R_0\left\{US_0(r,n) - (1-d)^{n+1} US_0\left(\dfrac{r-d-rd-g}{1+g}, n\right)\right\}$	n.a.
6. Combined growth and decay series with growth parameter g and decay parameter d	$R_0\left[US_0\left(\dfrac{r-g}{1+g}, n\right) - (1-d)^{n+1} US_0\left(\dfrac{r-d-rd-g}{1+g}, n\right)\right]$	n.a.

7. Summarize the two series described in (6), using $US_0(r,n)$ notation.

8. Referring to question (6a), describe the relationship between the geometric factor b and the discount rate r. How is this relationship used to obtain sums of geometric series?

9. Are geometric growth and decay series geometric series? Defend your answer. Are linear growth series geometric series? If not, how can they be solved using geometric series summation tools?

10. How can the present value sum of the linear cash flow series be used to find the percentage change in the present value of an asset in response to a 1 percent change in the one plus the discount rate?

11. Describe the conditions under which the generalized growth and decay model represents: (1) the uniform series; (2) the constant growth rate series; and (3) a convex decay series.

12. Can you give five examples of durables that are never idled? (Hint: the human heart is one.) Would you say that most durables are idled on a regular basis?

Application Questions

1. Two important geometric series, used repeatedly throughout the remainder of this book, are:

$$V_0^a = \frac{R}{(1+r)} + \frac{R}{(1+r)^2} + \dots + \frac{R}{(1+r)^n}.$$

and:

$$V_0^b = Rb + Rb^2 + \dots + Rb^n.$$

Financial calculators and tables available in most financial textbooks can be used to calculate the value of V_o^a, where r and n are known. How can the numeric solution for V_o^a be used to find the numeric solution for V_0^b?

2. This chapter demonstrated that the relationship between r and b was:

$$r = (1-b)/b.$$

Referring to application question number 1, if $V_o^a = RUS_0(r,n)$, write the solution for V_o^b using the US_0 notation.

Write the geometric series sum $US_0(1\text{-}b/b,n)$ in expanded form. Note that for various values of $(1\text{-}b/b)$ and n, the sum is calculated in Appendix 1 of this book or can be calculated using most financial calculators.

3.   An expression of the form $V_0 = R/r$ where V_0 represents a price, R represents the periodic net cash flow, and r is the opportunity cost of capital, is called an algebraic model. Were numbers substituted for the symbols, the expression would become numeric. Compare and contrast investment analysis problems where algebraic and numeric models would be useful.

4.   Identify which of the following series are geometric. For each series that is geometric or that can be transformed into a geometric series, find the geometric factor b.

(a) $V_0 = \dfrac{R}{(1+r)} + \dots + \dots \dfrac{R}{(1+r)^n}$

(b) $V_0 = R(1+r) + \dots + R(1+r)^n$

(c) $V_0 = \dfrac{R(1+g)}{(1+r)} + \dots + \dfrac{R(1+g)^n}{(1+r)^n}$

(d) $V_0 = \dfrac{R\left[1 - \dfrac{1}{(1+d)^n}\right]}{(1+r)} + \dfrac{R\left[1 - \dfrac{1}{(1+d)^{n-1}}\right]}{(1+r)^2} + \dots + \dfrac{R\left[1 - \dfrac{1}{(1+d)}\right]}{(1+r)^n}$

(e) $V_0 = \dfrac{R_0+\alpha}{(1+r)} + \dfrac{R_0+2\alpha}{(1+r)^2} + \dots + \dfrac{R_0+n\alpha}{(1+r)^n}$

(f) $V_0 = R + \dfrac{R}{(1+r)^3} + \dfrac{R}{(1+r)^6} + \dots$

(g) $V_0 = \dfrac{R(1+g)}{(1+r)} + \dfrac{R(1+g)}{(1+r)^2} + \dfrac{R(1+g)^2}{(1+r)^3} + \dfrac{R(1+g)^2}{(1+r)^4} + \dfrac{R(1+g)^3}{(1+r)^5} + \dfrac{R(1+g)^3}{(1+r)^6}$

$\qquad + \dfrac{R(1+g)^4}{(1+r)^7} + \dfrac{R(1+g)^4}{(1+r)^8} + \dots$

5. Using either Appendix 1 or a financial calculator, use the data described below and the geometric summation tool, $US_0[(1-b)/b,n]$, to find the numerical answer for each of the problems described in question (4).

    (a) $R = \$50$, $r = 10$ percent, $n = 15$
    (b) $R = \$50$, $r = 10$ percent, $n = 15$
    (c) $R = \$75$, $g = 3$ percent, $r = 9$ percent, $n = 20$
    (d) $R = \$100$, $d = 18$ percent, $r = 12$ percent, $n = 15$
    (e) $R_0 = \$5$, $a_1 = 22$, $r = 10$ percent, $n = 5$
    (f) $R = \$100$, $r = 10$ percent, $n = $ unlimited
    (g) $R = \$10$, $g = 4$ percent, $r = 10$ percent, $n = 10$

6. Express the sum of the geometric series below as a simplified algebraic expression:

$$V_0 = \frac{R}{(1+r)} + \frac{R}{(1+r)^2} + \dots + \frac{R}{(1+r)^n}.$$

7. Please solve the following puzzle. Consider the series:

$$V_0 = \frac{R_0(1+g)}{(1+r)} + \frac{R_0(1+g)^2}{(1+r)^2} + \dots = \frac{R_0(1+g)}{r-g}.$$

    Each individual element of the series is positive for R_0, g, $r>0$. But $R_0(1+g)/(r-g)<0$ if $r<g$. Explain this contradictory result.

References

Aplin, R.D., G.L. Casler, and C.P. Francis. *Capital Investment Analysis: Using Discounted Cash Flows,* 3rd edition. Columbus, OH: Grid Publishing, 1984.

Barry, P.J., P.N. Ellinger, J.A. Hopkin, and C.B. Baker. *Financial Management in Agriculture,* 5th edition. Danville, IL: Interstate Publishers, Inc., 1995.

Martin, J.D., S.H. Cox, and R.D. McMinn. *The Theory of Finance: Evidence and Applications.* New York: The Dryden Press, 1988.

Penson, J.B., Jr., D.W. Hughes, and G.L. Nelson. "Measurement of Capacity Depreciation Based on Engineering Data." *American Journal of Agricultural Economics* 59(1977):321-29.

Robison, L.J. and S.R. Koenig. "Cash Rents, Speculation, Illiquidity and Land Value in U.S. Agriculture." Michigan State University Working Paper, July 1990.

Van Horne, J.C. *Fundamentals of Financial Management,* 4th edition. Englewood Cliffs, NJ: Prentice-Hall, 1980.

Chapter 6

Ranking Investments

Key words: capital rationed investment constraints, internal rate of return (*IRR*), investment opportunity schedule (*IOS*), investment portfolios, marginal cost of capital schedule (*MCC*), mutually-exclusive investment constraints, net present value (*NPV*), rate-of-return restricted investments.

Introduction

Every day firms and individuals choose among alternative investments. Consumers choose among different models, sizes, and service capacities of cars; home buyers choose among different houses; workers choose among different occupations; firms choose among different capital structures, capital/labor mixes, etc. Because these choices often require large sums of money, they are important to the agents involved. How should investment choices be evaluated? They are usually not the continuous choices emphasized in economic theory textbooks — whose solutions are found by maximizing objective functions. Instead, they are solved using present value (*PV*) models. Investment analysis does not come in tidy packages. Real world investments are generally available in lumpy units and provide services over long periods of time.

While net present value (*NPV*) and internal rate of return (*IRR*) are clearly the preferred methods of evaluating investment choices, they can occasionally lead to inconsistent rankings of mutually-exclusive investments. Such inconsistencies are the result of violating one of the principles for constructing present value models described in Chapter 4. When the principles are carefully followed, *NPV* and *IRR* criteria produce identical rankings.

The next two sections show how conflicts between *IRR* and *NPV* criteria are resolved by applying the principles discussed in Chapter 4. Consistency requires that ranked investments obey the homogenous measures principle. The aspects of homogeneity emphasized in this chapter involve size and timing differences. The remainder of this chapter focuses on how rankings are handled under increasingly restrictive assumptions.

Conflicts Between *IRR* and *NPV* Criteria

The potential conflicts in rankings between the *NPV* and *IRR* models are illustrated as follows. Consider two investments, *A* and *B*, which are identical except for the reversed sign of their cash flows. Table 6.1 indicates that these two investments have the same *IRR*, but different *NPV*s. Thus, the *IRR* criterion in this example cannot distinguish between two clearly different investments even though the *NPV* criterion valued project *A* at $2,500 and would have rejected *B* with a negative $2,500 *NPV*.

The distinction between the two investments is that *A* is equivalent to a one-period investment that earns an interest rate of 50 percent, while *B* is equivalent to a loan at an interest rate of 50 percent. Clearly, investors are not indifferent. High rates of return are desirable for investments, while low interest rates are desirable for loans. Graphically, the relationship between projects *A* and *B* is evaluated using *IRR* and *NPV*. Simply stated, project *A*'s *NPV* is inversely related to its discount rate, while *B*'s *NPV* is directly related to its discount rate.

Table 6.1 implies that decision makers need to know more than investment *IRR*s to rank investment choices. The relationship between the discount rate and the *NPV*s of the investment must also be known.

A drawback of the traditional *IRR* method discussed in Chapter 2 is that more than one *IRR* may exist. Or, in extreme cases, an *IRR* may not exist (see Chapter 2). Another limitation is that the *IRR* criterion represents a percent, not a dollar value. For example, consider two mutually-exclusive investments,

Table 6.1 *IRR* and *NPV* Conflicts

Project	Initial Cash Flow	Cash Flow in Period 1	*NPV* at 20%	*IRR*
A	$-10,000	$+15,000	$+2,500	50%
B	$+10,000	$-15,000	$-2,500	50%

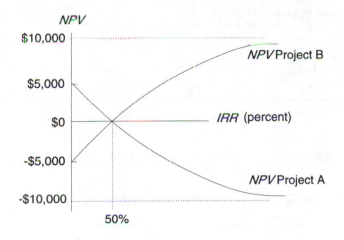

Figure 6.1
*NPV*s for Projects A and B
Described in Table 6.1

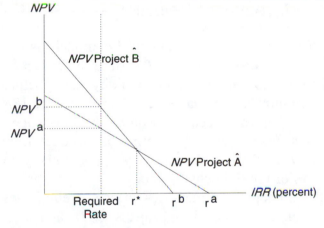

Figure 6.2
Comparing Projects Â and B̂
Using *IRR*s and *NPV*s

$\hat{A}$ and $\hat{B}$. If wealth is the goal, then the dollars earned and not just the percentages earned on the investments are relevant. Graphically, the problem is illustrated in Figure 6.2. Even though A has a higher *IRR*, r^a, its *NPV* is clearly less than that of project B when a "required rate" less than r^* is used as the discount rate.

A numerical example of the problem described in Figure 6.2 is shown in Table 6.2. Assume a firm must rank three mutually-exclusive investments, C, D, and E, whose initial outlay and cash flows are described below. Also assume that the opportunity cost of capital is 10 percent, and each investment has an economic life of one period.

The rankings for investments C, D, and E using the *NPV* criterion are (3), (1), and (2), while the *IRR* criterion ranks them (1), (2), and (3). With significant differences in the amount invested, inconsistent rankings using *NPV* and *IRR* can be expected.

Table 6.2 Ranking Investments of Unequal Size

Project	Initial Outlay	Cash Inflow One Period Later	NPV @ 10% (Rankings)	IRR (Rankings)
C	$1000.00	$1200.00	$90.91 (3)	20% (1)
D	$2000.00	$2360.00	$145.45 (1)	18% (2)
E	$3000.00	$3450.00	$136.36 (2)	15% (3)

Homogenous Measures and Investment Selection

One principle discussed in Chapter 4 for constructing *PV* models is the homogenous measures principle. It requires that the *IRR* of a defender be calculated for an investment of the same size, duration, and liquidity, using before or after-tax units, and real or nominal units as the challengers. Otherwise, the *IRR* will incorrectly measure what is being sacrificed to acquire the challenger. Although the homogenous measures were discussed in terms of the cash flow stream of the challenger and the *IRR* of the defender, they apply equally to comparisons between the cash flows of multiple challengers.

Table 6.3 illustrates how the homogenous measures principle eliminates conflicts between *IRR* and *NPV* rankings. Reconsider projects *C, D,* and *E* in Table 6.2. Since the discount rate is 10 percent, it is assumed that funds not invested in *C, D,* or *E* earn at that rate. That is, if funds available at 10 percent are not invested, it can only mean they continue to earn at the opportunity cost of capital. By adding $2,000 to the initial investment *C,* $1,000 to *D,* $2,000(1+r)=$2,200 to the cash flow of *C,* and $1,000(1+r)=$1,100 to the cash flow of *D,* a proper comparison is possible. With these adjustments, each project describes a $3,000 investment. This is shown in Table 6.3.

Notice that the *NPV*s did not change after making the investments comparable. Since the reinvestment rate was assumed to equal the discount rate, the *NPV*s could not change. However, the *IRR*s did change. When the investments were made comparable, the *IRR* and *NPV* rankings are the same. Of course, since the *NPV* gives the correct answer even without adjusting for size, assuming the reinvestment rate is also the discount rate, the adjustment for the *IRR*s really is not needed — just

Table 6.3 Adjusting for Size Differences

Project	Initial Outlay	Cash Inflow in Period 1	NPV @ 10% (Rankings)	IRR (Rankings)
C+$2000	$3000	($1200+$2200)	$90.91 (3)	13.3% (3)
D+$1000	$3000	($2360+$1100)	$145.45 (1)	15.3% (1)
E	$3000	$3450	$136.36 (2)	15.0% (2)

Table 6.4 Different Cash Withdrawals

Project	Initial Outlay	Cash Inflow in Period 1	Cash Inflow in Period 2	NPV @ 10% (Rankings)	IRR (Rankings)
F	$1000	$880	$354.00	$92.56 (2)	18% (1)
G	$1000	$160	$1160.00	$104.13 (1)	16% (2)

Table 6.5 Adjusting Differences in Cash Withdrawals

Project	Initial Outlay	Cash Flow in Period 1	Cash Flow in Period 2	NPV @ 10% (Rankings)	IRR (Rankings)
F*	$1000	0	$968+$354= $1322	$92.56 (2)	15.0% (2)
G*	$1000	0	$176+$1160= $1336	$104.13 (1)	15.6% (1)

use the *NPV*s. However, rate-of-return measures are very popular among business people, and if calculated correctly, provide correct rankings. The point is that *IRR* and *NPV* will always provide consistent rankings unless the homogenous measures principle is violated.

The homogenous measures principle may be applied in other circumstances to remove *NPV* and *IRR* ranking conflicts. To illustrate, suppose two investments, *F* and *G*, start out with equal amounts, and each investment has two periods of returns. Then, assume the two projects have funds withdrawn in unequal amounts over time. That is, they exhibit time disparity in their cash flows. In Table 6.4, project *F* withdraws $880 in period one, and project *G* withdraws $160.

Both projects begin with an initial outlay of $1,000. But at the end of period 1, project *F* earning at a rate of 18 percent has invested only $300 [$1,000(1.18)-880], after withdrawing $880, while project *G* has still invested $1,000 [$1,000(1.16)-160]. Clearly, the comparison in the second period violates the homogenous measures principle.

One way to make the comparison consistent with the homogenous measures principle is to account for the funds withdrawn in period 1. This is done by reinvesting the funds at the opportunity cost of capital equal to 10 percent. Thus, the investments added to cash flows in period 2 are $880(1.10)=$968 for project *F* and $160(1.10)=$176 for project *G*. Now the example can be rewritten (as shown in Table 6.5).

Once again, the initial *NPV*s did not change with the adjustments. However, the *IRR*s did change once the reinvestment assumption was made explicit. After making the correction, the *IRR* and *NPV* rankings are consistent.

Making Investments Term Compatible

The appropriate term for an investment is its economic life. This was the point of "the life of the investment principle" described in Chapter 4. On the other hand, two investments to be compared must satisfy the homogenous measures principle of equal terms between the investment alternatives. In Table 6.6, the sizes of two investments, *H* and *I*, are the same, but their terms or economic lives differ, and the opportunity cost of funds is still 10 percent. Also assume that project *H* is not repeatable.

The term disparity problem created by differences in the length of time funds are invested could be handled in the usual way by multiplying $1,180 by 1.10 for project *H*, and then by multiplying $160 by 1.10 and adding the product to period 2's cash flow for project *I*. If this is done, the example becomes a comparison of homogenous projects H^* and I^* described in Table 6.7.

Table 6.6 Investments with Different Terms

Project	Initial Outlay	Cash Flow in Period 1	Cash Flow in Period 2	NPV @ 10% (Rankings)	IRR (Rankings)
H	$1000	$1180	0	$72.73 (2)	18% (1)
I	$1000	$160	$1160	$104.13 (1)	16% (2)

Table 6.7 Rationalizing Term Differences

Project	Initial Outlay	Cash Flow in Period 1	Cash Flow in Period 2	NPV @ 10% (Rankings)	IRR (Rankings)
H*	$1000	0	$1180(1.1)= $1298	$72.73 (2)	13.9% (2)
I*	$1000	0	$160(1.1)+ $1160=$1336	$104.13 (1)	15.6% (1)

Table 6.8 Rationalizing Term Differences (cont'd)

Project	Initial Outlay	Cash Inflow in Period 1	Cash Inflow in Period 2	NPV @ 10% (Rankings)	IRR (Rankings)
$\hat{H}$	$1000	0	$1000(1.18)+ $180(1.1)= $1378	$138.84 (1)	17.8% (1)
I*	$1000	0	$160(1.1)+ $1160=$1336	$104.13 (2)	15.6% (2)

Again, the *NPV*s do not change as a result of the term adjustment. But the *IRR*s change and are made consistent with the *NPV* ranking.

An alternative approach to resolving timing differences is appropriate if project *H* is repeatable. Thus, of the $1,180 available at the end of the first period, $1,000 can be reinvested at 18 percent. If this alternative reinvestment assumption is made, then neither the *NPV* nor the *IRR* ranking is appropriate. To adjust the analysis for this reinvestment assumption while keeping the projects on comparable size and timing units, the following adjustments are made in project *H*, now called *Ĥ*. Of the $1,180 available in period one, $1,000 is reinvested to earn $1,180 in period two plus $180(1.10) or $198 from the earnings reinvested at the market rate of 10 percent. Thus, the total period 2 cash flow equals $1180+$198=$1378. Now the comparison is between projects *Ĥ* and *I** described in Table 6.8.

In this new comparison, project *Ĥ* is preferred over *I** because of the different reinvestment assumptions. When an investment is repeated, it earns at the *IRR*. The earnings from the first investment earn at the opportunity cost of capital. Thus, *Ĥ* is earning at both 18 percent (the investment's original *IRR*) and at 10 percent, the opportunity cost of capital.

When comparing investments of unequal lives, a key question is whether the investments can be repeated or is there some other investment for which the funds can be used that makes both investments equal in their terms? Only when the reinvestment rate is equal to the discount rate can the differences in the term of investments be ignored when calculating *NPV*s.

Another easily applied method for rationalizing time differences is the equivalent cost-per-year approach also known as the annuity equivalent method. This method is equivalent to finding the average amortized return for the different investments. This method assumes that the reinvestment and discount rate are equal and the investment is infinitely repeatable. Consider the *NPV* model:

$$NPV = -V_0 + \frac{R_1}{(1+r)} + \ldots + \frac{R_n}{(1+r)^n},$$

for which an annuity payment, *R*, exists such that:

$$NPV = -V_0 + \frac{R_1}{(1+r)} + \ldots + \frac{R_n}{(1+r)^n} = \frac{R}{(1+r)} + \ldots + \frac{R}{(1+r)^n},$$

or:

$$NPV = R\left[\frac{1}{(1+r)} + \ldots + \frac{1}{(1+r)^n}\right] = RUS_0\,(r,n),$$

and:

$$R = \frac{NPV}{US_0\,(r,n)}.$$

An important point to make is that the annuity equivalent is independent of the number of times the investment is repeated. For example, calculate:

$$NPV = -V_0 + \frac{R_1}{(1+r)} + \ldots + \frac{R_n}{(1+r)^n} = RUS_0(r,n).$$

Now calculate R over N investment cycles:

$$NPV = \left[-V_0 + \frac{R_1}{(1+r)} + \ldots + \frac{R_n}{(1+r)^n}\right]$$

$$+ \frac{1}{(1+r)^n}\left[-V_0 + \frac{R_1}{(1+r)} + \ldots + \frac{R_n}{(1+r)^n}\right]$$

$$+ \ldots + \frac{1}{(1+r)^{nN}}\left[-V_0 + \frac{R_1}{(1+r)} + \ldots + \frac{R_n}{(1+r)^n}\right].$$

Next, replace the bracketed expressions with $RUS_0(r,n)$ and write:

$$NPV = RUS_0(r,n) + \frac{R}{(1+r)^n}\,US_0(r,n)$$

$$+ \ldots + \frac{R}{(1+r)^{nN}}\,US_0(r,n)$$

$$= R\left[US_0(r,n) + \frac{US_0(r,n)}{(1+r)^n} + \ldots + \frac{US_0(r,n)}{(1+r)^{nm}}\right]$$

$$= RUS_0(r,nN).$$

Finally, solving for R, we establish that regardless of the number of replacements, the annuity for the series of identical replacements is always R:

$$R = \frac{NPV}{US_0\,(r,nm)}.$$

The result that the annuity calculation is independent of the number of times the investment is repeated is important. It is the basis of the claim that infinitely repeatable investments of unequal terms can be compared using the annuity equivalent approach. This is because if two infinitely repeatable investments of individual project length n and m are compared, there exists a common term of nm at which they could also be compared. But the annuity equivalent would be the same as if the annuities were calculated over terms n and m. The fact that both investments are repeatable in perpetuity means their terms are indeed equal. The annuity equivalent is simply a simplified means for making the comparisons.

Now consider another investment of the same size, V_0, where cash flow for $n \neq m$ periods could be written as:

$$NPV = -V_0 + \frac{\hat{R}_1}{(1+r)} + \dots + \frac{\hat{R}_N}{(1+r)^m} = \frac{\hat{R}}{(1+r)} + \dots + \frac{\hat{R}}{(1+r)^m},$$

or:

$$NPV = \hat{R}\left[\frac{1}{(1+r)} + \dots + \frac{1}{(1+r)^m}\right] = \hat{R}\,US_0\,(r,m),$$

and:

$$\hat{R} = \frac{NPV}{US_0\,(r,m)}.$$

In the annuity equivalent approach, one compares the annuities calculated for the two investments, R and $\hat{R}$, and selects the investment earning the larger annuity. To interpret $\hat{R}$ and R, recall that $US_0\,(r,n)$ is the present value sum of \$1 payments received for n periods. The expression $1/US_0\,(r,n)$ calculates the inverse. It finds the annuity value for \$1 in the present that would be paid for n periods in the future. Thus, $NPV/US_0\,(r,n)$ finds the annuity value of present dollars worth NPV.

If the investment were infinitely repeatable, the annuity of R or $\hat{R}$ would be available forever and the difference between n or m would be unimportant. While the assumption that the investment is infinitely repeatable may be appropriate in many cases, it is not always correct. When investments are not infinitely repeatable, investments may not end at a common point in time in which case the annuity equivalent should not be used to rationalize time differences. Table 6.9 illustrates the problem.

The rankings in Table 6.9 based on their annuity equivalents are not consistent with the rankings in Table 6.7 which have been adjusted for term differences. If the first period earnings are reinvested at the discount rate, consistency in timing is achieved. Once consistency in term has been achieved, investments can be

Table 6.9 Annuity Equivalent Rankings

Project	Initial Outlay	Cash Flow in Period 1	Cash Flow in Period 2	Annuity Equivalent 10% (Ranking)
H	$1000	$1180	0	$80 (1)
I	$1000	$160	$1160	$60 (2)

Table 6.10 Adjusted Annuity Equivalent Rankings

Project	Initial Outlay	Cash Flow in Period 1	Cash Flow in Period 2	Annuity Equivalent @ 10% (Ranking)
H*	$1000	0	$1180(1.10)= $1298	$41.90 (2)
I*	$1000	0	$1160+ [(160)1.10]= $1336	$60.00 (1)

ranked by their annuity equivalents, *IRR*s, or *NPV*s, as long as the discount and reinvestment rates are equal.

To demonstrate this last point, compare the annuity equivalent rankings in Table 6.10 with the *NPV* and *IRR* rankings in Table 6.7.

In sum, two points must be emphasized regarding the annuity equivalent method of ranking investments. First, it does not resolve inconsistency in investment sizes. Second, even without size differences, the annuity method correctly resolves term differences only under the assumption that investments are repeatable for *mn* periods.

Alternative Capital Budgeting Constraints

So far, the discussion has considered how investments can be ranked consistently using *NPV*s or *IRR*s. If the principles of formulating present value models are followed, the rankings cannot be in conflict, because the *IRR*s will be ranking returns on investments of the same size. Moreover, because each investment has only one average *IRR* when the reinvestment rate is specified, the larger the terminal cash return, the larger the *IRR*. Thus, the *IRR* rankings must be the same as those obtained by *NPV*.

Next, consider how to rank investments under alternative constraints. Investments can be restricted in many ways (Lorie and Savage). Some typical investment constraints are as follows:

1. *Rate-of-Return Restricted Investments*. Investments are rate-of-return restricted if their adoption requires their *IRR*s to exceed some required rate of return or their *NPV*s to exceed zero when discounted by the required rate of return. Otherwise, they are not rate-of-return restricted investments.

2. *Mutually-Exclusive Investment Constraints*. Investments *A* and *B* are mutually exclusive if the adoption of investment *A* precludes the adoption of investment *B*, or if the adoption of *B* precludes the adoption of *A*. Otherwise, they are not mutually-exclusive investments.

3. *Amount of Capital*. Investments are subject to capital rationing if the amount of investment funds is restricted to an absolute amount. Otherwise, the capital available for investing is not constrained.

4. *Increasing Cost of Capital*. As the investment size increases, so do the average and marginal costs of borrowing. This condition limits the amount that can be profitably invested.

Rate-of-Return Restricted Investments ⸻⸻⸻⸻⸻

First, consider ranking investment alternatives with the simplest restriction. The only requirement is that the *IRR*s exceed a required rate of return or that, when using a required rate of return as a discount rate, their *NPV*s are positive. The opportunity cost of capital, or required rate of return, is given. This restriction makes the implicit assumption that the firm has an unlimited supply of investment funds at an opportunity cost of capital determined in the market. Thus, the *IRR*s of alternative investments are not opportunity costs because they do not limit additional investments.

All investments with a rate of return exceeding their opportunity cost will be accepted. This criterion is indicated by an *NPV* that exceeds zero or by an *IRR* that exceeds the required rate of return. The question is: Should the restriction be implemented using the *NPV* criterion with the market rate of return as the discount rate, or should *IRR*s be calculated and compared to the required rate of return? Both approaches will give the same answer unless the homogenous measures principle is violated.

Mutually-Exclusive Investment Constraints

The next class of investment constraints is more restrictive than the case just considered. This investment case usually considers two constraints simultaneously: only one investment can be adopted and it must also pass the rate of return criterion. In rare cases, only the mutually-exclusive constraint is applied. When only the mutually-exclusive constraint is applied, the investor must choose a preferred investment from those available, regardless of its rate of return.

Examples of mutually-exclusive investments include the selection of a family car, the location for one's business or home, and the choice of pollution control equipment required by local zoning laws. In each example, a mutually-exclusive choice must be made: Requiring that one of the mutually-exclusive investments be adopted is a strong assumption. This constraint does not allow the choice to be "none of the above."

If investments are not mutually-exclusive, adopting individual projects with positive *NPV*s or *IRR*s above the required rate of return increases the present value or equity of the firm. However, if the investments are mutually-exclusive, then the optimal choice is the investment with the largest positive *NPV*.

Capital-Rationed Investments

Now, suppose that the firm is limited in the amount of capital it can invest to a capital budget restriction of *B*. The firm is also assumed to face a constant cost of capital over the range of possible investments whose sum does not exceed *B*. The question is: What criterion should be used? The situation is further complicated because investments are usually available in lumpy amounts.

This investment problem is illustrated using an example. Suppose the firm has three possible investments: *J, K*, and *L*. The total investment fund available is $500 and the required rate of return is 10 percent. These investment choices are described in Table 6.11.

All three investments, *J, K*, and *L*, have positive *NPV*s and all pass the required rate of return test. But because of the capital constraint, the adoption of *J, L*, or *J* and *L* precludes the investment of *K*. However, if selection were based on *NPV, K* would be selected and its *NPV* would equal $45.45. If *J* and *L* were selected, a feasible alternative since their investments sum to $500, *NPV* increases to $47.27 ($18.18+$29.09). Thus, the order in which profitable investments are selected influences the total return from the investment. If the investor based the selection of investments in Table 6.11 on descending *IRR*s, the *NPV* of the investment package would not be maximized. Plotting the two feasible investment *IRR*s against their investment amounts results in the relationship described in Figure 6.3.

Table 6.11 Capital Budgets and Investment Choices

Project	Initial Cash Flow	Cash Flow in Period 1	NPV @ 10%	IRR
J	$-100	$130	$18.18	30%
K	$-500	$600	$45.45	20%
L	$-400	$472	$29.09	18%
J+L	$-500	$602	$47.27	20.4%

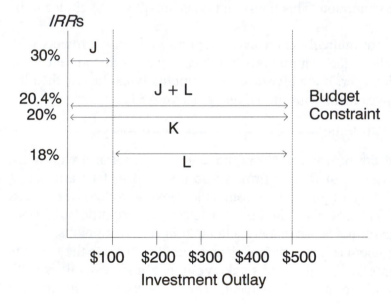

Figure 6.3
Investment Choices J, K, and L and J+K Plotted Against their Respective *IRR*s

The case described in Table 6.11 is easily solved by inspection because of the limited investment choices. Investment problems with many choices are less easily solved. The approach is to organize all feasible investment portfolios and determine their *NPV*s. Then, select the portfolio with the largest *NPV*.

In practice, integer programming is a feasible way to complete these calculations. That is, in order to avoid the violation of the homogenous measures principle, all investments that sum to the capital limitation and pass the rate-of-return criterion must be summed and compared. If the sum is less than the capital limitation, *NPV* comparisons are still correct, assuming the difference between the investment and capital limitation is invested at the opportunity cost of capital.

Increasing Cost of Capital Constraints

The most difficult constraint to analyze using present value techniques is the increasing cost of capital constraint. First, consider the validity of the increasing cost of capital assumption.

Proprietary firms have two sources of investment funds. They can liquidate other investments, including various types of financial investments, or they can reduce their credit reserves by borrowing.[1] If the funds used for the investment are obtained by liquidation, one would not expect all of the liquidated investments to yield the same rate of return. Nor would all investments held by the firm have the same degree of liquidity (measured by the cost of converting the assets to cash). So, the firm liquidating assets to fund new investments would likely begin by liquidating the least profitable and/or the most liquid ones. As additional invest-ments of larger size are funded, the cost of liquidating assets and the rate of return foregone on the liquidated assets will increase as more profitable and/or less liquid investments are converted to cash. In turn, these higher transactions costs and foregone rates of return imply increasing costs of financing the new investments.

On the other hand, when investments are funded by borrowing, the cost of borrowing likely increases for two reasons. First, lenders respond to the increasing risk of recovering their borrowed funds by charging higher interest rates and/or limiting the amount of credit extended. As the borrower's ratio of debt-to-equity (leverage) increases, the lender tends to increase the interest rate in response to the greater risk of loan loss. A second reason for an increasing cost of borrowing is attributed to increases in the implicit value of liquid credit reserves. These reserves are depleted by borrowing. Credit in reserve has value because it provides a liquid source of cash to cope with financial adversities or for responding to investment opportunities (Barry, Baker, and Sanint). As the credit reserve is depleted through borrowing, the marginal value of the remaining units of credit increases because a valuable source of liquidity is being depleted. Borrowing also enables the firm to avoid the higher liquidation costs associated with the alternative of liquidating investments. Thus, the cost of capital tends to increase whether the firm funds investments through the use of borrowed funds or with funds obtained from liquidating assets.[2]

The standard technique employed in corporate finance to determine the discount rate for capital budgeting when capital costs are not constant is to combine a firm's investment opportunity schedule (*IOS*) and its marginal cost of capital schedule (*MCC*) (e.g., Brigham and Gapenski). The firm's *IOS* can be represented by graphing the *IRR* of the firm's potential investments against the capital investment required for each project. Investments are graphed in order of decreasing *IRR*. The *MCC* is represented by graphing the firm's cost of capital as capital investment increases. The discount rate for capital budgeting is found at the intersection between the *IOS* and *MCC* schedules. Figure 6.4 illustrates the combined *IOS* and *MCC* schedules and the corresponding discount rate.

The discount rate, *kw*, is often the one used to analyze the set of investments available to the firm. Except for mutually-exclusive investments, the firm will invest in all projects with *IRR*s greater than *kw*. For mutually-exclusive projects, the firm will choose the project with the highest *NPV* using *kw* as the discount rate.[3]

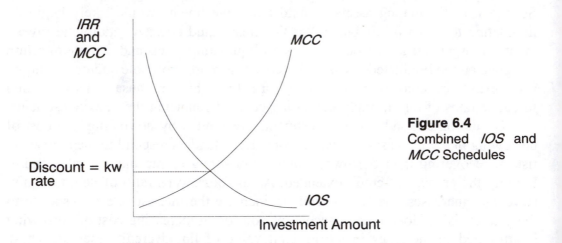

Figure 6.4
Combined *IOS* and *MCC* Schedules

Several practical problems prevent applying the method described by Figure 6.4 when the firm's investment opportunity schedule *(IOS)* and marginal cost of capital schedule *(MCC)* are equated. Most projects are not available in one unit intervals. Moreover, when they are lumpy and the cost of capital is rising, the intersection of the *IOS* curve and the *MCC* curve may be as shown in Figure 6.5, thus yielding an indeterminant investment amount.

Investment lumpiness must be dealt with. That is, the marginal cost of capital must be made consistent with the size of the investment being considered. For example, if an investment of size, I_1, is being considered, then the marginal cost of capital averaged over amount I_1 should be considered the marginal cost of capital for this investment. Thus, assuming that funds are acquired in continuously divisible amounts with increasing costs, the match-up of the average of the amount of funds required for each individual investment is shown in Figure 6.6.

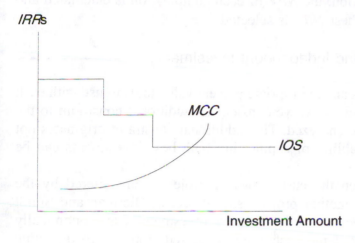

Figure 6.5
MCC and *IOS* Schedules When Investments are Available in Lumpy Amounts

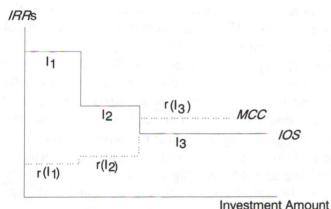

Figure 6.6
MCC and *IOS* Schedules When Costs of Funds Are Calculated in a Way Consistent with Lumpy Investment Choices

   The match-up of cost functions for applying the marginal cost approach must satisfy the homogenous measures principle. To use the cost of the last dollar invested in the project to evaluate a lumpy project would violate the homogeneity of size principle. The average cost of dollars for the investment, not the last dollar, should be used in the evaluation.

   In practice, a separate cost of capital curve must be calculated for each possible investment combination to determine the appropriate mix of assets. After having obtained all combinations of investment portfolios, the work is still not done. The next step is to find the average cost of capital for the combination of investments and use it as the required rate of return. Finally, with all possible combinations of feasible portfolios identified, and the required rate of return established for each combination, the *NPV* of each combination is calculated and the combination with the highest *NPV* is selected.

Economically Dependent and Independent Investments

So far, capital constraints and appropriate present value tools to use with each constraint have been described. Now, we consider an additional constraint to the way in which investments are analyzed. This additional constraint originates not with limitations on the availability of capital, but with how investments can be considered for adoption.

The problem arises when the cash flows of project *A* are altered by the adoption or non-adoption of another project, say project *B*. Bierman and Smidt referred to this condition as economic dependence. Investment *A* is economically independent of investment *B* if the cash flows expected from *A* are the same regardless of whether investment *B* is accepted or rejected. Otherwise, investments *A* and *B* are dependent.

When evaluating economically independent investments, no alterations in the procedures described above are needed. However, economically dependent investments require a change in the evaluation procedures.

A special case of economically dependent investments has already been described. This is the case of mutually-exclusive investments. In this case, the dependence was absolute. One investment was a perfect or required substitute for the other. At the other extreme, investment *A* may be a prerequisite for investment *B*. One would not consider investing in a building without simultaneously acquiring control of the land on which the building is to be constructed. Thus, for purposes of analysis, the investment in the land and the building would be considered one project. Similarly, the evaluation of alternative combinations of land and buildings would be considered alternative projects.

Between the extremes of perfect substitutes and perfect complements are combinations of investments that are neither required nor mutually exclusive, but still have interdependent cash flows. These dependencies are handled by referring to the total costs and returns principle. That principle requires that all costs and returns associated with a project's adoption be included in its projected cash flows.

Thus, if the adoption of project *B* reduces the cash flow of an existing project *A*, then the cash flow difference must be subtracted as a cost from *B*'s cash flow. If, on the other hand, *A*'s cash flow increases when project *B* is added, the additional cash flow must be credited to project *B*. In this manner, the evaluation of each project is based on the project's marginal contributions to the firm.

Summary

This chapter has focused on ranking investment alternatives using the *NPV* and *IRR* criteria, and on the procedures for attaining consistency between these two evaluative criteria. When investments are being compared, the homogenous measures principle is important to consider. For example, only investments of the same size can be compared. This chapter showed how differences in rankings produced by *NPV* and *IRR* models can be attributed to violations of the homogenous measures principle.

Unique problems are encountered when investments are lumpy. When faced with the discrete investment choices and a limited amount of capital, the solution requires an exhaustive comparison of all possible combinations of choice. When the number of investment combinations is large, this evaluation can best be performed using a computerized technique such as integer programming.

Finally, when faced with increasing costs of capital, and assuming continuity, maximization with respect to the level of investment indicates a selection criterion in which the marginal costs of capital are equal to the marginal rates of return on investments. This marginal result is familiar to economists. However, the rule must be modified when dealing with discrete choices.

In sum, this chapter has addressed the realistic world of discrete choices and business investments varying in duration, size, and timing of cash flows. Each of these situations was presented under conditions of mutual exclusiveness, capital limitations, rate-of-return constraints, and increasing costs of capital.

Endnotes

1. A large corporate firm would have the potential to seek equity capital funding through the sale of additional shares of stock.

2. Modigliani and Miller suggested that arbitrage in perfect capital markets would assure the result that the opportunity cost of capital is independent of the firm's debt/asset ratio. Since we are not assuming that investors face perfect capital markets, the opportunity cost of capital is not assumed to be independent of the debt/asset ratio.

3. The *IOS=MCC* method of finding the optimal portfolio of investments is justified as follows. In the process, it will become clear that selecting the investment portfolio using an average discount rate (as is frequently done) will likely produce incorrect *NPV* calculations. Let $R(I)$ be the marginal return earned on an investment of I amount. Let $r(I)$ equal the opportunity cost of the last dollar invested. Let V_0 equal the total quantity of funds invested. Then, the present value of a one-period project equals:

$$NPV = \int_0^{V_0} R(I)\,e^{-r(I)}\,dI - V_0.$$

Maximizing the expression above for V_0, the first-order conditions are found to equal:

$$R(V_0)\,e^{-r(V_0)} - 1 = 0,$$

or:

$$\left[\frac{R(V_0)}{1}\right] - 1 \approx r(V_0),$$

since $e^{r(V_0)}$ can be approximated by $[1 + r(V_0)]$.

The expression $R(V_0)/1$ is one plus a percent. The expression $[R(V_0)/1-1]$ is also the *IRR* of the last dollar invested. When I is at its optimal level (i.e., maximum *NPV*), $[R(V_0)-1]$ equals $r(V_0)$, the cost of the last dollar invested and homogeneity of measures is maintained.

Moreover, having found an optimal investment level, V_0^{*}, *NPV* can be calculated as:

$$NPV = \int_0^{V_0^{*}} R(I)\,e^{-r(I)}\,dI - V_0^{*}.$$

One may want to find the average cost of capital $\bar{r}$ where:

$$\int_0^{V_0^{*}} R(I)\,e^{-r(I)}\,dI = e^{-\bar{r}} \int_0^{V_0^{*}} R(I)\,dI = e^{-\bar{r}}\,S,$$

where S equals total returns from V_0. Then $\bar{r}$ is simply:

$$\bar{r} = -\ln\left[\int_0^{I_0^{*}} \frac{R(I)}{S}\,e^{-r(I)}\,dI\right].$$

It should be clear that $\bar{r}$ is a weighted function of $r(I)$. It is not a simple arithmetic average. Thus, for practical purposes, *NPV* should be calculated as the sum of the individual projects — each with a different discount rate.

The question may arise: Why use the *MCC* as the discount rate when calculating the *NPV* when higher return investments exist? The answer is because these higher return investments are not being sacrificed. Only the investment whose return is equal to the *MCC* is being sacrificed. Hence, its return is the discount rate and the reinvestment rate as well. Moreover, since units of an additional investment and *MCC* are consistent, the homogenous measures principle is preserved.

Review Questions

1. What prevents the application of the calculus of maximization to most investment problems?

2. Explain the investment ranking conflict between *NPV* and *IRR* criteria described in Table 6.1. How can such a conflict exist for two reasonable investment ranking criteria?

3. Review the limitations often associated with the use of the *IRR* criteria.

4. Refer to Table 6.2. Since the *IRR* and *NPV* rankings are inconsistent, which criteria would you follow — or which ranking best matches your preferred ranking?

5. Refer to Tables 6.6 and 6.7. When does making investments homogenous in size resolve the ranking conflict between *NPV* and *IRR*?

6. As Table 6.4 points out, if periodic cash flows are different, the homogeneity of size requirement is violated even if investments require the same initial investment. But if they produce identical cash flows, the investments are equally valued. How can we maintain homogeneity of size and still evaluate and rank different investments?

7. Describe two approaches for making the term of investments homogenous. What determines which method should be used to achieve term homogeneity?

8. Describe four ways in which an investor's capital budget may be restricted. Give realistic examples of the four cases of capital budget restrictions.

9. When is it necessary to make size and term adjustments to achieve homogeneity of size and term?

10. Can you be sure that *IRR* will rank mutually-exclusive investments consistent with the *NPV* criterion? Please explain.

11. Assume you have a capital budget, *B*, and it is possible to invest in $V_0^1, ..., V_0^n$, all of different sizes. Recommend an approach for maximizing the investment's *NPV* for a given capital budget, *B*.

12. Explain the steps required to rank investments under the increasing cost of capital assumption.

13. Define economically dependent and independent investments. What investment principle is most relevant for evaluating economically dependent investments?

Application Questions

1. Assume an investment of $2,500 would produce the following cash inflows:

$$R_1 = \$\ 800$$
$$R_2 = -\$1,200$$
$$R_3 = \$1,000$$
$$R_4 = -\$\ 600$$
$$R_5 = \$1,500$$
$$R_6 = \$1,800$$

With an opportunity cost of capital equal to 10 percent, would you approve the investment? For what discount rate is *NPV*=0?

2. Consider the following investments:

		Cash Flows				
Project	Initial Investment	(1)	(2)	(3)	(4)	(5)
A	$1000	$300	$600	$850		
B	$1000	$700	$500	$200	$100	$150
C	$1000	$400	$300	$100	$600	

(a) Without adjusting for differences in term or size of investment:
   (1) Rank the projects according to their *IRR*s.
   (2) Rank the projects according to their *NPV*s assuming a required rate of return of 18 percent.
   (3) Discuss the similarities or differences in the rankings.
(b) Repeat part (a) adjusting for term and size differences assuming a reinvestment rate of 18 percent. How do these adjustments affect the rankings?

3. Evaluate the four investment projects shown below. Consider that in the financial markets, the firm can raise up to $250,000 at a constant cost of 15 percent. Which investment(s) should the firm take? Discuss your results. Assume there are no taxes.

		Cash Flows in Periods 1-5				
Project	Initial Outlay	(1)	(2)	(3)	(4)	(5)
K	$120,000	$40,000	$60,000	$70,000	-$50,000	$80,000
L	$90,000	$20,000	$60,000	$60,000		
M	$150,000	$50,000	-$20,000	-$20,000	$60,000	$40,000
N	$100,000	$10,000	$30,000	$30,000	$80,000	$50,000

4. In Table 6.1, project *A* represents an investment and project *B* represents a loan. What do the results of Figure 6.1 suggest when the firm is calculating a maximum-bid price?

5. Demonstrate with a simple example how to rank repeatable investments of the same size consistent with the homogenous measures principle.

6. This chapter discussed how investments can be constrained by rates of return, mutual exclusiveness, capital rationing, and by increasing cost of capital. Consider investing in a perfectly competitive financial market. Which, if any, of the investment constraints would apply when investing in a perfectly competitive financial market? Defend your answer.

7. Suppose projects *A* and *B* require the same amount of funds, but *A*'s economic life is two periods while *B*'s economic life is three periods. Describe how to achieve term consistency if:

   (a) Neither *A* nor *B* is repeatable and the opportunity cost of capital is given.
   (b) If *B* can be repeated once and *A* can be repeated any number of times.
   (c) If *A* and *B* are both infinitely repeatable.

References

Alchian, A.A. "The Rate of Interest, Fisher's Rate of Return Over Cost and Keynes' Internal Rate of Return." *American Economic Review* 45(1955):938-42.

Barry, P.J., C.B. Baker, and L.R. Sanint. "Farmer's Credit Risks and Liquidity Management." *American Journal of Agricultural Economics* 63(1981):216-27.

Barry, P.J., P.N. Ellinger, J.A. Hopkin, and C.B. Baker. *Financial Management in Agriculture*, 5th edition. Danville, IL: Interstate Publishers, 1995.

Bierman, H., Jr. and S. Smidt. *The Capital Budgeting Decision*, 4th edition. New York: MacMillan Publishing Company, 1975.

Brealey, R. and S.C. Myers. *Principles of Corporate Finance*. New York: McGraw-Hill Series in Finance, 1981.

Brigham, E.F. and L.C. Gapenski. *Financial Management: Theory and Practice*, 5th edition. Chicago, IL: Dryden Press, 1988.

Dorfman, R. "The Meaning of Internal Rates of Return." *Journal of Finance* 46(1981):1011-21.

Johnson, R.W. *Capital Budgeting.* Dubuque, IA: Kendall/Hunt Publishing Company, 1977.

Levy, H. and M. Sarnat. *Capital Investment and Financial Decisions*, 3rd edition. United Kingdom: Prentice-Hall International, 1986.

Lorie, J.H. and L.J. Savage. "Three Problems in Rationing Capital." *Journal of Business* 28(1955):229-39.

Modigliani, F. and M.H. Miller. "The Cost of Capital, Corporation Finance and the Theory of Investment." *American Economic Review* 48(1958):261-97.

Van Horne, J.C. *Financial Management and Policy*, 3rd edition. Englewood Cliffs, NJ: Prentice-Hall, 1974.

Part 3

Economic Analysis Using Present Value Models

Chapter 7

Cash Flows, Capital Gains, and Liquidity[1]

Key words: capital gains, cash flows, coverage ratios, current-to-total-return (CT) ratios, debt/asset ratios, depreciation patterns, inflation, interest rates, liquidity.

Introduction

An asset may earn two types of returns for investors: (1) time-dated cash flows (called current returns); and (2) capital gains (or capital losses). As shown in this chapter, the relative importance of current returns versus capital gains under equilibrium asset pricing conditions is directly related to the time pattern of the cash flows—growing, constant, or declining—and to the magnitude of the growth or decline rates. In turn, the combination of current returns versus capital gains (losses) has important liquidity implications for investors, especially when an investment is financed with debt capital. Debt-financed investments in assets whose earnings are expected to grow over time may experience a cash shortfall, called a financing gap. This gap is most likely to occur early in the investment's life, or when the cash returns are less than the scheduled payments of principal plus interest. As time passes, the cash returns grow in size until they eventually exceed the repayment obligation and the liquidity problem is solved.

The term liquidity is used to describe "near cash assets" because of the similarity between liquids and liquid assets. A liquid such as water can fill the shape of its container and is easily transferred from one container to another. Similarly, liquid funds easily fulfill the financial needs of their owners. That is, liquid funds are easily transferred between the parties to an exchange. Illiquid assets such as land and buildings (like solids) are not easily used to fulfill financial needs because their ownership and control are not easily transferred.

A firm's liquidity reflects its capacity to generate sufficient cash to meet its financial commitments as they come due. A firm's failure to meet its financial commitments results in bankruptcy, even though the firm might be profitable and has positive equity. Consequently, firms must account for an investment's liquidity in addition to measuring its net present value (*NPV*).

There are several measures that reflect a firm's or an investment's liquidity. One measure is the *current ratio*, the ratio of current assets divided by current liabilities. Because current assets can be quickly converted to cash, they are an important source of liquidity for the firm. A similar ratio is the *acid test ratio*, the ratio of a firm's cash plus government securities and other cash equivalents divided by current liabilities.

The liquidity measures described above, while helpful, do not satisfy the need for a liquidity measure specific to an investment. Moreover, the measures described above relate to the firm's liquidity, not to the contributions of a particular investment to the liquidity of the firm or how these contributions may change over time. Furthermore, any investment-specific liquidity measure must include cash flows.

The liquidity measure explored in this chapter that provides investment-specific liquidity information over time is the current-to-total-return (*CT*) ratio. The *CT* ratio is derived from market equilibrium conditions where *NPV* is zero and represents the ratio of current (cash) returns to total returns. A related liquidity measure is the coverage (*C*) ratio. A coverage ratio is the ratio of cash returns to loan payments or other debt obligations in any particular period.

In this chapter, present value (*PV*) models are used to explore the relationship between the mix of current returns versus capital gains and the time pattern of an asset's earnings. Then, we relate the mix of returns to the level of debt claims on an investment. The *CT* and *C* ratios are derived and illustrated. Finally, important interrelationships between the two ratios are considered.

Current-to-Total-Returns Ratio

The *CT* ratio is a financial measure derived from the relationship in a given period between an asset's current (cash) returns, its capital gains (or losses), and its total return or the sum of current returns and capital gains (or losses). To derive the *CT* measure, we begin with the expression:

total rate of return=current rate of return + capital gains (losses) rate of return

The above relationship is expressed by letting V_0 and V_1 equal the investment's beginning and end-of-period values, respectively. Then, R_1 is defined as the asset's net cash or current returns earned at the end of the first period. Finally, an investment's total rate of return is defined in period one as r_1, which is the sum of capital gains $(V_1-V_0)/V_0$ plus the current rate of return (R_1/V_0):

$$r_1 = \underbrace{\frac{R_1}{V_0}}_{\substack{\text{current} \\ \text{rate of} \\ \text{return}}} + \underbrace{\frac{(V_1-V_0)}{V_0}}_{\substack{\text{capital gains} \\ \text{(loss) rate} \\ \text{of return}}}. \tag{7.1}$$

A useful measure obtained from equation (7.1) is the ratio of net cash returns, or current cash returns, R_1, divided by total returns, $r_1 V_0$. This ratio indicates the percentage of total returns the firm receives as cash. The higher this ratio, the greater the likelihood that the firm has the liquidity required to meet its debt obligations. Rearranging (7.1) yields the ratio of current to total returns in the first period equal to CT_1:

$$CT_1 = \frac{R_1}{r_1 V_0} = 1 - \frac{(V_1-V_0)/V_0}{r_1}, \tag{7.2a}$$

or:

$$CT_1 = 1 - \frac{\eta_1}{r_1}, \tag{7.2b}$$

where $\eta_1=(V_1-V_0)/V_0$, or the capital gains (loss) rate in period one.

The *CT* measure is now derived for two commonly used geometric series: the geometric growth series and the geometric decay series.

CT Ratio for the Geometric Growth Series

Consider an asset that is expected to generate a perpetual series of cash flows that grow at rate g per period. If R_0 is the initial cash payment and r is the discount rate, then the growth model is expressed as:

$$V_0 = \frac{R_0(1+g)}{1+r} + \frac{R_0(1+g)^2}{(1+r)^2} + \dots = \frac{R_0(1+g)}{r-g}. \tag{7.3}$$

Solving (7.3) for r, the total rate of return is expressed as the sum of a current rate of return plus a rate of capital gain:

$$r = \frac{R_0(1+g)}{V_0} + g.$$

$\underset{\substack{\text{current}\\\text{rate of}\\\text{return}}}{\qquad\qquad} \underset{\substack{\text{capital gains}\\\text{rate of}\\\text{return}}}{\qquad\qquad}$ (7.4)

To express the rate-of-return model in proportional terms, both sides are divided by r, yielding:

$$1 = \frac{R_0(1+g)}{rV_0} + \frac{g}{r}.$$

$\underset{\substack{\text{percentage}\\\text{of returns}\\\text{in cash}}}{\qquad\qquad} \underset{\substack{\text{percentage}\\\text{of returns}\\\text{earned as}\\\text{capital gains}}}{\qquad\qquad}$ (7.5)

Corresponding to (7.2a), the *CT* ratio in period 1 is the first term to the right of the equals sign in (7.5), or the percentage of returns received as cash:

$$CT_1 = \frac{R_0(1+g)}{rV_0}.$$

After substituting for V_0 using (7.3), CT_1 can be expressed as:

$$CT_1 = 1 - \frac{g}{r},$$ (7.6)

which corresponds to (7.2b).

Example 7.2 will help illustrate the practical importance of the *CT* ratio as a measure of the firm.

CT Ratio for the Geometric Decay Series

Now consider an asset that is expected to generate a series of cash flows that decline at rate d per period. If R_0 is the initial cash payment and r is the discount rate, then the asset-pricing model is expressed as:

$$V_0 = \frac{R_0(1-d)}{1+r} + \frac{R_0(1-d)^2}{(1+r)^2} + \dots,$$

Example 7.1: *CT* **Ratio for the Geometric Growth Series**

If $R_0 = \$100$ earned in perpetuity, $r = 0.10$, and $g = 0.05$, then the asset's *PV* is:

$$V_0 = \frac{R_0(1+g)}{r-g} = \frac{\$100(1.05)}{0.10-0.05} = \$2,100.$$

The current rate of return is:

$$\frac{R_0(1+g)}{V_0} = \frac{\$100(1.05)}{\$2,100} = 0.05,$$

and the rate of capital gain is:

$$g = 0.05.$$

The *CT* ratio then is:

$$CT_1 = \frac{r-g}{r} = \frac{0.10-0.05}{0.10} = 0.50,$$

or:

$$CT_1 = 1 - \frac{g}{r} = 1 - \frac{0.05}{0.10} = 0.50.$$

Example 7.2: Financing Farmland and the *CT* Ratio

It is frequently assumed that farmland values can be explained by equation (7.3) (Robison, Lins, and VenKataraman). If so, then inflation that increases future cash flows and creates capital gains is likely to reduce the firm's *CT* ratio and possibly create cash flow problems for persons who purchase long-term durables. To compare this theory with "real world" data, we construct an enterprise budget for one acre of land capable of producing medium yield corn grain. The data used to construct the table were reported by Michigan farmers as part of Michigan State University's record-keeping system, Telfarm, during 1979 (a year chosen because of high levels of inflation).

Example 7.2, Cont'd.: Financing Farmland and the *CT* Ratio

According to the budget estimates in Table 7.1, an acre of medium yield corn land at 1979 corn prices would have earned $61.69 ($R_1$). Letting ($r$-$g$) equal 5 percent and using equation (7.3), an acre of medium yield corn grain land would have had a market value of $1,233.80 ($61.69/.05). In 1979, Federal Land Banks (FLBs) in Michigan were offering interest rates (adjusted for stock purchases required by the banks) of 9.5 percent for farm real estate loans. If 100 percent of the land were financed, interest costs in the first year would have been $117.21 (9.5 percent x $1,233.80) and the cash flow deficit would have equaled $55.52 ($61.69 - $117.21).

If we let r be the FLB rate of 9.5 percent and let g equal 4.5 percent, the *CT* ratio (see (7.2b)) is:

$$CT_1 = 1 - \frac{0.045}{0.095} = 0.53.$$

This low *CT* measure is consistent with the cash flow shortage of $55.52.

Table 7.1 Enterprise Budget for One Acre of Medium-Yield Corn Grain

Gross Income	
(100 bushels x $2.00)	$200.00
Expenses:[a]	
Labor (6.1 hours x $5.00)	30.50
Repairs and Maintenance	9.80
Seeds	11.33
Fertilizer	38.25
Insecticides and Herbicides	12.40
Fuel	6.00
Utilities	2.30
Harvesting, Trucking	6.20
Corn Drying	14.00
Other Expenses (including interest operating debt)	7.53
	$138.31
Net Income (Gross Income - Expenses)	$61.69
Interest Expense on Real Estate Loan (IRR x V_{t-1})	$117.21
(9.5% x $1,233.80)	
Net Cash Shortage	($55.52)

[a]Source: Nott, S.B.

or:

$$V_0 = \frac{R_0(1-d)}{r+d}, \tag{7.7}$$

and the total rate of return, r, is the sum of the current cash rate of return minus the rate of capital loss or depreciation:

$$r = \underbrace{\frac{R_0(1-d)}{V_0}}_{\substack{\text{current} \\ \text{rate of} \\ \text{returns}}} - \underbrace{d.}_{\substack{\text{capital loss} \\ \text{rate of} \\ \text{returns}}} \tag{7.8}$$

The CT ratio in period 1 is the cash return $[R_0(1-d)]$ divided by the total return, rV_0, corresponding to (7.2b):

$$CT_1 = \frac{R_0(1-d)}{rV_0}. \tag{7.9}$$

After substituting for V_0 using (7.7), CT_1 can be expressed as:

$$CT_1 = 1 + \frac{d}{r}, \tag{7.10}$$

which corresponds to equation (7.2b).

Liquidity Implications

From expressions (7.4) and (7.8), it is clear that the mix of capital gain (loss) versus current return depends directly on the rates of growth (g) and decline (d), as do the CT ratios. Under conditions of growth, a higher value of g decreases the proportion of total return that is current return. (Note that r remains constant under higher growth, but the asset value, of course, increases.) The result is a reduction in the liquidity of earnings as the growth rate of earnings increases because the current cash returns have declined in importance relative to capital gains. (See Table 7.2 for a numerical illustration of the changing mix of total returns as the growth rate of earnings changes from 0 percent to 8 percent.)

Example 7.3: *CT* Ratio for the Geometric Decay Series

If R_0=100, r=0.10, and d=0.05, then the asset's value is $V_0 = R_0(1-d)/(r+d)$ = \$633.33, the current rate of return $R_0(1-d)/V_0$ is \$100(1-0.05)/\$633.33 or 15 percent. The value of the asset equals:

$$V_0 = \frac{R_0\,(1-d)}{r+d} = \frac{\$100\,(1-0.05)}{(0.10+0.05)} = \$633.33.$$

The *CT* ratio can be calculated as:

$$CT_1 = 1 + \frac{d}{r} = 1 + \frac{0.05}{0.10} = 1.5.$$

Table 7.2 Total Return, Current Return, and Capital Gain (Loss) for Different Growth (Decay) Rates of Earnings with r=0.10

Growth (Decay) Rate, %	Total Rate of Return, r, %	Current Rate of Return, $R_1/r_1 V_0$, %	Capital Gain (Loss), $(V_1 - V_0)/V_0$, %	Proportion of Total	
				Current Return	Capital Gain (Loss)
g=8	10	2	8	20	80
g=6	10	4	6	40	60
g=4	10	6	4	60	40
g=2	10	8	2	80	20
0	10	10	0	100	0
d=2	10	12	-2	120	-20
d=4	10	14	-4	140	-40
d=6	10	16	-6	160	-60
d=8	10	18	-8	180	-80

Under conditions of geometric decay, a higher value of d (a negative capital gain) increases the proportion of total returns that is current returns. The result is an increase in the liquidity of earnings. This result occurs because as d increases, the current cash returns have increased in importance relative to capital loss or depreciation. (Again, see Table 7.2 for a numerical illustration of the changing mix of total returns as the rate of decline in earnings changes from $d=0$ to $d=0.08$.)

These results clearly show the paradoxical conditions that growth in projected earnings can weaken the liquidity due to the increasing relative importance of capital gains. In contrast, a decline in projected earnings can strengthen the liquidity due to the increasing relative importance of current cash returns. At the same time, the wealth effects are as expected. Asset values increase as earnings increase, while asset values fall for declining cash flow streams.

Relationships to Challengers and Defenders

The CT ratios in (7.2a) and (7.2b) can be interpreted using the descriptions of challengers and defenders introduced in earlier chapters. In equation (7.3), r is the defender's period one internal rate of return while $R_0(1+g)$ is the challenger's first period net cash return. Equation (7.4) reflects an equilibrium condition in which the defender's opportunity cost of capital is equal to the sum of the challenger's current cash rate of return plus the rate of return in capital gain, g. If an asset does generate a capital gain ($g>0$), then net cash flow, $R_0(1+g)$, will be less than the opportunity cost of capital, rV_0. If no capital gains occur ($g=0$), net cash flows will equal the opportunity cost of capital.

When capital gains are incurred, the challenger's cash earnings in the first period are less than its opportunity cost by an amount equal to the capital gains earned in that period. If the shortfall between the opportunity cost of capital and the cash earned in the first period were deducted from the investment and converted to cash, the dollar amount invested in the capital good would stay constant. This cash deficit is analogous to a capital gain reserve. If the reserve were liquidated, the cash proceeds would cover the difference between the cash earnings and the investment's total returns.

When a capital loss occurs ($d>0$), the challenger's cash earnings exceed the investment's opportunity cost by the amount of the capital loss. If cash earnings in excess of the investment's opportunity cost were reinvested in the capital good, the amount invested in the capital good would remain constant. The difference between the cash return and the opportunity cost, under capital loss conditions, is equal to a reserve for capital loss or depreciation; reinvesting it restores the capital good to its original value.

Example 7.4: Capital Gains (Losses), Land Values, and *CT* Ratios

Capital gains and losses associated with changing land values produce time-varying *CT* ratios. To illustrate how *CT* ratios have differed over time, we graph CT_t for the State of Michigan for the period from 1950 to 1989. The opportunity cost measures (r in the *CT* formula) are found by multiplying the Federal Land Bank's interest rate on new loans times the market value of Michigan farmland. Cash returns are measured by cash rents paid for the use of land.

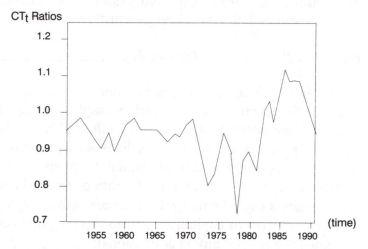

Figure 7.1 *CT* Ratios for the State of Michigan from 1950 to 1989

Source: Various Issues of *Farm Real Estate Market Developments* and USDA unpublished data.

As the data indicate, during the 1970's, Michigan's *CT* ratios for land were consistently below one, contributing to illiquidity in the farming sector. During the 1980's, however, cash returns consistently exceeded the cost of capital.

In summary, *CT* ratios combine cash flows and asset values obtained from the balance sheet. Standard liquidity measures obtained from the balance sheet alone are the current ratio (current assets/current liabilities) or working capital (current assets minus current liabilities). The balance sheet measures of liquidity provide important information about reserves available at a point in time for meeting cash flow requirements. In contrast, the *CT* ratio indicates the importance of current cash returns relative to total returns during a period of time when the difference between the two types of returns is a capital gain or loss.

Financial Feasibility, Coverage Ratios, and *CT* Ratios

Investments in assets can be evaluated according to both profitability and financial feasibility criteria. Profitability analysis focuses on whether the acceptance of an asset will increase the investor's present wealth position. Financial feasibility analysis considers whether an investment will generate cash flows consistent with the terms of financial capital, especially debt capital, that are used to finance the investment. Is an investment expected to generate sufficient net cash flow in each period to satisfy the requirements for repayment of the loan principal plus interest? If not, then the investment is financially infeasible in and of itself; part of the cash needed to serve the debt obligation must come from other sources of earnings or from additional borrowing. Thus, a simple test of financial feasibility is to compare the cash generated by the investment in a given period (e.g., the first period of the investment's life) with the debt servicing requirement. Various forms of coverage ratios can be used to conduct these tests.

Coverage Ratios

Firms faced with cash flow obligations are primarily concerned with the relationship between their net cash income and debt obligations. The accepted measure of this relationship is the coverage ratio. In the tth period, the coverage ratio, C_t, is equal to the net cash return, R_t, divided by the debt payment obligation A_t:

$$C_t = \frac{R_t}{A_t}. \tag{7.11}$$

If the coverage ratio is equal to or exceeds 1.0, then financial feasibility occurs. If coverage is less than one, infeasibility is the case.

In most cases, the debt obligation is a constant annuity payment, "*A*," that depends on the price of the purchased asset, V_0; the financed proportion of the purchase price γ; the term of the loan n; and the interest rate charged on the loan r^f. The relationship between the amount financed, the fixed annuity payment, and the $US_0(r^f,n)$ factor is expressed as:

$$\gamma V_0 = A \, US_0 \, (r^f, n),$$

and solving for A:

$$A = \frac{\gamma V_0}{US_0 \, (r^f, n)}. \tag{7.12}$$

Loan payments need not be constant. For example, a graduated payment loan requires increasing (decreasing) payments. A graduated payment loan requires that the payments grow at a constant rate, g, and fully amortize the loan by the end of period n. Under these conditions, the loan payment in any loan period t is $A_t = A_0(1+g)^t$. For this case, the relationship between loan payments, A_t; the interest rate, r^f; and the amount borrowed, γV_0, is:

$$\gamma V_0 = \frac{A_0(1+g)}{(1+r^f)} + \frac{A_0(1+g)^2}{(1+r^f)^2} + \dots + \frac{A_0(1+g)^n}{(1+r^f)^n} = A_0 \, US_0 \left(\frac{r^f - g}{1+g}, \, n \right). \tag{7.13}$$

Solving for the base payment yields:

$$A_0 = \frac{\gamma V_0}{US_0 \left(\dfrac{r^f - g}{1+g}, \, n \right)}, \tag{7.14}$$

while the payment in the tth period is $A_0(1+g)^t$. The effect of graduated and constant loan payments on C_t is demonstrated in Example 7.5.

Coverage Ratios and *CT* Ratios

The usefulness of the coverage ratio can be enriched by showing its relationship to *CT* ratios and debt obligations. Then, the coverage ratio simultaneously accounts for: (1) the relationship between the cash flow and the debt repayment obligation; and (2) the portion of the asset's total return that is a current cash return.

To show the relationship between the coverage ratio and *CT* ratios, we use equation (7.2a) to first solve for R_t:

$$R_t = r_t \, V_{t-1} \, CT_t, \tag{7.15}$$

Example 7.5: Coverage Ratios and Loan Payments

Consider an asset generating a cash flow of $100 per period that increases each period by 5 percent ($g=0.05$) over 10 periods. Assume 80 percent of the asset's purchase price is financed with a loan to be repaid in equal annual payments over 10 years at an interest rate of 10 percent which is assumed to also equal the firm's opportunity cost of capital. The asset's present value is:

$$V_0 = \$100 \ US_0 \left(\frac{r-g}{1+g}, 10 \right) = \$100 \ US_0(0.0476, 10) = \$781.18.$$

The annual loan payments are:

$$A = \frac{(0.8)(\$781.18)}{US_0(0.10, 10)} = \$101.71.$$

The coverage ratio in period one is:

$$C_1 = \frac{\$105.00}{\$101.71} = 1.03.$$

If loan payments increase by 5 percent, then:

$$A_0 = \frac{(0.8)(\$781.18)}{US_0(0.0476, 10)} = \$79.99 \text{ and } A = \$83.99.$$

The coverage ratio in period one is:

$$C_1 = \frac{\$105}{\$83.99} = 1.25.$$

and substitute the result into equation (7.11) so that:

$$C_t = \frac{r_t \ V_{t-1} \ CT_t}{A_t}. \tag{7.16}$$

The coverage ratio is now shown to depend jointly on the measure of cash flow relative to debt obligations and on the level of current return relative to total return.

Interest Payments Only

To explore further the properties of the coverage ratio and its relationship to CT ratios, consider the special case where the debt obligation consists only of the interest payment paid in perpetuity on an asset financed 100 percent ($\gamma=1$) with debt capital at an interest rate equal to the opportunity cost of capital r. Under these simplifying assumptions, $A_t=r_tV_0$ in (7.16), and the coverage ratio equals the CT ratio:

$$C_t = \frac{rV_{t-1} CT_t}{rV_0}.$$

The above expression emphasizes the direct relationship between C_t and CT_t ratios. Moreover, if V_{t-1} equals V_0, then C_t equals CT_t.

Example 7.6: Coverage Ratio With Interest Payments Only

Assume an infinitely lived asset where $R_t=R_0(1+g)^t$, $g=0.05$, $R_0=\$100$, $r=0.10$, and $V_0=R_0(1+g)/(r-g)=\$2,100$. Then:

$$C_1 = CT_1 = \frac{R_1}{rV_0} = \frac{\$105}{(0.10)(\$2,100)} = 0.50.$$

In this example, even under the most lenient repayment schedule (interest payments only), cash returns only pay for 50 percent of the interest charge.

Financing Gaps

Earlier in this chapter, it was demonstrated that with a growing payment series, a portion of an asset's total returns are capital gains so that the CT ratio is less than 1.0. Moreover, since financial requirements are closely related to total returns, an asset with growing returns often has small coverage ratios initially. The result is a financing gap and a financially-infeasible investment situation during the early years of the investment. In the specific case of Example 7.6, the

$C_t=CT_i=0.50$ measures indicate that the investment itself is generating cash equal to only half of the interest obligation in the initial period. This condition reflects adverse liquidity, not adverse profitability. The total return on the investment is still $r=0.10$, or 10 percent, although half of the 10 percent total return comes as a current rate of return, or 5 percent, while the other half comes as an unrealized capital gain of $g=0^{***}.05$. In contrast, the interest obligation of 10 percent that is due to the lender must be fully paid in cash, thus causing the liquidity problem.

This liquidity problem will diminish over time and eventually disappear as the cash flow in each period grows at the designated rate, while the debt payment obligation remains constant. The particular period at which the cash flow is equal to the interest obligation occurs when:

$$C_t = \frac{R_t}{A} = 1.0.$$

To illustrate, if:

$$C_t = \frac{R_0(1+g)^t}{r_1\,V_0},$$

as in Example 7.6, then C_t equals one when:

$$(1+g)^t = \frac{r_1\,V_0}{R_0},$$

and:

$$(1+g)^t = (1.05)^t = \frac{(r_1)(V_0)}{R_0} = \frac{(0.10)(\$2{,}100)}{\$100} = 2.1.$$

$$t = 15.21 \text{ periods}\,^2$$

Financing gaps and surpluses are described graphically in Figure 7.2.

Generalizing the Relationship Between Coverage and *CT* Ratios

The preceding section showed that $C_t=CT_t$ under the restrictive assumptions of perpetual debt equal to the asset's value and only interest payments required on the debt obligation. In practice, however, debt must be repaid within some finite period of time, and asset values may change over time so that $C_t \neq CT_t$ in general.

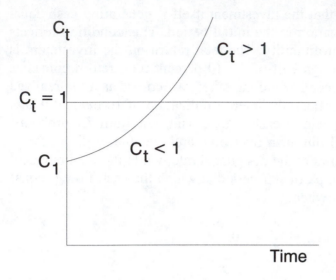

Figure 7.2
Financing Gaps for $C_t<1$ and
Financing Surpluses for $C_t>1$

Under these more general conditions, we can return to the amortized loan case of equation (7.14) and express a more general relationship between C_t and CT_t:

$$C_t = B_t \, CT_t. \tag{7.17}$$

Recall the basic formula for the coverage ratio of $C_t = R_t/A_t$. Then, substituting $r_t V_{t-1} \, CT_t$ for R_t [see equation (7.15)] and $\gamma V_0/US_0 \, (r^f, n)$ for A_t [see equation (7.12)] yields:

$$C_t = \frac{R_t}{A_t} = \frac{r_t \, V_{t-1} \, CT_t}{\gamma \, V_0/US_0 \, (r^f, n)} = \frac{US_0(r^f, n) r_t \, V_{t-1} \, CT_t}{\gamma \, V_0}, \tag{7.18}$$

or:

$$C_t = B_t \, CT_t, \tag{7.19}$$

where:

$$B_t = \frac{US_0(r^f, n) \, r_t \, V_{t-1}}{\gamma \, V_0}. \tag{7.20}$$

Thus, the coverage ratio is a weighted function of the *CT* ratio, where the weight is a composite measure of cash flow relative to the amortized debt obligation.

Example 7.7: Coverage Ratios and *CT* Ratios

Similar to the preceding examples, and assuming an infinite time horizon, suppose $R_0=100$, $g=0.04$, $\gamma=1.0$, $n=20$, $r=0.10$, and $r^f=0.10$.
The asset value is then:

$$V_0 = \frac{R_0(1+g)}{r-g} = \frac{100\,(1.04)}{.10-.04} = \$1,733.33.$$

The *CT* ratio is:

$$CT_1 = \frac{r-g}{r} = \frac{.10-.04}{.10} = .60,$$

or:

$$CT_1 = 1 - \frac{(V_1-V_0)/V_0}{r} = 1 - \frac{g}{r} = 1 - \frac{.04}{.10} = .60.$$

The loan amortization payment is:

$$A = \frac{\gamma\,V_0}{US_0(r^f,n)} = \frac{(1)(\$1,733.33)}{US_0(.10,20)} = \$203.60.$$

The coverage ratio in period one is:

$$C_1 = \frac{R_1}{A} = \frac{\$104}{\$203.60} = .511.$$

Or, using the coverage ratio expressions in (7.19) and (7.20):

$$C_1 = B_1\ CT_1 = \frac{US_0(r^f,n)\ rV_0\ CT_1}{\gamma\,V_0}$$

$$= \frac{(8.5136)(0.10)(\$1,733.33)(0.60)}{(1)(\$1,733.33)} = 0.5111.$$

Suppose now that a 40 percent downpayment is made so that $\gamma=0.60$. The new coverage ratio in period one is:

Example 7.7, Cont'd.: Coverage Ratios and *CT* Ratios

$$C_1 = \frac{(8.5136)(0.10)(\$1,733.33)(0.60)}{(0.6)(\$1,733.33)} = 0.8514.$$

And, suppose further that the financing terms are revised to include a 40 percent downpayment, a 30-year loan, and an interest rate of 9 percent. The new coverage ratio is:

$$C_1 = \frac{US_0(0.09,30)\, rV_0\, CT_1}{\gamma\, V_0}$$

$$= \frac{(10.2737)(0.10)(\$1,733.33)(0.60)}{(0.6)(\$1,733.33)} = 1.0274,$$

and financial feasibility has been attained.

Targeting a Coverage Ratio of *C*=1.0

Now consider the case in which an investor is aware that the asset he intends to purchase has a growing income stream, and thus will have a *CT* ratio less than one. The investor wishes to know the level of equity capital (or downpayment) he must provide to make the investment financially feasible — that is, to yield an initial coverage ratio of C_1=1.0. To find the level of γ that yields C_1=1.0, we recognize the definition of the coverage ratio:

$$C_1 = \frac{R_1}{A} = 1.0.$$

Therefore, $R_1=A$.

To find the value of R_1, we assume the asset value is:

$$V_0 = \frac{R_1}{r-g},$$

so that:

$$R_1 = V_0(r-g).$$

Next, the value of the amortized debt payment is:

$$A = \frac{\gamma V_0}{US_0(r^f, n)}.$$

Setting R_1 equal to A yields:

$$V_0(r-g) = \frac{\gamma V_0}{US_0(r^f, n)},$$

and solving for γ:

$$\gamma = (r-g) \, US_0(r^f, n). \tag{7.21}$$

Example 7.8: Breakeven Financial Feasibility

Find the level of downpayment (γ) yielding a coverage ratio of 1.0 in period one when $r=0.10$, $r^f=0.10$, $g=0.04$, $n=20$, $R_0=100$, and $V_0=\$1,733.33$. And using (7.21), we find:

$$\gamma = (r-g) \, US_0(r^f, n)$$
$$= (0.10-0.04)(8.5136) = 0.5106.$$

Time Patterns of Coverage Ratios

An explicit time pattern for the coverage ratio under conditions of growth and decline in the earnings series can be established by making some straightforward adjustments to the relationship between the coverage ratio and the CT ratio. For the growth case, recall the coverage ratio model from expressions (7.16) of:

$$C_t = \frac{r_t V_{t-1} CT_t}{A_t},$$

and the CT_t measure for the geometric growth model from expression (7.6) of:

$$CT_t = 1 - \frac{g}{r}.$$

Then, substituting for CT_t in the coverage ratio yields:

$$C_t = \frac{r_t V_{t-1}}{A_t} \left[1 - \frac{g}{r} \right]. \qquad (7.22)$$

A general relationship for the change in the asset value over time is:

$$V_{t-1} = V_0 (1+g)^{t-1}.$$

Substituting $V_0(1+g)^{t-1}$ for V_{t-1} in (7.22) yields:

$$C_t = \frac{r_t V_0 (1+g)^{t-1}}{A_t} \left(1 - \frac{g}{r} \right). \qquad (7.23)$$

Then, if $A_t = A$ and $r_t = r$, all of the variables to the right of the equal sign in (7.23) are constants except $(1+g)^{t-1}$. We can express (7.23) as:

$$C_t = K_g (1+g)^{t-1}, \qquad (7.24)$$

where:

$$K_g = \frac{V_0 (r-g)}{A}. \qquad (7.25)$$

The graph of the coverage ratio over time under these specifications is given in Figure 7.3.

On the other hand, if the cash flow stream is declining over time at rate d, so that $V_{t-1} = V_0(1-d)^{t-1}$, then the counterpart to (7.24) for the geometric decay series is the coverage ratio:

$$C_t = \frac{V_0 (1-d)^{t-1} (r+d)}{A}, \qquad (7.26)$$

or:

$$C_t = K_d (1-d)^{t-1}, \qquad (7.27)$$

where:

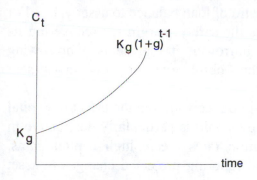

Figure 7.3 The Coverage Ratio for an Infinitely-Lived Asset Increasing in Value at Rate *g*

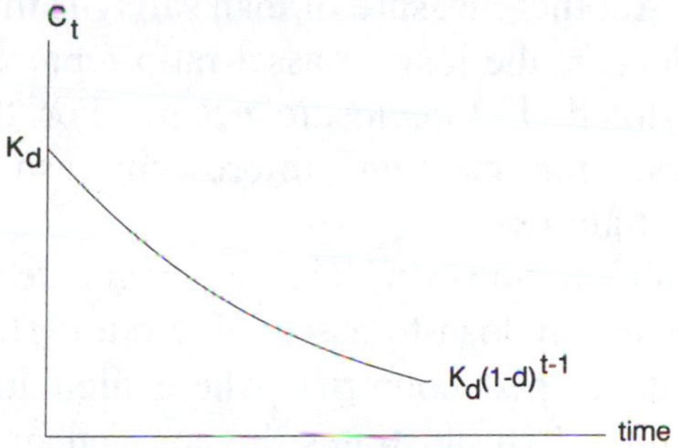

Figure 7.4 The Coverage Ratio for a Depreciating Durable Declining in Value at Rate *d*

$$K_d = \frac{V_0(r+d)}{A}. \tag{7.28}$$

The graph of the coverage ratio over time in the case of declining earnings is given in Figure 7.4.

Clear relationships emerge between changes in the coverage ratio and increases and decreases in asset values caused by growth and decline, respectively, in the earnings series. Assets with growing earnings have coverage ratios that increase over time, assuming a fixed payment amortization program on debt used to finance the asset. Assets with declining earnings initially may have higher coverage ratios than appreciating assets, but these coverage ratios decline over time. The solution to changing coverage ratios, largely resulting from time-varying earnings is to adjust the loan repayment program to coincide with the time pattern of the asset's earnings. A graduated payment loan would correspond to the case of earnings growth, while a declining payment loan would correspond to the case of declining earnings.

CT Ratios and Loan/Value Ratios

The coverage ratio is one indication of the liquidity firms face as they meet their cash flow obligations. It describes an important vital sign for both borrower and lender. For the lender, it represents the safety of the loan from remedial action such as increased loan supervision or possibly foreclosure. For the borrower, it represents the financial viability and staying power of the firm.

Another measure of loan safety is the ratio of loan balance to asset value. For the lender, the loan-to-asset ratio represents the safety margin for recovering its investment if foreclosure occurs. For the borrower, it represents a borrowing reserve for meeting unforeseen cash flow obligations or new investment opportunities.

Often, however, loans are negotiated without considering the effect of capital gains on the loan-to-asset value ratio. This oversight is particularly destructive in less-developed countries where high inflation rates create high capital gains. Example 7.10 illustrates the consequence of ignoring projected changes in asset values.

In economies with high inflation rates, liquidity problems associated with low CT rates are often addressed by mandating lower interest rates. This policy disturbs the proper functioning of the financial markets, since those who receive loans are are being subsidized. In addition, the lenders providing loans at subsidized credit rates often find their lending institution decapitalized.

The alternative to offering subsidized interest rates is to increase the borrower's loan by requiring less than full interest payments. Interest payments can be arranged such that the ratio L_t/V_t is a constant or decreasing and still not require full interest payments.

The essence of such a reduced interest payment arrangement is to allow the loan initially to increase.

One way to analyze the problem is by asking: At what rate could the loan increase and still maintain the initial loan/value ratio? The answer is: at the capital gains rate or at the rate: $(1-CT)$. To illustrate, if the initial loan-to-value ratio were one, then the full interest payment required in the first period is $r_1 V_0$. If the firm increases its loan by the amount of capital gains, then the remaining interest to be paid is $r_t V_{t-1} - (V_t - V_{t-1})$. But, $r_t V_{t-1} - (V_t - V_{t-1}) = R_t$. This implies that the firm could have a 100 percent financed asset and by paying only R_t, the loan/value ratio could be maintained at one.

If the firm had a loan/value ratio less than one and paid R_1, the loan/value ratio would decrease. The ratio of R_t to the total interest payment $r_t V_{t-1}$ is, of course, equal to CT_t and if the capital gains rate equals the inflation rate, then CT equals the real interest rate.

The relationship between the loan-to-asset value ratio and the CT ratio is easily derived. Let the loan value at the beginning of the tth period be:

$$L_{t-1} = A\,US_0(r^f, n-t+1),$$

Example 7.9: Increasing Payment Loans

Smartr. N. Bfor (known as Smarty around the bank) has just completed a course in present value (*PV*) models. She recognizes the liquidity problems created when financing an asset that grows in value at a constant rate *g* with a constant annuity. As a senior VP at her bank, she has an opportunity to implement improved lending practices.

Consequently, when one of her valued customers asks for a loan to purchase land at $1,000 per acre which is expected to grow at 5 percent, Smarty offers the following loan terms. She proposes a 20-year loan with payments that increase at 5 percent per year. Assume that the interest rate r^f equals the opportunity cost of capital of 12 percent. The coverage ratio for this loan over its 20-year life is:

$$C_t = \frac{r V_{t-1} CT_{t-1}}{A_t} = \frac{(0.12) V_0 (1.05)^{t-1}}{A_0 (1.05)^{t-1}} \left(1 - \frac{0.05}{0.12}\right).$$

The initial loan payment is expressed as:

$$A_0 = \frac{\gamma V_0}{US_0\left(\frac{r-g}{1+g}, n\right)} = \frac{\gamma V_0}{US_0\left(\frac{0.07}{1.05}, 20\right)}.$$

Then, if $\gamma = 0.8$:

$$C_t = \frac{0.12 \; US_0\left(\frac{0.07}{1.05}, 20\right)}{0.8} \left(1 - \frac{0.05}{0.12}\right) = \frac{(0.12)(10.874)\left(1 - \frac{0.05}{0.12}\right)}{0.8} = 0.95.$$

The coverage ratio is nearly equal to 1, implying near financial feasibility. If Smarty had not been so far-sighted, the initial coverage ratio with a fixed debt obligation would have been:

$$C_1 = \frac{r V_0 CT_0}{A_0} = \frac{(0.12) V_0 \left(1 - \frac{0.05}{0.12}\right) US_0(0.12, 20)}{0.8 V_0} = \frac{(0.12)\left(1 - \frac{0.05}{0.12}\right) 7.469}{0.8} = 0.65.$$

An initial coverage ratio of .65 will place the borrower under greater liquidity pressures for the early life of the loan. No wonder business is booming at Smarty's bank.

Example 7.10: Inflation and Loan/Value Rates

A common problem facing most developing economies is a high inflation rate that produces high interest rates. In response to high interest rates, the governments of these countries, often with international support, offer subsidized interest rates on loans. The problem, however, is not the interest rate, but the illiquidity of the loans created by high inflation rates. To demonstrate, consider the following.

Suppose an investment having a constant real value, V_0 (e.g., land), inflates in nominal dollars at rate i so that t periods later $V_t = V_0(1+i)^t$. In addition, suppose a loan is made that requires no principal repayment, only interest, and that initially the ratio of the loan-to-asset value (L_0/V_0) is 1. Then, at the end of the first period, the ratio is $L_0/V_0(1+i)$. At the end of the second period, the ratio is $L_0/V_0(1+i)^2$, and so on.

The rate of capital gains determines the loan-to-asset value ratio, even when no loan principal is repaid. Knowing this, it is possible to show the half life of a loan (How many periods before $L_0/V_t \le 50$ percent?) as a function of "i".

As Table 7.3 demonstrates, the lender's security position can be protected during inflationary periods even though no principal is repaid. The lender could even offer to increase the principal balance and still find the ratio of the loan-to-asset value increasing.

Table 7.3 Number of Periods Required for the Loan-to-Asset Value to Reach 50 Percent When the Durable's Value is Increasing at Rate i, No Loan Principal is Repaid, and 100 Percent Debt Financing.

$i=$1%	3%	5%	8%	10%	13%	15%	18%	20%	25%
$t=$69.7	23.4	14.2	9.0	7.3	5.7	5.0	4.2	3.8	3.1

Example 7.11: Reduced Interest Payments

The developing country of Enflayshun has a problem: Its inflation rate i is currently at 50 percent. Moreover, this inflation rate is expected to continue. Ineeda Loan wants to purchase a brick kiln. The kiln will earn \$5,000 a year for 20 years in real dollars. Ineeda's real opportunity cost of capital is r^*, equal to 5 percent. The National Development Bank of Enflayshun directed by a progressive president will increase the loan amount during early periods. The bank does, however, expect the loan-to-value ratio to decrease over time and to have the loan retired in 20 years.

The kiln's maximum-bid price is:

$$V_0 = \frac{R_0(1+i)}{(1+r^*)(1+i)} + \frac{R_0(1+i)^2}{[(1+r^*)(1+i)]^2} + \dots + \frac{R_0(1+i)^{20}}{[(1+r^*)(1+i)]^{20}}$$

$$= R_0\, US_0(r^*,20) = (\$5,000)(12.4622) = \$62,311.$$

The bank offers a loan of \$50,000. Ineeda agrees to pay γ percent of its net cash flows to repay its loan over the next 20 years. To find a γ that is consistent with Ineeda's cash flows and still retires the loan, we set L_0 equal to the *PV* of the loan payments and r_b^* equals the bank's real opportunity cost:

$$L_0 = \frac{\gamma\, R_0(1+i)}{(1+r_b^*)(1+i)} + \frac{\gamma\, R_0(1+i)^2}{[(1+r_b^*)(1+i)]^2} + \dots + \frac{\gamma\, R_0(1+i)^{20}}{[(1+r_b^*)(1+i)]^{20}}$$

$$= \gamma\, R_0\, US_0(r_b^*,20),$$

and:

$$\gamma = L_0 / R_0\, US_0(r_b^*,20).$$

If $r_b^* = 6$ percent, then γ equals:

$$\gamma = \$50,000 / (\$5,000)(11.4699) = 87.2 \text{ percent.}$$

If inflation is 50 percent and $r_b^* = 0.06$, then the interest rate must equal $(1.50)(1.06)-1 = 59$ percent. If only interest is charged, the first loan payment is $(0.59)(\$50,000) = \$29,500$. This amount exceeds income in

Example 7.11, Cont'd.: Reduced Interest Payments

the first period equal to ($5,000)(1.50) = $7,500. Allowing payments to increase with inflation allows the first payment to equal (0.87)($7,500) = $6,525, which is feasible for the firm.

Offering the borrower an increasing payment loan (requiring less than full interest payments) solves Ineeda's liquidity problem while maintaining the bank's security measured by its loan/value ratio.

and let the value of the asset financed be V_{t-1}. Then, the ratio of loan-to-asset value equals:

$$\frac{L_{t-1}}{V_{t-1}} = \frac{A\,US_0(r^f, n-t+1)}{V_{t-1}}. \tag{7.29}$$

Then, since $V_{t-1} = R_t/r_t CT_t$, we substitute for V_{t-1} in (7.29) and obtain:

$$\frac{L_{t-1}}{V_{t-1}} = \frac{A\,US_0(r^f, n-t+1)}{R_t}\, r_t CT_t. \tag{7.30}$$

But A/R_t is simply the reciprocal of the coverage ratio, so that:

$$\frac{L_{t-1}}{V_{t-1}} = \left(\frac{CT_t}{C_t}\right) \frac{r_t}{r^f} \left(1 - \frac{1}{(1+r^f)^{n-t+1}}\right). \tag{7.31}$$

Firm survival requires $C_t = 1$. If this restriction is imposed on equation (7.31), then the loan-to-asset value ratio that is consistent with a coverage ratio of one is:

$$\frac{L_{t-1}}{V_{t-1}} = CT_t \frac{r_t}{r^f} \left(1 - \frac{1}{(1+r^f)^{n-t+1}}\right). \tag{7.32}$$

Clearly, the loan-to-asset value ratio consistent with $C_t = 1.0$ is directly related to CT ratios, i.e., higher CT_t ratios allow higher loan-to-value ratios while lower CT_t measures require lower loan-to-value ratios.

One of the advantages of the CT ratio is that it provides an index for managing cash flows. Assuming coverage ratios of less than one ($C_t < 1$), CT_t values less than one at age t suggest other liquid funds, such as earnings from another

---

Example 7.12: Loan/Value Ratios and a Coverage Ratio of One

Tred N. Waters is considering the purchase of a depreciable durable whose value declines at a rate of 6 percent per year. Waters' opportunity cost of capital is 12 percent and the loan interest rate is 10 percent. For a loan of 8 years, Waters wants to find the loan-to-value ratio consistent with an initial coverage ratio of one.

Using equation (7.32), Waters calculated:

$$\frac{L_0}{V_0} = CT_1 \frac{r_1}{r^f}\left(1 - \frac{1}{(1+r^f)^n}\right)$$

$$= \left(1 + \frac{0.06}{0.12}\right)\left(\frac{0.12}{0.10}\right)\left(1 - \frac{1}{(1.10)^8}\right) = 96 \text{ percent.}$$

If instead of purchasing a depreciable asset, Waters considered the purchase of an asset growing at 6 percent, the loan/value ratio consistent with a coverage ratio of one would equal:

$$\frac{L_0}{V_0} = \left(1 - \frac{0.06}{0.12}\right)\left(\frac{0.12}{0.10}\right)\left(1 - \frac{1}{(1.10)^8}\right) = 32 \text{ percent.}$$

---

investment or additional borrowing, must be committed to manage the investment's liquidity. Hence, a close relationship is expected between CT_t measures and the use of debt. The relationship between CT ratios and debt is described next.

Liquidity and the Use of Debt

To show the relationship between CT_t measures and the use of debt funds, consider an infinite geometric growth model. Moreover, assume the coverage ratio is one, $R_0(1+g)=A_1$. Assume L_0 is the beginning period debt level financed at rate r^f for n periods. Then:

$$L_0 = A_1 \, US_0(r^f, n), \tag{7.33}$$

and:

$$A_1 = L_0 / US_0(r^f, n).$$

Setting R_1 equal to A_1 in the expression for the infinite geometric growth model $V_0 = R_0(1+g)/r-g$, we can write:

$$V_0 = \frac{R_0(1+g)}{r-g} = \frac{A_1}{r-g} = \frac{L_0/(r-g)}{US_0(r^f,n)}. \qquad (7.34)$$

This result, of course, implies $R_0(1+g)=A_1$ or a coverage ratio of one. Following similar procedures, V_1 can be expressed as:

$$V_1 = \frac{R_2}{r-g} = \frac{A_2}{r-g} = \frac{L_1/(r-g)}{US_0(r^f,n)}. \qquad (7.35)$$

Finally, we substitute (7.33), (7.34), and (7.35) into the equation for CT_0 below and after cancelling obtain:

$$CT_0 = 1 - \left(\frac{V_1 - V_0}{rV_0}\right) = 1 - \frac{L_1 - L_0}{rL_0}. \qquad (7.36)$$

It can easily be shown that the expression in (7.36) holds generally for coverage ratios not equal to one as well. The expression points out the close relationship between percentage change in debt, opportunity costs of capital, and *CT* ratios.

Summary

This chapter has considered the important relationships between the time patterns of asset earnings, asset values, and the forms of returns, which together determine an investor's liquidity position. Two significant liquidity concepts were used: (1) *CT* ratio, measured by the proportion of an asset's total returns that are current returns; and (2) coverage, measured by the ratio of current returns to debt payment obligations in any period. In addition, relationships between these two liquidity concepts were established by expressing the coverage ratio as a weighted function of an asset's *CT* ratio in order to simultaneously account for: (1) the relationship between current cash returns and the debt repayment obligation; and (2) the portion of an asset's total return that is a current cash return.

Extensions of the analyses indicated the important paradox involving greater wealth from higher rates of earnings growth versus lower liquidity when a higher proportion of total returns occurs as capital gains. The resulting illiquidity

Example 7.13:   Debt and Liquidity in Michigan and Indiana

To test the hypothesis implied in (7.36), we calculated CT_1 using real estate values in Michigan and Indiana. Then, we calculated the percentage change in outstanding farm mortgage debt $[(L_t\text{-}L_{t-1}/L_{t-1}]$ and multiplied it by $(1/r)$ using the Federal Land Bank rate on new farm mortgage loans as a proxy for r. Then, the data series on CT_t was regressed on the data multiplied by $1/r$ in order to measure the closeness of fit between these relationships. The regression results with t statistics below the estimated coefficients were:

Michigan

$$CT_t = \frac{1.01}{(65.6)} - \frac{1.03}{(6.4)} \left(\frac{L_t\text{-}L_{t-1}}{r_t L_{t-1}} \right).$$

$$\bar{R}^2 = 0.54 \quad DW = 1.63 \quad F = 40.45$$

Indiana

$$CT_t = \frac{1.05}{(62.9)} - \frac{1.03}{(8.7)} \left(\frac{L_t\text{-}L_{t-1}}{r_t L_{t-1}} \right).$$

$$\bar{R}^2 = 0.68 \quad DW = 1.45 \quad F = 76.04$$

From these results, we would not reject the hypothesis that periodic liquidity measures and percent changes in debt are related by equation (7.36).

combines with repayment obligations on highly-leveraged investments to create financing gaps early in the life of assets experiencing earnings growth. The opposite effects occur for assets with declining earnings over time. Designing loan repayment programs that synchronize the time patterns of the asset's earnings with the repayment obligations is one way to resolve the financing gaps and liquidity problems. In Chapter 9, we will extend the consideration of asset pricing, forms of returns, and liquidity to include their relationships to commonly-used accounting rates of return.

Endnotes

1.   This chapter has benefitted from discussions with Knut Walstedt. His contributions are gratefully acknowledged.

2.   We solve for *t* with the expression:

$$t = \ln \left[\frac{(0.10)(2,100)}{100} \right] / \ln(1.05).$$

Review Questions

1.   Define the terms: liquidity, current-to-total-returns ratio, current (cash) returns, and capital gains.

2.   As the proportion of an asset's returns earned in the form of capital gains increases, describe the effect on the firm's *CT* ratio.

3.   Consider two firms that purchase identical durables at the same price and each expects to earn the same rate of returns and proportion of returns in the form of capital gains. Why is liquidity of more concern for the firm that used more debt to purchase the durable?

4.   Find the portion of returns in the first period earned as capital gains and use that rate to find the *CT* ratio for the durables whose net cash return is described as:

$$V_0 = \frac{R_0(1+g)}{(1+r)} + \frac{R(1+g)^2}{(1+r)^2} + \cdots,$$

and:

$$V_1 = \frac{R_0(1+g)^2}{(1+r)} + \frac{R_0(1+g)^3}{(1+r)^2} + \cdots.$$

5.   Provide numerical examples for CT_0 ratios for the infinite life geometric growth and decay series (e.g., compare *CT* ratios in periods 0, 10, and 20 for specific values of *r*, *g*, and *d*).

6.   Interpret the coverage ratio, C_t, and suggest reasons why it might be useful for firms to consider coverage ratios before they make durable asset purchases.

7.   Under what conditions are coverage ratios and *CT* ratios equal?

8. Assume $CT_i=(1-g/r)$ where $g,r>0$ and are defined as the perpetual growth rate and opportunity cost of capital, respectively. Assume the debt repayment obligation is constant. How will the coverage ratio, C_t, change over time for the asset described above? How would the coverage ratio change over time if the asset's CT ratio were:

$$CT = 1 + \frac{d}{r},$$

where $d,r>0$ and d is the asset's perpetual decay rate?

9. An important liquidity measure is the loan/value ratio. Discuss its usefulness for borrowers and lenders.

10. If the firm's coverage ratio is one, $CT=0.8$, $r'=0.08$, and $r=0.12$, find the loan-to-value ratio if there are 10 years left to loan maturity on a constant payment loan.

11. In the case described above, what will be the percentage change in debt in each period?

Application Questions

1. Describe how V_t changes over time for durables whose cash flows are described as: (a) a constant cash flow stream with a constant discount rate over an infinite life; and (b) a constant cash flow with a constant discount rate over a finite life. Then, relate how changes in $=(V_t-V_{t-1})/V_{t-1}$ affect CT ratios. Demonstrate your results numerically for $r=0.07$, $R=\$100$, and for part (b) set $n=10$.

2. (a) Use η_t to describe how a durable's value would change over time if the cash flow earned by the durable followed a geometric decay pattern for an infinite number of time periods.
    (b) Use η_t to describe how a durable's value would change if the earnings followed a geometric decay pattern for n periods and then earned a constant return in perpetuity.

3. Suppose you purchase a durable that never wears out. Moreover, assume that its nominal returns increase with the rate of inflation implicit in the discount rate. If the only payments the owner has to make are constant interest payments on the original value of the durable, calculate the coverage ratio over time. Please illustrate your answer with a numerical example for the case where $\dot{r}=0.05$ and $i=0.10$.

4. It has been observed that, with increases in inflation and interest rates on loans, the ratio of net cash flow to land values does not change. Some have used this observation to suggest that land is not a good investment. Do you agree or disagree? Assuming the observation that the ratio of net cash flow

to land values is nearly constant is correct, can you explain why the ratio is nearly constant even when inflation rates vary?

5.   Assume a constant opportunity cost of capital r and a geometric series $V_0 = Rb + Rb^2 + \ldots + Rb^n$. Find η_t when n is infinite and when n is finite. Use your general results to find η_t for the growth and decay series when n is infinite.

6.   In developing countries with high rates of inflation, investors often experience cash flow difficulties, especially during the early periods of the investment. For an investment whose real returns are constant, calculate the ratio of the loan (without refinancing and no with principal payments) to the durable's value during the first three periods of the loan assuming the rate of inflation is 100 percent. Assume that 90 percent of the purchase price is financed so that the original loan-to-value ratio is .9. Can you use your results to explain why subsidized interest programs may be ineffective in solving the liquidity problems for investments in countries suffering from high rates of inflation?

7.   State whether you agree or disagree with the following statement. Then, defend your answer logically and with a numerical example. "All depreciable durables whose values decline over time ($V_t < V_{t-1}$) have CT measures greater than one."

8.   Find η_t and CT_t for a durable whose infinite income stream is:

$$R_t = R + Q(1-d)^t,$$

where R is some constant and $Q(1-d)^t$ is a decreasing income stream. Evaluate your results numerically by setting R=$50, Q=$100, d=0.2, t=1, and r=0.08.

References ——————————————————————————————

American Society of Agricultural Engineers. *Asymmetrical Engineering Yearbook.* St. Joseph, MO, 1986.

Ellinger, P.N., P.J. Barry, and D.A. Lins. "Farm Financial Performance Under Graduated Payment Mortgages." *North Central Journal of Agricultural Economics* 5(1983):47-53.

Leatham, D.J. and T.G. Baker. "Empirical Estimates of the Effects of Inflation on Salvage Value, Cost, and Optimal Replacement of Tractors and Combines." *North Central Journal of Agricultural Economics* 3(1981):109-17.

Nott, S.B. "Revised Michigan Crops and Livestock Estimated 1979 Budgets." *Agricultural Economics Report No. 350* (revised), Michigan State University, January 1979, p. 5.

Peacock, D.L. and J.R. Brake. *What Is Used Farm Machinery Worth?* Michigan State University Agricultural Experiment Station Research Report No. 109, March 1970.

Perry, G.M., A. Bayaner, and C.J. Nixon. "The Effect of Usage and Size on Tractor Depreciation." *American Journal of Agricultural Economics* 72(1990):317-25.

Reid, D.W. and G.L. Bradford. "Machinery Investment Decisions." *American Journal of Agricultural Economics* 69(1987):64-77.

Robison, L.J. and J.R. Brake. "Inflation, Cash Flows, and Growth: Some Implications for the Farm Firm." *Southern Journal of Agricultural Economics* 12(1980):131-37.

Robison, L.J., D.A. Lins, and R. Venkataraman. "Cash Rent and Land Values in U.S. Agriculture." *American Journal of Agricultural Economics* 67(1985):794-805.

Chapter 8

Tax Adjustments

Key words: after-tax internal rates of return, after-tax real rates of return, average after-tax rates of return, before-tax internal rates of return, challengers, defenders, percentage effective tax rates, real rates of return, tax adjustment coefficients, tax-free investments.

Introduction

Present value (PV) models compare two investments: a challenger, described by time-dated cash flows, and a defender, whose return characteristics are summarized by discount rates. Consistency is needed between the measures describing the cash flows of the challenger and the discount rate of the defender. Consistency in PV models requires that when cash flows of the challenger are adjusted for taxes, the discount rates of the defender must also be adjusted for taxes.

This chapter shows how to maintain tax consistency in PV models. It shows that the correct tax adjustment to the discount rate in PV models depends on both the defender's capital gains or losses and allowable tax depreciation in each period. This chapter also shows that multiplying the discount rate by $(1-T)$ achieves tax consistency only for special cases. Finally, variations in effective tax rates over time and their dependency on capital gains (losses) are demonstrated using historical data for investments in farmland, stocks, and bonds.

PV Models For Defenders and Challengers ———————

The goal is to find the after-tax *IRR*(s) associated with a defender. The first step is to find the defender's before-tax *IRR*(s). Recall that the before-tax *IRR*(s) is that rate of return such that *NPV* of before-tax net cash flows is zero. After-tax *IRR*(s) are before-tax *IRR*(s) adjusted for taxes. The after-tax *IRR*(s) discount the defender's after-tax cash flows so that its *NPV* remains equal to zero.

There is an easy test to determine if the before-tax *IRR* has been adjusted for taxes in a way consistent with the introduction of taxes into the cash flow stream. If the defender's *NPV* or the maximum (minimum) sell price is changed in response to an increase in taxes, then the discount rate cannot be the after-tax *IRR*. Because if it were, *NPV* or maximum-bid prices would be unaffected by the introduction of taxes.

Example 8.1: After-Tax *IRRs*

Constance Income is considering an investment that earns constant net cash flow R per period in perpetuity. The maximum-bid (minimum-sell) price V_0 for her investment is:

$$V_0 = \frac{R}{(1+r)} + \frac{R}{(1+r)^2} + \ldots = \frac{R}{r},$$

where $r=R/V_0$ is the before-tax *IRR*. Constance's constant marginal income tax rate T allows her to write the after-tax maximum-bid price as:

$$V_0 = \frac{R(1-T)}{1+r(1-T)} + \frac{R(1-T)}{[1+r(1-T)]^2} + \ldots = \frac{R(1-T)}{r(1-T)} = \frac{R}{r}.$$

Income R and the before-tax *IRR* r are adjusted for taxes in the after-tax model by multiplying by $(1-T)$. Constance is sure that $r(1-T)$ is the after-tax *IRR* since V_0 is the same in the before- and after-tax models. However, Constance should be aware that only in the special case of constant infinite income will multiplying r by $(1-T)$ produce the after-tax *IRR*.

Example 8.2: Growth Model Tax Adjustments

Gregory Growth is considering an investment in which last period's income R_0 grows geometrically at rate g. His before-tax model for calculating the investment's maximum-bid price equals:

$$V_0 = \frac{R_0(1+g)}{(1+r)} + \frac{R_0(1+g)^2}{(1+r)^2} + \ldots = \frac{R_0(1+g)}{r-g},$$

and the before-tax *IRR* equals:

$$r = \frac{R_0(1+g)}{V_0} + g.$$

Gregory introduces taxes into the above model in the same manner as Constance did in the previous example; he multiplies income and the before-tax *IRR* by $(1-T)$. The result is:

$$V_0 = \frac{R_0(1+g)(1-T)}{[1+r(1-T)]} + \frac{R_0(1+g)^2(1-T)}{[1+r(1-T)]^2} + \ldots = \frac{R_0(1+g)(1-T)}{r(1-T)-g}.$$

But note that an increase in T increases V_0:

$$\frac{dV_0}{dT} = \frac{R_0(1+g)g}{[r(1-T)-g]^2} > 0.$$

Since $dV_0/dT>0$, Gregory knows that $r(1-T)$ cannot equal the after-tax *IRR* for the investment under consideration. To find out what the after-tax *IRR* does indeed equal, Gregory enrolls in a present value course and reads the remainder of Chapter 8 (this chapter).

A general approach for finding after-tax *IRR*s follows. Consider a defender that has a market-determined value of V_{t-1}^d and earns a before-tax cash flow stream of $R_t, R_{t+1}, \ldots$. A before-tax *PV* model for this defender in period $t-1$ is:

$$V_{t-1}^d = \frac{R_t}{(1+r_t)} + \frac{R_{t+1}}{(1+r_t)(1+r_{t+1})} + \cdots$$

$$= \frac{R_t}{(1+r_t)} + \frac{1}{(1+r_t)}\left[\frac{R_{t+1}}{(1+r_{t+1})} + \frac{R_{t+2}}{(1+r_{t+1})(1+r_{t+2})} + \cdots\right],$$

(8.1)

where the before-tax discount rates (the defender's *IRR*s) for each period are denoted by r_t, r_{t+1}, ... Note that r_t can take different values each period. Similarly, V_t^d can be expressed as:

$$V_t^d = \frac{R_{t+1}}{(1+r_{t+1})} + \frac{R_{t+2}}{(1+r_{t+1})(1+r_{t+2})} + \cdots.$$

(8.2)

Substituting V_t^d for the bracketed expression in (8.1) and then solving for V_t^d yields:

$$V_t^d = V_{t-1}^d(1+r_t) - R_t,$$

(8.3)

and capital gains (losses) equal:

$$V_t^d - V_{t-1}^d = r_t V_{t-1}^d - R_t.$$

(8.4)

Solving (8.3) for the before-tax discount rate in the tth period yields:

$$r_t = \frac{V_t^d + R_t}{V_{t-1}^d} - 1.$$

(8.5)

The value of r_t in (8.5) represents the tth period's before-tax internal rate of return (*IRR*) for the defender described in (8.1). Estimating the values of r_{t+1}, . . . requires that values be observed or assumed for V_t^d, V_{t+1}^d, and R_{t+1}.

Now suppose that for the same observed or assumed values of V_t^d, V_{t+1}^d, and R_{t+1}, the goal is to find the tth period after-tax *IRR* for the defender described in (8.1). To do so, the discount rates and cash flows must be adjusted for taxes in (8.1) so that V_{t-1}^d is not changed. The defender's cash flows are adjusted for taxes by multiplying them by $(1-T)$. The before-tax discount rate, r_t, in the tth period is adjusted for taxes by multiplying it by $(1-\theta_t T)$. The tax rate adjustment coefficient, θ_t, adjusts r_t to its after-tax equivalent without changing V_{t-1}^d. Besides these tax adjustments, let T_g be the tax rate applied to allowable depreciation which equals $f(V_{t-1}^d)$ in the tth period, and $f(V_t^d)$ in the $(t+1)^{st}$ period, etc.[1]

The after-tax *PV* model corresponding to (8.1) that leaves V_{t-1}^d unchanged can be written as:

$$V_{t-1}^d = \frac{R_t(1-T) + T_g f(V_{t-1}^d)}{[1+r_t(1-\theta_t T)]} + \frac{1}{[1+r_t(1-\theta_t T)]} \left[\frac{R_{t+1}(1-T) + T_g f(V_t^d)}{[1+r_{t+1}(1-\theta_{t+1} T)]} + \dots \right]. \tag{8.6}$$

Similarly, V_t^d can be expressed as:

$$V_t^d = \frac{R_{t+1}(1-T) + T_g f(V_t^d)}{[1+r_{t+1}(1-\theta_{t+1} T)]} + \frac{R_{t+2}(1-T) + T_g f(V_{t+1}^d)}{[1+r_{t+1}(1-\theta_{t+1} T)][1+r_{t+2}(1-\theta_{t+2} T)]} + \dots. \tag{8.7}$$

Substituting V_t^d in (8.7) for the bracketed expression in (8.6) and solving for V_t^d yields:

$$V_t^d = V_{t-1}^d [1+r_t(1-\theta_t T)] - \left[R_t(1-T) + T_g f(V_{t-1}^d) \right], \tag{8.8}$$

which is analogous to equation (8.3), except that it is expressed on an after-tax basis.

The after-tax rate of return for period t is found by solving equation (8.8) for $r_t(1-\theta_t T)$:

$$r_t(1-\theta_t T) = \frac{V_t^d + R_t(1-T) + T_g f(V_{t-1}^d)}{V_{t-1}^d} - 1. \tag{8.9}$$

The value for θ_t in (8.9) is found by substituting the right-hand side of equation (8.5) for r_t. Solving for θ_t, the result is:

$$\theta_t = \frac{R_t - \left(\dfrac{T_g}{T}\right) f(V_{t-1}^d)}{R_t + \left(V_t^d - V_{t-1}^d\right)}. \tag{8.10}$$

The value for θ_t in equation (8.10) adjusts the defender's before-tax *IRR* to obtain consistency with tax adjustments made to the cash flows in equation (8.6). Adjusting for taxes using θ_t from equation (8.10) means that the tax adjustments made to the defender's cash flows and before-tax discount rates are equivalent; as a result, taxes have the same effect on cash flows and before-tax *IRRs*. Thus, by adjusting the before-tax discount rate, r_t, by $(1-\theta_t T)$, tax consistency is maintained in the model.

Consider a *PV* model that finds the maximum-bid price to purchase a challenger and still earn the after-tax rate of return on the defender. Let V_{t-1}^c be the maximum-bid price of the challenger at the beginning of the tth period, which on an after-tax basis equals:

$$V_{t-1}^c = \frac{R_t^c(1-T)+T_g\,f(V_{t-1}^c)}{\left[1+r_t(1-\theta_t T)\right]} + \frac{R_{t+1}^c(1-T)+T_g\,f(V_t^c)}{\left[1+r_t(1-\theta_t T)\right]\left[1+r_{t+1}(1-\theta_{t+1} T)\right]} + \dots, \tag{8.11}$$

where r_t, r_{t+1}, ... and θ_t, θ_{t+1} ... are obtained from equations (8.5) and (8.10), and are specific to the defender being liquidated to purchase the challenger.

Example 8.3: Finding θ for Gregory Growth

Suppose that, in Example 8.2, R_0=\$100, g=0.03, and r=0.10. It follows that:

$$V_0 = \frac{\$100(1.03)}{0.10-0.03} = \$1,471.43.$$

We also found earlier for the geometric growth model that V_1=$(1.03)V_0$ or that V_1-V_0=\$44.14. Substituting \$44.14 for $\left(V_t^d - V_{t-1}^d\right)$, zero for T_g, and \$103 for R_t in equation (8.10), we find θ equal to:

$$\theta = \frac{\$103}{\$103+\$44.14} = 0.7.$$

To check that θ is indeed 0.7, Gregory makes the following substitution for V_0:

$$V_0 = \frac{R_0(1+g)(1-T)}{[1+(1-\theta T)r]} + \frac{R_0(1+g)(1-T)}{[1+(1-\theta T)r]^2} + \dots = \frac{R(1+g)(1-T)}{(1-\theta T)r-g}$$

$$= \frac{\$103(1-T)}{(1-0.7\,T)0.10-0.03} = \frac{\$103(1-T)}{0.07(1-T)} = \$1,471.43,$$

proving that θ for this problem is indeed 0.7.

Calculating Tax Rate Adjustment Coefficients ────────────

Many authors, (e.g., Modigliani and Miller, and Adams) have assumed that the tax rate adjustment coefficient, θ_t, equals one. It is clear from (8.10), however, that values for θ_t will depend on allowable depreciation, cash flow R_t, the amount of capital gains (losses) the defender is expected to earn during each period, and on tax rates for ordinary income versus capital gains. In general, θ_t will not equal one.

For some defenders, such as land and stocks, allowable depreciation, $f(V_{t-1}^d)$, for an investor is zero except when the asset is sold. For these defenders, whether or not θ_t equals one depends on capital gains or losses, $(V_t^d - V_{t-1}^d)$. For other defenders, $f(V_{t-1}^d)$ is nonzero, and θ_t depends on both capital gains, $(V_t^d - V_{t-1}^d)$ and allowable depreciation, $T_g f(V_{t-1}^d)$. The next step is to consider the value of θ_t for various combinations of capital gains and allowable depreciation.[2]

Case 8.1: $(V_t^d - V_{t-1}^d) = 0$ and $f(V_{t-1}^d) = 0$.

In this case, the defender earns neither capital gains nor suffers capital losses, and the depreciation allowance is zero. Using (8.10), we see that θ_t equals one. This defender's return in each period is equal to its cash income which is fully taxed at income tax rate T. Therefore, the entire before-tax rate of return must be adjusted by $(1-T)$. An infinite constant cash flow series characterizes this case.

Case 8.2: $(V_t^d - V_{t-1}^d) > 0$ and $f(V_{t-1}^d) = 0$.

Capital gains that are not taxed lower the defender's effective tax rate. Thus, $\theta_t < 1$ and $(1-\theta_t T) > (1-T)$. The greater the capital gains during period t, the lower the effective tax rate in period t.

Case 8.3: $(-R_t < V_t^d - V_{t-1}^d < 0)$ and $f(V_{t-1}^d) = 0$.

In this case, the defender experiences capital losses in period t that are not deducted from current income for tax purposes. Thus, the defender's effective tax rate exceeds the tax rate on cash income and $\theta_t > 1$ and $(1-\theta_t T) < (1-T)$.

Case 8.4: $(V_t^d - V_{t-1}^d < -R_t < 0)$ and $f(V_{t-1}^d) = 0$.

In this case, the firm experiences capital losses that are not tax deductible, and exceed taxable cash income. The firm has a positive tax obligation, assuming $R_t > 0$, even though the firm's total returns in each period after accounting for capital losses are negative. Using (8.5), the total before-tax rate of return, r_t, is negative in this case. Since the total before-tax return is negative, but taxes are still paid, the effective tax adjustment, θ_t, must be negative, reflecting further decreases in the rate of return when taxes are considered. Consequently, $r_t \theta_t T > 0$ and taxes are still paid on current income despite a negative investment rate of return.

Stated another way, when capital losses exceed cash income, the rate of return on the defender is negative. Yet, because the capital losses do not shield income from taxes, the firm must still pay taxes, further reducing the rate of return. Such a situation occurred for some farmland owners who experienced large capital losses from declining land values and negative rates of return from land ownership during the early 1980's.

Case 8.5: $(V_t^d - V_{t-1}^d \lesseqgtr 0)$ and $T_g f(V_{t-1}^d) = T(V_{t-1}^d - V_t^d)$.

If capital gains (losses) and realized cash income are taxed equally, θ_t equals one. The effective tax rate on the total return in period t will be the same as the marginal income tax rate.

Case 8.6: $(V_t^d - V_{t-1}^d) = -R_t$ and $f(V_{t-1}^d) \lesseqgtr 0$.

In this case, the investment experiences capital losses, $(V_t^d - V_{t-1}^d) < 0$, equal to the cash income. In this case, the effective tax rate adjustment in equation (8.10) is undefined because the denominator is zero. Recognizing this difficulty, we will assume in the discussion to follow that $(V_t^d - V_{t-1}^d) \neq -R_t$.

Case 8.7: $(V_t^d - V_{t-1}^d) > 0$ and $f(V_{t-1}^d) > 0$.

Tax laws often allow depreciation that is not tied directly to actual capital losses. As a result, $f(V_{t-1}^d)$ may be positive even when capital gains are earned. For this case, θ_t is smaller than would be the case if $f(V_{t-1}^d)$ were zero. This relationship holds because this defender creates tax shields from tax deductible depreciation tied to book value of the asset.

The Importance of θ_t

As these cases show, θ_t depends on the properties of the defender and, in general, is not equal to one. *PV* models often adjust the defender's before-tax *IRR*(s) by multiplying them by $(1-T)$, the firm's constant marginal income tax rate. Since θ_t equals one only in special cases, this adjustment usually gives inappropriate after-tax discount rates. Then, as a result of incorrectly assuming $\theta_t = 1$, the *NPV* of the after-tax cash flows of the challenger are estimated incorrectly.

Finding θ_t is also important when investments are compared using after-tax *IRR*(s). This knowledge of θ_t permits more effective analysis of tax policy effects on asset values. Finally, knowledge about θ_t is needed to perform comparative static analysis; otherwise, inferences about the effects on asset values of increases in tax rates and changes in other variables may be incorrect.

Finding θ_t for Specific *PV* Models

In order to calculate the before-tax returns, $r_t, r_{t+1}, \ldots$ and effective tax rate adjustments, $\theta_t, \theta_{t+1}, \ldots$ for a defending asset, the values of the cash return series $R_t, R_{t+1}, \ldots$, the value series $V_t, V_{t+1}, \ldots$, and the allowable depreciation series $f(V_{t-1}), f(V_t), \ldots$ must be known.[3] If these values are known, then (8.5) and (8.10) can be used to calculate the values of r_t, and θ_t. It is common in most applications of *PV* models to estimate the return series, $R_t, R_{t+1}, \ldots$, using past, current, and projected data. The $f(V_{t-1}), f(V_t), \ldots$ series may or may not be known depending on the capital gains and tax characteristics of a particular investment. The value series $V_{t-1}, V_t, \ldots$, is usually not specified in applications of *PV* models. In most cases, however, the characteristics of the investment lend some insights into the likely behavior of the value series.

Suppose the defending asset has a stream of perpetual constant cash flows, i.e., $R_t = R_{t+1} = \ldots = R$. By making assumptions about the type of return generated by the defending asset, future values of the asset can be characterized. For example, suppose the before-tax return from the defending investment is constant over time and equal to r.[4] With this knowledge of r, the value of the defending investment can be characterized by the following expression:

$$V_{t-1}^d = \frac{R}{(1+r)} + \frac{R}{(1+r)^2} + \ldots = \frac{R}{r}. \tag{8.12}$$

From (8.12), it is clear that the capital gains $(V_t - V_{t-1})$ during each period for the defending investment equal zero. Assuming that $f(V_{t-1})$ is zero and using (8.10), θ_t is found to equal one for all t. This result is consistent with Case 8.1 and Example 8.1 where all returns are taxable cash income. Thus, the after-tax return for this defending investment is $r(1-T)$, and the typical θ_t of one is appropriate.

Next, consider a defender with an infinite stream of cash flows growing at a constant rate in each period. This model is often used in studies of farmland values (e.g., Alston; Baker; Robison, Lins, and Venkataraman).[5] Assuming a constant growth rate of g, the value of the investment on a before-tax basis is:

$$V_{t-1}^d = \frac{R_{t-1}(1+g)}{(1+r)} + \frac{R_{t-1}(1+g)^2}{(1+r)^2} + \ldots = \frac{R_{t-1}(1+g)}{r-g}, \tag{8.13}$$

where r is the constant before-tax rate of return. The change in value each period is:

$$V_t^d - V_{t-1}^d = gV_{t-1}^d. \tag{8.14}$$

To find θ_t, substitute the right-hand side of (8.14) for $V_t^d - V_{t-1}^d$ in (8.10). Then, substitute the right-hand side of (8.13) for V_{t-1}^d. The result is:

$$\theta_t = \frac{R_{t-1}(1+g)}{R_{t-1}(1+g) + gV_{t-1}^d} = \frac{R_{t-1}(1+g)}{R_{t-1}(1+g) + \dfrac{gR_{t-1}(1+g)}{r-g}} = \frac{r-g}{r} < 1 \tag{8.15}$$

for $r, g > 0$.

Moreover, if g increases holding r constant, θ_t decreases:

$$\frac{d\theta_t}{dg} = \frac{-1}{r} < 0.$$

Example 8.4: θ_t for Perpetual Growth Investments

Investn ThFuture can invest in a growth stock whose return is expected to increase at a 5 percent rate in perpetuity. With a before-tax discount rate of 10 percent, Investn calculates her tax adjustment coefficient, using equation (8.15), which equals:

$$\theta_t = \frac{.10 - .05}{.10} = 50 \text{ percent.}$$

Since Investn is in the 32 percent income tax bracket, she calculates that the effective tax rate for this investment is (.32)(.5) or 16 percent. She calculates her after-tax rate of return as 10 percent times (1-.16) or 8.4 percent. Had she adjusted her before-tax rate of return with the income tax rate, her after-tax rate of return would have been mistakenly calculated as 10 percent times (1-.32), or 6.8 percent.

This model resembles Case 8.2 discussed earlier. The result, $\theta_t < 1$, occurs because the capital gains earned each period are not taxed until the asset is liquidated. Moreover, θ_t is a constant in this model because capital gains are a fixed proportion of the investment's value in the previous period. As the growth rate in cash flows increases, θ_t declines because a larger portion of each period's returns is non-taxable capital gains. Clearly, adjusting the before-tax rate of return by (1-T) is not appropriate in this case as was demonstrated in Examples 8.2 and 8.3.

An alternative expression for θ_t in (8.15) is obtained by letting $V_{t-1}^d = R_t/(r-g)$ in (8.13). Then, after substituting R_t/V_{t-1}^d for $(r-g)$ in (8.15), θ_t can be expressed as:

$$\theta_t = \frac{R_t}{rV_{t-1}^d}. \tag{8.16}$$

Expressed in the form above, θ_t is recognized as the CT_t ratio described in Chapter 7. In other words, if $T_g = 0$, the tax adjustment coefficient equals the percentage of returns received as cash.

Tax Adjustment Coefficients and Loans

In many applications, the defender is a loan. When a loan is the defender, its associated tax adjustment coefficient can be easily calculated. Let r be the interest rate, let V_{t-1}^d be the original amount of the loan, and let A be the loan payment. Then, on a before-tax basis:

$$V_{t-1}^d = \frac{A}{(1+r)} + \ldots + \frac{A}{(1+r)^n}. \tag{8.17}$$

On an after-tax basis, interest (the difference between A and the principal portion of the payment) is adjusted for taxes. Assume this adjustment occurs at rate T. Then, the after-tax payment A_t^T in the tth period is:

$$A_t^T = A - T\left[A - \frac{A}{(1+r)^{n-t}}\right] = A(1-T) + \frac{TA}{(1+r)^{n-t}}, \tag{8.18}$$

where $A/(1+r)^{n-t}$ is the principal portion of the payment made in the tth period. In addition, $(V_t^d - V_{t-1}^d)$ also equals $A/(1+r)^{n-t}$. Making the appropriate substitutions into (8.10) by letting $f(V_{t-1}^d)$ equal $A/(1+r)^{n-t}$, A equal R_t, $(V_t - V_{t-1})$ equal $A/(1+r)^{n-t}$, and T_g equal T, θ_t is found to equal one:

$$\theta_t = \frac{A - \dfrac{A}{(1+r)^{n-t}}}{A - \dfrac{A}{(1+r)^{n-t}}} = 1. \tag{8.19}$$

θ_t equals one for loans because all interest paid creates a tax shield. Thus, the effective rate paid on loan funds is $r(1-T)$. These results characterize the conditions described by Case 8.5.

In general, if in equation (8.10) allowable depreciation $f(V_{t-1}^d)$ equals actual depreciation and T_g equals the income tax rate T, then $\theta_t = 1$:

$$\theta_t = \frac{R_t - \left(\dfrac{T}{T_g}\right)(V_t^d - V_{t-1}^d)}{R_t - (V_t^d - V_{t-1}^d)} = 1.$$

Example 8.5: After-tax Loan Payments

To illustrate equation (8.18), consider a loan of $1,000 to be repaid in four equal annual installments at an interest rate of 10 percent. The annual installment payment is found to be $315.47. In the second year, the $315.47 payment is comprised of interest of $78.45 and principal of $237.02. For an income tax rate of 20 percent, the after-tax loan payment is $299.78=$237.02 plus (1-0.2)($78.45).

The same result is found using equation (8.18):

$$A_t^T = A(1-T) + \frac{TA}{(1+r)^{n-t}} = (\$315.47)(1-0.2) + \frac{(0.2)(\$315.47)}{(1.10)^{4-1=3}}$$

$$= \$252.38 + \$47.40 = \$299.78.$$

Example 8.6: When θ_t Equals One

To demonstrate another example when θ_t may equal one, consider the model whose before-tax expression for V_{t-1} is written as:

$$V_{t-1} = \frac{R(1-d)}{(1+r)} + \frac{R(1-d)^2}{(1+r)^2} + \ldots = \frac{R(1-d)}{r+d}.$$

Since V_t can be expressed as $R(1-d)^2/(r+d)$, then $V_t - V_{t-1}$ can be found to equal $-dV_{t-1}$. Substituting into equation (8.10), θ_t is equal to:

$$\theta_t = \frac{R_t - \left(\dfrac{T_g}{T}\right)dV_{t-1}}{R_t - dV_{t-1}},$$

and $\theta_t=1$ if $T_g=T$.

Comparative Static Results

When valuing a challenger or performing sensitivity analysis on a challenger, values for θ_t associated with the relevant defender are required. Otherwise, incorrect values for V_{t-1}^d and inappropriate inferences about changes in V_{t-1}^c with respect to T and other variables might be inferred. For example, consider an infinite life investment with cash flows that grow at a constant rate g. Alston, and Robison, Lins, and Venkatarman, and others have suggested that V_{t-1}^c should increase as the marginal tax rate, T, increases. This result is obtained by assuming that θ_t equals one. As discussed earlier, this assumption is restrictive. A more flexible formulation of the problem incorporates the effective tax rate into the model. Accordingly, the after-tax value of the challenger is determined by:

$$V_{t-1}^c = \frac{R_{t-1}(1+g^c)(1-T)}{[1+r^d(1-\theta^d T)]} + \frac{R_{t-1}(1+g^c)^2(1-T)}{[1+r^d(1-\theta^d T)]^2} + \ldots = \frac{R_{t-1}^c(1-T)(1+g^c)}{r^d(1-\theta^d T) - g^c}, \qquad (8.20)$$

where g^c is the constant growth rate of the challenger, r is the defender's constant before-tax discount rate, and θ_t is the defender's constant effective tax rate adjustment coefficient. Taking the derivative of (8.20) with respect to T yields:

$$\frac{dV_{t-1}^c}{dT} = \frac{R_{t-1}^c(1+g^c)\left[r^d(\theta^d - 1) + g^c\right]}{[r^d(1-\theta^d T) - g^c]^2}. \qquad (8.21)$$

It is clear from (8.21) that the change in V_{t-1}^c in response to changes in T depends on θ^d. Suppose the defender is also an infinitely-lived investment with cash flows that grow at rate g^d. Then, we can replace θ^d with $(r^d - g^d)/r^d$ because we have assumed a series of earnings for the defender consistent with the one described in (8.20). After substituting for θ^d in equation (8.21), the change in V_{t-1}^c in response to an increase in T is found equal to:

$$\frac{dV_{t-1}^c}{dT} = \frac{R_{t-1}^c(1+g^c)\left[g^c - g^d\right]}{[r^d(1-\theta^d T) - g^c]^2} \gtrless 0 \text{ as } (g^c - g^d) \gtrless 0. \qquad (8.22)$$

If g^c is greater than g^d, the standard result is that the challenger's value and the marginal tax rate are positively related. But, if g^d is greater than g^c, V_{t-1}^c will be negatively related to the marginal tax rate T. If the growth rates of the challenger and defender are equal, then a change in the marginal tax rate has no effect.

Example 8.7: After-tax Present Value

To illustrate equation (8.20), suppose that the cash flow (R_{t-1}^c) is $100.00, the growth rate (g) is 0.05, the before-tax discount rate (r^d) is 0.10, the tax rate (T) is 0.20, and $\theta=1$. Then, the asset's value is:

$$V_{t-1}^c = \frac{R_{t-1}^c(1-T)(1+g^c)}{r^d(1-\theta^d T)-g^c} = \frac{\$100(1-0.2)(1.05)}{0.10(1-(1)(0.2))-0.05}$$

$$= \frac{\$84}{0.03} = \$2,800.$$

The important result here is that effects of changes in the marginal tax rate depend upon the relative rates of capital gains and losses of defenders and challengers. Failure to accurately adjust tax rates for capital gains and losses and allowable depreciation of the defender leads to incorrect inferences from comparative static analysis of economic models.

A problem frequently encountered by durable asset owners is that depreciation is claimed on a book value, but inflation reduces the nominal depreciation. Under such circumstances, one might wish to calculate the after-tax *IRR*. This requires, of course, that θ_t be calculated. On a before-tax basis, we describe a depreciating durable under inflationary conditions:

$$V_{t-1} = \frac{R_{t-1}(1-d)(1+i)}{(1+i)(1+r_t^*)} + \frac{R_{t-1}(1-d)^2(1+i)^2}{(1+i)^2(1+r_t^*)(1+r_{t+1}^*)} + \ldots$$

$$= R_{t-1}(1-d)/(r^*+d),$$

where i is the inflation rate and r_t^*, r_{t+1}^*, . . . are real rates. So, using (8.3), we obtain:

$$V_t = (1+r_t^*)(1+i)V_{t-1} - R_{t-1}(1-d)(1+i). \tag{8.23}$$

Next, we write V_{t-1} on an after-tax basis:

$$V_{t-1} = \frac{(1-d)R_{t-1}(1+i)(1-T)+dTV_{t-1}}{\left[1+(r_t^*+i+ir_t^*)(1-\theta_t T)\right]}$$

$$+ \frac{(1-d)^2 R_{t-1}(1+i)^2(1-T)+dTV_{t-1}(1-d)}{\left[1+(r_t^*+i+ir_t^*)(1-\theta_t T)\right]\left[1+(r_{t+1}^*+i+ir_{t+1}^*)(1-\theta_{t+1} T)\right]} + \dots,$$

and V_t can be written as:

$$V_t = \left[1+(r_t^*+i+ir_t^*)(1-\theta_t T)\right] V_{t-1} - (1-d)R_{t-1}(1+i)(1-T) - TdV_{t-1}. \qquad (8.24)$$

Finally, equating (8.23) and (8.24) and solving for θ, we obtain:

$$\theta_t = \frac{(1-d)R_{t-1}(1+i)}{V_{t-1}(r_t^*+i+ir_t^*)} - \frac{d}{(r_t^*+i+ir_t^*)}.$$

Then, after replacing V_{t-1} with $R_{t-1}(1-d)/(r^*+d)$, we find:

$$\theta = \frac{r_t^* + i(r_t^* + d)}{r_t^* + i(1+r_t^*)}.$$

To demonstrate the effect of increased inflation on the effective tax rate for the above model, θ_t is differentiated with respect to i. The result is:

$$\frac{d\theta_t}{di} = \frac{-r_t^{*2}}{[r_t^* + i(1+r_t^*)]^2} < 0. \qquad (8.25)$$

The effect on θ_t of an increase in inflation is affected two ways: inflation increases the capital gains tax shield from inflation but reduces the present value of book value depreciation. The overall effect, however, is to decrease θ_t.

Taxes and Real Rates of Return

As shown above, the nominal rates of return for investments with different return characteristics are affected differently by taxes. The real rates of return for investments with different types of return streams are also affected differently by inflation.

Example 8.8: Real After-tax Rates of Return on Financial Investments

Suppose Mr. Im Pak has savings which earn r percent returns taxed at rate $T(\theta=1)$. Mr. Pak calculated his real after-tax rate of return to be:

$$\frac{r(1-T)-i}{(1+i)} = \frac{(r^*+i+ir^*)(1-T)-i}{(1+i)} = r^*(1-T) - \frac{iT}{(1+i)} < r^*(1-T).$$

Mr. Pak finds his real after-tax rate of return decreases with increases in inflation. He also finds his real after-tax return to be less than the real rate of return r^* times $(1-T)$. To illustrate, suppose that the nominal rate of interest is $r=0.1024$, or 10.24 percent; the inflation rate is $i=0.06$, or 6 percent; and the tax rate is $T=0.20$. Then, using (8.26), the real rate of return is:

$$r^* = \frac{0.1024-0.06}{1.06} = 0.04 \text{ or } 4 \text{ percent.}$$

And, in the absence of inflation, the real after-tax return is $(.04)(1-0.2)=0.032$ or 3.2 percent.

Assuming inflation of $i=.06$, Mr. Pak calculates his real after-tax rate of return to be:

$$\frac{r(1-T)-i}{(1+i)} = 0.04(1-0.2) - \frac{(0.06)(0.20)}{1.06} = 0.0320 - 0.0113$$

$$= 0.0207 \text{ or } 2.07 \text{ percent} < r^*(1-T) = 3.2 \text{ percent.}$$

To begin, let $r=r^*+i+ir^*$ be a nominal rate of return earned by a tax-free financial investment that produces a perpetual stream of constant cash flows, where r^* is the real rate of return and i is the rate of inflation. The real rate of return for any investment is found by subtracting i from the nominal return and then dividing by $(1+i)$.

For the tax-free financial investment, the real return is:

$$\frac{r-i}{(1+i)} = r^*. \tag{8.26}$$

The real before-tax return is clearly independent of inflation.

Finally, consider an investment such as land whose cash flows grow at some constant rate i and are taxed at rate T. If the growth rate in the cash flows is equal to the inflation rate, then $\theta=(r-i)/i$ and the nominal after-tax rate of return adjusted for inflation equals:

$$\frac{r(1-\theta T)-i}{(1+i)} = r^*(1-T).$$

The above results answer an important question: Should capital gains be taxed? The answer depends on the taxing goal. If the goal is to administer the tax so that:

$$\frac{r(1-T)-i}{(1+i)} = r^*(1-T),$$

then the answer is clear. Do not tax capital gains if they are produced by inflation. Do tax them if they are not a product of inflation. To support this last case, suppose inflation is zero and:

$$V_0 = \frac{R(1+g^*)}{(1+r^*)} + \ldots = \frac{R(1+g^*)}{r^*-g^*}.$$

We know from earlier work that:

$$r^* = \frac{R(1+g^*)}{V_0} + g^*,$$

so that if the effective tax is to be $r^*(1-T)$, then capital gains must be taxed. That is:

$$r^*(1-T) = \left[\frac{R(1+g^*)}{V_0} + g^*\right](1-T).$$

It is, of course, a recognized fact, that in the U.S. and in many other countries, capital gains are taxed even when they are a result of inflation.

An Application

In this section, the realized tax adjustment coefficient θ_t is calculated for investments in farmland, stocks, and bonds during 1950 to 1985. Data required to analyze the realized values of θ_t are the after-tax values of the assets in each period, the cash income produced in the period for each investment, and the constant marginal tax rate on current income.

For farmland, annual land and service building values and cash rent values in Minnesota, Iowa, Illinois, Indiana, and Michigan are taken from various issues of *Farm Real Estate Market Developments* published by the USDA. Values in each state were then averaged to produce composite annual values. For stocks, total return and dividend yields of common stocks were taken from Ibbotson and Associates. Long-term government bond total return and interest yields were also collected from Ibbotson and Associates.

Our purpose here is to find the realized values of θ_t for individuals who held the above assets during the 1950 to 1985 time period. Realized values of θ_t were calculated from (8.10). Assuming $f(V_{t-1})$ or the depreciable base was zero each period, calculated values for θ_t are shown in Table 8.1. It is clear that realized values of θ_t differ across the three types of investments and are quite variable. Visual examination of the realized values of θ_t suggests little support for the assumption that θ_t equals one or that it is constant over time. Moreover, the magnitude and variation in θ_t suggest it is too important to assume θ_t is not significantly different than one.

Because the realized before-tax rate of return, r_t, changes over time, θ_t realizations are not very informative unless evaluated relative to the corresponding r_t. Using (8.5) and (8.10), we calculate $r_t \theta_t T$, which equals the realized percentage effective tax rate or the percent of the investment value paid as a tax. As such, it reflects the varying influences of both r_t and θ_t over time. Figure 8.1 shows the realized values of $r_t \theta_t T$ of land, stocks, and bonds. For illustrative purposes, a constant marginal tax rate of 30 percent was assumed for realized income. The realized percentage effective tax rate on land ranged from 1.43 percent to 2.23 percent. The percentage effective tax rate was fairly constant during the 1950's and 1960's, then dropped in the late 1970's because of large capital gains in land values.

The percentage effective tax rate on stocks ranged from 0.86 to 2.63 percent of stock value. There was a drop in the early 1950's, followed by a period of stability during which the effective rate in the 1960's was nearly one percent. Falling stock prices in the late 1970's increased the effective tax rate on stocks.

The percentage effective tax rate on bonds ranged from 0.64 to 2.63 percent of the bond's value. The rate increased in consistent fashion throughout the time period until the mid-1980's because of the general increase in interest rates, which resulted in capital losses on bonds.

The average of realized values of θ_t during the 1980 to 1988 period equals 0.53, 0.33, and 1.25 on land, stocks, and bonds, respectively. Thus, over the period

Table 8.1 Realized Values of the Effective Tax Rate Adjustment Coefficient (θ_t) for Farmland, Stocks, and Bonds

Year	Investment Types		
	Farmland	Stocks	Bonds
1950	0.29	0.28	35.33
1951	0.46	0.29	-0.61
1952	0.83	0.32	2.29
1953	1.05	-5.52	0.78
1954	0.62	0.12	0.39
1955	0.54	0.14	-2.13
1956	0.45	0.58	-0.53
1957	0.59	-0.36	0.46
1958	0.47	0.10	-0.54
1959	0.72	0.28	-1.77
1960	1.70	6.94	0.31
1961	0.67	0.13	3.95
1962	0.65	-0.34	0.58
1963	0.59	0.16	3.21
1964	0.57	0.20	1.18
1965	0.40	0.26	5.92
1966	0.46	-0.31	1.23
1967	0.56	0.15	-0.50
1968	0.62	0.29	-21.15
1969	0.89	-0.36	-1.17
1970	0.81	0.85	0.56
1971	0.56	0.23	0.48
1972	0.36	0.16	1.03
1973	0.23	-0.20	-5.86
1974	0.28	-0.14	1.67
1975	0.24	0.14	0.87
1976	0.17	0.18	0.47
1977	0.35	-0.60	-10.35
1978	0.26	0.81	-6.81
1979	0.25	0.31	-7.20
1980	0.32	0.18	-2.52
1981	-4.13	-1.00	6.21
1982	-1.38	0.26	0.33
1983	1.40	0.22	15.97
1984	-0.39	0.73	0.76
1985	-0.89	0.16	0.36
1986	-3.20	0.20	0.37
1987	0.38	0.70	-2.92
1988	0.44	0.25	0.92

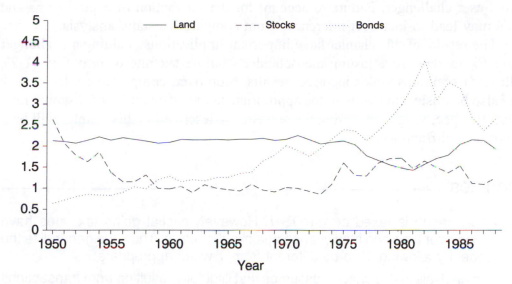

Figure 8.1 Percentage Effective Tax Rate $r_t\theta_t$T)

considered in this study, stocks produced the lowest average effective tax rate, equivalent to 33 percent of the marginal tax rate, followed by farmland at 53 percent of the marginal tax rate. On the other hand, bonds exhibited an average effective tax rate equivalent to 125 percent of the marginal tax rate, a result of the general capital losses on bonds over the period. This evidence demonstrates the importance and necessity of calculating θ_t values when comparing after-tax ratios or competing investments.

Summary

This chapter has examined the effects of capital gains and allowable depreciation on the after-tax internal rates of return on defenders. These defender *IRR*s are important because they serve as the discount rate for finding the net present values of new challenger investments. The correct tax adjustment to the defender's before-tax rate of return was found to equal one for the general case, the common assumption, only when the investment earned no capital gains or losses, when there was no depreciation allowance for tax purposes, or when capital gains were taxed the same as ordinary income.

Using the results developed in this chapter, effective tax rate adjustments were calculated for several defenders with different cash flow patterns. The effects of comparative statics were illustrated using the standard constant growth valuation model as a challenger. Failure to account for the interaction of capital gains and taxes may lead to incorrect inferences from comparative static analysis.

The results of this chapter have important implications. Valuing a challenger using *PV* models by adjusting the defender's before-tax rate of return by (1-*T*), with few exceptions yields incorrect results. Moreover, comparative static results may also be misleading without the appropriate tax adjustment to the discount rate. Correctly specifying θ_t following the procedures described in this chapter will help avoid these difficulties.

Endnotes

1. Depreciation is taxed at rate $T_g=T$. However, capital gains tax rates have varied over time and may change again in the future. Thus, we generalize the model by allowing T_g to be different from *T* when appropriate.

2. The analysis in this chapter assumes that illiquidity resulting from transactions costs, immovable investments (land), and imperfect information reduces the choices of challengers to a subset of those available in the complete markets. Therefore, the market facing the investor is considered imperfect.

3. While one normally calculates V_t based on values of R_t, *T*, *g*, and *d*, etc., one may think of a problem where one projects values of V_t or observes them to be fixed by contract.

4. A variety of assumptions help specify the value stream of the asset over time. Specifying some structure on the before-tax or after-tax return expected from the asset is a logical choice. The examples in this section assume the defending assets produce a constant before-tax return. In examples included in the text, this assumption is also consistent with the assumption at a constant after-tax rate of return. The return structure could also incorporate more sophisticated specifications such as allowing for term structure effects.

5. The model developed by Alston assumes that the risk premium is not taxed and that the market interest rate is a function of the marginal tax rate. Otherwise, it fits the framework described here.

Review Questions

1. If *PV* models result in the same maximum-bid price calculated on a before-tax or after-tax basis, what must be true of the tax adjustments applied to the cash flow stream and to the discount rate?

2. Explain why the tax adjustment coefficient for a durable asset that earns constant income in perpetuity has a value of one while the tax adjustment

coefficient for a durable asset whose cash flow stream increases at rate *g* in perpetuity has a value less than one.

3. Consider an investment described by the *PV* model below:

$$V_0 = \frac{R_0(1+g)(1-T)}{[1+r(1-\theta T)]} + \frac{R_0(1+g)^2(1-T)}{[1+r(1-\theta T)]^2} + \ldots$$

Calculate $\theta_t = \theta$ and V_0 if $g=.03$, $T=.25$, $R_0=100$, and $r=.12$.

Application Questions

1. Assume a tax-free rate of return, (r^*+i+ir^*) on government securities was chosen as a discount rate. Adjusting it for inflation by subtracting *i* and dividing by $(1+i)$ produces r^*, a real rate independent of inflation:

$$\frac{(r^*+i+ir^*) - i}{(1+i)} = r^*.$$

Now define r^* as a real rate charged on loans, (r^*+i+ir^*) as the nominal (inflation adjusted) rate, and $(r^*+i+ir^*)(1-T)$ as the after-tax nominal interest rate. Adjusting this rate for inflation, yields:

$$\text{real rate on financial investments} = \frac{(r^*+i+ir^*)(1-T) - i}{(1+i)} = r^*(1-T) - \frac{iT}{(1+i)}.$$

This result indicates that the real rate on financial investments is not constant, but varies with the inflation rate *i* or tax rate *T*. Solve for θ such that the real after-tax interest rate is independent of the inflation rate. Hint: Find θ in the expression:

$$\frac{(r^* + i + ir^*)(1 - \theta T) - i}{(1+i)} = r^*(1-T).$$

2. Samuelson showed that if capital gains were taxed at the income tax rate, then $\theta=1$. This result implies that taxes would be neutral. Prove Samuelson's results for the geometric growth model used in Examples 8.2 and 8.3. (Hint: Calculate capital gain and tax it at the income tax rate *T*.)

3. Define the following variables as:
   R = net cash income in period zero
   d = rate of nominal decay in *R*
   T = income tax rate, a percentage

r = before-tax nominal discount rate
V_0 = maximum-bid price
g = rate of nominal growth in R

Consider two functions:

Function (a) is characterized by a constant rate of growth in its perpetual payment series.

(a)

$$V_0^g = \frac{R(1+g)(1-T)}{[1+r(1-T)]} + \frac{R(1+g)^2(1-T)}{[1+r(1-T)]^2} + \ldots = \frac{R(1+g)(1-T)}{r(1-T) - g},$$

and:

$$\frac{dV_0^g}{dT} = \frac{gR(1+g)}{[r(1-T) - g]^2} > 0.$$

Function (b) is characterized by a constant rate of decline in its perpetual earnings series.

(b)

$$V_0^d = \frac{R(1-d)(1-T)}{[1+r(1-T)]} + \frac{R(1-d)^2(1-T)}{[1+r(1-T)]^2} + \ldots = \frac{R(1-d)(1-T)}{r(1-T)+d},$$

and:

$$\frac{dV_0^d}{dT} = \frac{-dR(1-d)}{[r(1-T)+d]^2} < 0.$$

Explain why an increase in the tax rate, T, increases V_0^g but decreases V_0^d. Does this suggest that not all durables are affected equally by changes in tax laws?

4.   Calculate θ for the durable asset whose after-tax cash flows are:

$$V_0 = TV_0 + \frac{R(1-d)(1-T)}{[1+r(1-\theta T)]} + \frac{R(1-d)^2(1-T)}{[1+r(1-\theta T)]^2} + \ldots$$

(Hint: Note that taxes do not enter into the cash flow stream as they did in equation (8.6). Thus, equation (8.10) cannot be used to find θ.)

5. Consider an investment that yields five equal payments of $100 ($R$) each. G. Deal, the purchaser of the investment, is currently in the 25 percent tax bracket (T). If Mr. Deal's before-tax opportunity cost of capital is 10 percent, calculate his tax adjustment coefficients $\theta_1, \ldots, \theta_5$. Use equation (8.10) to find your answer and assume $T_g = 1.2T$ and $f(V_{t-1}^d)$ equals $V_{t-1} - V_t$.

6. An investment to be studied in Chapter 13 (a bond) pays no cash return to the purchaser until it is sold. Moreover, the tax rate T_g applied to the earnings may be less than the investor's income tax rate T. The before-tax maximum-bid price for the bond is:

$$V_0 = \frac{V_n}{(1+r)^n}.$$

The after-tax maximum-bid price is:

$$V_0 = \frac{V_n - T_g(V_n - V_0)}{[1 + r(1 - \theta T)]^n}.$$

For this investment, find both the before-tax *IRR* and θ. Finally, find the value of θ when $T_g = T$ and $n = 1$. Explain your result.

7. Suppose that investment one has cash flows that are a multiplicative constant of investment two. How will θ_1 for investment one compare with θ_2 for investment two? (Hint: Observe that multiplying income in each period by a positive constant changes the asset's value by the same multiplicative constant.) Construct an example to verify your results.

References

Adams, R.D. "The Effect of Income Tax Progressivity on Valuations of Income Streams by Individuals." *American Journal of Agricultural Economics* 59(1977):538-42.

Alston, J.M. "An Analysis of Growth of U.S. Farmland Prices, 1963-82." *American Journal of Agricultural Economics* 68(1986):1-9.

Feldstein, M. "Inflation, Portfolio Choice, and the Prices of Land and Corporate Stock." *American Journal of Agricultural Economics* 62(1980):911-16.

Hirshliefer, J. *Investment, Interest and Capital.* Englewood Cliffs, NJ: Prentice-Hall, Inc., 1970.

Ibbotson and Associates. *Stocks, Bonds, Bills, and Inflation*. 1991 Yearbook, Ibbotson and Associates, Inc., 1991.

Mishkin, F.S. "Understanding Real Interest Rates." *American Journal of Agricultural Economics* 70(1988):1058-72.

Modigliani, F. and M.H. Miller. "Corporate Income Taxes and the Cost of Capital: A Correction." *American Economic Review* 53(1963):433-43.

Robison, L.J. and S.D. Hanson. "Capital Gains and After-Tax Internal Rates of Return." *American Journal of Agricultural Economics* 64(1992):663-71.

Robison, L.J., D.A. Lins, and R. Venkataraman. "Cash Rents and Land Values in U.S. Agriculture." *American Journal of Agricultural Economics* 67(1985):794-805.

Samuelson, P.A. "Tax Deductibility of Economic Depreciation to Insure Invariant Valuations." *Journal of Political Economy* 72(1964):604-06.

Shiller, R.J. "The Volatility Debate." *American Journal of Agricultural Economics* 70(1988):1057-63.

Thurman, W.N. "Understanding Real Interest Rates: Discussion." *American Journal of Agricultural Economics* 70(1988):1076-77.

U.S. Department of Agriculture. *Farm Real Estate Market Developments*. Various issues.

U.S. Department of Commerce. *Business Statistics*. Various Issues.

Chapter 9

Interpreting Rate-of-Return Measures

Key words: accounting rates of return, book value depreciation, book values, depreciable investments, economic depreciation, economic rates of return, market values, nondepreciable investments.

Introduction

Accounting rates of return are considered important indicators of a firm's profitability. However, the accounting measures have been subject to several criticisms. Included are conceptual difficulties both in comparing accounting rates of return among firms and enterprises, and in relationship to economic rates of return. The difficulties occur in part because accounting rates of return generally are ex post measures of financial performance in which book (or cost-based) values of investments are adjusted for depreciation. In contrast, economic rates of return are based on market values of investments that depend on the present values of expected future earnings.

In this chapter, we will use present value (*PV*) models to explore differences in pricing and rate-of-return relationships for different types of investments, and demonstrate these differences using simulated investments.[1]

Economic and Accounting Rates of Return

The economic rate of return is defined as the discount rate that equates the present value of an investment's projected net cash flows to its initial value. Thus, the economic rate of return is the internal rate of return (*IRR*) of an investment. We can use earlier results to define the economic rate of return as follows. For the general series:

$$V_0 = \frac{R_1}{(1+r_1)} + \frac{R_2}{(1+r_1)(1+r_2)} + \dots, \tag{9.1}$$

we can write the sum (see equation 5.45) as:

$$V_1 = V_0(1+r_1) - R_1. \tag{9.2}$$

V_0 and V_1 are the investment's present value at the beginning of the first and second periods; R_1, R_2,... are expected net cash flows; and r_1, r_2,... are periodic economic rates of return. We can solve for the economic rate of return for time period one using (9.2). It equals:

$$r_1 = \frac{R_1}{V_0} + \frac{(V_1 - V_0)}{V_0}. \tag{9.3}$$

Period one economic rate of return, r_1, is made up of two parts. The first part is the rate of current returns, (R_1/V_0). The second is an economic rate of depreciation (gain) in the investment's value, $(V_1-V_0)/V_0$.

The rate of economic depreciation or gain depends on the amount of economic depreciation, V_1-V_0. Economic depreciation is defined as the change in the investment's present value as time passes, given the remaining, but shorter series of earnings and given the economic rate of return.

The practical difficulty that most firms face in the calculation of r_1 is that most of their investments are not traded in the market each period. Consequently, few firms know the market value of their investments in each period. Therefore, it is difficult to calculate economic depreciation measures. The exception is when well-defined markets for used investments provide market values as is the case for used cars. But in reality, the market value for most used machines and buildings is not readily available. Generally, the only hard data most firms have about the value of their investments is original acquisition prices.

This data difficulty leads firms to calculate accounting rates of return based on adjustments to the original value of the investment. These adjustments reflect the commonly used accounting methods for depreciation: straight-line, sum-of-the-years digits, and declining balance. Let V_0^A and V_1^A represent the accounting-adjusted price of a used investment at the beginning of the first and second period. Then, the first period's accounting rate of return, r_1^A, can be written as:

$$r_1^A = \frac{R_1}{V_0^A} + \frac{V_1^A - V_0^A}{V_0^A}. \tag{9.4}$$

The difference between period one's economic rate of return, r_1, and period one's accounting rate of return, r_1^A, is the estimate of book value rather than economic depreciation (gains). The economic rate of return uses an economic depreciation measure based on market values, $(V_1 - V_0)/V_0$. The accounting rate of return uses a book value depreciation based on the accounting-adjusted prices, $(V_1^A - V_0^A)/V_0^A$.

In Examples 9.1 and 9.2 that follow, economic and accounting rates of return are calculated for a simple *PV* model. The point of the examples is to illustrate how differences in accounting depreciation measures and economic depreciation measures can create differences between measures of economic and accounting rates of return.

Economic and accounting rates of return are equal only when the accounting measure of depreciation is based on true economic depreciation. However, neither the economic rates of return nor the economic depreciation are easily observable values because they are based on expectations of future earnings, time patterns of earnings, and uncertain lengths of planning horizons, each of which can change frequently and significantly.[2]

In practice, accounting profits are generally measured as net operating profit (excluding interest expenses) realized by a firm minus depreciation measured by the application of selected depreciation rules (e.g., straight-line, declining balance, sum of the years digits) to the book (cost less accumulated depreciation) values of investments in each year. The accounting rate of return is then found by dividing accounting profits by the investment value, measured at the beginning or end of the year, or averaged over the beginning and end of the year. Thus, it is not surprising that accounting and economic rates of return would differ from one another, and careful studies of the situation suggest that the differences can be substantial.

In particular, Fisher and McGowan; Solomon; Barry and Robison; and others have shown that economic and accounting rates of return for depreciable and nondepreciable investments bear little, if any, systematic relationship to one another as earnings patterns, growth rates, investment lives, depreciation methods, and other investment characteristics are allowed to vary. The accounting rates of return on individual investments may vary substantially over time and are only stabilized if ". . . somehow averaged out by the firm's investment behavior over time. . . ." (Fisher and McGowan, p. 83). Even then, Fisher and McGowan argued

Example 9.1: Economic Rates of Return

Consider an investment generating a series of $100 annual returns over a four-year period. The present value of the investment is $316.99 and its economic rate of return, r, is 10 percent; i.e.:

$$\$316.99 = \frac{\$100}{1.1} + \frac{\$100}{(1.1)^2} + \frac{\$100}{(1.1)^3} + \frac{\$100}{(1.1)^4}.$$

Economic depreciation is calculated in Table 9.1 given the remaining but shorter series of earnings and the economic rate of return.

Table 9.1 Economic Depreciation and Economic Rates of Return

Time, t	Payment Series, R_t	Investment Value, V_t	Economic Depreciation (Gain) $(V_t - V_{t-1})$	Profit (2+4)	Economic Rates of Return (5/3)
(1)	(2)	(3)	(4)	(5)	(6)
0	n.a.	$316.99	n.a.	n.a.	n.a.
1	$100	$248.69	$-68.30	$31.70	0.10
2	$100	$173.55	$-75.14	$24.86	0.10
3	$100	$90.91	$-82.64	$17.36	0.10
4	$100	0	$-90.91	$9.09	0.10

The investment values shown in column 3 are the present values of the $100 series of earnings over planning horizons of 4, 3, 2, and 1 years, respectively. The economic depreciation (gain) in column 4 is the difference in the declining investment values between the successive time points. Column 5 indicates economic profits in the respective years, defined as the $100 payments in column 2 plus economic depreciation (gain) in column 4. The measure of economic rates of return in column 6 is economic profit divided by the respective beginning-of-year investment values. As the values in column 6 indicate, the economic rates of return equal 10 percent in each period.

Example 9.2: Accounting Rates of Return

Reconsider Example 9.1 and suppose the firm does not know the market value of its investment over time. Instead, it uses a straight-line depreciation method. In this depreciation method, depreciation in each of the four periods is equal to $316.99/4=$79.25. Using the straight-line depreciation and investment book value, the firm calculates its accounting rates of return.

Table 9.2 Straight-Line Depreciation and Accounting Rates of Return

Time, t	Payment Series, R_t	Investment Book Value, V_t^A	Book Value Depreciation (Gain) $(V_t^A - V_{t-1}^A)$	Accounting Profit (2+4)	Accounting Rates of Return (5/3)
(1)	(2)	(3)	(4)	(5)	(6)
0	n.a.	$316.99	n.a.	n.a.	n.a.
1	$100	$237.74	$-79.25	$20.75	0.065
2	$100	$158.50	$-79.25	$20.75	0.087
3	$100	$79.25	$-79.25	$20.75	0.131
4	$100	0	$-79.25	$20.75	0.262

Notice that the accounting rates of return underestimate the economic rates of return in the first two periods, and overestimate it in the last two periods. Nor does the average of the accounting rates of return [(0.065+0.087+0.131+0.26)/4=13.6 percent] or the geometric mean of the accounting rates of return $([(1.065)(1.087)(1.131)(1.26)]^{1/4}-1=13.3$ percent) equal the economic rate of return.

that the accounting rate of return for the firm depends on its rate of growth from the reinvestment of earnings and will only equal an economic rate of return by accident. These arguments will be demonstrated numerically later.

Another difficulty associated with both economic and accounting rates of return is inflation. Since inflation varies over time, comparing rates of return without controlling for inflation leads to incomparable rates-of-return measures. During periods of high inflation, a firm may show "paper profits" — positive rates of return — even though these are inflation-based. So, in the next section, "real" or inflation-corrected rates-of-return measures are developed.

Real Rates of Return

As equation (9.3) demonstrates, the economic rate of return, r, is made up of a current rate of return (R_1/V_0) plus the rate of economic depreciation (gain) of ($V_1 - V_0$)/V_0. Accounting rates of return estimate the rate of accounting depreciation (gain) from accounting measures of the investment's values $(V_1^A - V_0^A)/V_0^A$. Both the accounting and economic rates of return can be adjusted to equal real rates of return, r_1^{*A} and r_1^*, respectively. We next calculate the real economic rate of return r_1^*.

In equation (9.3) we derived the rate of return in period one, r_1, as the sum of current rate of return plus capital gains rate. Moreover, decomposing the current return into a real portion, r^*, and an inflation component, i, we write:

$$(1 + r_1) = (1 + r_1^*)(1 + i),$$

so that:

$$r_1^* = \frac{(1 + r_1)}{(1 + i)} - 1 = \frac{r_1 - i}{(1 + i)}.$$

Applying this decomposition measure to our general rate-of-return measure that includes current returns and capital gains (losses), we write:

$$r_1^* = \left(\frac{R_1}{V_0} + \frac{V_1 - V_0}{V_0} - i \right) / (1 + i). \tag{9.5}$$

Calculating Real Rates of Return

Real or inflation adjusted rates of return often must be calculated for valid comparisons across time periods because nominal rates vary with inflation. We illustrate how this is done for three *PV* models: the infinite constant real return series, the infinite decay model, and the infinite growth model.

Case 1: Infinite Constant Real Return Series

Assume $i_t = i$, $r_t^* = r^*$, and $R_t = R_0(1+i)^t$. Then:

$$V_0 = \frac{R_0(1+i)}{(1+r^*)(1+i)} + \frac{R_0(1+i)^2}{(1+r^*)^2(1+i)^2} + \ldots = \frac{R_0}{r^*}.$$

Furthermore:

$$r^* = \frac{R_0}{V_0}. \tag{9.6}$$

Case 2: Infinite Decay Model

Assume $r_t^* = r^*$, $i_t = i$, and $R_t = R_0(1-d)^t$ where d is a nominal decay measure and d^* is the real decay rate. Then, letting:

$$V_0 = \frac{R_0(1-d^*)(1+i)}{(1+r^*)(1+i)} + \frac{R_0(1-d^*)^2(1+i)^2}{(1+r^*)^2(1+i)^2} + \ldots = \frac{R_0(1-d^*)}{r^* + d^*}.$$

Furthermore:

$$r^* = \frac{R_0(1-d^*)}{V_0} - d^*. \tag{9.7}$$

For the infinite decay model, R_0/V_0 does not measure the real economic rate of return. Instead, $[R_0(1-d^*)/V_0]-d^*$ is the appropriate measure.

Case 3: Infinite Growth Model

Assume r^* is the real discount rate, $i_t = i$, and $R_t = R_0(1+g^*)^t(1+i)^t$ where g^* is the real growth measure. Then:

Example 9.3: Real and Nominal Depreciation Measure

Payper Profits calculates the value of his investments at the beginning of the period to be $100,000. Net cash returns last period, R_0, were $10,000. At the end of the current period, R_1 is expected to equal $8,000. Moreover, the current inflation rate, i, is 8 percent. Assuming the return pattern follows an infinite geometric decay pattern, Payper calculates the ratio of $R_1=R_0(1-d)$ to R_0 to be:

$$\frac{R_0(1-d)}{R_0} = \frac{\$8,000}{\$10,000} = 0.8,$$

from which d is found equal to 0.2. Furthermore:

$$d = d^* + d^*i - i = 0.2,$$

from which Payper calculates d^* to equal:

$$d^* = \frac{(d+i)}{(1+i)} = \frac{0.28}{1.08} = 0.26.$$

Finally, using equation (9.7), Payper calculates his real rate of return to be:

$$r^* = \frac{\$10,000(0.74)}{\$100,000} - 0.26 = -18.6 \text{ percent.}$$

$$V_0 = \frac{R_0(1+g^*)(1+i)}{(1+r^*)(1+i)} + \frac{R_0(1+g^*)^2(1+i)^2}{(1+r^*)^2(1+i)^2} + \ldots = \frac{R_0(1+g^*)}{r^*-g^*}.$$

Furthermore:

$$r^* = \frac{R_0(1+g^*)}{V_0} + g^*. \tag{9.8}$$

Example 9.4: Real and Nominal Growth Measures

Betern Before (her friends call her Betty) calculates the value of her investments at the beginning of the period to be $100,000. Net cash returns last period, R_0, were $8,000. At the end of the current period, R_1 is expected to equal $9,000. Moreover, the current rate of inflation is 8 percent. Assuming the return pattern follows an infinite geometric growth pattern, Betty calculates $R_0=\$8,000$ and $R_0(1+g^*)(1+i)=\$9,000$ and:

$$\frac{R_0(1+g^*)(1+i)}{R_0} = \frac{\$9,000}{\$8,000} = 1.125,$$

from which g is found to equal 12.5 percent. Furthermore, $g = g^* + g^*i + i = 0.125$, from which Betty calculates g^* to equal:

$$g^* = \frac{g-i}{1+i} = \frac{0.045}{1.08} = 0.042.$$

Finally, Betty calculates her real rate of return using equation (9.8) to be:

$$r_1^* = \frac{R_0(1+g^*)}{V_0} + g^* = \frac{\$8,000\,(1.042)}{\$100,000} + 0.042$$

$$= 12.5 \text{ percent.}$$

Earnings-to-Value Ratio

An important rate-of-return measure referred to frequently is the earnings-to-value (price) ratio. This ratio is equal to R_0/V_0 and is calculated next for the three investments whose real rates of return were described in equations (9.6), (9.7), and (9.8). The earnings-to-value ratio for the infinite constant real return series is calculated from equation (9.6) and is equal to $R_0/V_0=r^*$. Notice that for this series, the ratio changes only in response to a change in r^* and is unaffected by changes in inflation that increase current income and capital gains at the same rate.

The earnings-to-value ratio for the infinite decay model is calculated from equation (9.7) and is equal to:

Example 9.5: Earnings-to-Value Ratios

Dee Sisions wants to compare the economic performance of three different investments. The first investment is expected to earn a constant real cash return in perpetuity and has maintained in the past an earnings-to-value ratio of 4 percent. Based on these expectations, Dee calculates the real rate of return r^* to be 0.04.

A second investment is expected to experience a decline in its *real* net cash flow in perpetuity at the rate of 10 percent. This investment, however, has maintained an impressive earnings-to-value ratio of 13 percent. Dee understands, however, that earnings-to-value ratios do not accurately measure real rates of return for durables that experience real growth or decay in their net cash flow streams. So Dee uses equation (9.7) to find r^* equal to:

$$r^* = \frac{R_0}{V_0}(1-d^*) - d^* = (0.13)(0.9) - 0.1 = 1.17 \text{ percent.}$$

A third investment is expected to experience an increase in its *real* net cash flow in perpetuity at the rate of 2 percent. This investment, however, has in the past maintained a low earnings-to-value ratio of 3 percent. Dee calculates r^* for this investment using equation (9.8) to equal:

$$r^* = \frac{R_0}{V_0}(1+g^*) + g^* = (0.03)(1.02) + 0.02 = 5.06 \text{ percent.}$$

Based on her calculations and assuming liquidity is not her overriding consideration, Dee chooses to invest in the one with real cash flows growing at a real rate of return equal to 2 percent.

$$\frac{R_0}{V_0} = \frac{(r^* + d^*)}{(1-d^*)}.$$

Notice that for depreciable investments, the ratio of earnings-to-value will be greater than r^*. This is because there are no capital gains. Thus, current returns must pay for depreciation plus earn a real return of r^* on the investment. However, like the constant real return series, inflation does not affect the earnings-to-value ratio.

Finally, consider the infinite growth model. Its earnings-to-value ratio is calculated from equation (9.8) and is equal to:

$$\frac{R_0}{V_0} = \frac{(r^* - g^*)}{(1 + g^*)}.$$

Notice that for investments whose earnings increase in real terms, the ratio of earnings-to-value will be less than r^*. This is because the firm earns capital gains in addition to a current return. Thus, the earnings-to-value ratio is expected to be less for the growth in income series than for those investments that earn no capital gains or suffer capital losses. Notice that the inflation rate does not influence the ratio.

Because the earnings-to-value ratios vary depending on the expected future cash flow stream earned by the investment, they should be interpreted cautiously.

Income Tax Effect

The effects of income taxes are introduced by specifying the payment series on an after-tax basis, and by valuing the tax shield of the depreciable investment over its anticipated life. Recall the after-tax series from Chapter 8 described as:

$$V_0 = \frac{R_1(1-T) + T_g f(V_0,1)}{[1 + r_1(1 - \theta_1 T)]} + \frac{R_2(1-T) + T_g f(V_0,2)}{[1 + r_1(1 - \theta_1 T)][1 + r_2(1 - \theta_2 T)]} + \ldots, \tag{9.9}$$

where T is the constant marginal income tax rate, T_g is the tax rate applied to allowable depreciation, and allowable depreciation is described as a function of the original value of the durable and the age of the durable t, $f(V_0,t)$. Finally, θ_t is the tax rate adjustment coefficient applied to the discount rate. All these elements of the after-tax income expression are described in detail in Chapter 8.

The sum of (9.9) after solving for V_1 is found in equation (8.8) and can be expressed as:

$$V_1 = V_0[1 + r_1(1 - \theta_1 T)] - R_1(1-T) - T_g f(V_0,1),$$

and the after-tax economic rate of return can be written as:

$$r_1(1 - \theta_1 T) = \frac{V_1 - V_0}{V_0} + \frac{R_1(1-T) + T_g f(V_0,1)}{V_0}. \tag{9.10}$$

The allowable depreciation will not only affect the nominal after-tax economic rate of return, but will also affect the present value of the investment. This is because the allowable rate of depreciation determines the tax shield which in turn affects the cash flows associated with the investment, and therefore its value.

There is an important link between the allowable depreciation and the after-tax accounting rate of return. Economic depreciation (gain) must be consistent with allowable depreciation. We reflect this consistency in the calculation of the after-tax accounting rate of return by specifying that:

$$f(V_0,1) = V_1^A - V_0^A.$$

Then, we write the after-tax accounting rate of return as:

$$r_1^A(1-\theta_1^A T) = \frac{V_1^A - V_0^A}{V_0^A} + \frac{R_1(1-T) + T_g(V_1^A - V_0^A)}{V_0^A}.$$

Now it becomes clear that additional opportunities exist for differences to arise between accounting and economic rates of return. For accounting and economic rates of return to be the same, not only must $V_1^A=V_1$ and $V_0^A=V_0$, but $T_g f(V_0,1)$ must equal $T_g f(V_1^A - V_0^A)$ as well.

Implications for Accounting Rates of Return

As the previous analysis has shown, investment values depend on their depreciability, even though these investments are valued using the same economic rates of return. In turn, the accounting rates of return for depreciable investments differ as well, depending on their depreciability.

It is useful to explore some of the differences in pricing models for depreciable and nondepreciable investments (or, more generally, for investments with different rates of depreciability) using some relatively simple assumptions about the parameters involved. The pricing models will highlight the effects of the various variables, including the effects of differences in investment life and growth pattern of earnings. And, the models will provide insight about differences in the rate-of-return measures for the various types of investments.

The approach generally taken to evaluate the implications of investment depreciability for rates of return is based on a simulated numerical analysis (Fisher and McGowan; Solomon; Barry and Robison). The investing firm is considered to have reached a steady state in the sense of maintaining a constant real value of nondepreciable or depreciable investments, net of the replacement of depreciated investments. In this framework, the accounting rates of return at the firm level are weighted averages of the rates of return on the individual investments comprising the firm with the book values of investments in each year serving as the weights. The steady state allows the accounting rates of return on individual investments to converge to a weighted average accounting rate of return for the firm.

Steady States

It is possible to deduce steady state results when investments have certain regular depreciation patterns. The analytic results provide a benchmark for later use in evaluating numerical simulations.

The point of the steady state analysis is that firms are concerned with more than the economic rate of return for a single investment. Firms are concerned with the rate of return on a portfolio of investments. When the firm matures, the real value of its investments remains constant so that the real value of replacements equals the real value of economic depreciation.

Suppose a particular type of investment depreciates at age t by real amount $D_t^* = V_{t-1}^* - V_t^* > 0$. Moreover, assume that $D_n^* = V_{n-1}^*$ so that the investment's economic life is n periods. If the initial value of the investment were V_0, then it follows that:

$$V_0 = D_1^* + D_2^* + \ldots + D_n^*. \tag{9.11}$$

If the firm purchases an investment each year for n years, the real value of the new investment purchased would just equal the real amount of depreciation and the total real value of the firm's investments or assets, A_0, would equal:

$$A_0 = V_0 + (V_0 - D_1^*) + (V_0 - D_1^* - D_2^*) + \ldots + (V_0 - D_1^* - D_2^* \ldots - D_n^*)$$

$$= nV_0 - (n-1)D_1^* - (n-2)D_2^* - \ldots - D_n^*. \tag{9.12}$$

Without inflation, the value of the firm's investments, A_0, is constant over time. Moreover, the ratio of real depreciation to the real value of new investment purchases is one. Under such ideal conditions, one might expect the accounting rate of return to equal a constant. However, even if the accounting rate of return is a constant, differences may still exist between the accounting and economic rate of return.

Now suppose that inflation increases the value of each investment purchased by i percent per period. Then, the book value of the firm's investments at the beginning of the first period is:

Example 9.6: Infinite Depreciation and Steady States

A. Sets desires to know the rate of return earned on his investments and selects the help of a trained *PV* analyst to make the calculation. Assume A. Sets purchases depreciable investments at a constant real price of V_0. The investments depreciate at a real rate of d^*. After a very long time, the value of A. Sets' investments in current period dollars, A_0, equals:

$$A_0 = V_0 + (1-d^*) V_0 + (1-d^*)^2 V_0 + \ldots = V_0/d^*.$$

Moreover, the economic depreciation in current period dollars equals *Dep*:

$$Dep = d^* V_0 + d^*(1-d^*) V_0 + d^*(1-d)^2 V_0 + \ldots = V_0.$$

As n becomes large, the value of A. Sets' investment equals a steady state solution and the value of the new purchase, V_0, just equals depreciation.

The rate of return for A. Sets' investment can be calculated in the following way. First, assuming inflation is zero; and second, that book value and economic depreciation are equal, total cash returns, *TCR*, equal:

$$TCR = R(1-d^*) + R(1-d^*)^2 + \ldots = \frac{(1-d^*)}{d^*} R.$$

The return, r, defined in equation (9.3), equals:

$$r = \frac{TCR - Dep}{A_0} = \frac{\left[(1-d^*) \dfrac{R}{d^*}\right] - V_0}{V_0/d^*} = \frac{(1-d^*)R}{V_0} - d^*.$$

$$A_0^a = V_0 + \frac{(V_0 - D_1^*)}{(1+i)} + \frac{(V_0 - D_1^* - D_2^*)}{(1+i)^2} + \ldots$$

$$+ \frac{(V_0 - D_1^* - D_2^* - \ldots - D_n^*)}{(1+i)^n}.$$

$$(9.13)$$

Investments purchased during periods of inflation have book values less than their market values. This is because book values are fixed to their values at the time of purchase and not adjusted for inflation. The implication of this result is that the book value depreciation claimed in any one period in a steady state (constant real value of investments) is less than the value of the investments purchased. Thus:

$$V_0 > \frac{D_1^*}{(1+i)} + \frac{D_2^*}{(1+i)^2} + \ldots + \frac{D_n^*}{(1+i)^n}.$$

This causes the ratio of accounting depreciation to the investments' book values to decrease as the inflation rate increases. This result will be demonstrated for different depreciation formulas later in this chapter. The point is that the new investment purchase, V_0, although equal in real value to the sum of depreciation, is greater than the sum of the book values of depreciation for investments already purchased. As a result, a steady state investment level is not reached after n periods even though a steady state of real values is obtained. So accounting rates of return are greater than economic rates of return during inflation as long as the firm maintains its constant real investment base.

Next, consider how inflation alters accounting and economic rates of return. Inflation alters accounting rates of return because it fixes book values and depreciation measures to the investment's value at the time of purchase. In Example 9.7, a real depreciation rate of d^* and economic rate, r, are assumed along with inflation rate, i.

The important implication of this steady state analysis is the following. Book value depreciation will understate actual depreciation during inflationary periods while cash returns will reflect inflationary pressures. As a result, accounting rates of return will be greater (and misleading) compared to economic rates of return especially during inflationary periods.

An Application

Having derived analytic results for the steady state with the geometric decay model, we now create numerical examples with more general depreciation patterns.

Example 9.7: Infinite Depreciation, Steady States, and Inflation

Assume that a depreciating investment in the current period is valued according to:

$$V_0 = \frac{R(1-d^*)(1+i)}{(1+r^*)(1+i)} + \frac{R[(1-d^*)(1+i)]^2}{[(1+r^*)(1+i)]^2} + \dots$$

$$= \frac{R(1-d^*)}{r^* + d^*}.$$

Then, the same investment purchased a year earlier would have cost $V_0/(1+i)$ and after one period of depreciation would equal $V_0(1-d^*)/1+i$. Similarly, a durable purchased two periods earlier would have cost $V_0/(1+i)^2$ and be valued in the current period at $V_0(1-d^*)^2/(1+i)^2$. Consequently, the book value of Sets' investments in the current period is:

$$A_0^a = V_0 + \frac{V_0(1-d^*)}{(1+i)} + \frac{V_0(1-d^*)^2}{(1+i)^2} + \dots = \frac{(1+i)V_0}{(i+d^*)}.$$

Then, substituting $R(1-d^*)/r^* + d^*$ for V_0, we find A_0^a equal to:

$$A_0^a = \frac{(1+i)(1-d^*)R}{(i+d^*)(r^*+d^*)}.$$

Meanwhile, book value depreciation can be written as:

$$Dep^a = \frac{d^* V_0}{(1+i)} + \frac{d^* V_0(1-d^*)}{(1+i)^2} + \frac{d^* V_0(1-d^*)^2}{(1+i)^3} + \dots$$

$$= \frac{d^* V_0}{(i+d^*)} = \frac{d^* R(1-d^*)}{(i+d^*)(r^*+d^*)}.$$

Example 9.7, Cont'd.: Infinite Depreciation, Steady States, and Inflation

Because of inflation the book value depreciation is now less than the value of the new purchase, V_0, even though the real value of Sets' investment is constant. In fact, the ratio of accounting depreciation to the new purchase (Dep^a/V_0) is equal to $d^*/(d^*+i)$. If $d^*=0.1$ and $i=0.08$, the ratio is 55.5 percent. The result is that Sets finds the value of his investments increasing in nominal values with inflation and his ratio of depreciation to investment values declining.

Finally, Sets calculates total cash returns as:

$$TCR = R(1-d^*)(1+i) + R[(1-d^*)(1+i)]^2 + \ldots$$

$$= \frac{R(1-d^*)(1+i)}{d^*(1+i)-i}.$$

Having available current returns, book value depreciation, and book values of investments, Sets calculates his accounting rate of return, r^a, as:

$$r^a = \frac{TCR - Dep^a}{A_0^a} = \frac{\dfrac{R(1-d^*)(1+i)}{d^*(1+i)-i} - \dfrac{d^* R(1-d^*)}{(i+d^*)(r^*+d^*)}}{\dfrac{(1+i)(1-d^*)R}{[(i+d^*)(r^*+d^*)]}}$$

$$= \frac{(r^*+d^*)(i+d^*)}{d^*(1+i)-i} - \frac{d^*}{(1+i)}.$$

Note that $dr^a/di > 0$ and $dr^a/dd^* < 0$; that is, increasing inflation increases the accounting rate of return. Moreover, increasing the real rate of depreciation decreases the accounting rate of return. To make this point numerically, consider values of $d^*=0.1$, $i=0.04$, and $r^*=0.03$. We find the economic rate of return $r=(1.04)(1.03)-1=7.12$ percent. Comparing r to r^a, we find:

$$r^a = \frac{(0.03+0.1)(0.04+0.1)}{(0.1)(1.04)-0.04} - \frac{0.1}{1.04} = 18.8 \text{ percent.}$$

Example 9.7, Cont'd.: Infinite Depreciation, Steady States, and Inflation

For shorter-lived investments, say $d^*=0.2$. Then:

$$r^a = \frac{(0.03+0.2)(0.04+0.2)}{(0.2)(1.04)-0.04} - \frac{0.2}{1.04} = 13.6 \text{ percent.}$$

Thus, as the investment life is reduced, the accounting rate of return is also reduced. On the other hand, if $d^*=0.1$ as in the original problem and inflation increases from 4 percent to 8 percent, the economic rate of return increases to $(1.08)(1.03)-1=11.24$ percent. Meanwhile, the accounting rate of return equals:

$$r^a = \frac{(0.03+0.1)(0.08+0.1)}{(0.1)(1.08)-0.08} - \frac{0.1}{1.08} = 74.3 \text{ percent.}$$

The following illustration is taken from a study by Barry and Robison in which accounting rates of return for depreciable and nondepreciable investments are derived under various assumptions about investment lives, depreciation methods, inflation, and taxation. The data for this situation include real rental payments of $100 per period ($R_0=\$100$) for both investments; a real before-tax required return of 5 percent ($r^*=0.05$); an ordinary income tax rate of 40 percent, $\theta_i=1$; a capital gains tax rate, T_g, of 20 percent; an anticipated inflation rate of 6 percent; a real growth rate, g^*, of zero; and depreciable investment lives of 3, 5, 10, 15, and 20 years. Thus, the before-tax real interest rate of 5 percent is equivalent to an after-tax real rate of 3 percent ($r^*(1-T)=0.05(1-0.4)$). In turn, the 3 percent real after-tax rate is equivalent to a nominal after-tax rate of 6.78; $[(r^*+i+ir^*)(1-T)]=[(0.05+0.06+0.003)(1-0.4)]$ percent and a nominal before-tax rate of 11.30 percent, given the 6 percent inflation rate.

For the depreciable investment, Tables 9.3 and 9.4 show financial data and accounting rates of return for three depreciation methods: straight-line, sum-of-the-years digits, and double declining balance. The analysis begins by excluding the effects of inflation and taxation in order to illustrate the calculation procedures, and then these effects are included in determining the accounting rates of return. The first row of Table 9.3, for example, represents a three-year investment. The investment's present value of $272.32 is found using the payments of $100, a three-year horizon, and the 5 percent discount rate. A steady state for the firm occurs when three investments are held. Thus, total annual depreciation is $272.32, which implies the annual replacement of one investment, and the average annual net cash flow from the three investments is $300. Average annual accounting profits are $27.68—total net cash flow less depreciation.

Columns 8, 9, and 10 indicate the average annual book values for the three depreciation methods. These values are found as the product of three measures: (1) the average percentage of remaining life per dollar of the investment's initial value; (2) the investment's initial value; and (3) the number of investments. The percentages of average investment are found by taking the average of the remaining value per dollar of initial investment for the beginning time point and at the end of each year of the investment's life. For straight-line depreciation, these remaining values are 1.00 at present, 0.67 at year 1, 0.33 at year 2, and 0.00 at year 3. The average value is 0.50 or 50 percent. The average values for the double declining balance and the sum-of-the-year digits methods are 36 percent and 41.67 percent, respectively. Thus, the average annual investment for straight-line depreciation is one-half of the investment's present value multiplied by the number of investments ($408.49=(0.50)($272.32)(3)). The average annual investments for the declining balance and the sum-of-the-years methods are $294.11 and $340.40, respectively.

The accounting rates of return in Table 9.4 are found by dividing the measures of accounting profits by the appropriate beginning and end-of-year levels of average investment. As panel *I* of Table 9.4 shows, the accounting rates without inflation and taxation differ moderately among the investment lives and the depreciation methods, and are higher for the accelerated depreciation methods. In all cases, the accounting rates exceed the economic rate of return of 5 percent, although without inflation, the differences are relatively small.

When inflation and taxation are introduced, the accounting rates increase considerably due to the inflation-induced growth in cash flows and accounting profits measured relative to the depreciated book value of investments. For inflation alone (panel *II*), the accounting rates tend to increase with the length of investment life, are slightly higher for beginning-of-year investment values, and range from a low of 10.93 percent for the three-year investment life under straight-line depreciation to 17.22 percent for the 20-year life under sum-of-the-years digits depreciation, even though the nominal economic rate of return is 11.30 percent (0.1130=(1.05)(1.06)-1) in all cases. The effects of taxation (panel *III*), at a 40 percent rate, have a substantial moderating effect on the range of accounting rates as well as reducing the rate levels relative to the case of inflation alone. The accounting rates again increase with the length of the investment life, and range from a low of 8.88 percent to 11.73 percent, even though in all cases the nominal value of the after-tax economic rate of return is 9.18 percent.

Table 9.3 Financial Data for Depreciable Investments, No Taxation, or Inflation

Invest-ment Life	Average Annual Net Cash Flow	Invest-ment Values	Number of Investments for Steady State	Total Annual Net Cash Flow	Total Depreci-ation	Total Annual Accounting Profits	Average Annual Book Value of Investment		
							Straight-Line Depreci-ation	Sum of Years Digits Deprec.	Declining Balance Deprec.
(1)	(2)	(3)	(4)	(5)	(6)	(7)	(8)	(9)	(10)
3	$100	$272.32	3	$300	$272.32	$27.68	$408.49	$340.40	$294.11
5	$100	$432.95	5	$500	$432.95	$67.05	$1,082.37	$841.85	$833.43
10	$100	$772.17	10	$1,000	$772.17	$227.83	$3,860.87	$2,807.89	$3,102.72
15	$100	$1,037.95	15	$1,500	$1,037.95	$462.05	$7,784.74	$5,514.11	$6,433.06
20	$100	$1,246.22	20	$2,000	$1,246.22	$753.78	$12,462.20	$8,703.76	$10,417.21

Source: Barry and Robison.

Table 9.4 Accounting Rates of Return for Depreciable Investments with Different Investment Lives, Depreciation Methods, Taxation and Inflation

Investment Life	Straight-Line Depreciation		Sum of Years Digits Depreciation		Declining Balance Depreciation	
	Beginning of Year	End of Year	Beginning of Year	End of Year	Beginning of Year	End of Year
(1)	(2)	(3)	(4)	(5)	(6)	(7)
I. No Inflation or Taxation						
3	6.78	6.78	8.13	8.13	9.41	9.41
5	6.19	6.19	7.96	7.96	8.05	8.05
10	5.90	5.90	8.11	8.11	7.34	7.34
15	5.94	5.94	8.38	8.38	7.17	7.17
20	6.05	6.05	8.66	8.66	7.24	7.24
II. Inflation at 6 Percent; No Taxation						
3	11.59	10.93	12.85	12.12	13.62	12.85
5	11.90	11.22	13.44	12.68	13.55	12.78
10	12.69	11.98	14.85	14.01	14.16	13.36
15	13.58	12.81	16.06	15.15	15.04	14.19
20	14.51	13.69	17.22	16.25	16.06	15.16
III. Inflation at 6 Percent; Tax Rate at 40 Percent						
3	9.41	8.88	9.70	9.16	10.06	9.49
5	9.45	8.92	10.03	9.46	10.07	9.50
10	9.82	9.26	10.65	10.05	10.36	9.77
15	10.22	9.65	11.19	10.56	10.78	10.17
20	10.66	10.06	11.73	11.06	11.22	10.59

Source: Barry and Robison.

Nondepreciable Investments

Table 9.5 shows accounting rates of return and other financial data for a farmland investment under the same inflation and tax conditions for the first period in the planning horizon. The accounting rates of return will remain constant in subsequent time periods.

As row *I* indicates, excluding inflation and taxation, yields an investment value of $2,000 and earns an accounting rate of return of 5 percent at the end of the period which equals the economic rate of return. Including inflation alone at a 6 percent rate again yields a present investment value of $2,000 and accounting rates of 5.30 percent and 5.00 percent on beginning and end-of-year investment values, respectively. The end-of-year rate is the same as the real economic rate of return (r^*=0.05), although both accounting rates are well below the nominal economic rate of return of 11.30 percent. The margin of difference is comprised of an inflationary capital gain that is not reflected in the accounting measures. Similar results occur when both inflation and taxation are introduced, as indicated by rows *III* and *IV* in Table 9.5. That is, the accounting rates of return on the nondepreciable investment are below the nominal economic rates of return under inflationary conditions, and are below the accounting rates of return on depreciable investments for all of the conditions evaluated, even though the economic rates of return are the same in all cases for the two types of investments.

Summary

As this chapter has indicated, commonly used accounting rates of return for depreciable and nondepreciable investments may vary even though they have the same economic rate of return. Accounting rates of return on nondepreciable investments have a downward bias relative to nominal economic rates of return, and the bias increases with inflation.

A significant problem for investors in non- (or low) depreciable investments is the liquidity crunch or financing gap that occurs when investment purchases are financed with debt capital (see Chapter 7). Higher inflation magnifies the repayment problems, especially early in the repayment period, since lenders require all of their scheduled compensation in a cash payment of which part is a real return and part is an inflation premium. The leveraged investors, however, experience only part of their return as a current payment; the rest is capital gain. The current payment tends to grow over time as a result of inflation, but the financing gaps still remain early in the horizon. Thus, liquidity management and a clear understanding of one's financial position take on increased importance in these circumstances.

Table 9.5 Accounting Rates of Return for a Constant Real Return Investment for Different Inflation and Tax Conditions

Situation	Annual Net Cash Flow (R_t)	Investment Value			Accounting Rates of Return	
		Beginning of Year (V_{t-1})	End of Year (V_t)	Accounting Profit	Beginning of Year	End of Year
	(1)	(2)	(3)	(4)	(5)	(6)
I. No Taxation or Inflation	$100	$2,000	$2,000	$100	5.00	5.00
II. Inflation at 6 Percent; No Taxation	$106	$2,000	$2,120	$106	5.30	5.00
III. Inflation at 6 Percent; Ordinary Income Taxes at 40 Percent	$63.60	$2,000	$2,120	$63.60	3.18	3.00
IV. Inflation at 6 Percent; Ordinary Income Taxes at 40 Percent; Capital Gains Taxes at 20 Percent	$63.60	$1,428	$1,514	$63.60	4.45	4.20

Source: Barry and Robison.

Endnotes

1. The material in this chapter draws heavily on the article: Barry, P.J. and L.J. Robison, "Economic Versus Accounting Rates of Return for Farmland," *Land Economics* 62(1986):388-401.

2. See Gustafson, Barry, and Sonka for an illustration of these points.

Review Questions

1. Explain the concept of economic depreciation. How is economic depreciation related to accounting depreciation?

2. Explain the concept of an economic rate of return, its relationship to accounting rates of return, and its relationship to internal rates of return.

3. Explain why accounting measures of depreciation (appreciation) may differ from economic depreciation (appreciation).

Application Questions

1. Identify the annual economic depreciation for an investment yielding a return of $100 in year 1, $200 in year 2, $300 in year 3, $400 in year 4, and $500 in year 5. Use a discount rate of 10 percent. Explain any unusual patterns in the estimated economic depreciation series.

2. Consider an investment whose current income is $1,000, the cost of capital is 10 percent, the nominal growth rate of earnings is 5 percent, and the inflation rate is 4 percent. Assuming the earnings series lasts in perpetuity, find the following:

    a. The investment's current market value
    b. The investment's market value one and two years in the future
    c. The investment's rate of capital gain in the first period
    d. The investment's real rate of return

3. Evaluate the statement: depreciable investments tend to have higher accounting rates of return than nondepreciable investments.

4. Explain how the choice of depreciation method affects the comparison of accounting rates of return and economic rates of return.

5. Calculate the total value of Sets' investments (A_0) and actual depreciation (*Dep*) in period zero values (see Example 9.6). Assume V_0=$100 and

d^*=0.1. (Hint: The value of V_0 after one period is $V_0(1-d^*)$. You need to calculate the undepreciated value of Sets' investments: $V_0+(1-d^*)V_0+(1-d^*)^2 V_0+....$

6.   In question 5, you were asked to calculate the current value of Sets' undepreciated investments. Now calculate the book value of Sets' investments (A_0^a), assuming $i = 0.08$. (Hint: You need to calculate:

$$\sum_{t=1}^{\infty} V_{-t}^{A} = V_0 + \frac{(1-d)V_0}{(1+i)} + \frac{(1-d)^2 V_0}{(1+i)^2} + \ldots ,$$

to answer this question.) Compare your calculated book value of investments (A_0^a) to the market value (A) of the undepreciated investments calculated in question 5. Which is larger? Explain why.

7.   Explain how a firm's accounting rate of return, calculated for its total investment base, can exceed its economic rate of return.

References

Barry, P.J. and L.J. Robison. "Economic Versus Accounting Rates of Return for Farmland." *Land Economics* 62(1986):388-401.

Fisher, F.M. and J.J. McGowan. "On the Misuse of Accounting Rates of Return to Infer Monopoly Profits." *American Economic Review* 73(1983):82-97.

Gustafson, C.R., P.J. Barry, and S.T. Sonka. "Utilizing Expectations to Measure Economic Depreciation and Capital Gains of Farm Machinery." *Agribusiness: An International Journal* 6(1990):489-503.

Solomon, E. "Alternative Rate of Return Concepts and Their Implications for Utility Regulation." *Bell Journal of Economics* 2(1971):65-81.

Chapter 10

Market Equilibrium Prices and Rates of Return for Durables

Key words: aggregation, market clearing prices, maximum (minimum) bid (sell) price models, *NPV* model, single sector, two-sector *NPV* models

Introduction

Previous chapters have developed methods for estimating and analyzing present value (*PV*) models for individuals. A relevant question is whether or not the *PV* models used to find maximum-bid and minimum-sell prices for individuals can be used to describe the market price of durables such as land. The answer is yes, and this chapter shows how insights about market prices can be obtained from *PV* models.

To integrate traditional market concepts and *PV* models, a two-sector model is included in the chapter in which land is traded between an agricultural and a nonagricultural sector. Equilibrium prices are influenced by returns earned in both sectors. Finally, this chapter shows how future demand for land for nonagricultural uses affects the current price of agricultural land.

A Single-Sector Land Value Model

To begin, we reintroduce the simple capitalization formula for a durable (e.g., land). As before, the opportunity cost is r, the tax-free rate of return or opportunity cost. Variable R_t^i is the initial cash return for the ith firm in the tth

period which grows at rate g. Taxes and transactions costs are ignored in order to focus on the problem of aggregation.

Let the maximum-bid (minimum-sell) price for the unit of land described for the ith firm at the time of purchase be V_0^i. Then:

$$V_0^i = \frac{R_0^i(1+g)}{(1+r)} + \frac{R_0^i(1+g)^2}{(1+r)^2} + \ldots$$

(10.1a)

$$= \frac{R_0^i(1+g)}{r-g}.$$

Solving for R_0^i, the net cash rent that justifies a maximum-bid or minimum-sell price of V_0^i is found. It equals:

$$R_0^i = \frac{V_0^i(r-g)}{(1+g)}.$$

(10.1b)

An important simplification was assumed in the derivation of equation (10.1a) and earlier *PV* models. The assumption was that the income stream, R_0^i, was independent of the quantity of land held by the ith firm. This assumption is an oversimplification because distances to markets, access to roads, and managerial skills cannot expand in the same proportion as land is acquired. Thus, at some point, R_0^i must diminish with increases in the quantity of land, Q_0^i, controlled by the ith firm.

To relate R_0^i to Q_0^i while keeping the model relatively simple, let the ith firm's returns be linearly and inversely related to the quantity of land it controls. This relationship is expressed as:

$$R_0^i = \alpha_0^i - \alpha_1 Q_0^i,$$

(10.2a)

and:

$$Q_0^i = \frac{\alpha_0^i - R_0^i}{\alpha_1},$$

(10.2b)

where α_0^i and α_1 are parameters used to estimate the marginal return per unit of additional land for the ith firm.

Next, suppose that the ith firm holds a quantity of land equal to $\overline{Q}_0^i$ at the beginning of the present period. Thus, the firm's marginal return on the last unit of land it holds is:

$$\overline{R}_0^i = \alpha_0^i - \alpha_1 \overline{Q}_i,$$

or, solving for $\overline{Q}_0^i$:

$$\overline{Q}_0^i = \frac{\alpha_0^i - \overline{R}_0^i}{\alpha_1}. \tag{10.3}$$

Finally, suppose the ith firm observes a market price of V_0^m and a market interest rate of r percent. Based on this observed price, the ith firm calculates its demand for additional land. To find the quantity of land that justifies the market price of V_0^m, the firm substitutes V_0^m for V_0^i in equation (10.1b), and substitutes the result into equation (10.2b). Then, it solves for the quantity of land demanded, Q_0^i, consistent with the ith firm's earning expectation and market price, V_0^m. The quantity of land demanded by the ith firm, Q_0^i, equals:

$$Q_0^i = \frac{\alpha_0^i - \left[V_0^m (r-g)/(1+g) \right]}{\alpha_1}. \tag{10.4}$$

The mathematically-derived relationship is now graphically described. Panel *a* of Figure 10.1 graphs the relationship described in equation (10.2a). Panel *b* graphs the relationship described in equation (10.1b). In both graphs, the vertical axes represent net cash returns in the current period. The horizontal axis in panel *a* represents quantity of land desired (Q_0^i) or currently controlled ($\overline{Q}_0^i$). The horizontal axis in panel *b* represents the market price of land (V_0^m), or the value of the last unit of land to the ith firm (V_0^i).

In Figure 10.1, a line is drawn from the market price of land, V_0^m, found on the axis in panel *b*, to panel *a* that identifies the quantity of land desired by the ith firm, Q_0^i, located on the horizontal axis of panel *a*. Then, from panel *a* a line is drawn from the current quantity of land controlled by the ith firm, ($\overline{Q}_0^i$), to the value of the last unit of land controlled by the ith firm V_0^i located on the horizontal axis of panel *b*.

The difference between $\overline{Q}_0^i$ and Q_0^i represents excess demand if $Q_0^i > \overline{Q}_0^i$, and excess supply if $Q_0^i < \overline{Q}_0^i$. If market price exceeds the value of the land to the current owner, he or she has excess supply of land and enters the market as a seller. If the market price is less than the value of the land to the current owner, he or she has excess demand for land and enters the market as a buyer.

Clearly, all market participants in the land market do not view their income opportunities for land in the same way as does the ith firm. If they did, all would

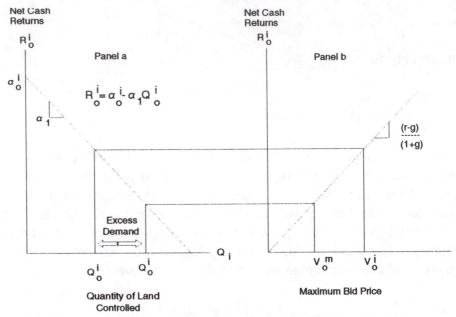

Figure 10.1   Panel *a*. The Relationship for the *I*[th] Firm between Cash Returns R_o^I and Quantity of Land $\bar{Q}_o^I$ Controlled by the *I*[th] Firm

Panel *b*. The Relationship Between the Market Price for Land V_o^m, the Firm's Maximum Bid (Minimum Sell Price) V_o^I and its Expected Net Cash Returns R_o^I

seek to expand their holdings of land. But, this would drive up the price so that it could not represent an equilibrium because no sellers would be willing to satisfy the excess demand for land. In order for V_0^m to represent an equilibrium price, the combined excess demand and excess supply of land must equal zero at the prevailing price of V_0^m. If this occurs, the market-clearing condition for N agricultural land users can be expressed as:

$$\sum_{i=1}^{N} \left(Q_0^i - \overline{Q}_0^i\right) = 0. \tag{10.5}$$

To find the market clearing price and its relationship to the demand curves of N participants in the land market, the right-hand sides of equations (10.4) and (10.3) are substituted into equation (10.5). The result is:

$$\sum_{i=1}^{N} \left[\frac{\alpha_0^i - \left[V_0^m(r-g)/(1+g)\right]}{\alpha_1} - \frac{\left(\alpha_0^i - \overline{R}_0^i\right)}{\alpha_1} \right] = 0. \tag{10.6}$$

Based on the information in equation (10.6), we can find the market clearing price for land that equates excess supply and demand. First, in equation (10.6), we cancel and sum to obtain:

$$\sum_{i=1}^{N} \overline{R}_0^i - \frac{NV_0^m(r-g)}{1+g} = 0.$$

Then, we solve for the market clearing price, V_0^m, to obtain:

$$V_0^m = \sum_{i=1}^{N} \frac{\overline{R}_0^i(1+g)}{N(r-g)} = \frac{\overline{\overline{R}}_0(1+g)}{(r-g)}, \tag{10.7}$$

where $\overline{\overline{R}}_0$ is $\sum_{i=1}^{N} \overline{R}_0^i/N$ or the average land rents. Thus, the market price equals the capitalization of average rents earned on the last unit of land held by each of the N land market participants.

A Two-Sector Land Model

Like many durables, land has many uses: agricultural, residential, recreational, and road location services. Thus, the use of land depends on its returns in alternative uses. It will be used in its highest and best use if economic forces are allowed to rule.

To show how competing demands for land determine land prices, consider a two-sector land market. The first sector is the traditional demand for the agricultural production services of land. The second sector involves a nonagricultural use.

Consider the net cash returns, R_0^j, from land held for nonagricultural uses in the current period by the jth nonagricultural firm. As before, assume R_0^j is a function of the quantity of land controlled by the jth firm, Q_0^j. The relationship is expressed as:

$$R_0^j = \beta_0^j - \beta_1 Q_0^j, \tag{10.8}$$

where β_0^j and β_1 are parameters used to estimate the marginal return per unit of additional land for the jth firm.

Because the jth firm holds a quantity of land at the beginning of the period equal to $\overline{Q}_0^j$, its actual return on the last unit of land equals:

$$\overline{R}_0^j = \beta_0^j - \beta_1 \overline{Q}_0^j,$$

Example 10.1: Market Price of Land

In an isolated hill country, the 100-unit land market is controlled by Jack and Jill. Each owns 50 acres of land at the beginning of the period. Each faces an opportunity cost of capital of $r = 0.10$, and Jill's current net return function [equation (10.2a)] is:

$$R_0^{Jill} = 100 - 1.0 \ Q_0^{Jill},$$

while Jack's net return function [equation (10.2a)] is:

$$R_0^{Jack} = 75 - 1.0 \ Q_0^{Jack}.$$

Using their net return equations, and substituting 50 for Q_0^{Jill} and Q_0^{Jack}, Jack and Jill calculate:

$$\overline{R}_0^{Jill} = (\$100 - \$50) = \$50,$$

and:

$$\overline{R}_0^{Jack} = (\$75 - \$50) = \$25.$$

Both Jack and Jill expect net cash returns to increase at a 6 percent rate. Using equation (10.7), the market price of land is determined to be:

$$V_0^m = \frac{\left(\overline{R}_0^{Jill} + \overline{R}_0^{Jack}\right)(1.06)}{2(0.10 - 0.06)} = \frac{(\$50 + \$25)(1.06)}{2(0.04)} = \$993.75.$$

To confirm that this price clears the market, we use equation (10.4) to find Q_0^{Jill} equal to:

$$Q_0^{Jill} = 100 - (993.75)(0.04)/(1.06) = 62.5 \text{ acres,}$$

while Q_0^{Jack} equals:

$$Q_0^{Jack} = 75 - (993.75)(0.04)/(1.06) = 37.5 \text{ acres.}$$

Since $Q_0^{Jack} + Q_0^{Jill} = 100$, the market clears.

and solving for $\overline{Q}_0^j$:

$$\overline{Q}_0^j = \frac{\beta_0^j - \overline{R}_0^j}{\beta_1}. \tag{10.9}$$

Finally, suppose the jth nonagricultural firm, like the ith agricultural firm, observes a market price of V_0^m and a market rate of return of r percent. Based on this observed price, the jth firm calculates its desired quantity of land, Q_0^j. To justify the market price of V_0^m, the firm solves for R_0^j in a capitalization formula which equals:

$$R_0^j = \frac{V_0^m(r-h)}{(1+h)}, \tag{10.10}$$

where h is the nominal growth rate of nonagricultural land rents.

Substituting the right-hand side of equation (10.10) for the left-hand side of equation (10.8), the quantity of land desired, Q_0^j, is found to equal:

$$Q_0^j = \frac{\beta_0^j - \left[V_0^m(r-h)/(1+h) \right]}{\beta_1}. \tag{10.11}$$

As before, if $Q_0^j > \overline{Q}_0^j$, then the jth firm enters the market as a demander. If $Q_0^j < \overline{Q}_0^j$, then the jth firm enters the market as a seller.

If there is both an agricultural demand for land by N agricultural firms as well as a nonagricultural demand for land by M nonagricultural firms, then the influence of both must be accounted for in determining the market clearing land price. Stated another way, equation (10.7) can represent the market price for land only if no demand exists for land for nonagricultural uses, and equally important, all land is currently used only for agricultural purposes.

The nonagricultural and agricultural demands for land can be accounted for simultaneously by rewriting the market clearing equation. The new market clearing equation requires that the total excess demand for land by N agricultural and M nonagricultural land users equals the supply of land offered for sale by the N agricultural and M nonagricultural land owners. The market clearing equation is:

$$\sum_{i-1}^{N} \left(Q_0^i - \overline{Q}_0^i \right) + \sum_{j=1}^{M} \left(Q_0^j - \overline{Q}_0^j \right) = 0. \tag{10.12}$$

This new market clearing equation requires that the demand for land for agricultural and nonagricultural uses equal the sum of land available.

Graphically, the solution to this problem is described in Figure 10.2. Panel *a* is comparable to panel *a* in Figure 10.1. Panel *c* is also the equivalent graph to panel *a* in Figure 10.1, only it is drawn to represent the relationship between returns and quantity of land held by the jth firm for nonagricultural uses. The graphs are drawn so that the excess supply of agricultural land $\overline{Q}_0^i - Q_0^i$ equals the excess demand for nonagricultural land $Q_0^j - \overline{Q}_0^j$.

Notice that the excess demand in panel *c* equals the excess supply of land in panel *a* and is equated by a common market price of V_0^m. This equality occurs despite the different rents expected on the last unit of land held. Rents in this case need not be the same when the capitalization factors are assumed unequal. In panel *b*, the capitalization factor for agricultural land, $(r-g)/(1+g)$, exceeds the capitalization factor for the nonagricultural demand for land $(r-h)/(1+h)$.

We now solve for the market clearing price that equates excess demand and excess supply for both agricultural and nonagricultural uses. The solution process begins by substituting expressions for $\overline{Q}_0^i, Q_0^i, \overline{Q}_0^j,$ and Q_0^j, respectively, into equation (10.12).

These expressions are obtained from equations (10.3), (10.4), (10.9), and (10.11). It is important to note that the market price for land, V_0^m, which appears in the agricultural equation (10.4), is the same as the market price that appears in

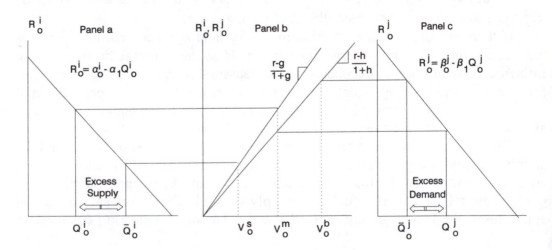

Figure 10.2 A Two-Sector Equilibrium Land Market Equating the Excess Nonagricultural Demand for Land $\overline{Q}^j - Q^j$ to the Excess Supply of Agricultural Land $Q_o^i - \overline{Q}_o^i$

the nonagricultural equation (10.11). After the necessary substitution is made into equation (10.12), we write:

$$\sum_{i=1}^{N} \left[\frac{\alpha_0^i - \left[V_0^m (r-g)/(1+g) \right]}{\alpha_1} - \frac{\left(\alpha_0^i - \overline{R}_0^i \right)}{\alpha_1} \right] +$$

$$\sum_{j=1}^{M} \left[\frac{\beta_0^j - \left[V_0^m (r-h)/(1+h) \right]}{\beta_1} - \frac{\left(\beta_0^j - \overline{R}_0^j \right)}{\beta_1} \right] = 0. \tag{10.13a}$$

Then, solving for V_0^m, we find:

$$V_0^m = \frac{\overline{\overline{R}}_0^i}{\left(\dfrac{r-g}{1+g} \right) + \left(\dfrac{M\alpha_1}{N\beta_1} \right) \dfrac{(r-h)}{(1+h)}}$$

$$+ \frac{\overline{\overline{R}}_0^j}{\left(\dfrac{r-h}{1+h} \right) + \left(\dfrac{N\beta_1}{M\alpha_1} \right) \left(\dfrac{r-g}{1+g} \right)}, \tag{10.13b}$$

where $\overline{\overline{R}}_0^j = \sum_{j=1}^{M} \overline{R}_0^j / M$.

Land Values When Diversions in Use Are Expected

In the analysis just completed, land values were determined as though the influences of agricultural use and nonagricultural use simultaneously affected the market clearing price of land. Equilibrium was obtained by setting the sum of excess demand equations equal to zero. This section considers a different way in which agricultural and nonagricultural demands for land influence the price of land. Understanding this alternative model may help explain the widely divergent land value-to-rent ratios of agricultural land reported by the *USDA*.

The market equilibrium inherent in this alternative model is expressed through the discount rates. If the market is efficient, then assets in the market are expected to earn the same rate of return. If an asset is earning more than the market rate of return, its price is expected to increase; on the other hand, if the

Example 10.2: Additional Demand for Land

In Example 10.1, Jack and Jill were assumed to control the agricultural land market. Now assume that D. Vel O'fers foresees some potential benefit for developing Jack and Jill's land into a new shopping center and golf course. Vel's net cash return is:

$$R_0^{Vel} = \$120 - 2Q_0^{Vel},$$

where $r=0.10$ and the expected growth rate of $h=0.05$. Since Vel begins without any holdings of land, $\overline{Q}_0^{Vel} = 0$. Moreover, since $\overline{Q}_0^{Vel} = 0$, $\overline{R}_0^{Vel} = \$120$. Using equation (10.13b) plus the results of Example 10.1, the new market price is equal to:

$$V_0^m = \cfrac{(\$50+\$25)/2}{\cfrac{0.04}{1.06} + \left(\cfrac{1}{2}\right)\left(\cfrac{1}{2}\right)\left(\cfrac{0.05}{1.05}\right)} + \cfrac{\$120}{\left(\cfrac{0.05}{1.05}\right) + (2)(2)\left(\cfrac{0.04}{1.06}\right)}$$

$$= \$755.43 + \$604.34 = \$1,359.77.$$

As a result of Vel's influence on the land market, the market price of land increased from $993.75 (see Example 10.1) to $1,359.77, an increase of nearly 37 percent.

To confirm that the new price of $1,359.75 clears the market, we calculate the post transactions holdings of land using equation (10.4), remembering that α_1 for Jill and Jack is 1 and for Vel, α_1 equals 2:

$$Q_0^{Jill} = 100 - \frac{(1359.77)(0.04)}{1.06} = 48.69 \text{ acres,}$$

$$Q_0^{Jack} = 75 - \frac{(1359.77)(0.04)}{1.06} = 23.69 \text{ acres,}$$

$$Q_0^{Vel} = \frac{120 - \dfrac{1359(0.05)}{1.05}}{2} = 27.64 \text{ acres.}$$

Clearly, the sum of $Q^{Jill} + Q^{Jack} + Q^{Vel} = 100$ and the market clears.

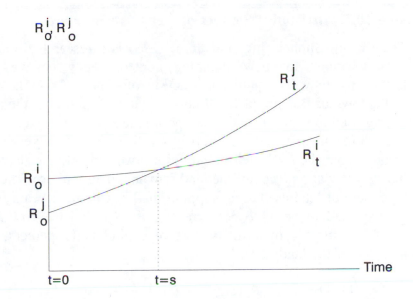

Figure 10.3   The Relationship between Expected Future Net Cash Income from Agricultural Uses of Land (R_t^j) and Nonagricultural Uses of Land (R_t^j)

asset is earning less than the market rate of return, the asset's price is expected to fall until all assets earn the same market rate of return.

In the model to be described, suppose the ith agricultural firm holds a quantity of land whose earnings in the current period exceed its potential earnings in nonagricultural uses. Thus, one would not expect the land to be diverted from its agricultural use, at least in the current period. But, suppose that beginning s periods in the future, the nonagricultural return from the land is expected to exceed the agricultural use return.

Figure 10.3 graphically describes the relationship between expected income from agricultural and nonagricultural uses of land. Net cash returns from agricultural use of land are represented as R_t^i and nonagricultural returns from land are represented as R_t^j. In period $t=s$, the returns from the two mutually-exclusive uses are equal; thereafter $R_t^j > R_t^i$.

To model the relationship described in Figure 10.3, one need not be more specific in the relationship between income earned in both agricultural and nonagricultural uses than to specify that beginning in period $t=s$, the use of the land shifts from agricultural to nonagricultural uses. Up to period t, the land earns agricultural income. After period t the land earns nonagricultural income. This relationship is expressed as:

Example 10.3: Alternative Sources of Net Cash Returns

The firm of Shoppe, Ing, and Spree (SIS) is a research firm that identifies locations for new shopping centers. They believe that population growth will require construction of a new shopping mall outside the town of Boomingdale, Illinois. A site acceptable for the mall is currently used to grow corn. Current population growth suggests that construction for the new mall should begin in five years. Last year's net cash returns from the land used in agriculture were $100; and they are expected to grow at 5 percent if the land remains in agriculture. The net return per acre of land used as a shopping mall beginning 5 years from now, is expected to be $406 per acre and is expected to grow at 6 percent. Assuming the opportunity cost of capital is 12 percent, the current value of the land equals:

$$
V_0 = \frac{R_0^i(1+g)}{(1+r)} + \dots + \frac{R^i(1+g)^5}{(1+r)^5} + \frac{R_0^j(1+h)}{(1+r)^6} + \frac{R_0^j(1+h)^2}{(1+r)^7} + \dots
$$

$$
= R_0 \, US_0 \left(\frac{r-g}{1+g}, 5 \right) + \frac{R_0^j(1+h)}{(1+r)^5(r-h)}
$$

$$
= (\$100)(4.1371) + \frac{(\$400)(1.06)}{(1.12)^5(.06)} = \$4,490.99.
$$

SIS calculates the ratio of land value to rent for the next 8 years. These ratios are reported below:

	1	2	3	4	5	6	7	8
V_t	$4854	$5337	$5877	$6483	$7067	$7491	$7940	$8417
R_t	$105	$110	$116	$122	$400	$424	$449	$476
V_t/R_t	46.2	48.5	50.7	53.1	17.7	17.7	17.7	17.7

For years one to four, the ratio of land value to rent is very high. This is because agricultural rents are below the land's long-term earnings when used as a shopping center. Thus, the ratio of land value to net cash returns to land is high until the land is converted to its nonagricultural use.

$$V_0 = \frac{R_1^i}{(1+r_1)} + \frac{R_2^i}{(1+r_1)(1+r_2)} + \ldots + \frac{R_s^i}{(1+r_1)\ldots(1+r_s)}$$

$$+ \frac{R_{s+1}^j}{(1+r_1)\ldots(1+r_{s+1})} + \frac{R_{s+2}^j}{(1+r_1)\ldots(1+r_{s+2})} + \ldots . \qquad (10.14)$$

In equation (10.14), the price of land is determined as in *PV* models introduced earlier. Absent in equation (10.14), however, is the relationship assumed earlier between returns and quantity of land controlled. Still, the allocation of land between agricultural and nonagricultural uses is determined by returns in the two sectors.

One of the important consequences of future uses of land with different current earnings expectations is that the ratio of value-to-rent will vary significantly over time and among states. The previous example illustrated such a result. The table of land values to rent ratios reported by Robison, Lins, and VenKataraman also confirm that alternative future uses of land are affecting the current value of farmland, particularly in densely populated states such as New Jersey (NJ), Delaware (DE), and Maryland (MD). Ratios tend to be lower in states whose land values reflect less pressure for nonagricultural uses such as Indiana (IN), Illinois (IL), and Iowa (IA) (see Table 10.1 below).

Land Values When Land Earns Agricultural and Non-Agricultural Income in the Same Period

In the previous section, we showed how alternative uses of land in the future different than the current use can affect an individual's evaluation of the present worth of land. Moreover, the ratio of land value to rent could be affected as a result of expected diversion of the land to other uses. Now the model introduced in the previous section is generalized. The generalization allows land to earn returns from agricultural and non-agricultural uses in the same time period. One might think of joint uses of land to include crop production in warm weather, and hunting and recreation during the season when no crops are being grown.

The generalized model has the following characteristics: Not only is land allowed to be diverted to an alternative use in the future and earn returns R_i^j, but land may also earn in the same period agricultural returns, R_t^i, and nonagricultural returns R_t^j. The framework used to analyze this process is again the *PV* model introduced in earlier chapters.

Table 10.1 Land Value-to-Cash Rent Ratios, 1960-92, Selected States

	State					
Year	NJ	DE	MD	IN	IL	IA
1960	26.8	16.6	15.3	14.9	18.4	16.1
1965	26.4	17.4	19.6	14.3	18.1	15.0
1970	32.8	22.0	33.8	14.8	17.2	13.9
1971	40.7	⸰23.0	27.4	14.5	16.4	13.7
1972	95.1	21.1	33.0	14.1	16.5	13.5
1973	95.9	21.0	41.3	14.3	17.2	14.1
1974	62.5	28.0	31.1	14.4	16.7	13.7
1975	84.1	28.0	42.1	13.6	17.9	14.5
1976	86.0	24.3	43.2	15.0	19.2	16.5
1977	94.0	31.7	99.7	17.3	21.3	18.4
1978	79.5	32.5	53.2	19.7	23.6	19.1
1979	72.9	34.8	35.9	19.1	23.1	20.0
1980	66.2	32.4	42.8	20.5	23.2	21.5
1981	66.1	33.6	40.3	19.7	22.6	21.4
1982	55.6	28.6	38.5	18.5	20.0	20.0
1983	47.6	28.6	29.4	17.2	17.9	17.5
1984	71.4	26.3	30.3	16.1	17.2	15.4
1985	76.9	27.8	41.7	14.1	14.1	11.8
1986	90.0	27.8	31.3	13.0	12.8	11.1
1987	125.0	32.3	40.0	13.5	13.2	10.8
1988	200.0	34.5	47.6	13.9	14.7	11.9
1989	333.3	47.6	43.5	14.3	15.9	12.1
1990	--	23.8	30.3	14.7	14.9	12.7
1991	500.0	31.3	40.0	15.2	14.9	11.8
1992	200.0	26.3	--	14.1	15.2	12.5

Sources: Various issues of *Farm Market Real Estate Development*.

To begin, assume that farmland produces a stream of cash flows from agricultural activities of R_t^i, R_{t+1}^i, R_{t+2}^i, ... in periods t, $t+1$, $t+2$, ... Moreover, assume that the opportunity costs of capital for periods t, $t+1$, $t+2$,... equal r_t, r_{t+1}, r_{t+2},.... The *PV* of future returns from agricultural activities generated from the farmland, V_{t-1}^a, can be written as:

$$V_{t-1}^a = \frac{R_t^i}{(1+r_t)} + \frac{1}{(1+r_t)}$$

$$\left[\frac{R_{t+1}^i}{(1+r_{t+1})} + \frac{R_{t+2}^i}{(1+r_{t+1})(1+r_{t+2})} + \; ... \right],$$

(10.15)

and V_t^a can be written as:

$$V_t^a = \frac{R_{t+1}^i}{(1+r_{t+1})} + \frac{R_{t+2}^i}{(1+r_{t+1})(1+r_{t+2})} + \; ....$$

(10.16)

Substituting V_t^a for the bracketed expression in equation (10.15), we can solve for V_t^a and write:

$$V_t^a = (1+r_t) \; V_{t-1}^a - R_t^i.$$

(10.17)

Suppose another stream of net cash income or expenses, R_t^j, R_{t+1}^j, R_{t+2}^j,... is associated with nonagricultural uses of the farmland for periods t, $t+1$, $t+2$,... whose *PV* equals:

$$V_{t-1}^0 = \frac{R_t^j}{(1+r_t)} + \frac{1}{(1+r_t)} \left[\frac{R_{t+1}^j}{(1+r_{t+1})} + \frac{R_{t+2}^j}{(1+r_{t+1})(1+r_{t+2})} + \; ... \right].$$

(10.18)

Following the same procedures used to find equation (10.18), equation (10.19) is written as:

$$V_t^0 = (1+r_t) \; V_{t-1}^0 - R_t^j.$$

(10.19)

The market value of farmland, V_t, can then be expressed as:

$$V_t = V_t^a + V_t^0 = V_{t-1}(1+r_t) - R_t^i - R_t^j.$$

(10.20)

It is important to observe that the model just introduced is the same as the model introduced in equation (10.14) in the previous section except that it allows for two sources of income. To see this, set $R_1^j, \ldots, R_s^j$ and $R_{s+1}^i, \ldots$ equal to zero. The earlier model will be the result. The amount of nonagricultural earnings in the tth period can be found by solving for R_t^j in equation (10.20). This amount equals:

$$R_t^j = V_{t-1}(1+r_t) - V_t - R_t^i. \tag{10.21}$$

Agricultural versus Nonagricultural Values of Land ——————

There are several reasons why it may be important to separate farmland's agricultural use value from its market value. Many states have enacted laws that encourage the continued use of farmland for agricultural purposes near urban centers. To do so, farmland used in agricultural production near urban centers is assessed for tax purposes at its (lower) agricultural use value rather than its (higher) market value. In these instances, the agricultural use value of farmland must be distinguished from its market value.

Another reason for separating farmland's agricultural use value from its market value is to better understand and interpret the relationships between the market value of farmland and agricultural rents from farmland. Without such information, the ratios of farmland value to agricultural rents reported in Table 10.1 are hard to explain. The challenge is to estimate V_t^a/V_t, the proportion of the farmland's value attributable to agricultural activities.

To estimate V_t^a/V_t, suppose that in the tth period, a tract of land earns agricultural income, R_t^i, that grows at rate g_t and nonagricultural income, R_t^j, that grows at rate h_t while the market rate of return in the tth period is r_t. Given these assumptions, V_t can be written as:

$$V_t = V_t^a + V_t^0 = R_t^i \left[\frac{(1+g_t)}{(1+r_t)} + \frac{(1+g_t)(1+g_{t+1})}{(1+r_t)(1+r_{t+1})} + \ldots \right]$$
$$+ R_t^j \left[\frac{(1+h_t)}{(1+r_t)} + \frac{(1+h_t)(1+h_{t+1})}{(1+r_t)(1+r_{t+1})} + \ldots \right]. \tag{10.22}$$

Substituting α_t and β_t for the bracketed expressions in equation (10.22) allows us to write:

$$V_t = \alpha_t R_t^i + \beta_t R_t^j. \tag{10.23}$$

Example 10.4: Rates of Return for Land With Joint Products

Agricultural policy makers frequently ask: what is the rate of return on agricultural farmland, and do farmers receive part of their returns from land in the form of nonagricultural income? To answer these questions, equation (10.21) is rearranged to obtain the expression:

$$V_t + R_t^i = (1+r_t) V_{t-1} - R_t^j.$$

We now attempt to estimate empirically the above relationship for Michigan farmland to measure non-agricultural income influences on land used in agriculture.

Letting V_t be the Michigan average agricultural land price in year t and letting R_t^i be the net cash return from agriculture in year t allows us to estimate the regression equation for years 1955-65:

$$y_t = \beta_0 + \beta_1 V_{t-1} + \epsilon,$$

where $y_t = V_t + R_t^i$ and β_0 estimates non-agricultural returns R_t^j, β_1 estimates $(1+r)$ and $\epsilon \sim N(0,1)$. The result is:

$$y_t = 15.75 + 1.047 \ V_{t-1},$$
$$(2.1) \quad (25.3)$$

with $\overline{R}^2 = 99$, $D.W. = 2.2$ where t statistics are reported in parentheses underneath the estimates of β_0 and β_1. That $\beta_0 = -R_t^j = \$15.75 \neq 0$ suggests that in equilibrium, other income equals an average -$15.75 per acre, indicating perhaps other costs that are deducted from net cash rents such as property taxes. Moreover, the coefficient $\beta_1 = 1.047$ suggests the average rate of return on Michigan farmland over the period 1955 to 1965 has been 4.7 percent. Both β_0 and β_1 estimates are significantly different from zero at the five and one percent levels, respectively.

Repeating this regression for the period 1966-1976, yields:

$$y_t = -8.95 + 1.18 \ V_{t-1},$$
$$(0.72) \quad (18.16)$$

with $\overline{R}^2 = .97$ and $D.W. = 1.41$. The t-statistics suggest that other income was not significantly different from zero during the period 1966-1976 while the average rate of return during the period was 18 percent.

Example 10.4, Cont'd: Rates of Return for Land With Joint Products

The point of these empirical results is that the influence of nonagricultural income or income other than farmland rent varies over time.

Suppose the right-hand side of equation (10.21) is substituted into equation (10.23). Then, if we approximate α_t with α and β_t with β, we obtain:

$$V_t = \left[\frac{\alpha - \beta}{1 + \beta} \right] R_t + \left[\frac{\beta}{1 + \beta} \right] V_{t-1}(1 + r_t). \qquad (10.24)$$

We empirically estimate the equation:

$$V_t = k_1 R_t^i + k_2 V_{t-1}(1 + r_t), \qquad (10.25)$$

where:

$$\frac{\alpha - \beta}{1 + \beta} = k_1,$$

and:

$$\frac{\beta}{1 + \beta} = k_2.$$

We then use k_1 and k_2 to find estimates of α and β. The result is:

$$\beta = \frac{k_2}{1 - k_2},$$

and:

$$\alpha = k_1(1 + \beta) + \beta = \frac{k_1 + k_2}{(1 - k_2)}.$$

Since $V_t^a = \alpha R_t^i$ and $\alpha = (k_1 + k_2)/(1 - k_2)$, it is possible to estimate V_t^a/V_t. The results of the estimation and calculations are reported in Robison and Koenig, and a summary of empirical estimates of V_t^a/V_t is reported in Table 10.2.

Table 10.2 Percentage of Agricultural Land's Market Value Attributed to Agricultural Rents, by State, 1960-86

Year	State						
	NJ	MD	MI	OH	IN	IL	IA
1960	20	143	138	87	113	91	63
1961	22	141	134	91	118	95	66
1962	18	114	134	88	119	91	68
1963	18	94	130	93	119	93	69
1964	18	109	129	91	119	91	69
1965	15	105	129	89	118	91	69
1966	14	103	130	93	131	92	72
1967	14	84	141	86	113	92	69
1968	16	90	119	91	116	99	72
1969	13	83	97	87	117	97	76
1970	14	76	91	89	120	101	78
1971	14	75	114	93	122	104	79
1972	11	79	100	101	126	98	79
1973	11	71	92	93	120	97	77
1974	12	67	93	88	116	94	81
1975	10	62	96	92	129	93	76
1976	8	59	96	92	121	89	70
1977	8	64	87	83	108	77	58
1978	8	55	81	83	97	73	58
1979	8	66	78	79	88	69	54
1980	9	58	79	71	83	68	49
1981	9	55	75	74	82	67	48
1982	10	64	75	85	90	78	52
1983	12	80	80	89	97	85	59
1984	11	78	85	89	99	86	65
1985	10	84	79	102	114	105	84
1986	11	83	82	99	117	113	89

Summary

In this chapter, the *NPV* model was extended in several ways. First, market equilibrium results consistent with individual maximum-bid and minimum-sell models were derived. Important in the results was that differences in supply and demand functions for land were recognized in deriving the market clearing equations. The result was a market clearing equation that capitalized average rent variables in the usual way.

Next, the traditional firm-level maximum-bid and minimum-sell equations were extended to include two sectors, one with *N* firms demanding land for use in agriculture, and another with *M* other firms demanding land for nonagricultural uses. Setting excess demand for land equal to zero allowed us to sum the excess demand and supply equations across both agricultural and nonagricultural sectors to find a market clearing equation.

Next, the traditional maximum-bid and minimum-sell equations were extended by allowing nonagricultural uses in the future to affect the current price of agricultural land. In this model, what equilibrated the demand for land to its expected returns and market price was the discount rate, reflecting equilibrium rates of return in both the agricultural and nonagricultural sectors. The result was an equation strongly resembling the equation derived earlier for the two-sector model.

Finally, the maximum-bid equation was extended still further by allowing land to earn agricultural returns and nonagricultural returns in the same period. Methods were then developed to determine what portion of the *PV* of land could be attributed to its agricultural uses. Generalizing the traditional *PV* models allows us to explain value-to-rent ratios that otherwise would appear unreasonable and to increase confidence in the practical usefulness of *PV* models. Much work, however, remains to be done to identify which *PV* model best describes market values for land.

Review Questions

1.   Explain the difference between a *PV* model calculated for an individual (an individual's maximum-bid or minimum-sell price) and a market value for the same asset. Should they be equal?

2.   Explain why individuals must calculate their own maximum-bid or minimum-sell price even though the market price is known.

3. Describe how equilibrium conditions for the model described graphically in Figure 10.2 are obtained.

4. Explain why land value to net cash return ratios may vary widely among states in the U.S. depending on the population densities and nonagricultural returns to land.

5. Why is it of practical interest to identify the portion of land's market value that is attributed to its agricultural use?

6. Can nonagricultural returns influence the market value of farmland? Identify some of the sources of nonagricultural returns.

Application Questions

1. This chapter extended the traditional *PV* equation to derive market values for durables and to account for simultaneous influences on the value of an asset. The models were applied to land. Identify another investment whose market clearing price could also be estimated using the methods derived in this chapter; that is, an asset whose value may be subject to future demands different than its current use. Defend your answer.

2. A market clearing equation for a single sector, equation (10.7), was derived by assuming firms possessed downward sloping demand curves with equal capitalization rates. Demonstrate that one could derive a market clearing equation for a single-sector model allowing each of the N market participants to hold different capitalization rates.

   (Hint: $Q_0^i = \dfrac{\left[\alpha_0^i - V_0^m(r^i - g^i)/(1+g^i)\right]}{\alpha_1}$ where r^i is the ith firm's opportunity cost of capital and g^i is the ith firm's expected rate of increase in cash flows.)

3. Would the extended model described in equation (10.20) apply to an investment whose use would alternate every four years? That is, for the first four years, it would earn returns according to R_t^j. For the next four years, it would earn returns according to the schedule R_t^j; please defend your answer.

4. Describe the similarities and differences between equations (10.23) and (10.13b). What additional assumption might be added to result in equations (10.23) and (10.13b) being identical?

5.   Suppose a farmer located near an urban center recognized that his land was influenced by nonagricultural uses. Unless the farmer is willing to consider selling his land, he need not be concerned about nonagricultural influences on its price. Do you agree or disagree? Please explain why you agree or disagree.

6.   Suppose that in the two-sector geometric growth model, the number of agricultural participants and nonagricultural participants both equal 1. Moreover, assume that $\alpha_1 = \beta_1$. Under these very restrictive conditions, solve for V_0^m and interpret your results. Then, also assume that $g=h$ and solve for V_0^m. Interpret your results. Finally, set $M=1$, $N=50$, $g=h$, and $\alpha_1 = \beta_1$ and solve for V_0^m. Interpret and compare this solution with those derived earlier.

References

Castle, E.N. and I. Hoch. "Farm Real Estate Price Components, 1920-78." *American Journal of Agricultural Economics* 64(1982):8-18.

Espel, T.K. and L.J. Robison. *A Conversation Between Buyers and Sellers of Land, or a Market-Equilibrium Approach for Estimating Land Values.* Agricultural Economics Report No. 403, Michigan State University, December 1981.

Pope, C.A. "Agricultural Productive and Consumption Use Components of Rural Land Values in Texas." *American Journal of Agricultural Economics* 67(1985):81-86.

Robison, L.J. and S.R. Koenig. "Market Value Versus Agricultural Use Value of Farmland." Chapter 13 in *Costs and Returns for Agricultural Commodities*, ed. by Mary C. Ahearn and Utpal Vasavada. Westview Press, 1992, pp. 207-28.

Robison, L.J., D.A. Lins, and R. VenKataraman. "Cash Rents and Land Values in U.S. Agriculture." *American Journal of Agricultural Economics* 67(1985):794-805.

U.S. Department of Agriculture. *Farm Real Estate Market Development.* Washington D.C., various issues.

Chapter 11

Risk and Present Value Analysis

Key words: beta values, CAPM, certainty equivalents, expected values, risk-adjusted discount rates, risk attitudes, risk measures, risk premiums, single index approach, stand-alone risk.

Introduction

In this chapter, the effects of risk on present value (*PV*) models are introduced and analyzed. As will become clear, the methods of conducting *PV* analysis under risk are relatively straightforward. The two most widely used approaches are: (1) to add a risk premium to the discount rate to reflect the risks associated with the asset or investment under consideration; or (2) to adjust the series of risky cash flows so that they represent a series of "certainty equivalent" returns. Other approaches may involve Monte Carlo simulation, decision trees, and sensitivity analysis.

While the methods are straightforward, this aspect of the problem is only the tip of an analytical iceberg. Underlying the methods is a host of conceptual and measurement issues associated with decision making and asset valuation under risk. The following sections of this chapter illustrate the methods of accounting for risk in *PV* models, and then address some of the major conceptual and measurement issues. These issues are considered within the context of investment analysis; however, the concepts, measurement approaches, and methods apply to other applications of *PV* models as well. But first, important risk concepts are introduced.

Risk Concepts

Risk analysis is based on the concepts of: (1) risk attitudes; (2) risk measures; (3) risk premiums; and (4) certainty equivalents. *Risk attitudes* represent an individual decision maker's personal feelings about the amounts and types of risk he or she is willing to accept. Such attitudes are embodied in the decision maker's goal function, or utility function, that is defined with respect to some meaningful object(s) (i.e., profits, rate of return, consumption levels, wealth) of utility. While such attitudes are unique among individuals, it is common to classify individuals according to whether they are risk averse, risk neutral, or risk preferring. These risk attitude classes are distinguished by the relationship between risk and financial compensation a decision maker would require to accept the risk involved. Thus, risk averse means that an individual anticipates receiving compensation for taking risk, risk preferring means that an individual is willing to provide compensation or to pay a premium for taking risks, and risk neutrality means that an individual expects no compensation or premium for taking risks. In general, the risk-averse category is believed to dominate these attitudinal characteristics of decision makers, as indicated by the results of most empirical studies of risk attitudes and because positive risk premiums are observed to occur in the levels of returns for various types of risky assets.

Risk measurement is usually based on probabilistic concepts. That is, the expectations of decision makers generally are expressed as *probability distributions* based either on objective or subjective concepts of probability. The *distribution* reflects the range of possible outcomes for an investment or other actions of the decision maker. The *probabilities* reflect the likelihood or relative weight of occurrence for the possible outcomes. The amount of risk (or measure of risk) is then determined by the characteristics (mean, variance, skewness) of the probability distribution in question. Likelihood of loss, for example, could be estimated in terms of the probabilities at the lower end of the probability distribution. Relative dispersion could be measured by a coefficient of variation (standard deviation divided by the mean). Viewed in this way, decision analysis under risk essentially involves choosing among probability distributions based on the conformance between the characteristics of the distributions and the risk attitudes of the decision makers.

A *risk premium* is the difference between the expected return on a risky investment and the return on a risk-free investment. If a risky investment has an expected return that indeed equals the risk-free rate plus the appropriate risk premium, then the investor would be indifferent between the two investments (i.e., the risky and the risk-free investment). Finally, the *certainty equivalent* is the level

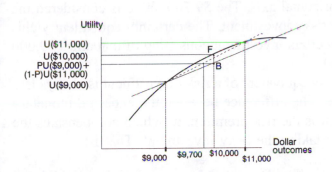

Figure 11.1 An Expected Utility Decision where Probability of Outcomes $9,000 and $11,000 are P and (1-P), Respectively

of return on a risky investment that is equivalent in utility terms to a completely certain return. the relationships among expected returns, risk premiums, certainty equivalents, risk attitudes, and risk levels can be expressed in terms of an investor's utility function applied to the evaluation of a decision situation under conditions of risk. The general characteristics of the utility function reflect the risk attitude of the investor. That is, a linear utility function implies risk neutrality, a function concave to the origin implies risk aversion, and a convex function implies a risk-preferring attitude. Thus, the utility function of a risk averter is characterized by diminishing marginal utility. This decision maker will prefer an investment with a perfectly certain return to another investment with an equal, but uncertain, expected return. This preference occurs because the loss of utility from a loss of returns exceeds the gain in utility from a gain in returns when the loss and gain in returns are of equal magnitude and likelihood.

To illustrate, consider the decision situation portrayed in Figure 11.1 in which a risky investment offers two possible payoffs–$11,000 and $9,000–with probabilities of $P=0.50$ in each case (analogous to the toss of a coin). The basic question is how much would a risk-averse decision maker, whose utility function is expressed in Figure 11.1, be willing to pay to participate in this risky investment? The expected monetary value of the investment is $10,000. The expected utility, $EU=(1-P)U(9,000)+ (P)U(11,000)$, of the risky investment is represented by point B. However, the utility, $U(10,000)$, of having the $10,000 for certain (risk-free) is point F; the utility at F exceeds the expected utility at B of the risky investment having $10,000 as its expected value. Thus, a risk averter would not purchase the risky investment at a price equal to its expected monetary value, because the shape (concave) of the utility function would translate the zero monetary gain into a utility loss; i.e., $PU(\$9,000)+(1-P)U(\$11,000)-U(\$10,000)<0$.

The risk averter would be willing, however, to pay a price for the risky investment that would yield the same utility as the investment's expected utility. The expected utility of the risky investment is $EU(B)$ on the vertical axis. The price the investor is willing to pay for certain, that yields a utility value of $EU(B)$, is indicated as $9,700 on the horizontal axis. The $9,700 value is considered the *certainty equivalent (CE)* of the risky investment. The certainty equivalent yields the same utility as owning an uncertain investment consisting of outcomes $9,000 and $11,000, with mean $10,000.

For a risk averter, the certainty equivalent of a risky investment is always less than its expected monetary value. The difference between the expected monetary value and the certainty equivalent is the risk premium, π, which compensates the investor in utility terms for undertaking the risky investment. That is:

The Risk Premium (π) equals **The Expected Monetary Value (*EMV*)** minus **The Certainty Equivalent (*CE*)** or $\pi = EMV - CE$

The concepts of certainty equivalent and risk premium are valuable in various types of risk analysis. If an investment's expected monetary value is known, then the certainty equivalent can be found, thus determining the risk premium. Or, if a certainty equivalent is known (i.e., a risk-free rate of return), then an appropriate risk premium can be added to it to obtain the required expected return for a risky investment. Finally, consistent with the principles of the capital asset pricing model (see a later section), the combined effects of actions in the market place by risk-averse investors should result in assets or investments with different risks having different expected returns. The margins of difference among these returns represent their risk premiums relative to one another. The margins of difference between their expected returns and the risk-free rate of return represent their risk premiums relative to the risk-free asset.

The magnitude of the risk premium for an individual investor depends jointly on the investor's level of risk aversion, as expressed by the bending rate of the utility function, and on the level of risk as determined by the probability distribution of the investment in question. In general, risk premiums increase as risk aversion increases, as the level of risk increases, or as both events occur together.

In the context of Figure 11.1, greater risk aversion is indicated by a more rapid bending of the utility function. Greater risk is indicated by a wider dispersion of outcomes on the horizontal axis. The reader can confirm that both of these actions, taken separately or together, are associated with greater risk premiums and lower certainty equivalents. Alternatively, as the bending rate declines, so does the level of risk aversion, until the utility function becomes a straight line (i.e., linear) and thus implies a risk premium of zero (i.e., risk neutrality).

Risk Adjustment Methods ———————————————————————

Adjusting the Discount Rate ———————————————————

To this point in the book's coverage of *PV* models, the discount rate has solely represented the opportunity cost of an investor's capital under conditions of certainty, expressed either in real or nominal terms. Thus, the discount rate has been considered risk-free. However, under conditions of risk, a simple method of accounting for the effects of risk is to add a risk premium to the risk-free rate and to discount the expected (or mean) values of the cash flows to a present value at this risk-adjusted discount rate. The risk premium is presumed to reflect the combined effects of the amount of risk added by the investment to an existing portfolio of assets and the risk attitude of the investor. Thus, the risk premium represents the investor's anticipated reward for risk bearing.

Adding the risk premium increases the discount rate, thereby reducing the *PV* of an asset or reducing the net present value (*NPV*) of a prospective investment. Thus, the risk premium represents a cost of risk bearing and, like other costs, it reduces an investment's profitability.

Certainty Equivalent Approach ———————————————————

The certainty equivalent approach is based on the use of a risk-free discount rate with the adjustment for risk occurring in the numerator or cash flows of the *PV* model. This adjustment can be expressed by multiplying the expected cash flow (R_t) by a coefficient (α_n) having a value that varies inversely between zero and 1.0 with the degree of risk:

$$NPV_0 = V_0 + \sum_{t=0}^{n} \frac{\alpha_t R_t}{(1+r)^t},\qquad (11.1)$$

where V_0 is the initial investment outlay and r is the risk-free discount rate derived from the defender's *IRR* of a certainty equivalent cash flow stream.

The adjustment coefficient (α_t) is selected in order to make the expected cash flows of the investment equivalent to a completely certain cash flow. Hence, this method is called the certainty equivalent approach. It, too, makes implicit use of the concept of a risk premium. That is, the difference between the expected value of the cash flows and their certainty equivalent is considered to be the risk premium that is required by the investor for undertaking investment risk (see the

Example 11.1: Adjusting the Defender for Risk

To illustrate how we adjust the defender for risk, consider a proposed investment requiring a $10,000 initial outlay of funds and returning $2,000 per year for 10 years. At a risk-free discount rate of 8 percent, the *NPV* is:

$$NPV_0 = -\$10,000 + \$2,000 \; US_0(.08,10)$$

$$= \$3,420.16.$$

The positive *NPV* signifies a profitable or acceptable investment relative to the required, risk-free opportunity cost of 8 percent. Alternatively, the investment's *IRR* of 15.10 percent also exceeds the required risk of 8 percent.

Suppose, however, that an evaluation of the investment's risk and the investor's risk attitude suggests that a risk premium of 8 percent should be added to the 8 percent risk-free rate, yielding a risk-adjusted discount rate of 16 percent. The *NPV* then declines to -$333.55, an unacceptable level, and the risk-adjusted required rate of return of 16 percent now exceeds the *IRR* of 15.10 percent.

Example 11.2: Adjusting the Challenger to Its Certainty Equivalent

To illustrate how the challenger is adjusted to be homogenous in risk to the defender, consider the example introduced above in which the expected value of the risky annual net cash flows is $2,000 per year for 10 years and the risk-free discount rate is 8 percent. The investor must designate a completely certain cash flow which is regarded as equivalent to this expected level of risky cash flow. If $2,000 were designated, then $\alpha=1.0$, and the investment would be considered risk-free. If $1,300 were designated, then $\alpha=1,300/2,000=0.65$. The smaller value of α indicates the perceived riskiness of the investment and represents a $700 risk premium deducted from the expected value of the cash flows in each period. If $\alpha=0.65$ were the case for each year, then the *NPV* for the investment under the certainty equivalent approach is:

$$NPV_0 = -10,000 + \frac{(0.65)(2,000)}{1.08} + \frac{(0.65)(2,000)}{(1.08)^2}$$

$$+ \frac{(0.65)(2,000)}{(1.08)^3} + \dots + \frac{(0.65)(2,000)}{(1.08)^{10}} = -1,276.89.$$

preceding section for a conceptualization of the risk premium and certainty equivalent).

An alternative to adjusting the cash flows of the challenger and defender to their certainty equivalent is to leave the cash flows of the challenger at their mean levels and add a risk premium to the certainty equivalent *IRR* associated with the defender.

If the risk-adjusted discount rate and certainty equivalent approaches are applied in a consistent fashion by the investor, then they should yield the same results for the *PV* models in investment analysis under risk. However, several factors may work against the similarity of results. Both approaches are based on data reflecting the amounts of risk and the risk attitude of the investor, and imperfections in the methods of eliciting behavioral data from investors, measuring investment risks, and translating these data into useful decision information work against the exact equivalence of numerical results for the two methods. That is, both the certainty equivalent and risk-adjusted discount rate methods consider the adjustment in returns needed to make an investor feel indifferent between a risky and a risk-free investment. Hence, the designation of a certainty equivalent income is as subjective as the choice of a risk-adjusted discount rate.

Applications to Investment Analysis

The conceptual and procedural material discussed in the preceding sections basically indicate that the fundamental approach to investment analysis under risk is to first determine the amount of risk that a prospective investment will *add* to a firm, portfolio, or other economic unit, and then to determine whether the risk attitude of the investor must be explicitly considered. Knowledge about these issues is essential in choosing the level of risk premium to either add to a risk-free discount rate or to deduct from the expected values of the risky cash flows in order to determine certainty equivalent values in the respective periods of the planning horizon. As will be shown, only under the specific conditions of the capital asset pricing model (*CAPM*) can a market-determined risk premium be found and even then, most analysts suggest caution and judgment in choosing the exact discount rate to use.

The basic question involving the measurement of relevant investment risk is whether all of a project's risk should be considered or whether some of the risk can be diversified away when the project is undertaken. That is, will the principles of diversification and the characteristics of the economic unit and its investors be such that the net addition of a new investment's risk to the economic unit is less than the investment's total risk? In responding to these types of questions, it has been common in the finance literature to identify several types of investment risk. For example, Brigham and Gapenski (page 390) cited three types of risk:

(1) stand-alone risk which views the risk of a project in isolation,...;

(2) within-firm risk, also called corporate risk, which views the risk of a project within the context of the firm's portfolio of projects; and

(3) market risk, which views a project's risk within the context of the firm's stockholders diversification in the general stock market.

A project's market risk is expected to be less than its within-firm risk, which is expected to be less than its stand-alone risk.

To illustrate these risk measurement issues, we can array the degrees of diversity of a firm's assets and the claims held by investors on these assets. At one extreme, a firm that invests in only one asset and whose owner only invests in the firm would have the same risk at the asset, firm, and ownership levels. The relevant risk for investment analysis, then, would be total asset risk. At the other extreme, a firm (generally large, incorporated, and with publicly-traded common stock) that invests in many assets, none of which is very large relative to total assets, and whose owners have portfolios that are well diversified need only consider an investment's net contribution of risk to the investor's portfolio. Diversification at the firm level, then, has little or no value in terms of the firm's own risk-return position, because investors can adjust for risk through the diversity of their own portfolios. In this case, the net contribution to risk is represented by the investment's systematic (or nondiversifiable) risk as measured by the *CAPM* in which a beta value representing systematic risk is determined by regressing the investment's historic returns against those of a market portfolio.

An intermediate point in this range is a firm that holds a relatively large number of assets, but whose owners concentrate their investments in the firm. This situation might characterize many small businesses and retail outlets, farms, and ranches, and other units in which various enterprises, investments, and marketing procedures are employed, but ownership is concentrated in the hands of one or more families whose assets are heavily committed to the business. Under these conditions, the investment analysis essentially occurs at the firm level, rather than at the investor level, and the risk of a new investment is represented by its contribution to the firm's risk. With limited diversity and nonmarketability of equity claims, the investment's contribution to the firm's risk probably is less than the investment's total risk, but likely involves some degree of nonsystematic risk. This risk might be measured by computing a beta for the new investment in terms of the firm's total return or some other relevant factor, rather than the market portfolio.

In the following sections, we will demonstrate how these concepts can be applied to express and estimate risk premiums.

CAPM Approach

In corporate capital budgeting, one of the approaches to estimating the risk premium on a firm's cost of capital is based on the Capital Asset Pricing Model (*CAPM*). The *CAPM* is a market equilibrium concept which shows that rates of return on individual assets or portfolios of assets adjust to levels that reflect the risk that each asset contributes to a market portfolio of all assets. Investors holding a portion of the market portfolio need only require compensation for the total market or systematic risk that is common to all assets in the portfolio and that cannot be diversified away. Thus, the risk premiums on individual assets need only compensate for their systematic risk.

CAPM Components

In market equilibrium, the *CAPM* expresses the relationship between an asset's expected return and its systematic risk in a linear fashion as the sum of a risk-free rate r_s, and a risk premium reflecting the product of the price and quantity of risk:

$$r_j = r_s + \left[\frac{E(r_m) - r_s}{\sigma_m^2} \right] \rho \sigma_m \sigma_j, \tag{11.2}$$

where r_j is the expected return of asset j, r_s is a risk-free rate, $E(r_m)$ and σ_m^2 are the expected return and variance, respectively, of a market portfolio, and $\rho \sigma_m \sigma_j$ is the covariance of returns between asset j and the market portfolio, with σ_j as the standard deviation of returns for asset j and ρ as the correlation coefficient. The bracketed term in equation (11.2) is the price per unit of risk and $\rho \sigma_m \sigma_i$ is the quantity of risk.

In empirical analysis, the model is modified to the familiar beta approach:

$$r_j = r_s + \left[E(r_m) - r_s \right] \beta_j, \tag{11.3}$$

or:

$$r_j - r_s = \left[E(r_m) - r_s \right] \beta_j, \tag{11.4}$$

where $\beta_j = \rho\sigma_m\sigma_j/\sigma_m^2$. In equation (11.4), the excess returns (above r_s) on asset j are expressed as a function of the excess returns $[E(r_m) - r_s]$ on the market portfolio where β_j measures asset j's systematic risk. Thus, an asset with $\beta > 1.0$ has returns that are more volatile than those of the market portfolio, and an asset with $\beta < 1.0$ will have less volatile returns than the market portfolio. An asset with $\beta = 0$ is a risk-free asset—its expected returns equal risk-free rate r_f, and its excess returns above r_f are zero.

The notion of pricing to cover the risk an asset *adds* to the market portfolio is clearly shown by the correlation coefficient (ρ). If $\rho = 0.00$, for example, then β also is zero and the asset is considered risk-free, even though the asset's own variability (σ_j) may be large. Thus, stand-alone risk is a part of the *CAPM*, but the main focus is on the correlation between the asset's return and that of the market portfolio.

CAPM Assumptions and Tests

Like other economic theories, the *CAPM* is based on an extensive set of assumptions about the behavior of investors and the characteristics of markets in which assets are traded. The markets are assumed highly efficient so that the expected returns quickly and fully reflect available information; no transactions costs, tax obligations, or asset indivisibilities exist; and for risk-free assets, lending and borrowing rates are equal. Investors are assumed risk-averse, well-diversified,

---

Example 11.3: *CAPM* and Stand-Alone Risk

To illustrate, suppose that the risk-free rate is 8 percent ($r_s = 0.08$) and the expected return on the market portfolio is 12 percent ($r_m = 0.12$). If an individual asset has a beta of 1.5 ($\beta_j = 1.50$), then the asset's expected return is 14 percent, and its risk premium is 6 percent:

$$r_j = 0.08 + (0.12 - 0.08)(1.5) = 0.08 + 0.06 = 0.14.$$

If $\beta_j = 0.50$, then:

$$r_j = 0.08 + (0.12 - 0.08)(0.5) = 0.10,$$

and the asset's risk premium is 2 percent. If $\beta_j = 1.00$, then the asset's expected return is 12 percent and its risk premium is 4 percent, the same as that of the market portfolio.

and to hold homogenous expectations that are fully characterized by means and variances over a single period horizon. Finally, the input-output relationships for the assets involved are linear. That is, every dollar invested in asset j will earn rate of return r, regardless of the level of investment.

Much attention has been given to the *CAPM*'s explanatory capacity and to the consequences of modifying these assumptions (Jensen; Modigliani and Pogue; Levy and Sarnat; Van Horne; Roll). Appraisals have been mixed, caused in part by problems with data and testing procedures. On the one hand, many of the assumptions do not appear realistic, but if the implications of the theory are reasonable approximations to actual observations, then the theory is worthwhile.

Empirical tests of the *CAPM* have considered the stability of beta estimates over time, the accuracy of estimating betas for individual assets versus portfolios of assets, and the consistency of empirical measures with expected relationships suggested by the theoretical framework. In general, the tests appear to support the view that beta is a useful risk measure and that high beta securities are priced to yield high rates of return. The results also appear to indicate that beta estimates are more stable and accurate for portfolios of assets than for individual assets, and the evidence generally shows a significant positive relationship between realized returns and systematic risk, even though the *CAPM* theory is based on an asset's future risk position.

CAPM and Capital Budgeting

In terms of corporate capital budgeting, the *CAPM* approach basically implies that the cost of equity capital to use in evaluating a prospective investment project is a linear function of the project's systematic risk; that is:

$$r_{ej} = r_s + \beta_j \left(r_m - r_s\right), \tag{11.5}$$

where r_{ej} is the equity capital cost for asset (project) j. The value of β in equation (11.5) represents the case of a firm with all equity capital. If, however, the firm employs financial leverage or another similar firm is being evaluated that has a different level of leverage, then an adjusted beta is needed in order to reflect the additional financial risk for the return on equity that is attributed to financial leverage. Assuming that debt is risk-free (i.e., a zero beta on debt), the adjustment to the cost of equity to account for leverage can be shown as (Van Horne):

$$r_{ej} = r_s + \beta_{uj} \left(r_m - r_s\right) \left[1 + \frac{D}{E}\left(1-T\right)\right], \tag{11.6}$$

where β_{uj} is the unlevered beta value and T is the firm's tax rate. Now the firm's risk premium includes the effects of business risk (the unlevered beta) and financial risk as represented by the adjustment in beta due to financial leverage. Thus, the leverage-adjusted beta (β_j) can be expressed as:

$$\beta_j = \beta_{uj} \left[1 + \frac{D}{E} \ (1-T) \right]. \tag{11.7}$$

Within this framework, one can go from an observed beta for a leveraged firm to an unlevered beta by solving equation (11.7) for β_{uj}:

$$\beta_{uj} = \frac{\beta_j}{\left[1 + \dfrac{D}{E} \ (1-T) \right]}. \tag{11.8}$$

Then, the beta for a different level of leverage can be estimated using equation (11.8). This practice is sometimes employed when a firm is undertaking a new investment that differs from the firm's current mix of activities. In this case, the investing firm might estimate the new investment's systematic risk by using the beta on the stock of another firm that utilizes the same investment, when the second firm has a different level of financial leverage than the investing firm.

The adjusted beta is used to determine the cost of equity capital for the investment project. The equity cost, then, is combined with the after-tax cost of debt to determine the weighted average cost of capital for capital budgeting. This approach assumes that the risk of a new investment depends only on its systematic risk and that all nonsystematic risk is diversified away or otherwise not important to corporate investors.

Several other points also need careful consideration for using the *CAPM* to evaluate risk premiums on equity capital for corporate capital budgeting. One consideration involves the extension of the single period *CAPM* concepts to the multi-period case. This appears strictly valid as long as the beta values are expected to remain constant over time. Even then, however, it has been shown that using a constant risk-adjusted discount rate implies that risk is increasing at a constant rate over time. Assuming that beta is constant in each period means that the risk carried per period is constant, but the cumulative risk will grow steadily at a constant rate (Brealey and Myers). Thus, the risk-adjusted discount rate is strictly applicable only for investments whose risks meet these characteristics. Finally, the commonly followed procedures for estimating beta values all rely on historic relationships between the return on individual assets and a market portfolio. Since relationships expected in the future are the important ones, a close match between past and future conditions is needed for the *CAPM* to be valid.

CAPM and Certainty Equivalents

Equations (11.5) through (11.8) and the above discussion are oriented toward the use of the *CAPM* in estimating the risk-adjusted cost of capital to use in corporate capital budgeting. However, the *CAPM* can also be applied in the certainty equivalent approach to capital budgeting in which an asset's *PV* is found by discounting certainty equivalent returns at a risk-free discount rate (Haley and Schall). The resulting single period valuation model for asset *j* is:

$$V_j = \frac{\bar{y}_j - \lambda\ cov\ (y_j, r_m)}{1 + r_s},$$
(11.9)

where $\bar{y}_j$ is the expected earnings and $\lambda\ cov\ (y_j, r_m)$ is the risk premium where $\lambda = \dfrac{E(r_m) - r_s}{\sigma_m^2}$. Expression (11.9) represents the discounted *PV* of the asset's returns one period in the future, where the expected returns (in the numerator) are reduced by an appropriate risk premium. Thus, the net value of the numerator represents the certainty equivalent of the random return y_j. If the risk premium, $\lambda\ cov\ (y_j, r_m)$ is zero, then expression (11.9) is reduced to $V_j = \bar{y}_j / 1 + r_s$, which is the same as the single period *PV* model under conditions of certainty.

Single Index Approach

When the conditions justifying the use of the *CAPM* do not hold, then the focus is on the measurement and pricing of risk at either the firm level or the stand-alone risk for the asset itself. As indicated earlier, the risk added by an individual investment might be measured by computing a beta for the new investment in terms of the firm's total return or some other relevant factor, rather than the market portfolio. This approach basically involves the application of the single index model rather than the *CAPM*, and it is likely that some level of nonsystematic risk is still added to the firm. Moreover, no market mechanism is now at work to quantify the risk premium and the risk attitude of the individual investor comes into play as well.

One approach to illustrating these points was followed by Collins and Barry who developed an adoption criterion for investment projects by a proprietary firm that is based on measurement of beta at the firm level. This approach utilizes the Sharpe single index portfolio model and standard mean-variance analysis. According to expected utility theory based on the mean-variance approach, the objective of the proprietary firm's owner can be expressed as:

$$Max\ EU = \bar{r}_e - \left(\frac{\lambda}{2}\right) \bar{\beta}^2 \sigma_f^{\ 2}, \tag{11.10}$$

where λ is the Arrow-Pratt risk aversion coefficient for income or wealth, $\bar{r}_e$ is the weighted average expected rate of return of the firm's m projects, σ_f^2 is the variance of the factor (i.e., the firm's income or another factor) used in the single index approach and $\bar{\beta}$ is the average beta of the firm's existing portfolio of m assets. Using equation (11.10), the acceptability of a new project for the proprietary firm may be evaluated in terms of its ability to increase EU. That is, a new investment project (project $m+1$), whose net after-tax cash flows increase the first term more than the second term, will increase expected utility and thus be adopted. Collins and Barry showed that this intuition yields an adoption criteria of:

$$r_{e,\ m+1} > \bar{r}_e + \lambda \sigma_f^{\ 2} \bar{\beta}\ (\beta_{m+1} - \bar{\beta}). \tag{11.11}$$

Expression (11.11) indicates that the required rate of return for a new project ($m+1$) is the sum of the rate of return ($\bar{r}_e$) on the existing assets of the firm plus a risk premium (discount) that depends on the systematic risk of the new project (β_{m+1}). If the new project has a beta equal to the firm's weighted beta ($\bar{\beta}$), its hurdle rate of return (to use as a discount rate in PV analysis) is the weighted rate of return on previous projects ($\bar{r}_e$). If, however, $\beta_{m+1} > \bar{\beta}$, then the hurdle rate exceeds the firm's existing expected rate of return. In general, then, if β_{m+1} does not equal $\bar{\beta}$, the relevant price of risk is $\lambda \sigma_f^2 \bar{\beta}$ that reflects the proprietor's risk attitude, the riskiness of the external environment, and the riskiness of previous investment decisions ($\bar{\beta}$).

An extension of the analysis to consider debt financing of projects and the increased financial risk results in the following acceptance criteria:

$$r_{m+1} > r_s + \frac{\lambda}{1-\delta}\ \sigma_a^{\ 2} + \frac{\lambda}{1-\delta}\ \bar{\beta}\sigma_f^{\ 2}\left(\beta_{m+1} - \bar{\beta}\right), \tag{11.12}$$

where r_s is the risk-free borrowing rate, σ_a^2 is the variance of returns on the firm's assets, and δ is the debt-to-asset ratio. The criterion now states that, for debt-financed projects, the hurdle rate is the sum of the borrowing rate plus a risk premium for the effect project $m+1$ has on the riskiness of the portfolio of investments.

In general, then, interesting analogies can be developed between investment analysis under risk for corporate and proprietary firms. However, the absence of a pricing mechanism for the risk premium and the explicit presence of the risk attitude are important differences between the two approaches. As Collins and Barry (pages 144-145) concluded:

> The analogies that can be drawn between investment analysis under risk for corporate and proprietary firms are especially interesting. In both cases, the principle focus is on adjusting the adoption criterion (or hurdle rate) for a new investment project to account for the risk that is added either to the firm or to the portfolios of the firm's investors. Major differences occur between the marketability of equity claims and the degrees of diversity for these types of firms and their investors, making the *CAPM* not directly applicable to the proprietary firm.
>
> Still, however, this analysis shows that the risk premiums for new projects in proprietary firms depend on elements of nonsystematic risk as well as on the risk-return attitudes of the firm's investors and on the firm's leverage position. The resulting adoption criterion is expressed in a form similar to that used in cases where the *CAPM* is directly applicable. However, we cannot escape the need for quantitative measures or benchmarks about the individual investor's risk attitudes. This, of course, is the long-standing dilemma in developing risk-adjusted hurdle rates for proprietary firms and closely held corporations.

Stand-Alone Risk

Stand-alone risk refers to the riskiness of an individual investment project that is considered either as the sole activity of a firm or in isolation of the rest of a firm's projects or activities. Again, the calculation procedures are relatively straightforward and basically involve an extension of the calculations for finding *NPV*s under conditions of certainty. That is, under conditions of risk, the net cash flows in each period of the investment horizon are presumed to come from an underlying probability distribution in each of the respective periods. Thus, the basic approach is to discount to a present value the relevant properties of the probability distribution of cash flows in each period, using a risk-free discount rate. The resulting measures, expressed in *PV* terms, can then be evaluated according to the properties of the investor's utility function.

As in other types of risk analyses, a major hurdle to this approach is the estimation of the underlying probability distribution. The basic alternatives still are two-fold. That is, subjective judgments may be used, or probability distributions anticipated to hold in the future may be based on variability measures estimated from historic data.

The typical approach is to simplify the situation by characterizing the underlying distributions as normal, so that they can be fully described by their expected values and variances (or standard deviations) (Levy and Sarnat). Even if the distributions are not normal, however, the summation of each period's discounted values together with the central limit theorem suggest that the *PV* can be approximated by a normal distribution (Hillier).

The calculations then involve solving for: (1) the *expected NPV* measured as the sum of the discounted *expected values* of the net cash flows in each year of the horizon; and (2) the *variance* of the *NPV*, measured as the sum of discounted *variances* of the net cash flows in each year of the horizon. These calculations are followed whether the cash flows are statistically independent over time (i.e., a zero correlation among periods) or dependent (a nonzero correlation among periods), although the dependence case results in a much more complex set of calculations (Levy and Sarnat; Hillier).

Assuming independence of the net cash flows over time, the expected *NPV* ($\overline{NPV}$) of the expected cash flows ($\overline{R_t}$) can be expressed as:

$$\overline{NPV}_0 = -V_0 + \frac{\overline{R}_1}{1+r} + \frac{\overline{R}_2}{(1+r)^2} + \frac{\overline{R}_3}{(1+r)^3} + \dots + \frac{\overline{R}_N}{(1+r)^N}, \tag{11.13}$$

where V_0 is the initial outlay of funds and r is the discount rate.

The variance (σ_{NPV}^2) of the *NPV* can be expressed as:

$$\sigma_{NPV}^2 = \frac{\sigma_1^2}{(1+r)^2} + \frac{\sigma_2^2}{(1+r)^4} + \frac{\sigma_3^2}{(1+r)^6} + \dots + \frac{\sigma_N^2}{(1+r)^{2N}}, \tag{11.14}$$

where σ_n^2 is the variance of the net cash flows in period n. Note that the discount factor in the variance equation is expressed with the exponent doubled (i.e., $2n$). This expression occurs because the variance rather than the standard deviation is used as the measure of dispersion. If standard deviation were used, the expression for period two, for example, would be $\sigma_2/(1+r)^2$.

These measures of expected value and variance (or standard deviation) of *NPV* can be directly evaluated by the investor. If the properties of the mean-variance utility function are known, then the utility associated with the investment could be calculated. The coefficient of variation ($\sigma_v/\overline{V}_0$) also could be calculated to indicate the relative variability or average *NPV* per unit of risk. Alternatively, confidence limits can be found that indicate the likelihood of the *NPV* exceeding zero or some other threshold value.

To illustrate, consider the probability distribution of V_0 in Figure 11.2. It is fully characterized by its mean, $\overline{V}_0 = 1,000$ and standard deviation, 400, yielding a coefficient of variation of 0.40. Typical confidence limit statements are that the chances are about 66 percent that V_0 will fall between 600 and 1,400 (minus or plus one standard deviation from the mean), 84 percent that V_0 will exceed 600 (the area under the curve to the right of 600), and 99 percent that V_0 will exceed zero (the area to the right of zero, or above 2 1/2 standard deviations below the mean).

If the net cash flows of the investment were statistically dependent over time (e.g., a high cash flow in one period invariably is followed by a high or low cash flow in the next period), then the variance expression for the *NPV* is extended to account for the correlations between periods. Similarly, if more than one project is to be evaluated, and the cash flows of each project are correlated with one another and over time, then the combined effects on total variance of all these factors must be considered. Now, however, multiple projects and covariances place the problem in a portfolio setting, remove the focus on stand-alone risk, and bring

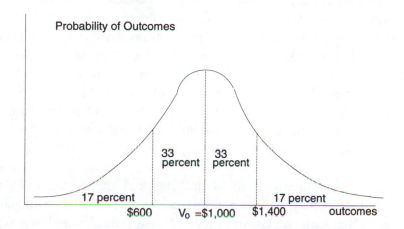

Figure 11.2   Probability Distribution of V_o with Mean $1000 and Standard Deviation of $400

us back to the *CAPM*, single index, and beta issues discussed earlier in the chapter.

Using the *IRR* criterion under conditions of risk is hampered by the inability to solve a variance equation for the series of cash flows. The expected value of *IRR* can be found in the usual way by solving for the discount rate that equates the expected *NPV* of the expected net cash flows to zero. However, no comparable expression is possible for the variance measure (Hillier). One approach is for the analyst to resort to Monte Carlo simulation analysis to repetitively sample net cash flows from the underlying probability distributions in each period, and then to solve for an *IRR* for each run of the simulation model (Hertz). The result would be a probability distribution of internal rates of return, from which a mean and variance could be calculated. As shown in a landmark article by Hertz, this approach could be disaggregated by specifying probability distributions for each of the major components of net cash flow (e.g., sales, prices, expenses) and applying Monte Carlo simulation to the full set of distributions in order to develop a probability distribution of the *IRR* for the firm or project.

Summary

As suggested in the introduction to the chapter, the methods of conducting *PV* analysis under risk are relatively straightforward. However, the procedures for quantifying the degree of risk adjustment (i.e., the risk premium) for either the discount rate or the future cash flows are not straightforward. These procedures introduce challenging conceptual and measurement issues associated with the types of risk to consider, the measurement of risk, and the role of risk attitudes of managers, owners, and investors. Risk identification involves the degree of risk that is added to the economic unit, the unit's debt capacity, and the effects of risk that are less easily analyzed (e.g., litigation and abandonment values). Risk measurement involves the distinction between subjective and objective concepts of probability and the effects of diversification at the firm and investor levels on systematic and nonsystematic risk. Risk attitudes need not be considered in approaches based on the *CAPM*, but are important in other types of investment situations.

Given the lack of precision in identifying and measuring risks and risk attitudes, it is not surprising that leading textbooks in financial management and *PV* analysis (e.g., Brigham and Gapenski; Van Horne; Brealey and Myers) suggest a combined approach that is based on one or more of the *PV* models, as well as on subjective factors and the judgment of the analyst. Moreover, in practical applications of investment analysis under risk, it is common to observe the use of less formal approaches such as sensitivity analysis (the responses of *NPV*s or *IRR*s to changes in a key variable affecting cash flows) and scenario analysis (responses of *NPV*s or *IRR*s to changes in the underlying probability distributions). The general objective is the same, however, regardless of the comprehensiveness and formality of the risk analysis—that is, to account for the effects of risk in the most valid fashion possible in order to enhance the quality of decision making.

Review Questions

1. Contrast and critique the risk-adjusted discount rate and certainty equivalent methods of investment analysis under risk.

2. Identify the major classes of risk attitudes. How would you distinguish among these classes?

3. Explain the concept of a risk premium. What determines the size of a risk premium? Can a risk premium be negative?

4. Find the certainty equivalent for an investment situation in which the expected value is 15 percent and the risk premium is 6 percent.

5. Define and distinguish among stand-alone risk, firm risk, and market risk. Which type of risk is addressed by the capital asset pricing model?

6. Is the capital asset pricing model applicable to estimating risk premiums for smaller-scale, proprietary firms? Why or why not?

7. Find the expected return of an asset whose beta value is 1.40 when the risk-free rate is 10 percent and the market's risk premium is 5 percent.

8. Does the use of leverage increase or decrease a firm's risk premium estimated using the *CAPM*?

9. Under what conditions is an asset's stand-alone risk appropriate to estimate? How is information about stand-alone risk used in investment analysis under risk?

Application Questions

1. Determine the risk premium on an investment that has an expected *NPV* of $15,000 and a certainty equivalent of $10,000.

2. Find the expected value of an investment yielding three possible payoffs—$12,000 with a 0.40 probability, $8,000 with a 0.35 probability, and $2,000 with a 0.25 probability.

3.   Find the *NPV* and *IRR* for an investment requiring an initial outlay of $20,000 and net cash flows of $6,000 per year for five years, where the risk-free rate is 8 percent and the risk premium is 7 percent. Is the investment profitable?

4.   Evaluate the profitability of the investment in question (3) under the certainty equivalent approach where δ = 0.80 in each year.

5.   Determine the expected rate of return on an asset that has a beta value of 1.30 when the risk-free rate is 10 percent and the expected rate of return on the market portfolio is 15 percent. What is the asset's risk premium?

6.   Find the cost of equity capital for a leveraged firm with an unlevered beta value of 0.80, a risk-free rate of 10 percent, an expected rate of return on the market portfolio of 15 percent, a tax rate of 20 percent, and a debt-to-equity ratio of 1.0. What is the leverage-adjusted beta?

7.   Find the expected *NPV* and standard deviation of an investment requiring an initial outlay of $10,000 and yielding an expected net cash flow of $5,000 for three years with an annual standard deviation of $2,000. The risk-free discount rate is 10 percent.

References

Brealey, R. and S.C. Myers. *Principles of Corporate Finance*. New York: McGraw-Hill, 1981.

Brigham, E.F. and L.C. Gapenski. *Financial Management: Theory and Practice*, 6th ed. Chicago: Dryden Press, 1991.

Collins, R.A. and P.J. Barry. "Beta-Adjusted Hurdle Rates for Proprietary Firms." *Journal of Economics and Business* 40(1988):139-45.

Haley, C.W. and L.D. Schall. *The Theory of Financial Decisions*. New York: McGraw-Hill, 1979.

Hertz, D.B. "Risk Analysis in Capital Investment." *Harvard Business Review* 42(January-February 1964):95-106.

Hillier, F. "The Derivation of Probabilistic Information for the Evaluation of Risky Investments." *Management Science* 9(1963):443-57.

Jensen, M.C. "Capital Markets: Theory and Evidence." *Bell Journal of Economics and Management Science*, Autumn 1972.

Levy, H. and M. Sarnat. *Capital Investment and Financial Decisions*, 3rd ed. Englewood Cliffs, NJ: Prentice-Hall, 1986.

_____. *Portfolio and Investment Selection: Theory and Evidence*. Englewood Cliffs, NJ: Prentice-Hall, 1984.

Modigliani, F. and G.A. Pogue. "An Introduction to Risk and Return." *Financial Analysts Journal* 30(March-April):68-80, (May-June):69-86.

Robison, L.J. and P.J. Barry. *The Competitive Firm's Response to Risk*. New York: McGraw-Hill, 1986.

Roll, R. "A Critique of Asset Pricing Theory Tests." *Journal of Financial Economics* 4(1977):129-76.

Ross, S.A. "The Current Status of the Capital Asset Pricing Model." *Journal of Finance* 33(1978):885-902.

Van Horne, J.C. *Financial Management and Policy*, 6th ed. Englewood Cliffs, NJ: Prentice-Hall, 1989.

Part 4

Applications of Present Value Models

Chapter 12

Loan Analysis[1]

Key words: actuarial interest rate, annual percentage rate (*APR*), balloon payment loans, compensating balance loans, constant payment loans, constant principal loans, disguised interest rate loans, effective interest rate, moderated payment loans, net present value (*NPV*) of constant payment loans, refinanced loans, term elasticity, variable interest rate loans

Introduction

Loan formulas have many characteristics of the present value (*PV*) models analyzed earlier. Interest rates and loan payments are like opportunity costs and investment cash flows. These and other similarities between *PV* models and loan formulas allow applications of *PV* tools to analyze different aspects and types of loans. The next section focuses on alternative interest rate definitions. Later sections will describe various types of loans. This chapter will help in identifying loan payments and interest costs, and in calculating effective interest rates for a wide variety of loans.

Comparing the Actuarial Rate, Annual Percentage Rate (*APR*), and Effective Interest Rate

Various interest rate definitions are found in finance literature. To avoid confusion, the most common definitions will be used here. Three major interest rate definitions are needed to understand interest rate calculations and *PV* techniques. Although they often have different names, these three rates are closely related to each other. These rates and their commonly used synonyms are listed below. The most common name of each of the interest rates and the ones used in this chapter are italicized. They are: (1) *Actuarial rate*, compound rate, true rate, or periodic rate; (2) *Annual percentage rate (APR)*, nominal rate, annual rate, or nominal annual rate; and (3) *Effective rate* or effective annual rate.

In financial transactions, interest may be computed and charged more than once a year. For example, interest on savings deposits is usually calculated on a daily basis while many corporate bonds pay interest on a semiannual basis. The interest rate used in computations for periods of less than one year is called the actuarial rate. The actuarial rate is defined as the interest rate per compounding period or the interest rate per period of conversion. It is the actuarial rate at which the principal sum is charged interest during each successive conversion period. For example, a 1 percent actuarial rate charged monthly on $1,000 means that in the first month of the loan, 1 percent of $1,000 or $10 of interest is computed. In the second month, interest is charged on $1,010 equal to $10.10, etc.

The small letter r^f usually stands for the *APR*. The small letter m stands for the number of times during the year the interest is calculated or charged. Thus, m equals the number of compounding periods per year. The ratio of r^f/m is the actuarial rate, the compound rate, the true rate, or the periodic rate.

Actuarial rates are usually converted to *APR* to simplify comparisons among different quoted rates. The *APR* is determined by expressing the actuarial rate on an annual basis. The annual rate is found by multiplying the actuarial rate by m. In the previous example, the actuarial rate of 1 percent per month was multiplied by 12 to yield an *APR* of 12 percent. When the compound period or conversion period is one year in length, then the actuarial rate and the *APR* are equal.

Consider two savings institutions, both offering the same *APR*. The only difference is that institution *A* offers monthly compounding of interest while institution *B* offers only annual compounding. Which one should the saver prefer? Obviously, monthly compounding is preferred because the saver earns interest on the interest earned during the same year. With institution *B*, interest is earned only on the principal saved, and on interest earned in previous years. Dividing the interest earned during the year by the principal invested produces an effective rate or an effective annual rate (r^e). When *APRs* have different numbers of compound periods per year, the different rates should be converted to their effective interest rates for comparison. The effective rate is obtained by compounding the actuarial rate for a period of one year. As the frequency of compounding periods increases, the difference between the *APR* and the effective rate increases. Also, as the actuarial rate increases, so does the relative difference between the *APR* rate and the effective rate.

These relationships between an actuarial rate, an *APR*, and an effective rate can be easily summarized using the notation already described. To review, let *m* be the conversion periods per year and let r^f be the *APR*. Then, r^f/m is the actuarial rate and r^e is the effective rate. The relationship between effective rate r^e, *APR* rate r^f, and actuarial rate r^f/m is found by dividing the interest earned during the year by the amount *A* invested. The result is:

$$r^e = \left[\left(1 + \frac{r^f}{m}\right)^m - 1\right]. \tag{12.1}$$

When *m* equals 1, the *APR* rate (r^f), the effective rate r^e, and the actuarial rate r^f/m are equal. To illustrate equation (12.1) numerically, let r^f be 0.12 and *m* be 4 representing quarterly compounding; then the effective rate is:

$$0.1255 = \left[\left(1 + \frac{0.12}{4}\right)^4 - 1\right].$$

And if *m* is increased to 12 or monthly compounding periods, the effective rate is:

$$0.1268 = \left[\left(1 + \frac{0.12}{12}\right)^{12} - 1\right].$$

A special compounding formula is obtained by allowing the number of periods compounded to be very large. This idea is expressed with the notation, *limit* $m \to \infty$, which means as *m* approaches infinity, the effective rate, r^e, under such conditions is:

$$\lim_{m \to \infty} r^e = \left[\left(1 + \frac{r^f}{m}\right)^m - 1\right] = e^{r^f} - 1.$$

To complete the example, let r^f equal 0.12 and calculate r^e. The answer is $r^e = 0.1275$ or 0.75 percentage points greater than the *APR*.

Types of Loans

The following six types of loans are considered: (1) constant payment loan: (2) balloon payment loan; (3) moderated payment loan; (4) constant principal loan; (5) disguised interest rate loan; and (6) compensating balance loan. In addition, the blending and refinancing of constant payment loans are discussed.

Constant Payment Loans

Having defined interest rates in financial models, *PV* tools are applied to the first loan type, the constant payment loan. Constant payment loans are repaid by a series of equal payments *A* at equal time intervals. These payments may occur *m* times during a year over *n* years, yielding a total of *mn* payments.

The fundamental equality is that the loan payments discounted at the actuarial interest rate equal the amount loaned. Thus, the interest rate in loan analysis is like the *IRR* in maximum-bid price models.

The relationship between loan L_0 extended in time period zero with payments of amount *A* made for *mn* periods at actuarial interest rate r^f/m is:

$$L_0 = \frac{A}{\left(1 + \frac{r^f}{m}\right)} + \frac{A}{\left(1 + \frac{r^f}{m}\right)^2} + \dots + \frac{A}{\left(1 + \frac{r^f}{m}\right)^{mn}} = A\left[US_0\left(\frac{r^f}{m}, mn\right)\right]. \tag{12.2}$$

From this fundamental equality, any of the five variables L_0, *A*, r^f, *m*, and *n* can be found if the other four variables are known. For example, if all the variables but *A* are known, then *A* can be found from the expression of:

$$A = \frac{L_0}{US_0\left(\frac{r^f}{m}, mn\right)}. \tag{12.3}$$

If all of the variables but *n* are known, one can solve the equation:

$$US_0\left(\frac{r^f}{m}, mn\right) = \frac{L_0}{A}. \tag{12.4}$$

Use a financial calculator or look up the value for $US_0(r^f/m, mn)$ in Appendix 1. Look up the value for r under the approriate column and then find n in the corresponding row.

If all of the variables but r^f are known, it too can be found with the aid of a financial calculator or Appendix 1 and equation (12.4). To find r^f using Appendix 1, search across the appropriate row value for mn in Appendix 1. Then, read the column heading value that indicates the r^f/m value associated with $US_0(r^f/m, mn)$, and multiply by m to find r^f. Or more simply, solve for r^f using a financial calculator.

Total Interest Costs.   There may be many reasons for wanting to know what part of a loan payment covers interest costs. For example, when interest payments are tax deductible, interest must be separated from principal payments. In the case of the constant payment loan, the total interest costs can be calculated by subtracting from total payments (mnA) the loan principal L_0. Denoting total interest costs as TI, this subtraction equals:

$$TI = (mnA - L_0).$$

(12.5)

The total interest cost in Examples 12.1 and 12.2 equals:

Example 12.1: Constant Payment Loan Annuities

Suppose $5,000 is borrowed from a bank for five years. The loan is to be repaid with 60 equal monthly installments at an *APR* of 12 percent or a monthly actuarial rate of 1 percent. What is the payment or annuity necessary to retire the loan?

Using equation (12.3) we can solve for the payment that repays the $5,000 loan:

$$A = \frac{L_0}{US_0(0.01, 60)} = \frac{\$5,000}{44.9550} = \$111.22.$$

Notice that the number 44.9550, the $US_0(0.01, 60)$ value, is from Appendix 1 at the end of the book.

Example 12.2: Constant Payment Loan Amounts

Now suppose A is known to be \$111.22, r^f/m is 0.01, and mn is 60. The loan supported by payments at these terms can be found using equation (12.2):

$$L_0 = A\,US_0(0.01, 60) = (\$111.22)(44.9550) = \$5,000.$$

Finally, assume that L_0=\$5,000, A=\$111.22, and r^f/m=0.01, but mn is not known. To find mn, use equation (12.5) and scan Appendix 1 under the 1 percent column until the $US_0(0.01, mn)$ value corresponding to 44.9550 is found. The mn value at which that occurs is 60.

$$TI = [60(\$111.22) - \$5,000] = \$1,673.20.$$

Besides determining total interest costs, one may need to calculate the accumulated interest and principal paid as of some date. Early loan repayment and the need to calculate the tax savings associated with interest payments are possible reasons for such calculations.

The formula for calculating principal paid, $PP(t)$, in the tth period equals the difference in the outstanding loan balance at the beginning of the tth and $(t+1)$ period. That is:

$$PP(t) = \left[\frac{A}{\left(1+\dfrac{r^f}{m}\right)} + \dots + \frac{A}{\left(1+\dfrac{r^f}{m}\right)^{mn-(t+1)}} \right]$$

$$- \left[\frac{A}{\left(1+\dfrac{r^f}{m}\right)} + \dots + \frac{A}{\left(1+\dfrac{r^f}{m}\right)^{mn-t}} \right] = \frac{A}{\left(1+\dfrac{r^f}{m}\right)^{mn-(t-1)}}. \tag{12.6}$$

In the example of the \$111.22 payment (where $r^f/12$=0.01 and mn=60), principal paid in period one, $PP(1)$, equals:

$$PP(1) = \frac{\$111.22}{(1.01)^{60}} = \$61.22.$$

The interest portion of the t payments, $I(t)$, is simply:

$$I(t) = A - PP(t).$$

In the previous example, $I(1)$ is:

$$I(1) = \$111.22 - \$61.22 = \$50.00,$$

which equals the loan rate ($r^f/m = 0.01$) times the outstanding loan balance of $5,000.

Accumulated principal $AP(t)$ paid after t payments equals:

$$AP(t) = L_0 - A\,US_0\left(\frac{r^f}{m}, mn - t\right). \tag{12.7}$$

After six payments, the result is:

$$AP(6) = \$5,000 - \$111.22\ US_0\,(0.01, 60-6) = \$5,000 - \$4,623.27 = \$376.73.$$

The accumulated interest $AI(t)$ payments formula follows:

$$AI(t) = tA - AP(t). \tag{12.8}$$

After six payments, the result is:

$$AI(6) = \$667.32 - \$376.73 = \$290.59.$$

Finally, principal due $PD(t)$ to retire the loan after t payments is:

$$PD(t) = L_0 - AP(t). \tag{12.9}$$

After six payments, the result is:

$$PD(6) = \$5,000 - \$376.73 = \$4,623.27.$$

Comparing Term and Payment Size of Constant Payment Loans. An important relationship exists between loan maturity and total interest paid. To illustrate, consider a $30,000 loan at 15 percent *APR* to be repaid in monthly payments over 30 years. Monthly payment is $379.33, while total interest paid equals $106,560. Increasing the payment amount by 10 percent to $417.27 reduces the term of the loan to just over 15.36 years and total interest paid is reduced to $46,911.

These results are not always so significant. For example, if the above loan had an *APR* of 8 percent, the monthly payment would equal $220.13 instead of $379.33. Increasing the payment 10 percent would only decrease the term of the loan from 30 years to 21.93 years, and total interest paid would be decreased only from $49,247 to $33,722.

It would be useful to know how changing loan maturity affects loan payment size and total interest paid. It can be shown that as *mn* becomes large, the payment *A* approaches the interest cost; i.e., the smallest payment possible equals the interest charged on the outstanding loan balance.

If the borrower wished to minimize his or her payment, the appropriate term is the one that permits the borrower to repay only interest. The shortest repayment period, on the other hand, is one. There is a trade-off between the size of the loan payment and the length of the loan.

The point elasticity of term n with respect to the payment A, $E_{n,A}$, measures the percentage change in term that occurs with a 1 percent increase in A. The elasticity formula equals:

$$E_{n,A} = \frac{-\left(e^{r^f n} - 1\right)}{rn} < 0. \tag{12.10}$$

Since $E_{n,A} < 0$, the term is reduced as A is increased. It is generally true (and always true when $nr^f > 1$) that $-E_{n,A}$ increases as n and r^f increase. A table of selected values for $-E_{n,A}$ is given below (Table 12.1).

The elasticity measure described in Table 12.1 can be a useful guide in selecting loan terms when liquidity concerns are being balanced against the desire for shorter-term loans.

NPV and Constant Payment Loans. Thus far, the constant loan payments have been discounted by the interest rate charged on the loan. These calculations assume the opportunity cost (*IRR*) equals the interest rate and the *NPV* of the loan is zero. Suppose, however, that the borrower's opportunity cost of capital is not equal to the interest rate associated with the loan. This may result from a concessionary interest rate offered the borrower, or it may be the result of changes in inflation after the loan was negotiated.

Table 12.1 Tabled Values of $-E_{n,A}$

n	r^f=0.005	0.01	0.03	0.05	0.075	0.10	0.15	0.20
1	1.00	1.01	1.01	1.03	1.04	1.05	1.08	1.11
2	1.01	1.01	1.03	1.05	1.08	1.11	1.17	1.23
3	1.01	1.02	1.08	1.08	1.12	1.17	1.26	1.37
4	1.01	1.02	1.05	1.11	1.17	1.23	1.37	1.53
5	1.01	1.03	1.08	1.14	1.21	1.30	1.49	1.72
10	1.03	1.05	1.17	1.30	1.49	1.72	2.32	3.19
15	1.04	1.08	1.26	1.49	1.85	2.32	3.77	6.36
20	1.05	1.11	1.37	1.72	2.32	3.19	6.36	13.40
25	1.07	1.14	1.49	1.99	2.94	4.47	11.07	29.48
30	1.08	1.17	1.49	2.32	3.77	6.36	19.78	67.07
60	1.17	3.04	2.99	6.36	19.78	67.07	900.23	13,562.82

Example 12.3: Term and Loan Payment Trade-Offs

Lucy Landlord is financing the renovation of a property. She needs a loan for $28,000. Her lender offers her a loan for 20 years at the current interest rate of 15 percent. She calculates her annual payment to be $4,473.32. If she increases her payment by 1 percent to $4,518.05, her term is reduced to 19 years or a reduction of 5 percent. This percentage reduction is nearly equal to the $-E_{n,A}$ value in Table 12.1 found at the intersection of the row labeled 20 and the column labeled 0.15. Large percentage increases in A, such as a 10 percent increase, may cause a percentage decrease in n, not accurately reflected by values in Table 12.1. This is because the percentage changes in n with respect to A are large compared to very small changes in n with respect to A used to calculate Table 12.1.

When the interest rate is not equal to the opportunity cost of capital, the *PV* of loan repayments no longer equals the loan amount received in the present. We now examine the relationship between interest rates, opportunity cost of capital, loan amounts, and the *PV* of the loan. Then, the *NPV* of the loan, if L_0, m, n, r, and r^f were known, is:

$$NPV = L_0 - \left[\frac{A}{\left(1+\dfrac{r}{m}\right)} + \frac{A}{\left(1+\dfrac{r}{m}\right)^2} + \ldots + \frac{A}{\left(1+\dfrac{r}{m}\right)^{mn}} \right] \tag{12.11}$$

$$= L_0 - A\, US_0\left(\frac{r}{m}, \ mn\right).$$

From equation (12.3) we know that A equals $L_0/US_0(r^f/m, \ mn)$. Making the substitution into equation (12.11) for A using equation (12.3) allows us to express the *NPV* of the constant payment loan as:

$$NPV = L_0 \left[1 - \frac{US_0\left(\dfrac{r}{m}, \ mn\right)}{US_0\left(\dfrac{r^f}{m}, \ mn\right)} \right]. \tag{12.12}$$

Example 12.4: *NPV* for a Constant Payment Loan

We return now to the example of the constant payment loan. The amount borrowed was assumed to be \$5,000. The actuarial rate of the loan was 1 percent repaid over five years of monthly payments. From Appendix 1, $US_0(0.01,60)$ was found to equal 44.9550. Now suppose the borrower's opportunity cost of capital $r/12$ is not 1 percent but 1.25 percent, an *APR* of 15 percent. Using equation (12.12), the *NPV* of his \$5,000 loan is calculated to be:

$$\$324.81 = \$5,000 \left[1 - \frac{42.0346}{44.9550} \right].$$

Balloon Payment Loans

While the constant payment loan, or the installment loan, is the loan most frequently used, many other types of loans have been developed. One reason for their development is volatile interest rates and the need to fit repayments to the borrower's cash flows. When interest rates are volatile, lenders assume greater risk by offering fixed rate loans, particularly on longer term loans. The risk they incur with fixed rate lending is from a future increase in interest rates above the existing rate. In this situation, the lender is caught with fixed rate investments while his costs of funds are rising. Borrowers may also be at risk from volatile interest rates if lenders charge fees to renegotiate loan terms.

One response to higher interest rate risk has been to offer balloon payment loans. The balloon payment loan is like the constant payment loan except for the last payment. That is, the loan maturity is shorter than the amortization period, and the balloon payment represents the outstanding, unpaid loan balance at maturity time. Thus, the balloon payment is used to pay off a loan before its normal term is complete and the last payment need not equal the amount of the other payments. The advantage to the lender (and borrower) is that it provides an opportunity to renegotiate the interest rate on the remaining balance should the borrower decide to refinance the balloon payment. In this regard, it resembles a variable rate loan except that the repricing intervals are longer and match the shorter maturity.

The questions to answer with a balloon payment loan are the same as those for the constant payment loan: What payments (constant and balloon) are required to repay the loan? What loan amount can be supported by known (constant and balloon) payments? And how many constant payments and a known balloon are required to retire a balloon payment loan?

Consider the relationship between the amount of loan L_0 to be retired using a series of payments A made at regular intervals over $(mn-1)$ periods at an interest rate of r^f/m percent, with a final balloon payment B made in the mn^{th} period. The equality between the borrower loan (L_0) and the present cost (discounted series of payments A plus balloon) is:

$$L_0 = \frac{A}{\left(1+\dfrac{r^f}{m}\right)} + \ldots + \frac{A}{\left(1+\dfrac{r^f}{m}\right)^{mn-1}} + \frac{B}{\left(1+\dfrac{r^f}{m}\right)^{mn}}. \tag{12.13}$$

Since $mn-1$ payments of A constitute a uniform series, equation (12.13) can be written as:

$$L_0 = A\,US_0\left(\frac{r^f}{m},\ mn-1\right) + \frac{B}{\left(1+\dfrac{r^f}{m}\right)^{mn}}. \tag{12.14}$$

To illustrate the formula, suppose a borrower could afford payments of $150 per month for 9 years and 11 months at an actuarial rate of 1 percent. After 119 payments, the borrower could then make a balloon payment of $5,000. What loan would such a payment arrangement support? The answer is obtained by substituting the appropriate values into equation (12.14). Substitute 150 for A, 69.3975 for $US_0(0.01,119)$, $5,000 for B, and 0.3030 for $1/(1+0.01)^{120}$. The answer is:

$$\$11,924.63 = (\$150)(69.3975) + (\$5,000)(0.3030).$$

If the amount of the loan and the size of the balloon payment are known, then the regular payment to be made over n periods at an interest rate r^f can be found by solving for A in equation (12.14). It equals:

$$A = \frac{L_0 - B\left(1+\dfrac{r^f}{m}\right)^{-mn}}{US_0\left(\dfrac{r^f}{m},\ mn-1\right)}. \tag{12.15}$$

Example 12.5: Balloon Payment Loan

Balloons Galore takes out a balloon payment loan for $75,000 to finance an expansion of their birthday catering business into wedding services. The loan has a balloon payment of $25,000 due in 11 years. The loan terms include quarterly payments for 10 years and nine months (43 payments) at an actuarial rate of 3 percent or 12 percent *APR*. What is the payment necessary to meet these requirements? Using equation (12.15) and Appendix 1 or a financial calculator, the constant payment is found to equal:

$$A = \frac{\$75,000 - \$25,000(1+.03)^{-44}}{US_0(.03,43)}$$

$$= \frac{\$75,000 - \$25,000(.2724)}{23.9819} = \$2,843.40.$$

Another loan payment calls for a $50,000 loan to be repaid with $900 payments every month for four years and 11 months (59 payments) at an actuarial rate of 1 percent plus a balloon payment at the end of five years. What balloon payment or principal will remain after five years?

Solving, using equation (12.16), yields:

$$B = [\$50,000 - \$900 \ US_0(.01,59)] \ (1+.01)^{60}$$

$$= \$18,232.11.$$

Balloons Galore wants to determine total interest paid after five years. Equation (12.18) is used to give:

$$TI = (59)(\$900) + \$18,232.11 - \$50,000 = \$21,332.11.$$

And, if A and L_0 are known, the balloon payment can be easily found. It equals:

$$B = \left[L_0 - A\,US_0 \left(\frac{r^f}{m},\ mn{-}1 \right) \right] \left(1 + \frac{r^f}{m} \right)^{mn}. \qquad (12.16)$$

Finally, suppose L_0, A, B, and r^f/m are known. Can we find mn? The answer is yes! It equals:

$$mn = \frac{\ln \left[\dfrac{B - A \left(\dfrac{r^f}{m} \right)^{-1} \left[1 + \left(\dfrac{r^f}{m} \right) \right]}{L_0 - A \left(\dfrac{r^f}{m} \right)^{-1}} \right]}{\ln \left(1 + \dfrac{r^f}{m} \right)}. \qquad (12.17)$$

Thus, total interest paid under the terms of a balloon loan is:

$$TI = (mn - 1)\,A + B - L_0. \qquad (12.18)$$

Moderated Payment Loans

Another category of loans designed to mitigate the cash flow problems of borrowers is moderated payment loans. Such loans are designed to reduce cash flow requirements of the borrower in early periods of the loan in anticipation of increased payment ability later. As discussed in Chapter 7, inflationary expectations tend to add to the cost of borrowing money by increasing interest rates. This relationship between inflation and interest rates on loans creates a problem for borrowers. With a constant payment loan, interest costs are a large percentage of the loan, especially during the early payment periods. But if the loan is for the purchase of an investment whose earnings will also benefit from inflation, cash flows later on may be more than adequate for the constant payment, while cash flows early in the life of the loan may not.

Graduated Payment Loans. One type of moderated payment loan is the graduated payment loan. To introduce the formula for the graduated payment loan, consider the following. Assume a uniform or constant payment loan with annuity payments A_0 and with interest rates charged at the rate of r^f. Then, mn

Example 12.6: A Graduated Payment Loan

To illustrate the formula, suppose a borrower could initially afford a payment of $150. He is willing to make semiannual payments ($m=2$) that increase at 2 percent ($i/m=2$ percent). The actuarial interest rate is 7 percent ($r^f/2=7$ percent) for 5 years. The borrower wants to know what loan amount such a repayment schedule would permit. The answer is found by first solving for:

$$r^{*f} = \frac{0.07 - 0.02}{1.02} = 4.9 \text{ percent.}$$

Then, substituting $150 for A_0, 1.02 for $(1+i/m)$ and 10 for mn, and using equation (12.20) the borrower finds that:

$$L_0 = \$150 \ US_0 \left(\frac{0.05}{1.02}, 10 \right) = \$150 \, (7.7586) = \$1163.79.$$

The borrower may wish to know the size of the last loan payment. It equals:

$$A_0 \left(1 + \frac{i}{m} \right)^{mn} = \$150 \, (1.02)^{10} = \$182.85.$$

Finally, without a graduated payment plan (equation (12.19)) constant loan payments of $150 would have repaid a loan of $\hat{L}_0$ equal to:

$$\hat{L}_0 = \$150 \ US_0 (0.07, 10) = \$1,053.54.$$

loan payments of amount A_0 at interest rate r^f can repay a loan amount L_0, a relationship expressed as:

$$L_0 = \frac{A_0}{\left(1 + \dfrac{r^f}{m} \right)} + \ldots + \frac{A_0}{\left(1 + \dfrac{r^f}{m} \right)^{mn}} \tag{12.19}$$

$$= A_0 \left[US_0 \left(\frac{r^f}{m}, \ mn \right) \right].$$

Next, we recognize that r^f is equal to an inflationary component i and a real component r^{*f}. Since $r^f = r^{*f} + i + ir^{*f}$, $r^{*f} = (r^f - i)/(1 + i)$, and if we allow loan payments to increase at inflation rate i, then equation (12.19) is rewritten as:

$$L_0 = \frac{A_0^*\left(1 + \dfrac{i}{m}\right)}{\left(1 + \dfrac{r^{*f}}{m}\right)\left(1 + \dfrac{i}{m}\right)} + \frac{A_0^*\left(1 + \dfrac{i}{m}\right)^2}{\left[\left(1 + \dfrac{r^{*f}}{m}\right)\left(1 + \dfrac{i}{m}\right)\right]^2} + \cdots$$

$$+ \frac{A_0^*\left(1 + \dfrac{i}{m}\right)^{mn}}{\left[\left(1 + \dfrac{r^{*f}}{m}\right)\left(1 + \dfrac{i}{m}\right)\right]^{mn}} = \frac{A_0^*}{\left(1 + \dfrac{r^{*f}}{m}\right)} + \frac{A_0^*}{\left(1 + \dfrac{r^{*f}}{m}\right)^2} + \cdots \qquad (12.20)$$

$$+ \frac{A_0^*}{\left(1 + \dfrac{r^{*f}}{m}\right)^{mn}} = A_0^*\, US_0\left(\frac{r^{*f}}{m}, mn\right).$$

Since $r^{*f} < r^f$, it should be obvious that $A_0^* < A$ so that if A_0^* in equation (12.20) were increased to A_0, the graduated plan would support a larger loan.

It turns out that the graduated payments will fully repay the loan during the maturity period, even though the rate of principal reduction is low, or even negative (i.e., negative amortization) during the early period of the loan.

During periods of inflation, borrowers face the *CT* ratios described in Chapter 7. This problem has been addressed by Ellinger, Barry, and Lins; Robison and Brake; and Tweeten. The simple solution is to allow the borrower to repay the loan principal using increasing payments.

It may be that the loan payments increase at some rate $g \neq i$. Then, the loan supported by payments increasing at rate g is found using equation (12.20) with i replaced by g and $r^{*f} = r^f - g / 1 + g$.

Skip Payment Loans.

Another type of moderated payment loan is the skip payment loan. As its name implies, payments are not made during the first t periods of the loan. The relationship between the loan amount L_0, the payments A, the actuarial interest rate on the loan r^f/m, the term of the loan mn, and the $(t+1)^{st}$ period in which the first payment occurs is:

$$L_0 = \frac{A}{\left(1+\dfrac{r^f}{m}\right)^{t+1}} + \ldots + \frac{A}{\left(1+\dfrac{r^f}{m}\right)^{mn}}$$

(12.21)

$$= \frac{1}{\left(1+\dfrac{r^f}{m}\right)^{t}} \left[\frac{A}{\left(1+\dfrac{r^f}{m}\right)} + \ldots + \frac{A}{\left(1+\dfrac{r^f}{m}\right)^{mn-t}} \right].$$

Since the bracketed series is a uniform series equal to $US_0(r/m, mn-t)$, equation (12.21) can be written as:

$$L_0 = \frac{A}{\left(1+\dfrac{r^f}{m}\right)^{t}} \, US_0\left(\frac{r^f}{m}, \, mn-t\right).$$

(12.22)

From this relationship, the payment A can be found to equal:

$$A = \frac{L_0 \left(1+\dfrac{r^f}{m}\right)^{t}}{US_0\left(\dfrac{r^f}{m}, \, mn-t\right)}.$$

(12.23)

Given L_0, A, r^f, and t, the term of the loan can be easily found:

$$mn = \frac{-\ln\left[1-\left(\dfrac{r^f}{m}\right)\left(\dfrac{L_0}{A}\right)\left(1+\dfrac{r^f}{m}\right)^{t}\right]}{\ln\left(1+\dfrac{r^f}{m}\right)} + t.$$

(12.24)

Total interest costs can be calculated much as before; namely, total payments *(mn-t)A* less principal:

$$TI = (mn-t) A - L_0.$$

(12.25)

Example 12.7: Skip Payment Loans

a)   The purchasers of a home could afford monthly payments of $500 a month; however, they will not be able to begin payments for one year. If the lender agrees to forego the first year's payments and loan terms include an interest rate of 14 percent *APR* for 20 years, how large a loan can the purchaser afford?

Solving, using equation (12.22), yields:

$$L_0 = \left[\frac{\$500}{\left[\left(1 + \frac{0.14}{12} \right)^{12} \right]} \right] \left[US_0 \left(\frac{0.14}{12}, 240 - 12 \right) \right]$$

$$= [434.8582]\,[79.6257] = \$34,625.89.$$

b)   The purchaser of a car is not required to make the first six monthly payments on the loan. If the loan is for $10,000 at 18 percent *APR* for four years, what is the monthly payment amount necessary to retire the loan?

Solving, using equation (12.23), yields:

$$A = \frac{\$10,000(1+.015)^6}{US_0\,(0.015, 42)} = \frac{\$10,000\,(1.0934)}{30.9941} = \$352.79.$$

Skip Principal Loans. A loan similar to the skip payment loan is the skip principal loan. This loan requires interest payments for the first few t periods, but does not require principal payments. After t periods, payments include both principal and interest. The relationship between the original loan L_0, the payment A, the term of the loan mn, the interest rate on the loan r^f/m, and the period of the first principal and interest payment $t+1$ is:

$$L_0 = \left[\frac{\left(\frac{r^f}{m}\right)L_0}{\left(1+\frac{r^f}{m}\right)} + \cdots + \frac{\left(\frac{r^f}{m}\right)L_0}{\left(1+\frac{r^f}{m}\right)^t}\right]$$

$$+ \left(1+\frac{r^f}{m}\right)^{-t}\left[\frac{A}{\left(1+\frac{r^f}{m}\right)} + \cdots + \frac{A}{\left(1+\frac{r^f}{m}\right)^{mn-t}}\right]. \qquad (12.26)$$

Since the first bracketed sum is a uniform series of payments $(r/m)L_0$ made for t periods at interest rate r/m, and the second bracketed series is the one associated with the skip payment loan, L_0 can be written as:

$$L_0 = \frac{r^f L_0}{m} US_0\left(\frac{r^f}{m}, t\right) + \frac{A\,US_0\left(\frac{r^f}{m}, mn-t\right)}{\left(1+\frac{r^f}{m}\right)^t}. \qquad (12.27)$$

Solving for L_0 in equation (12.27) obtains:

$$L_0 = A\,US_0\left(\frac{r^f}{m}, mn-t\right). \qquad (12.28)$$

From the above equation, A is found to equal:

$$A = \frac{L_0}{US_0\left(\frac{r^f}{m}, mn-t\right)}. \qquad (12.29)$$

The term of the loan can be determined using equation (12.29). Assuming L_0, r^f, A, and t are all known, mn can be expressed as:

$$mn = \frac{-\ln\left(1-\frac{r^f}{m}\frac{L_0}{A}\right)}{\ln\left(1+\frac{r^f}{m}\right)} + t, \qquad (12.30)$$

Example 12.8: Skip Principal Loans

a)   In order to moderate cash flow problems in the early part of a five-year loan, the principal portion of the loan payment is skipped for two years. If the terms of the $20,000 loan include monthly payments at 13 percent *APR*, or an actuarial rate of 1.08 percent, what is the payment necessary to retire the loan?

Solving, using equation (12.29), gives:

$$A = \frac{\$20,000}{US_0\ (0.0108, 36)} = \$673.88.$$

For 24 months of the loan, payments are $216.00 or ($20,000) .13/12. Payments for the next 36 periods are $673.88. A payment of $673.88 is, of course, larger than $455.06, $20,000/$US_0$(0.13/12, 60), the payment necessary to retire the loan if no skips were made in the five-year amortization.

b)   A borrower can afford monthly payments of $500 after the first year of the loan. Suppose the lender agrees to permit the borrower to pay only interest costs the first year of his loan and principal and interest payments of $500 per month for the next 19 years. At an *APR* rate of 14 percent, how large a loan can the borrower obtain?

The question is solved using equation (12.28), so that:

$$L_0 = \$500\ US_0\ (.0117, 228) = \$39,812.85.$$

or using the $US_0\ (r^f/m, mn)$ approach as:

$$US_0\left(\frac{r^f}{m}, mn{-}t\right) = \frac{L_0}{A}. \tag{12.31}$$

When $mn{-}t$ is found from the above expression, t is added to obtain mn.

Finally, total interest costs can be calculated as:

$$TI = t\,\frac{r^f}{m}\,L_0 + (mn{-}t)\,A - L_0. \tag{12.32}$$

Buy-Down Loans. A third moderated payment type loan is the buy-down loan. This type of loan moderates or reduces the interest charged on early payments. For example, assume the *APR* interest rate is r^f percent. The lender offering a buy-down loan agrees to place in escrow a fund that pays part of the first t payments sufficient to reduce the actuarial interest rate charged during the first t periods to an *APR* rate of $(r^f - \Delta r)$ percent. This program is often attractive to buyers who anticipate improved cash flows in the future.

The relationship between the principal amount borrowed L_0, the *APR* interest rate r^f, the subsidized rate $(r^f - \Delta r/m)$, the terms of the loan mn, the subsidized payment A_s, and the regular payment A is:

$$L_0 = \frac{A_s}{\left(1+\dfrac{r^f-\Delta r}{m}\right)} + \ldots + \frac{A_s}{\left(1+\dfrac{r^f-\Delta r}{m}\right)^t} + \frac{A}{\left(1+\dfrac{r^f}{m}\right)^{t+1}} + \ldots + \frac{A}{\left(1+\dfrac{r^f}{m}\right)^{mn}}. \qquad (12.33)$$

Since the sum contains two uniform series, it can be rewritten as:

$$L_0 = A_s \, US_0\left(\frac{r^f-\Delta r}{m}, \, t\right) + \frac{A \, US_0\left(\dfrac{r^f}{m}, \, mn-t\right)}{\left(1+\dfrac{r^f}{m}\right)^t}. \qquad (12.34)$$

If the interest rate over mn periods remained at $(r-\Delta r)$, a constant payment of A_s would fully repay the loan. Similarly, if the interest rate remained at r^f, a constant payment of A would fully repay the loan. Thus, A_s and A can be calculated using equation (12.3) for the same L_0:

$$A_s = \frac{L_0}{US_0\left[\left(\dfrac{r^f-\Delta r}{m}\right), \, mn\right]}, \qquad (12.35)$$

and:

$$A = \frac{L_0}{US_0\left(\dfrac{r^f}{m}, \, mn\right)}. \qquad (12.36)$$

Example 12.9: Buy-Down Loans

A lender offers a buy-down loan to moderate cash flow problems on a new business. Suppose the lender holds sufficient funds in an escrow account to lower the stated *APR* interest rate of 12 percent to 6 percent for a period of two years. If the new loan is for $100,000 and is to be repaid with monthly payments for 10 years, what will be the payments necessary to fully amortize the loan?

Solving, using equations (12.35) and (12.36), gives:

$$A_s = \frac{\$100,000}{US_0 \ (0.005,120)} = \$1,110.20,$$

and:

$$A = \frac{\$100,000}{US_0 \ (0.01,120)} = \$1,434.71.$$

The *PV* of the reduced loan payment provided by the lender can be found using equation (12.37). Assume $r=.12$ and $r/m=0.01$. Then:

$$NPV = (\$1,434.71 - \$1,110.20) \ US_0(0.01,24) = \$6,893.70.$$

Now consider a similar situation in which the subsidized payment amount is $2,500 and the unsubsidized amount is $3,000. Using the same payment schedule and interest rates as described in the previous example, what loan amount will these payments support?

Solving, using equation (12.34), gives:

$$L_0 = \$2,500 \ US_0 \ (0.005,24) + \frac{\$3,000 \ US_0 \ (0.01,96)}{(1.01)^{24}}$$

$$= \$201,782.75.$$

One might also like to know the *PV* of the reduced loan payments A_s compared to the full payment A for t periods. The answer can be found by comparing the *PV* to the difference between A and A_s. The *PV* of that difference is:

$$NPV = (A - A_s) \, US_0 \left(\frac{r}{m}, \, t \right). \tag{12.37}$$

The term of the buy-down loan can be found using either equation (12.35) or (12.36) above. Using equation (12.36), mn can be found from the expression:

$$US_0 \left(\frac{r^f}{m}, \, mn \right) = \frac{L_0}{A}. \tag{12.38}$$

Finally, total interest costs can be calculated as:

$$TI = tA_s + (mn-t) \, A - L_0. \tag{12.39}$$

Refinancing Constant Payment Loans. Borrowers often face the need to refinance their loans, perhaps due to changes in interest rates. But restrictions and costs associated with refinancing loans complicate the borrower's decision.

For example, many mortgage loans are written with a due-on-sale clause so that the interest rate on the mortgage loan is refinanced if the mortgaged property is sold. In other cases, any time a loan amount is increased, the lender reserves the right to adjust the interest rate on the outstanding amount of the existing loan as well as on the increased loan amount. All of these interest rate adjustment possibilities protect the lender against fluctuating interest rates.

On the other hand, a borrower may protect himself or herself against fluctuating interest rates by refinancing existing loans if interest rates fall. But the lenders may discourage a borrower from refinancing by charging a fee to close the new loan. The borrower needs to know the trade-off between the refinancing fee versus the advantage of lower interest rates. This subject is discussed next.

Whether to refinance a loan depends on a number of factors. At a minimum, these include the interest rate on the old loan r_0^f, the remaining term to maturity on the loan $m_0 n_0$, and the amount to be refinanced L_0 which represents the outstanding portion of the original loan.

From earlier calculations, the annuity A_0 on the old loan is:

$$A_0 = \frac{L_0}{US_0 \left(\dfrac{r_0^f}{m_0}, \, m_0 \, n_0 \right)}. \tag{12.40}$$

Corresponding to the annuity on the old loan is the annuity on the new loan A_α which depends on the loan closing fees π_α, the interest rate on the new loan r_α^f, and the new term of the loan $m_\alpha n_\alpha$. This relationship is expressed as:

$$A_\alpha = \frac{(L_0 + \pi_\alpha)}{US_0\left(\frac{r_\alpha^f}{m_\alpha}, \ m_\alpha \ n_\alpha\right)}. \tag{12.41}$$

What loan closing fee π_α would leave the decision-maker indifferent between refinancing or continuing with the old loan? The answer is the value of π_α which leaves the *PV* of the two loans the same.

The *PV* of the two loans is found by discounting using the firm's opportunity cost of capital r. In this case, since no new loan funds are required, the opportunity cost of capital may be tied to the *IRR* of a liquidated investment or, if lower, the interest rate plus the liquidity premium on the credit reserve charged on new loans. The *PV* of the old loan before and after substituting for A_0, and using equation (12.40), is:

$$PV(L_0) = A_0 \ US_0\left(\frac{r}{m_0}, \ m_0 \ n_0\right) = \frac{L_0 \ US_0\left(\frac{r}{m_0}, \ m_0 \ n_0\right)}{US_0\left(\frac{r_0^f}{m_0}, \ m_0 \ n_0\right)}. \tag{12.42}$$

The *PV* of the new loan, $PV(L_0 + \pi_\alpha)$ before and after substituting for A_α, and using equation (12.41), is:

$$PV(L_0 + \pi_\alpha) = A_\alpha \ US_0\left(\frac{r}{m_\alpha}, \ m_\alpha \ n_\alpha\right)$$

$$= \frac{(L_0 + \pi_\alpha) \ US_0\left(\frac{r}{m_\alpha}, \ m_\alpha \ n_\alpha\right)}{US_0\left(\frac{r_\alpha^f}{m_\alpha}, \ m_\alpha \ n_\alpha\right)}. \tag{12.43}$$

The break-even value for π_α is that value such that the *PV* of the old loan $PV(L_0)$ and the *PV* of the new loan $PV(L_0 + \pi_\alpha)$ are equal. Equating equations

(12.42) and (12.43) and solving the equation for break-even points expressed as a percentage of the original loan are equal to:

$$\frac{\pi_\alpha}{L_0} = \frac{US_0\left(\dfrac{r}{m_0}, m_0\, n_0\right)\; US_0\left(\dfrac{r_\alpha^f}{m_\alpha}, m_\alpha\, n_\alpha\right)}{US_0\left(\dfrac{r_0^f}{m_0}, m_0\, n_0\right)\; US_0\left(\dfrac{r}{m_\alpha}, m_\alpha\, n_\alpha\right)} - 1. \tag{12.44}$$

Equation (12.44) is simplified if the terms on the old and new loans are the same. In that case, equation (12.44) simplifies to:

$$\frac{\pi_\alpha}{L_0} = \frac{US_0\left(\dfrac{r_\alpha^f}{m_0}, m_0\, n_0\right)}{US_0\left(\dfrac{r_0^f}{m_0}, m_0\, n_0\right)} - 1. \tag{12.45}$$

The solutions of equations (12.44) and (12.45) are expressed as an *IRR* model. If π_α were given, there is no reason to expect that $PV(L_0)$ would equal $PV(L_0 + \pi_\alpha)$. In this case, we would solve for the *NPV* and write the result as the difference between $PV(L_0)$ and $PV(L_0 + \pi_\alpha)$:

$$NPV = PV(L_0) - PV(L_0 + \pi_\alpha). \tag{12.46}$$

Implicit in the above analysis is the assumption that r, the firm's opportunity cost of capital, is independent of term and size differences. Clearly, this is a strong assumption, but one frequently made.

Constant Principal Loans

Another type of loan is the constant principal payment loan. As the name implies, it requires a constant principal payment each period plus interest on the remaining loan balance. As a result, interest costs and total loan payment decrease over time.

The principal payment in each period is L_0/mn; the interest cost in the tth payment is $r^f[L_0-(t-1)L_0/mn]$. Thus, the total payment in the tth period is:

Example 12.10: A Refinance Problem

Jane Doe has an outstanding balance of \$4,500 on her car loan. The interest rate on her loan is 15 percent. She makes monthly payments on her loan and it matures in 30 months.

Now assume that Jane can refinance her car loan at 12 percent with monthly payments over three years. Assuming that the *IRR* of a liquidated asset is 10 percent, Jane's opportunity cost of capital is 10 percent. She asks: "What is the maximum number of points I could pay to close the new loan and break even?"

To find the break-even points (π_α/L_0), we solve equation (12.44):

$$\frac{\pi_\alpha}{L_0} = \frac{US_0\left(\frac{0.10}{12}, 30\right)}{US_0\left(\frac{0.15}{12}, 30\right)} \frac{US_0\left(\frac{0.12}{12}, 36\right)}{US_0\left(\frac{0.10}{12}, 36\right)} - 1$$

$$= \frac{26.4470}{24.8889} \frac{30.1075}{30.9912} - 1 = 3.23 \text{ percent.}$$

Jane, however, is not interested in just breaking even. She wants to know how much money she will save if the lender agrees to close for one and one-half points (1.5 percent of \$4,500) which is a value of π_α equal to \$67.50.

We solve this problem for Jane by substituting into the *NPV* formula in equation (12.46), for $PV(L_0)$ and $PV(L_0+\pi_\alpha)$:

$$NPV = \frac{\$4,500\ US_0\left(\frac{0.10}{12}, 30\right)}{US_0\left(\frac{0.15}{12}, 30\right)} - \frac{\$4,567.50\ US_0\left(\frac{0.10}{12}, 36\right)}{US_0\left(\frac{0.12}{12}, 36\right)}$$

$$= \frac{(\$4,500)(26.4470)}{(24.8889)} - \frac{(\$4,567.50)(30.9912)}{(30.1075)} = \$80.15.$$

Jane stands to gain \$80.15 if the assumptions underlying her analysis are correct.

Example 12.11: Payments for a Constant Principal Payment Loan

To illustrate equation (12.47), suppose a $50,000 loan offers annual constant principal payments for 20 years at 14 percent *APR*. The principal payment each year is:

$$\frac{L_0}{n} = \frac{\$50,000}{20} = \$2,500.$$

To determine the interest cost in the eighth period, use:

$$r^f\left[L_0 - \frac{(t-1)L_0}{n}\right] = 0.14\left[\$50,000 - \frac{(7)(\$50,000)}{20}\right] = \$4,550,$$

so that the payment in the eighth period equals:

$$A_8 = \$2,500 + \$4,550 = \$7,050.$$

$$A_t = \frac{L_0}{mn} + r^f L_0 \left[1 - \frac{(t-1)}{mn}\right]. \tag{12.47}$$

Disguised Interest Rate Loans

Disguised interest rate loans have effective interest rates increased by methods other than increasing the interest rate on the loan. For example, interest costs can be subtracted in the initial period, reducing the actual loan amount received by the borrower (a discount loan). Interest can be charged as though the original loan balance was outstanding throughout the life of the loan (an add-on loan). Alternatively, the lender can charge a loan closing fee, reducing the actual loan balance received by the borrower. Or, the interest can compound more frequently than loan payments occur. Each of these methods will increase the effective interest rate above the stated interest rate. Several types of disguised interest rate loans are now discussed.

The Discount Loan. A borrower approaches his lender for a loan of L_0 for mn periods. The borrower learns that the stated interest rate or disguised interest rate is r^d percent. When the borrower picks up the check for his loan, the amount he receives equals only:

$$L_0^d = L_0 (1 - r^d n). \qquad (12.48)$$

The amount of the loan actually received has had the interest cost subtracted in advance. The discount was the stated interest times the number of years for which the loan will be outstanding.

Meanwhile, the periodic loan payments are calculated as:

$$A = \frac{L_0}{mn}. \qquad (12.49)$$

To calculate the actuarial interest rate r^f associated with this loan, treat payments A as if they were associated with a constant payment loan that retires a principal amount of L_0^d equal to $L_0(1 - r^d n)$. The relationship is expressed as:

$$L_0^d = A\, US_0 \left(\frac{r^f}{m}, mn \right). \qquad (12.50)$$

Next, substitute for A using equation (12.49) and adjust terms to obtain the expression:

$$\frac{mn L_0^d}{L_0} = US_0 \left(\frac{r^f}{m}, mn \right). \qquad (12.51)$$

The actuarial interest rate r^f in equation (12.51) will always be higher than the disguised interest rate r^d because: (1) the interest costs are subtracted at the beginning of the loan; and (2) the interest cost for the loan term is calculated on the original loan balance.

The Add-On Loan. An add-on loan adds interest costs as though the entire loan were to be outstanding for the life of the loan. To illustrate, the borrower applies for a loan of L_0 for n periods at a disguised interest rate of r^d percent. In this case, the borrower actually receives the loan amount of L_0, but loan payments are calculated as:

$$A = \frac{(1 + r^d n)\, L_0}{mn}. \qquad (12.52)$$

Example 12.12: A Discount Loan

A consumer obtains an installment loan for $10,000 from which $2,500 is deducted for interest costs. The loan is to be repaid over 2 years with monthly payments equal to $416.67 ($10,000/24). Using equation (12.51), $US_0 (r^f/12, 24)$ associated with this loan is calculated to equal:

$$US_0\left(\frac{r^f}{m}, mn\right) = \frac{(24)(\$7{,}500)}{\$10{,}000} = 18.0000.$$

Associated with $US_0\left(\frac{r^f}{m}, mn\right) = 18.0000$ is an actuarial monthly rate of 2.46 percent or after multiplying by 12 equals an *APR* rate of:

$$r^f = 29.5 \text{ percent.}$$

The effective rate is:

$$r^e = (1.0246)^{12} - 1 = 33.9 \text{ percent.}$$

The actual rate r^f/m, however, is calculated from the relationship:

$$L_0 = A\,US_0\left(\frac{r^f}{m}, mn\right), \tag{12.53}$$

from which one can find $US_0(r^f/m, mn)$ equal to:

$$US_0\left(\frac{r^f}{m}, mn\right) = \frac{L_0}{A} = \frac{mn}{(1+r^d n)}. \tag{12.54}$$

The interest rate corresponding to $US_0(r^f/m, mn)$ can be found by using financial calculators or Appendix 1.

Example 12.13: Add-On Loan

A bank offers a consumer loan that uses an add-on method of interest calculation with a stated interest rate of 10 percent. On a $2,000 loan, the borrower repays the loan in 24 monthly installments. What is the *APR* interest rate r^f for this loan plan?

The payment is determined by equation (12.52) and equals:

$$A = \frac{(1+r^d n)\,L_0}{mn} = \frac{[1+(0.10)(2)]\,\$2,000}{24} = \$100.00.$$

The $US_0(r^f/12, 24)$ value is calculated using equation (12.54):

$$US_0\left(\frac{r^f}{12},\ 24\right) = \frac{\$2,000}{\$100} = 20.000.$$

Associated with $US_0\left(\frac{r^f}{12}, 24\right) = 20.00$ is a monthly actuarial interest rate of 0.0151. The *APR* rate equals 0.0151 times 12 or 18.2 percent. The effective rate $r^e = (1.0151)^{12} - 1 = 19.7$ percent.

Points Added Loan. Sometimes lenders charge points to close a loan. For example, let p be the percent of the loan charged as a closing fee. The fee has the effect of increasing the interest rate on the loan since the lender earns more than the stated rate suggests. The *APR* rate for such a loan can be calculated by first computing the payment which retires the loan, plus the points added at rate p. The payment equals:

$$A = \frac{(1+p)\,L_0}{US_0\left(\dfrac{r^d}{m},\ mn\right)}. \tag{12.55}$$

Next, express the relationship between the payment A, the *APR* rate r^f, and the actual amount of the loan received as:

$$A = \frac{L_0}{US_0\left(\dfrac{r^f}{m},\ mn\right)}. \tag{12.56}$$

Example 12.14: Points Added Loan

A bank offers a loan rate of 12 percent with monthly payments for three years with a 3 percent loan closing fee. What is the *APR* interest rate r^f?

Using equation (12.57), $US_0(r^f/m, mn)$ is found to equal:

$$US_0\left(\frac{r^f}{m}, mn\right) = \frac{US_0(0.01, 36)}{1.03} = \frac{30.1075}{1.03} = 29.2306.$$

A $US_0(r^f/m, mn)$ value of 29.2306 corresponds to an actuarial interest rate of 1.17 percent. An *APR* rate equals 12 times 1.17 or 14.04 percent. The effective interest rate $r^e = (1.0117)^{12} - 1 = 14.98$ percent.

Equating equations (12.55) and (12.56), we find r^f from the equality:

$$US_0\left(\frac{r^f}{m}, mn\right) = \frac{US_0\left(\frac{r^d}{m}, mn\right)}{1 + p}. \tag{12.57}$$

Compensating Balance Loans

The final type of loan considered in this chapter is called the compensating balance loan. Compensating balance loans require the borrower to deposit with the lender a percentage p of his loan L_0. In many cases, this compensating balance of pL_0 earns interest at rate r^c. To evaluate this loan, assume it is repaid in equal installments. The relationship between L_0, r^c, r^d, p, and the term of the loan mn is:

$$L_0 = \frac{A}{\left(1+\frac{r^d}{m}\right)} + \ldots + \frac{A}{\left(1+\frac{r^d}{m}\right)^{mn}} + \frac{pL_0\left(1+\frac{r^c}{m}\right)^{mn}}{\left(1+\frac{r^d}{m}\right)^{mn}}. \tag{12.58}$$

This formulation suggests that annuity payments A plus the *PV* of the compensating balance plus earned interest equal the original loan. This relationship can, of course, be simplified once the geometric series is summed and L_0 is isolated. This simplified expression is:

$$L_0 = \frac{A\, US_0\left(\dfrac{r^d}{m},\ mn\right)}{\left[1 - \dfrac{p\left(1+\dfrac{r^c}{m}\right)^{mn}}{\left(1+\dfrac{r^d}{m}\right)^{mn}}\right]}. \tag{12.59}$$

The *APR* interest rate r^f can be found by first solving for A in equation (12.59). It equals:

$$A = \frac{L_0\left[1 - p\left(1+\dfrac{r^c}{m}\right)^{mn}\Big/\left(1+\dfrac{r^d}{m}\right)^{mn}\right]}{US_0\left(\dfrac{r^d}{m},\ mn\right)} = \frac{L_0(1-\hat{p})}{US_0\left(\dfrac{r^d}{m},\ mn\right)}. \tag{12.60}$$

Example 12.15: A Compensating Balance Loan

Suppose a lender requires a compensating balance of 5 percent on his loans. Moreover, assume the lender pays no interest rate on the balance ($r^c=0.0$) and advertises a five-year loan with monthly payments charged at the disguised interest rate r^d of 12 percent, or a monthly rate of 1 percent.

To find the *APR* interest rate r^f, we use equation (12.63). To calculate $US_0(r^f/m, 60)$, we find $US_0(0.01, 60)=44.9550$. Then:

$$US_0\left(\frac{r^f}{12},\ 60\right) = \frac{(0.95)(44.9550)}{\left[1 - \dfrac{0.05}{(1.01)^{60}}\right]} = 43.9159.$$

Associated with a $US_0(r^f/m, mn)$ value of 43.938 is an actuarial rate of 1.084 percent or an *APR* rate of 13.01 percent. The effective rate is $r^e = (1.0109)^{12} - 1 = 13.84$ percent.

Next, we recognize that the loan available to the borrower was not L_0 but $(1-p)L_0$. So, the *APR* interest rate depends on the relationship:

$$(1-p)L_0 = \frac{A}{\left(1+\dfrac{r^f}{m}\right)} + \ldots + \frac{A}{\left(1+\dfrac{r^f}{m}\right)^{mn}} \tag{12.61}$$

$$= A\, US_0\left(\frac{r^f}{m},\, mn\right),$$

and substituting for A from equation (12.60), we obtain:

$$(1-p)L_0 = \frac{L_0\,(1-p)\, US_0\left(\dfrac{r^f}{m},\, mn\right)}{US_0\left(\dfrac{r^d}{m},\, mn\right)}. \tag{12.62}$$

Solving for $US_0(r^f/m,\, mn)$, we obtain:

$$US_0\left(\frac{r^f}{m},\, mn\right) = \frac{(1-p)\, US_0\left(\dfrac{r^d}{m},\, mn\right)}{(1-p)}. \tag{12.63}$$

Summary

This chapter has introduced and analyzed major types of loans using *PV* techniques. Loan types included in the analysis were: constant payment loans, moderated payment loans, refinanced constant payment loans, constant principal loans, disguised interest rate loans, and compensating balance loans. Because of its importance, the constant payment loan was discussed in the most detail.

Moderated payment loans reduce the size of loan payments during the early periods of the loan. Different loan plans achieve this objective. Several plans, including skip payment and skip principal loans, buy-down loans, concessionary interest rate loans, and graduated payment loans were analyzed. Moreover, the *NPV* of refinancing constant payment loans was also analyzed.

Disguised interest rate loans were also discussed. Discount, add-on, and points added loans all have one feature in common: they increase the *APR* interest rate above the stated or disguised interest rate. One loan plan not reviewed is the adjustable rate mortgage (*ARM*). The essential feature of *ARMs* is that the interest rate changes according to some previously agreed upon signal. Unfortunately, there is such a wide variety of *ARMs* that they are difficult to typify.

Endnotes

1. This chapter is based on a report by Robison, Koenig, and Brake. Appreciation is expressed for permission to reproduce some of the material contained in the report.

2. To calculate the elasticity of *n* with respect to *A*, call it $E_{n,A}$, we write:

$$E_{n,A} = \frac{dn}{dA} \frac{A}{n}.$$

Recall that in continuous time:

$$L_0 = \int_0^n A\, e^{-r^f t}\, dt = \frac{A\left(1 - e^{-r^f n}\right)}{r^f},$$

and:

$$A = \frac{r^f L_0}{\left(1 - e^{-r^f n}\right)},$$

from which we find:

$$\frac{dA}{dn} = \frac{-(r^f)^2 L_0 e^{-r^f n}}{\left(1 - e^{-r^f n}\right)^2}.$$

Furthermore, *dn/dA* equals the inverse of *dA/dn*.
   Substituting for *dn/dA* and for *A* into the formula for $E_{n,A}$, we find:

$$E_{n,A} = \frac{-\left(e^{r^f n} - 1\right)}{r^f n}.$$

Review Questions ────────────────────────────────

1. Distinguish among the following:
   a. Actuarial interest rate
   b. Annual percentage rate (*APR*)
   c. Effective rate

2. What are the similarities and differences between loan models and *NPV* models? Can a loan formula be included in an *NPV* model?

3. Different loans serve different purposes. List three factors that borrowers might consider when choosing among different loan types.

4. Describe the borrowers and the conditions that would result in the following loans being preferred:
   a. A constant payment loan
   b. A balloon payment loan
   c. A skip payment loan
   d. A graduated payment loan
   (Hint: Consider periodic liquidity, *PV* of tax deductible interest payments, etc.)

Application Questions ────────────────────────────

1. Which would you prefer to earn on your savings? An annual interest rate of 12.5 percent or 1 percent compounded monthly? Given an *APR* of *r* percent, what is the most that the effective rate can earn above the *APR* rate if it is compounded continuously?

2. Sometimes we approximate $ln(1+r)$ with *r*. Show that $ln(1+r^e)=r$ exactly. (Hint: $1+r^e = \underset{m\to\infty}{limit}\left(1+\dfrac{r}{m}\right)^m$.) Can you show when this is a reasonable approximation? (Hint: $ln\ e^r=r$, but $e^r\neq(1+r)$)

3. A loan of $80,000 has a balloon payment of $20,000 due in 10 years. The loan terms include monthly payments for nine years and 11 months at an actuarial interest rate of 1 percent, or 12 percent *APR*. What is the loan payment required to repay the loan under the existing conditions? What is the total interest paid?

4. A carpet company advertised free credit for six months after the purchase of its carpets. If the carpet costs $1,500 and after six months the carpet buyer makes monthly payments at an *APR* rate of 14 percent, what is the

monthly payment required to repay the loan in 12 payments? What is the effective rate paid on this loan?

5. Mr. and Mrs. Say Burr have a $54,000 loan that paid for a new addition to their home. The existing loan requires monthly payments at an *APR* of 11 1/4 percent. For a 3 percent closing fee, the Burrs could obtain a loan at 11 percent for 21 years. Assuming interest rates won't change, which loan is preferred?

6. A consumer obtains an installment loan of $12,000 from which $2,700 is deducted for interest costs. The loan is to be repaid over two years with monthly payments equal to $500 ($12,000/24). Please determine the effective interest rate r^e on this loan.

7. Discuss in general terms how the effective interest rate is figured on:
    a.   Add-on loans
    b.   Points added loans
    c.   Compensated balance loans

8. A loan customer intends to borrow $25,000 and the *APR* is 12 percent. Suppose the bank offers the borrower a 15-year term. By what percent will her term decrease if she increases her loan payment by 5 percent? Calculate $E_{n,A}$ for this problem for $n=15$.

9. One of the important ways lenders can mitigate periodic liquidity effects of inflation (see Chapter 7) is to offer graduated loan repayment plans (*GPP*s). To show how *GPP*s increase the amount lenders are willing to loan, compare the loan amounts supported by a fixed payment plan:

$$L_0 = \frac{R}{(1+r)} + \dots + \frac{R}{(1+r)^n},$$

with a *GPP* plan in which payments increase at rate g:

$$L_0^g = \frac{R(1+g)}{(1+r)} + \dots + \frac{R(1+g)^n}{(1+r)^n},$$

where r is the interest rate. Calculate the ratio of L_0^g/L_0 in general and specifically for the case where $n=10$, $r=0.13$, and $g=0.04$.

10. A farm supply store offers its customers 30 days same as cash arrangements. That is, for bills paid within 30 days after purchases are made, no interest is charged. On the other hand, to encourage early payment, the supply store offers a 2 percent discount on bills paid within

10 days. Please calculate the effective interest rate the store offers its buyers for giving up 20 days of free credit.

References

Ellinger, P.N., P.J. Barry, and D.A. Lins. "Farm Financial Performance Under Graduated Payment Mortgages." *North Central Journal of Agricultural Economics* 5(1983):47-53.

Robison, L.J. and J.R. Brake. "Inflation, Cash Flows, and Growth: Some Implications for the Farm Firm." *Southern Journal of Agricultural Economics* 12(1980):131-37.

Robison, L.J. and S.R. Koenig. "Wrap-Around Mortgages and Blended Interest Rates: A Technical Note." *Engineering Economist* 32(1986):51-5.

Robison, L.J., S.R. Koenig, and J.R. Brake. "An Analysis of Interest and Principal Payments, Interest Rates and Time in Common and Uncommon Loans Using Present Value Tools." Agricultural Economics Report No. 459, Michigan State University, November 1984.

Slater, K. "The 15-Year Mortgage: Its Savings Often Fall Short of Backers' Claims." *The Wall Street Journal*, November 6, 1985.

Tweeten, L.G. "Farmland Pricing and Cash Flow in an Inflationary Economy." Oklahoma State University Agricultural Experiment Station Research Report P-811, June 1981.

Chapter 13

Stocks, Bonds, and Other Financial Investments

Key words: bonds, coupons, duration, financial investment, options, portfolios, real investment, stocks, yield

Introduction

In its broadest meaning, to invest means to give up something in the present for something of value in the future. Investments can differ greatly. They may range from the purchase of lottery tickets and burial plots to municipal bonds and corporate stocks. It is helpful to categorize these investments into two general categories: real and financial investments. Real investments involve the exchange of money for nonfinancial investments that produce services. Financial investments involve the exchange of money for a future money payment.

This chapter applies present value PV models developed earlier to financial investments such as stocks and bonds. Large corporations and other business organizations require financial investments of a large number of small investors to provide funds for operation and growth. The collection of these funds would be impossible if each investor were required to exercise a managerial role in the organization. Moreover, the collection of investment funds from a large number of small investors would be impossible unless the investors could be assured of investment safety and limited liability. A number of financial investments have been designed to overcome these and other obstacles.

The market in which financial investments are traded is called the securities market or financial market. Activities in the financial markets are facilitated by brokers, dealers, and financial intermediaries. A broker acts as an agent for investors in the securities markets. The securities broker brings two parties together to obtain the best possible terms for his or her customer and is compensated by a commission. A dealer, in contrast to a broker, buys and sells securities for his or her own account. Thus, a dealer also becomes an investor. Similarly, financial intermediaries (e.g., a bank, savings and loan association, insurance company) play important roles in the flow of funds from savers to ultimate investors. The intermediary acquires ownership of funds loaned or invested by savers, modifies the risk and liquidity of these funds, and then either loans the funds to individual borrowers or invests in various types of financial assets.

Numerous books discuss the institutional arrangements associated with securities trading. In this chapter, the focus is not on the details of trading in the securities market but on how to value financial investments or securities.

Valuation of Riskless Securities

The price of financial investments, like other prices, is set by the market. The characteristics of markets, however, may differ significantly for various types of financial investments. Common to all markets, though, is that a market price is established by matching the desires of buyers and sellers. Moreover, in equilibrium there is neither excess demand nor excess supply. However, equilibrium does not mean that all prospective buyers and sellers agree that an investment's price is equal to its value. It only means that a price has been found that in a sense balances the different goals of buyers and sellers.

Bonds

One type of financial asset frequently traded in financial markets is a bond. Bonds represent debt claims on the assets and income of the entity issuing the bond. A bond's value is equal to the present value of its future cash flows (interest and principal) discounted at an appropriate interest rate. Bonds usually have a known maturity date at which the bond holder receives the bond's face value or par value. Bonds are unique because their redemption or salvage value is fixed. Typical amounts are $1,000 or $10,000.

Consider the following example. Suppose a bond can be purchased at a price of V_0 (an initial cash outflow) and redeemed n periods later at a cash value of V_n (salvage value, a cash inflow to the bond holder). Moreover, suppose that it generates no cash return except when it is sold. Further, assume that the before-tax

Example 13.1: Minimum-Sell Bond Prices

The Corporation of General Motors (*CGM*) is planning to issue a new series of bonds with no interest payments and a maturity of 10 years in order to finance a new joint venture with a Japanese company for the assembly of light trucks at a new plant in California.

CGM estimates that it can earn 12 percent on the funds it receives from sale of its bonds. Considering that the face value of the bonds in 10 years is $1,000, *CGM* calculates its minimum price using equation (13.1):

$$V_0 = \frac{\$1,000}{(1.12)^{10}} = \$321.97.$$

discount rate is r percent. Ignoring any tax consequences, the *NPV* of this bond is the sum of the cash outflow $-V_0$ plus the present value of the cash inflow:

$$NPV = -V_0 + \frac{V_n}{(1+r)^n}. \tag{13.1}$$

Those who purchase bonds want to calculate the "yield" on a bond, which is the discount rate that equates the present value of the bond's cash flows to its present market value. If, for example, the bond's market value is $321.97 and its cash flow of $1,000 occurs at the end of year 10 (see Example 13.1), then the bond's yield is 12 percent. Clearly, the yield of the bond is the same as its internal rate of return (*IRR*).

Now consider the effect of taxes. First, assume capital gains taxes are paid by the bond purchaser at rate T_g and income taxes are paid at rate T. The after-tax *NPV* of the bond is calculated by adjusting the discount rate to its after-tax equivalent and by subtracting the amount of capital gains tax from the cash flow:

$$NPV = -V_0 + \frac{V_n - T_g(V_n - V_0)}{[1 + r(1 - \theta T)]^n}, \tag{13.2}$$

when θ is the tax adjustment coefficient defined in Chapter 8 calculated by the buyer using a *defending* investment (see Example 13.2).

Example 13.2: Taxes and Maximum-Bid Prices for Bonds

The effect of taxes on *CGM*'s bond price is found by assuming that T is 15 percent for income and capital gains, that $\theta=1$, and that $r=0.12$. Using equation (13.2) *NPV* is equal to:

$$NPV = -\$321.97 + \frac{\$1,000 - 0.15(\$1,000 - \$321.97)}{[1+0.12(1-0.15)]^{10}}$$

$$= \$18.13.$$

We can find the bond's after-tax *IRR* in Example 13.2 by setting *NPV*=0 and solving for θ. The result is:

$$NPV = -\$321.97 + \frac{\$1,000 - 0.15(\$1,000 - \$321.97)}{[1+0.12(1-0.15\theta)]^{10}} = 0.$$

Solving for θ, we find:

$$\theta = \frac{1.12 - \left[\dfrac{\$1,000 - 0.15(\$1,000 - \$321.97)}{\$321.97} \right]^{\frac{1}{10}}}{(0.12)(0.15)} = 0.66.$$

For $\theta=0.66$ the effective tax rate is reduced from 0.15 to $(0.66)(0.15)=0.10$.

The Tax Reform Act of 1986 in the U.S. equated T_g to T (for $T \leq 0.28$). Many experts believe that in the future, part of capital gains will be excluded from taxation. Suppose the capital gains tax is set equal to αT. Then, the *NPV* of the bond is that described in equation (13.3) and illustrated in Example 13.3:

$$NPV = -V_0 + \frac{V_n - \alpha T(V_n - V_0)}{[1+r(1-\theta T)]^n}. \qquad (13.3)$$

Example 13.3: Capital Gains Taxes and Maximum-Bid Bond Prices

What is the effect on *CGM*'s bond price if capital gains T_g=3 percent while income taxes remain fixed at T=15 percent, n=10, and θ=1?

Calculating the maximum-bid price for a bond purchaser using equation (13.3):

$$0 = -V_0 + \frac{\$1,000 - 0.03(\$1,000 - V_0)}{[1 + 0.12(1 - 0.15)]^{10}},$$

$$2.6413 \ V_0 = \$1,000 - 30 + 0.03 \ V_0,$$

$$2.6113 \ V_0 = \$970,$$

$$V_0 = \$371.46.$$

Now consider the yield to maturity available from a particular bond (see Example 13.4). That is, let *NPV* be zero and solve for the after-tax *IRR* on the investment. Solving for $r(1-\theta T)$ from (13.3) equals:

$$r(1 - \theta T) = \left\{ \left[\frac{V_n - (V_n - V_0) T_g}{V_0} \right]^{\frac{1}{n}} - 1 \right\}. \tag{13.4}$$

Coupons and Bonds

Most bonds, in addition to capital gains (or losses), provide "coupon" (interest) payments. The number and amount of the coupon payments will alter the *NPV* as well as the price of the bond. Usually the coupon rate r^c is a percentage of the redemption or par value of the bond.

The before-tax *NPV* of a bond with n coupon payments (see Example 13.5) is:

$$NPV = -V_0 + \frac{r^c V_n}{(1+r)} + \ldots + \frac{r^c V_n}{(1+r)^n} + \frac{V_n}{(1+r)^n}$$

$$= -V_0 + r^c V_n US_0(r, n) + \frac{V_n}{(1+r)^n}, \tag{13.5}$$

Example 13.4: Yield to Maturity Calculations

Suppose an investor seeks the yield-to-maturity of a bond that can be purchased for $942.50 and sold 3 years later for $1,000. The investor's tax bracket is 28 percent, $\theta=1$ and $T_g=T$. Using equation (13.4), $r(1-\theta T)$ is calculated to be:

$$r(1-0.28) = \left[\frac{\$1,000-(\$1,000-\$942.50)0.28}{\$942.50}\right]^{\frac{1}{3}} - 1 = 1.44 \text{ percent},$$

and:

$$r = \frac{1.44}{0.72} = 2.00 \text{ percent}.$$

---

or if *NPV* is set equal to zero, the solution for the maximum-bid price V_0 is:

$$V_0 = r^c V_n US_0(r, n) + \frac{V_n}{(1+r)^n}.$$

Taxes, of course, affect the *NPV* of bonds with coupon payments. Only now, taxes may or may not be paid on the coupon payments and capital gains. For example, coupon payments of many municipal bonds are not taxed but their capital gains are taxed. Tax exemption, of course, raises the *NPV* of the bonds for all investors but especially for higher tax bracket investors. The after-tax present value of the bond (see Example 13.6) is written as:

$$V_0 = r^c(1-T^*)(V_n) US_0[r(1-\theta T), n] + \frac{V_n-(V_n-V_0)T_g^*}{[1+r(1-\theta T)]^n}, \tag{13.6}$$

where $T_g^* = \begin{cases} 0 \text{ for tax-exempt bonds} \\ T \text{ for non-tax-exempt bonds} \end{cases}$

Bond Theorems

This chapter now will focus on how bond values are influenced by changes in the discount rate, asymmetric valuation responses, and initial level of yield. These relationships are demonstrated by employing a set of bond theorems

Example 13.5: Maximum-Bid Prices and Coupon Payments

Calculate the maximum-bid price for a three-year bond if it offers semi-annual coupon payments of 5 percent, $r=14$ percent and $r/2=7$ percent.

Using equation (13.5) and recognizing that the coupon payments equal $r^c V_n = .05(\$1{,}000)=\$50$ and the 14 percent annual rate is equivalent to a 7 percent semi-annual rate, we calculate V_0 equal to:

$$V_0 = \$50\ US_0(0.07,6) + \frac{\$1{,}000}{(1.07)^6}$$

$$= \$283.33 + \$666.34 = \$949.67,$$

where $283.33 is the present value of the coupon payments and $666.34 is the present value of the liquidated bond.

Example 13.6: Coupon Payments and Taxes

In this example, the data in Example 13.5 are used except that taxes are added (i.e., the discount rate (r) equals 14 percent, r^c equals 5 percent, and the redemption value (V_n) equals $1,000). Let n equal 3. Let T_g and T equal 0.28 and assume θ equals 1. Making the necessary substitutions in equation (13.6) obtains:

$$V_0 = \$50\ US_0(0.0504,6) + \frac{\$1{,}000 - 0.28(1{,}000 - V_0)}{[1+0.14(1-0.28)]^3}$$

$$= \$253.46 + \frac{\$1{,}000 - 0.28(1{,}000 - V_0)}{1.3339} = \$1{,}003.98.$$

proposed and proven in an important article by Malkiel. The theorems are stated and illustrated below.

Consider a bond (or other fixed-payment loan) that has been issued at a face value of V_n, a coupon interest rate of r^c percent, and coupon payments of $r^c V_n$. The return from the bond consists of coupon payment $r^c V_n$ received each year plus V_n received at the end of the nth year. The maximum-bid model is formulated as:

$$V_0 = \sum_{t=1}^{n} \frac{r^c V_n}{(1+r)^t} + \frac{V_n}{(1+r)^n} = r^c V_n\, US_0(r,n) + \frac{V_n}{(1+r)^n}. \qquad (13.7)$$

Suppose the coupon payment is a constant equal to $r^c V_n = r V_n$. Then, replacing r^c with r in equation (13.7) produces the result:

$$V_0 = V_n.$$

Example 13.7: Changes in Coupon Payments

Consider a bond that has been issued for a five-year term ($n=5$), at a face value of $1,000 ($V_n=\$1,000$), and at a coupon rate of $r^c=9$ percent. If the discount rate is 10 percent, then using equation (13.7), the maximum-bid price equals:

$$V_0 = r^c V_n\, US_0(r,n) + \frac{V_n}{(1+r)^n}$$

$$= \$90\, US_0(0.1,5) + \frac{\$1,000}{(1.1)^5} = \$962.09.$$

If $r^c=10$ percent, then:

$$V_0 = \$100\, US_0(0.1,5) + \frac{\$1,000}{(1.1)^5} = \$1,000,$$

and, if $r^c=11$ percent, then:

$$V_0 = \$110\, US_0(0.1,5) + \frac{\$1,000}{(1.1)^5} = \$1,037.91.$$

When the market discount rate r is the same as the coupon rate (r^c), the bond is priced to sell at its par value of $1,000. However, if the market rate differs from the coupon rate, then the bond's price will also differ from its par value, yielding a premium or discount when the bond is sold.

Using the above specifications as the base case, the bond theorems are introduced and illustrated as follows:

Theorem 13.1: In the absence of tax considerations, the bond price V_0 is inversely rated to the discount rate r.

To understand this theorem, note that the discount factor of the earnings series $US_0(r,n)$ and the discount applied to the bond's terminal value $1/(1+r)^n$ are inversely related to r; that is, the higher the discount rate, the smaller the present value of future payments. Thus, in equation (13.7):

$$\frac{dV_0}{dr} = r^c V_n \frac{\partial US_0(r, n)}{\partial r} + \frac{\partial \left[\frac{V_n}{(1+r)^n}\right]}{\partial r} < 0,$$

since:

$$\frac{\partial US_0(r, n)}{\partial r} < 0 \text{ and } \frac{\partial \left[\frac{V_n}{(1+r)^n}\right]}{\partial r} < 0.$$

Example 13.7 illustrated the conclusions of Theorem 13.1 that as r increases relative to r^c, V_0 decreases. Theorems 13.2 through 13.5 are from Malkiel and are stated without proof.

Theorem 13.2: Holding the coupon rate constant for a given change in market interest rates, the percentage change in bond prices is greater the longer the term to maturity.

Theorem 13.2 indicates that an investment's present value becomes increasingly sensitive to a given change in interest rates as the term to maturity (or asset life or planning horizon) lengthens and other factors remain the same. To illustrate, suppose the term to maturity is lengthened in five-year increments from five to 20 years. The resulting present values are shown in panel *a* of Table 13.1 for the base rate of 10 percent and for coupon rates of 8 and 12 percent, respectively. Also shown in panel *b* of Table 13.1 are the percentage changes in present value from the $1,000 par value.

If the interest rate declines to 8 percent, the percentage gain in the investment's present value increases from 7.9 percent for the five-year term to 19.6 percent for the 20-year term. Similarly, for an increase in the interest rate from 10 percent to 12 percent, the percentage loss in the investment's present value increases from 7.2 percent for the five-year term to 14.9 percent for the 20-year term. These results demonstrate that for a given change in interest rates, percentage changes in bond prices increase with the bond's term.

Table 13.1 Numerical Illustrations of Malkiel's Bond Theorems

Panel *a*: Present values when $r^c=0.1$ and $V_0=\$100\ US_0(r,n)+\$1,000/(1+r)^n$

$$V_0 = \$100\ US_0(r,n) + \$1,000/(1+r)^n$$

Term	$r=0.08$	$r=0.10$	$r=0.12$
5	$1,079.85	$1,000	$927.90
10	$1,134.20	$1,000	$887.00
15	$1,171.19	$1,000	$863.78
20	$1,196.36	$1,000	$850.61

Panel *b*: Percentage changes in present values in response to increases in the opportunity costs of capital for various terms

Term	$\%\Delta V_0 = \dfrac{V_0(0.08,n) - V_0(0.1,n)}{V_0(0.1,n)}$	$\%\Delta V_0 = \dfrac{V_0(0.12,n) - V_0(0.1,n)}{V_0(0.1,n)}$
5	7.9%	−7.2%
10	13.4%	−11.3%
15	17.2%	−13.6%
20	19.6%	−14.9%

Table 13.1, Cont'd.

Panel *c*: Percentage changes in present values in response to increases in terms and opportunity costs of capital

Term	$\dfrac{[V_0(0.08,n+5) - V_0(0.1,n+5)] - [V_0(0.08,n)-V_0(0.1,n)]}{V_0(0.08,n) - V_0(0.1,n)}$	$\dfrac{[V_0(0.12,n+5)-V_0(0.1,n+5)]-[V_0(0.12,n)-V_0(0.1,n)]}{V_0(0.12,n)-V_0(0.1,n)}$
5-10	68%	57%
10-15	28%	21%
15-20	15%	10%

Panel *d*: Percentage changes in present values for increases in opportunity costs of capital for given coupon rates

Coupon Rate r^c	$\%\Delta V_0 = \dfrac{V_0(r=0.08,n=15,r^c) - V_0(r=0.10,n=15,r^c)}{V_0(r=0.10,n=15,r^c)}$
10	$\dfrac{\$1,171.19-\$1,000}{\$1,000} = 17.1\%$
15	$\dfrac{\$1,599.16-\$1,380.30}{\$1,380.30} = 15.9\%$
20	$\dfrac{\$2,027.14-\$1,760.61}{\$1,760.61} = 15.1\%$

Theorem 13.3: The percentage changes described in Theorem 13.2 increase at a diminishing rate as the term to maturity increases.

Theorem 13.3 qualifies the relationship described in Theorem 13.2 by indicating that the relative magnitude of the fluctuation in an investment's present value (for a given change in interest rates) increases at a decreasing rate as maturity lengthens. This relationship is illustrated in panel *c* of Table 13.1 by showing the declining margins of difference between the percentage changes for the five- to 10-year interval, the 10- to 15-year interval, and the 15- to 20-year interval. These margins of difference are 0.68, 0.28, and 0.15 if the interest rate equals 8 percent; and 0.57, 0.21, and 0.10 if the rate equals 12 percent.

Theorem 13.4: Price movements resulting from equal absolute (or proportionate) increases or decreases in market interest rates are asymmetric; in particular, a decrease in yield increases price more than an equal increase in yield lowers price.

Theorem 13.4 indicates that symmetric changes in market interest rates (or yields) cause asymmetric variations in the asset's price, with the relatively greater price change occurring in response to reductions in yield. This relationship is demonstrated in panel *b* of Table 13.1 by comparing the absolute values and percentage changes in an asset's price for each of the terms to maturity. In each case, the percentage change in asset value is greater for the decline in market interest rate when the increase and decrease in the market interest rate are the same.

Theorem 13.5: Holding term-to-maturity constant and starting from the same market yield, the higher the coupon rate, the smaller the percentage change in price for a given change in yield (except for perpetuities and bonds with one period to maturity).

Theorem 13.5 indicates that the sensitivity of the investment's price to a change in yields diminishes as the bond's original yield (coupon rate) increases, holding the term to maturity constant. This theorem is illustrated in panel *d* of Table 13.1. Panel *d* assumes a base coupon rate of 10 percent for the 15-year term to maturity with $100 annual payments, then yields changes from 10 percent to 8 percent, respectively. The asset's value changes from $1,171.11 to $1,000 or an increase of 17.1 percent. For a coupon rate of 20 percent, the same change in the yields increases the bond price by only 15.1 percent.

Common Stocks

In contrast to bonds, common stocks have neither a fixed return nor a fixed cost. The terminal value of bonds is usually fixed, but the terminal value of stocks depends on the market value of the stock on the sale date. The equity capital generated by the sale of stock is an alternative to debt capital generated by the sale of bonds. It also is a means of sharing risk among numerous investors.

Debt capital must be repaid regardless of the financial fortunes of the business. However, the return to stockholders depends critically on the performance of the company. This makes *NPV* analysis of stock investments subject to considerable uncertainty.

Stocks offer significant benefits for stockholders as well as the companies issuing the stocks. Stockholders have the opportunity for ownership in the major businesses of the world with the consequent share in profits, while their liability is limited to their investments. Moreover, stock ownership frees them from decision-making responsibility in the management of the company, although common stock allows its owner to vote for directors and sometimes other matters of significance facing the company.

Stock owners receive dividend payments on their stocks, usually on a quarterly basis. The amount of dividends paid on stocks is determined by a corporation's board of directors. The board of directors' dividend policies may influence the kinds of stock they issue and the kinds of investors they attract.

The relevant question for a potential stock purchaser is: What is the maximum-bid price for a particular stock? If r is the nominal discount rate and R_1, R_2... are dividends paid on the stock in periods 1, 2,..., the maximum-bid price on the stock is:

$$V_0 = \frac{R_1}{(1+r)} + \frac{R_2}{(1+r)^2} + \ldots \tag{13.8}$$

The model above assumes an infinite life. This assumption is consistent with the "life of the investment" principle discussed in Chapter 4 because to know the terminal value of the stock, V_n, dividends in periods $(n+1)$, $(n+2)$... must be known. But knowing all future dividends converts the problem to one in which the number of periods equals the life of the firm.

A simplified form of equation (13.8) is possible if expected dividends are constant; i.e., $R=R_1=R_2=$.... Then V_0 equals:

$$V_0 = R\,US_0(r,\infty) = \frac{R}{r}, \tag{13.9}$$

and r, the stock's *IRR*, is R/V_0. Thus, with long-term constant dividends of $100 and the stock valued at $1,000, the rate of return is 10 percent.

One problem with evaluating stocks in this manner is that dividend payments do not accurately reflect earnings potentials. For example, some companies may retain a larger portion of their earnings to acquire sufficient capital. This strategy allows them to take advantage of high earning potentials on investments in later periods. For such a firm, if one simply calculated the investment's value based on the capitalization of the current period's dividend, the true value of the stock might not be reflected because a higher retention rate leads to more rapid growth in dividends in the future.

Suppose a firm earns $R_1, R_2, R_3,...$ in each period, but decides to return to its stockholders only $(1-k_1), (1-k_2), (1-k_3),$ ... percent of the earnings in periods 1, 2, 3, ... where k_t is the percentage of the firm's earnings retained and reinvested by the firm. Then, in the tth period, the stockholders' dividend equals d_t where:

$$d_t = R_t(1-k_t) + r^r \sum_{i=1}^{t-1} k_i R_i,$$

where r^r is the rate of return on reinvested funds. Under this arrangement, the value of the stock is still:

$$V_0 = \frac{d_1}{(1+r)} + \frac{d_2}{(1+r)^2} + \text{....} \tag{13.10}$$

To simplify the results, assume that earnings are a constant R each year and $k_i = k$. Then:

$$d_1 = (1-k)R,$$
$$d_2 = (1-k)R + r^r kR,$$
$$d_3 = (1-k)R + 2r^r kR.$$

Now, making the substitutions for $d_1, d_2, d_3,...$ in equation (13.10), the value of the stock is:

$$V_0 = \frac{(1-k)R}{(1+r)} + \frac{(1-k)R + r^r kR}{(1+r)^2} + \frac{(1-k)R + 2r^r kR}{(1+r)^3} + \text{...}$$

$$= \frac{(1-k)R}{r} + \frac{1}{(1+r)}\left[\frac{r^r kR}{(1+r)} + \frac{2r^r kR}{(1+r)^2} + \text{...}\right]. \tag{13.11}$$

The bracketed expression is a linear-growth series whose sum is $r'kR/r^2$. Thus, V_0 can be written as:

$$V_0 = \frac{(1-k)R}{r} + \frac{r'kR}{r^2} = \frac{d_1}{r} + \frac{r'kR}{r^2}. \qquad (13.12)$$

Clearly, the capitalized dividend in period zero, d_1/r, would not give the true value of the stock when earnings are growing due to retention and reinvestment of the firm's earnings.

Some insights into valuing stocks by the capitalization of dividends are gained by rearranging equation (13.12). Solving for the internal rate of return r, we obtain (if $r'=r$):

$$r = \frac{d_1}{V_0} + \frac{kR}{V_0}. \qquad (13.13)$$

One implication of equation (13.13) is that the *CT* ratio defined in Chapter 7 is less than one because the stock is increasing in value as a result of the retained and reinvested earning.

These models give plausible results that can be used to evaluate stocks. Growth stocks should have low dividend-to-price ratios, all other things being equal. On the other hand, stocks that represent companies in decay with disinvestment occurring may actually have $k>1$ and very high dividend-to-price ratios. Such companies in decay may be attractive take-over opportunities for other companies wishing to improve their cash flows.

Example 13.8: Valuing Stocks

Sunset Company's stock and dividends have been growing over the past several years. Last year's dividend was $100 per share of stock values at $2,000. Recognizing that the firm reinvests 40 percent of its earnings means the rate of return for this growth firm is greater than $100/$2,000. Using equation (13.13) and the relationship between R and d, Sunset calculates its rate of return. First, since $R(1-k)=d$ and since $k=0.4$ and $d=$100$, $R=$100/0.6=166.67. Therefore:

$$r = \frac{\$100}{\$2,000} + \frac{(0.4)(\$166.67)}{\$2,000} = 8.33 \text{ percent.}$$

Duration Concepts and Measures

The concepts and measures of duration are widely used in finance. Duration measures can be used to: (1) summarize the time patterns of an investment's cash flows; (2) measure the responsiveness of an investment's price to changes in interest rates; and (3) develop financial strategies for responding to interest rate risks. Most duration measure applications have involved fixed-payment securities such as long-term bonds; however, the principles and procedures apply to any type of investment. The duration concept has received extensive use in the portfolio management of financial institutions where interest rate risks are a major source of concern; however, the concepts are applicable to other types of firms as well.

The purpose here is to review the fundamentals of duration, show its relationship to investment pricing, and illustrate its application to managing interest rate risk. The literature in this area is extensive, although applications of the duration concept to nonfinancial assets and firms other than financial institutions are rare.

What is Duration?

The duration concept was developed in the late 1930s by Frederick Macauley as a means of measuring the time pattern of an investment's cash flow in a fashion that gives more information than the term to maturity. Maturity only gives information about the date of the final payment. Thus, a maturity of 20 years for a long-term bond (or other type of investment) only tells the time span between the initial date and the final payment. Nothing is conveyed about the frequency, level, time pattern, and other characteristics of the cash flows occurring within the maturity period.

Duration is similar to maturity, but it is designed to represent a weighted average of the maturities of each of the cash flows that comprise the earning series of the asset, using present values as the weights. While a number of duration formulas have been developed, the most commonly-used one is expressed as follows:

$$D = \frac{\sum_{t=1}^{n} t \left[\frac{R}{(1+r)^n} \right]}{\sum_{t=1}^{n} \frac{R_t}{(1+r)^t}} = \frac{\sum_{t=1}^{n} \frac{tR_t}{(1+r)^t}}{V_0}, \qquad (13.14)$$

where D is duration, R_t is the cash payment in period t, (t) is the length of time from the present to the payment, and r is the discount or yield to maturity. The denominator of equation (13.14) is the present value of the series of cash flows or V_0. The numerator is the summation of the present values of each cash flow multiplied by its individual maturity. Thus, the duration of an investment's cash flow stream is simply the weighted average of the maturities of the individual cash flows where each period n is weighted by the present value of that period's payment.

Equation (13.14) shows that the duration of an investment is based on the interaction among the cash payments, their timing, and the interest rate or yield. If any of these factors change, so will the measure of duration. However, because duration is measured by the length of period (years in this case), one can compare the durations of several assets even if their yields, cash flows, or maturities differ. It is also possible for two assets with very different characteristics to have the same duration. Equation (13.14) is illustrated in Example 13.9.

Example 13.9: Duration Measures

Find the duration of a loan that has a five-year maturity with equally amortized principal and interest payments of $1,000 at an interest rate of 10 percent. The denominator of equation (13.14) is simply the present value of the five-year series of $1,000 payments discounted at 10 percent:

$$V_0 = \sum_{t=1}^{5} \frac{R_t}{(1+r)^n} = \frac{\$1,000}{1.10}$$

$$+ \frac{\$1,000}{(1.10)^2} + \dots \frac{\$1,000}{(1.10)^5} = \$3,790.79.$$

The duration model is then expressed as:

$$D = \frac{(1)\left(\frac{\$1000}{1.10}\right) + (2)\left(\frac{\$1000}{(1.10)^2}\right) + (3)\left(\frac{\$1000}{(1.10)^3}\right) + (4)\left(\frac{\$1000}{(1.10)^4}\right) + (5)\left(\frac{\$1000}{(1.10)^5}\right)}{\$3,790.79}$$

$$= 2.81.$$

Thus, the duration of the loan is 2.81 years.

Duration is always shorter than an investment's maturity (with one exception), because it accounts for the timing of the cash flows within the maturity period. The one exception is an investment yielding a single payment (i.e., zero coupon bonds) at maturity. In this case, maturity and duration are the same. Usually, duration and maturity are positively related to one another—that is, longer maturities are associated with longer duration—but the relationship is complex and exceptions may occur.

Simplified Duration Measures

Consider the duration measure for a series of payments $R_t=(1+g)^t R_0$ for n periods (Boquist, Racette, and Schlarbaum). The duration measure in this case is:

$$D = \frac{R_0 \sum_{t=1}^{n} t(1+g)^t/(1+r)^t}{V_0} = \frac{S}{V_0}, \tag{13.15}$$

which can be expressed as:[1]

$$D = \frac{1+r}{r-g} - \frac{n}{\left[\left(\frac{1+r}{1+g}\right)^n - 1\right]}. \tag{13.16}$$

In the limit, as n becomes large, D in equation (13.16) reduces to:

$$\lim_{n \to \infty} D = \frac{1+r}{r-g}, \tag{13.17}$$

and where n is large and $g=0$, D reduces to:

$$D = \frac{1+r}{r}. \tag{13.18}$$

Finally, if $g=0$ and n is finite, D equals:

$$D = \frac{(1+r)}{r} - \frac{n}{\left[(1+r)^n - 1\right]}. \tag{13.19}$$

Duration and Price Elasticity

It is sometimes helpful to be able to measure the response of an investment's price (present value) to a change in the interest rate with other variables (e.g., cash payment, length of series) held constant. While the bond theorems in an earlier section of this chapter reflect general relationships between present values and interest rates, no explicit measure of this relationship can be found using the maturity periods of an investment's cash flows. However, a simple relationship can be found using the duration concept.

The relationship between duration and the price of an investment is based on the observation by Hicks (1939) that the duration of a cash flow stream is also the absolute interest rate elasticity of its present value. That is, the measure of duration represents the proportional change in an investment's present value for a one unit change in the interest rate (yield); this relationship holds exactly for very small changes in the interest rate, but is only an approximation for larger changes. Moreover, to be precise, the interest rate elasticity is measured with respect to a change in one plus the rate of interest, rather than the rate interest itself.

This relationship, described by Hicks, is expressed as:

% change in asset price	equals	minus duration	times	proportional change in one plus the interest rate
$\dfrac{\Delta V_0}{V_0}$	=	$(-D)$	X	$\left[\dfrac{\Delta(1+r)}{1+r}\right]$

$$\tag{13.20}$$

or:

% change in asset price	divided by	proportional change in one plus the interest rate	equals	minus duration
$\dfrac{\Delta V_0}{V_0}$	÷	$\left[\dfrac{\Delta(1+r)}{1+r}\right]$	=	$(-D)$

$$\tag{13.21}$$

To illustrate, consider the numerical example introduced in Example 13.9 in which a duration of 2.8101 years was found for a $1,000 annuity over five years at an interest rate of 10 percent. Suppose the interest rate increases by 100 basis points to 11 percent. Using equation (13.21), the percentage change in the investment's price is estimated as:

$$\frac{\Delta V_0}{V_0} = (-2.8101) \left[\frac{1.11 - 1.10}{1.10} \right]$$

$$= 0.02555 \text{ or } 2.555 \text{ percent.}$$

The same percentage change in investment price would occur for a decline in the interest rate of 100 basis points—that is, from 10 percent to 9 percent.

Now, compare this estimate of the investment's price response to the true changes in present value. Recall from Example 13.9 that the present value of a $1,000 series of payments for five years is $3,790.79 using a 10 percent discount rate. If the discount rate increases to 11 percent, the present value declines to $3,695.90, a 2.5032 percent decline. If the discount rate declines to 9 percent, the present value increases to $3,889.65, a 2.6080 percent increase. The difference in these percentage changes reflects the asymmetric price response indicated by Malkiel's Bond Theorem 13.4. However, the average of these percentage changes is 2.5556 percent, indicating that the duration-based estimate of price volatility closely approximates the average percentage change in the asset's present value. The smaller the interest rate change, the more accurate the approximation.

Deriving the Duration and Elasticity Measures

One investment price elasticity measure is derived by computing the differential of the asset price with respect to one plus the rate of interest (Hopewell and Kaufman). In the usual fashion, the investment's present value is equal to the sum of the present values of the series of payments:

$$V_0 = \sum_{t=1}^{n} \frac{R_t}{(1+r)^t}. \tag{13.22}$$

Taking the differential:

$$\frac{dV_0}{d(1+r)} = -\sum_{t=1}^{n} \frac{tR_t}{(1+r)^{t+1}}. \tag{13.23}$$

Multiplying both sides of equation (13.23) by $-(1+r)/V_0$ yields:

$$\frac{-dV_0}{d(1+r)} \frac{(1+r)}{V_0} = \sum_{t=1}^{n} \frac{tR_t}{(1+r)^t} \Big/ V_0 = D. \tag{13.24}$$

But:

$$\frac{dV_0}{d(1+r)} \frac{(1+r)}{V_0} = -D,$$

also defines the elasticity of V_0 with respect to $(1+r)$, $E_{V_0,1+r}$. (See Chapter 5 for a discussion of elasticity measures.) Therefore, $-D = E_{V_0,1+r}$.

Another measure related to duration is the change in V_0 with respect to a change in r divided by V_0. This measure is called the price volatility measure. Define:

$$\frac{dV_0}{dr} = -\left[\sum_{t=1}^{n} \frac{tR_t}{(1+r)^t}\right] \Big/ (1+r), \tag{13.25}$$

and:

$$-\left(\frac{dV_0}{dr}\right) \Big/ V_0 = \frac{D}{(1+r)},$$

which is the price volatility relationship.

Values of duration and price volatility are shown in Table 13.2 for alternative specifications of the characteristics of the cash flow series. Columns 2 and 3 indicate the duration and price volatility values for a uniform series of cash flows received in perpetuity. The duration measures are calculated using simplified duration equations derived from equation (13.16). For example, for an interest rate of $r=0.06$ and $g=0$, duration is:

$$D = \frac{1+r}{r} = \frac{1.06}{0.06} = 17.67,$$

and the price volatility measure is:

$$\frac{D}{(1+r)} = \frac{17.67}{1.06} = 16.67.$$

Table 13.2 Duration and Elasticity Measures for Alternative Interest Rates and Payment Characteristics

Interest Rate	Level Perpetuity (g=0)		Growing Perpetuity (g=0.02)		Level Finite Annuity (n=15, g=0)		Growing Finite Annuity (n=15, g=.02)	
	Duration $D = -E_{V_0, 1+r}$	Price Volatility $D/(1+r)$	Duration $D = -E_{V_0, 1+r}$	Price Volatility $D/(1+r)$	Duration $D = -E_{V_0, 1+r}$	Price Volatility $D/(1+r)$	Duration $D = -E_{V_0, 1+r}$	Price Volatility $D/(1+r)$
(1)	(2)	(3)	(4)	(5)	(6)	(7)	(8)	(9)
0.06	17.67	16.67	26.50	25.00	6.93	6.54	7.29	6.88
0.08	13.50	12.50	18.00	16.67	6.59	6.10	6.95	6.44
0.10	11.00	10.00	13.75	12.50	6.28	5.71	6.62	6.02
0.12	9.33	8.33	11.20	10.00	5.98	5.34	6.31	5.64
0.14	8.14	7.14	9.50	8.33	5.70	5.00	6.01	5.27
0.16	7.25	6.25	8.29	7.15	5.44	4.69	5.74	4.95

Columns 4 and 5 indicate duration and price volatility for an investment whose cash returns increase at the rate of 2 percent in perpetuity. The duration measures are calculated using equation (13.17). For example, for an interest rate of $r=0.06$, duration is:

$$D = \frac{1+r}{r-g} = \frac{1.06}{0.06-0.02} = 26.50,$$

and the price volatility is:

$$\frac{D}{(1+r)} = \frac{26.50}{1.06} = 25.00.$$

Thus, the growth in earnings increases both the duration of the asset's earnings series and the degree of volatility.

Columns 6 and 7 indicate duration and elasticity values for a uniform series (annuity) of payments over 15 years. These duration measures are calculated using equation (13.19). For example, for $r=0.06$, duration is:

$$D = \frac{1+r}{r} - \frac{n}{(1+r)^n-1} = \frac{1.06}{0.06} - \frac{15}{(1.06)^{15}-1} = 6.93,$$

and the price volatility is:

$$\frac{D}{(1+r)} = \frac{6.93}{1.06} = 6.54.$$

Finally, columns 7 and 8 indicate the duration and elasticity measures for a series of payments that grows at a constant rate of 2 percent for 15 years.

Duration and the Management of Interest Rate Risks ─────

Holders of financial investments with a fixed series of payments (e.g., a bond) are subject to two types of interest rate risk.[2] First, changes in market interest rates during the holding period will change the investment's market value and create uncertainty about the level of the proceeds if the investment is sold prior to maturity. The price relationship is an inverse one in that increases in market interest rates reduce the investment's market value. Moreover, as shown above, the relative magnitude of the price change increases as duration increases.

The second type of interest rate risk involves changes in the earnings rate on the reinvestment of the payments received on the investment. Thus, the investor is uncertain about the future value of the series of reinvested payments. The earnings relationship is a positive one in that increases in interest rates increase the future value of the reinvested payments.

To illustrate, consider the value of an investment t periods in the future that earns a constant cash flow R. Then, V_t equals $V_0(1+r)^t$ and if r increases, V_0 decreases but the increase in $(1+r)^t$ may offset the decrease in V_0. Thus:

$$\frac{dV_t}{dr} = \frac{\partial (1+r)^t US_0(r, n-t)}{\partial r} \underset{>}{\overset{<}{=}} 0.$$

These two sources of interest rate risk yield offsetting effects on the investor's wealth position because, for example, an increase in the market interest rate will reduce the investment's market value, but increase the value of the reinvested earnings. However, with one exception, the effects are only partially offsetting, leaving the investor in an uncertain position about the future wealth (or yield) from holding the financial asset. The exception is when the length of the holding period equals the duration of the asset (Fisher and Weil; Hopewell and Kaufman). In this case, interest rate risks are reduced to zero—or nearly so, because it is often impossible to exactly match a holding period with an asset's duration. In addition, the duration relationship becomes less exact for larger changes in interest rates and duration itself is subject to change as time passes.

A rule-of-thumb that has sometimes been used by financial institutions to manage interest rate risk is to match the maturities of the major sources (e.g., deposits or bonds) and uses (e.g., loans) of funds. However, this approach may not be valid in immunizing the effects of the institution's net worth against interest rate risk. Rather, as indicated above, a more exact approach is to match as closely as possible the durations of the sources and uses of funds—that is, to match the durations of assets and liabilities (see Example 13.10).

Active Portfolio Management

The above examples illustrating the use of duration concepts to manage interest rate risks are based on the assumptions of a flat initial yield curve and only one parallel shift in the curve immediately after the beginning of the period. Under these conditions, matching the duration of the asset with the length of the holding period will assure that the realized returns equal the target returns.

Example 13.10: Changes in Market Interest Rates

Consider the numerical example introduced in Example 13.9 in which a five-year loan with $1,000 annual payments was found to have a present value of $3,790.79 and a duration of 2.81 years. The investor's goal is to maintain a target yield of 10 percent and to sell the loan at the end of two years.

If market interest rates stay at 10 percent and the sale occurs at the end of year two, then the investor's wealth position at the end of this time is the sum of the future value of the two $1,000 payments reinvested at 10 percent plus the market value of the loan as represented by the present value of the three remaining loan payments:

$$V_2 = \$1,000 \left[US_0(0.10,5)(1.10)^2 \right] = \$4,586.85.$$

Discounting $4,586.85 over two years at 10 percent interest yields the present value of $3,790.79, indicating that the 10 percent yield is attained.

Now suppose that the market interest rate is subject to unanticipated variation and either increases to 12 percent or decreases to 8 percent immediately after the loan contract is established. If the market rate increases to 12 percent and the sale occurs at the end of year two, the investor's wealth position at that time is:

$$V_2 = \$1,000 \left[US_0(0.12,5)(1.12)^2 \right] = \$4,521.83.$$

Note that the reinvested value of the first two payments increased from $2,100 to $2,120 while the discounted value in period two of the last three payments declined from $2,486 to $2,401.83. The yield of the loan fell from 10 percent to 9.22 percent on the loan. That is, 9.22 percent is the discount rate that equates the $4,521.83 value at the end of year two to the present value of $3,790.79.

If the market rate decreases to 8 percent and the sale occurs at the end of year two, the wealth at that time is:

Example 13.10, Cont'd.: Changes in Market Interest Rates

$$V_2 = \$1,000 \left[US_0(0.08, 5)(1.08)^2 \right] = \$4,657.10,$$

which is equivalent to a yield of 10.84 percent. Thus, for these numerical specifications and this length of holding period, the changes in market interest rates cause the yield on the loan to vary from 9.22 percent to 10.84 percent.

As a hedge against interest rate risk, suppose the investor adjusts the length of the holding period to equal the duration of the asset, 2.81 years. In this case, if the market interest rate increases to 12 percent, the wealth after 2.81 years is:

$$V_{2.81} = \$1,000 \ US_0(0.12, 5)(1.12)^{2.81}$$

$$= \$4,956.57,$$

which also is equivalent to a yield of 10 percent since:

$$\left(\frac{\$4,956.57}{\$3,790.79} \right)^{\frac{1}{2.81}} = 10 \ \text{percent.}$$

Similarly, if the market interest rate declines to 8 percent, the wealth effect for a holding period of 2.81 years is:

$$V_{2.81} = \$1,000 \ US_0(0.08, 5)(1.08)^{2.81}$$

$$= \$4,956.65,$$

which is equivalent to a yield of 10 percent since:

$$\left(\frac{\$4,956.55}{\$3,790.79} \right)^{\frac{1}{2.81}} = 10 \ \text{percent.}$$

Thus, by utilizing the duration approach to establish the holding period for the loan, the investor largely offsets the risk attributed to unanticipated changes in market interest rates.

Example 13.11: Difference in Bond and Loan Maturities and Duration

Consider a long-term lender who makes 30-year loans funded by the sale of 10-year bonds. Is this mismatch of maturities serious? Suppose the terms of the loan include a total amount of $10,000 and 30 annual amortized payments of principal and interest at a rate of 11 percent. The terms of the $10,000 bond are annual interest payments at 8 percent plus redemption of the bond at the end of year 10.

Using equation (13.19), the duration of the loan is:

$$D = \left[\frac{1+r}{r}\right] - \left[\frac{n(1+r)}{(1+r)^{n-1}}\right]$$

$$= \frac{1.11}{0.11} - \frac{30(1.11)}{(1.11)-1} = 8.57 \text{ years.}$$

Using equation (13.14), the duration of the bond is:

$$D = \frac{(1)\left(\dfrac{800}{1.08}\right) + (2)\left(\dfrac{800}{1.08^2}\right) + \dots + (10)\left(\dfrac{10,800}{(1.08)^{10}}\right)}{10,000}$$

$$= 7.25 \text{ years.}$$

Thus, while the durations differ by about 1.4 years, the mismatch is much less than is implied by the maturities of 10 and 30 years. Moreover, the reader can confirm that shortening the loan maturity from 30 to 25 years would yield a loan duration of 8.05 years.

Clearly, however, these assumptions are highly simplified in a world characterized by frequent changes in interest rates and by the passage of time. Both of these factors—multiple changes in interest rates and the passage of time—cause changes in the duration of assets and call for periodic restructuring of the asset holdings to maintain the hedge (immunization) against interest rate risk. Thus, immunization based on duration concepts is an active rather than a passive strategy (Elton and Gruber). Moreover, the computation of duration measures utilizes detailed information on maturity dates, payment patterns, and interest rates for all of the assets involved. Further adjustments are involved if a mortgage or bond is prepaid, called, or subject to repricing. Thus, the practical use of these techniques may not be feasible for all financial market participants.

As Leibowitz demonstrated, even active duration management in a volatile interest rate environment can never assure that a target level of returns can be exactly assured. However, techniques for periodic rebalancing of portfolio holdings will minimize the vulnerability of the target returns across a wide range of interest rates. The purpose of such rebalancing is to engage in appropriate financial asset transactions in order to keep the duration of an asset (a portfolio of assets) equal to the length of the investment period. For example, after five years of a 10-year holding period have passed, during which interest rates have changed significantly, the asset-holder could sell the asset and reinvest the proceeds in another asset whose duration (based on the revised interest rate) equals five years.

The more frequent the restructuring, the closer are the realized returns to the target returns. While the demands of active duration management can be high, empirical studies of both duration and maturity strategies suggest that the dispersion of realized returns is consistently smaller when duration rather than maturities is matched with holding periods, and when portfolio management is active rather than passive (Bierwag and Kaufman; Yawitz).

Active immunization strategies also apply to asset-liability management by financial institutions. In this case, the object is to insulate the institution's net worth against the effects of changes in interest rates on the market values of both assets and liabilities (Mitchell; Gardner and Mills). This is accomplished by setting the average duration of rate-sensitive assets equal to the average duration of rate-sensitive liabilities. Changes in market interest rates then have equal and offsetting effects on the values of assets and liabilities, leaving net worth the same. Because numerous categories of assets and liabilities are involved, and interest rates may change frequently, the use of duration concepts as part of an immunization strategy often becomes complex.

Option Values

For the most part, investment decisions require choosing between a challenger and a defender in the present time. An additional investment opportunity may be to postpone making the investment decision until a later period (Pindyck). Several reasons might exist for postponing an investment decision. By waiting, the decision maker may gain information that improves his or her ability to evaluate an investment's *NPV*. Information that may be acquired by waiting includes:

performance data about the investment, the resolution of unresolved legal issues affecting the investment's performance, the demand and price paid for services produced by the investment, and the development of new products that may provide an improved alternative to the investment in question.

Waiting has costs, however, including the return the new investment would have earned during the waiting periods. A second cost of waiting is possible increases in the investment's cost in the future. Finally, some investments are profitable only to innovators who invest early so that waiting precludes making a profitable investment.

In well-developed markets, investors may purchase legal instruments called options that guarantee them the right to buy or sell an investment at a stated price during a specified period. Option contracts exist for many kinds of investments including investments, common stock, land, and agricultural commodities. Option contract specifics vary depending on who sells the contracts and the type of contracted investment.

The concern here is not with the purchase of an option contract, but with the value that is added to an *NPV* model when the decision maker has the possibility of investing in the future. Nevertheless, one can easily relate the discussion that follows to the analysis of options because the value added to an *NPV* model by postponing the investment decision is equal to the value of an options contract for the right to purchase (sell) the investment in the future.

Suppose a decision maker has amount V_0 invested in a defending investment that earns a risk-free rate of return of r. If investing in the challenger is postponed one period, the investor will earn return rV_0 on the defender and give up the return on the challenger. Furthermore, waiting one period may also change the capitalized value of future returns that may be earned on the challenger.

The *NPV* of waiting one period can be expressed by adopting the following notation. Let the random net cash flow be $\tilde{R}_1 \sim (R_1, \sigma_{R_1})$ where R_1 and σ_{R_1} are the mean and standard deviation of R_1. Let the certainty equivalent income for the stochastic income described in Chapter 11 be reflected by $R_1 - \frac{\lambda}{2} \sigma_{R_1}^2$ where λ is the decision maker's absolute risk aversion coefficient.

The *NPV* of the certainty equivalent cash flow stream can be expressed as:

$$NPV = -V_0 + \frac{R_1 - \frac{\lambda}{2} \sigma_{R_1}^2}{1+r} + \frac{R_1 - \frac{\lambda}{2} \sigma_{R_1}^2}{(1+r)^2} + \ldots = -V_0 + \frac{R_1 - \frac{\lambda}{2} \sigma_{R_1}^2}{r}. \quad (13.26)$$

Now assume that in the present period, future returns are viewed as equal to the stochastic income, $\tilde{R}_1$. One period later, however, an outcome of the random variable is realized and its net cash return will take on a particular value of $\tilde{R}$. At time zero, the decision maker does not know what value $\tilde{R}$ will assume. However, at time period one, he knows that its value must exceed rV_0; otherwise, investment in the defender that earns rV_0 will be continued. Thus, the mean of the distribution of possible outcomes must be greater than or equal to the mean of the ex ante random variable $\tilde{R}_1$. Let the mean of the realized outcomes be $R \geq R_1$.

The realization of the random variable means that no risk costs will be subtracted from R_1 in the future period cash flows since the actual value will be known. Under these conditions, *NPV* for the delayed investment equals:

$$NPV^d = -\frac{V_0}{1+r} + \frac{R}{(1+r)r}. \tag{13.27}$$

The difference between NPV^d, the *NPV* of the delayed investment, and *NPV*, the *NPV* of investing now is the option value of postponing the decision. Let *OV* be the option value of postponing the investment decision one period. Then, $OV>0$ if:

$$OV = \frac{rV_0 + R/r}{1+r} - \frac{\left(R_1 - \frac{\lambda}{2}\sigma_{R_1}^2\right)}{r} \geq 0. \tag{13.28}$$

The firm should delay investment by one period if the present value of next period's income earned on the defender plus the capitalized value of the realized income exceeds the capitalized value of the certainty equivalent of the challenger. Another interpretation of *OV* is that it equals the maximum price that could be paid to guarantee the right to purchase the investment at price V_0 one period in the future.

Summary

This chapter has applied *PV* tools to financial investments. Financial investments are characterized by exchanges of time-dated cash flow streams modified by taxes, transactions costs, interest rates, risk, and the size and term of the investment commitments. One of the features peculiar to financial investments is that their attractiveness can be specialized to specific investors. That is, the opportunity for returns, the degree of liquidity, and the tax consequences can all be tailored to meet the needs of specific investor groups.

Entire books have been written on the subject introduced in this chapter. One of the many differences between these books and this chapter is the attention they pay to risk. Risk, it turns out, is one of the main concerns when making financial investments. Instead, this chapter has focused on the time dimension.

Endnotes

1. Multiplying S by $(1+r)/(1+g)$ results in:

$$\frac{S(1+r)}{(1+g)} = R_0 + \frac{2R_0(1+g)}{(1+r)} + \cdots + \frac{nR_0(1+g)^{n-1}}{(1+r)^{n-1}}.$$

Then, subtracting S from $S(1+r)/(1+g)$:

$$\frac{S(1+r)}{(1+g)} - S = \frac{(r-g)}{(1+g)}S = R_0 + \frac{R_0(1+g)}{(1+r)} + \cdots + \frac{R_0(1+g)^{n-1}}{(1+r)^{n-1}} - \frac{nR_0(1+g)^n}{(1+r)^n}$$

$$= \frac{(1+r)}{(1+g)} US_0\left(\frac{r-g}{1+g}, n\right) - \frac{nR_0(1+g)^n}{(1+r)^n}.$$

Solving for S:

$$S = \frac{(1+r)}{(r-g)} RUS_0\left(\frac{r-g}{1+g}, n\right) - \frac{nR_0(1+g)^{n+1}}{(1+r)^n(r-g)}.$$

Finally, substituting for S and V_0 in the expression $D=S/V_0$ gives:

$$D = \frac{1+r}{r-g} - \frac{n}{\left[\left(\frac{1+r}{1+g}\right)^n - 1\right]}.$$

2. Also see M.J. Gardner and D.L. Mills. *Managing Financial Institutions: An Asset/Liability Approach*. New York: The Dryden Press, 1988, pp. 175-79.

Review Questions

1. Distinguish between real and financial investments. Give examples of your own real and financial investments.

2. Compare the salvage values of stocks and bonds. What is the relationship between the present value of bonds and stocks and their terminal values?

3. Explain how capital gains and capital gains taxes are computed for bonds.

4. Describe the condition such that a bond's present value V_0 equals its terminal value V_n. Rework Example 13.7 setting r^c equal to 10 percent.

5. Explain why the present value of a bond is inversely related to r and directly related to r^c.

6. Other things being equal, how would you expect the present value of bonds to change as their maturity date increases? Find examples from the *Wall Street Journal* to support your claim.

7. Give an explanation for why a firm may desire to delay the distribution of earnings to its stockholders.

8. Define duration and illustrate how it is calculated.

9. In what way is duration related to the elasticity of an asset's price with respect to a change in interest rate?

10. What are the major effects of interest rate risk and how can the duration concept be used to manage interest rate risk?

Application Questions

1. Assume a defender is a one-year tax-exempt bond described in equation (13.6). (Only the coupon payment is tax-exempt.) Using methods developed in Chapter 8, find θ. Hint: The before-tax value of the bond is:

$$V_0 = \frac{(1+r^c)V_1}{(1+r)}.$$

    Find the after-tax value of the bond and solve for θ.

2. Would you expect the market value of a 20-year bond to vary more, the same, or less than a 10-year bond of similar quality? Defend your answer.

3. Suppose an investor desires to calculate the yield to maturity of a bond that can be purchased for $871 and sold four years later for $1,000. The investor's tax bracket is 30 percent, $\theta=1$, and $T_g=T$. Find the bond's yield.

4. Calculate the maximum-bid price for a five-year bond assuming it offers semiannual coupon payments of 6 percent and the firm's opportunity cost of capital is 14 percent.

   a. Describe the numerical effects on the bond's price calculated above of an increase of 1 percent to 15 percent in the firm's opportunity cost of capital.

   b. Next, calculate the maximum-bid price for the bond described in the introduction to this problem if it were a 10-year bond instead of a five-year bond.

   c. Holding coupon rates constant, calculate the percentage change in the five-year bond and the 10-year bond resulting from an increase of 1 percent in the firm's opportunity cost of capital. Explain the differences.

5. Find the duration of a loan that has an eight-year maturity with equally amortized annual principal and interest payments of $1,000 at an interest rate of 10 percent.

6. Using the simplified duration measures derived in this chapter, calculate duration and price volatility measures for: (a) a level perpetuity series; (b) a growing perpetuity series; (c) a level finite annuity; and (d) a growing finite annuity. In your calculations let $r=0.09$, $g=0.03$ when appropriate, and $n=14$ when appropriate.

7. Collect bond prices that demonstrate the conclusions of Theorem 13.2. State the source of your data.

References

Bierwag, G.O. and G.G. Kaufman. "Duration Gap for Financial Institutions." *Financial Analysts Journal* 41(March/April 1985):68-71.

_____, G.G. Kaufman, and A. Toeva. "Bond Portfolio Immunization and Stochastic Process Risk." *Journal of Bank Research* 13(Winter 1983):282-91.

Boquist, J.A., G.A. Racette, and G.G. Schlarbaum. "Duration and Risk Assessment for Bonds and Common Stock." *Journal of Finance*, December 1975, pp. 1360-65.

Elton, E.J. and M.J. Gruber. *Modern Portfolio Theory and Investment Analysis*, 2nd Edition. New York: John Wiley and Sons, 1984.

Fisher, L. and R.L. Weil. "Coping with the Risk of Interest-Rate Fluctuations: Returns to Bondholders from Naive and Optimal Strategies." *Journal of Business* 44(October 1971):408-31.

Gardner, M.J. and D.L. Mills. *Managing Financial Institutions: An Asset/Liability Approach*. New York: The Dryden Press, 1988, pp. 175-79.

Haugen, R.A. *Modern Investment Theory*. New Jersey: Prentice-Hall, 1986.

Hicks, J.R. *Value and Capital*, 2nd Edition. Oxford: The Clarendon Press, 1946.

Hopewell, M.H. and G.G. Kaufman. "Bond Price Volatility and Term to Maturity: A Generalized Respecification." *American Economic Review* 73(1973):749-53.

Kaufman, G.G. "Measuring and Managing Interest Rate Risk: A Primer." *Economic Perspectives*. Federal Reserve Bank of Chicago 8(1984):16-29.

Liebowitz, M.L. "Bond Immunization: A Procedure for Realizing Target Levels of Return." *Financial Markets: Instruments and Concepts*. Memorandum reprinted in John R. Brick, ed. Richmond, Virginia: Robert F. Dame, Inc., 1981, pp. 443-54.

Macauley, F.R. *Some Theoretical Problems Suggested by the Movements of Interest Rates, Bond Yields, and Stock Prices in the United States Since 1865*. New York: National Bureau of Economic Research, 1938.

Malkiel, B. "Expectations, Bond Prices and the Term Structure of Interest Rates." *Quarterly Journal of Economics* 76(1962):197-218.

Martin, J.D., S.H. Cox, and R.D. McMinn. *The Theory of Finance: Evidence and Applications*. New York: The Dryden Press, 1988.

Mitchell, K. "Interest Risk Management at Tenth District Banks." *Economic Review*. Federal Reserve Bank of St. Louis, May 1985, pp. 3-19.

Pindyck, R.S. "Irreversibility, Uncertainty, and Investment." *Journal of Economic Literature* 29(September 1991):1110-48.

Reilly, F.K. and R.S. Sidhu. "The Many Uses of Bond Duration." *Financial Analysts Journal* 36(July/August 1980):58-72.

Yawitz, J.B. "The Relative Importance of Duration and Yield Volatility on Bond Price Volatility." *Journal of Money, Credit, and Banking* 9(February 1977):97-102.

Chapter 14

Transaction Costs and Land Purchase/Sale Decisions

Key words: adjustment flexibility, capital gains taxes, income taxes, investment fixity, land, maximum-bid price model, minimum-sell price model, property taxes, seller-financed land sales, transactions costs, value in use

Introduction

Land is unique among investments and thus warrants special attention in present value (PV) analysis. Two unique characteristics of land are its immobility and durability. Immobility means that land cannot be moved and limits the extent of the land market so that land is infrequently traded. On average, only 2 to 3 percent of the privately-owned farmland in the United States is sold each year. The thinness of the land market is a direct consequence of land's immobility. Durability means the service potential of land changes slowly. Lenders prefer land as collateral for loans because of its durability, and special institutions and programs have developed for financing residential and farm real estate.

The immobility and durability of land also make it a popular object on which to assess taxes. Taxing agencies have easy and indisputable records of the amount of land subject to tax and who owns the land. Thus, most land owners pay property taxes on land and buildings, but pay no similar tax on other more mobile and less durable investments. Consequently, land is one of the few investments on which taxes are based on the value of the investment at the beginning of the period as well as on the earnings of the investment during the period.

Land's durability also suggests it will have low ratios of current to total returns during periods of inflation because it will earn capital gains at a faster rate

Percent change

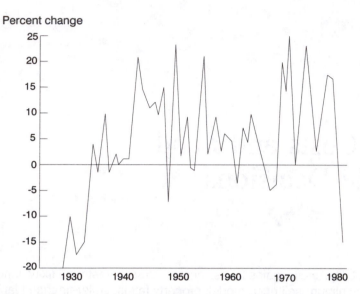

Figure 14.1
Percent Change in Michigan Farmland Prices, 1950 to 1985

Source of Primary Data: U.S. Department of Agriculture, Economic Research Service.

than depreciable investments. The illiquidity of land is also indicated by relatively wide spreads between bid and ask prices of land investors (see Chapter 2). The absolute elasticity values of land with respect to changes in interest rates will also be large relative to elasticities for depreciable durables. Thus, percentage fluctuations in land values may be greater than for other classes of durables. Figure 14.1 illustrates the volatility of land prices in Michigan over the period 1950 to 1985.

The objectives of this chapter are to develop *PV* models to estimate maximum-bid prices, value in use, and minimum-sell prices for land investments and to describe the factors and institutions that contribute to valuation and liquidity of these investments.

Maximum-Bid Prices for Land

This section will build on earlier studies by Alston; Baker; Castle and Hoch; Lee and Rask; and Robison and Burghardt to develop *PV* models that value land based on projected cash flows. These projections include cash flows associated with: (1) land as a productive investment; (2) taxes including income taxes, property taxes, and capital gains taxes; (3) the sale or purchase of the land; and

(4) financing. The goal is to begin with the simplest model and then to add details until the quest for realism is offset by the burden of analytical complexity. The analysis begins with the standard capitalization formula for land under the assumptions of no transaction costs, constant net cash flows R, a discount rate of r, no taxes, and 100 percent financing with equity funds. The initial model is represented in equation (14.1) where V_0 is the PV of the land:

$$V_0 = \frac{R_0}{(1+r)} + \frac{R_0}{(1+r)^2} + \ldots = \frac{R_0}{r}. \tag{14.1}$$

Without transaction costs, V_0 is both the maximum-bid price and the minimum-sell price. Land value V_0 is also the same price for the current owner of the land who will neither sell the existing land nor purchase additional land.

Suppose, next, that the income stream is specified by $R_t = (1+g)^t R_0 = (1+g^*)^t (1+i)^t R_0$. Where g^* is a real growth rate and i is the inflation rate, the value of land to potential buyers and sellers and existing owners is:

$$V_0 = \frac{R_0(1+g)}{(1+r)} + \frac{R_0(1+g)^2}{(1+r)^2} + \ldots = \frac{R_0(1+g)}{r-g}. \tag{14.2}$$

Using equation (14.2), the land value-to-earnings ratio is:

$$\frac{V_0}{R_0} = \frac{(1+g)}{r-g} = \frac{(1+g^*)(1+i)}{(r^*-g^*)(1+i)} = \frac{(1+g^*)}{r^*-g^*}, \tag{14.3a}$$

where r^* is the real interest rate. If g^* is zero, then:

$$\frac{V_0}{R_0} = \frac{1}{r^*}. \tag{14.3b}$$

If in equation (14.3b), r^* were 3, 4, or 5 percent, the ratio of land value-to-earnings would be 33, 25, or 20, respectively. Assuming that equations (14.3a) or (14.3b) accurately describes ratios of land value to rent, the evidence in Table 14.1 suggests that the real interest rate r^* or g^* has fluctuated considerably.

Table 14.1 Land Value-to-Cash Rent Ratios, 1960 to 1992, Selected States[a]

Year	PA	MI	WI	MN	OH	MO	ND	NC	KY	GA	AR
1960	16.6	15.7	11.5	14.1	18.2	13.7	11.2	12.4	12.4	9.3	10.0
1965	21.1	16.6	13.0	13.4	17.8	14.9	11.7	12.5	14.7	9.6	11.8
1970	26.6	18.6	14.5	13.0	18.5	15.8	11.2	17.1	15.5	15.3	16.8
1971	24.6	16.1	14.7	13.3	18.6	20.0	11.2	18.0	12.7	14.0	14.5
1972	27.1	19.8	13.6	13.1	18.1	15.2	11.7	18.5	14.0	16.2	14.0
1973	28.8	19.7	14.6	13.9	19.3	16.4	11.3	20.8	15.0	20.3	14.7
1974	32.9	21.5	14.9	14.0	21.5	15.5	11.4	20.9	16.0	22.9	16.4
1975	39.4	17.9	14.2	13.8	21.5	15.0	12.1	21.5	16.8	21.2	16.4
1976	37.6	18.5	15.0	14.0	21.5	16.4	12.0	19.4	18.2	22.0	18.2
1977	37.4	18.3	14.9	16.0	21.5	15.8	13.0	23.4	14.9	20.3	16.7
1978	38.1	20.2	15.9	17.9	20.0	15.9	13.6	24.4	18.3	19.8	18.7
1979	43.4	22.1	17.8	18.9	24.3	16.8	16.1	22.1	21.3	21.4	21.1
1980	47.4	22.4	19.5	20.5	25.1	17.2	16.6	26.5	20.7	23.2	19.2
1981	41.6	23.6	19.3	21.0	23.8	17.0	16.9	24.4	20.0	22.7	21.8
1982	40.0	23.8	18.9	20.4	21.3	17.2	17.2	25.6	20.0	24.4	23.3
1983	35.7	21.7	19.2	18.2	18.9	15.6	15.9	25.0	20.0	23.8	23.8
1984	37.0	20.4	16.1	16.4	18.5	14.9	15.6	25.0	19.6	23.3	20.8
1985	43.5	19.6	15.4	13.2	16.4	12.5	13.5	27.0	21.3	22.2	*
1986	41.7	18.2	14.9	11.1	15.4	12.2	12.4	29.4	18.2	25.6	20.8
1987	40.0	16.4	14.7	11.0	16.7	13.5	13.0	38.5	16.1	31.3	17.2
1988	40.0	17.9	12.8	11.8	16.4	12.1	12.4	41.7	20.4	28.6	16.7
1989	47.6	16.7	12.8	11.9	16.7	12.2	12.4	40.0	20.0	30.3	17.0
1990	43.5	17.0	12.5	12.8	17.0	11.1	11.4	38.5	18.9	28.6	14.7
1991	52.6	15.2	12.7	13.2	17.0	11.9	12.1	34.5	18.2	26.3	14.5
1992	55.6	16.7	12.4	13.0	19.2	13.7	12.1	34.5	20.0	33.3	14.7

*Insufficient information

[a]Various issues of "Farm Real Estate Market Development," USDA unpublished data.

Maximum-Bid Price Model

To increase realism in the model, variables that distinguish between buyers and sellers are introduced. Two costs that differentiate the maximum-bid price for buyers and the minimum-sell price for sellers are taxes and transactions costs. Let s equal the percentage of the real estate's acquisition price paid to a realtor by the seller. Let c equal the percent of the real estate's acquisition price paid as closing fees including loan closing fees, title examination and registration fees, attorney's costs, and closing points paid by the buyer. Denote V_0^s as the minimum-sell price and V_0^b as the maximum-bid price.

Ignoring taxes and assuming that the land will never be sold again, the expression for V_0^b can be written as:

$$(1+c)\, V_0^b = \frac{R_0(1+g)}{(1+r)} + \frac{R_0(1+g)^2}{(1+r)^2} + \ldots = \frac{R_0(1+g)}{r-g}. \tag{14.4}$$

Expression $(1+c)\, V_0^b$ represents the maximum-bid price, including the effect of closing costs. To isolate the maximum-bid price, we solve for V_0^b:

$$V_0^b = \frac{R_0(1+g)}{(r-g)(1+c)}. \tag{14.5}$$

Example 14.1: Finding the Maximum-Bid Price

What is the maximum-bid price of a parcel of land if the buyer pays 6 percent of the acquisition price as a closing fee? To solve the problem, assume last year's net cash flow was \$22,000 which is expected to grow in perpetuity at 4.5 percent. The buyer's opportunity cost of capital is 12 percent. The maximum-bid price is calculated using equation (14.5):

$$V_0^b = \frac{R_0(1+g)}{(r-g)(1+c)} = \frac{22{,}000(1.045)}{(0.12-0.045)(1.06)} = \$289{,}182.$$

If closing costs as a percentage of the price increase from 6 percent to 9 percent, V_0^b decreases to \$281,223.

Minimum-Sell Price Model

Realtor fees and other closing costs paid by the seller are now introduced into the minimum-sell price model. To build the minimum-sell price model, let s be the percent of the sale price paid to realtors who assisted in the sale and let sV_0^s be subtracted from the seller's proceeds. The result is the minimum-sell model which is written as:

$$(1-s)\ V_0^s = \frac{R_0(1+g)}{(1+r)} + \frac{R_0(1+g)^2}{(1+r)^2} + \dots = \frac{R_0(1+g)}{(r-g)}. \qquad (14.6)$$

Solving for V_0^s, the minimum-sell price is:

$$V_0^s = \frac{R_0(1+g)}{(r-g)(1-s)}. \qquad (14.7)$$

The differences between the maximum-bid price and the minimum-sell price models are best explained by recognizing that the discount rate represents the rate of return from a challenger in the minimum-sell price model and the rate of return for a defender in the maximum-bid price model. In the buyer model, the land to be purchased is the challenging asset. If adopted, it will require the liquidation of other assets or the liquidation of credit reserves to provide the funds to acquire the land. These liquidated funds come from defending investments and their average cost is reflected by the discount rate.

Example 14.2: Finding the Minimum-Sell Price

Letting $s=2$ percent and using the data from Example 14.1, the minimum-sell price is found using equation (14.7):

$$V_0^s = \frac{R(1+g)}{(r-g)(1-s)} = \frac{22,000(1.045)}{(0.12-0.045)(0.98)} = \$312,789.12.$$

Now, suppose s increases from 2 percent to 3 percent. In turn, V_0^s increases to \$316,014. In contrast to the effects of an increase in c that reduced the maximum-bid price, an increase in s increases the minimum-sell price:

$$dV_0^s/ds > 0.$$

The reverse is true in the minimum-sell price model. The defender is the land to be sold. It is described by the potential cash flow streams. The challenger's rate of return is the discount rate because it represents the rate of return the seller expects to earn by investing the proceeds from the sale of land in the challenging investment.

The other important difference between the maximum-bid and minimum-sell price models is the land price. For the seller, it is a return; for the buyer, it is a cost. Any decrease in the price of land is welcomed by the buyer. Any reduction in the price of land is a penalty for the seller. Thus, buyers reduce their maximum-bid prices to compensate for increased transactions costs while sellers increase their minimum sales price to accomplish the same goal.

Land Values and Asset Liquidity

Adjustment Flexibility or Liquidity

Adjustment flexibility or liquidity of an investment is reflected by differences between its acquisition or maximum-bid price and its salvage or minimum-sell price. We now describe why differences between the maximum-bid and the minimum-sell price may exist. We also demonstrate how liquidity may influence the amount and price of durables sold.

For a given maximum-bid price, decreasing the minimum-sell price increases the investment's liquidity. That is, increasing an investment's liquidity makes its trade more likely.

A dollar bill whose maximum-bid price equals its minimum-sell price is perfectly liquid for almost any two potential exchange partners. But for used cars and machinery, agreement over the maximum-bid price and the minimum-sell price is less likely. Hence, they are less liquid than dollar bills.

Adjustment flexibility or liquidity is not a significant consideration in choosing a design unless one expects the investment to be traded in a short time. In the event a trade is anticipated in the short run, firms may purchase or design durables with greater liquidity.

The maximum-bid price of a perfectly liquid durable, such as a dollar bill, equals its salvage price. To describe a durable as liquid means that a ready market exists in which there is general agreement that the maximum-bid price equals or exceeds its minimum-sell price.

For illiquid durables, the minimum-sell price exceeds the durable's maximum-bid price; therefore, the current owner of the durable is not likely to find a willing buyer at a price equal to or above the minimum-sell price. Thus, the durable will not be sold and is described as illiquid or fixed in its current use.

Some of the spread between maximum-bid and minimum-sell prices is due to transactions costs paid by the buyer (seller) and not received by the seller (buyer). Examples of such transactions costs are sales commissions, title documentation, capital gains tax, title and other ownership transfer fees, and loan closing costs.

Differences in opportunity costs between buyers and seller also create transactions costs. For example, a loan tied to the ownership of durables at a below market interest rate may create a wedge between the maximum-bid price and the minimum-sell price. If the loan has a due-on-sale clause, then the seller gives up something of value that is not received by the buyer when the investment is sold. Thus, interest rates may create illiquidity. The relationship between transactions costs and durable liquidity for land investments is treated in detail in this chapter.

Differences in information between buyer and seller may create illiquidity. When two trusted friends exchange a durable, the information costs are insignificant—they freely exchange information. However, when two strangers exchange a durable, the buyer must commit resources to discover the quality of the information provided by the seller. If an investment's service capacity is easily observed, as with certified seed or fertilizer, then the information cost is small and the investment will be more liquid. Durables like used cars or tractors, whose remaining service capacity is not easily observed, will be less liquid. The issuance of a warranty is a signal of higher quality and, thus is an attempt to reduce information costs for the perspective buyer.

A durable's age is often related to the cost of acquiring information about its service capacity. A standard durable, with which many have had experience, tends to have greater liquidity. Once used, however, the uncertainty associated with the intensity of use and care of the durable creates an immediate decline in the value of the durable. On the other hand, a used durable whose service extraction is nearly depleted is more liquid because there is nearly perfect information about the durable's remaining capacity.

The liquidity of durables is also affected by disposal costs. Disposal cost is the cost of removing durables from service to its current owner. Most durables are mobile. Buildings, however, must be disassembled at considerable cost. In some cases, the investment is so valuable that assembly and disassembly are warranted. An example is the "London Bridge." Most durables with high disposal costs become completely illiquid and remain in service to their first owner until destroyed. Often it is easier to transfer the owner rather than the investment itself. Examples of durables with high disposal costs are land and houses.

Liquidity of durables may also be related to changes in the value of the durable. Durables whose values increase with time and use are called appreciating durables. Durables whose values decrease with time and use are called depreciating durables. A durable whose value increases with time and use will be more liquid than one whose value declines with time and use, with all other liquidity attributes held constant. Appreciating durables provide greater security for lenders than depreciating durables because their value and the lender's security are increasing. Finally, liquidity is affected by whether or not time or use determines the durable's service capacity. Durables whose service capacity is determined by time have a fixed pattern of changes in service capacity and cannot adjust to changes in the market. Durables whose change in service capacity is determined by use can adjust to changes in the marketplace. Thus, durables whose service capacity is tied to use are more liquid than those whose service capacity is linked to time.

The liquidity of durables is also influenced by the number of services the durable can provide. Durables become more liquid if the buyer has opportunities for the durable's services that are not available to the seller. A durable is more likely to have multiple uses when it is not fixed geographically. Multiple use is also tied to the acquisition characteristics of the durable. If the durable is lumpy in acquisition, potential buyers must take it or leave it. Durables divisible in acquisition, on the other hand, provide options for prospective buyers. They can buy a gallon or a tankful of gas, or a sack of seeds or a truckful.

Finally, durables whose service extraction rate is fixed, and hence irreversible, are less liquid than durables whose service extraction rate is variable. Variations in service capacity provide greater adjustment potentials, and thus reduce the differences in perceptions between buyers and sellers. Moreover, durables whose service extraction rates vary tend to have multiple use while those with fixed service extraction rates tend to be single-use durables.

Table 14.2 summarizes the liquidity characteristics of durable assets. Durable characteristics described in Table 14.2 are ranked according to their liquidity from low to high.

Transaction Costs

At the beginning of this chapter, it was stated that land is infrequently traded. A reason for this is now given. An investment is fixed (illiquid) if its value in use (V_0) is bounded by its acquisition price (V_0^b) and its salvage price (V_0^s) (Edwards). We can easily show that for individuals with identical expectations of land earnings, land's value in use exceeds its minimum-sale price and is less than its maximum-bid price due to the existence of closing costs and realtor fees.

Compare equations (14.2), (14.5), and (14.7). It should be clear that:

$$V_0^b = \frac{R_0(1+g)}{(r-g)(1+c)} = \frac{V_0}{(1+c)}. \tag{14.8}$$

Then, for $c>0$, $V_0^b<V_0$. Moreover:

$$V_0^s = \frac{R_0(1+g)}{(r-g)(1-s)} = \frac{V_0}{(1-s)}.$$

Then, for $s>0$, $V_0<V_0^s$. Combining these results allows us to express the effects of transactions costs on the maximum-bid, minimum-sell, and value-in-use models:

$$V_0^b < V_0 < V_0^s.$$

Table 14.2 Liquidity Ranking of Durables

Source of Liquidity/ Illiquidity	Liquidity Ranking		
	low	medium	high
1. Transactions costs	high costs		low costs
2. Divisibility	lumpy		divisible
3. Use characteristics	fixed		variable
4. Service potential	single service		many services
5. Changes in capacity	time		use
6. Uniqueness	one of a kind		standardized
7. Information costs	high costs		low costs
8. Durable's age	middle-aged		new or old
9. Location	fixed		movable
10. Number of potential buyers or sellers	few.		many

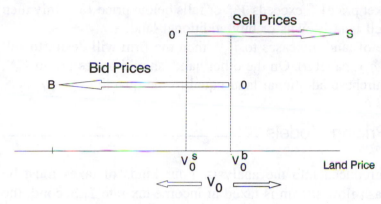

Sell Prices

Bid Prices

Figure 14.2
A Representation of
Conditions that Must
Exist for Land to be
Traded

Land Price

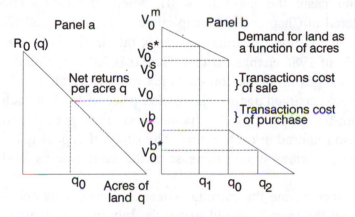

Panel a

Panel b

Demand for land as
a function of acres

Net returns
per acre q

Transactions cost
} of sale

Transactions cost
} of purchase

Acres of
land q

Figure 14.3
The Relationship between
the Firm's Demand for
Land (Panel b) and the
Net Earnings in the Current
Period as a Function of
Acres Owned (Panel a)

For a land sale to occur, land's value must be liquid; that is, $V_0^s \leq V_0^b$. Investment liquidity is represented with Figure 14.2.

Line segment OB represents acceptable bid prices, while V_0^b is the maximum bid. Similarly, line segment $O'S$ represents acceptable sell prices for the seller, while V_0^s is the minimum bid the seller would accept. The intersection region of prices, $V_0^s \leq V_0 \leq V_0^b$, represents acceptable prices for buyer and seller that allow land to be traded. When no intersection exists, land is illiquid.

To graphically show the illiquidity of land, let $R_0 = R_0(q)$ be the firm's net profit function over acres q. Let q_0 be the current acres owned by the decision-maker. This relationship is described in panel *a* of Figure 14.3. The downward sloping nature of the relationship reflects the firm's diminishing marginal productivity for additional acres.

Holding acres q_0, the firm finds the value in use of the last unit of land is V_0. Because of transactions costs, the firm is relatively unresponsive to market changes unless the market price V_0^m exceeds V_0^s or falls below price V_0^b. Only then is the firm willing to sell land it owns or buy additional land.

If the market price of land increases to V_0^{s*}, then the firm will desire to sell a quantity of land $(q_0 - q_1)$ (panel *a*). On the other hand, should prices fall to V_0^{b*}, the firm will want to purchase additional land equal to the quantity $(q_2 - q_0)$.

Taxes and Land Pricing Models

Taxes are now introduced into the analysis. Four kinds of taxes must be considered. First, the cash flow stream is taxed at income tax rate T. Second, the opportunity cost of capital is expressed on an after-tax basis. Because the discount rate may reflect the opportunity cost of capital associated with investments that earn both capital gains and cash, the tax rate is θT where $0 < \theta < 1$. The calculation of θ was considered in Chapter 8. The capital gains tax rate T_g is αT. Historically, the value of α that defines a capital gains tax rate in the U.S. was (0.4), but the Tax Reform Act of 1986 changed α to 1. Here α is left in the model in order to reflect possible changes in the capital gains tax rate in the future.

Property taxes (T_p) are also charged against the market price of land in each period. Thus, the maximum-bid price must be included in each period. An estimate of land values is also required in each period. The study of capital gains in Chapter 7 indicated that land prices should increase at the same rate as land earnings.

Three land models that incorporate the earnings streams, transactions costs, and taxes will be constructed: the maximum-bid price, the minimum-sell price, and the value-in-use models. A land price is determined in each model, assuming *NPV* is zero. Thus, the discount rate in each model must equal the *IRR*. Before specifying cash flow streams and solving the models, an important simplification must be made. The buyer of land in the maximum-bid price model never considers selling. Thus, he or she avoids paying the capital gains tax. The seller in the minimum-sell price model considers selling only once in the current period. Finally, in the value-in-use model, the current owner neither considers selling nor buying and thus avoids all transactions costs.

The Maximum-Bid Price Model

The expanded maximum-bid price model is written as:

$$V_0^b(1+c) = \frac{R_0(1+g)(1-T) - V_0^b T_p(1-T)}{[1+r(1-\theta T)]}$$

(14.9)

$$+ \frac{R_0(1+g)^2(1-T) - V_0^b(1+g) T_p(1-T)}{[1+r(1-\theta T)]^2} + \dots ,$$

where θ defined in Chapter 8 is the tax adjustment coefficient. The cash flow stream contains two geometric series. In both series, the geometric factor b is $(1+g)/[1+r(1-\theta T)]$. The constant in the first series is $R_0(1-T)$. In the second series, the constant is $-V_0^b T_p(1-T)/(1+g)$. Once the constants and the geometric factor b are known, the geometric sum for the series in equation (14.9) can be written as:

$$S_1 = \frac{R_0(1+g)(1-T)}{[1+r(1-\theta T)]} + \frac{R_0(1+g)^2(1-T)}{[1+r(1-\theta T)]^2} + \dots = \frac{R_0(1+g)(1-T)}{r(1-\theta T) - g},$$

and:

$$S_2 = \frac{-V_0^b(1-T)(1+g)}{(1+g)[1+r(1-\theta T)]} + \frac{-V_0^b T_p(1-T)(1+g)^2}{(1+g)[1+r(1-\theta T)]^2} + \dots = \frac{-V_0^b T_p(1-T)}{r(1-\theta T) - g}.$$

Finally, setting $(1+c)V_0^b$ equal to the sum of S_1 and S_2, $(1+c)V_0^b = S_1 + S_2$; and solving for $V_0^b{}_1$, the maximum-bid price of land is:

$$V_0^b = \frac{R_0(1+g)(1-T)}{[r(1-\theta T)-g](1+c) + T_p(1-T)}.$$

(14.10)

Table 14.1 showed the ratio of V_0^b/R_0 and demonstrated that this ratio varied considerably by state. Equation (14.10), illustrated in Example 14.3, demonstrates that the ratio depends critically on the growth rate for future earnings (g), property tax rate (T_p), opportunity cost of capital (r), closing costs (c), income tax rate (T), and the importance of capital gains earned by the investment described by the tax adjustment coefficient (θ). To summarize, the qualitative relationships between the price/earnings ratio and these variables are expressed as follows:

Example 14.3: Maximum-Bid Price with Taxes

An investor is interested in buying a crop farm. According to the financial statements, last year the farm generated a net cash income of $48,000. Past data indicated that net cash returns have been growing at 6 percent per year. The investor's opportunity cost of capital is 11 percent, and closing fees for the transaction are 3 percent. The investor's income tax bracket is 30 percent, the property tax is 2 percent, and $\theta = 0.75$. Using equation (14.10), the maximum-bid price for the farm is:

$$V_0^b = \frac{48,000\,(1.06)\,(1-(0.30))}{\{0.11\,[1 - (0.75)(0.30)] - 0.06\}\,(1.03) + 0.02\,(1-(0.30))}$$

$$= \frac{35,616}{0.0260 + 0.0140} = \$890,400.$$

$$\frac{d(V_0^b / R_0)}{dc} < 0,$$

$$\frac{d(V_0^b / R_0)}{dT_p} < 0,$$

$$\frac{d(V_0^b / R_0)}{dg} > 0,$$

$$\frac{d(V_0^b / R_0)}{dr} < 0,$$

and $\dfrac{d(V_0^b / R_0)}{dT}$ depends on the magnitude of θ.

In Table 14.1, notice the high ratios of $\dfrac{V_0^b}{R_0}$ for New Jersey and Maryland. One explanation is that the expected value for "g" in these states is much higher because of urban and other pressures on land values.

The Minimum-Sell Price Model

The minimum-sell price model is constructed similar to the maximum-bid price model. The exceptions include the following. First, assume the seller originally bought his or her land t periods earlier at a price of V_{-t}^b. Then, if V_{-t}^b is less than (more than) the current selling price of V_0^s, the seller pays (earns) capital gains taxes (credits).

Another difference is the transaction costs. These costs affect taxable capital gains because the capital gains tax is only paid on the net gain from the sale of land. Like the maximum-bid price model, however, the property tax rate is assessed against the inflating maximum-bid price since the market price can never exceed the most a buyer is willing to pay. The minimum-sell price model net of taxes and transaction costs is expressed as:

$$V_0^s(1-s) - [V_0^s(1-s) - V_{-t}^b(1+c)]\alpha T$$

$$= \frac{R_0(1+g)(1-T) - V_0^b T_p(1-T)}{[1+r(1-\theta T)]}$$

$$+ \frac{R_0(1+g)^2(1-T) - V_0^b(1+g) T_p(1-T)}{[1+r(1-\theta T)]^2}$$

$$+ \dots = S_1 + S_2.$$

$$(14.11)$$

The term to the left of the equal sign represents the selling price, V_0^s, adjusted for sales costs and capital gains taxes. The term V_{-t}^b represents the original price paid by the seller t periods earlier. The terms to the right of the equal sign represent the nominal values of the series of projected net cash flows minus the property tax obligation in each period.

Having already solved equation (14.9), it can be recognized that the two geometric series on the right-hand side of equation (14.11) equal S_1 and S_2.

So, $S_1 + S_2$ is replaced by $(1+c)V_0^b$ in equation (14.11) and can be written as:

$$V_0^s(1-s)(1-\alpha T) = (1+c) V_0^b - (1+c) V_{-t}^b \alpha T,$$

and solving for V_0^s:

$$V_0^{\,s} = \frac{\left[V_0^{\,b} - \alpha TV_{-t}^{\,b}\right](1+c)}{(1-s)(1-\alpha T)}.$$ (14.12)

Example 14.4: Calculating Land's Liquidity

ABC Corporation wants to sell a large farm. They want to know the minimum-sell price to accept. *ABC* bought the farm 12 years ago for $600,000, and paid 3 percent closing fees. The financial statements show that last year's pre-tax return was $48,000. Thanks to good technical and managerial practices, the *ABC* returns have grown steadily at a rate equal to 6 percent per year.

Last year, *ABC* paid 30 percent of its pre-tax returns as income tax, 2 percent of their land's market value as a property tax, and used $\theta=0.75$ and $\alpha=0.4$ for similar investments. The funds they can obtain from the sale can be invested in money market securities with a yield of 11 percent. *ABC* estimates that the closing fees are 5 percent. Summarizing the information associated with the possible sale: $R_0=\$48,000$; $V_{-t}^{\,b}=\$600,000$; $c=3$ percent; $g=6$ percent; $T=30$ percent; $T_p=2$ percent; $\theta=0.75$; $\alpha=0.4$; $r=11$ percent; and $s=5$ percent.

Using equation (14.10), $V_0^{\,b}$ is:

$$V_0^{\,b} = \frac{(\$48,000)(1.06)(.7)}{\{(.11)\,[1-(.3)(.75)]\,-\,.06\}\,(1.03)\,+\,(.02)(.7)}$$

$$= \$890,400.$$

Then, using equation (14.12), $V_0^{\,s}$ is:

$$V_0^{\,s} = \frac{[\$890,400\,-\,(.4)(.3)(\$600,000)]\,(1.03)}{(.95)[1-(.4)(.3)]}$$

$$= \$1,008,316.$$

Recall that $V_0^{\,s}$ is the smallest price acceptable to the seller. A change in a variable on the right-hand side of equation (14.12) that increases $V_0^{\,s}$ implies the seller requires increased compensation to sell.

Useful comparative static results include:

$$\frac{dV_0^{\,s}}{dR_0} > 0, \quad \frac{dV_0^{\,s}}{ds} > 0, \quad \frac{dV_0^{\,s}}{dV_{-t}^{\,b}} < 0, \quad \frac{dV_0^{\,s}}{dT_p} < 0,$$

$$\frac{dV_0^{\,s}}{dT} \quad \text{depends on } \theta, \quad \frac{dV_0^{\,s}}{d\alpha} \quad \text{depends on } V_{-t}^{\,b},$$

$$\frac{dV_0^{\,s}}{dg} > 0, \quad \frac{dV_0^{\,s}}{dr} < 0, \quad \frac{dV_0^{\,s}}{dc} < 0, \text{ and } \quad \frac{dV_0^{\,s}}{d\theta} < 0.$$

To summarize, variables that increase selling costs and capital gains taxes increase the minimum-sell price. Variables that increase the rate of return on the land relative to the rate of return on the challenger also increase the minimum-sell price. An increase in α, (depending on $V_{-t}^{\,b}$), and a decrease in c all reduce the net selling price and force the minimum-sell price to increase. Meanwhile, an increase in R_0 and g, a decrease in T_p, or an increase in θ all increase the returns from land relative to $r(1-\theta T)$, and thus increase $V_0^{\,s}$.

The Land-in-Use Model

Land is considered a fixed investment if its value-in-use is bounded by its maximum-bid and minimum-sell prices. Knowing the difference between value-in-use and land's maximum-bid and minimum-sell prices helps to measure the liquidity of land. Thus, a measure of land's liquidity requires us to calculate not only maximum-bid and minimum-sell prices, but also value-in-use.

The value-in-use model asks: What is the value of land to an owner who is not motivated to buy more land or sell off land now owned? Because land is not sold in this model, no capital gains tax is paid. Nor are transaction costs considered. It is the simplest of the three models. The model can be written as:

Example 14.5: Value of Land in Use

Assuming the same data used in Example 14.4 and using equation (14.14), find the value of land-in-use for *ABC* Corporation. Making the appropriate substitutions:

$$V_0 = \frac{48,000\,(1-(.3))\,(1.06)}{\{[.11(1-(.75)(.3))] - .06\} + .02(1-(.3))}$$

$$= \$907,414.$$

$$V_0 = \frac{R_0(1-T)(1+g) - V_0^b T_p(1-T)}{[1+r(1-\theta T)]}$$

$$+ \frac{R_0(1-T)(1+g)^2 - V_0^b(1+g)T_p(1-T)}{[1+r(1-\theta T)]^2} + \dots \qquad (14.13)$$

$$= S_1 + S_2 = \frac{R_0(1-T)(1+g)}{[r(1-\theta T)-g] + T_p(1-T)}.$$

Because $(1+c)V_0^b = S_1 + S_2$, then V_0 can be expressed as:

$$V_0 = (1+c)\,V_0^b. \qquad (14.14)$$

Because the comparative static analyses of the variables in equation (14.12) (except for c) are the same as those in the model describing V_0^b, they are not repeated here.

In summary, then, the three examples indicate that the maximum-bid price is $890,400 and the minimum-sell price is $1,008,316, yielding a bid-ask spread of $117,916. The value-in-use is $907,414, indicating for the examples used here that no land transaction would occur.

Any changes that affect transactions costs of buying and selling land (including changes in tax laws) will affect land's liquidity. For example, consider the difference between V_0^s and V_0^b. This difference can be expressed as:

$$V_0^s - V_0^b = \frac{\left[V_0 - \alpha\, TV_{-t}^b\right](1+c)}{(1-s)(1-\alpha T)} - \frac{V_0}{(1+c)}. \qquad (14.15)$$

Example 14.6: Increasing the Capital Gains Tax Rate

Recent tax laws (Tax Reform Act of 1986 (*TRA*)) increased α from 0.4 to 1. To see the effect on the liquidity of land, we compute the derivative for the change in bid-ask spread relative to a change in α:

$$\frac{d\left[V_0^s - V_0^b\right]}{d\alpha} = \left[V_0^b - V_{-t}^b\right]\left[\frac{T(1+c)}{(1-s)(1-\alpha T)^2}\right] \gtrless 0, \text{ if } V_0^b \gtrless V_{-t}^b.$$

Note that $\dfrac{d\left[V_0^s - V_0^b\right]}{d\alpha} < 0$ implies an increase in both the liquidity of land and in the number of farmland sales. Because $V_0^b < V_{-t}^b$ was true following the *TRA* of 1986, an increase in the number of acres of land transfers was expected. In Minnesota, land sales increased from 113,714 acres in 1985 to 150,696 acres in 1986 and 206,995 acres in 1987 (Schwab and Raup). Other factors, of course, could have influenced the increase in acres sold.

If s or c is increased, transaction costs are increased and liquidity falls as:

$$\frac{d(V_0^s - V_0^b)}{dc} = \frac{V_0}{(1-s)(1-\alpha T)} + \frac{V_0}{(1+c)^2} > 0,$$

and:

$$\frac{d(V_0^s - V_0^b)}{ds} = \frac{[V_0 - \alpha T V_{-t}^b](1+c)}{(1-s)^2(1-\alpha t)} > 0.$$

Seller Financing

As discussed in the introduction, the characteristics of land make it ideally suited for use as security for loans. This advantage, plus the opportunity to negotiate interest rates on loans offered by sellers and the exchange price, make seller financing an important part of the land market. The advantages of seller financing for both buyer and seller are now considered.

Under the current tax laws, a land buyer may not deduct the price paid for real estate from his or her taxable income. Improvements on real estate, such as fences, buildings, and drainage tile, are tax deductible through depreciation charges. Similarly, interest paid on loans is fully tax deductible. From the buyer's perspective, taxes can be reduced if the land could be purchased at a low price in exchange for an above-market interest rate. On the other hand, before the capital gains rate was increased to the ordinary income tax rate, the seller would have preferred to lower interest income by offering a below-market interest rate while offering an increased land sale price. Interest income is fully taxable, while a portion of capital gains was sheltered from taxation. Which of these arrangements would have occurred before the *TRA* depended on the amount of capital gains or losses and the relative income tax positions of the buyer and seller?

Seller financing also allows the seller to spread the payment of capital gains taxes over time because capital gains taxes are only paid in proportion to the amount of principal payments received each period. On the other hand, seller financing also delays the receipt of any tax savings that result from capital losses on the sale of the land because the tax savings are also received in proportion to the amount of principal received each period. Thus, seller financing becomes relatively more (less) desirable if capital gains (losses) are incurred by the sale of the land. The potential benefits from deferring capital gains depend upon the progressivity of the income tax rates and on earnings rates from reinvesting the payments as they are received. The higher the reinvestment rates and the lower the progressivity of tax rates, the lower the benefit will be in *PV* terms of deferring capital gains. Thus, the substantial reduction in progressivity of tax rates in 1985 and elimination of the capital gains tax shelter substantially diminished the tax advantages of deferring capital gains.

Buyer's Perspective

For simplicity, suppose the borrower must repay only interest expenses plus make a down payment. While this is an abstraction, if the growth in land values (g) is positive, the abstraction approaches reality. If $g>0$, the ratio of amount loaned to the current value of land decreases over time because V_t^b increases at a rate of g percent. Thus, the real balance of the investment financed decreases even though no principal payments are made.

Assume that the buyer pays D percent of the purchase price as a down payment and finances the remaining amount through the seller. If $(1-D)V_0^{bf}$ is financed at r^f percent, the *PV* of the interest payments, $PV\left[(1-D)V_0^{bf}\right]$, equals:

$$PV\left[(1-D)\,V_0^{bf}\right] = \frac{r^f(1-T)\,V_0^{bf}(1-D)}{(1+r(1-\theta T))} + \frac{r^f(1-T)\,V_0^{bf}(1-D)}{(1+r(1-\theta T))^2} + \cdots$$

$$= \frac{r^f(1-T)\,V_0^{bf}(1-D)}{r(1-\theta T)}.$$

(14.16)

Clearly, neither the buyer nor the seller will agree to a seller-financed land purchase unless they are at least as well off as without it. If $r^f(1-T) < r(1-\theta T)$, then the *PV* of the loan will be less than the loan value. To offset this, the land's sale price with financing, V_0^{bf}, must be greater than without financing, V_0^b. On the other hand, the buyer will agree because on an after-tax *PV* basis he or she pays less than the sale price, V_0^{bf}.

The maximum amount the buyer will pay is found by setting the value of the seller-financed sale equal to the discounted value of the land's cash flows:

$$V_0^{bf}(D+c) + \frac{(1-D)\,V_0^{bf}\,r^f(1-T)}{r(1-\theta T)} = V_0^b(1+c).$$

(14.17)

Then, solving for V_0^{bf}:

$$V_0^{bf} = \frac{V_0^b(1+c)\,r(1-\theta T)}{(D+c)\,r(1-\theta T) + (1-D)\,r^f(1-T)}.$$

(14.18)

Example 14.7: Maximum-Bid Price and Financing

Assume Al B. Broke has calculated that the maximum-bid price per acre of land he intends to purchase is $1,000. For Al, $r=13$ percent, $c=4$ percent, $\theta=1$, and $T=32$ percent. The seller of the land, Hav I. Gotadeal, offered Al a loan requiring 20 percent down payment at $r^f=9$ percent for a price of $1,200. Should Al accept? To respond to Hav, Al calculates V_0^{bf} using equation (14.18). It equals:

$$V_0^{bf} = \frac{(1000)(1.04)(0.13)(0.68)}{(0.24)(0.13)(0.68) + (0.8)(0.09)(0.68)} = \$1,310,$$

and Al concludes he should accept Hav's offer.

Clearly, if $D=1$, or $r^f(1-T) = r(1-\theta T)$, V_0^{bf} in equation (14.17) reduces to V_0^b. It should also be clear that V_0^{bf} and r^f in equation (14.17) are inversely related.

Seller's Perspective

The seller's goals may be consistent with those of the buyer if between them they can adjust financing and the exchange price to minimize the *PV* of tax payments. If this is possible, both will benefit. However, the tax-reducing incentives for the buyer and seller do not always occur in the same direction. Moreover, recent changes in the tax laws have altered the potential for tax reduction.

Specifically, consider a seller when the capital gains tax rate was less than the income tax rate (i.e., $0<\alpha<1$). For the land seller who finances the buyer, all interest received is taxed at the income tax rate T.

To find the trade-off acceptable to the seller between r^f and V_0^{sf}, the seller-financed land price, the net after-tax *PV* of the buyer's interest payments to the seller must be included. To analyze this relationship between V_0^{sf} and r^f for the seller, assume the seller requires a down payment of D percent, and thus, the loan offered to the buyer is $(1-D)V_0^{sf}$.

To calculate the seller's minimum-sell price when offering to finance the buyer, all of the assumptions and notations employed in the buyer model are used. Let V_0^{sf} be the minimum-sell price. Assume sV_0^{sf} is the seller's closing fees. Since D percent is paid as a down payment, only $D\left[V_0^{sf}(1-s) - V_{(-t)}(1+c)\right]$ is subject to the capital gains tax at the rate of αT. Finally, assume that $(1-D)V_0^s$ earns interest in perpetuity for the seller. Thus, his or her *PV* of the interest income equals:

$$\frac{(1-D)\,V_0^{sf}\,r^f(1-T)}{r(1-\theta T)}.$$

The seller-financed minimum-sell price can be expressed as:

$$-sV_0^{sf} - D\left[V_0^{sf}(1-s) - V_{-t}^b(1+c)\right]\alpha T + DV_0^{sf}$$

$$+\frac{(1-D)\,V_0^{sf}\,r^f(1-T)}{r(1-\theta T)} = S_1 + S_2 = V_0^b(1+c). \tag{14.19}$$

Then, solving for V_0^{sf}, we obtain:

$$V_0^{sf} = \frac{\left[V_0^b - V_{-t}^b\alpha TD\right](1+c)\,r(1-\theta T)}{r(1-\theta T)[(D-s) - D(1-s)\alpha T] + (1-D)r^f(1-T)}. \tag{14.20}$$

Example 14.8: Minimum-Sell Prices and Financing

Mr. Gotadeal, introduced in Example 14.7, wonders if his minimum sale price of $1,200 is consistent with *PV* principles. Fortunately, his accountant, Adam Up is trained in *PV* analysis. Using equation (14.20) and setting $\alpha=1$, $s=3$ percent, and $V_{-t}^{b}=\$600$, he finds V_0^{sf} equal to:

$$V_0^{sf} = \frac{[1,000-(600)(0.32)(0.2)]\,(1.04)(0.13)(0.68)}{(0.13)(0.68)[(0.2-0.03)-0.2(0.97)(0.32)] + (0.8)(0.09)(0.68)}$$

$$= \$1,511.$$

Clearly, based on the calculations of his accountant, Mr. Gotadeal should hope his offer to sell the land for $1,200 is refused since he has agreed to sell for less than V_0^{sf}, and hence will earn a return less than his opportunity cost of capital.

An Application

Table 14.3 reports average prices of farmland sold from 1980 to 1990 by region. In most areas, capital losses occurred following 1982. Should these price trends have affected the percentage of land transferred financed by sellers?

To find the answer, equations (14.10), (14.12), (14.18), and (14.20) are used to calculate the effects of reduced capital gains and capital gains taxes:

$$\frac{d\left(V_0^s - V_0^b\right)}{dV_{-t}^b} = \frac{-\alpha T(1+c)}{(1-s)(1-\alpha T)} < 0, \tag{14.21}$$

$$\frac{d\left(V_0^{sf} - V_0^{bf}\right)}{dV_{-t}^b} = \frac{-\alpha TD(1+c)}{(1-s)(1-D\alpha T)} < 0, \tag{14.22}$$

and:

$$\left|\frac{d\left(V_0^s - V_0^b\right)}{dV_{-t}^b}\right| > \left|\frac{d\left(V_0^{sf} - V_0^{bf}\right)}{dV_{-t}^b}\right|. \tag{14.23}$$

Table 14.3 Average Price Per Acre of Farmland Transferred from 1980 to 1990 by Region

Region	Year										
	1980	1981	1982	1983	1984	1985	1986	1987	1988	1989	1990
	Dollars Per Acre										
Corn Belt	1890	2006	1819	1468	1459	1187	944	870	955	1088	1097
Lake States	1217	1257	1329	1201	1119	945	806	666	644	744	800
North Plains	529	565	536	505	525	408	265	265	260	294	323
South Plains	592	581	528	678	647	598	792	448	321	379	324
48 States	856	886	919	858	888	747	725	607	566	639	654

Source: "Agricultural Resources: Agricultural Land Values and Markets, Situation and Outlook Report," USDA, ERS, AR-10, June 1988 and June 1990.

Table 14.4 Percentage of Credit Volume Extended by Sellers for Farmland Transfers from 1980 to 1990 by Region

Region	Year										
	1980	1981	1982	1983	1984	1985	1986	1987	1988	1989	1990
	Percent										
Corn Belt	34	38	37	37	32	27	30	20	17	20	21
Lake States	55	59	60	44	44	49	53	41	39	38	33
North Plains	41	44	35	32	27	25	49	24	19	24	31
South Plains	30	43	43	31	23	24	30	15	14	27	35
48 States	38	40	41	33	28	33	32	30	24	24	28

Source: "Agricultural Resources: Agricultural Land Values and Markets, Situation and Outlook Report," USDA, ERS, AR-10, June 1987 and June 1990.

To interpret equations (14.21), (14.22), and (14.23), consider the following. When transactions costs paid by the seller to someone other than the buyer (such as the government) are reduced, the likelihood of the maximum-bid price being greater than the minimum-sell price increases. Increasing V_{-t}^b in equations (14.21) and (14.22) reduces capital gains (and therefore, capital gains taxes), and thus increases the likelihood of a land sale. If there are capital losses as occurred during the 1980's, tax savings are only available when the land is sold. This effect further increases the liquidity of land. But when seller financing is involved, tax savings associated with capital losses apply only to principal portions of the seller-financed loan payments and the downpayment. Thus, seller financing reduces the tax savings created by capital losses (see equation (14.23)). Consequently, sellers will be reluctant to offer seller financed loans during periods of capital losses. If $D=0$, no change in liquidity occurs as a result of an increase in V_{-t}^b.

As Table 14.4 demonstrates, corresponding to declines in land prices, the portion of financing supplied by sellers declined from its peak in 1982 in all parts of the country.

Summary

This chapter has reviewed land value models and demonstrated the effects of transactions costs on buyers, sellers, and those who intend to continue ownership and use. Adding taxes showed how tax obligations could be minimized if sellers and buyers cooperated in arranging the terms for sale and finance.

Many more specifications could be added to the land models. For example, income from land was independent of the quantity of land held by one owner. Income could be represented as a function of production and other investment decisions. Or land could be resold every n periods making the holding period an important variable. Or, multiple sources of income from the land—increasing or decreasing at different rates—could be considered. Some of these problems are left for the reader to address in the problem set at the end of this chapter.

Review Questions

1. What characteristics of land make it especially useful as collateral for loans?

2. Explain why land prices may fluctuate more than prices of other shorter lived durables.

3. Explain why a land seller and land buyer are unlikely to find an acceptable exchange price if they both have the same earnings expectations.

4. Define: investment fixity or investment liquidity. How do transactions costs affect investment liquidity?

5. Describe the various taxes affecting the bid, sell, and use values of land. How do these taxes affect land's liquidity?

6. Give several explanations for the different price/earnings ratios for land in the several states reported in Table 14.1.

7. How does the direction of land prices (capital gains or capital losses) affect the liquidity of land?

8. What incentives exist for sellers financing the buyer's purchase?

9. How do land price trends influence the incentive for seller financing?

10. What other features besides those described in this chapter could be added to the land models to increase the realism of the models?

Application Questions

1. Under what conditions will a buyer's maximum-bid price exceed a seller's minimum-sell price?

2. Compare and interpret the discount rates in a maximum-bid price model and a minimum-sell price model.

3. Explain how increasing the frequency of land sales affects the maximum-bid price of land. Prove your results using a *PV* model. To simplify the analysis, you may ignore taxes and assume $s=0$.

4. Assume that $g=i$ so that $V_0/R_0=1/r^*$. Calculate the implied values for r_t^* in Table 14.1 for PA and OH. Compare the implied real rate with ex post real rates. Use the r_t^* values of your choice obtained from any acceptable reporting source.

5. Why do increased closing costs for the buyer reduce the buyer's maximum-bid price while increasing closing costs for the seller increase the seller's minimum-sell price? (See Examples 14.1 and 14.2.)

6. Find the maximum-bid price of a parcel of land if the buyer pays 4 percent of the acquisition price as a closing fee, net cash flow from the land is expected to grow at 3 percent and last year's net cash flow was $15,000. Finally, assume the buyer's opportunity cost of capital is 10.5 percent. (For this question, you may ignore the effect of taxes.)

7. Find the minimum-sell price of the parcel of land described in the earlier question if the seller is required to pay 3 percent of the sale price to a realtor. Describe the effects on the minimum sale price if the realtor's fee increases to 4 percent. (For this question, you may ignore the effect of taxes.)

8. Find tax-adjusted maximum-bid prices and minimum-sell prices using data contained in questions (6) and (7) and the following tax related data. Let $V_{-t}^{b}=\$8,000$, $T=32$ percent, $T_{p}=2$ percent, $\theta=0.8$, and $\alpha=0.4$.

9. For Example 14.7, calculate the values of V_{0}^{bf} for alternative values of $r^{f}=7$, 10, and 12 percent. Explain the relationship between V_{0}^{bf} and r^{f}.

10. Suppose a land seller has a loan, L_{0}, at a concessionary interest rate of $r^{f}<r$ where r is the firm's opportunity cost of capital and the rate at which the net proceeds of the land sale can be reinvested. Also suppose that the loan has a clause that requires it be paid in full if the current owner sells the land. If last period's net cash returns from the seller's land, R_{0}, were expected to grow in perpetuity at rate g; if the firm's income tax rate, property and capital gains rates were T, T_{p}, and T_{g}, respectively; and, if $r(1-\theta T)$ is the after-tax discount rate and V_{-t}^{b} was the acquisition price, find the minimum-sell price.

    What happens to the minimum-sell price as L_{0} increases? How is land liquidity affected by the seller's holding concessionary interest rate loans with due on sale clauses? (For simplicity, assume that the loan requires only interest payments of $r^{f}L_{0}$ and can be held in perpetuity.)

11. Solve for θ in equation (14.10) subject to the constraint that the before-tax *IRR* must satisfy the expression:

$$V_{0}^{b} = \frac{R_{0}(1+g)}{(r-g)(1+c)}.$$

Then, show how much θ increased as a result of property taxes.

References

Alston, J.M. "An Analysis of Growth of U.S. Farmland Prices, 1963-82." *American Journal of Agricultural Economics* 68(1986):1-9.

Baker, T.G. "An Income Capitalization Model of Land Values with Income Tax Considerations." *Journal Paper No. 47907*. Purdue Agricultural Experiment Station, June 1981.

Castle, E.N. and I. Hoch. "Farm Real Estate Price Components, 1920-78." *American Journal of Agricultural Economics* 64(1982):8-18.

Edwards, C. "Resource Fixity and Farm Organization." *Journal of Farm Economics* 41(1959):747-59.

Lee, W.F. and N. Rask. "Inflation and Crop Profitability: How Much Can Farmers Pay for Land?" *American Journal of Agricultural Economics* 58(1976):984-90.

Robison, L.J. and W.G. Burghardt. "Five Principles for Building Present Value Models and Their Application to Maximum (Minimum) Bid (Sell) Price Models for Land." *Michigan Agricultural Experiment Station Journal Article No. 11051*, November 1983.

_____, S.D. Hanson, and D.A. Lins. "A Present Value Analysis of Land Transactions and the Proportion of Seller Financing." *Agricultural Finance Review* 50(1990):26-34.

_____, D.A. Lins, and R. Venkataraman. "Cash Rents and Land Values in U.S. Agriculture." *American Journal of Agricultural Economics* 67(1985):794-805.

Schwab, A. and P.M. Raup. "The Minnesota Rural Real Estate Market in 1987: With an Analysis of Three Decades of Land Price Changes." *Economic Report ER 88-7*. University of Minnesota, September 1988.

U.S. Department of Agriculture. *Agricultural Resource*. ERS, RA-6, July 1987.

_____. *Agricultural Resource*. ERS, AR-10, June 1988.

_____. *Farm Real Estate Market Development*. Washington, D.C., various issues.

Chapter 15

Farm Management Applications
by Mark Krause[1]

Key words: alternatives to ownership, custom hiring, limited information, private management consultants, replacement rules, simplified present value models, tax depreciation, tax shields, taxes, uncertain remaining values, uncertain repair costs

Introduction

U.S. farmers usually manage large investments in farmland, farm buildings and storage structures, and farm machinery. Many U.S. farmers also manage large investments in breeding livestock, dairy cows, and perennial crops. For example, on January 1, 1989, the average U.S. cash grain farm managed land and buildings valued at $234,621 and farm equipment valued at $72,657 to obtain a net farm income of $20,641 (Morehart, Johnson and Banker). The average U.S. dairy farm managed land and buildings valued at $283,186, farm equipment valued at $69,438, and a livestock inventory valued at $87,564 to obtain a net farm income of $28,765 (Morehart, Johnson, and Banker). These asset values are net of depreciation, but they indicate the importance of durable investments. Deciding whether to invest in a production durable, when to replace a production durable, and choosing between alternative durables each involve present value (*PV*) analysis. Another important application of *PV* analysis is to determine annual costs of durables for use in budgets.

---

[1]Mark Krause is an Assistant Professor in the Department of Agricultural Economics at North Dakota State University.

Unfortunately, few farmers have been trained in *PV* analysis. *PV* analysis is taught in agricultural finance and farm management classes at land grant universities, but many farmers have not attended college. The recent availability of low-cost personal computers has also made *PV* analysis more accessible to farmers. However, many farmers have not yet purchased computers. Hence, while large commercial farm operations are often managed by farmers who use *PV* analysis, many more farmers are unable or unwilling to use it.

As a result, *PV* analyses of farm management problems are usually done by extension specialists, private management consultants, or professional farm managers and land appraisers.[1] This situation raises two problems. First, *PV* analysis is limited by the type and amount of information a farmer is willing or able to provide, and by the time in which the farmer expects an answer to his or her investment or replacement question. A farmer may withhold information because it is none of the analyst's business, or because of poor bookkeeping. A farmer may also expect an immediate answer and be unwilling to wait for a *PV* analysis that considers all of the principles in Chapter 4. The second problem is that the analysis must be understandable to the farmer; the farmer takes the risks and responsibility for the outcome, not the consultant or extension specialist. These two problems result in slippage between the theory of *PV* analysis and its typical application to farm management.

Farm management specialists often conclude that *PV* analysis is too difficult for most farmers to understand and instead, have used rules of thumb or other simple approaches. One rule of thumb, found in almost every farm management textbook, is the DIRTI 5 rule that annual depreciation, interest, repair, tax, and insurance costs total about 20 percent of a farm machine's original value. Another traditional budgeting technique is to calculate depreciation and opportunity cost based on the mid-life value of the machine (Watts and Helmers). A simple budgeting technique, which uses some *PV* concepts, is to calculate a capital recovery charge based on the difference between the initial cost and salvage value, with an interest charge added to the salvage value (Boehlje and Eidman). The payback and average rate of return methods for comparing investments (Chapter 2) are other examples of simple analyses.

This chapter illustrates how *PV* analysis can be applied to farm management decisions, with and without simplifications. The chapter also discusses the difficulties in forecasting future cash flows and errors introduced by the simplified approaches.

Farm Management Defined

In general, farm management consists of making and implementing the financial, production, and marketing decisions that generate farm income, plus monitoring the farm business, new technologies, and relevant markets to identify problems and new opportunities. Although there are many different types of farm organizations, usually the same person (or persons in a partnership) owns, operates, and manages the farm (Luening and Jones). Because operating farm machinery and caring for livestock require skill and judgment, it is difficult to separate management from the operator's labor (Milligan and Stanton). However, many of the most important management decisions clearly transcend day-to-day farm operation. Such management decisions may be called "strategic planning" (White); they include choosing what to produce, allocating acreage among different enterprises, hiring and firing laborers, and setting marketing plans.

Strategic planning also includes investment, replacement, and financing decisions. Furthermore, strategic planning includes whole-farm budget analysis, for which estimates of annual costs for production durables are needed. *PV* analysis is applied to the strategic planning part of farm management.

Investment in Production Durables

In addition to the different production durables that a farmer may purchase, at least three kinds of financial decisions should be considered. These decisions include: (1) whether to purchase a production durable or rely on variable input substitutes; (2) choosing between alternative durables; and (3) choosing between alternative financing plans. These three kinds of financial decisions are discussed here in relation to farm machinery.

For each of these financial decisions, tax shields in the years following the purchase and opportunities to spread payments over a period of years are important in determining the most profitable choice. (The farmer's primary goal is to maximize the *PV* of profits.) The magnitude of these tax shields is one of the primary reasons for using *PV* analysis, because neither the rules of thumb nor traditional budgeting methods take the tax shields into account. Most rules of thumb and simple budgeting methods also do not effectively handle the time patterns of cash flows.

There often are several alternatives to purchasing farm machinery. Most machinery can be leased for one or more years, rented for short periods, or custom hired. Non-durable substitutes for farm machinery are also possible. For example, chemical herbicides often can substitute for tillage implements. Labor is still an effective substitute for some machinery in some situations. For example, the hay baling equipment that forms large rectangular bales or round bales and automatic stacking equipment for small rectangular bales are nearly essential for large hay enterprises; however, labor-intensive handling systems are still competitive for small hay enterprises. Similarly, some of the services provided by a front-end loader on a tractor can be provided by laborers with a pickup truck. Recently, farmers have been encouraged to buy computers for record-keeping and automated feed rationing systems, both of which are substitutes for labor.

The choice between buying farm machinery or substituting a variable input generally involves a comparison of their annual costs.[2] In order to maximize profits, machinery should only be purchased if its annual cost is less than the annual cost of variable input substitutes. *PV* analysis is the preferred technique for estimating the annual cost of ownership.

Application of *PV* analysis to machinery investments is straight forward. First, all of the cash flows associated with ownership should be listed in a table with a description and the timing of each cash flow in relation to the present. An immediate payment has a timing of 0 and a payment a year from the present has a timing of 1. The list of cash flows must include each loan repayment, including principal and interest, if the purchase is financed, each tax deduction or tax credit that results from the purchase, and any salvage or trade-in value. If another machine is traded in at the time of purchase, then the investment is either a replacement model discussed below, or the liquidation of an unrelated durable asset.

Any other cash flows that would not occur if the machinery is not purchased should also be included in the list, following the *Total Costs and Returns Principle* of Chapter 4. For example, if a storage shed must be built or modified for the new machinery, its cash cost and subsequent tax depreciation deductions should be included. However, costs that are approximately constant each year, such as insurance, property taxes, and operating costs, can be considered later.

The second step is to determine *PV* discount factors for each cash flow. Third, the discount factors are multiplied by the corresponding cash flows to determine the *PV* of each cash flow. The *PV* of the investment is the sum of the *PV* of all cash flows. Finally, the *PV* is multiplied by an annuity factor to convert it to an annual equivalent value. If constant annual costs associated with ownership were previously omitted from the analysis, they would be added to the annual equivalent value at this point. The result is the annual cost of owning the machinery which may be compared to the annual cost of variable input substitutes.

An illustration of these concepts and procedures for a combine investment is provided in Example 15.1 and in the accompanying Table 15.1.

The importance of considering all cash flows related to the combine purchase is seen by comparing the capital recovery charge, which ignores tax shields, to the annual cost calculated in Table 15.1. The annual capital recovery charge formula (Boehlje and Eidman, p. 143) is:

Annual Capital Recovery Charge =

$$\left[\left(\begin{array}{c}\text{Purchase } \text{Salvage} \\ \text{Price - Value}\end{array}\right) \text{x} \left(\begin{array}{c}\text{Capital} \\ \text{Recovery}\end{array}\right)\right] + \left[\left(\begin{array}{c}\text{Salvage} \\ \text{Value}\end{array}\right) \text{x} \left(\begin{array}{c}\text{Interest} \\ \text{Rate}\end{array}\right)\right]$$

Using the same real, after-tax discount rate of 4 percent, the capital recovery factor equals 0.1233. This value is the same as the factor Willie used to convert the *PV* of all cash flows to an annual equivalent value after taxes. Plugging in the purchase price, salvage value, and interest rate (the discount rate of 4 percent), the annual capital recovery charge is $6,993.06 + $931.20 = $7,924.26. In order to make this value comparable to the annual cost estimated using *PV* analysis (Table 15.1), the annual equivalent value of repair costs, which equal $533.75, must be added. After adding the same $2,010 operating cost and dividing by 600 acres, the annual capital recovery charge provides an estimated annual cost of $17.45 per acre. The capital recovery charge is 4 percent higher than the before-tax annual cost estimated using *PV* analysis because it implies the use of straight-line tax depreciation. In contrast, the *PV* method is able to consider accelerated depreciation rules. The *PV* method can also consider the effect of repair costs that increase over the life of the combine.

Now suppose Willie finds a suitable used combine and wants to know whether the used combine or the new combine is a better investment. The four-year-old, used combine costs $48,000, but has higher expected repair costs and fuel costs. Because the combine is already four years old and because Willie hates breakdowns, he would keep the combine only the eight years required to receive the full benefit of tax depreciation before selling for an estimated $24,634 (Bowers). Calculating the annual cost for purchasing the used combine (Table 15.2) and comparing it to the annual cost of a new combine

Example 15.1: Purchase versus Custom Hiring

A common example of an investment problem is the choice between purchasing a combine for wheat harvest or hiring a custom combining operator to harvest wheat each year. In the Great Plains, custom combine operators are readily available, so it is feasible to avoid purchasing a combine. Suppose Willie the Wheat Grower has 600 acres of wheat to harvest each year, and the standard custom-hire rate for combining wheat is $14.00 per acre.

For simplicity, we will ignore the cost of purchasing and repairing a truck to haul the grain. Average fuel and labor costs for the truck are included because the custom operator hauls the harvested wheat to Willie's farm. After shopping around, Willie finds no acceptable used combines but he can buy a new combine for $80,000 (list price $100,000). Willie has just received a large deficiency payment from the government, so he can pay cash for the combine or invest the money in Treasury bonds for an annual yield of 8.4 percent. Because he is in the 15 percent marginal tax bracket, his after-tax yield is 7.14 percent. Willie figures that price inflation will average 3 percent for the next several years, so the discount rate that reflects his real, after-tax opportunity cost is 4 percent $((1.0714/1.03) - 1 = 0.04)$.

The list of cash flows for Willie's problem (Table 15.1) includes the single purchase payment at time 0, estimated repair costs for each year, depreciation tax shields for years one to eight, and an expected salvage value 10 years from the present of $29,100 (Bowers). Each cash flow must be a real, inflation-adjusted value in order to maintain consistency with the inflation-adjusted discount rate. Often, no inflation adjustment is needed because available estimates for these cash flows are current values at the time the decision is made rather than projected future values. However, any projected nominal values of cash flows must be adjusted for inflation in order to maintain consistency. The depreciation shields are calculated as 15 percent of the Modified Accelerated Cost Recovery System (MACRS) annual depreciation percentages that apply to farm machinery placed into service in 1991 (*IRS Farmer's Tax Guide*), multiplied by the initial cost and converted to real values.

Many estimates of the annual cost of machinery ownership only consider an average real repair cost, even though real repair costs

Example 15.1, Cont'd.: Purchase versus Custom Hiring

generally increase with use. This simplification is often justified
because repair costs are difficult to predict. However, trends
in repair costs over time will be important in the next
example, so repair cost estimates based on formulas by Rotz
and Bowers (1991) and 118 hours of use per year are
included in Table 15.1.

Willie finds that the depreciation shields and salvage value
substantially reduce the net present cost of the combine. After
converting the net present cost after taxes to an annual value before
taxes and adding expected fuel and labor costs, the per acre, before-
tax cost of harvesting wheat with Willie's own combine is $16.82.
The custom harvest rate is $14.00 per acre, so owning a combine
costs Willie $2.82 more before taxes than custom hiring. On the other
hand, if Willie harvested 800 acres of wheat, the before-tax cost of
harvesting with his own combine would be $13.45 per acre, 55 cents
less than the before-tax cost of custom-hiring.

(Table 15.1) is an example of using *PV* analysis to choose between alternative
durables.

Using the same procedure as before, Willie finds that the annual cost of
purchasing the used combine is only $12.60 per acre (Table 15.2), versus a cost
of $16.82 per acre for the new combine. Based on the variables considered in
the *PV* analysis and the estimates of repair costs and trade-in value, the used
combine appears to be a much less costly option. However, some possible
problems should be noted. First, no additional costs for breakdowns were
considered for the used combine. Second, new machinery often has superior
technology that increases its effectiveness (e.g., less grain left in the field)
and/or reduces costs. In this example, the technology was assumed the same.
Third, estimates for repair costs and remaining values vary widely, and using
alternative estimates can produce strikingly different results. For example, using
Bowers' (1987) formulas for estimating repair costs instead of Rotz and
Bowers' (1991) formulas raises the annual cost per acre of the new combine by
$1.40 and the cost per acre of the used combine by $1.99. The uncertainty
regarding such estimates is discussed in greater detail below.

Table 15.1 Calculation of Willie's Annual Costs for Owning a Combine

Cash Flow Item	Cash Flow	Timing	Discount Factor	*PV* of Cash Flow
Combine Purchase	80,000	0	1.0000	$80,000.00
Repairs, Year 1	45	0.5	0.9802	$43.98
Depreciation, Year 1	(1,248)	1.0	0.9608	($1,198.84)[1]
Repairs, Year 2	147	1.5	0.9418	$138.89
Depreciation, Year 2	(2,164)	2.0	0.9231	($1,997.46)[1]
Repairs, Year 3	258	2.5	0.9048	$233.75
Depreciation, Year 3	(1,651)	3.0	0.8869	($1,463.91)[1]
Repairs, Year 4	374	3.5	0.8694	$325.06
Depreciation, Year 4	(1,306)	4.0	0.8521	($1,112.96)[1]
Repairs, Year 5	493	4.5	0.8353	$411.70
Depreciation, Year 5	(1,268)	5.0	0.8187	($1,038.18)[1]
Repairs, Year 6	615	5.5	0.8025	$493.23
Depreciation, Year 6	(1,231)	6.0	0.7866	($968.42)[1]
Repairs, Year 7	739	6.5	0.7711	$569.46
Depreciation, Year 7	(1,195)	7.0	0.7558	($903.35)[1]
Repairs, Year 8	864	7.5	0.7408	$640.38
Depreciation, Year 8	(581)	8.0	0.7261	($421.67)[1]
Repairs, Year 9	992	8.5	0.7118	$706.08
Repairs, Year 10	1,121	9.5	0.6839	$766.68
Trade-In	(29,100)	10.0	0.6703	($19,506.31)[1]
Sum				$55,718.11
Annual cost after taxes, excluding fuel and labor				$6,869.54
Annual cost before taxes, excluding fuel and labor				$8,081.81
Fuel and labor costs, before taxes ($3.35/A x 600 A)				$2,010.00[2]
Total Annual Cost before taxes				$10,091.81
Total Annual Cost per Acre before taxes				$16.82[3]

[1] For simplicity, the example assumes that Willie has already used his Section 179 expensing deduction that allows him to treat up to $10,000 per year of property subject to depreciation as an annual expense. See the *Farmer's Tax Guide*, IRS Publication 225 for details.

[2] The fuel cost in this example is based on 1 gallon per acre of diesel fuel for wheat harvesting (Bowers) plus 0.2 gallons per acre for hauling wheat. It is assumed that diesel fuel is priced at $1.00 per gallon, and lubrication costs equal to 15 percent of fuel costs are included. Labor is priced at $6.00 per hour. It is assumed that 1.67 laborers are needed per acre and 5.09 acres are harvested per hour.

[3] It is instructive to note the effects on Willie's decision of using alternative compounding rates (see Chapter 12). The discount factors in Table 15.1 are calculated using continuous compounding of the discount rate. However, few farmers have sufficient mathematics training to be comfortable with the continuous compounding formula for the discount factor, e^{-rt}. The annual compounding formula for the discount factor, $1/(1+r)^t$, is more familiar and easier to explain (e.g., Boehlje and Eidman). Furthermore, the differences in *PV* and their annual equivalent values when using annual compounding rather than continuous compounding are usually small. For example, if annual compounding were used to recalculate Willie's annual costs per acre for owning a combine, the result would be $16.78, just 4 cents per acre less than the continuous compounding result.

Table 15.2 Willie's Annual Costs for Buying a Used Combine

Cash Flow Item	Cash Flow	Timing	Discount Factor	*PV of* Cash Flow
Combine Purchase	48,000	0	1.0000	$48,000.00
Repairs, Year 1	493	0.5	0.9802	$483.14
Depreciation, Year 1	(749)	1.0	0.9608	($719.30)[1]
Repairs, Year 2	615	1.5	0.9418	$578.81
Depreciation, Year 2	(1,298)	2.0	0.9231	($1,198.48)[1]
Repairs, Year 3	739	2.5	0.9048	$668.27
Depreciation, Year 3	(990)	3.0	0.8869	($878.34)[1]
Repairs, Year 4	864	3.5	0.8694	$751.50
Depreciation, Year 4	(784)	4.0	0.8521	($667.78)[1]
Repairs, Year 5	992	4.5	0.8353	$828.59
Depreciation, Year 5	(761)	5.0	0.8187	($622.91)[1]
Repairs, Year 6	1,121	5.5	0.8025	$899.70
Depreciation, Year 6	(739)	6.0	0.7866	($581.05)[1]
Repairs, Year 7	1,252	6.5	0.7711	$965.02
Depreciation, Year 7	(717)	7.0	0.7558	($542.01)[1]
Repairs, Year 8	1,383	7.5	0.7408	$1,024.76
Depreciation, Year 8	(348)	8.0	0.7261	($253.00)[1]
Trade-In	(24,634)	8.0	0.7261	(17,887.70)
Sum				$30,849.22
Annual cost after taxes, excluding fuel and labor				$4,581.97
Annual cost before taxes, excluding fuel and labor				$5,390.55
Fuel and labor costs, before taxes ($3.50/A x 600 A)				$2,172.00[2]
Total Annual Cost before taxes				$7,562.55
Total Annual Cost per Acre before taxes				$12.60

[1] For simplicity, the example assumes that Willie has already used his Section 179 expensing deduction that allows him to treat up to $10,000 per year of property subject to depreciation as an annual expense. See the *Farmer's Tax Guide*, IRS Publication 225 for details.

[2] The fuel cost in this example is based on 1 gallon per acre of diesel fuel for wheat harvesting (Bowers) plus 0.2 gallons per acre for hauling wheat. It is assumed that diesel fuel is priced at $1.00 per gallon, and lubrication costs equal to 15 percent of fuel costs are included. Labor is priced at $6.00 per hour. It is assumed that 1.67 laborers are needed per acre and 5.09 acres are harvested per hour.

Another problem with comparing a new and a used combine is that wheat harvesting services are provided for 10 years in the former case but only eight years in the latter. The use of annual equivalent values makes the costs comparable, but if Willie will continue to grow wheat after trading in his current combine, the effects of his current choice on longer-term harvesting costs should also be considered. This is the subject of durable replacement analyses, that will be discussed in the next section.

PV analysis is not only useful for comparing investments in alternative durables, but also for comparing alternative financing arrangements for the same durable. Machinery dealers usually offer a variety of financing plans. Options include leasing, varying the loan length and/or payment frequency, alternative down-payment percentages, interest-free periods, and ballooning payments. The machinery dealers or their financing companies have used *PV* analysis to ensure that all of these financing plans provide them with roughly equivalent net profits. However, cash flow and tax considerations often make one payment plan more desirable for an individual farmer than other plans.

An example of a combine purchase with a five-year payment plan is shown in Table 15.3 to illustrate the advantages and disadvantages of purchasing with borrowed capital versus equity capital. The durable being purchased is the same new combine considered in Table 15.1. However, this time Willie is offered the option of making a 15 percent down payment and paying the balance over five years with an interest rate of 10 percent. It is assumed that payments are made annually, a common arrangement for crop farmers. The timing of payments within the year is arbitrarily set at the same time taxes are paid.

In order to calculate the *PV* and annual cost of purchasing the combine with financing, additional lines for loan payments and interest expense deductions are added to the table. Since loan payments and interest expense deductions are nominal values, they must be converted to real values before their real *PV* can be calculated. For farms with large taxable income, the tax shield from interest expense deductions is often large. Since Willie has only a 15 percent marginal tax rate, the tax shield from interest expense deductions lowers the net present cost by only $2,577.40.

The annual cost per acre for purchasing the combine with financing in this example is $17.44, which is 62 cents more than the annual cost per acre of purchasing with equity capital. This difference occurs because Willie's discount rate is much less than the interest rate on the loan, even on an after-tax basis. When the after-tax interest rate for financing is higher than the discount rate (opportunity cost of capital), purchasing with equity capital is more profitable than purchasing with financing.

Table 15.3 Willie's Annual Costs for Buying a Combine with Financing

Cash Flow Item	Cash Flow	Timing	Discount Factor	*PV* of Cash Flow
Combine Down Payment	12,000	0	1.0000	$12,000.00
Repairs, Year 1	45	0.5	0.9802	$43.98
Depreciation, Year 1	(1,248)	1.0	0.9608	($1,198.84)
Payment, Year 1	17,416	1.0	0.9608	$16,732.87
Repairs, Year 2	147	1.5	0.9418	$138.89
Interest Ded. (Pmt. 1)	(961.45)	2.0	0.9231	($887.53)
Depreciation, Year 2	(2,164)	2.0	0.9231	($1,997.46)
Payment, Year 2	16,909	2.0	0.9231	$15,608.51
Repairs, Year 3	258	2.5	0.9048	$233.75
Interest Ded. (Pmt. 2)	(780.55)	3.0	0.8869	($692.29)
Depreciation, Year 3	(1,651)	3.0	0.8869	($1,463.91)
Payment, Year 3	16,416	3.0	0.8869	$14,559.70
Repairs, Year 4	374	3.5	0.8694	$325.06
Interest Ded. (Pmt. 3)	(594.53)	4.0	0.8521	($506.62)
Depreciation, Year 4	(1,306)	4.0	0.8521	($1,112.96)
Payment, Year 4	15,938	4.0	0.8521	$13,581.37
Repairs, Year 5	493	4.5	0.8353	$411.70
Interest Ded. (Pmt. 4)	(402.83)	5.0	0.8187	($329.81)
Depreciation, Year 5	(1,268)	5.0	0.8187	($1,038.18)
Payment, Year 5	15,474	5.0	0.8187	$12,668.77
Repairs, Year 6	615	5.5	0.8025	$493.23
Interest Ded. (Pmt. 5)	(204.86)	6.0	0.7866	($161.15)
Depreciation, Year 6	(1,231)	6.0	0.7866	($968.42)
Repairs, Year 7	739	6.5	0.7711	$569.46
Depreciation, Year 7	(1,195)	7.0	0.7558	($903.35)
Repairs, Year 8	864	7.5	0.7408	$640.38
Depreciation, Year 8	(581)	8.0	0.7261	($421.67)
Repairs, Year 9	992	8.5	0.7118	$706.08
Repairs, Year 10	1,121	9.5	0.6839	$766.68
Trade-In	(29,100)	10.0	0.6703	($19,506.31
Sum				$58,291.95
Annual cost after taxes, excluding fuel and labor				$7,186.87
Annual cost before taxes, excluding fuel and labor				$8,455.14
Fuel and labor costs, before taxes ($3.35/A x 600 A)				$2,010.00
Total Annual Cost before taxes				$10,465.14
Total Annual Cost per Acre before taxes				$17.44

Durable Replacement Analyses _____

Farmers often ask when is the best time to trade in old, worn-out equipment for new equipment. In theory, if the new equipment is identical to the old equipment, the optimal time to trade is when the cost of keeping the equipment an additional year to year $t+1$ just equals or exceeds the annual equivalent cost of replacing the equipment every t years (Perrin; Bradford and Reid; Bowers). This replacement criterion has been a popular topic for journal articles among farm management economists, but it is difficult to apply to real farm management problems (Bradford and Reid). This rule and others will be discussed in more detail in Chapter 16. The principal difficulty with the identical replacement model is that it is based on the assumption that cash flows for all successive replacement machines are identical to those of the current machine. It has been shown (Watts and Helmers) that the optimal replacement interval is not affected by uniform inflation in all parameters, but uniform inflation is highly unusual. Furthermore, the technology of new machines usually is improved, resulting in lower fuel usage, lower repairs, or other improvements in machine performance (Bradford and Reid). Therefore, Bradford and Reid proposed a *PV* model for replacing three successive machines that allows for changes in initial costs, remaining values, repair and operating costs, prices, and discount rates. They suggest that the time horizon for the three machines is sufficient for making a good replacement decision in the current period.

Epplin et al. suggested using a variation of the identical replacement model to determine when to replace one set of durables with another. They determined that a reduced-tillage system would be more profitable in the long run for an Oklahoma wheat farm than a plow system, but went on to ask when it is most profitable to replace the machinery set for the plow system with the machinery set for the reduced-tillage system. In this case, the identical replacement rule is modified to: When is the annual (marginal) cost of keeping the plow system another year greater than the average (annual equivalent) cost for the reduced-tillage system, assuming infinite identical replacement of the reduced-tillage system once it is adopted? Epplin et al. found that the marginal cost of keeping the plow system was higher than the average cost of the reduced-tillage system in the first three years of use, but then remained lower until the plow system equipment was worn out. They concluded that it is often optimal to delay adoption of a technology that requires new equipment until the old equipment is worn out.

Although they present a useful application of *PV* analysis, three limitations in Epplin et al.'s analysis should be noted. First, they used an identical replacement analysis to calculate the average cost of the reduced-tillage machinery, which is subject to all of the objections of Bradford and Reid. In particular, new technology generally continues to improve for many years, so the second set of reduced-tillage machinery will likely be more efficient than the first set. Also, farmers typically experience an adjustment period in which they learn how to use the new technology more efficiently. Technological improvements and learning curves are inconsistent with identical replacement analysis, but Epplin et al. ignored these factors.

Second, Epplin et al. considered the machinery for each tillage system to be a single unit that is all replaced at once. In practice, even if machinery for the plow system were purchased all at once, the rates of depreciation in remaining values and increases in repair costs would not be equal for all machines in this set. It probably would be optimal to replace some durable components of the plow system before others, which greatly complicates the analysis.

Third, Epplin et al.'s calculation of the marginal cost of keeping the plow system depends critically on a specific pattern of remaining value changes in the early years of ownership. There is much disagreement about remaining value estimates and little empirical evidence to support them, as will be discussed below.

In practice, most farm management economists use the identical replacement analysis to find the optimal replacement interval for machinery, then use their best judgment to adjust the replacement interval for technology changes, inflation, or other factors. Technological improvements reduce the optimal replacement interval (Bowers). The effects of inflation on the optimal replacement interval depend on which prices inflate faster than others and the impact of inflation on tax payments. Farm management economists also might recommend lengthening the optimal replacement interval to reduce debt exposure and financial risk, as they did in the mid-1980's. This procedure is ad hoc and subjective. However, it is probably better to use informed judgment than to rely completely on numerical analyses that are based on parameters with little empirical foundation, such as repair costs and remaining value.

When a farm has many units of a production durable that are replaced routinely, *PV* analysis often can be avoided. Examples of such production durables are dairy cows and fruit trees. If the total number of units and the rate of replacement over time are expected to remain approximately constant, the costs of durable replacement can be included in enterprise budgets. A detailed example for dairy cow replacement is presented by Luening et al. Even when the number of units and rate of replacement are expected to fluctuate, the additional time required to optimally manage these fluctuations using *PV* analysis is rarely justified.

Considering All Relevant Costs and Returns ——————————

The question of how much analysis is justified is frequently encountered in farm management investment and replacement problems. Often, if the consultant or extension specialist does not answer an investment or replacement question quickly, the farmer will not wait for the answer and will not benefit from the results of *PV* analysis. This is particularly true if the farmer must provide detailed information from a poor record-keeping system. Farm management consultants and extension specialists also must allocate their own scarce time among many problems. The opportunity cost of a thorough analysis is often greater than the expected benefit. For example, even the most committed *PV* analyst will usually not do a *PV* analysis before investing in a $15 wrench, although it probably will provide services for several years.

The total costs and returns principle stated in Chapter 4 is important in farm management applications of *PV* analysis. Because investment and replacement decisions usually affect more than one farm enterprise, a whole-farm analysis is often needed to determine the most profitable option. The profitability of durable investment and replacement decisions usually depends on the production technologies used in the various enterprises, but the optimal choice of production technology depends on the design and capabilities of the production durables. Therefore, durable investment and replacement decisions should be made jointly with the choices of technology, as argued by Bradford and Reid.

Consider replacing a six-row planter with an eight-row planter. The larger planter will tend to increase average corn and/or soybean yields because some fields can be planted earlier. It may allow more corn or soybean acreage to be planted. The larger planter may increase hay and dairy production by freeing fixed labor resources to work on other enterprises. Or, it may increase off-farm income by allowing the farmer to hold a full-time job and plant in the evenings and on weekends. The larger planter may accelerate physical depreciation of the tractor. Switching to an eight-row planter also may force other equipment to be changed or modified. Particularly in regions where rows follow curves, having the same number of rows on the planter, row cultivator, and corn head of the combine may be desirable.

Another example is replacing a conventional planter with a no-till planter. This change usually eliminates the need for plowing and harrowing operations, but tends to increase the need for herbicide spraying. The change may force use of other, more expensive formulations of fertilizer and require more frequent applications of lime. The no-till planter may also free labor resources to work on other enterprises, although changes in operation dates might create new time conflicts with other enterprises. Finally, if plowing and harrowing are no longer needed, a smaller tractor can be used, which links the question of whether and when to replace the planter to the question of when to replace a tractor.

Whole-farm analyses and joint selection of production technologies and durable equipment are time-consuming and data-intensive. It is relatively easy to state qualitatively how other costs and returns are affected by durable investment and replacement decisions, but much more difficult to quantify these relationships. In theory, a mathematical programming technique such as multi-period mixed-integer programming should be used to consider all of the substitution and resource competition relationships across enterprises and over time. However, mathematical programming models require a large number of numerical coefficients to represent these relationships, many of which may be difficult to validate. Extensive model validation is needed before the model results should be used to make recommendations to farmers. Furthermore, it is not obvious in most cases that the profits gained by considering all related costs and returns are greater than the cost of the analysis, when the opportunity cost of the farm management economist's time is considered.

Estimating Future Cash Flows and Opportunity Costs _____

In the investment and replacement analyses cited earlier, the decisions that minimize the *PV* of costs or maximize the *PV* of net profits are determined by the level and timing of cash flows and by the discount rate. As seen in the examples, the relevant cash flows often occur many years into the future. Some of these future cash flows are very predictable, but others are highly uncertain. It is important to consider how alternative estimates of cash flow amounts or timing affect *PV* analysis. Similarly, as explained in Chapter 3, the discount rate is determined by the decision maker's opportunity cost of capital which usually changes over time. The accuracy of cash flow estimates and the discount rate are also influenced by the quality of available information.

The timing and amounts of financial payments and tax shields are predictable. Financial payments usually are specified in a signed contract which may be broken under only heavy penalty (e.g., seizure of collateral). Interest rates for financial payments sometimes vary, but opportunities to fix interest rates are usually available. The timing and amounts of tax deductions are specified by federal law according to when a durable is placed in service; thus, tax deductions also are predictable. The amount that tax payments are reduced will depend on taxable net income for each year and the marginal tax rate for that level of income. Annual tax planning offers many possibilities for reducing the variation of farmers' taxable income.

The services from agricultural production durables are used to produce commodities that often have uncertain yields and prices. Yield uncertainty can be reduced by risk-reducing inputs, intensive management, and insurance. However, it may be difficult to reduce yield uncertainty when new technologies are used in conjunction with the durable. Short-term price uncertainty can be reduced by using futures markets and forward contracting. Prices in the medium term can be forecasted using econometric techniques. However, long-term prices are often subject to major policy changes and structural changes in markets that are difficult to predict. Because of yield and price uncertainty, farm management applications of *PV* analysis frequently include sensitivity analyses for yield and price variation. *PV* analysis also may be used to calculate break-even yields and prices as explained in Chapter 2.

Some costs are also more predictable than others. Costs for fuel, fertilizer, and chemical pesticides have been reasonably constant after the 1970's, although the deregulation of natural gas prices has often been an important factor to consider in the analysis of irrigation investments. Labor costs have not varied greatly, although many agricultural laborers are paid near the minimum wage, which changes according to an unpredictable political process. Labor costs also vary with unpredictable immigration laws and their variable enforcement. The costs of intermediate agricultural products, such as feed and livestock, are highly variable, although their variability often can be reduced as explained above for product prices in general. However, one highly variable cost that was very important in all of the investment and replacement examples above is repair cost. In fact, accumulated repair costs over the life of many types of agricultural equipment exceed 80 percent of the initial list price (Rotz and Bowers).

According to Rotz and Bowers, not only are repair costs variable, but little empirical research has been conducted to estimate how average repair costs change with time and usage. A few empirical studies have estimated repair costs as exponential functions of use. The parameters of these functions have been adjusted by the consensus judgments of agricultural engineers and published annually in the yearbook of the American Society of Agricultural Engineers (ASAE).

There are several problems with the agricultural engineers' consensus repair cost estimates. Most of the large-sample empirical work was done so many years ago that technologies have often changed significantly since then. In addition, the large-sample empirical work was done at a time when farmers changed equipment more frequently than most farmers do now, so that there were few observations on equipment with many accumulated hours of use. Finally, there is a logical problem caused by estimating repair costs based on accumulated hours of use. Since hours of use is an inverse function of speed of operation, operating equipment at a lower speed results in higher estimates of repair costs, which is counter-intuitive. Also, large equipment has smaller repair cost estimates relative to list price than small equipment, even though large equipment usually has more hydraulic parts and flexible joints than small equipment.

Remaining value estimates are also highly variable and generally have a weak empirical base (Bradford and Reid). Perry, Bayaner, and Nixon provided large-sample econometric results for tractor remaining values that are consistent with agricultural engineering estimates (e.g., Bowers). They also included useful estimates for the effects of size, manufacturer, and condition, while most earlier estimates only considered the effects of age or accumulated hours. Potentially large errors in remaining value estimates can be caused by using formulas that are functions of age or accumulated hours alone, as occurred in the examples above. Econometric results using simple functional relationships have been published for combine remaining values, but sound econometric results for the remaining values of other equipment are lacking.

Uncertainties regarding the appropriate discount rate to use are mostly due to an individual farmer's reluctance to provide information about his or her financial position. As explained in Chapter 3, the discount rate reflects the farmer's opportunity cost of capital, the return that could be earned by other investments, or by liquidating debt. Because most U.S. farmers operate with a mix of equity capital and borrowed capital that can easily be substituted for each other, Aplin, Casler, and Francis argued that the discount rate should be a weighted average of the opportunity cost of equity capital and the interest rates on borrowed capital. The weights are the proportions of capital provided by each source. The use of a weighted average cost of capital may also be easier than getting a farmer to specify the alternative investments and principal payments that would occur if the investment in question is not made.

Summary

Although some difficulties are encountered in the application of *PV* models to farm management problems, *PV* models are commonly used to evaluate investment and replacement decisions for durables used in agricultural production. The timing of cash flows and the opportunity cost of capital are important considerations in farm management, and *PV* analysis is usually better than any alternative technique for analyzing them. Other techniques for evaluating investments ignore important cash flows and sometimes lead to recommendations that are clearly not in a farmer's best interest.

Some simplification of *PV* analysis for farm management applications is justified. Using annual compounding to calculate discount factors instead of continuous compounding leads to negligible errors in most cases, and is much easier to explain to a clientele that has little mathematical training. Some related costs and returns can justifiably be omitted from a *PV* analysis when their *PV* is expected to be small and the cost of obtaining reliable estimates is large. This omission is particularly justified when the *PV* of related costs and returns is less than the margin of error for estimates of highly uncertain cash flows, such as salvage values and repair costs. It is also appropriate to use personal judgment to make adjustments in *PV* results when some of the estimates for large future cash flows are suspect, or when assumptions of that model are not realistic (e.g., the identical replacement model).

In all applications of *PV* analysis to farm management problems, the preferences of the decision maker are more important than an analyst's desire to consider all relevant aspects of the problem. The preferences of the decision maker are paramount because he or she accepts responsibility for the outcome, not the farm management consultant or extension specialist. These preferences often include the desires to make a decision quickly, to avoid spending a lot of time hunting through records for information, and to protect privacy. The farm management consultant or extension specialist also has to consider his or her own opportunity cost of time before deciding how thorough to make the *PV* analysis of a particular problem. For all of these reasons, slippage between the theory of *PV* analysis and its application to farm management problems is unavoidable.

Endnotes

1. A professional farm manager is paid a salary or a percentage of gross receipts to manage one or more farms (usually many) without contributing labor to those farms. Professional farm managers are usually hired by banks, trust funds, and absentee landlords, although a few are hired directly by very large farms. The professional distinction is important because all farmers are farm managers, but professional farm managers are specialists and usually have more business training.

2. The choice may also be based on the minimum *PV* of net cash outflows over the relevant planning horizon. However, farmers are more accustomed to comparing annual costs, since enterprise budgets are almost always presented in annual terms.

3. However, farm managers who are comfortable with *PV* analysis, have good records, and can quickly complete *PV* analyses using a computer will not need to share private information. Furthermore, these farm managers are usually willing and able to consider more aspects of the problem than farmers who are not comfortable with *PV* analysis and have poor record-keeping systems.

Review Questions

1. Explain why the information required for building *PV* models may not be available to the analyst.

2. Why do analysts simplify *PV* procedures when solving applied *PV* problems for farm firms?

3. Define farm management. Are there definitions or considerations beyond those described in this chapter?

4. Define "strategic planning." Describe how *PV* models may be useful in strategic planning.

5. How might the duties of a farm manager differ from those of a fast food restaurant manager? (Hint: What factors are the most significant in determining the success of a farm manager and a fast food restaurant manager?)

6. What factors influence the farm manager's decision to rent versus buy?

7. Compare the identical replacement rule to that proposed by Epplin et al. Under what conditions is the identical replacement rule most likely to produce valid results?

8. What practical advice would you give to farm managers who must allocate their time between keeping records, building *PV* models, and plowing, planting, and maintaining buildings and equipment, etc.?

9. How should farm managers account for risk as they perform *PV* analysis? What types of uncertainty or risk are most important in *PV* analysis?

10. Which farm management decisions commonly utilize *PV* analysis?

Application Questions

1. Explain how Willie's analysis of a new versus a used combine purchase would be changed if the reinvestment rate did not equal the discount rate.

2. Assume that Willie's real after-tax reinvestment rate is 2.5 percent. Reevaluate which is the preferred investment: the purchase of a used or new combine.

3. Is it necessary to adjust interest charges for inflation if the analysis is conducted in real units? Defend your answer.

4. Why does using simplifying assumptions for *PV* analysis of farm management decisions produce better recommendations than simple rules of thumb?

5. What kinds of information for farm management applications of *PV* analysis are the most difficult to obtain; the most uncertain?

6. What economic principle can be used to justify the simplification of *PV* analysis for farm management problems?

References

Aplin, R.D., G.L. Casler, and C.P. Francis. *Capital Investment Analysis.* 2nd edition. Columbus, Ohio: Grid Publishing, 1977.

Boehlje, M.D. and V.R. Eidman. *Farm Management.* New York: John Wiley and Sons, 1984.

Bowers, W. *Farm Machinery Management.* East Moline, Illinois: Deere and Company, 1987.

Bradford, G.L. and D.W. Reid. "Theoretical and Empirical Problems in Modeling Optimal Replacement of Farm Machines." *Southern Journal of Agricultural Economics* 14(1982):109-16.

Epplin, F.M., T.F. Tice, A.E. Baquet, and S.J. Handke. "Impacts of Reduced Tillage on Operating Inputs and Machinery Requirements." *American Journal of Agricultural Economics* 64(1982):1039-46.

Leuning, R.A., R.M. Klemme, and W.T. Howard. "Wisconsin Farm Enterprise Budgets: Dairy Cows and Replacements." *Agricultural Bulletin A2731*. Madison, Wisconsin: Cooperative Extension Service, University of Wisconsin-Madison, 1987.

Leuning, R.A. and B.L. Jones. "Characteristics of U.S. Farm Managers." In Deborah T. Smith (editor), *Farm Management: 1989 Yearbook of Agriculture*. Washington, D.C.: U.S. Department of Agriculture, 1989.

Milligan, R.A. and B.F. Stanton. "What Do Farm Managers Do?" In Deborah T. Smith (editor), *Farm Management: 1989 Yearbook of Agriculture*. Washington, D.C.: U.S. Department of Agriculture, 1989.

Morehart, M.J., J.D. Johnson, and D.E. Banker. "Financial Characteristics of U.S. Farms, January 1, 1989." *Agriculture Information Bulletin No. 579*. Washington, D.C.: Economic Research Service, U.S. Department of Agriculture.

Perrin, R.K. "Asset Replacement Principles." *American Journal of Agricultural Economics* 54(1972):60-67.

Perry, G.M., A. Bayaner, and C.J. Nixon. "The Effect of Usage and Size on Tractor Depreciation." *American Journal of Agricultural Economics* 72(1990):317-25.

Rotz, C.A. and W. Bowers. "Repair and Maintenance Cost Data for Agricultural Equipment." *ASAE Paper 911531*, presented at the 1991 Winter Meeting of the American Society of Agricultural Engineers. East Lansing, Michigan: Department of Agricultural Engineering, Michigan State University, 1991.

U.S. Department of Treasury, Internal Revenue Service. *Farmer's Tax Guide*. Publication 225. Washington, D.C.: Internal Revenue Service, 1990.

Watts, M.J. and G.A. Helmers. "Inflation and Machinery Cost Budgeting." *Southern Journal of Agricultural Economics* 11(1979):83-88.

White, G.B. "Using Strategic Planning to Prepare for the Future." In Deborah T. Smith (editor), *Farm Management: 1989 Yearbook of Agriculture*. Washington, D.C.: U.S. Department of Agriculture, 1989.

Chapter 16

Privately-Owned
Natural Resources[1]

Key words: exhaustible resources, expected price trends, extraction rates, finite horizons, harvest rates, Hotelling's rule, infinite horizons, renewable resources, site value, stocks of remaining resources, time between harvests

Introduction

Present value (*PV*) models are versatile tools with widespread applications to intertemporal problems. In this chapter, *PV* models are applied to the study of natural resources. One chapter can only introduce the well-developed literature devoted to natural resources and must be narrowly focused. Therefore, this chapter focuses on finding preferred extraction rates of privately-owned natural resources. It also applies Hotelling's rule to describe extraction rate patterns over time.

Two kinds of natural resources are studied in this chapter: exhaustible and renewable. Studies of exhaustible and renewable resources are illustrated in Carlson, Zilberman, and Miranowski. An exhaustible resource, like oil, coal, minerals, ground water, or natural gas, exists within the earth's crust. The most important feature of this resource is that its supply cannot be increased or replenished. Once the supply is exhausted, it cannot be replaced or reproduced. Some groups have organized to express concerns over the rate at which exhaustible resources are being depleted.

Renewable natural resources include wildlife, rivers, trees, and plants. The renewal rate of these resources is biologically determined and need not be depleted if properly managed. An important issue in managing renewable resources is to find harvest rates that maximize their net present value (*NPV*).

The issue of whose *NPV* to maximize separates the study of privately-owned natural resources from benefit-cost analysis and the study of publicly-owned natural resources. This chapter focuses on the management and extraction of privately-owned natural resources. But the larger issue of managing natural resources for future generations is also important. Because the current owners did not create the exhaustible resource, can they claim the right to exhaust its supply simply because they have the opportunity to do so?

The debate over who has the right to extract natural resources has no immediate answer. Nor is there a clear answer of how to weigh the well being of current versus future generations. One approach is to consider the future generations to be close family members. Then, the management of the resource for their use is balanced against the needs of current family members. For now, we will assume that the decision of whose *NPV* matters most has already been made and the opportunity now exists to employ *PV* tools to assist the decision maker in the management of privately-owned resources.

An important concept related to the extraction of exhaustible resources and the harvest of renewable resources is Hotelling's rule. This topic is discussed next. Then, the remainder of the chapter applies *PV* tools to find optimal extraction rates of exhaustible and renewable natural resources.

Hotelling's Rule

In a landmark article, the economist Harold Hotelling identified an important principle that has come to be known as Hotelling's rule. To explain Hotelling's rule, consider an investment problem with an obvious solution. Assume an investor has two investment opportunities, *A* and *B*, that earn marginal returns $r^A(x)$ and $r^B(y)$, respectively, depending on the amounts of x and y invested. Also assume the investor has an amount $V_0=x+y$ to invest. If the rates of return earned in investments *A* and *B* are concave down functions of the amounts invested and assuming interior solutions exist, the optimal investment rule is to allocate x and y such that $r^A(x)=r^B(y)$. If this equality were not satisfied, one could always shift resources from the investment earning the lower rate of return to the investment earning the higher rate of return and increase total earnings.

The obvious rule of equating marginal investment returns in any given period can be applied to intertemporal investment problems. Assume cash returns in the tth period, $R_t(x)$, to depend on the investment of resource x. Assume cash returns in the $(t+1)^{st}$ period, $R_{t+1}(y)$, to depend on the investment of resource y. If $x+y=V_0$, then the optimal allocation of x and y requires that:

$$R_t'(x) = \frac{R'_{t+1}(y)}{(1+r)},$$

or:

$$\frac{R'_{t+1}(y)}{R'_t(x)} = (1+r),$$

where $R'_t(x)$ and $R'_{t+1}(y)$ are marginal cash returns in the tth and $(t+1)^{st}$ periods, respectively.

The implication of this rule is that marginal cash returns in each period must increase over time at the opportunity cost of capital. This required pattern of returns will be used to determine the optimal extraction rates of exhaustible resources.

The Extraction of Exhaustible Resources

Exhaustible natural resources already exist. As a result, economic considerations of exhaustible natural resources focus on the cost of extraction as opposed to their creation or production. Two assumptions often made regarding the cost of extraction are that the cost of extraction depends on the extraction rate per period or on the amount of the resource remaining. If the amount of the resource extracted this period affects the cost of later resource extractions, then a new opportunity cost is introduced into the problem and Hotelling's rule applies. If there are no interperiod dependencies, Hotelling's rule does not apply. Next we consider an extraction problem in which no interperiod dependencies exist.

Case 1: Unconstrained Extraction of an Exhaustible Resource Rate

Let s_t be the amount of an exhaustible resource extracted in the tth period. Assume a constant price p is paid per unit of the resource extracted. Furthermore, let $C(s_t)$ be the cost of extracting s_t in the tth period such that $C'(s_t) > 0$ and $C''(s_t) > 0$. Then, cash returns $R_t = ps_t - C(s_t)$. Assume that the total stock of the resource is S_0 and that the firm has purchased a permit costing V_0 that allows it n periods to complete its extraction. Then, the *NPV* model is:

$$\max_{s_1,\ldots,s_n} NPV = -V_0 + \frac{ps_1 - C(s_1)}{(1+r)} + \ldots + \frac{ps_n - C(s_n)}{(1+r)^n}. \qquad (16.1)$$

If the resource stock $S_0 > s_1 + \ldots + s_n$ is not a binding constraint, then optimal extraction rates depend only on the opportunity costs of extracting the resource and no interperiod opportunity costs exist. Consequently, in the tth period, the optimal level of extraction satisfies the first-order condition:

$$p - C'(s_t) = 0.$$

Case 2: Interperiod Dependent Extractions

Suppose an additional constraint is added to the unconstrained extraction problem that creates a new opportunity cost. Assume that the stock S_0 must be extracted in n periods. This constraint is introduced into the *PV* model by replacing s_n with $S_0 - s_1 - \ldots - s_{n-1}$ obtained by solving for s_n in the constraint $S_0 = s_1 + \ldots + s_n$. Now, the *NPV* model can be expressed as:

$$\max_{s_1,\ldots,s_{n-1}} NPV = -V_0 + \frac{ps_1 - C(s_1)}{(1+r)} + \ldots + \frac{ps_{n-1} - C(s_{n-1})}{(1+r)^{n-1}}$$

$$+ \frac{p(S_0 - s_1 - \ldots - s_{n-1}) - C(S_0 - s_1 - \ldots - s_{n-1})}{(1+r)^n}. \qquad (16.2)$$

First-order conditions for $s_1,\ldots,s_{n-1}$ (which when found can be used to find $s_n = S_0 - s_1 - \ldots - s_{n-1} \geq 0$) equal:

$$p - C'(s_1) - \frac{[p - C'(S_0 - s_1 - \ldots - s_{n-1})]}{(1+r)^{n-1}} = 0,$$

$$p - C'(s_2) - \frac{[p - C'(S_0 - s_1 - \ldots - s_{n-1})]}{(1+r)^{n-2}} = 0,$$

$$\cdot$$
$$\cdot$$
$$\cdot$$

$$p - C'(s_{n-1}) - \frac{[p - C'(S_0 - s_1 - \ldots - s_{n-1})]}{(1+r)} = 0.$$

The difference between the first-order conditions for $s_1, \ldots, s_{n-1}$ is the power of the discount factor applied to marginal cash returns in the nth period. Optimality with the additional constraint of $S_0 = s_1 + \ldots + s_n$ requires the *PV* of marginal cash returns in each period be equal.

The opportunity costs created by the constraint $S_0 = s_1 + \ldots + s_n$ leads to the relationship between marginal cash returns in the tth and $(t+1)^{st}$ period equal to:

$$\frac{p - C'(s_{t+1})}{p - C'(s_t)} = (1 + r).$$

Thus, the *PVs* of marginal cash revenues in each period are equal and consistent with Hotelling's rule.

Now, consider an alternative constraint on the problem just described. Let the salvage value V_n be a function of the remaining stock of the resource such that $V_n = V_n(S_0 - s_1, \ldots, s_n)$. Also assume that the amount extracted per period is not limited by S_0. Now, the *NPV* model can be expressed as:

$$\max_{s_1, \ldots, s_n} NPV = -V_0 + \frac{ps_1 - C(s_1)}{(1 + r)} + \ldots$$

$$+ \frac{ps_n - C(s_n)}{(1 + r)^n} + \frac{V_n(S_0 - s_1 - \ldots - s_n)}{(1 + r)^n}. \tag{16.3}$$

This new constraint creates a different kind of interperiod dependency. The first-order conditions can be expressed as:

$$\frac{dNPV}{ds_1} = p - C'(s_1) - \frac{\partial V_n(S_0 - s_1 - \ldots - s_n)/\partial s_1}{(1 + r)^{n-1}} = 0,$$

.
.
.

$$\frac{dNPV}{ds_2} = p - C'(s_2) - \frac{\partial V_n(S_0 - s_1 - \ldots - s_n)/\partial s_2}{(1 + r)^{n-2}} = 0,$$

.
.
.

$$\frac{dNPV}{ds_n} = p - C'(s_n) - \partial V_n(S_0 - s_1 - \ldots - s_n)/\partial s_n = 0.$$

The difference between the first-order conditions for $s_1, \ldots, s_n$ is the power of the discount factor applied to the change in salvage value resulting from a unit increase in the resource extracted. It is assumed that second-order conditions hold.

The reason for the difference between the *PV* of marginal salvage costs can easily be explained. Extracting the last unit of resource in period one reduces the salvage value by $\partial V_n / \partial s_1$ n-1 periods in the future. Extracting an additional unit of resource in the nth period reduces the salvage value by $\partial V_n / \partial s_n = \partial V_n / \partial s_1$ immediately. Thus, the *PV* of extracting an additional unit of resource in period n is higher than extracting the same unit of resource in earlier periods.

When the salvage value depends on the amount of resources extracted, Hotelling's rule or relationship exists between marginal cash returns as before:

$$\frac{p - C'(s_{t+1})}{p - C'(s_t)} = (1 + r).$$

However, another obvious relationship exists. To satisfy Hotelling's rule in the above relationship, $C'(s_{t+1}) < C'(s_t)$. This relationship requires that $s_1 > s_2 > \ldots > s_n$. Thus, extraction levels decrease over time unless offset by other cost considerations.

Another version of the extraction problem with interperiod dependent opportunity costs is to require as before that $S_0 = s_1 + \ldots + s_n$, and in addition, assume that the price depends on the amount of the resource extracted. The firm desires as before to choose $s_1, \ldots, s_n$ such that its *NPV* is maximized.

The *NPV* model just described can be written as:

$$\max_{s_1, \ldots, s_n} NPV = -V_0 + \frac{p(s_1)s_1}{(1+r)}$$
$$+ \ldots + \frac{p(s_n)s_n}{(1+r)^n}, \qquad (16.4)$$

subject to $S_0 = s_1 + \ldots + s_n$.

Substituting the constraint into the model, thereby creating an opportunity cost for postponing extraction, the *NPV* model can be written as:

$$\max_{s_1,\ldots,s_{n-1}} NPV = -V_0 + \frac{p(s_1)s_1}{(1+r)} + \ldots$$

$$+ \frac{p(s_{n-1})s_{n-1}}{(1+r)^{n-1}} + \frac{p(S_0 - s_1 - \ldots - s_{n-1})(S_0 - s_1 - \ldots - s_{n-1})}{(1+r)^n}. \tag{16.5}$$

First-order conditions can be written as:

$$\frac{dNPV}{ds_1} = p(s_1) + s_1 p(s_1) - \frac{p(s_n) + s_n p'(s_n)}{(1+r)^{n-1}} = 0,$$

$$\cdot$$
$$\cdot$$
$$\cdot$$
$$\cdot$$

$$\frac{dNPV}{ds_2} = p(s_2) + s_2 p'(s_2) - \frac{p(s_n) + s_n p'(s_n)}{(1+r)^{n-2}} = 0,$$

$$\cdot$$
$$\cdot$$
$$\cdot$$

$$\frac{dNPV}{ds_{n-1}} = p(s_{n-1}) + s_2 p'(s_{n-1}) - \frac{p(s_n) + s_n p'(s_n)}{(1+r)} = 0.$$

From the first-order conditions just obtained, we verify that marginal cash returns increase at rate r:

$$\frac{p(s_{t+1}) + s_{t+1} p'(s_{t+1})}{p(s_t) + s_t p'(s_t)} = (1+r).$$

Finally, assume that only price changes between periods are allowed. Then, to equate the *PV* of returns in each period would require that:

$$\frac{p(s_t)s_t}{(1+r)^t} = \frac{p(s_{t+1})s_{t+1}}{(1+r)^{t+1}},$$

or that:

$$p(s_{t+1}) = p(s_t)(s_t/s_{t+1})(1+r).$$

Assuming that $p'(s) < 0$, then again we deduce the result that $s_t > s_{t+1}$. However, if $s_t > s_{t+1}$ and the equality holds, then:

$$\frac{p(s_{t+1})}{p(s_t)} = \frac{s_t}{s_{t+1}} (1+r) < (1+r).$$

Or, in other words, prices of the resource would increase over time but at a rate less than r.

Case 3: Extraction Rates and Disposal Constraints[2]

Now, we consider a constraint that imposes an opportunity cost of extraction depending on the extraction time. To illustrate this problem, consider a strip mine operation. Suppose the land committed to the mine operation has a recreational use that cannot be realized until the mining operation is completed. Furthermore, suppose the *PV* of the land that could be used for recreation depends on the period it is converted from mining to recreation, a value equal to $V(n)$ such that $V'(n) > 0$ and $V''(n) < 0$. Finally, to facilitate differentiating with respect to n, $(1+r)^{-t}$ is replaced by its continuous equivalent e^{-rt} and the summation sign Σ is replaced with the continuous summation sign or integral $\int$. This continuous time *NPV* model is expressed as:[3]

$$\max_{n} NPV = -V_0 + \int_0^n [ps - C(s)]e^{-rt}dt + V(n)e^{-rn}. \qquad (16.6)$$

As in the earlier unconstrained case, there is no interperiod dependence or opportunity costs. Thus, extraction levels in the tth period are independent of extraction levels in the $(t+1)^{st}$ period. However, the opportunity of revenue from discontinuing mining and converting the land to recreation creates a new opportunity cost. It is the opportunity cost associated with postponing by one period the revenue from the land used for recreation.

The two first-order conditions taken with respect to extraction rate s and length of horizon n set equal to zero are:

$$\frac{dNPV}{ds} = [p - C'(s)] = 0, \qquad (16.7a)$$

$$\frac{dNPV}{dn} = [ps - C(s)] - rV(n) + V'(n) = 0. \tag{16.7b}$$

Second-order conditions require that:

$$NPV_{nn} = [-rV'(n) + V''(n)] < 0, \quad \text{and:}$$

$$NPV_{ss} = -\int_0^n C''(s)\, e^{-rt}\, dt < 0, \text{ and } NPV_{nn}\, NPV_{ss} - [p - C'(s)]\, e^{-rn}[p - C(s)] > 0.$$

Equation (16.7a) implies that within each period the extraction amount is chosen to equate marginal revenue and marginal cost. Equation (16.7b) implies that extraction continues until the profit per period of extraction equals the opportunity cost of postponing the alternative use of the site for another period.

If $V(n) = 0$, then extraction would continue, possibly until the resource is exhausted because of the absence of opportunity costs. Otherwise, extraction will stop while some level of resource still exists.

Another way to view equations (16.7a) and (16.7b) is to solve for p on the left-hand side of equation (16.7b). Then, by equating the left-hand sides of equation (16.7a) with p solved for in equation (16.7b), we obtain the result:

$$C'(s) = \frac{rV(n) - V'(n) + C(s)}{s}. \tag{16.8}$$

This equation says another unit expenditure on s, $C'(s)$, should be equal to the average cost per period which includes inventory control costs, variable costs, and capital loss (gains). Stated another way, extraction should increase to the point where the marginal cost of intensifying extraction equals the average cost of extending the time of extraction.

Income Streams from Exhaustible Resources

One way to resolve the conflict over present and future payments received from the extraction of exhaustible resources is to save. For example, a worker has a finite period over which he or she is an active participant in the work force. Income after retirement must, therefore, be provided from savings made during the worker's career. Likewise, future generations may benefit from a

Example 16.1: Extraction of an Exhaustible Resource

Harder N. Roc owns a quarry containing gravel stock S_0. The price per unit of gravel is p. Extraction of the gravel requires a shovel with which u units of gravel per period can be extracted. Production per period can be increased by purchasing more shovels. The acquisition cost per shovel is F_x and the number of shovels purchased is x. Meanwhile, the variable cost for operating each shovel is p_x.

The question is: how many shovels should be purchased? The question is important because the number of shovels determines the length of time gravel is extracted. Shortening the extraction period reduces the time cost, but increases shovel acquisition costs. Assuming the extraction exhausts the resource reduces the problem to finding the number of shovels to purchase, since $n=S_0/xu$ and u is a constant. In this problem, the extraction per period is $s=xu$. NPV is expressed as:

$$\max_{x,n} NPV = \int_0^n (pxu - p_x x)\, e^{-rt} dt - xF_x,$$ (16.9)

$$s.t. \quad n = S_0/xu.$$

Substituting for n at the top of the integral sign, NPV is rewritten as:

$$\max_x NPV = \int_0^{S_0/xu} (pxu - p_x x)\, e^{-rt} dt - xF_x$$ (16.10)

$$= (pxu - p_x x)\, US_0(r, S_0/xu) - xF_x.$$

The first-order condition equals:

$$\frac{dNPV}{dx} = (pu - p_x)\, US_0(r, S_0/xu) + (pxu - p_x x) \frac{\partial US_0(r, S_0/xu)}{\partial x} - F_x = 0,$$

and:

Example 16.1, Cont'd.: Extraction of an Exhaustible Resource

$$pu - p_x = F_x / US_0(r, S_0/xu) - \frac{(pxu - p_x x)\dfrac{\partial\, US_0(r, S_0/xu)}{\partial x}}{US_0(r, S_0/xu)}.$$

The solution reveals that shovels should be purchased until the marginal return equals the annualized cost of an additional shovel less the change in the annualized return earned during a reduced period of extraction. (Adapted from Greenberg, Kim, and Manes.)

current extraction of exhaustible resources if part of the revenue from the sale of the exhaustible resources is saved, reinvested, and paid to future generations.

El Serafy considered how much of the net cash returns from the extraction and sale of exhaustible natural resources should be invested to provide an infinite stream of constant real income. Call this infinite stream of constant real income, permanent income generated from the capital stock. In other words, permanent income equals income from capital that can be consumed without reducing the durable's potential to provide income in the future. We now ask: what level of investment is required to obtain a permanent income stream from nonrenewable natural resources?

To answer the question, assume a nonrenewable natural resource will provide a stream of net cash returns R for n periods, after which the resource is exhausted and no further income can be generated. Obviously, R is not a permanent income. But suppose some portion of R, call this amount I, were invested in each period at interest rate r. Thus, during the n periods of extraction, R dollars of income are generated, of which y is consumed and $I = (R - y)$ is reinvested. El Serafy asked: What level must I equal to sustain consumption at level y in perpetuity?

The ratio of permanent income y divided by total cash returns R provided by the resource during the extraction period is now calculated. To find y/R, define the PV of the exhaustible natural resource V_0 as the PV of the net cash returns R earned over n periods. V_0 is written as:

$$V_0 = \frac{R}{(1+r)} + \ldots + \frac{R}{(1+r)^n} = \frac{R}{r}\left[1 - \frac{1}{(1+r)^n}\right]. \tag{16.11}$$

Similarly, the *PV* of the exhaustible natural resource can be expressed as the capitalized value of the infinite income stream y or:

$$V_0 = \frac{y}{(1+r)} + \frac{y}{(1+r)^2} + \ldots = \frac{y}{r}. \qquad (16.12)$$

Equating the right-hand sides of equations (16.11) and (16.12), y/R is found to equal:

$$y/R = 1 - \frac{1}{(1+r)^n}.$$

Similarly, the ratio I/R equals $1-(y/R)$ or:

$$I/R = 1/(1+r)^n.$$

The ratio of consumed income to net cash returns in each of the n periods, y/R, depends only on the length of the extraction period n and the discount rate r. Increasing r or n reduces the savings rate required to maintain consumption at y in perpetuity. The relationships among I/R, r, and n are summarized in Table 16.1.

The problem just solved can be generalized. Suppose that an individual owns an exhaustible resource, but does not require an infinite earnings stream from the resource. Instead, the individual requires only an income stream y^* for n^* periods. To find the percentage of returns that must be invested to earn income y^* for n^* periods, equation (16.12) is replaced with the expression:

$$V_0 = \frac{y^*}{(1+r)} + \ldots + \frac{y^*}{(1+r)^{n^*}} = \frac{y^*}{r}\left[1 - \frac{1}{(1+r)^{n^*}}\right]. \qquad (16.13)$$

Then equating the right-hand side of equation (16.13) with the right-hand side of equation (16.11), the new ratio of y^*/R is found to equal:

$$\frac{y^*}{R} = \left[1 - \frac{1}{(1+r)^n}\right] / \left[1 - \frac{1}{(1+r)^{n^*}}\right]. \qquad (16.14)$$

Public versus Private Resources Extraction Rates ————

Another important question related to the extraction of exhaustible resources involves the difference between optimal private versus public extraction rates. The difference can be illustrated graphically.

Suppose the demand for a resource is expressed as $p=D(q)$ while the constant marginal cost of extracting the resource is p_q. Graphically, the market equilibrium would be q^* as shown in Figure 16.1.

The net social benefit (*NSB*) is the triangle PP_q^*A in Figure 16.1 equal to the area above the p_q^* line and below the demand curve and to the left of q^*. *NSB* is the worth of the resource in excess of its cost p_q. The consuming public's preferred level of extraction is q^*.

Table 16.1 Portion of Cash Returns That Must Be Invested (*I/R*) to Produce Consumption Possibilities of *y* in Perpetuity

Extraction Periods (*n*)	Discount Rate (*r*)									
	1	2	3	4	5	6	7	8	9	10
					-percent-					
2	98	96	94	92	91	89	87	86	84	83
3	97	94	92	89	86	84	82	79	77	75
4	96	92	89	85	82	79	76	73	71	68
5	95	91	86	82	78	75	71	68	65	62
6	94	89	84	79	75	70	67	63	60	56
7	93	87	81	76	73	67	62	58	55	51
8	92	85	79	73	68	63	58	54	50	47
9	91	84	77	70	64	59	54	50	46	42
10	91	82	74	68	61	56	51	46	42	39
11	89	80	72	65	58	53	48	43	39	35
15	86	74	64	56	48	42	36	32	27	24
20	82	67	55	46	38	31	26	21	18	15
30	74	55	41	31	23	17	13	10	8	6

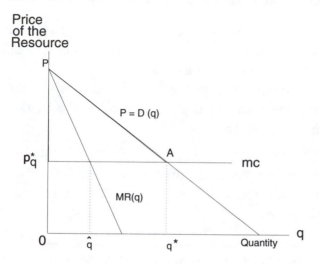

Price
of the
Resource

P = D (q)

A

mc

p_q^*

MR(q)

0        $\hat{q}$ q^* Quantity   q

Figure 16.1
Net Social Benefit of Extracting q^* of an Exhaustible Resource; Optimal Extraction Rate if the Resource is Privately Owned

Example 16.2: Investing Returns of an Exhaustible Resource

Eaze E. Street owns a gravel pit that is expected to earn $100,000 net of extraction costs for 15 years. Eaze has a current life expectancy of 40 years and wants to know: What percentage of the $100,000 may be consumed and still have a constant annuity over the next 40 years of his life that completely exhausts the value of his investment? Mr. Street calculates that any amount of money invested can earn a rate of return of 7 percent.

Using equation (16.14), Mr. Street calculates y^*/R equal to:

$$y^* / R = \left[1 - (1.07)^{-15}\right] / \left[1 - (1.07)^{-40}\right]$$
$$= .64 / .93 = 68 \text{ percent.}$$

Thus, 32 percent of the $100,000 must be reinvested in each period or 68 percent of the returns can be consumed.

On the other hand, if the resource is privately owned, then the firm maximizes the profit from extracting the resource instead of maximizing *NSB*. The firm's profit function equals:

Example 16.3: Managing Water Resources

Farmers who face water management problems must consider their feasible water sources; the investment, financing, and operating costs of alternative distribution and drainage systems; crop responses to water; and legal controls. Irrigation water typically comes from ponds, reservoirs, lakes, streams, canals, or wells. Drilling wells and establishing water distribution systems require large, lumpy capital investments, and relatively high annual operating costs. Even with higher, more stable yields, payback periods for the initial investment may cover many years.

Special problems arise when groundwater is the primary source of an area's irrigation water. Groundwater has accumulated over long geological ages, although some is replaced by current rainfall as it is used. Heavy pumping reduces the permanent supply and lowers the water table. The results are increasingly costly irrigation and expected depletion of that water supply within a finite planning horizon.

Many groundwater formations do not receive appreciable recharge of water supply relative to annual withdrawals for irrigation. Moreover, groundwater is generally considered a common property resource, since many users may tap from the same reservoir. Thus, as pumping becomes increasingly costly, resources committed to irrigated crop production will revert to dryland farming. The result will be reduced annual returns to individual producers, lower land values, and lower economic activity in these areas.

Several studies have utilized *PV* models and farm-level or regional optimization (e.g., linear programming, dynamic programming) models to project groundwater withdrawal rates under alternative irrigation practices and have derived optimal (i.e., *PV* maximizing) time patterns of water use for variations in discount rates, crop market conditions, technologies for water handling systems, and other business constraints. Not surprisingly, rates of water use tend to increase for higher levels of discount rates and for changes in crop conditions that increase near term returns relative to future returns.

The results of such studies provide important managerial insight to private decision makers about strategies for water use over time, and they provide important policy insights to public-sector decision

---

Example 16.3, Cont'd.: Managing Water Resources

makers who may wish to constrain or otherwise influence water allocation by private decision makers for the benefit of future generations or for regional development purposes. Furthermore, such analyses may stimulate the development of new techniques and technologies for water conservation that will prolong the availability of the exhaustible groundwater supplies (Lacewell and Grubb; Burt; Bekure and Eidman).

$$\max \, \pi = p(q)\,q - p_q\,q = D(q)\,q - p_q\,q.$$

The solution from maximizing firm profits equals:

$$D'(q)\,q + D(q) = p_q,$$

where $D'(q)q + D(q)$ is the marginal revenue from q, $MR(q)$.

Since $D'(q) < 0$, the solution for the individual will not be $D(q)=p_q$ but $MR(q)=p_q^*$. This solution is represented in Figure 16.1 as $\hat{q} < q^*$.

In this case, the resource is conserved more when it is privately owned than if it were publicly owned. This is not always the case.

Example 16.3 describes a practical extraction problem facing farmers in many arid areas. It points out the importance of solving for optimal resource extraction rates.

Harvest Rates of Renewable Resources —————————

Renewable resource owners and managers most often face two kinds of decision problems. In one, the harvest rate is fixed and the time between harvests must be determined. In the second, the time between harvests is fixed, and the harvest rate must be determined.

Examples of the first case include trees and growing livestock for slaughter where the complete tree is harvested or the animal is slaughtered. Partial harvest or slaughter is not considered. Examples of the second case include: (1) the harvest of perennial crops, where growth in the current period is a function of harvest in the previous period; (2) fish harvests; and (3) in developing countries, the level of services to extract per day from oxen, knowing that today's performance is a function of the previous day's exertion. These alternatives can be considered in two cases of renewable resources.

It will be helpful later on to represent the net cash returns as a neoclassical production function defined over the variable input harvest time (n). This production function is represented in Figure 16.2 as having returns that increase at an increasing rate ($R'(n) > 0$ and $R''(n) > 0$), then increase at a decreasing rate ($R'(n) > 0$ and $R''(n) < 0$), and then decrease at an increasing rate ($R'(n) < 0$ and $R''(n) < 0$).

Case 1: Harvest Rate Dependent on Time between Harvests

In this case, the entire stock is harvested all at once. An example is the harvest of a forest or the slaughter of feed animals. The harvest is completed to make room for replacements. However, the amount of harvest depends on the length of growing time between harvests.

Let $R'(n)$ be marginal cash returns associated with growth in the nth period and $R(n)$ be the net return from harvest in the nth period. The opportunity cost in this case is not a different use of the resource, but repetition of the same use of the resource which will continue to earn returns $R(n)$ every n periods. Thus, the *NPV* for this problem is written as:

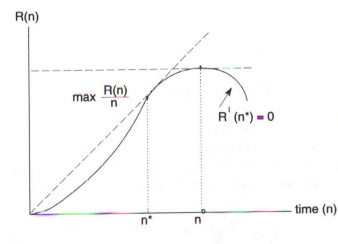

Figure 16.2
Neoclassical Production Functions Converted to Cash Units Defined over Harvest Time

$$\max_{n} NPV = -V_0 + R(n)\left[e^{-rn} + e^{-r2n} + e^{-r3n} + \ldots\right]$$

$$= -V_0 + \frac{R(n)}{(e^{rn}-1)}. \tag{16.15}$$

After maximizing *NPV* with respect to n, we find n that satisfies the first-order condition:

$$R'(n) = \frac{rR(n)}{(1-e^{-rn})}. \tag{16.16}$$

Expressing the solution as the ratio of marginal to average cash returns, we write:

$$\frac{R'(n)}{R(n)/n} = \frac{nr}{(1-e^{-rn})}. \tag{16.17}$$

Call the value for n that satisfies equations (16.16) or (16.17) $\hat{n}$.

The interpretation of equation (16.6) is straightforward. Keep the renewable resource growing until the marginal cash return $R'(\hat{n})$ equals the annualized average cash return of the replacement. To show that $rR(\hat{n})/(1-e^{-r\hat{n}})$ is the annualized average cash return, we find the annualized average A such that:

$$R(\hat{n}) = \int_0^{\hat{n}} Ae^{-rt}\,dt = \frac{A(1-e^{-r\hat{n}})}{r}.$$

Solving for A, yields:

$$A = \frac{rR(\hat{n})}{(1-e^{-r\hat{n}})} = R'(\hat{n}).$$

The optimal solution for $\hat{n}$ is illustrated graphically in Figure 16.3.

An alternative objective function to the one that maximizes *NPV* might be to maximize the average cash return per harvest, $R(n)/n$. This solution can be written as:

$$\max_{n} \frac{R(n)}{n}.$$

R'(n̂),A(n̂)

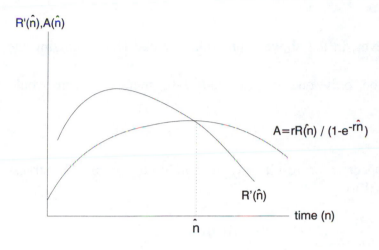

A=rR(n) / (1-e^{-rn̂})

R'(n̂)

time (n)

n̂

Figure 16.3
Optimal Harvest Period
n̂ where Marginal Cash
Return R'(n̂) Equals An-
nualized Cash Returns
A = rR(n)/(1-e^{-rn})

Differentiating average returns with respect to *n*, we find:

$$\frac{nR'(n) - R(n)}{n^2} = 0.$$

And the average profit maximizing *n* satisfies:

$$R'(n) = \frac{R(n)}{n}. \tag{16.18}$$

The ratio of marginal to average cash returns for the solution in equation (16.18) can be expressed as:

$$\frac{R'(n)}{R(n)/n} = 1. \tag{16.19}$$

Call the value for *n* that satisfies equations (16.18) or (16.19) n^*.

A relevant question is: Why would a decision maker ever maximize average returns? The answer is: When $r=0$ and the total growing time *N* is fixed, then $n=n^*$ maximizes average returns and also maximizes *NPV*. To demonstrate this point, let $r=0$ in equation (16.15) and assume there will be *N/n* harvests. Then, total returns equal:

$$\max_{n} \ NPV = \frac{N}{n} R(n) = N \left[\frac{R(n)}{n} \right].$$

Maximizing *NPV*, however, in the above expression is equal to maximizing the average cash returns.

If there were to be only one harvest and $n>0$, then the firm would maximize:

$$\max_{n} \ NPV = R(n) e^{-rn}.$$

Differentiating with respect to *n* results in the condition for single harvest return maximization equal to:

$$\frac{dNPV}{dn} = R'(n) e^{-rn} - rR(n) e^{-rn} = 0,$$

and expressing the result as a ratio of marginal to average returns, we write:

$$\frac{R'(n)}{R(n)/n} = rn.$$

We represent the optimal solution for *n* above as $n = \bar{n}$.

If the firm wants to merely maximize returns at harvest, then its objective function is:

$$\max_{n} \ R(n),$$

and:

$$\frac{dR(n)}{dn} = R'(n) = 0.$$

This solution is represented as $n=n^0$.

When would a decision maker ever choose to maximize total returns per harvest? The answer is: When $r=0$ and when harvest time is unrestricted. To demonstrate this point, let $r=0$ in equation (16.15) and assume there will be *m* harvests of unrestricted length. Then, total returns equal:

$$\max_{n} \ NPV = mR(n). \tag{16.20}$$

Maximizing *NPV* with constant *m*, however, in the above expression is equal to maximizing *R(n)* which is obtained at $R'(n)=0$.

The alternative solutions for harvest dates are summarized in Table 16.2. In Table 16.2, the solution symbols ($\hat{n}$, n^*, $\bar{n}$, and n^0) are given along with their solutions, and the conditions under which the solutions are consistent with *NPV* maximums.

The alternative solutions are represented graphically in Figure 16.4. The solution that maximizes total return per harvest is represented as n^0 in Figure 16.4. It is that solution for which $R'(n)$ equals zero. The solution that maximizes average returns is represented by finding the tangency of a line drawn from the origin to R(n). At this point of tangency, $R'(n)$ equals $R(n)/n$ and is represented in Figure 16.4 as point n^*.

Points n^* and n^0 serve as reference points for other solutions. For example, suppose that $nr=1$. Under this assumption, the single harvest solution is $\bar{n}=n^*$. If $nr<1$, then $R'(n)<[R(n)/n]$ and $\bar{n}<n^*$. Similar reasoning for $nr>1$ leads to the conclusion that $n^*<\bar{n}<n^0$.

We represent the solution to equation (16.17) in Figure 16.4 as $n=n^*$.

Finally, if $nr/(1-e^{-rn})$ is one, then $n^*=\hat{n}$. However, if $n^*=\hat{n}$, then $nr<1$ and $\bar{n}>n^*$. For all $r>0$, it follows that $\bar{n}>\hat{n}$—or that increasing the number of replacements increases opportunity costs and shortens the time between harvests.

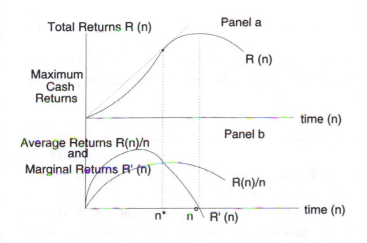

Total Returns R (n)   Panel a

R (n)

Maximum
Cash
Returns

time (n)

Average Returns R(n)/n
and
Marginal Returns R' (n)

Panel b

R(n)/n

n^* n^0 R' (n)   time (n)

Figure 16.4
Total Cash Returns
(Panel *a*) and Average
Cash Returns, R(*n*)/n,
and Marginal Cash
Returns $R'(n)$, (Panel *b*)

Table 16.2 Harvest Rate Solutions (*n*) under Alternative Conditions

	Satisfies	Comments
$\hat{n}$: maximizes *NPV* of infinite number of harvests	$\dfrac{R'(\hat{n})}{R(\hat{n})/\hat{n}} = \dfrac{\hat{n}r}{(1-e^{-r\hat{n}})}$	Appropriate when *r*>0 and the number of harvests is infinite
n^*: maximizes average return	$\dfrac{R'(n^*)}{R(n^*)/n^*} = 1$	Appropriate when *r*=0 and total growing time is fixed
$\tilde{n}$: maximizes *NPV* of a single harvest	$\dfrac{R'(\tilde{n})}{R(\tilde{n})/\tilde{n}} = \tilde{n}r$	Appropriate when there is only one harvest and *r*>0
n^0: maximizes returns at harvest	$R'(n^0) = 0$	Appropriate when *r*=0 and unlimited time is available for harvesting *m* harvests

---

Now, compare solutions $\tilde{n}$ in equation (16.17) with $\hat{n}$ in equation (16.16). Only if:

$$(1 - e^{-rn})/r = n,$$

will the solutions that maximize *NPV* of a single harvest equal the solutions that maximize *NPV*. But, $\int_0^n e^{-rt}dt = (1-e^{-rn})/r = n$ only if *r*=0. So, for all positive values of *r*, *n* will always be greater than $\int_0^n e^{-rt}dt$. This condition implies that for the usual case of $R'(n)>0$ and $R''(n)<0$, the optimal harvest date will be $\hat{n} < \tilde{n}$, or earlier than the harvest date that maximized an individual harvest.

Summary

This chapter has shown that the derivation of optimal extraction rates of natural resources is based on the use of familiar *PV* tools. These tools developed in the context of solving disposal, replacement, and rotation problems apply equally well to solving natural resource problems, which themselves are problems of disposal, replacement, and rotation. The study of exhaustible resource use is, indeed, a disposal problem. Because the resource

Example 16.4: Finding Optimal Harvest Time

Peter and Paula Pulp grow trees for use as paper products. They estimate the net cash return per stand of trees is:

$$R(n) = 10n - 0.1n^2.$$

Their opportunity cost of capital is 18 percent. Since $R'(n) = 10 - 0.2n = 0$ or $n=5$, to maximize net returns per period they would harvest at age five. (This solution corresponds to $\bar{n}$.) On the other hand, if they maximized average harvest per period, they would harvest trees at year n that satisfied the expression:

$$R'(n) = R(n)/n,$$
$$\text{or} \quad 10 - 0.2n = 10 - 0.1n.$$

The only value of n that satisfies the above expression is $n=0$. (This solution corresponds to n^*.) If harvest occurred according to the replacement rule satisfying equation (16.16), they would harvest at age n that satisfies:

$$10 - 0.2n = \frac{(10n - 0.1n^2)(0.13)}{1 - e^{-0.13n}}.$$

The value of n that satisfies this expression (found by searching) is $n=3.4$. (This solution corresponds to $\hat{n}$.) Thus, $n^* \approx 0 < \hat{n} = 3.4 < \bar{n} = 5$.

cannot be replenished or the extraction cycle repeated, the only real choice is to dispose of (or conserve by limited use) the exhaustible resource. The main task is to derive an optimal intertemporal disposal path.

Renewable resources, on the other hand, are a different matter. In this case, the regeneration property of renewable resources makes their analysis resemble a replacement problem. Moreover, a renewable resource problem takes on some of the properties of a rotation model because the level of its initial production can be altered by adjusting the harvest date. If the harvest date is fixed, as occurs for some renewable resources, the level of harvest can achieve the same result of altering the level of output or production at which the cycle begins.

The analysis of publicly- and privately-owned resources may lead to quite different solutions. When resources are not privately owned, or in the case of unborn users unable to reflect their desires for optimal resource use, one cannot always rely on the market determined price to allocate resource use over time. The evaluation of public versus private projects will be considered in Chapter 19. For now, remember that *PV* analysis is needed to solve for optimal resource use over time for both nonrenewable and renewable resources.

Endnotes

1. We thank Ted Graham-Tomasi for his review and comments on this chapter.

2. Readers may benefit from reviewing continuous time concepts discussed in Chapter 21 before completing this section of the chapter.

3. The derivative of e^{-rn} with respect to n is $-re^{-rn}$. The derivative of $\int_0^n [ps - C(s)] e^{-rt} dt$ with respect to n is $[ps - C(s)] e^{-rn}$. The derivative of $\int_0^n [ps - C(s)] e^{-rt} dt$ with respect to s is:

$$[p - C'(s)] \int_0^n e^{-rt} dt.$$

A more general discussion of differentiating integrals is provided in Chapter 21.

Review Questions

1. Distinguish between exhaustible and renewable natural resources. Give examples of each.

2. Why might some groups or individuals object to a time path of natural resource use that maximizes the *NPV*s of resource owners?

3. Why was it important to use the continuous time discount factor e^{-rt} to solve the *NPV* harvest problem?

4. How would the optimal harvest time of a renewable resource, whose stock depends on its age, vary if the discount rate were: (a) zero; or (b) positive; and if the resource could only be harvested once?

5. Explain why the optimal extraction of a privately-owned exhaustible resource may differ from the optimal extraction of a publicly-owned exhaustible resource.

Application Questions

1. Suppose you must determine the optimal level of extraction of an exhaustible resource and the length of time over which extraction is to occur. Use equations (16.7a) and (16.7b) to find the optimal extraction amount per period s and the period of time over which extraction is to occur (assume the resource is not exhausted) if:

$$C(s) = 10s + 0.01 s^2 ; \; r = 0.13, \; p = 15,$$

and:

$$V(t) = 5 + 3t.$$

2. Compare the solution to equation (16.8) with the solution to equation (16.16). Describe the similarities. How does one intensify versus extensify the extraction of resources?

3. Resolve the problem described in problem (1), only now let the cost of resource extraction depend on the amount already extracted. That is, the cost function in (1) is modified to:

$$C(s, t) = 10s + 0.01 s^2 + 0.001 (ts).$$

Explain the differences in answers to the problems described in this question and question (1).

4. You expect to be employed for 30 years during which time you will contribute to a retirement fund. Your retirement contributions will be reinvested at a rate of 9 percent. If you expect to live for 25 years beyond retirement, at what level should you save to maintain a constant level of consumption during your working and retirement years?

5. Suppose income from an exhaustible resource is initially expected to grow at rate g for n periods. Assume the investor desires a perpetual income

stream initially at y_0 but which grows at rate h. Find the ratio of y_t/R_t for periods $y_1/R_1,\ldots,y_{10}/R_{10}$ using hypothetical numbers: g=0.08, h=0.05, r=0.1, and n=10 where:

$$V_0 = \frac{R(1+g)}{(r-g)}\left[1 - \left(\frac{1+g}{1+r}\right)^n\right] = \frac{y_0(1+h)}{(r-h)}.$$

Furthermore, let $R_t=R(1+g)^t$ and $y_t=y_0(1+h)^t$.

6. Assume you are faced with two opportunities to prepare for retirement. The first is a supplemental retirement plan that allows you to invest R before-tax dollars for n_1 periods. Then, for the next n_2 periods, the invested funds plus earnings are withdrawn and taxed at the constant income tax rate T. The second investment opportunity allows you to invest after-tax dollars $R(1-T)$ for n_1 periods. Then, for the next n_2 periods, the invested funds plus earnings are withdrawn with no tax obligation—which, if either, plan is preferred if r is both the discount rate and the reinvestment rate?

References

Bekure, S.E. and V.R. Eidman. "Intertemporal Allocation of Ground Water in the Central Ogalla Formation." *Southern Journal of Agricultural Economics* 3(1971):155-60.

Burt, O.R. "The Economics of Conjunctive Use of Ground and Surface Water." *Hilgardia* 36(1964):31-111.

_____. "Economic Control of Groundwater Reserves." *Journal of Farm Economics* 48(1966):632-47.

Carlson, G.A., D. Zilberman, and J.A. Miranowski, eds. *Agricultural Resources and the Environment.* New York: Oxford University Press, 1993.

El Serafy, S. "The Proper Calculation of Income from Depletable Natural Resources." *Environmental and Resource Accounting and Their Relevance to the Measurement of Sustainable Income.* Washington, DC: World Bank, 1988.

Greenberg, R., S.K. Kim, and R. Manes. "Optimal Exploitation of a Stock Resource." *The Engineering Economist* 28(1982):293-309.

Hotelling, H. "The Economics of Exhaustible Resources." *Journal of Political Economy* 30(1931):137-75.

Lacewell, R.D. and H.W. Grubb. "Economic Implications of Alternative Allocations of an Exhaustible Irrigation Water Supply." *Southern Journal of Agricultural Economics* 3(1971):149-54.

Lee, W.F. and P.J. Barry. "The Setting for Firm Growth: Market, Institutional and Legal Issues." *Economic Growth of the Agricultural Firm*. College of Agriculture Research Center, Washington State University, February 1977.

Chapter 17

Enterprise Budgets

Key words: capital budgets, capital gains, cash flow budgets, cost of production estimates, depreciation, economic life, enterprise or traditional budgets, opportunity cost, ownership costs, real interest rate

Introduction

Significant attention is given to estimating budgets. For example, a recent task force sponsored by the Economic Research Service of the U.S. Department of Agriculture, the American Agricultural Economics Association (AAEA), and many universities devoted much time and effort to defining procedures for estimating and calculating costs and returns for growing crops and other commodities (Ahern and Vasavada). Much of the debate in that project involved the proper allocation of costs of using durables. This chapter uses present value (*PV*) tools to guide the construction of budgets with emphasis on the allocation of the costs of using durables. This chapter demonstrates that an enterprise budget can be viewed as an application of *PV* analysis where durable(s) are components of the net present value (*NPV*) model.

Definition of Budgets

Budgeting methods involve an orderly approach to assembling and analyzing information about investments in durable and nondurable assets. These investment alternatives may differ not only in the durable to be purchased, but also in the means of financing. The investment being considered defines the unit of analysis for capital budgeting or investment analysis. In some cases, this may be for an individual enterprise (acre, cow, etc.) or for an aggregate of investments that produce a single or joint products. Firm budgets frequently are designed to describe the economic activities of an economic unit such as a single-owner business, a partnership, or corporation. Some typical budgets are described next.

Cash Flow Budgets. In financial management, the emphasis is on cash flow budgets. These budgets are projections and ex-post summaries of cash transactions associated with a particular enterprise. Cash flow budgets are helpful to firms as they plan for the resources needed to cover their cash needs.

Capital Budgeting or Investment Analysis. Capital budgeting is a procedure for evaluating how a firm's investment choices affect a business's equity, risk, and liquidity. The process of capital budgeting includes identifying alternative investments, collecting relevant data, assuring consistency in comparisons, and evaluating the data. The analysis part of capital budgeting is based on *PV* models.

Enterprise Budgets. Sometimes referred to as traditional budgets, enterprise budgets include both cash and noncash elements. Enterprise budgets give decision makers a periodic check on the economic performance of their investments. Their short-run focus represents a snapshot of the contribution of durables during a period of time rather than considering the contribution of durables over their economic lives. Therein lies the problem. How does one allocate returns to the durable or durables contributing to the enterprise?

The questions raised above have realistic implications. The U.S. Congress passes appropriation bills and determines price supports for some commodities produced by the U.S. agricultural sector based on enterprise budgets estimated by the ERS, sometimes aided by universities. These budgets may in turn affect the costs and returns of growing crops and the capitalized value of durables. Individual owners of durables need periodic checks on the profitability of their investments. Constructed enterprise budgets can provide the needed investment information.

A significant problem in constructing enterprise budgets is the estimation of changes in durable values not evaluated by sales in the market place. The discussion that follows suggests methods deduced from *PV* models to build enterprise budgets. When appropriate, this chapter will point out methods used to approximate durables' use costs and explain why budget builders may sometimes disagree about budget formulations.

Theoretical Basis for Enterprise Budgets ⎯⎯⎯⎯⎯⎯⎯⎯

Consider a durable purchased at price V_0 that provides s units of services per period for n periods, after which the durable disintegrates into nothing. To produce a product, the durable's services must be combined with a variable input x purchased each period at price p_x. In addition, the budgets must allow for fixed cash costs F (independent of depreciation) to be subtracted from returns. In some economic applications F includes noncash as well as cash costs. We restrict F to cash costs for consistency with PV construction principles described in Chapter 4. Were taxes included, F would include real estate taxes on land. The purchase of x, its transformation into an output, and the sale of the output are, for the moment, assumed to occur at the same time. Assuming instantaneous production that combines services s from a durable and an expendable input x, the NPV of the enterprise with one durable is expressed as:

$$NPV = -V_0 + \frac{pf(x, s) - p_x x - F}{(1+r)} + \dots + \frac{pf(x, s) - p_x x - F}{(1+r)^n}. \tag{17.1}$$

The firm determines its optimal input level x^* that satisfies:

$$pf'(x^*; s) = p_x,$$

(assuming $f''(x^*; s) < 0$).

To determine the durable's profitability in each period, the firm calculates:

$$R = pf(x^*, s) - p_x x^* - F. \tag{17.2}$$

The firm could separate cash returns from cash operating costs, $p_x x^*$, in each period and construct the cash operating budget described in Table 17.1. Expenses F, not included as part of cash operating expenses, will be referred to as ownership costs or time costs.

Table 17.1 A Single-Period Cash Operating Budget

Cash Receipts	Cash Operating Costs
$pf(x^*; s)$	$p_x x^*$

Example 17.1: Cash Operating Expenses of Soybeans in Ohio and Michigan

The Governors of Ohio and Michigan have requested that cash operating expenses be calculated on a per acre basis for soybeans for the year 1989. The results are presented below:

Cash Operating Expenses	1989
Seed	$15.56
Fertilizer	$76.02
Chemicals	$51.02
Custom Operations	$23.85
Fuel, Lube, and Electricity	$25.52
Repairs	$39.83
Hired Labor	$49.25
Noncash Benefits	$ 1.81
Freight and Dirt-Hauling Charges	$10.13
Miscellaneous	$ 2.10
Hauling Allowance	$-0.73
Total Cash Operating Expenses	$294.37

Source: "Costs of Production–Major Field Crops, 1989," *Economic Indicators of the Farm Sector.* USDA, ERS, ECIFS 9-5, April 1991.

Defining Costs of Using Durables

One of the important critiques of the static neoclassical production function is that it ignores time. Ignoring time when describing production processes has led to a confused concept of fixed costs in production models. What are fixed costs? Costs that are independent of output in a single period can only be a function of time. That is, what are commonly referred to as fixed costs must in reality be costs associated with inventory costs, depreciation associated with the passage of time, or other services that vary with time. All these costs plus fixed cash costs are included in what are traditionally called ownership costs.

Depreciation

Durables can be distinguished by their changes (losses) in service capacity. Service capacities may change as a result of use, time, or the interaction of time and use. Moreover, the value of a durable changes as a result of both changes in the durable's service capacity and with the market value of the durable's services.

Enterprise budgets generally assume that the values of durables decline over time. Thus, most enterprise budgets include a cost category called depreciation that lumps together the changes in the values of durables attributed to time, use, and changes in the market.

The major cost considered here is the value of the durable's service capacity lost through use. We call this "direct user cost." This cost is measured by the expenditure required to restore the durable to its original level of service capacity in the current period. Or, one might conceptualize this cost as the difference between two durables that are identical except for the services extracted in the most recent period. Because this cost depends on use, it is a variable cost to the firm.

The value of the durable's service capacity lost through time is called capacity time cost. Examples of capacity time cost have already been given. Because these costs are beyond control of the durable's owner, except during the durable design stage, they are not considered variable costs. Nonetheless, the durable's owner still may have some degree of control over capacity time costs.

Altering the rate of service extraction changes both the life of the durable and the number of periods in which the durable's service capacity is reduced by the passage of time. If the service capacity depends on use and time, use decisions can affect capacity time costs.

The final depreciation category of durable ownership costs is imposed by the market. The value of the durable depends on the value of its services. Changes in market demand and supply of these services expose the firm to the possibility of gains or losses in the durable's value. If the durable's value declines, as a result of changes in its service, the resulting cost is considered a capital loss. This loss in value is often referred to as economic depreciation (see Chapter 9).

Opportunity Costs

Durables, like any inventory, experience holding costs. If the firm's capital were not committed to the inventory of durable services, it could be invested elsewhere to earn its opportunity cost. The opportunity cost of holding durable services is "inventory time cost." Inventory time costs will decrease as the durable ages and its inventory of potential services is reduced. To reduce inventory time costs, one might anticipate heavier durable use earlier in its life than later. Opportunity costs may also be associated with expendables purchased at the beginning of the period.

Other Time (Fixed) Costs

Other time (fixed) costs are another cost category. Insurance costs are often referred to as a fixed cost. But insurance costs depend on the level and duration of the coverage so they are really a cost associated with time. Taxes, especially property taxes on land and in some states on durables, are also used to exemplify fixed costs. But taxes like insurance are assessed per unit of time and are referred to as other time costs.

The characteristics of the durable just described lead to the following description of costs associated with using durable services. These costs are described below.

PV Bases for Enterprise Budgets

To construct an accurate measure of the total costs and returns of the enterprise during a period, recall from Chapter 5 that when *NPV* is zero, the value of the durable V_t can be written as:

$$V_t = (1+r) \, V_{t-1} - R_t. \tag{17.3}$$

Substituting for R_t, equation (17.2) and solving for cash returns, we write:

$$pf(x^*,s) = p_x x^* + (V_{t-1} - V_t) + r V_{t-1} + F. \tag{17.4}$$

With returns and costs described above, an enterprise budget that represents the durable's cost is now described in Table 17.3. The cost term $p_x x^*$ represents the cost of purchasing expendables or cash operating expenses. Depreciation or changes in the durable's value associated with use, time, or changes in the market equal $(V_{t-1} - V_t)$. Opportunity costs associated with holding an inventory of durable services equal the opportunity cost of capital times

Table 17.2 Durable Ownership Costs

Type of Cost	Definition
Depreciation	
Direct user cost	Value of service capacity (inventory) lost by use.
Capacity time cost	Value of service capacity lost by the passage of time.
Market induced capital gains (losses)	Change in value of asset (not a change in service capacity) resulting from changes in the demand for the asset's services or the cost of supplying services.
Opportunity Costs	
Opportunity cost of durables	Cost of funds committed to holding an inventory of durable asset services.
Opportunity cost of expendables	Cost of funds committed to holding an inventory of expendables.
Other Time Costs Insurance, taxes, licenses, and others	Other cash costs of production not affected by durable use.

Table 17.3 Single-Period Enterprise Budget

Returns		Expenses	
Sale of product	$pf(x^*,s)$	Cash operating expenses	$p_x x^*$
		Depreciation	$V_{t-1} - V_t$
		Opportunity cost of durables	rV_{t-1}
		Other time costs	F
Total returns	$pf(x^*,s)$	Total costs	$p_x x^* + F + r_t V_{t-1} + (V_{t-1} - V_t)$

$$\text{profit } \pi = pf(x^*,s) - p_x x^* - (V_{t-1}-V_t) - rV_{t-1} - F$$

the value of the inventory at the beginning of the period: $r_t V_{t-1}$. Finally, other time (fixed) costs, F, may be associated with insurance, taxes, licenses, and some types of maintenance required by the passage of time. All of these costs are summarized in Table 17.3.

If total returns equal total costs in each period, then *NPV* is zero. If not, the enterprise earns a profit (loss) equal to π_t where π_t equals:

$$\pi_t = pf(x^*, s) - p_x x - F - rV_{t-1} - (V_{t-1} - V_t). \tag{17.5}$$

Estimating Depreciation and Opportunity Costs ——————————

It is a standard practice among accountants to combine time and use cost into a single depreciation measure. Measurement difficulties prevent most accountants from attempting to divide depreciation measures into time and use depreciation measures. Moreover, tax laws often dictate the depreciation measure to be used. The depreciation measure depends on the class of durable in use, use rates, and the market in which it is bought and sold. All of these notions are intertemporal and consistent with *PV* model formulations.

One difficulty with constructing enterprise budgets is the lack of empirical data. Lack of good data often requires that accountants and others utilize approximations for actual values. For example, opportunity costs of durables are often approximated by interest charges paid for the use of the durable. Whether or not opportunity costs are accurately estimated depends on how well the interest rate reflects the firm's opportunity cost of capital. It also depends on how well the durable's book value estimates the durable's actual value. Another often used approximation is to substitute the straight-line depreciation method for actual depreciation $V_{t-1} - V_t$. Thus, an accountant might use V_0/n, to approximate $V_{t-1} - V_t$, assuming $V_n = 0$.

Even in the simplest cash flow relationships, however, straight-line depreciation may not be a good approximation (see Example 17.2). For example, assume the cash flow pattern is $R_t = R$, a constant. The exact measure of $V_{t-1} - V_t$ is calculated by taking the difference between V_{t-1} and V_t:

$$V_{t-1} = \frac{R}{(1+r)} + \dots + \frac{R}{(1+r)^{n-t}} + \frac{R}{(1+r)^{n-t+1}}, \tag{17.6}$$

and:

Example 17.2: Straight-Line Estimates of Economic Depreciation

Adam Wright is an accountant working for the firm whose enterprise budget was described in Table 17.3. Instead of charging $V_{t-1} - V_t$ for its depreciation costs, the accountant uses straight-line depreciation or V_0/n. Assume $R=\$50$, $r=0.12$, and $n=15$. Then:

$$V_0 = \$50 \; US_0 \, (0.12, 15) = \$340.54.$$

In the first period, actual depreciation is equal to:

$$V_0 - V_1 = \frac{R}{(1+r)^n} = \frac{50}{(1.12)^{15}} = \$9.13.$$

And, in the last period, depreciation is:

$$V_{14} - V_{15} = \frac{R}{(1+r)} = \frac{50}{1.12} = \$44.64.$$

But, according to the straight-line depreciation method, depreciation entered in traditional budgets in each period would equal $\$340.54/15=\$22.70$.

$$V_t = \frac{R}{(1+r)} + \dots + \frac{R}{(1+r)^{n-t}},$$

so that:

$$V_{t-1} - V_t = \frac{R}{(1+r)^{n-t+1}}, \tag{17.7}$$

which is not necessarily equal to V_0/n. Only when $r=0$ will $V_{t-1} - V_t$ always equal V_0/n.

The straight-line method of calculating depreciation does provide the correct depreciation measure on average. That is:

$$\sum_{t=1}^{n} \left(\frac{V_{t-1} - V_t}{n} \right) = (V_0 - V_n) / n. \tag{17.8}$$

But, $(V_{t-1} - V_t)$ need not equal $(V_0 - V_n)/n$ or any other ex ante determined depreciation value in any particular period.

Capital Recovery

Depreciation and opportunity cost of durables in Table 17.3 make up what is often referred to as capital recovery, often assumed to be constant over the economic life of the durable. For example, the durable whose PV or present cost is \$340.54 in Example 17.2 has a capital recovery cost each period equal to:

$$R = (V_{t-1} - V_t) + rV_{t-1} = V_0 / US_0(r, n),$$

or:

$$\$340.54 / US_0(.12, \ 15) = \$340.54 / 6.8109 = \$50.00.$$

Boehlje and Eidman, for example, calculated capital recovery in this manner (see pp. 142-44).

Ownership Costs

The summation of depreciation, $\left(\sum_{t=1}^{n} (V_{t-1} - V_t) \right)$, other time (fixed) costs F, and opportunity costs rV_{t-1}, equal what many refer to as ownership costs. When profit π_t is zero, the relationship from equation (17.5) can be expressed as:

$$\sum_{t=1}^{n} \left[pf(x^*, s) - p_x x \right] = \sum_{t=1}^{n} \left[(V_{t-1} - V_t) + rV_{t-1} + F \right]. \tag{17.9}$$

Moreover, if we let $\hat{R} = pf(x^*,s) - p_x x$, then after completing the summation and noting that the summation of depreciation equals $(V_0 - V_n)$ and the sum of opportunity costs equals:

$$r \sum_{t=1}^{n} V_{t-1}.$$

We obtain:

$$n\hat{R} = V_0 - V_n + r \sum_{t=1}^{n} V_{t-1} + nF,$$

and:

$$\hat{R} = (V_0 - V_n)/n + r\overline{V} + F,$$

where $\overline{V}$ is the average value of the durable. $(V_0 - V_n)/n$ and $r\overline{V}$ are both commonly used as approximations of depreciation and opportunity costs (Watts and Helmers). Again, they are best defended as an approximation when the net cash returns from the durable are constant over its life.

Charging the depreciation and opportunity costs in the traditional approach, while on average is correct, requires knowledge about the value of V_n and $\sum_{t=1}^{n} V_t/n$ as well as requiring r to be constant. Often the midpoint $(V_0 + V_n)/2$ is used instead of $\sum_{t=1}^{n} V_t/n$ as an approximation. Thus, ownership costs in traditional enterprise budgets often depend on approximations.

Timing of Inputs

In most cases, the variable inputs used in a production activity are purchased one period before the sale of the output. The difference between the timing of the variable input purchase and the sale of the output means that the variable costs are in different time units than the returns. The same interest cost considerations apply to other time costs as well.

One way to rationalize the timing difference between receipts and costs is to discount the cash receipts or to compound forward the cash costs by $(1+r)$. The approach most often followed is to include an interest cost associated with the funds extended to purchase the variable input and to pay for other time costs. Assuming that the reinvestment rate equals the discount rate, the interest cost (really the opportunity cost associated with the variable input) equals $r(p_x x^* + F)$. To reflect this timing sequence, the *PV* model can be written as:

$$NPV = -V_0 + \frac{1}{(1+r)} \left[pf(x^*, s) - (1+r)(p_x x^* + F) \right]$$

$$+ \frac{1}{(1+r)^2} \left[pf(x^*, s) - (1+r)(p_x x^* + F) \right] \qquad (17.10)$$

$$+ \dots + \frac{1}{(1+r)^n} \left[pf(x^*, s) - (1+r)(p_x x^* + F) \right].$$

Now, the net cash flow associated with a cycle of productive activities is:

$$R_t = pf(x^*, s) - (p_x x^* + F)(1+r),$$

and x^* satisfies the equation:

$$pf'(x^*, s) = (1+r) p_x.$$

Table 17.4 includes this added consideration of purchase timing. It is described next.

Enterprise Budgets with Land

Land represents a particular challenge for enterprise budgets because its value is not assumed to change through time or use. Its value may change, however, because of maintenance or other value-enhancing investments such as tilling or leveling, and changes in the land and capital markets. The only assumption on net cash returns consistent with no capital gains or losses is a constant net cash return from land. Under this assumption, V_0^l, the *PV* of land, equals:

$$V_0^l = \frac{R^l}{(1+r)} + \dots = \frac{R^l}{r}, \qquad (17.11)$$

Table 17.4 An Enterprise Budget Accounting for Timing, Differences Between Output Sale and Variable Input Purchase

Returns		Expenses	
Sale of product	$pf(x^*,s)$	Cash operating expenses	$p_x x^*$
		Depreciation	$V_{t-1} - V_t$
		Opportunity cost of durables	rV_{t-1}
		Opportunity cost of variable inputs and other time costs	$r(p_x x^* + F)$
		Other time costs	F
Total returns	$pf(x^*,s)$	Total costs	$(1+r)p_x x^* + V_{t-1}$ $-V_t + rV_{t1} + (1+r)F$

Table 17.5 An Enterprise Budget with Land Assuming an Infinite, Constant Stream of Nominal Net Cash Flows from Land

Returns		Expenses	
Sale of product	$pf(x_x, s^l)$	Cash operating expenses	$p_x x^*$
		Opportunity cost of land	rV_0^l
		Opportunity cost of variable inputs and other time costs	$r(p_x x + F)$
		Other time costs	F
Total returns	$pf(x_x, s^l)$	Total costs	$(1+r)p_x x + rV_0^l +$ $(1+r)F$

and the opportunity cost for land is the current interest rate r times V_0^l, or rV_0^l and where cash returns from land in the tth period are $R_t^l = pf(x, s^l) - p_x x - F$ and s^l are services from land. Under these conditions, the traditional enterprise budget with land is presented in Table 17.5.

To extend the analysis, suppose a growth rate g for all revenues and expenses is introduced into the model so that:

$$V_0^l = \frac{(1+g)}{(1+r)} \left[pf(x^*, s') - (1+r)(p_x x^* + F) \right]$$

$$+ \frac{(1+g)^2}{(1+r)^2} \left[pf(x^*, s') - (1+r)(p_x x^* + F) \right]$$

$$+ \ldots = \frac{R_0^l(1+g)}{r-g}, \tag{17.12}$$

where:

$$R_0^l = pf(x^*; s') - (p_x x + F)(1+r).$$

Under these conditions, land experiences a rate of capital gain (or loss) over time that depends on the rate of growth (decline) g in the series of earnings generated by the land investment; that is, $V_t^l = (1+g)V_{t-1}^l$ or $(V_t^l - V_{t-1}^l) = gV_{t-1}^l$, not zero. So, when $g \neq 0$, the opportunity cost calculation of rV_{t-1}^l exaggerates the true sum of depreciation plus opportunity cost because of land's appreciation. The actual sum of opportunity costs less capital gains in period one is easily calculated. We find:

$$R_0^l(1+g) = (r-g)V_0^l = \text{opportunity cost less capital gains.}$$

If the inflation rate i equals g and r^* is the real opportunity cost of capital, then $(r-g)V_{t-1}^l = (r-i)V_{t-1}^l = (r^* + i + ir^* - i)V_{t-1}^l = r^*(1+i)V_{t-1}^l$ or the real rate r^* times the value of land at the end of the period. A practical approximation of this cost is the rental rate of land that reflects a current rate of return to the land user, but excludes any capital gains (losses). If the rent is paid at the end of the period, it equals $(r-g)V_0^l = R_0^l(1+g)$.

From these results comes the usually applied, and almost defensible approach of estimating the ownership costs of land equal to its opportunity costs plus change in value by multiplying its end of period value by the real interest rate and ignoring capital gains or losses. Alternatively, one may use the rental rate for land as an estimate of ownership costs. A similar approach is sometimes followed for machinery. Table 17.6 illustrates an enterprise budget for land with opportunity costs and capital gains combined.

Enterprise Budget with Cash Rents

Suppose the enterprise budget with land earns rent at the rate:

$$\hat{R}_t^l = [pf(x^*, s^l) - (1+r)(p_x x^* + F)](1+g)^t.$$

Then, the *PV* of land can be written as:

$$V_0^l = \frac{\hat{R}_0^l(1+g)}{(1+r)} + \frac{\hat{R}_0^l(1+g)^2}{(1+r)^2} + \dots = \frac{\hat{R}_0^l(1+g)}{r-g}.$$

Furthermore, substituting $\hat{R}_0^l(1+g)$ for R_t in equation (17.3) allows us to write:

$$V_1^l = (1+r) V_0 - \hat{R}_0^l(1+g),$$

and:

$$\hat{R}_0^l(1+g) = (V_0^l - V_1^l) + r V_0^l.$$

Table 17.6 An Enterprise Budget with Land Assuming an Infinite Net Cash Flow Stream that Grows at Rate *g* and Where No Separate Accounting for Depreciation Is Kept

Returns		Expenses	
Sale of product	$pf(x^*, s^l)(1+g)$	Cash operating expenses	$p_x x(1+g)$
		Opportunity cost less capital gains	$(r-g)V_0^l$
		Opportunity cost of variable inputs and other time costs	$r(p_x x + F)(1+g)$
		Other time costs	$F(1+g)$
Total returns	$pf(x^*, s^l)(1+g)$	Total costs	$(1+r)(1+g)(p_x x^* + F) + (r-g)V_0^l$

Or, we may write:

$$pf(x^*,s^I)(1+g) = (1+r)(1+g)(p_x x^* + F) + (V_0^I - V_1^I) + rV_0^I$$

$$= (1+r)(1+g)(p_x x^* + F) + \hat{R}_0^I(1+g).$$

It can be seen now that if rent equals the difference between cash returns and variable and other time costs (including their opportunity costs), it equals ownership costs of using land. If so, costs of using land can be approximated using cash rents and the enterprise budget for land can be written as shown in Table 17.7.

Inflation and Enterprise Budgets with Depreciable Durables

In Chapter 7, we showed how inflation may actually increase the market value of depreciable durables such as machines and buildings. Let V_{t-1}^m equal the *PV* of a depreciable durable at the beginning of the tth period. Suppose $V_{t-1}^m - V_t^m < 0$, signifying a capital gain has occurred. Depreciation charges, however, in the enterprise budget are based on the traditional estimation method of V_0^m/n (assuming zero salvage). Under this procedure, depreciation

---

Table 17.7 An Enterprise Budget with Land Assuming Cash Rents Approximate the Sum of Opportunity Costs, Depreciation, and Other Time Costs

Returns		Expenses	
Sale of product	$pf(x^*,s^I)(1+g)$	Cash operating expenses	$p_x x^*(1+g)$
		Opportunity cost of variable inputs and other time costs	$r(p_x x^* + F)(1+g)$
		Cash rents	$\hat{R}^I(1+g)$
		Other time costs	$F(1+g)$
Total returns	$pf(x^*,s^I)(1+g)$	Total costs	$(1+r)(p_x x^* + F)(1+g) + \hat{R}^I(1+g)$

charges will be greatly exaggerated. Again, the practical decision of how to estimate the ownership costs must be considered.

Let the real decay rate in the value of the durable's service be d^* percent and let the inflation rate be i. Then, ignoring other time costs for the moment:

$$V_0^m = \frac{R_0^m(1-d^*)(1+i)}{(1+r^*)(1+i)} + \dots = \frac{R^m(1-d^*)}{r^*+d^*}. \tag{17.13}$$

One period later:

$$V_1^m = \frac{R_0^m(1-d^*)^2(1+i)^2}{(1+r^*)(1+i)} + \dots = \frac{R^m(1-d^*)^2(1+i)}{r^*+d^*}$$

$$= V_0^m(1-d^*)(1+i).$$

This allows us to write:

$$V_0^m = \frac{R_0^m(1-d^*)(1+i)}{(1+r^*)(1+i)} + \frac{V_1^m}{(1+r^*)(1+i)}.$$

Ownership costs in the first period, $R_0^m(1-d^*)(1+i)$, equal:

$$R_0^m(1-d^*)(1+i) = V_0^m - V_1^m + (r^*+i+r^* i)\, V_0^m$$

$$= \text{depreciation} + \text{opportunity costs} \tag{17.14}$$

$$= \text{ownership costs.}$$

But the change in value can be written as:

$$V_0^m - V_1^m = V_0^m - V_0^m(1-d^*)(1+i) = V_0^m(d^*+d^* i-i),$$

so that an expanded ownership costs expression equals:

$$R_0^m(1-d^*)(1+i) = V_0^m(d^*+d^* i-i) + (r^*+ir^*+i)\, V_0^m$$

$$= \text{depreciation} + \text{opportunity costs} \tag{17.15}$$

$$= \text{ownership costs.}$$

The important point here is to note that for depreciables with explicit depreciation charges, opportunity costs are calculated with a nominal rate (as opposed to a nominal rate less a capital gains rate (r-g) used with land).

For intertemporal comparisons, one may wish to deflate the measure of ownership costs to some real base period measure. This is easily achieved by discounting by $(1+i)$ so that:

$$R_0^m(1-d^*) = V_0^m \frac{(d^*+ d^* i- i)}{(1+i)} + \frac{(r^*+i+r^* i)\, V_0^m}{(1+i)}.$$ (17.16)

Notice that $(r^*+i+r^* i)/(1+i)=r^*+i/(1+i)$ is not equal to the real rate r^*. Thus $r^* V_0^m$ is not a correct measure of the opportunity cost in base period dollars. Thus, it is not strictly appropriate to say the best estimate of the opportunity cost of depreciable durables such as machinery, is the real rate r^* times the value of the durable at the beginning of the period. On the other hand, if inflation i is zero, then:

$$R_0^m(1-d^*) = V_0^m - V_1^m + r^* V_0^m$$
$$= \text{depreciation} + \text{opportunity costs}$$ (17.17)
$$= \text{ownership costs,}$$

and $r^* V_0^m$ is indeed the correct measure of opportunity costs.

Example 17.3: Calculating Ownership Costs

Bud Ghet wants to evaluate an equipment investment. The equipment is used to shred tree limbs and depreciates at the rate of 15 percent per year ($d^*=0.15$). Last year net cash returns, R_0^m, were $300 and Ghet recognizes that inflation is 9 percent.

The machine's current value, V_0^m, is $4,000. At the end of one period of use, the expected market value is $3,800. Ghet wonders about the opportunity cost of holding the machine another period—especially since liquid funds are currently earning 13.5 percent. Using equation (17.14), Ghet calculates depreciation $V_0^m -V_1^m =$200 and opportunity costs as (0.135)($4000)=$540. Ownership costs, the sum of depreciation, and opportunity costs, equal ($200+$540)=$740. Net cash returns $R_0^m(1-d^*)(1+i)=$300(1-0.15)(1.09)=$277.95. Thus, net cash returns of $277.95 are less than ownership costs of $740 and the investment is not profitable.

Multiple Durables

The analysis can be extended to construct enterprise budgets for production processes that use more than one durable and perhaps more than one variable input. Consider two durables, a machine whose periodic services equals s^m and land, whose periodic services are represented by s^l.

Assuming the variable input is purchased at the beginning of the period and the product is sold at the end of the period, the *PV* model is written as:

$$NPV = -V_0^m - V_0^l + \frac{1}{(1+r)} \left[pf(x^*; s^m, s^l) - (1+r)(p_x x^* + F) \right]$$

$$+ \frac{1}{(1+r)^2} \left[pf(x^*; s^m, s^l) - (1+r)(p_x x^* + F) \right] + \dots \qquad (17.18)$$

$$+ \frac{1}{(1+r)^n} \left[pf(x^*; s^m, s^l) - (1+r)(p_x x^* + F) \right] + \frac{V_n^m + V_n^l}{(1+r)^n},$$

where $f(x^*; s^m, s^l)$ is the formula for describing the conversion of services from the machine and land plus the variable input, x^*, into an output.

As before we assume that the machine produces services s^m for n periods and then disintegrates. Then, we write an expression for the *PV* of the machine equal to:

$$V_0^m = \frac{\hat{R}^m}{(1+r)} + \dots + \frac{\hat{R}^m}{(1+r)^n},$$

and:

$$\hat{R}^m = V_0^m / US_0(r, n),$$

as before.

A similar expression for land assumes that land provides services in perpetuity. In such a world, we write:

$$V_0^l = \frac{\hat{R}^l}{(1+r)} + \dots = \frac{\hat{R}^l}{r},$$

where $\hat{R}^l$ is the net cash return for land's services and:

$$\hat{R}^l = r V_0^l.$$

Many writers have assumed, with some justification, that $\hat{R}^l$ can be estimated by the cash rent paid for the use of land. If so, the enterprise budget with land and machines as durables can be approximated as shown in Table 17.8.

Ownership costs for machinery and land can be decomposed into depreciation and opportunity costs. If r is the nominal discount rate, then:

$$V_t^m = (1+r) V_{t-1}^m - \hat{R}_t^m,$$

or:

$$\hat{R}_t^m = r V_{t-1}^m + (V_{t-1}^m - V_t^m)$$

$$= \text{opportunity} + \text{depreciation cost}$$ (17.19)

$$= \text{ownership costs}.$$

Likewise, the formula for land may be written as:

$$\underset{\substack{\text{ownership} \\ \text{costs}}}{\hat{R}_t^l} = \underset{\substack{\text{opportunity} \\ \text{cost}}}{r V_{t-1}^l} + \underset{\text{depreciation}}{(V_{t-1}^l - V_t^l)}$$

$$= \text{ownership costs}$$

Table 17.8 An Enterprise Budget that Includes Ownership Costs for Machinery Inputs, Land, and Costs of Using a Variable Input

Returns		Expenses	
Sale of product	$pf(x^*;s^m,s^l)$	Cash operating expenses	$p_x x^*$
		Opportunity cost of variable inputs and other time costs	$r(p_x x^* + F)$
		Ownership cost of machinery	$\hat{R}^m$
		Ownership cost for land	$\hat{R}^l$
		Other time costs	F
Total returns	$pf(x^*;s^m,s^l)$	Total costs	$(1+r)(p_x x^* + F) + \hat{R}^m + \hat{R}^l$

For machinery, the costs are usually decomposed into an opportunity cost plus a depreciation cost. Land, however, is not assumed to depreciate. Thus, depreciation is often assumed to equal zero and is not included in the enterprise budget.

Maintenance and Repairs

Associated with durables are maintenance and repairs. Routine maintenance associated with the passage of time is included in other time costs F. Repairs such as modifying the durable by replacing or improving a component part have offsetting effects on the cost side of the enterprise budget. First, they create an additional cost equal to RP_t. Then, if they change (increase), the value of the durable V_t^m, they may reduce expenses by reducing depreciation or increasing capital gains.

The complete enterprise budget is described now in Table 17.9.

Table 17.9 An Enterprise Budget that Includes Machinery Ownership Costs

Returns		Expenses	
Sale of product	$pf(x^*;s^m,s^l)$	Purchase of variable inputs	$p_x x$
		Opportunity cost of variable inputs and other time costs	$r(p_x x+F)$
		Machinery depreciation	$(V_{t-1}^m - V_t^m)$
		Depreciation (capital gains) for land	$(V_{t-1}^l - V_t^l)$
		Opportunity cost for machinery	rV_{t-1}^m
		Opportunity cost for land	rV_{t-1}^l
		Other time costs	F
		Repairs	RP_t
Total returns	$pf(x^*;s^m,s^l)$	Total costs	$(1+r)(p_x x^* + F) + (V_{t-1}^m - V_t^m) + RP_t + (V_{t-1}^l - V_t^l) + (rV_{t-1}^m + rV_{t-1}^l)$

Differences in Enterprise Budgets _____

So far in this chapter, we have provided a method for building enterprise budgets or cost of production (COP) estimates consistent with *PV* methods. However, theoretical purity rarely translates into feasible reality. As a result, considerable differences exist in the methods actually used to build enterprise budgets or COP estimates. In a useful article on the actual methods used to construct farm enterprise budgets, Klonsky noted the differences in budgeting procedures used in 41 states.

She noted that in all 41 states responding to her survey, enterprise budgets included fuel, repairs, interest on operating capital, and labor as operating costs in their crop budgets. Only 15 states included a management charge, 22 states included business ownership costs, and 31 states included property taxes on equipment.

Klonsky also noted important differences between investment or ownership costs, which has been the focus of this chapter. She noted that only two states included an explicit cost for buildings, 14 states did not calculate a land charge, and for those remaining states that did include a land charge, the majority used the cost of renting land as their opportunity cost of land estimate.

All but two states in Klonsky's survey included an ownership cost for equipment. Ninety percent of the states valued the ownership cost of equipment as the sum of depreciation and interest. Moreover, significant differences existed between states in their use of nominal or real interest rates in the calculation of machinery ownership costs.

The essence of Klonsky's survey is that considerable differences exist in the construction of enterprise and COP budgets. Some have argued that the differences can be justified because these budgets have different uses such as farm management analysis, determining regional and national competitiveness, supply response modeling, and determining commodity price supports. But, are these differences justified from a theoretical sense? The answer is: No! Then, the only other justification for the differences is that the availability or the cost of obtaining the theoretically-correct data prevents it from being used and requires approximations.

The issue of theoretical purity versus practical implementation of COP budgets is important. Correct evaluation of investments depends on consistent construction of *PV* models. The problem of incorrectly-constructed enterprise budgets is that the numbers from these budgets may be used in *PV* models and lead to misinformation. Knowing the relationship between consistently constructed *PV* models and enterprise budgets may preclude the publication of misinformation.

National Commodity Cost and Return Estimates

The U.S. Department of Agriculture (USDA) has estimated COP budgets for farm commodities since the early 1900's. In the early 1970's, ERS, in cooperation with several Land Grant Universities, established the Firm Enterprise Data System (FEDS). FEDS consists of farm and ranch enterprise budgets and whole farm budgets. FEDS calculates costs and return estimates as if all production for a commodity is represented by a single average acre in the state. It was hoped that the FEDS budgets would become a standardized set of budgets allowing comparable cost estimates to be developed across commodities and regions.

Differences, however, continue to exist between USDA and land grant university estimates of production costs. The differences stem primarily from the intended use of the budgets. In general, universities and other research institutions estimate cost of production to provide local farmers guidance in management planning. USDA budgets are estimated in response to a Congressional mandate to provide historical measures to guide policy decisions (Morehart, Johnson, and Shapouri). The point of this chapter, however, is that these differences may introduce inconsistencies between USDA and university budgets derived for calculating costs and returns.

Another USDA-ERS effort to develop commodity cost and returns estimates at the farm-level is the Farm Level Budget Model (FLBM). FLBM calculates costs and returns for each farm surveyed and summarizes these estimates at the state, regional, or national level based on the appropriate weight for each observation.

FLBM prepares two types of enterprise budgets. They differ primarily in their treatment of costs associated with durables. One budget is a cash budget. It charges for the use of durables based on cash generated expenses, such as interest costs of loans associated with the durables. The other budget attempts to account for the full economic cost of durables used in enterprises.

The cash operating expenses included in both the cash and full economic cost budgets are listed in Table 17.10.

Panel *a* of Table 17.11 lists the cash cost components of an enterprise budget. Panel *b* of Table 17.11 lists those items of FEDS budgets that account for full economic costs of ownership. Total enterprise costs are then estimated as the sum of variable cash expenses plus either fixed cash expenses or variable cash expenses plus full ownership costs. Panel *c* of Table 17.11 identifies cost categories consistent with *PV* models.

General farm overhead that includes expenses for farm shop and office equipment, accounting and legal fees, etc. and taxes and insurance are included in both fixed cash expenses and the full ownership costs. Interest costs associated with operating and real estate loans can be expected to correctly

Table 17.10 Typical Cash Cost Items Included in a Per Acre Crop Budget

Gross value of production
(excluding direct government payments):
  Primary crop
  Secondary crop
Total, gross value of production

Cash operating expenses:
  Seed
  Fertilizer
  Lime and gypsum
  Chemicals
  Custom operations
  Fuel, lube, and electricity
  Repairs
  Hired labor
  Purchased irrigation water
  Technical services
  Drying
  Ginning
Total cash operating expenses

measure opportunity costs associated with the durables only under special conditions.

Operating capital, land, and other nonland capital categories included in the full ownership cost approach attempt to measure the opportunity costs of land, capital, and inputs held over time. These categories are proper elements of an enterprise budget. In a similar way, opportunity costs associated with unpaid labor can be defended. Only the category of capital replacement is inconsistent with the theoretically-correct enterprise budget. This category should instead measure the difference in the beginning and ending value of the durables used in the enterprise. While capital replacement may in some instances adequately measure the change, it cannot be expected to adequately represent this category in general.

Unresolved Conflicts

If a market is in perfect equilibrium, each input is paid its *IRR*, and this allocation just exhausts the return. In the real world, however, *NPV*'s from enterprises are hardly zero and the rate of return-to-equity capital varies across

Table 17.11 Three Methods for Charging Costs Associated with Use of Durables

Panel a:

Fixed Cash Expenses
General farm overhead
Taxes and insurance
Interest on operating loans
Interest on machinery loans
Interest on real estate

Panel b:

Full Ownership Costs
General farm overhead
Taxes and insurance
Capital replacement
Operating capital
Other nonland capital
Land
Unpaid labor

Panel c:

NPV Consistent Costs
Purchase of variable inputs
(including labor) or cash
operating expenses
Opportunity cost of variable
inputs and other time costs
Depreciation and opportunity
cost of general farm capital
Depreciation and opportunity
cost of farm capital
Opportunity cost and
depreciation of land
Other time costs (taxes and
insurance)

investments. Moreover, some assets such as the right to produce have returns difficult to calculate. These conditions make it difficult to allocate the positive or negative *NPV* among investments. This allocation is particularly troublesome when more than one durable contributes services to the enterprise; or when a single durable contributes services to more than one enterprise.

Suppose, for example, that an enterprise absorbs services from machinery, land, and family labor. If these durables are credited with their opportunity costs and there is still a residual, to what input should it be assigned? In the FEDS budget, the residual is assigned to risk and management. But one could ask: Shouldn't the risk control and management services be charged the same as any other set of services from the durable? Or, if the services have already been properly accounted for, why not arrange some pro rata basis for assigning the returns to the existing classifications of durables?

Perhaps the most satisfying approach is to treat an enterprise as a composite durable. For example, a car is composed of several durables: tires, seats, pistons, tie rods, etc. and it uses variable inputs such as gas, oil, and labor. Yet, we would never think of trying to allocate returns from owning a taxi to the tires, radio, etc. The returns are simply assigned to the taxi business enterprise. And efforts to distribute the *NPV* to the component parts of the taxi are really not relevant to the more important question: Is the taxi business, after accounting for all expenses, profitable? Unfortunately, we still have to ask: Should we replace the tires or sell the taxis? And the answer to this question may require that we allocate returns to each component, a task that we wish to avoid.

Summary

The conflict between what is theoretically correct and practically possible meets in sharp contrast in the construction of enterprise budgets. From earlier chapters describing the relationship between durable values and cash flows, clear procedures have been developed for estimating capital budgets. But capital budgets are long-run tools and investors need short-term measures to check on the economic performance of their investments. These short-term checks are usually enterprise budgets and require the estimation and allocation of ownership costs.

In this chapter, *PV* models have been used to deduce a theoretically correct enterprise budget. The problem is that few firms have the data required to construct a theoretically correct budget and are, therefore, forced to use estimates. The estimation procedures are best in the absence of inflation since accountants usually use the purchase price of durables as the basis for depreciation estimates despite evidence in some cases that the durable's value may have actually increased. These overestimates of the depreciation charges are offset by calculating opportunity costs using a real interest rate rather than a nominal rate.

Since theoretically correct budgets can be defined, why not calculate them? These theoretically correct budgets are in nominal units and calculate actual changes in the value of the asset. Some argue that budgets in real units are preferred. However, theoretically correct budgets in real units are more difficult to calculate and they still require all of the information of nominally calculated budgets. Moreover, no single deflator is completely acceptable. Therefore, by calculating nominal budgets, the issue of the correct deflator can be separated from the issue of the theoretically correct way to calculate an *NPV* consistent budget.

It is likely that no easy compromise exists between the need for theoretically correct enterprise budgets and the lack of data to construct them. Thus, in the foreseeable future, economists will continue to debate how best to construct enterprise budgets.

Review Questions _____

1. What is a budget?
2. Distinguish between capital budgets, cash flow budgets, and enterprise budgets.
3. Why may firms require capital as well as enterprise budgets to determine the profitability of an investment?
4. Define depreciation (capital gains) and opportunity costs using the cost distinction found in Table 17.3.
5. Compare depreciation measures using the actual value V_{t-1}-V_t versus an approximation using the straight-line method $(V_0$-$V_n)/n$. Under what conditions would they give the same answer? Under what conditions would they be equal on average but not necessarily equal in any one year? Under what conditions would the two depreciation measures not be equal on average? (Hint: Assume inflationary pressures increase the durable price in at least one year.)
6. What is the likely basis for disagreement over how to construct enterprise budgets? (Hint: Is it because of theoretical disagreements deduced from *PV* models or practical problems collecting the required data?)

Application Questions _____

1. The Governors of Michigan and Ohio have asked you to prepare a cash-costs-of-production budget for an acre of sugar beets. You have been trained in *PV* methods and recognize that without estimates of durable costs, a clear picture of the sugar beet enterprise will not be revealed. So, you decide to produce full ownership cost estimates as well. But, the accountants on the governor's staff, while recognizing the need to account for durable costs, prefer a cash basis. So, you prepare both estimates of

fixed cash expenses and full ownership costs estimates following USDA procedures. Finally, you know that your colleagues and instructors of *PV* methods will read your report, and to please them, you prepare a theoretically correct budget including variable cash expenses, opportunity costs, and depreciation (gains).

a.   Your assignment is to prepare budgets including variable cash costs, fixed cash costs, full ownership costs, and opportunity costs and depreciation.

b.   Please comment on the differences between the various methods of estimating costs associated with the durables.

To aid you in your budgets, the following information has been collected from surveys on a per acre basis. The gross value of sugar beets produced is $718.29. Seed costs are $15.56, fertilizer costs are $76.02, chemicals costs are $51.02, custom operations are $23.85, variable costs associated with machinery use including fuel, lubes, and repairs equal $63.35. Hired labor costs including noncash benefits equal $51.06. Hauling and other miscellaneous variable cash costs equal $11.50. Taxes and insurance costs per acre are $68.09 and other ownership costs including accountant fees equal $39.65. Interest expenses on real estate and operating loans adjusted to a per acre basis equal $76.35. (Assume the real estate loan equals the value of the land.)

An acre of typical land used to grow soybeans can be rented for $84.72. Your spouse has helped in sugar beet production. The money value of this labor per acre equals $32.59. Many of the inputs were purchased and applied months before the harvest. You financed the use of these inputs with equity and borrowed funds at a cost of $11.86. Inventory control costs associated with other capital employed are $21.96. Your accountants have allocated $72.98 for capital replacement. But, you have estimated that the annuity value of the durable to be $83.00. Finally, you expect that the acre of land on which the sugar beets are grown has increased by $15.35.

Using the information above, please estimate your budgets for the governor and explain the differences.

References _____

Ahearn, M.C. and V. Vasavada (eds). *Costs and Returns for Agricultural Commodities.* Boulder, CO: Westview Press, Inc., 1992.

Barry, P.J. "Capital Asset Pricing and Farm Real Estate." *American Journal of Agricultural Economics* 62(1980):549-53.

Boehlje, M.D. and V.R. Eidman. *Farm Management.* New York: John Wiley and Sons, 1984.

Burt, O.R. "A Unified Theory of Depreciation." *Journal of Accounting Research* 10(1972):28-57.

_____. "Allocation of Capital Costs in Enterprise Budgets," Chapter 15 in *Costs and Returns for Agricultural Commodities,* ed. by M.C. Ahearn and V. Vasavada, pp. 259-72, Boulder, CO: Westview Press, Inc., 1992.

Casler, G.L. "Use of State Farm Record Data for Studying Determinants of Farm Size" in *Determinants of Size and Structure in American Agriculture.* Ames, IA: Iowa State University Press, 1991.

Gustafson, C.R., P.J. Barry, and M.B. Ali. "Estimating Costs of Durable and Operating Capital Services," Chapter 16 in *Costs and Returns for Agricultural Commodities*, ed. by M.C. Ahearn and V. Vasavada. Boulder, CO: Westview Press, Inc., 1992, pp. 273-87.

Hoffman, G. and C.R. Gustafson. "A New Approach to Estimating Agricultural Costs of Production." *Agricultural Economics Research* 35(1983):9-14.

Hottel, J.B. and B.L. Gardner. "The Rate of Return to Investment in Agriculture and Measuring Net Farm Income." *American Journal of Agricultural Economics* 65(1983):553-57.

Klonsky, K. "Results of National Survey on Data and Methods," Chapter 10 in *Costs and Returns for Agricultural Commodities,* ed. by M.C. Ahearn and V. Vasavada, pp. 147-64. Boulder, CO: Westview Press, Inc., 1992.

Morehart, M.J., J.D. Johnson, and H. Shapouri. "The National Commodity Cost and Return Estimates," Chapter 8 in *Costs and Returns for Agricultural Commodities,* ed. by M.C. Ahearn and V. Vasavada, pp. 103-27. Boulder, CO: Westview Press, Inc., 1989.

U.S. Department of Agriculture. "Economic Indicators of the Farm Sector: Costs of Production—Major Field Crops, 1988." ECIFS 8-4. Washington, DC: Economic Research Service, April 1990.

Walrath, A.J. "The Incompatibility of the Average Investment Method for Calculating Interest Costs with the Principle of Alternative Opportunities." *Southern Journal of Agricultural Economics* 5(1973):181-85.

Watts, M.J. and G.A. Helmers. "Inflation and Machinery Cost Budgeting." *Western Journal of Agricultural Economics* 11(1979):83-88.

Chapter 18

Leasing Decisions

Key words: comparative advantage, financial lease, investment control, investment financing, lease agreement, lessee, lessor, operating lease, sale and leaseback lease

Introduction

Control of a durable can be transferred between parties in several ways. One important way is a lease agreement. A lease is a contract by which control over the right to use a durable is transferred from one party, the lessor, to another party, the lessee. In exchange for the right to use or control a durable for a specified time period, the lessee pays to the lessor a rental payment or share in the output produced by the leased durable. This lease payment or shared output must cover the inventory costs and other time costs, and use depreciation of the durable and other incidental ownership costs incurred by the lessor. Thus, leasing is a method of financing the control of a durable that separates its use from its ownership.

There are several kinds of lease arrangements and several kinds of durables that are leased. Farmland is frequently leased. So are machinery, housing, cars, computers, buildings, breeding livestock, and many kinds of labor services including secretarial services, legal services, and office management services. In this chapter, we describe various types of leases, evaluate their advantages and disadvantages, and apply present value (*PV*) tools to analyze leasing benefits for both the lessee and the lessor.

Types of Lease Arrangements ⸻

Sale and Leaseback. Under the sale and leaseback agreement, a firm owning a durable to be leased sells the durable to a financial institution and simultaneously executes an agreement to lease the durable back. Thus, the lease becomes the alternative to a purchase with a specific advantage to the lessee; namely, it is allowed to write off the entire lease payment as an expense instead of just interest costs in the case of a mortgage. The lessor will not enter into this type of lease agreement unless the lease payments are sufficient to return the full purchase price to the investor, plus a return on the investment.

Operating Leases. Operating leases, sometimes called service leases, provide for both financing and maintenance. These leases ordinarily call for the lessor to maintain the leased equipment. The cost of the maintenance is built into the lease payment. Computers and office copiers, together with cars and trucks, are the primary types of equipment involved in operating leases.

In the case of operating leases, lease payments are often insufficient to recover the full cost of the equipment. To offset this feature, the lease is written for a time period considerably less than the expected life of the leased equipment, leaving the lessor to recover his or her investment in renewal payments of the lease or through disposal of the leased equipment.

One of the main advantages of the operating lease for lessees is the cancellation of the short lease period which allows them to adopt and bring into use more advanced equipment. Thus, for durables subject to rapid changes in technology, an operating lease is often a preferred method for gaining control of a durable.

Financial or Capital Leases. A financial lease is a fully amortized lease whose *PV* of the lease payments equals the full price of the leased equipment. It does not provide for maintenance service nor is it cancelable. The financial lease begins with a firm selecting the specific items it requires and agreeing with the seller about the price and the delivery of the item. The firm arranges with a bank or another financial institution to purchase the equipment and simultaneously executes a financial lease with the firm that intends to use the equipment. The purchaser of the equipment builds into the lease payments a rate of return equivalent to what would be charged on a loan and the lease is cancelled when the purchase price of the durable plus a return for the lessor is paid.

Under financial leases, lessees generally pay property taxes and insurance and in many cases can acquire ownership of the durable at the end of the lease. The significant difference between the sale and leaseback lease and the financial lease is that the lessor purchases the durable directly from the manufacturer rather than from the lessee under the terms of the financial lease.

Lease Agreements and Taxes

One of the major effects of the lease is to alter the tax obligations of the lessee and the lessor. Therefore, special attention is required to make sure that lease agreements are acceptable under current tax codes interpreted in the United States by the Internal Revenue Service. An important distinction for tax purposes is between a lease agreement and a loan. If the lease agreement cannot be distinguished from an ordinary loan agreement, then any special tax provisions associated with the lease agreement are lost.

To distinguish a lease from a sale agreement, the term over which the durable is leased must be less than 75 percent of the economic life of the durable. Nor should the lessee be granted any special repurchase option not available to others not involved in the lease. There are other conditions as well and tax codes are evolving documents that are constantly being updated.

Advantages of Leases

In the typical case, the firm decides to acquire a particular building or piece of equipment. Normally, the decision to acquire the durable is not at issue in the typical lease analysis. The issue at hand is whether to acquire control of the durable through purchase, often by borrowing some amount to finance the purchase, or through lease. The decision requires a careful examination of the advantages of leasing.

Leasing offers several possible advantages relative to owning a durable. Included are the following:

Release of Cash and Credit. When a firm leases or sells a durable on a leaseback arrangement, the lessee avoids the cash downpayment required to purchase the investment. If the investment is purchased, whether the lease payments or the loan payments are the most accelerated relative to the life of the investment will determine how the firm's liquidity is affected by leasing.

Some texts discuss in some detail the effect on the firm's credit reserve from leasing. If leasing uses up credit at a slower rate than does borrowing, there may be credit incentives for leasing rather than borrowing. However, lenders are likely to recognize that long-term lease agreements place the same requirements on future cash flows as do loans.

Risk Reduction. Investments may experience significant obsolescence risks; that is, there is a high likelihood of durables becoming obsolete or the need for durable's services changing before the durable's service capacity is exhausted. Part of this obsolescence risk may be reduced through a lease arrangement for a short time period, especially if the lessor is less subject to obsolescence risk than the lessee. This is likely the case where the leased equipment has alternative uses in other firms or industries, and where the risk can be spread over many lessees.

Idle Capacity Risk. Another risk that can often be reduced through lease arrangements is the risk of holding idle equipment. If the demand for services from a durable is not sufficient to employ the durable full time, the lessee can reduce idle capacity risk by leasing rather than owning the durable. From the lessor's point of view, the durable can be completely employed because many lessees will use the equipment.

Foreclosure Risk. In many respects, leasing is similar to borrowing because it represents an obligation of the firm to a series of future cash payments. But there is one significant difference between a lease and borrowing to purchase the durable. In the case of financial difficulties, the lessor simply takes back the equipment, because he or she holds the legal title. In the case of a loan, inability to meet loan payments may result in more complex foreclosure proceedings.

Tax Advantages. A tax advantage may be gained when the term of the lease is shorter than the allowable tax depreciation period for ownership. However, tax incentives for the lessee must be a result of a lower total tax burden for the lessee and lessor. This situation implies that the lease arrangement has legitimately allowed for a reduction in the total amount of taxes paid. Needless to say, the Internal Revenue Service imposes conditions on what does and does not constitute a legal lease.

Comparing Lease and Purchase

The decision to lease or buy depends on the net present values (*NPVs*) of the lease versus the purchase option. Because the investment size and timing of the two alternatives are consistent, the homogeneity of size requirement is likely met. On the other hand, Gordon and others have argued that the risks of the two options may not be comparable and suggest adjustments to account for these differences. In the following discussion, the cash flows are considered risk adjusted and the problem is treated as riskless. The resulting solution is similar to that proposed by Gordon and recommended by others (e.g., Levy and Sarnat; Ford and Musser; Robertson, Musser, and Tew).

To compare the lease with the purchase option, the market value of the durable leased or purchased is V_0, the lease payment at age t is C_t, T is the constant marginal income tax rate, and V_t^A is the book value of the depreciable durable at age t. Furthermore, r_t is the before-tax opportunity cost of capital for the firm at durable age t. With these definitions in place, the net present cost of a lease, NPC^L, for n periods is:

$$NPC^L = \frac{C_1(1-T)}{[1+r_1(1-\theta_1 T)]} + \ldots + \frac{C_n(1-T)}{\prod\limits_{t=1}^{n} [1+r_t(1-\theta_t T)]}. \tag{18.1}$$

For simplicity, assume that $C_t=C$, $r_t=r$, and $\theta_t=\theta$, then:

$$NPC^L = \frac{C(1-T)}{[1+r(1-\theta T)]} + \ldots + \frac{C(1-T)}{[1+r(1-\theta T)]^n} \tag{18.2}$$

$$= C(1-T)\ US_0[r(1-\theta T),n].$$

The net present cost of a cash purchase NPC^P, meanwhile, is:

$$NPC^P = V_0 - \frac{T(V_0^A - V_1^A)}{[1+r(1-\theta T)]} - \ldots - \frac{T(V_{n-1}^A - V_n^A)}{[1+r(1-\theta T)]^n}$$

$$- \frac{[V_n - T(V_n - V_n^A)]}{[1+r(1-\theta T)]^n}. \tag{18.3}$$

On the right-hand side of equation (18.3) is the purchase price V_0, n periods of tax savings from depreciation equal to $T(V_t^A - V_{t-1}^A)$ discounted to the present period, and at age n, the salvage value V_n minus a tax adjustment term $T(V_n - V_n^A)$ to account for any discrepancy between the book value and actual value of the durable. If the investment is completely depreciated by the nth period and the salvage value is zero, then the NPC^P can be written as:

$$NPC^P = V_0 - T \sum_{t=1}^{n} \frac{(V_{t-1}^A - V_t^A)}{[1+r(1-\theta T)]^t},$$

where $V_n^A = 0$.

Finally, if the NPC^L is equated to NPC^P, we can solve for the lease payment C which equates the two alternatives for controlling the services from the durable. If the investment is completely depreciated by the nth period and $V_n = 0$, the result is:

$$C(1-T) US_0 [r(1-\theta T), n] = V_0 - T \sum_{t=1}^{n} \frac{(V_{t-1}^A - V_t^A)}{[1+r(1-\theta T)]^t},$$

and:

$$C = \frac{V_0 - T \sum_{t=1}^{n} \{(V_{t-1}^A - V_t^A)/[1+r(1-\theta T)]^t\}}{(1-T) US_0 [r(1-\theta T), n]}.$$

If the salvage value is not zero and $V_n \neq V_n^A$, then:

$$NPC^P = V_0 - T \sum_{t=1}^{n} \frac{(V_{t-1}^A - V_1^A)}{[1+r(1-\theta T)]^t} - \frac{[V_n - T(V_n - V_n^A)]}{[1+r(1-\theta T)]^n}, \qquad (18.4)$$

and the break-even lease payment is:

$$C = \frac{NPC^P}{(1-T) US_0 [r(1-\theta T), n]}. \qquad (18.5)$$

Example 18.1: Leasing Trucks for Lawn Servicing

Go-Green is a lawn service that requires a new truck to service its customers. It wants to know the largest lease payment it could afford and still be as well off as it would be if it purchased the truck.

The truck in question has a new sticker price of $30,000 and can be depreciated using a straight-line method over five years. At the end of the lease, the truck has a salvage value of $5,000. To find the maximum lease payment, the following assumptions are used: $T=0.32$, $r=0.14$, $\theta=1$, $n=5$, $V_n=\$5,000$, and $V_n{}^A=0$. Using equation (18.4), NPC^P is calculated:

$$NPC^P = \left[\$30,000 - (0.32) \, \$6,000 \, US_0(0.095,5) - \frac{\$5,000\,(1-0.32)}{(1.0952)^5} \right]$$

$$= \$20,473.75,$$

and C is found using equation (18.5):

$$C = \frac{NPC^P}{(1-0.32)\,US_0(9.52,5)} = \frac{20,473.75}{2.6096} = \$7,845.38.$$

Lease versus Purchase Option with Concessionary Interest Rates

A standard practice among sellers of large equipment is to offer to finance the purchase of the durable, often at concessionary interest rates. Recall from Chapter 12, that a loan of amount γV_0 at a concessionary interest rate of r^f for n periods when r is the market rate or opportunity cost of capital, can be computed as follows. The annuity payment A required to repay the loan of γV_0 at r^f percent over n periods is:

$$\gamma \, V_0 = A \, US_0(r^f, n), \tag{18.6}$$

or:

$$A = \gamma \, V_0 / \, US_0(r^f, n).$$

The after-tax *NPC* can be found by separating the tth payment into an interest portion $[A-A/(1+r^f)^{n-t+1}]$ and principal portion $A/(1+r^f)^{n-t+1}$. Recall that the interest portion of the annuity is tax deductible so $(1-T)[A-A/(1+r)^{n-t+1}]$ is the after-tax interest payment. All of this allows us to write the after-tax present cost of the loan as $NPC^F(\gamma V_0)$:

$$NPC^F(\gamma \, V_0) = \frac{(1-T)\left[A - \dfrac{A}{(1+r^f)^n}\right]}{[1+r(1-\theta T)]} + \cdots + \frac{(1-T)\left[A - \dfrac{A}{1+r^f}\right]}{[1+r(1-\theta T)]^n}$$

$$+ \frac{A/(1+r^f)^n}{[1+r(1-\theta T)]} + \cdots + \frac{A/(1+r^f)}{[1+r(1-\theta T)]^n} \tag{18.7}$$

$$= A\left\{(1-T)\, US_0\,[r(1-\theta T), n] + \frac{T}{(1+r^f)^{n+1}}\, US_0\left[\frac{r(1-\theta T)-r^f}{1+r^f}, n\right]\right\}.$$

Finally, if $(1-\gamma)V_0$ is paid as a downpayment, and $\gamma V_0/US_0(r^f, n)$ is substituted for A in equation (18.7), then NPC^F is expressed as:

$$NPC^F(V_0) = (1-\gamma)\, V_0 + \left(\frac{\gamma \, V_0}{US_0(r^f, n)}\right)$$

$$\left\{(1-T)\, US_0[r(1-\theta T), n] + \frac{T}{(1+r^f)^n}\, US_0\left[\frac{r(1-\theta T)-r^f}{1+r^f}, n\right]\right\}. \tag{18.8}$$

Note that if $T=0$ and no payment is made, equation (18.8) is identical to equation (12.12), the *NPC* of a subsidized loan on a before-tax basis. To find *NPC* of the financed purchase $NPC^{P/F}$, the *PV* of the tax shield is subtracted from NPC^F and is written as:

$$NPC^{P/F}(V_0) = NPC^F - T\sum_{t=1}^{n} \frac{(V_{i-1}^A - V_i^A)}{(1+r-\theta T)^t} - \left\{\frac{[V_n - T(V_n - V_n^A)]}{[1+r(1-\theta T)]^n}\right\}. \tag{18.9}$$

Example 18.2: Present Cost of a Loan

Bank First With Us offers a 10-year, $30,000 machinery loan requiring a 30 percent downpayment to I. Am Greedy at an interest rate of 6 percent. Greedy's opportunity cost of capital is 12 percent and his constant marginal tax rate is 32 percent. The present cost of Greedy's loan is found using equation (18.8). Assuming $\theta=1$, it equals:

$$NPC^F = (0.3)(\$30,000) + \frac{(0.7)(\$30,000)}{US_0(0.06,10)}$$

$$\left\{ 0.68\ US_0[0.0816,10] + \frac{0.32}{(1.06)^{10}}\ US_0[0.0204,10] \right\}$$

$$= \$9,000 + \frac{\$21,000}{7.3601}\left[(0.68)(6.66192)+(0.16857)(8.96381)\right]$$

$$= \$9,000 + \$17,236.79 = \$26,236.79.$$

To find the maximum lease payment consistent with a concessionary interest rate purchase, the right-hand side of (18.9) is equated to the NPC^L of the lease (the right-hand side of equation (18.2)); then C is solved. The result is:

$$C = \frac{NPC^{P/F}}{(1-T)\ US_0[r(1-\theta T),n]}. \tag{18.10}$$

Example 18.3: Maximum Lease Calculation

Greedy has an opportunity to lease rather than purchase the machine. Greedy calculates the maximum lease payment he could afford and still break even using equation (18.10). The break-even lease payment C equals:

$$C = \frac{\$19,841.34}{(0.68)\ US_0[0.12(0.68),10]} = \$4,379.88.$$

Example 18.4: Machinery Purchase with a Subsidized Loan

Greedy calculates that at the end of 10 years the machine will have a salvage value equal to the removal cost. But, it will generate a $3,000 per year tax shield whose *PV* is:

$$TS_0 = \sum_{i=1}^{10} \frac{T(V_{i-1}^A - V_i^A)}{[1 + r(1 - \theta T)]^i}$$

$$= \frac{\$3,000(0.32)}{(1.0816)} + \dots + \frac{\$3,000(0.32)}{(1.0816)^{10}} = \$6,395.45.$$

Subtracting the tax shield savings from the cost of financing his purchase, Greedy calculates $NPC^{P/F}$ as:

$$NPC^{P/F} = NPC^F - TS_0$$

$$= \$26,236.79 - \$6,395.45 = \$19,841.34.$$

Maximum Lease Payment Under Inflation

In equation (18.3), the salvage value V_n of the durable and its depreciated book value V_n^A could be different. A difference could exist because it is not possible to accurately predict future durable values, and hence align book and market value of durables. Another reason why V_n and V_n^A may differ is that book value depreciation reduces the purchase price V_0 according to some predetermined schedule.

This approach to allowing for depreciation is most likely to be inaccurate in the presence of inflation. Inflation may not only slow the rate of the durable's decline in value, but may actually increase its value in nominal terms, at least during its early life.

The difference in the book value and actual value of durables has important influences on the tax savings from owning a durable and on the break-even lease payment. The effect of inflation on the *PV* of the tax shield from owning a durable is two-fold. First, inflation increases the difference between V_n and V_n^A; hence, inflation increases the tax obligation when the durable is sold.

On the other hand, inflating the price of a depreciable durable suggests a motive for frequent resale. Whenever $V_t > V_t^A$, resale allows the new owner to start calculating depreciation at a higher level V_t. The resale allows the inflationary increase in the durable's value to be captured as a tax shield. But, if the increase $(V_t - V_t^A)$ is taxed at the seller's income tax rate, reselling the durable creates an income tax obligation that reduces the motive for resale.

Inflation and the Tax Shield

Suppose the goal is to calculate the *PV* of the tax shield created by depreciation at the rate γ of the previous period's book value. Then, the *PV* of the shield, TS_0, for a durable whose initial purchase price was V_0 can be expressed as:

$$TS_0 = \frac{TV_0\gamma}{[1+r(1-\theta T)]} + \frac{TV_0\gamma(1-\gamma)}{[1+r(1-\theta T)]^2} + \ldots$$

$$= \frac{TV_0\gamma}{r(1-\theta T)+\gamma}. \qquad (18.11)$$

If inflation increases the discount rate and leaves V_0 unaffected, then TS_0 is unambiguously reduced. To show this condition, TS_0 is differentiated with respect to the discount rate:

$$\frac{dTS_0}{dr} = -\frac{TV_0\gamma(1-\theta T)}{[r(1-\theta T)+\gamma]^2} < 0.$$

Finally, as the allowable depreciation rate increases, so does TS_0:

$$\frac{dTS_0}{d\gamma} = \frac{r(1-\theta T)TV_0}{[r(1-\theta T)+\gamma]^2} > 0.$$

One way to mitigate the effects of inflation on TS_0 is to resell the depreciable durable. Because the maximum-bid price will exceed the durable's book value, the new book value allows the second buyer to claim an increased benefit from the tax shield. But selling the durable requires the payment of a capital gains tax. The question, then, is which will dominate, the capital gains tax or the increased tax shield?

Example 18.5: Inflation and Tax Shields

Consider the calculation of TS_0 assuming the marginal income tax rate is 32 percent, and the depreciable rate of the previous period's book value is 20 percent. Then, if the durable's PV is $30,000 and the nominal discount rate is 14 percent, we can calculate TS_0 using equation (18.11). The value is:

$$TS_0 = \frac{(0.32)(30,000)(0.20)}{(0.14)(1-0.32)+0.20} = \$6,504.$$

If inflation expectations fall lowering r to 11 percent, then TS_0 increases to:

$$TS_0 = \frac{(0.32)(\$30,000)(0.20)}{(0.11)(1-0.32)+20} = \$6,987.$$

An Application

Suppose the depreciable durable is sold at the end of the nth period at a price of $V_0^u(1-\gamma)^n(1+i)^n$. If T_g is the capital gains tax rate, then a capital gains tax must be paid on the difference between the market value $V_0^u(1-\gamma)^n(1+i)^n$ and the depreciation-adjusted durable's book value $V_0^u(1-\gamma)^n$. Thus, the value of a depreciable durable that is subject to a tax shield with a resale possibility, TS_0^R, is:

$$
\begin{aligned}
TS_0^R = &\left\{ \frac{\gamma TV_0^d}{[1+r(1-\theta T)]} + \frac{\gamma TV_0^d(1-\gamma)}{[1+r(1-\theta T)]^2} + \dots + \frac{\gamma TV_0^d(1-\gamma)^{n-1}}{[1+r(1-\theta T)]^n} \right\} \\
&+ \frac{(1+i)^{n+1}}{[1+r(1-\theta T)]^n} \left\{ \frac{\gamma TV_0^d(1-\gamma)^n}{[1+r(1-\theta T)]} + \frac{\gamma TV_0^d(1-\gamma)^{n+1}}{[1+r(1-\theta T)]^2} + \dots \right\} \\
&- \frac{T_g[V_0^d(1-\gamma)^n(1+i)^n - V_0^d(1-\gamma)^n]}{[1+r(1-\theta T)]^n}.
\end{aligned}
\tag{18.12}
$$

On the right-hand side of equation (18.12) is the *PV* of the tax shields claimed by the two owners after adjusting the durable's value to its market value after the nth period. Then, the last term subtracts off the capital gains tax.

Whether or not a tax advantage is associated with resale depends on the difference between equation (18.11), the *PV* of the tax shield without resale, and equation (18.12), the *PV* of the tax shield with resale. By comparing the *PV* of the tax shield with and without resale, we can determine which effect, the increase in the tax shield or the capital gains tax, dominates. Because the investments produce identical cash flows for the first *n* periods, they only need to be compared after period *n*.

The difference between $TS_0^R - TS_0$ is equal to the difference of the two series after *n* periods and is expressed as:

$$TS_0^R - TS_0 = \frac{T\gamma\, V_0^d (1-\gamma)^n \left[\dfrac{(1+i)^n - 1}{r(1-\theta T)+\gamma}\right] - T_g V_0^d (1-\gamma)^n \left[(1+i)^n - 1\right]}{[1+r(1-\theta T)]^n}$$

(18.13)

$$= \frac{V_0^d (1-\gamma)^n \left[(1+i)^n - 1\right]\left[\dfrac{T\gamma}{r(1-\theta)+\gamma} - T_g\right]}{[1+r(1-\theta T)]^n}.$$

For analytic convenience, T_g is expressed as αT where $0 \le \alpha \le 1$ so that if $\alpha=1$, then $T_g=T$; if $\alpha=0$, then $T_g=0$.

If resale is to reduce the total tax burden, then $TS_0^R > TS_0$ and equation (18.13) must be positive. Finding the value for γ that equates $TS_0^R = TS_0$ will indicate break-even conditions between the tax shield with and without resale. Substituting αT for T_g and solving for γ that sets equation (18.13) to zero implies:

$$\frac{\gamma}{r(1-\theta T)+\gamma} = \alpha,$$

(18.14a)

and:

$$\gamma = \frac{\alpha\, r(1-\theta T)}{(1-\alpha)}.$$

(18.14b)

Notice that if $\alpha=1$, there is no solution.

Example 18.6: Break-Even Capital Gains Tax Rate αT and Depreciation Rate γ

Suppose that the depreciation rate γ is 8 percent. Also, let $r=0.14$, $\theta=1$, and $T=0.32$. The break-even portion of capital gains excluded from taxation is calculated using equation (18.14a) to be:

$$\alpha = \frac{0.08}{0.14(1-0.32)+0.08} = 46 \text{ percent.}$$

On the other hand, if 40 percent of capital gains were excluded from taxation as occurred for much of the 1980s, the break-even depreciation rate γ can be calculated using equation (18.14b):

$$\gamma = \frac{(0.4)(0.14)(1-0.32)}{(1-0.4)} = 6.3 \text{ percent.}$$

The solution in equation (18.14b) indicates that if $\alpha=1$, no gain or reduction in the tax shield occurs as a result of resale. On the other hand, if a seller in a low tax bracket sold to a buyer in a high tax bracket, then the value of the tax shield increases. These results depend critically on the assumption that tax rates of the seller and buyer are equal.

Comparative Advantages and Leases

So far we have described the technical properties of leases, such as the types of leases and how to calculate maximum lease payments. Now we show why leases may be executed.

A fundamental principle of economics is that firms should specialize in tasks for which nature, institutions, or luck has granted them an advantage. Suppose two farmers, A and B, can both produce dry edible beans and carrots. Also assume A can grow dry edible beans and carrots better than B and B can grow carrots better than it can dry beans. If both beans and carrots must be produced, then A should produce beans and B should grow carrots. They could then trade to obtain what they did not produce and both be better off.

Example 18.7: Comparative Advantage

Bruce Bean and Leila Lettuce are both farmers (and the only ones in their market). Bruce can grow 120 units of lettuce or 240 units of beans per acre. Leila can grow 60 units of lettuce or 90 units of beans per acre. Suppose Bruce and Leila divided production between beans and lettuce. Then, on one acre of Bruce's land and one acre of Leila's land, total lettuce production would equal:

$$\frac{1}{2}(120) + \frac{1}{2}(60) = 90 \text{ units of lettuce,}$$

and:

$$\frac{1}{2}(240) + \frac{1}{2}(90) = 165 \text{ units of beans.}$$

For Bruce, the ratio of lettuce to beans that could be produced on an acre of land is one-half; for Leila, this ratio is two-thirds. Another way to express this ratio is that for Bruce, the opportunity cost for producing another unit of beans is one-half unit of lettuce. For Leila, the opportunity cost of an increased unit of bean production is two-thirds unit of lettuce. Because their opportunity costs are different, they can trade and both be made better off.

Suppose Bruce only grows beans. Then, on his acreage, 240 units of beans are grown. On the other hand, suppose Leila grows only lettuce; then, 60 units of lettuce would be produced. Now more beans are grown: 240 units compared to 165 units. On the other hand, less lettuce is grown: 60 units compared to 90 units. The acceptability of this changed production schedule depends on the relative price of beans and lettuce.

Suppose prices are such that it is important to maintain lettuce production. To do so efficiently, we assume Bruce agrees to grow one-fourth acre of lettuce producing 30 units which still leaves three-fourths acre bean production equal to:

$$\frac{3}{4}(240) = 180 \text{ units of beans.}$$

Now, lettuce production is still 90 units while bean production has increased from 165 to 180 units. This result demonstrates the law of comparative advantage and the importance of specialization and trade.

Even though A produced both beans and carrots more efficiently than B, it would still be to A's and B's advantage to specialize. They should decide in which product A had the greatest advantage in production or B had the least comparative disadvantage and then specialize and trade as before.

An application of the law of comparative advantage explains why two firms may lease. Suppose firm A is able to purchase a durable at a lower price than firm B. But firm B, not firm A, has need of the services of the durable. In this case, firm A's advantage is in purchasing, while B's advantage is in using the durable. Thus, A might purchase the durable and either sell or lease to B.

Another reason why A and B might both agree to lease has to do with relative taxes. Suppose A's tax rate T^P (A is the purchaser) is greater than B's (the lessee's) tax rate of T^L. As the durable is depreciated, the depreciation creates a tax shield of greater value to A than to B. Thus, we might say that A has a comparative advantage over B in claiming tax depreciation. The lease allows A and B to benefit from their comparative advantages associated with tax shields created by depreciation.

Still another reason why A and B might purchase and lease a durable is because A and B face different opportunity costs of capital, have different opportunities for using the durable's services, or face different marginal costs of credit.

Break-Even Leases

To demonstrate the idea of comparative advantage with a lease agreement, consider that B, the lessor, will not lease for more than it would cost to purchase. To simplify, assume the break-even lease payment is C, the purchase price of the asset is V_0, the book value depreciation rate is γ percent of the previous period's value, r^L is the lessee's opportunity cost of capital, and assume the tax adjustment coefficients for A and B equal one. Then, NPC^P is:

$$
\begin{aligned}
NPC^P &= V_0 - \frac{T^L \gamma V_0}{[1 + r^L(1-T^L)]} - \frac{T^L \gamma V_0(1-\gamma)}{[1 + r^L(1-T^L)]^2} - \cdots \\
&= V_0 - \frac{T^L \gamma V_0}{r^L(1-T^L) + \gamma}.
\end{aligned}
\tag{18.15}
$$

Similarly, assume NPC^L is:

$$NPC^L = \frac{C(1-T^L)}{[1+r^L(1-T^L)]} + \frac{C(1-T^L)}{[1+r^L(1-T^L)]} + \ldots = \frac{C}{r^L}. \tag{18.16}$$

Equating NPC^P and NPC^L, the break-even lease payment C is found to equal:

$$C = r^L V_0 - \frac{r^L T^L \gamma\, V_0}{r^L(1-T^L)+\gamma}. \tag{18.17}$$

The payment C above is the most B will pay for use of the investment. This is because any higher payment would mean B would be better off purchasing the investment.

The Buyer's Perspective

Now consider A's perspective: A has no use for the durable but finds its tax depreciation shield attractive. If A leases to B, A can claim the depreciation and earn a return C (the lease payment) from its services. Thus, A calculates his/her NPV as:

$$NPV = -V_0 + \left[\frac{T^P \gamma\, V_0}{[1+r^P(1-T^P)]} + \frac{T^P \gamma\, V_0(1-\gamma)}{[1+r^P(1-T^P)]^2} + \ldots \right]$$

$$+ \left[\frac{C(1-T^P)}{[1+r^P(1-T^P)]} + \ldots \right] = -V_0 + \frac{T^P \gamma\, V_0}{r^P(1-T^P)+\gamma} + \frac{C}{r^P}, \tag{18.18}$$

where r^P is the buyer's opportunity cost of capital.

Substituting for C, the right-hand side of equation (18.17), the lessor's maximum lease payment, NPV for A is:

$$NPV = -V_0 + \frac{T^P \gamma\, V_0}{r^P(1-T^P)+\gamma} + V_0 - \frac{T^L \gamma\, V_0}{r^L(1-T^L)+\gamma}$$

$$= \gamma\, V_0 \left[\frac{T^P}{r^P(1-T^P)+\gamma} - \frac{T^L}{r^L(1-T^L)+\gamma} \right]. \tag{18.19}$$

Example 18.8: Purchase and Lease Arrangements

Suppose Affordable Assets (*AA*) buys durables and leases them to other firms. As a well-to-do established firm, its tax rate T^P is a high 45 percent. On the other hand, the Unendowed User (*UU*), lacks capital and prefers to lease rather than own. *UU*'s tax rate T^L is 21 percent. In addition, assume that the leased durable wears out at the rate of $\gamma=10$ percent and the market rate of return, r, on securities is 14 percent. Finally, assume that the purchase price of the durable is $4,000.

UU calculates its break-even lease payment using equation (18.17) and finds it equal to:

$$C = (0.14)(\$4,000) - \frac{(0.14)(0.21)(0.10)(\$4,000)}{(0.14)(1-0.21)+0.10} \tag{18.20}$$

$$= \$504.16.$$

AA calculates its *NPV* assuming it could purchase the durable and lease it to *UU*. Using equation (18.19), *AA*'s *NPV* equals:

$$NPV = (0.10)\$4,000$$

$$\left[\frac{0.45}{(0.14)(1-0.45)+0.10} - \frac{0.21}{(0.14)(1-0.21)+0.10} \right] \tag{18.21}$$

$$= \$617.14.$$

If the lessee's tax bracket were 32 percent instead of 21 percent, *AA*'s *NPV* falls to:

$$NPV = (0.10)\$4,000$$

$$\left[\frac{0.45}{(0.14)(1-0.45)+0.10} - \frac{0.32}{(0.14)(1-0.32)+0.10} \right] = \$361.21. \tag{18.22}$$

On the other hand, suppose *AA*'s tax bracket fell to 32 percent while *UU*'s remained at 21 percent. *AA*'s *NPV* would drop from $617.14 to:

$$NPV = (0.10)\$4,000$$

$$\left[\frac{0.32}{(0.14)(1-0.32)+0.10} - \frac{0.21}{(0.14)(1-0.21)+0.10} \right] = \$441.26. \tag{18.23}$$

As the tax rate T^P of the purchaser increases relative to T^L the tax rate of the lessor, the purchaser's *NPV* increases. And, as the purchaser's *NPV* increases, so does the incentive to lease. Thus:

$$\frac{dNPV}{dT^P} = \frac{\gamma \, V_0(r+\gamma)}{[r(1-T^P)+\gamma]^2} > 0.$$

Similarly, if r^P increases relative to r^L, *NPV* and the incentive to lease decreases:

$$\frac{dNPV}{dr^P} = \frac{-\gamma \, V_0(1-T^P)}{[r^P(1-T^P)+\gamma]^2} < 0.$$

Summary

Trades occur when each party to the exchange gives up something of value in return for something of greater value. In most transfers, a physical object or service is exchanged for an agreed amount of cash. Moreover, in most cases, ownership is transferred along with the good or service.

This chapter has considered a different kind of transfer in which the control over the use of a good or service is transferred, not ownership of the good or service. Leasing exists because it provides benefits that might not be realized if the good were sold.

Different types of leases described in this chapter included: sale and leaseback, operating leases, and financial or capital leases. Leases offer particular advantages for lessees including the avoidance of capital requirements associated with purchase. As a result, lessees may use their limited credit reserves for other purchases. Obsolescence risk of ownership is also reduced for lessees. And leasing offers the chance to better match service requirements to the delivery of services. Ownership of durables may require holding idle capacity—less likely when services of a durable are leased.

Tax considerations are critical in the decision to lease or purchase. Ownership allows for tax depreciation shields. Leasing allows the entire lease payment to be claimed as an expense.

An important principle of comparative advantage is involved in the lease decision. If the tax depreciation from ownership is greater for one firm than another, leasing permits the firm to claim those tax advantages by purchasing the asset and leasing it to another firm. Not only can comparative tax advantages be optimally used but also comparative advantages in acquiring financing may be utilized through leasing. Comparative advantage and the incentive to lease may also result from differences in opportunity costs, access to credit, and use for the durable's services.

In essence, leasing is a critical tool that allows firms to take advantage of their comparative advantages.

Review Questions

1. List several durables that are frequently leased. Describe any characteristics these durables have in common.

2. Compare and contrast the following types of leases: sale and leaseback, operating leases, financial leases, and share leases.

3. Explain how leases may allow lessors and lessees to reduce their combined tax obligation.

4. List several advantages leases may offer the lessee over a purchase agreement. What advantages do they offer a lessor over a sale?

5. When does a lease agreement improve the credit position of a lessee relative to a purchase agreement?

6. Discuss how lease and purchase comparisons meet the homogeneity conditions described in Chapter 4.

7. Describe how inflation affects the *PV* of a tax shield resulting from book value depreciation.

8. Will increased inflation encourage the more frequent sale of durables? Defend your answer.

9. How can a lease agreement take advantage of tax rate differences applied to lessees and lessors to reduce their combined tax burdens?

Application Questions

1. Find the net present cost of a 10-year lease whose payments are $700 per year if the lessee's constant marginal tax rate $T=32$ percent and $r_i(1-\theta T)=10$ percent.

2. Assume $C=\$500$, $n=10$, $r_i(1-\theta T)=10$ percent, and $T=32$ percent. What is the most you would pay for a durable assuming zero salvage and straight-line depreciation? (Hint: the annual depreciation that creates a tax shield is $V_0/10$. Find V_0 in equation (18.5) given C).

3. Find the maximum lease payment one could afford in Example 18.2 if the concessionary interest rate were 7 percent instead of 6 percent. Explain why the maximum lease payment changed in the direction it did. (Hint: use equation 18.9.)

4. Calculate the maximum lease payment for a durable that is fully depreciated in 10 years using a straight-line depreciation method. Assume $T=0.21$, $r=0.14$, $\theta=1$, and $V_0=\$4,000$ and that $V_{11}=0$ so that after 10 years the asset can provide no service but that during each of the 10 years of use it provides the same level of service.

5. Calculate the purchaser's *NPV* for the durable described in the previous problem. That is, assume the durable is purchased and the buyer leases it for 10 years after which it can offer no services and has a zero salvage value. Also assume $T^P=0.45$.

6. Using the numbers assumed in the solution to equation (18.3), except for $r^P=14$, find r^P such that *NPV* is zero. Explain why increasing reduces to (decreasing) $r^L=14$ (r^P was required for *NPV* to be equal to zero).

References

Barry, P.J., P.N. Ellinger, J.A. Hopkin, and C.B. Baker. *Financial Management in Agriculture*, 5th ed. Danville, IL: Interstate Publishers, Inc., 1995.

Bierman, H., Jr. *The Lease Versus Buy Decision.* Englewood Cliffs, NJ: Prentice Hall, 1982.

Ford, S.A. and W.N. Musser. "The Lease-Purchase Decision for Agricultural Assets." *American Journal of Agricultural Economics* 76(1994):277-85.

Gordon, M.J. "A General Solution to the Buy or Lease Decision: A Pedagogical Note." *Journal of Finance* 29(1974):245-50.

Heaton, H. "Corporate Taxation and Leasing." *Journal of Financial and Quantitative Analysis* 21(1986):351-59.

Levy, H. and M. Sarnat. *Capital Investment and Financial Decisions*, 3rd ed. Englewood Cliffs, NJ: Prentice Hall, 1986.

Miller, M.H. and C.W. Upton. "Leasing, Buying, and the Cost of Capital Services." *Journal of Finance* 31(1976):787-98.

Myers, S.C., D.A. Dill, and A.J. Bontista. "Valuation of Financial Lease Contracts." *Journal of Finance* 31(1976):799-819.

Robertson, J.D., W.N. Musser, and B.V. Tew. "Lease Versus Purchase of a Center-Pivot Irrigation System: A Georgia Example." *Southern Journal of Agricultural Economics* 14(July 1982):37-42.

Chapter 19

Project Analysis
by Eric W. Crawford[1]

Key words: benefits, costs, discount rate, economic vs. financial analysis, investment constraints, measure of project worth, numeraire, objective function, project selection decision rule, ranking, risk, structure of present value (*PV*) model

Introduction

"Project analysis," as the term is used here, means the use of benefit-cost analysis (*BCA*) procedures to evaluate the net impact on public welfare of a project or set of projects. The major questions addressed in this chapter are: What are the differences between project analysis (*PA*) and other applications of present value (*PV*) models?; and how are those differences reflected in the choice and use of *PV* models? In answering these questions, we will examine the following topics: (1) objective function and definition of benefits and costs; (2) choice of discount rate; (3) structure of the *PV* models; (4) choice of project valuation (profitability) measure; (5) project selection decision rules; (6) ranking of alternative projects; and (7) treatment of risk.

Three of the *PV* models described in Chapter 2 are used in project analysis: the net present value (*NPV*) model, the *IRR* model, and the benefit-cost ratio (*BCR*) model. *BCA* can also be applied to policies, programs, and regulatory or other institutional changes. The vast literature on *BCA* began with a focus on public investment analysis in Western industrialized countries, but a

[1]Eric W. Crawford is a Professor in the Department of Agricultural Economics at Michigan State University.

substantial part of the more recent (post-1960) literature has addressed the application of *BCA* to development projects in Third World countries.

The distinguishing feature of project analysis (and of *BCA*) is its objective function. Although *PA* may include a financial analysis (*FA*), its primary purpose is to determine the *economic* or *social* profitability of alternative investments. The terms "economic" and "social" are often used interchangeably in the *BCA* literature. One may, however, use "economic" profitability to denote net *national income* benefits (sometimes called "efficiency benefits"), and "social" profitability to denote inclusion of non-efficiency benefits as well (e.g., improvements in income distribution).

Economic analysis (*EA*) values benefits and costs in terms of *real resource costs* or opportunity costs, not financial costs. For example, placing an import tariff on fertilizer increases the financial cost to the farmer but leaves national income unchanged. The tariff payment is just a transfer within the economy. Taxes, subsidies, and other transfers are counted in *FA* but not *EA*. Conversely, externalities and indirect effects should be considered in *EA* but not in *FA*, since they affect the overall economy but not (by definition) the direct participants in the project.

By contrast, financial analysis (*FA*), the subject of most other chapters of the book, seeks to determine profitability for the private investor (individual or firm). *FA* values benefits and costs in terms of actual prices paid or received. The purposes of *FA* in project analysis include: (1) to determine the attractiveness of the project to its intended participants; and (2) based on cash flow analysis, to identify credit needs and financing plans for individual participants (or for the project as a whole). Because the distinguishing feature of *BCA* is its focus on economic benefits and costs, and because the financial analysis methods used in project appraisal are similar to those discussed in other chapters, this chapter will concentrate on economic analysis.

The focus of *PA* on economic or social profitability leads to differences in: (1) objective function (definition of costs and benefits); (2) numeraire (unit of measure used to express benefits and costs); (3) the types of prices used to value benefits and costs; and (4) definition of an appropriate discount rate. *PA* applications also differ from other uses of *PV* models in the choice of profitability indicator and project selection decision rule.

Objective Function and Definition of Benefits and Costs

In order to identify desirable investments, *PA* requires an operational method for both measuring changes in public welfare and comparing alternative public investments. A variety of criteria for evaluating social welfare have been discussed in the literature (e.g., Randall, Ch. 7). The criterion most commonly used in *PA* is a variation of the one stated in the 1936 Flood Control Act, viz. that a project should be considered desirable if "the benefits to whomsoever they accrue are in excess of the estimated costs" (Pearce and Nash, p. 1). This is sometimes called the "economic efficiency" criterion; it involves a comparison of aggregate benefits to aggregate costs, expressed in terms of national income, without regard to the distribution of benefits (Randall). The criterion is based on the concept of "potential Pareto improvement," according to which welfare is improved when the aggregate gains resulting from a public investment exceed the aggregate losses, such that the gainers could in principle compensate the losers and still remain better off (e.g., Sugden and Williams).

Use of this criterion has several implications. One is that a dollar of benefits to the poor is assumed to have the same social value as a dollar of benefits to the rich. This implication is equivalent to assuming a social welfare function with unitary welfare weights for all individuals. A second implication is that some individuals may be made worse off by a public project, even though on balance the gains outweigh the losses. Third, one group may bear the costs of a new project while another group reaps the benefits. Or, implementation of a new project ("challenger") that benefits group *A* may entail liquidating an existing investment ("defender") that benefits group *B*.

Taking such inequitable project impacts into account requires the use of more complex evaluation criteria. The criterion of "maximum social well-being" (Randall, pp. 142-44), which assumes the existence of a social welfare function, allows for greater weight to be assigned to project impacts affecting some groups rather than others. While this criterion still allows some individuals to be made worse off, it can incorporate a more realistic (although difficult to estimate!) set of value judgments or welfare weights than the assumption of unitary weights.

Randall also discussed the criteria of "Pareto-safety" and "constant proportional shares." Pareto-safety requires that at least one person's welfare be increased, and no one's be reduced, by a change. In addition, the constant proportional shares criterion requires that each person's proportional share of income be maintained by a change.

Differential weights and other objectives, such as priority to investment and economic growth as opposed to current consumption, are incorporated in certain "social" *BCA* approaches for evaluating development projects in the Third World. Project effects on these objectives are added to net efficiency benefits to give an aggregate measure of net social benefits. While these approaches consider a wider range of objectives than just efficiency, they have been criticized for being too complex and for hiding more information than they reveal. Example 19.1 illustrates the latter point (See Amin).

Aggregate social benefits are the same for both projects, even though the patterns of efficiency benefits are quite different. The point is that weighting *per se*, as a means of incorporating "social" objectives such as equity, does not add more information than is conveyed by examining the distributional impacts of the projects concerned. In fact, distributional weights are only rarely included in practical applications of *PA* procedures by the World Bank and other international lending organizations (Little and Mirrlees 1991, pp. 359-62).

This lengthy discussion of the objective function is important because benefits and costs are defined in relation to it: benefits are changes that increase the value of the objective function, while costs are changes that reduce the value of the objective function. Because economic and financial analysis use different objective functions, financial and economic benefits and costs will in general not be the same.

The objective function (and other definitions and procedures) used in *PA* also differs according to the general approach used. Many governments and lending agencies have formulated manuals of *PA* procedures. The principal approaches include:

Example 19.1: Display of Aggregate Social Benefits

Item	Project *A* Rich	Project *A* Poor	Project *B* Rich	Project *B* Poor
Unweighted benefits	2	10	26	-2
Social weight	1	2	1	2
Weighted benefits	2	20	26	-4
Net social benefits	22		22	

Adapted from Amin.

1. U.S. government evaluation procedures applied to water and other natural resource development projects (U.S. Inter-Agency Committee on Water Resources; U.S. Congress);
2. The "traditional" World Bank approach, reflected in Gittinger;
3. The "revised" World Bank approach, as developed by Squire and van der Tak;
4. The Organisation for Economic Cooperation and Development (OECD) Guidelines developed by Little and Mirrlees (1968) and later revised (Little and Mirrlees, 1974);
5. The U.N. Industrial Development Organisation (UNIDO) Guidelines, developed by Dasgupta, Sen, and Marglin; and
6. The French "effects method," as outlined in Chervel and Le Gall.

Of the many differences among these approaches, two are worth mentioning here:

1. Each approach uses a slightly different *numeraire*, meaning the unit of account or common denominator that measures the objective being maximized:
   a. The Gittinger numeraire (in economic analysis) is the real net *national income* change valued at opportunity cost and expressed in domestic currency (at the shadow exchange rate). "Real" means expressed in constant dollars, excluding inflation.
   b. The Little-Mirrlees and Squire/van der Tak numeraire is "uncommitted *public sector* income" measured in terms of freely available foreign exchange (i.e., world prices) expressed in domestic currency at the official exchange rate. The premium on public income reflects a preference for projects that not only increase national income but also channel benefits to those who will save and reinvest part of them so as to increase the future rate of economic growth. The assumption, which may be empirically unfounded in a given country, is that the rate of savings and reinvestment in the public sector is higher than in the private sector. It is often assumed that unskilled workers and small farmers have low or zero savings rates.
   c. The UNIDO numeraire is *aggregate consumption*, expressed in domestic currency (at the shadow exchange rate). For practical purposes, this is equivalent to the Gittinger national income numeraire.
2. The Little/Mirrlees, UNIDO, and Squire/van der Tak approaches represent "social benefit-cost analysis," meaning that they incorporate

equity (income distribution) and growth objectives along with the standard economic efficiency objective. (For a thorough comparison of these three approaches, see Weiss.)

Discount Rate

As noted in Chapter 2, the discount rate is "the first essential element of any *PV* model" (Ch. 2, p. 1). In the context of *PA*, where each period's costs and benefits are expressed in terms of the numeraire, the discount rate is defined as "the rate of fall in the value of the numeraire over time" (Squire and van der Tak). Because of differences in numeraire, the appropriate discount rate will not be the same in economic and financial analysis, and in economic analysis will depend on the overall benefit-cost analysis (*BCA*) approach used (World Bank, OECD, UNIDO).

The three most common discount rates proposed are the opportunity cost of capital (*OCC*), the consumption rate of interest (*CRI*), and the accounting rate of interest (*ARI*). The definition and rationale of each rate are discussed below.

In the traditional World Bank approach, the discount rate is based on the concept of opportunity cost of capital, as follows (Gittinger, p. 314):

1. *Financial analysis*: the marginal cost of money to the farm or firm, which may be a weighted average of the costs of borrowed and equity capital.

2. *Economic analysis*: the *OCC*, or the return on the marginal investment in the economy. This definition is consistent with the principle given in Chapter 3, that the appropriate discount rate for evaluating the challenger is the *IRR* to the defender. The *OCC* is considered the real, risk-free rate, usually assumed to lie between 8 and 15 percent (Gittinger, p. 314).

In the UNIDO approach, where the numeraire is aggregate consumption, the discount rate is the consumption rate of interest (*CRI*), defined as "the rate at which the value of consumption, in terms of a social welfare function *W*, falls over time" (Ray, p. 77). The *CRI* may be derived as follows:

$$CRI = \eta g + \rho,$$

where η is the elasticity of marginal utility of consumption with respect to per capita income, g is the expected growth rate of average per capita consumption, and ρ is the rate of pure time preference. According to Markandya and Pearce, η and ρ are judgmental parameters, the former usually lying between one and two and the latter usually assigned a value of 2 percent or less.[1] In general, therefore, the *CRI* is not equal to either the rate of pure time preference or the market interest rate, because of capital market imperfections or differences in tax rates among consumers (Ray).

In the Little/Mirrlees and Squire/van der Tak approaches, the discount rate is the accounting rate of interest (*ARI*), which is the *CRI* adjusted to reflect the valuation of future as against present public income. The *ARI* is defined generally as follows (notation modified following Weiss):

$$ARI = CRI + \Delta v,$$

where Δv is the change over time in value of public income vs. private consumption.

An alternative formulation from Squire and van der Tak is:

$$ARI = sq + (1-s)q/v\beta,$$

where q is the marginal productivity of capital in economic prices; s is the marginal rate of savings, or fraction of q reinvested; v is the public income weight or value of public income relative to consumption; and β is a factor for expressing consumption in terms of public income equivalents. Since v may be expressed as $q/CRI \cdot \beta$, the above equation can be simplified to:

$$ARI = sq + (1-s)CRI.$$

Squire and van der Tak interpreted the two right-hand side components of this equation as the "rate of reinvestment" plus the "rate of consumption generation in terms of the numéraire" (p. 114). Bruce interpreted the equation as splitting "the marginal product of capital into its private consumption and savings elements and [revaluing] its consumption element in terms of public income by dividing it by v, the social value of public income" (p. 41). Example 19.2 illustrates the derivation of a numerical value for *ARI*.

Some authors (Little and Mirrlees, 1974; Bruce) suggested using the *ARI* as a *target rate of return*, chosen so that the selected projects just exhaust the supply of investible capital.[2] Weiss (p. 353, n. 52) criticized this practice as "burdening the discounting rate with the additional budgetary weapon function, . . . thus obscuring the problem of weighting present against future

Example 19.2: Calculation of Accounting Rate of Interest

$$ARI = sq + (1-s)q/v\beta,$$

$$CRI = \eta g + \rho,$$

$$v = q/CRI \cdot \beta.$$

Assume the following values (Squire and van der Tak, pp. 69-70):

$$q = s = 0.12; \; \eta = 1; \; g = \rho = 0.03; \; \beta = 0.8.$$

Then:

$$CRI = (1)0.03 + 0.03 = 0.06,$$

$$v = 0.12/(0.06)(0.8) = 2.5,$$

$$ARI = 0.12(0.12) + (1-0.12)(0.12)/(2.5)(0.8)$$
$$= 0.0144 + 0.1056/2 = 0.0672.$$

Thus, the *ARI* is greater than the *CRI*, reflecting the premium on public income, but less than q, the marginal productivity of capital.

events." Markandya and Pearce noted that "the available public funds are not exogenously given, but are rather the subject of choice on the basis of what projects meet a given rate of return" (p. 5). (See the section on ranking for further discussion of this issue.)

A concern sometimes expressed about projects generating natural resource or environmental benefits over a long time period is that normal discount rates (e.g., 8 to 12 percent) virtually eliminate from consideration any values occurring beyond 25 years into the future. For example, a project to reestablish teakwood forests in Thailand is unlikely to be profitable at a discount rate of 10 percent, given that teak trees take 60 years to mature. Conversely, the profitability of nuclear power projects is helped by the fact that the costs of decommissioning the plant and disposing of the radioactive waste may not be incurred until 50 years in the future.

Some propose using low or zero discount rates on the grounds that governments are more far-sighted than private capital markets, and want to take into account project impacts in the distant future. The desirability of ensuring intergenerational equity is also marshalled as an argument for low discount rates. The majority view, however, is that intergenerational equity and the value of maintaining environmental benefits over time should not be addressed by tinkering with the discount rate (Dixon and Meister). Arbitrarily lowering the discount rate would not only allow acceptance of economically inefficient projects, but perhaps also accelerate resource use in the near term by lowering the cost of capital (Norgaard, cited in Munasinghe).

Although the sustainability and intergenerational impacts of projects are issues receiving increasing attention, incorporating such aspects into the *PV* analysis of projects remains a challenge. Randall noted: "When considering events that may greatly restrict the opportunities of future generations, it seems that discounting theories based on the logic of ordinary investments are simply out of their depth" (p. 240). Possible solutions to this problem include: (1) designing projects that offset or compensate for environmental or capital stock degradation (Pearce); and (2) in the case of projects causing irreversible damage, modifying standard *PA* methodology by incorporating the value of foregone preservation benefits (Norgaard, cited in Munasinghe).

On both practical and theoretical grounds, the *OCC* is difficult to estimate in *LDC*s. Theoretically, private interest rates may differ among individuals. Also, the return on the marginal investment will differ across sectors of the economy and will differ from the market interest rate, which is not adjusted for risk, inflation, or price distortions (as would be necessary in economic analysis).

In general, it is assumed that the private discount rate will exceed the social discount rate (Ray).[3] Following Marglin and Sen, Boadway and Wildasin argued that if individual utility depends not only on own consumption, but also on the consumption of all members of the next generation, individual savings will yield external benefits. Since the individual saver does not take this externality into consideration, the social discount rate r^s will differ from the private rate r. Because a dollar available to the next generation will have a higher *PV* in social terms than in private terms, by implication, r^s will be lower than r.

Structure of the *PV* Model

In this section, the *PV* models used in *PA (PV/PA)* are briefly compared with the *PV* models presented in earlier chapters. This comparison will be organized in terms of the five principles given in Chapter 4 for constructing consistent *PV* models.

Cash flow principle. *PV/PA* models use the same general format (no depreciation or capital gains shown), but benefits and costs can include the *imputed or estimated monetary value of nonmarketed goods* and may be valued in terms of opportunity costs or shadow prices, not market prices. Examples of such nonmarketed goods include farm output consumed by the family (significant in many Third World agricultural development projects), payments made or received in kind rather than in cash, and the estimated value of external effects or environmental goods and services generated by the project but not marketed.

Homogenous measures principle.
1. **Measure.** *PV/PA* models adhere to this principle. Rather than comparing a "challenger" and a "defender," however, *PV/PA* models make a generally similar comparison between a "with project" scenario and a "without project" scenario, both constructed using the same units of measure.
2. **Taxes.** Generally not relevant in LDC applications. As transfers, taxes are excluded from the economic analysis. In most LDCs, income and capital gains taxes are rarely applied effectively in the industrial sector, much less in the agricultural sector. When taxes exist, however, they would be included in the financial analysis.
3. **Certainty.** This principle is followed, although certainty equivalents are generally not used. (See later section on uncertainty.)
4. **Inflation.** Economic analysis is generally done in real (constant) prices. Financial analysis is done in either real or nominal (current) prices, the latter when inflation is very rapid or when the objective is to estimate project-level credit needs or the project's impact on the government budget. Although seldom done, one can incorporate the impact of inflation on the real burden of debt service in a constant-price analysis by deflating loan repayment values over time by the inflation rate. Current-price and constant-price values of internal rate of return (*IRR*) can be derived from each other using the following expression:

$$(1 + \text{constant-price } IRR) = (1 + \text{current-price } IRR) /$$
$$(1 + \text{inflation rate})$$

where the *IRR*s and inflation rate are expressed in decimal form.

5. **Liquidity.** Differences between the "with" and "without project" scenarios in terms of the "nearness to cash" of costs and returns are not explicitly considered. Potential liquidity problems caused by negative incremental ("with" minus "without project") net returns in early years of the project would be regarded as a potential drawback of the project if they implied a need for substantial borrowing.

6. **Term.** "With" and "without project" scenarios always have the same terms. Alternative projects or variants of the same project would not necessarily have the same terms. One approximate solution to this problem is to compare a long-term project with two or more iterations of a short-term project, e.g., a 20-year project compared with two cycles of a 10-year project.

7. **Size.** Both the "with" and "without" scenarios, as well as alternative projects, are likely to be of unequal size. Few authors discuss adjustments needed to deal with this problem (exceptions are Mishan and Schmid). In practice, adjustments are rarely made except possibly when dealing with the situations of capital limitations or mutually exclusive investments.

Consistency in timing. This principle is followed in *PA*. Benefits and costs enter in the period in which they are received or incurred.

Life of the investment. Project time horizons are set somewhat arbitrarily. Gittinger stated: "The general rule is to choose a period of time that will be roughly comparable to the economic life of the project" (p. 355). Dixon and Meister stated that the appropriate time horizon for an investment project is: "the *shorter* of (1) the expected useful life of the project; or (2) the effective economic life of the project when discounting is taken into account." This condition recognizes that typical discount rates virtually erase values occurring more than 25 to 30 years in the future.

The final year of cash flow may include a salvage value reflecting the *PV* of anticipated future earnings of the asset. Duration and repeatability are given little attention in practice or in the *PA* literature (exceptions again are Mishan and Schmid).

Total costs and returns principle. This principle is incorporated in *PV/PA* models partly by defining the project at an appropriately inclusive level (in terms of geographical regions, individuals, and sectors affected), and partly by the inclusion (in theory) of externalities in economic analysis.

Other Structural Features ————————————————————————————

Several other characteristics of *PV/PA* models are worth noting:

1.   Because economic analysis looks at net returns to the overall economy, it focuses on estimating the *return to total assets* (*RTA*), i.e., determining the return to all resources invested in the project (inherent profitability), separate from the consideration of how best to finance the project. In financial analysis, as outlined in Gittinger, one may calculate the profitability of the project "before financing" (*RTA*) or "after financing" (return to equity, *RTE*). The latter is considered to be of more interest to the potential participant in the project.

2.   Various conventions are followed for time phasing and discounting of benefits and costs:

   a.   In the standard convention, initial investment costs are not discounted. This approach will be called the "year 0" format. Investment is shown in year 0; returns, operating costs, and production costs start in year 1 and are discounted by $1/(1+r)$.

   b.   In the convention used most commonly by the World Bank, investment costs are included in year 1 and discounted accordingly ("year 1" format).

   c.   A variation sometimes used by the World Bank shows only investment costs (and loan receipts in *FA*) in year 1, discounted by $1/(1+r)$. Other costs and benefits remain at their "without project" levels in year 1. Project-generated increases in production or operating costs (and benefits, if any) are shown beginning in year 2. Gittinger called this the "time-adjusted" format; it includes provision for increasing (or reducing) working capital in year t to cover the expected increases (or decreases) in production costs in year $t+1$. This format gives different *NPV*s compared to the other formats, but identical *IRR*s.

3.   In projects where part of the investment is financed by loans or grants from external donor agencies, the convention is to treat these funds as national capital, i.e., to assign to donor funds the same opportunity cost as that associated with use of domestic capital (Gittinger). The intention is to separate the decision about project worth from the decision about how to finance it. Where donor grants or low-interest loans are tied completely to a specific project (i.e., made available if and only if used for that project), this assumption overestimates the opportunity cost of that capital. However, such cases are uncommon.

Choice of Measure of Project Worth

In *PA*, the two major questions are: (1) is a given project economically profitable?; and (2) for a given set of alternative projects, which should be selected for investment? The second question implies that a set of alternative projects is waiting to be evaluated, which is not often the case.

In the *PA* literature, it is often stated that any of the *PV* measures (*NPV, IRR, BCR*) will identify the same set of projects as profitable if the measures are used in the same way to evaluate all project alternatives against a given opportunity cost of capital (*OCC*). It is not always acknowledged that the simple decision rules (*NPV*≥0, *IRR*≥*OCC*, *BCR*≥1) must be modified when project alternatives are mutually exclusive or capital is limited.

In spite of this supposed equivalence of project worth measures, the most commonly used measure is *NPV*. *BCR* is used more in the U.S. and other industrialized countries than in appraisal of Third World projects. The World Bank prefers *IRR* because it is more easily understood, and because use of *IRR* avoids the need to set world-wide or country-specific values of *OCC*, which might invite invidious comparisons (Gittinger).

In other respects, the discussion of the pros and cons of the various measures in the *PA* literature follows the standard finance literature, except for little thorough discussion of the *reinvestment rate assumption* issue other than in Mishan and Schmid.[4] A variant of the *BCR*, called the "net benefit to investment" (*N/K*) ratio, is recommended by Gittinger for ranking alternative projects when capital is limited. The *N/K* ratio is the *PV* of project net benefits after they turn positive, divided by the *PV* of the initial negative net benefits.

Project Selection Decision Rules

As explained in Chapter 6, the choice of project worth measure and the related decision rule depend on the assumptions about *investment constraints*. The common decision rules used in *PA* will be discussed in this framework.

The most common assumption is that projects are only *rate of return restricted*, i.e., that capital is unlimited and projects are independent. Here, one can calculate any of the three *PV* measures, and select any and all projects that are profitable using one of the following criteria: *NPV*≥0, *IRR*≥*OCC*, *BCR*≥1.

If project alternatives are *mutually exclusive*, the recommended approach is to select the alternative with the highest *NPV*. Another method outlined in Gittinger involves calculating the "incremental *IRR*," i.e., the *IRR* to the (large-small project) cash flow. If the incremental *IRR*≥*OCC*, the rule is to choose the larger alternative; otherwise, choose the smaller. This approach involves more computation than does calculation of *NPV*, and works only with pairwise comparisons.

Mutually-exclusive projects are common in Third World applications of *PA*. Some examples and their recommended profitability measures are:

1. **Entirely different projects.** Select the project giving the highest *NPV*.
2. **Different scales of project.** Select the project scale giving the highest *NPV*.
3. **Different project starting dates.** Compute *NPV* for all timing scenarios, using the same year as t_1, and pick the scenario (i.e., the starting year) with the highest *NPV*.
4. **Different technologies.** Select the technology giving the highest *NPV*, or, if the technologies provide equal benefits, the technology with the lowest *PV* of cost. Another method (Gittinger) is to calculate the discount rate at which the *PV*s of cost of two alternative technologies are equal (the *IRR* to the expensive-cheap technology cost flow, with "expensive" meaning higher undiscounted total cost). If this "crossover" or "equalizing" rate ≤ OCC, the rule is to accept the expensive technology, otherwise accept the cheap technology. The latter approach implies ignorance of the exact *OCC*.

Ranking

The *PA* literature makes the point that ranking is needed only for capital-rationed investments. If capital is unlimited, any profitable project would be implemented, other considerations aside. If capital is rationed, more projects may be evaluated as profitable than can be implemented. Various approaches have been suggested for handling this situation, most involving some form of ranking.

Although Gittinger observed that practitioners tend to use *IRR* and *BCR* to rank projects, he argued that only the *N/K* ratio is valid for ranking *per se*. The logic is that the denominator of the *N/K* ratio consists only of investment capital, which is the scarce resource to which the returns should be maximized. Use of *NPV*, *IRR*, or *BCR* for ranking can give inconsistent results when projects are of different size and duration. Schmid, drawing on Mishan, outlined a method for incorporating explicit assumptions about reinvestment rates and for calculating terminal values of the alternative investments to adjust for differences in size and duration. Values of *NPV*, *IRR*, and *BCR* calculated from these transformed or "normalized" values give consistent rankings. Chapter 6 discusses similar adjustments and summarizes the conditions in which *NPV* and *IRR* give identical rankings.

In *PA*, the normal assumptions in the capital-rationed investment case are that the *cost of capital remains constant* until available capital is exhausted, and that projects are *independent*. The case of the upward-sloping cost of capital curve is not discussed.

The following methods recommended by Gittinger for dealing with capital limitations differ from those discussed in Chapter 6. They are based implicitly on an *OCC* defined as the rate that equates the supply and demand of capital, rather than an *OCC* that is set *a priori* and used as a basic parameter of the analysis. Thus, an excess of profitable projects over the number that can be funded indicates too low an *OCC* used for discounting in the original analysis.

1. Calculate *NPV* using successively higher discount rates until one is left with a set of projects that pass the *NPV*≥0 criterion and just exhaust the capital available (fit within the budget constraint).

2. If using *IRR*, raise the cut-off rate until one is left with a set of projects that pass the *IRR*≥*OCC* criterion and just exhaust the available capital.

3. If using the *N/K* ratio, select projects in descending order of *N/K* ratio (highest first) until one is left with the set of projects that just exhaust available capital.

Given the illustrative projects in Example 19.3, methods (1) and (2) would lead to selection of project *J*. A discount rate of 20 percent or less leaves more profitable projects than can be funded. Methods (1) and (2), therefore, do not lead to the correct decision (for an *a priori* discount rate of 10 percent), which is to select projects *J* and *L* (maximizing the *NPV* obtained from investing 500 units of capital).

Method (3), selection by *N/K* ratio, also fails. Project *J* would be selected first, since it has the highest *N/K* ratio. Project *K* has the next highest *N/K* ratio, but cannot be selected since it requires more capital than the 400 units remaining. Method (3) only works if one can skip too-large projects and go to the next profitable and fundable one, or if one assumes perfectly divisible investments.

Thus, as noted in Chapter 6, the clearest decision rule to use in this situation is to select the set of independent project alternatives that maximize overall *NPV*.

Example 19.3: Ranking of Alternative Projects with Capital = $500

Project	R_0	R_1	NPV @10%	IRR	N/K
J	-$100	$130	$18.18	30.0%	1.18
K	-$500	$600	$45.45	20.0%	1.09
L	-$400	$472	$29.09	18.0%	1.07

Problem: All three projects are profitable at a 10 percent opportunity cost of capital, yet not all three can be implemented with only 500 units of capital available. Which project(s) should be selected?

Treatment of Risk

Considering risk is clearly an important issue in *PA*. Imperfect information about likely project impacts and uncertainty about future unit costs and prices undermine one's faith in profitability measures based on "best guess" estimates. Although a project's *IRR* might be estimated at 15 percent based on assumed levels of construction and imported input costs and on the value of exports, the stochastic nature of these costs and prices makes *IRR* a random variable.

The probabilistic nature of project performance raises several questions (Boadway and Wildasin). First, what is the likelihood of making an incorrect project selection decision? Second, what should be the criterion for measuring the riskiness of a project? Third, how should the *PV* analysis be adjusted to reflect the riskiness of a project?

Regarding the first question, the literature on applied *PA* mostly addresses the use of *sensitivity analysis* or *break-even analysis* to examine the sensitivity of estimated profitability levels to alternative yield, cost, or price assumptions, and the likelihood of the actual project being unprofitable. An example is calculation of "switching values," or the percentage by which a key variable must change to reduce project profitability to zero. Certainty equivalents are discussed by some authors (Markandya and Pearce; Schmid) but are rarely, if ever, used in practice.

More elaborate risk analysis involving Monte Carlo simulation has been proposed by Hertz and Pouliquen. The goal here is to estimate the probability distribution of the chosen outcome variable (e.g., *IRR, NPV*). The steps include:

1. Identify the uncertain variables.
2. Identify the probability distribution of each uncertain variable.
3. Determine the effect on project outcome of variation in each factor, using a model of the project cash flow.
4. Display the results in terms of expected value or cumulative probability distributions.
5. Apply a decision rule based on a measure of risk such as maximizing expected *IRR*, minimizing the probability of obtaining an unacceptable *IRR* or *NPV*, or a lexicographic or safety-first rule incorporating both aspects.

Such systematic risk analysis is not often carried out, which suggests that the perceived benefits are lower than the costs. The value of project appraisal itself, not necessarily including risk analysis, in reducing the likelihood of making an incorrect decision is examined by Little and Mirrlees (1991). Their analysis suggests that the approximate value of project appraisal is "at least 2 percent of the mean net value of projects appraised" (1991, p. 356).

Regarding the second question—how to assess the riskiness of projects—a common measure is the variability in rate of return of the project. This is one measure of the project's "stand alone" risk, as discussed in Chapter 11. Markandya and Pearce also discussed the risk of a project in terms of "its addition to the total variance of a portfolio of assets as well as its covariance with that portfolio," with the latter interpreted as the set of all investments in the economy. This approach is comparable to the concept of "systematic risk" discussed in Chapter 11.

Regarding the third question, several methods have been proposed to adjust for the riskiness of a project:

1. Express costs and benefits in certainty equivalents, and discount using the real risk-free discount rate. The usefulness of this approach is reduced by the difficulties of obtaining the certainty equivalent values.
2. Alternatively, use the expected values of costs and benefits and add a risk premium to the discount rate. Aside from the difficulties of estimating the risk premium empirically, its use implies that all benefits and costs are equally risky, and that the degree of risk increases exponentially through time. Neither of these two assumptions would usually be valid.

More ad hoc methods include:

1. "Subjective conservatism"—picking the most conservative values when estimating benefits and costs. The result depends on the analyst's risk

attitudes, and may lead to an unnecessarily pessimistic evaluation of the project.

2. Shortening the time horizon of the project. This approach is undesirable because it treats all benefits and costs as equally risky, and penalizes long-gestation projects.

Little and Mirrlees (1991) noted that flexible projects which can be reoriented to changing economic conditions are worth more than inflexible projects. They suggest that the benefits of flexibility should be added to other benefits; yet this is not done in practice.

In contrast to the above proposals, it is sometimes argued that the costs of risk need not be incorporated for public projects. Arrow and Lind, as summarized in Boadway and Wildasin, used the concepts of risk-spreading and risk-pooling in presenting this argument. First, as the number of individuals sharing the benefits and costs of a project rises, the costs of risks are spread more widely and the total cost of risk-bearing falls. Second, if there are many small public projects whose outcomes are uncorrelated, risks tend to offset each other. Thus, for the overall portfolio of public projects, the cost of risk-bearing is small and the risk premium low.

Summary

In this chapter, we have examined the differences between project analysis and other applications of *PV* models. We have reviewed how these differences affect the implied objective function and the definition of benefits and costs; the choice of discount rate; the structure of the *PV* models; the choice of project valuation (profitability) measure and of project selection decision rules; the ranking of alternative projects; and the treatment of risk.

The three *PV* models used in project analysis are the *NPV*, *IRR*, and *BCR* (benefit-cost ratio) models. The distinguishing feature of project analysis is its focus on the economic or social profitability of investments. The most noteworthy effects of this focus on economic rather than financial analysis are differences in the definition and valuation of benefits and costs, choice of discount rate, and treatment of risk. In other respects, the *PV* methods applied in project analysis are broadly similar to those found in the standard investment analysis literature.

Endnotes

1. See Markandya and Pearce for a discussion of efforts to estimate these two parameters empirically.

2. Squire and van der Tak stated that "the *ARI* is that rate of discount which balances the supply of and demand for public investible resources. As such, the *ARI* should equal the internal social rate of return on the marginally-acceptable project" (p. 114).

3. Mishan stated that in the presence of uncertainty and for Western economies with large private investment sectors and a substantial proportion of public funds used for investment, "it is appropriate to regard the highest actuarial [expected] rate of return ρ on the riskier private investments as the basis of the opportunity yield ρ for public investment" (p. 379).

4. See Crawford and Schmid for a spreadsheet model that allows explicit incorporation of alternative reinvestment rate assumptions.

5. As noted in Chapter 11, the estimation of risk premia is a common practice in the U.S. However, Markandya and Pearce noted that this approach is impossible in developing countries, since the necessary economy-wide information is not generally available.

Review Questions

1. In applying project analysis techniques, one often encounters mutually-exclusive projects. What are the different types of mutually-exclusive projects, and what problem(s) do they create in deciding which project to select?

2. What are the main differences between the application of *PV* methods in project analysis, and other applications of *PV* models?

3. What different conventions are followed for time phasing and discounting of benefits and costs in project analysis?

4. The discount rate is an important element of the *PV* calculations in project appraisal, as in any *PV* model.

   a. What is the appropriate discount rate to use in project appraisal?

   b. Discuss some of the alternative definitions of the social discount rate.

   c. Why might the social discount rate be lower than the private market interest rate?

5. Perhaps more often than with private investments, public projects aim to satisfy multiple objectives.

    a. What analytical problems result when projects have multiple objectives, and what methods are available for addressing those problems?

    b. What problems are associated with the use of differential weights to take account of social (non-efficiency) objectives?

6. Much of the conceptual basis of benefit-cost analysis comes from welfare theory.

    a. Define and contrast the following terms: Pareto improvement, potential Pareto improvement, and Pareto safety.

    b. Discuss the conditions for welfare maximization. Is Pareto optimality sufficient for welfare maximization? Explain.

7. Simplified methods of incorporating uncertainty into project appraisal are often used as an alternative to full-scale risk analysis.

    a. Illustrate these simplified methods and summarize their drawbacks.

    b. Discuss the disadvantages of using "best estimates" and sensitivity analysis in comparison to more formal risk analysis to deal with uncertainty in project analysis.

8. Define the following terms and briefly explain their role in project appraisal:

    a. Efficiency benefits.

    b. Numeraire.

    c. Switching value.

    d. *N/K* ratio.

9. When is it appropriate to rank project alternatives?

10. Explain why the choice of discount rate and the treatment of risk are significantly different in *PV* models used in project appraisal, compared to other applications of *PV* models.

Application Questions ─────────────────────────────────

1. Answer the questions below, using **only** the information given here:

| | Incremental Net Benefits | | | | NPV | NPV | IRR |
Project	Year 1	Year 2	Year 3	Year 4	10%	15%	
A	-$150	$10	$10	$170	---	---	9%
B	-$60	$25	$25	$40	$12	---	21%
C	-$290	$320	$10	$10	$15	$2	---

**The blanks in this table represent numbers which you may or may not need to calculate in order to answer the questions below.

	10%	15%	20%
Discount factor, year 1	0.909	0.870	0.833
Discount factor, year 2	0.826	0.756	0.694
Discount factor, year 3	0.751	0.658	0.579
Discount factor, year 4	0.683	0.572	0.482

a.   Under the assumption of unlimited capital and independent projects, which project(s) would you select if the opportunity cost of capital (*OCC*) were 10 percent? If it were 15 percent? Explain.

b.   Suppose now that you have only $300 to invest, and that the cost of capital remains constant until it is exhausted. Which project(s) would you select if the *OCC* were 15 percent?

c.   Suppose now that you again have unlimited capital, but that the three projects are mutually-exclusive. Which project would you select if the *OCC* were 10 percent? Explain.

2.   Given the following information on a particular project, use interpolation to estimate its *NPV* for a 10 percent discount rate:
   —   the *NPV* of the investment at 15 percent is -$100
   —   the *IRR* to the investment is either 16.5 percent or 11 percent (one or the other, not both)

3.   A project has the following incremental net benefit stream: ($600) in year 1; ($850) in year 2; ($150) in year 3; $150 in year 4; and $1,100 in each of years 5-10. Figures in parentheses are negative.

a. Calculate the *NPV* of this project using a discount rate of 20 percent. Discount factors at 20 percent are: 0.833 (year 1); 0.694 (year 2); 0.579 (year 3); and 0.482 (year 4). *PV* of annuity factors at 20 percent are 4.192 (year 10); 2.589 (year 4); and 2.991 (year 5).

b. Given your result, would the internal rate of return of this project be higher or lower than 20 percent?

4. Choose between the following two mutually-exclusive projects, assuming that the opportunity cost of capital is (a) 10 percent; and then (b) 15 percent.

Project	Year 1	Years 2-4	*IRR*
A	-$1,000	$500	24%
B	-$2,200	$1,000	17%

Use the following information in answering the question:

	10%	15%
Discount factor, year 1	0.909	0.870
Present value of an annuity factor, year 2	1.736	1.626
Present value of an annuity factor, year 4	3.170	2.855

5. Farmers in an East African country who are now growing maize are being encouraged to convert land to coffee production. Evaluate the profitability of this investment, based on the following data. All figures are in *shillings per hectare*.

    — Investment cost:
        · initial coffee tree establishment = $5,000 (year 0)
        · sprayer = $1,250 (purchased in year 1; replaced in year 4)
    — Fungicide spray = $300 per year
    — Hired labor = $500 in year 1, $1,000 subsequently
    — Fertilizer = $800 in year 1, $500 subsequently
    — Revenues from coffee sales = 0 in years 1 to 2, $5,000 in year 3, $10,000 in year 4, and $15,000 in years 5 to 10
    — Current net revenues from maize production = $5,000

a. Prepare a capital budget for the investment in coffee trees. Use a 10-year time horizon, and show one column for years 5 to 10.

b. Calculate the *NPV* of the investment at a 15 percent discount rate, and indicate whether the investment is profitable.

6. A project has been designed to provide farmers with horses to use as draft animals. Using the following information, evaluate the profitability of this investment for an individual farmer.

    –   purchase price of the horse = $90

    –   useful life = 6 years

    –   estimated straight-line depreciation per year = $12

    –   feed cost per year = $18

    –   veterinary costs per year = $5

    –   revenues earned by using the horse = $40 (year 1) and $50 (years 2 to 6)

a. Prepare a capital budget for this investment. Using the discount and *PV* of annuity factors given below, calculate the *NPV* of the investment.

    –   *Discount factors* at 15 percent are: 0.870 (year 1); 0.432 (year 6).

    – $US_0(0.15,1) = 0.870$ (year 1); $US_0(0.15,2) = 1.626$ (year 2); $US_0(0.15,5) = 3.352$ (year 5); and $US_0(0.15,6) = 3.784$ (year 6).

b. Assuming that the *NPV* at 10 percent is 5 and the *NPV* at 15 percent is -20, use interpolation to estimate the *IRR*.

References

Amin, G. "Project Appraisal and Income Distribution." *World Development* 6(1978):139-52.

Arrow, K.J. and R.C. Lind. "Uncertainty and the Evaluation of Public Investment Decisions." *American Economic Review* 60(1970):364-78.

Boadway, R.W. and D.E. Wildasin. *Public Sector Economics*, 2nd edition. Boston, MA: Little, Brown, 1984.

Bruce, C. "Social Cost-Benefit Analysis." Staff Working Paper No. 239. Washington, DC: World Bank, August 1976.

Chervel, M. and M. Le Gall. *Manuel d'Evaluation Economique des Projets—La Méthode des Effets*. Paris: République Française, Ministère des Relations Extérieures, Coopération et Développement, 1984.

Crawford, E.W. and A.A. Schmid. "User's Guide to BENCOS–Lotus 1-2-3 Templates for Benefit-Cost Analysis." MSU International Development Working Paper No. 37. East Lansing, MI: Department of Agricultural Economics, Michigan State University, 1990.

Dixon, J.A. and A.D. Meister. "Time Horizons, Discounting, and Computational Aids." In *Economic Valuation Techniques for the Environment*, ed. by J.A. Dixon and M.M. Hufschmidt, pp. 39-56. Baltimore, MD: Johns Hopkins University Press, 1986.

Gittinger, J.P. *Economic Analysis of Agricultural Projects*, 2nd edition. Baltimore, MD: Johns Hopkins University Press, 1982.

Hertz, D.B. "Risk Analysis in Capital Investment." *Harvard Business Review* 42(Jan./Feb. 1964):95-106.

Little, I.M.D. and J.A. Mirrlees. *Project Appraisal and Planning for Developing Countries*. New York, NY: Basic Books, 1974.

_____. Project Appraisal and Planning Twenty Years On." In *Proceedings of the World Bank Annual Conference on Development Economics, 1990*, pp. 351-82. Washington, DC: World Bank, 1991.

Marglin, S.A. "The Social Rate of Discount and the Optimal Rate of Investment." *Quarterly Journal of Economics* 77(1963):95-112.

Markandya, A. and D.W. Pearce. "Environmental Considerations and the Choice of the Discount Rate in Developing Countries." Environment Department Working Paper No. 3. Washington, DC: World Bank, May 1988.

Mishan, E.J. *Cost-Benefit Analysis*. Rev. Edition. New York, NY: Praeger, 1976.

Munasinghe, M. "Environmental Economics and Valuation in Development Decisionmaking." Paper presented at the CIDIE Workshop on Environmental Economics and Natural Resource Management in Developing Countries. Washington, DC: World Bank, 22-24 January 1992.

Norgaard, R.B. "Sustainability as Intergenerational Equity: The Challenge to Economic Thought and Practice." Internal discussion paper, Asia Regional Series, Report No. IDP 97. Washington, DC: World Bank, June 1991.

Organization for Economic Cooperation and Development (OECD). *Manual of Industrial Project Analysis in Developing Countries*, Vol. II. Paris: OECD Development Centre, 1968.

Pearce, D.W. "An Economic Perspective on Sustainable Development." *Development* 2/3(1989):17-20.

Pearce, D.W. and C.A. Nash. *The Social Appraisal of Projects: A Text in Cost-Benefit Analysis*. New York, NY: John Wiley, 1981.

Pouliquen, L.Y. *Risk Analysis in Project Appraisal*. Baltimore, MD: Johns Hopkins University Press, 1970.

Randall, A. *Resource Economics: An Economic Approach to Natural Resource and Environmental Policy*, 2nd edition. New York, NY: John Wiley, 1987.

Ray, A. *Cost-Benefit Analysis: Issues and Methodologies*. Baltimore, MD: Johns Hopkins University Press, 1984.

Schmid, A.A. *Benefit-Cost Analysis: A Political Economy Approach*. Boulder, CO: Westview Press, 1989.

Sen, A.K. "Isolation, Assurance and the Social Rate of Discount." *Quarterly Journal of Economics* 81(1967):112-24.

Squire, L. and H.G. van der Tak. *Economic Analysis of Projects*. Baltimore, MD: Johns Hopkins University Press, 1975.

Sugden, R. and A. Williams. *The Principles of Practical Cost-Benefit Analysis*. Oxford: Oxford University Press, 1978.

U.N. Industrial Development Organization (UNIDO). *Guidelines for Project Evaluation*. Project Formulation and Evaluation Series No. 2. New York: United Nations, 1972.

U.S. Congress, Joint Economic Committee. *The Analysis and Evaluation of Public Expenditures: The PPB System*. Vols. 1, 2, and 3. 91st Congress, 1st Session, 1969.

U.S. Inter-Agency Committee on Water Resources. *Proposed Practices for Economic Analysis of River Basin Projects*. Washington, D.C., May 1958.

Weiss, D. "Economic Evaluation of Projects: A Critical Comparison of a New World Bank Methodology with the UNIDO and the Revised OECD Approach." *Socio-Economic Planning Sciences* 12(1978):347-63.

Chapter 20

Valuation of Research
by James F. Oehmke[1]

Key words: cowpea, development, hungry season, productivity, research, Senegal, sensitivity analysis, social surplus, sorghum, Sudan, technology, technology transfer

Introduction ——————————————————————————

The goal of this chapter is to explain how present value (*PV*) models are used for the evaluation of public investments in agricultural research, development, and technology transfer (RD&TT). In agriculture, much RD&TT is publicly funded through government or donor agencies. This public funding is an investment in the process of finding and implementing improved production or processing inputs and practices. The public will realize a return to this investment if these new inputs or practices improve the quality of agricultural outputs, lower production costs, or develop new uses of agricultural commodities that enhance their value to consumers. However, these returns may not be realized until after many years of research and development. Hence, a *PV* model is necessary for accurate valuation of the investment in RD&TT.

———————————————————————

[1]James F. Oehmke is an Associate Professor in the Department of Agricultural Economics at Michigan State University.

What Are Research, Development, and Technology Transfer?

Research is "a search or investigation directed to the discovery of some fact by careful consideration or study of a subject; a course of critical or scientific inquiry" (*Oxford English Dictionary*). In agriculture, research is usually directed to the discovery of a fact that will improve agricultural production or processing, or the quality of agricultural output. For example, genetic research may be directed toward isolating those genes that control resistance to certain diseases.

Development is the process of transforming abstract knowledge into techniques and innovations that can be applied to production, processing, or distribution processes. Usually, the abstract knowledge has been generated by research. For example, suppose that research has determined that genes control soybean tolerance to herbicides, and how to incorporate alleles that increase this tolerance. Development is the stage at which a number of different genetic alterations are tested to see which alteration(s) is best in terms of least cost, herbicide tolerance, yields and yield stability, bean quality, and other characteristics that affect the cost and/or value of soybean production. As development progresses, one or more of the alterations will be chosen as socially and commercially viable. The developers must then produce seeds for the improved varieties embodying the genetic alterations. More generally, the final product of the development stage will be an input, technique, or innovation that farmers, processors, or distributors can use to increase productivity.

The technology transfer process begins where the development process ends. It transfers the new inputs, innovations, or techniques from the research and development laboratories to the farms or firms engaged in production, processing, and distribution. The largest economic impacts of RD&TT are usually felt after the inputs, innovations, or techniques are transferred to producers. At that time, the consequent cost reductions or quality improvements begin to affect the marketplace.

In its entirety, the RD&TT process involves formulating an idea, testing that idea for accuracy, developing new inputs or techniques based on the idea, and transferring these new inputs or techniques to farmers and producers.

The Typical Pattern of RD&TT Investment and Returns ———

The RD&TT process can be lengthy. Schweikhardt argued that "it is good for both the public and the scientist to be patient with research work" because "it takes 10 years at least to establish one agricultural fact."[1] Pardey and Craig found evidence that "long lags–at least thirty years–may be necessary to capture all of the impact of research on agricultural output."[2] The classic example of agricultural research is the development of hybrid corn in the United States. The time from the start of the research leading to successful hybridization techniques to the widespread adoption and use of hybrid corn in the United States was in excess of 40 years.[3]

Once the techniques are adopted by farmers or other agricultural producers, society reaps the benefits of improved product quality, lower production costs, or increased product availability. These benefits persist for as long as the new techniques or inputs are used. Eventually, however, techniques that were once new and state of the art will become obsolete as they are replaced by newer, better techniques. As this replacement occurs, the flow of benefits from the original RD&TT will taper off and eventually become zero when none of the original inputs or techniques are used.

Comparing the flow of costs to the flow of benefits shows that most of the RD&TT costs are incurred in the earlier years, while the benefits come in later years. Indeed, benefits generally start to accrue when costs decline. Consequently, as discussed in Chapter 6, the internal rate of return (*IRR*) provides an ordinal ranking of RD&TT projects that is consistent with the ranking provided by a net present value (*NPV*) analysis when certain consistency conditions are met. Because the *IRR* provides an easy comparison of returns across projects with different capitalization requirements, it has traditionally been used as the measure of returns to RD&TT. This chapter maintains that tradition, although some discussion of other *PV* models is provided toward the end.

Measuring the Benefits of RD&TT Investments ———

The social surplus paradigm is the traditional method for measuring research benefits; it has played a crucial role in the literature on research evaluation. The idea of social surplus can be expressed in terms of the standard supply and demand diagram of the market for an agricultural output, such as cassava.[4]

The cassava market is depicted in Figure 20.1. In this figure, we shall interpret S and D as "inverse" supply and demand curves, $S=S(Q)$ and $D=D(Q)$, respectively. The height of the inverse supply curve at quantity Q_0, $S(Q_0)$, represents the cost of producing the Q_0^{th} unit of cassava. Similarly, the height of the inverse demand curve at quantity Q_1, $D(Q_1)$, represents the amount that consumers are willing to pay for the Q_1^{th} unit of cassava. The market equilibrium is determined by the intersection of the supply and demand curves. The equilibrium quantity is Q_e, and the equilibrium price, P_e, reflects both the cost of producing the Q_e^{th} unit and the value to the purchaser of consuming the Q_e^{th} unit.

The net gain to the farmer or firm producing the Q_0^{th} unit of output is the price received less the cost of producing that unit, or $P-S(Q_0)$. The aggregate gain to all producers is the integral of $P-S(Q)$ from 0 to Q_e, and is represented by the area under the horizontal line at P_e and above the inverse supply curve. This area is known as producers' surplus. The net gain to the consumer eating the Qth unit of cassava is the value to the consumer of eating that unit less the price paid, $D(Q_1)-P$. The aggregate gain to all consumers from eating all Q_e units is equal to the integral of $D(Q)-P$ over all units from 0 to Q_e. This gain is represented by the area above the dashed line at P_e and below the demand curve D, and is called consumers' surplus.

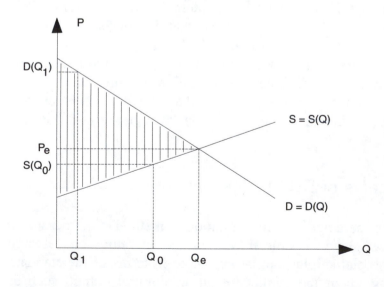

Figure 20.1
Consumers', Producers',
and Social Surplus

Social surplus is the sum of consumers' and producers' surplus; it represents the net gain to society from the production, trade, and consumption of cassava. Social surplus is represented by the entire shaded area in Figure 20.1.

Social surplus is measured in dollars, even though the investments in public RD&TT do not generate any cash return. For example, increases in consumers' surplus are captured by consumers who purchase agricultural products at market prices below what they are willing to pay. Hence, the benefits from an increase in consumers' surplus can be thought of as savings to consumers expressed in dollar terms. Two important points emerge. First, the fact that some portion of the benefits is captured by consumers is part of the reason why agricultural RD&TT is largely publicly sponsored—private firms are not able to capture these benefits, and hence may limit their investments in RD&TT. Second, for *PV* models, the increase in social surplus attributable to RD&TT can be treated as equivalent to cash, even though monetary returns do not accrue to the RD&TT organizations. Thus, the *PV* models developed in earlier chapters can be applied, treating social surplus as the equivalent of cash.

Successful RD&TT improves techniques and inputs used by farmers, as represented by a downward shift in the inverse supply curve from *S* to S_1 in Figure 20.2. As in Figure 20.1, social surplus is represented by the area between the inverse supply and demand curves. The downward shift in the inverse supply curve thus increases social surplus by an amount represented by the shaded area between *S* and S_1 and to the left of *D*. The increase in social surplus due to the shift of the inverse supply curve is considered a social benefit attributable to the RD&TT investment.

The diagrammatic representation of social surplus depicted in Figures 20.1, 20.2, and 20.3 is static. That is, the area between the supply and demand curves measures social surplus during the time period for which the borogove market is in effect. In most parts of the world, borogove is grown once a year, so that the static representation is sufficient to describe annual social surplus.

How can the static analysis be modified to capture research effects which may last for several years? The simplest way is to repeat the static analysis for each year that the research program affects the market. The result is a series of diagrams such as Figure 20.2, one for each year. Each diagram will depict the inverse supply curve, *S*, which would have occurred in the absence of the RD&TT, and the shifted inverse supply curve that incorporates the technical progress made possible by RD&TT. Thus, each diagram can be used to attribute to RD&TT the increase in social surplus achieved in the year for which the diagram is drawn. The result is a time series of social surplus values that measure the benefits in each year of the RD&TT.

Example 20.1: The Calculation of Social Surplus

The borogove market is characterized by linear inverse supply and demand curves: $S(Q)=(Q+20)/4$ and $D(Q)=(100-Q)/2$, where quantities are measured in tons and prices are in \$/ton (Figure 20.2). For the moment, ignore the curve $S_1>S_1(Q)$. Setting $S(Q)=D(Q)$ reveals the equilibrium quantity is 60 tons; using the definitions of the inverse supply and demand curves, it follows that the equilibrium price is determined by $S(60)=D(60)=\$20$.

Producers' surplus is represented by the area above the supply curve and below the horizontal line at $P=P_e=\$20/\text{ton}$. The base of this triangle has length P_e minus the point at which the supply curve intersects the price axis, or 20-5=\$15/ton. (This can be seen by rotating the figure 90° counterclockwise.) The height is equal to the equilibrium quantity, 60 tons. Hence, producers' surplus is (\$15/ton)x(60 tons)/2=\$450. Consumers' surplus is given by the area of a triangle whose base is that part of the price axis between P_e and the intercept of the inverse demand curve. The length of this base is 50-20=\$30/ton. The height of the triangle is equal to Q_e. Hence, consumers' surplus is (\$30/ton)x(60 tons)/2=\$900.

Social surplus in the borogove market is producers' surplus plus consumers' surplus, or \$450+\$900=\$1350. Alternatively, social surplus could be calculated as the area of the triangle whose sides are $S(Q)$, $D(Q)$, and the price axis. This triangle has area equal to (\$50/ton-\$5/ton)x(60 tons)/2=\$(45x30)=\$1,350, which is the same result obtained by adding consumers' and producers' surplus.

Example 20.2: Measuring the Change in Social Surplus from a Supply Shift

The new inverse supply curve is given by the equation $S(Q)=5+Q/16$ (Figure 20.3). Because of this shift, the new equilibrium quantities and prices are $Q'_e=80$ and $P'_e=10$. The producers' surplus in the borogove market after the supply shift is \$200, and consumers' surplus is \$1600. Thus, producer surplus declines but consumer surplus increases by a large amount. Social surplus is thus \$200+\$1,600=\$1,800, an increase of \$450 from before the introduction of the new technique. This change can also be measured by directly calculating the area between S and S', as shown in Figure 20.2.

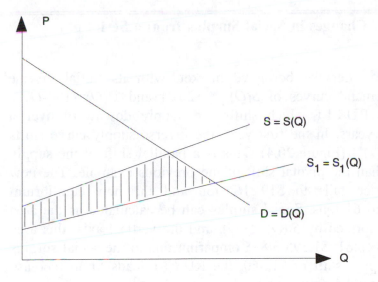

Figure 20.2
RD and TT Increase
Social Surplus

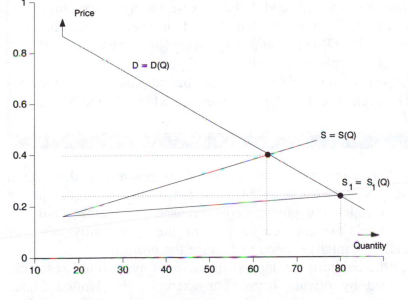

Figure 20.3
Social Surplus in the
Borogove Market

Measuring the Costs of RD&TT

For many RD&TT projects, the flow of costs equals the flow of yearly expenditures on the project. For publicly-sponsored projects, these expenditures are a matter of public record.

There are three important exceptions to the simple measurement of costs as expenditures. First, administrative or welfare costs may be associated with

Example 20.3: Changes in Social Surplus from a Series of Supply Shifts

Let's reconsider the borogove market, with its initial inverse supply and demand curves of $S(Q)=(Q+20)/4$ and $D(Q)=(100-Q)/2$. Now consider RD&TT which shifts the supply downward over a period of four years. In the first year, the inverse supply curve shifts to $S_1(Q)=(Q+17)/4$ (Figure 20.4). This is a parallel shift of the supply curve, rather than the pivotal shift of the previous example. The new equilibrium price falls to $19 1/2 ton and the new equilibrium quantity rises to 61 tons. Social surplus can be calculated as the area of the triangle formed by $S_1(Q)$, $D(Q)$, and the vertical axis: this area is $1/2x(50-17/4)x61=$1,395 3/8. Comparing this to the social surplus prior to the supply shift of $1,350, the RD&TT leads to an increase of $45 3/8 in social surplus in year 1.

Suppose that in years 2, 3, and 4 the inverse supply curve shifts downward by the same amount that it did in year 1, so that $S_2(Q)=(Q+14)/4$, $S_3(Q)=(Q+11)/4$, and $S_4(Q)=(Q+8)/4$. Calculation of equilibria and social surpluses reveals that in year 2, social surplus increases by $1,441 1/2-1350=$91 1/2 over the surplus before the supply shifts. For years 3 and 4, the increases are $138 3/8 and $186, respectively.

raising public funds. For example, to raise $1.00 of tax revenue in the United States, it may cost taxpayers as much as $1.35 in tax payments, higher prices for goods and services which the government purchases, and other "hidden" costs *t*. These costs should be counted as part of the opportunity costs of raising the public funding (capital) needed to finance the project.

Second, although the public is the largest financier of agricultural research, some research is funded by private firms. For example, the United States Department of Agriculture funds the maintenance of many different plant strains, but private companies do most of the development of the varieties that farmers actually plant. Hence, these private development costs should be included as part of the cost of RD&TT of improved variety seeds.

The third important consideration in quantifying the costs of RD&TT is the interaction with other public programs. In the U.S., many commodities have prices supported by the government. In essence, these supports guarantee to farmers that they will receive a government-specified price for their product—if

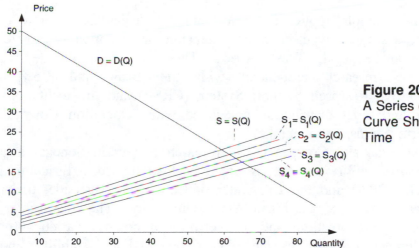

Figure 20.4
A Series of Supply
Curve Shifts over
Time

the market price is lower than the specified price, then the government makes up the difference. Thus, the government is often paying farmers something for each bushel they produce. RD&TT which shifts the inverse supply curve down increases the amount that farmers produce. The government then pays farmers the difference between the support price and the market price on a greater number of bushels, increasing the costs of the program. Although some of these increased costs should be attributed to the price support program, some are also attributable to the RD&TT program.

Utilizing the Data on Benefits and Costs

The benefits and costs of the project can be utilized to calculate the cash-equivalent flow associated with the RD&TT project. At each instant in time, this flow is equal to the benefits minus the costs. For the early years of the project, when the costs are large and the benefits are small, the flow will be negative. However, if the project successfully increases social surplus, then eventually the benefits will dominate the costs and the cash-equivalent flow will become positive.

Once the cash-equivalent flow has been calculated, it can be plugged into equation (2.4) for the flow $R(0)$, ..., $R(n)$, and the *IRR* can be calculated.

Although the most commonly used measure for valuation of RD&TT is the *IRR*, other valid measures are also used. These measures include benefit-cost analysis and *NPV*, when a good estimate of the opportunity cost of capital

Example 20.4: Cowpea Production in Senegal

This example applies the *IRR* method to calculate the rate of return to a set of cowpea research, extension, and technology transfer projects in Senegal, West Africa. These projects include the underlying research associated with the Bean and Cowpea Collaborative Research Support System (CRSP) and the technology transfer and input distribution associated with "Operation Cowpea" (Schwartz, Sterns, and Oehmke).

The Bean and Cowpea CRSP research project in Senegal is a collaborative effort of the Senegalese Institute for Agricultural Research (ISRA) and the University of California, Riverside, under the management of Michigan State University. The research is centered around breeding and maintenance of cowpea varieties for heat tolerance, drought resistance, yield potential and stability, and resistance to disease and insects. The Bean and Cowpea CRSP has been active in Senegal since 1981.

Operation Cowpea was implemented in 1985, after prolonged drought had decimated peanut crops and left the Government of Senegal without sufficient peanut seed for distribution for the 1985 planting season. Following the poor harvest in 1984, the Senegalese Minister of Rural Development urged the European Economic Community, the United States Agency for International Development, and the Government of Senegal to put together an emergency package to increase cowpea production as a replacement for peanut production. The result was Operation Cowpea, funded at US$ 1,000,000 in 1985 and US$ 600,000 in 1986, targeted at those peanut-growing regions most severely stricken by drought. Based on previous research, ISRA and the Bean and Cowpea CRSP recommended in 1985 that the Operation purchase seed for the CB-5 cowpea variety and distribute this seed to farmers along with insecticides, sprayers, and explanations of farm management and production practices. These recommendations (slightly modified in 1986) were carried out under the auspices of the Senegalese extension service).

A follow-up impact study quantified the benefits and costs of Operation Cowpea and the underlying CRSP research (Table 20.1). The benefits are zero before 1985, since from 1981 to 1984 there was

Example 20.4, Cont'd.: Cowpea Production in Senegal

no transfer of technology from the experiment stations to the farmers. The benefits began to accrue with the onset of Operation Cowpea and its transfer of research results to farmers in the form of seeds, insecticides, and farm management practices. These benefits are estimated to have been US$ 3,185,000 in 1985 and US$ 3,188,000 in 1986. Since Operation Cowpea ended with the 1986 season, the impact assessment stops with the 1986 season.

The costs of the projects include the costs directly associated with Operation Cowpea plus the cost of the CRSP and ISRA research upon which the program was based. Research costs were incurred in all years from 1981 through 1986, ranging from US$ 286,000 in 1986 to US$ 395,000 in 1983. Total costs are shown in Table 20.1, and peak in 1985 when Operation Cowpea costs were at their peak.

The annual cash-equivalent flows associated with the investment in CRSP research and Operation Cowpea are the annual benefits less the annual costs. These cash-equivalent flows can then be used in equation (2.4) to calculate the *IRR* to the research, development, and technology transfer investments. This calculation shows the *IRR* to be 38 percent.

The 38 percent *IRR* is a nominal rate of return in the sense that the cash-equivalent flows are denominated in current dollars. In the U.S., where much of the program funding originated, nominal capital costs were in the 15 to 20 percent range in the 1981 to 1986 period, so that by comparison the 38 percent *IRR* indicates a moderately successful program.[5]

If a real *IRR* were desired, the researcher could deflate the cash-equivalent flows, or adjust the nominal rate of return by subtracting the rate of inflation (the two procedures may give different results).

is available. For example, Ahmed and Sanders analyzed RD&TT investments in improved sorghum technology for irrigated farmland in Sudan. They found an *IRR* of 22 to 34 percent, and a *NPV* of $20 to $51 million at a 13 percent discount rate. Policy makers who had little economics background preferred a different type of presentation. Ahmed and Sanders used *NPV* analysis to find that an annuity paying $2.6 to $6.8 million per year for 30 years had the same *NPV* as the RD&TT project. Since the annual operating budget for all research

Table 20.1 Benefits, Costs and Net Cash-Equivalent Flows Associated with the Senegalese Cowpea Projects

Year	Benefits	Costs	Net Cash-Equivalent Flow
	Current US$	Current US$	Current US$
1981	0	350,000	-350,000
1982	0	360,000	-360,000
1983	0	395,000	-395,000
1984	0	390,000	-390,000
1985	3,185,000	1,325,000	1,860,000
1986	3,188,000	866,000	2,322,000

Source: Schwartz, Sterns, and Oehmke

by Sudan's Agricultural Research Corporation, the main agricultural research institute in Sudan, is $0.8 million of Sudanese-generated funds, the project was viewed as quite successful.

Sensitivity Analysis

Often the perfect data set is not available and the researcher must make some assumptions in order to quantify the benefits and costs of the RD&TT. These assumptions could involve the shape of the inverse supply and demand curves (e.g., linear or constant elasticity), the form of the supply shift (e.g., pivotal or parallel), the role of exogenous factors, the accuracy of the data, etc. These assumptions can affect the outcome of the *IRR* calculation. For example, the assumption that the shift in the inverse supply curve is small will lead to a small measured benefit, and hence to a low calculated *IRR*. Some assumptions affect the calculated *IRR* more than others. Sensitivity analysis measures how sensitive the *IRR* is to the assumptions made; that is, it measures how much the calculated *IRR* would change if a different assumption were used. It gives a feeling for how much uncertainty is involved in the assessment of RD&TT. If the *IRR* does not change much in response to changing assumptions, then the researcher can feel reasonably certain that the estimated *IRR* is accurate.

Example 20.5: The *NPV* of Senegalese Cowpea Projects

The last column in Table 20.1 shows the current value of the net cash-equivalent flow associated with Senegalese cowpea projects. To obtain the *NPV* of these projects, the value of the net cash-equivalent flow at time t is substituted for R_t in equation (2.2). That is, the *NPV* formula becomes:

$$NPV = \sum_{t=0}^{T} R_t/(1+r)^t,$$

where R_t denotes net cash-equivalent flow at time t. If the opportunity cost of capital is 15 percent, then the *NPV* of the cowpea projects is $869,351. The positive *NPV* indicates that the projects have been successful, which is consistent with the *IRR* analysis.

For historical reasons, investigators of agricultural RD&TT have tried to be overly conservative—that is, not to make assumptions that impose an upward bias in the estimated *IRR*. Early analyses of the impact of agricultural research (Schultz; Griliches; Evenson) used strong assumptions to simplify the calculation of benefits, and found high *IRR*s. For example, Lindner and Jarrett criticized the assumptions Griliches used to generate the external rate of return of 500 to 600 percent, claiming that accurate assumptions could cut the estimated returns in half (which is still an exceptional return). Because *IRR*s are sometimes used to justify funding of public agricultural research, critics of agricultural research are vocal in denouncing the *IRR* literature as overly optimistic. In response, economists calculating *IRR*s have painstakingly tried to prevent an upward bias in *IRR* calculations, using conservative assumptions and methodologies whenever possible—and still find high *IRR*s to agricultural research.

The conservative assumptions used in the assessment of agricultural research can be relaxed in a sensitivity analysis. By making less conservative (and sometimes more realistic) assumptions, the sensitivity analysis can determine the range in which the true *IRR* probably falls, and can isolate factors such as adoption rates or yield increases that influence the magnitude of the *IRR*.

Example 20.6: Sensitivity Analysis for Cowpeas

The previous example was based on a "conservative" scenario. One assumption in this scenario was that all of the cowpeas were consumed as shelled peas after the traditional harvest. It is likely that some of the cowpeas are consumed before the harvest in the form of green pods. In Senegal (and many developing countries), the period immediately before the harvest is a period of extreme hunger when farmers try to make last year's crops last until this year's harvest comes in. In some areas, malnutrition and related disease are real possibilities during the pre-harvest, "hungry" season. Consequently, increased production of a crop that can be consumed during this period is quite important. Cowpeas, with their possibilities for green pod production, are such a crop. However, these benefits were not accounted for in the conservative estimate of the *IRR*.

Through sensitivity analysis, it is possible to relax the strict assumption that all production was in the form of peas after the traditional harvest. Although data are of poor quality, Schwartz, Sterns, and Oehmke estimated that if greenpod production during the hungry season were included, benefits were increased in 1985 and in 1986. Subtracting the costs and using the net benefits as a cash-equivalent flow in equation (2.4) yields an estimated *IRR* of 96 percent. This sensitivity analysis shows that the *IRR* could be nearly three times that found in the conservative scenario.

Summary

Two characteristics of public RD&TT make it amenable to *IRR* analysis. First, the intertemporal nature of RD&TT means that a *PV* model is required. Second, the cash-equivalent flow from public investments in RD&TT is usually negative at first, then becomes positive and remains non-negative. These characteristics mean that the ordinal ranking of projects by *IRR* is consistent with that provided by an *NPV* ranking. Because the *IRR* allows easy comparison of returns to projects having different capitalization requirements, it has traditionally been the measure of choice for assessing investments in RD&TT. Calculation of the *NPV* of an RD&TT project or program, or benefit-cost analysis, is also possible if the researcher has an acceptable estimate of the opportunity cost of capital.

The benefits from RD&TT often occur as improved quality, increased output, or lower production and processing costs. These benefits are usually captured by consumers or producers, and not returned directly to the investors. However, the social surplus paradigm provides a way to quantify these benefits in cash-equivalent terms.

The costs of RD&TT are the expenditures generating RD&TT services. However, some care must be taken to ensure that all relevant costs are included. Subtracting the costs from the benefits yields a cash-equivalent flow from the investment in RD&TT. This flow is used in equation (2.4) to calculate the *IRR*. Sensitivity analysis shows how the *IRR* changes as the assumptions change. When a range of assumptions is plausible, sensitivity analysis shows the range in which the "true" *IRR* lies.

Endnotes

1. See Schweikhardt.
2. H.H. Goodell as quoted in Schweikhardt, p. 92.
3. See P.G. Pardey and B. Craig.
4. This section is based on Oehmke et al.
5. Based on prime rates. Alternatively a 35 percent welfare cost of raising funds could be used for comparison.

Review Questions

1. What is the definition of research?
2. What is technology transfer?
3. How long does it take to establish one agricultural fact?
4. Are public funds an important contributor to agricultural research?
5. What does the height of the supply curve represent?
6. What does the height of the demand curve represent?
7. What does social surplus represent?
8. What is sensitivity analysis?

Application Questions

1. Suppose that an RD&TT project achieves the supply shifts and benefits discussed in Example 20.3 (for simplicity, assume that benefits accrue for only four years). Suppose that to achieve these benefits RD&TT expenditures of $10/year were required for 10 years before any benefits were obtained, and expenditures of $20/year were required during the four years in which benefits were obtained.

    (a) Complete the following table:

Year	Cost	Benefit	Net Benefit
1	$10	0	-10
2			
3			
4			
5			
6			
7			
8			
9			
10			
11	$20	45 3/8	25 3/8
12			
13			
14			

    (b) Calculate the *IRR*.

    (c) If the opportunity cost of capital is 12 percent, what is the benefit-cost ratio?

    (d) What is the *NPV* of this project at a 12 percent discount rate?

    (e) Would you recommend this project? Why or why not? By what criterion?

2. Suppose that the inverse supply and demand curves in the borogove market are $S(Q)=(Q+20)/4$ and $D(Q)=(100-Q)/2$, as in Example 20.I. Successful RD&TT causes a parallel shift in the inverse supply curve to $S'(Q)=(Q+5)/4$.

    (a) Calculate the new equilibrium price and quantity.

(b) Calculate the change in consumers', producers', and social surplus due to the RD&TT.

(c) Now, suppose that instead of the parallel shift, the RD&TT has caused a pivotal shift from $S(Q)=(Q+2)/4$ to $S^2(Q)=5Q/26+5$. Calculate the new equilibrium price and quantity, and the increase in consumers', producers', and social surplus.

(d) Compare the effects of the parallel and pivotal shifts on consumers', producers', and social surplus.

3. Suppose that supply and demand are constant elasticity: $S = aP^\alpha, D = dP^\epsilon$; where S is quantity supplied, D is quantity demanded, α and ϵ are the elasticities, a and d are parameters, and P is price. Suppose that research shifts the supply curve in a pivotal fashion from $S = a_0 P^\alpha$ to $S = a_1 P^\alpha$, where a_0 and a_1 are the particular values the parameter takes on before and after the research shift. Assume that equilibrium $(S=D)$ holds both before and after the shift. Under what conditions does research increase producer surplus? Under what conditions does producer surplus decrease? Explain the latter conditions.

4. In calculating RD&TT costs, only equilibrium conditions have been considered. Now, suppose that some input (e.g., water or fertilizer) is subsidized by the government, and that research develops a new variety that is particularly responsive to this input. As this new variety is adopted, input use increases, raising the costs to the government of maintaining the subsidy.

   How much of these increased costs should be attributed to the research program? The subsidy program? How much is a result of interactions between these programs, and cannot be easily divided between them? (Further readings include Alston et al., 1988 and Oehmke, 1988.)

5. Suppose that only two inputs are used in agriculture, land, and seeds. Land is in fixed supply (perfectly inelastic), but the supply of seeds is perfectly elastic. The demand curve for the agricultural output is perfectly inelastic. Assume that RD&TT causes the supply curve for agriculture production to shift down and to the right. Do land owners or seed producers gain from this shift? How much relative to the change in producers' surplus?

6. How would you explain why a supply curve might have a parallel shift? A pivotal shift? A change in curvature? (For further reading, see Linder and Jarrett; Rose.)

7. Over time, each of a sequence of innovations shifts the supply curve down and to the right. Can you distinguish the social benefits of one innovation

from another? In evaluating an RD&TT program, is this necessary? How do you determine when a particular innovation is no longer generating social benefits?

8.   Suppose you must evaluate an RD&TT investment using *NPV*. If the investment funds are taken from public revenues, should the opportunity cost of capital reflect the social cost or the private cost? Why? What are the differences between social and private costs? How would you measure the appropriate opportunity cost?

References

Ahmed, M. and J. Sanders. "The Impact of Hageen–Dura I in Sudan." Presented at the Symposium on the Impact of Technology on Agricultural Transformation in Africa, Washington, DC, October 14-16, 1992.

Alston, J.M., G. Edwards, and G. Freebairn. "Market Distortions and Benefits from Research." *American Journal of Agricultural Economics* 69(1990):281-88.

Evenson, R.E. "The Contribution of Agricultural Research to Production." *Journal of Farm Economics* 49(1967):1415-25.

Griliches, Z. "Research Costs and Social Returns: Hybrid Corn and Related Innovations." *Journal of Political Economics* 60(1958):419-31.

Lindner, R. and Jarrett, F. "Supply Shifts and the Size of Research Benefits." *American Journal of Agricultural Economics* 60(1978):48-56.

Oehmke, J.F. "The Calculation of Returns to Research in Distorted Markets." *Agricultural Economics* 1(1988):53-65.

Oehmke, J.F., L., Daniels, J.A. Howard, M. Maredia, and R. Bernstein, "The Impact of Agricultural Research: A Review of the Ex-Post Assessment Literature with Implications for Africa." Michigan State University, 1990, 38 pages.

Pardey, P.G. and B. Craig, 1989. "Causal Relationships Between Public Sector Agricultural Research Expenditures and Output." *American Journal of Agricultural Economics* 71:9-19, quote appears on page 18.

Rose, R.N. "Supply Shifts and Research Benefits: Comment." *American Journal of Agricultural Economics* 62(1980):834-37.

Schultz, T.W. "The Economic Organization of Agriculture." New York: McGraw-Hill, 1953.

Schwartz, L.A., J.A. Sterns, and J.F. Oehmke. "Economic Returns to Cowpea Research, Extension, and Input Distribution in Senegal." *Agricultural Economics* 8(1993):161-71.

Schweikhardt, D.B., 1983. "The Role of Nonmonetary Values in Induced Institutional Innovation: The Case of the State Agricultural Experiment Stations." M.S. thesis, Department of Agricultural Economics, Michigan State University, p. 92.

Part 5

Optimization and Present Value Models

Chapter 21

Replacement Principles

Key words: average performance, average returns, capital recovery factor, continuous time, disposal cost, economic life, investment tax credits, opportunity cost of capital, replacement models, rotation, salvage values, transaction costs

Introduction

Most durables wear out. After use and the passage of time, durables do not provide the same quality and reliability of services as they did earlier. Sometimes the difference in the quality of service is small enough to be ignored—a light bulb is an example. But if reliability of services is important, even a light bulb's services change over time as the likelihood of its failure increases. Other durables' services may change over time because the quality and reliability of supporting durables change.

In some cases, a "main" durable may require replacement because its "supporting" durables fail. Main durables consist of several supporting durables. Supporting durables are required to maintain a "main" durable in use. Tires on cars, batteries in flashlights, firebrick in blast furnaces, and roofs on houses are examples of supporting durables. When a supporting durable fails, the owner of the durable must ask: Is it time to dispose of, replace, or to rotate the use of supporting durables or the main durable?

Sometimes the optimal economic life of a durable investment may be unrelated to the physical characteristics of the durable. For example, investment tax credits available in the early life of a durable may stimulate replacement independent from the services available from the durable. Increasing costs of inputs required by the durable may also influence the investment decision; for example, rising gas prices in the 1970s shortened the economic life of many large, fuel inefficient cars.

Disposal, replacement, and rotation models contain two unknowns: net present value (*NPV*) and *n*, the economic life of the durable. The disposal, replacement, and rotation models are developed in this chapter in continuous time using continuous compounding. We use continuous time because of the need to differentiate *NPV* models with respect to time to find the optimal replacement time n^*.

Replacement models belong to the class of more complicated *PV* models described in Chapter 2. What distinguishes replacement models apart from other *PV* models is their opportunity costs. In replacement models, extraction of services from the replacement(s) cannot occur until services from the current durable are ended. Thus, the opportunity cost of extending use of the current durable is related to postponing returns and services from its replacement(s).

In this chapter, we introduce measures of continuous compounding that aid in the evaluation of replacement decisions. Then, these measures are applied first to the case of disposal models without replacement and then to a set of increasingly complex, yet realistic, replacement models.

Required Calculus and Continuous Compounding ——————

In a previous chapter, alternative investments were compared and selected based on either their *NPV*s or internal rates of return (*IRR*s). Solutions for the *NPV* or *IRR* models were provided by the single-equation *PV* model. In an earlier chapter, single-equation models that can be solved for a single unknown were called less complicated *PV* models. In this chapter, we seek the solution to at least two unknowns, *NPV* and the economic life of the durable, *n*. The result is a model requiring more than one equation to solve.

The second equation for finding the optimal *n*, n^*, is found by maximizing the *NPV* equation for *n*. This first-order expression is the second equation used to find *n*. Calculus techniques are most easily applied when the variable being maximized is continuous. Because time is a continuous variable, the *PV* model must be converted from discrete time to continuous time to apply the maximizing techniques of calculus.

Under the continuous-time formulation, the *PV* model can be maximized with respect to time to obtain the second equation needed to find the optimal replacement time. Replacement rules for discrete *NPV* models can be inferred from the replacement rule used to solve continuous-time replacement models.

To convert discrete time problems into continuous-time problems, begin by writing a standard discrete time problem as:

$$NPV = -V_0 + \frac{R_1}{(1+r)} + \frac{R_2}{(1+r)^2} + \dots + \frac{R_n}{(1+r)^n}. \qquad (21.1)$$

Now suppose that time is divided into *m* shorter time periods. The model becomes:

$$NPV = -V_0 + \frac{R_1/m}{(1+\frac{r}{m})} + \dots + \frac{R_1/m}{(1+\frac{r}{m})^m} + \frac{R_2/m}{(1+\frac{r}{m})^{m+1}} + \dots + \frac{R_2/m}{(1+\frac{r}{m})^{2m}}$$

$$+ \dots + \frac{R_n/m}{(1+\frac{r}{m})^{m(n-1)+1}} + \dots + \frac{R_n/m}{(1+\frac{r}{m})^{mn}}.$$

A well-known result in calculus is that as *m* approaches an infinitely large (undefined) number, the value of $(1+r/m)^m$ approaches the value e^r, where $e=2.7182818...$ The result is:

$$\lim_{m \to \infty} (1+\frac{r}{m})^m = e^r.$$

It is recognized, of course, that:

$$e^r = 1 + r^e \neq 1 + r,$$

and that:

$$\ln e^r = \ln (1 + r^e) = r.$$

The difference between r^e and r is attributed to continuous compounding. Thus, $e^{0.05}-1$ equals 5.127 percent and ln (1.05127) equals 5 percent.

The unusual property of the number e is that the derivative of e^t is itself. Moreover, for $y = e^{-rt}$, $\dfrac{dy}{dt} = -re^{-rt}$ while the integral of e^{-rt} equals:

$$\int_0^n e^{-rt}dt = \frac{1}{r}(1-e^{-rn}).$$

Having defined a continuous-time discount factor, the equivalent to $US_0(r/m,mn)$ in continuous time can be expressed as:

$$\lim_{m\to\infty} US_0(r/m,mn) = \int_0^n e^{-rt}dt = \frac{1}{r}(1-e^{-rn}).$$

Moreover, because e^{-r} equals $1/(1+r^e)$, then:

$$\lim_{m\to\infty} US_0\ (r/m,\ mn) = \frac{1}{r}\left(1 - \frac{1}{(1+r^e)^n}\right).$$

Finally, the discounted present value (PV) of an annuity A is:

$$A \lim_{m\to\infty} US_0(r/m,mn) = \int_0^n Ae^{-rt}dt = \frac{A}{r}(1-e^{-rn}).$$

Having introduced continuous discounting and letting income be a continuous function of time, the continuous-time equivalent of equation (21.1) is now maximized to obtain the second equation of the PV model needed to solve for n:

$$\max_n\ NPV = -V_0 + \int_0^n R(t)e^{-rt}dt. \tag{21.2}$$

The general formula for differentiating the integral $y = \int_{p(x)}^{q(x)} f(s,x)ds$ with respect to x can be written as:

$$\frac{dy}{dx} = \int\limits_{p(x)}^{q(x)} \frac{\partial f}{\partial x} + f[q(x),x] \frac{dq}{dx} - f[p(x),x] \frac{dp}{dx}.$$

Differentiating equation (21.2) with respect to n produces the result:

$$\frac{dNPV}{dn} = R(n)\,e^{-rn} = 0.$$

Thus, the optimal finite value of n is that which equates $R(n)$ to zero. Moreover, it is a global maximum if (see Example 21.1 for an application):

$$\frac{d^2 NPV}{dn^2} = -rR(n) + R'(n) < 0.$$

Disposal Models and Salvage Values

In the previous discussion and in Example 21.1, value from the ownership of the durable could only occur by extracting services. However, owners of durables often can sell their durables at the end of the economic life for a price of $V(n)$. Sometimes $V(n)$ is negative representing a disposal cost. Consider a disposal problem where the durable considered for disposal has a positive salvage value. For this case, NPV is written as:

$$NPV = -V_0 + \int\limits_0^n R(t)\,e^{-rt}\,dt + e^{-rn}\,V(n). \tag{21.3}$$

The salvage value $V(n)$ discounted to the present by the continuous-time discount factor e^{-rn} distinguishes equation (21.3) from equation (21.2).

To find the optimal n for this case, equation (21.3) is maximized with respect to n:

$$\frac{dNPV}{dn} = R(n) + V'(n) - rV(n) = 0,$$

and second-order conditions are met if:

Example 21.1: Optimal Life Without Replacement, Disposal, or Salvage Values

Roll'm Tight Tissue Company decided to purchase a roller whose maintenance requirements increase linearly over time. The machine produces 100 units of service per time period. Each unit of service is valued at $1. Maintenance has been increasing at the rate of $10 per time period. The firm's opportunity cost of capital is 10 percent. The firm wants to know the machine's *NPV* and optimal economic life. The purchase price of the machine is $750.

The firm expresses its *NPV* for the roller as:

$$NPV = -\$750 + \int_{0}^{n} (100 - 10\,t)\, e^{-rt} dt.$$

First-order conditions for this problem are:

$$\frac{dNPV}{dn} = (100 - 10\,n)\, e^{-0.10\,t} = 0,$$

and *NPV* maximizing *n* is n^* and equals 10. Thus, the investment should be held by the firm until maintenance costs drive net returns to zero. Moreover, since:

$$\frac{d^2 NPV}{dn^2} < 0,$$

second-order conditions guarantee that this solution is a global optimum.

To find *NPV*, *n* is replaced by *10* and *NPV* is found to be positive:

$$NPV = -\$750 + \int_{0}^{10} (100 - 10\,t)\, e^{-0.10\,t} dt \approx \$249.$$

Note that n^* is found for the existing investment without consideration of disposal or salvage values of the durable being liquidated. The effects of disposal or salvage values on the economic life of a durable are considered next.

$$\frac{d^2NPV}{dn^2} = R'(n) + V''(n) - rV'(n) < 0.$$

The first-order condition can be rewritten as:

$$R(n) + V'(n) = rV(n). \tag{21.4}$$

Equation (21.4) is interpreted as follows. On the left-hand side of the equation is the last period's income, $R(n)$, plus capital gains or losses $V'(n)$. On the right-hand side of the equal sign is an annuity. The annuity occurs from the sale of the durable. That is, if the durable is sold for $V(n)$ and the sale proceeds are invested at the firm's opportunity cost of capital, it could pay the firm the annuity of $rV(n)$ each period. The optimal disposal time occurs when the annuity equals the net return in the last period.

Graphically, this equilibrium is described as follows. The top line in Figure 21.1 represents the declining salvage value of the asset $V(t)$ that depends on the age of the durable t. The net returns line $R(t)$ plus capital gains (losses) is also decreasing because of increasing maintenance costs. The rate of change (loss) in salvage value is $V'(t)$. The sum of $R(t)$ and $V'(t)$ identifies net return to the durable over time. Its intersection with opportunity cost $rV(t)$ identifies the point in time where net returns equal the opportunity cost and salvage should occur. The optimal age for disposal in Figure 21.1 is n^*.

Now consider a different version of the salvage value problem. Suppose at the end of n periods the firm must pay a disposal fee or a transaction cost of amount D.

In the previous example, $V(n)$ was assumed to equal the *PV* of earnings expected by the buyer. For this model, the *NPV* of the durable is represented by the expression:

$$NPV = -V_0 + \int_0^n R(t)\, e^{-rt}\, dt - De^{-rn},$$

where $R(t)$ represents the net cash flow in the tth period and De^{-rn} is the *PV* of the disposal cost in the nth period. The first-order conditions are:

$$\frac{dNPV}{dn} = R(n) + rD = 0.$$

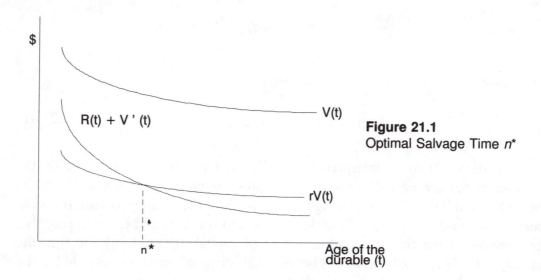

Figure 21.1
Optimal Salvage Time n^*

Second-order conditions are satisfied if $R'(n) < 0$. To maximize the *NPV* of the durable, disposal should occur only if $R(n) < 0$. This result explains the rather common sight of old, unused buildings occupying land that could be used for other purposes. These unused buildings have no value in other uses. They require no additional costs even though they may generate no net cash return. But, their disposal may cost the firm amount D. By postponing their disposal, their owners save the opportunity cost of disposal expense, rD, which is preferred to disposal as long as $R(n) < -rd$ (see Example 21.2).

Buyers and Sellers with Identical Expectations

Until now, the salvage or disposal value of the durable $V(n)$ was treated as exogenous. Now suppose the salvage value equals the discounted *PV* of future income. This assumption is essentially the "life of the investment" principle.

We begin by writing:

$$NPV = -V_0 + \int_0^{n_1} R(t)\,e^{-rt}dt + e^{-rn_1}\,V(n_1).$$

Now $V(n_1)$ is specified to depend on its future earnings and $e^{-rn_1}V(n_1)$ is replaced with:

Example 21.2: The "Greenbelt" Tax Laws and Disposal

"Greenbelt" tax laws provide some tax savings for land used for agricultural purposes and impose some penalties if the conversion to nonagricultural uses occurs within a specified time period. To modify the model to account for these transactions costs, let $S(t)$ be the tax savings for continued production by the first owner and let $TC(n)$ be the transactions cost which is reduced by increases in n. Finally, let $Q(t)$ be the income that could be earned from land in nonagricultural uses after the agricultural land is converted to nonagricultural uses in period n. *NPV* can be written as:

$$NPV = -V_0 + \int_0^n [R(t) + S(t)]e^{-rt} - TC(n)e^{-rn} + \int_n^\infty Q(t)e^{-rt}dt. \quad (21.5a)$$

The first-order condition is written as:

$$[R(n) + S(n)] + rTC(n) = TC'(n) + Q(n). \quad (21.5b)$$

The first-order condition in equation (21.5b) says that to maximize *NPV*, use land for agricultural purposes until the return in the last period plus tax savings, plus the interest saved on the payment of the transactions cost equals the change in the transactions cost by postponing the sale one period plus the income that could be earned in the nth period from nonagricultural uses of the land.

To find an explicit value for n, let $R(n)$ equal 100, and $S(n)$ equal 10. Let $rTC(n)$ equal $0.10e^{-0.01n}$ and $TC'(n)$ equal $0.01e^{-0.01n}$. Finally, let $Q(n)$ equal $20e^{0.1n}$. Then, the first-order condition is expressed as:

$$[100+10] + 0.10\,e^{-0.01n} = 0.01e^{-0.01n} + 20\,e^{0.1n}$$

$$(110) + 0.09\,e^{-0.01n} = 20\,e^{0.1n}.$$

At n equal to 0, the left-hand side of the expression is 110.09, while the right-hand side equals 20. As n increases, the larger quantity declines toward 100. At the same time, the right-hand side increases. By trial and error, the equality is satisfied for n equal to 17.

$$\int_{n_1}^{n_2} R(t)\, e^{-rt} dt.$$

Similarly, if the investment is sold again at age n_2, its price will depend on the earning stream:

$$\int_{n_2}^{n_3} R(t)\, e^{-rt} dt,$$

etc. Then, *NPV* can be written as:

$$NPV = -V_0 + \int_0^{n_1} R(t)\, e^{-rt} dt + \int_{n_1}^{n_2} R(t)\, e^{-rt} dt + \int_{n_2}^{n_3} R(t)\, e^{-rt} dt + \dots \qquad (21.6)$$

The first-order conditions for n_1 are:

$$\frac{dNPV}{dn_1} = R(n_1)\, e^{-rn_1} - R(n_1)\, e^{-rn_1} = 0,$$

for which there is an infinite number of solutions. That is, since *NPV* is unaffected by the trade, trade yields no advantages as long as buyers and sellers have the same income prospects. Consequently, the economic life of a durable is not affected by trade. Therefore, trades occur only if the buyer derives some advantage from its ownership not available to the seller at the time of the sale. Only then will the buyer willingly offer a price equal to or exceeding the seller's minimum-sell price. Alternatively, the seller must have an opportunity to invest the proceeds of the sale that exceeds the *IRR* of the durable to be liquidated.

Replacement Models

The disposal model discussed in the previous section serves to introduce replacement models. In the disposal model just discussed, a seller disposed of his/her investment to a buyer. However, the acquisition of a replacement investment for the original owner was not tied to the sale. Another purchase, for example, would have simply expanded the firm's capital investment. In a replacement situation, the acquisition of a new investment coincides with the disposal of an old one. In addition, the opportunity costs change as does the optimal life of investments because the disposal is tied to the replacement decision.

The assumption behind replacement models is that a replacement cannot be purchased unless the existing durable is liquidated. This situation would characterize poultry producers, beef feedlots, and other investments whose replacements cannot be acquired until the current investments are replaced. However, this situation would not characterize a firm whose retiring machines will be kept for spare parts or as a reserve.

A shorthand notation is needed to analyze this model. Instead of distinguishing the cash flows associated with durable service flows from the purchase and sale of the durable, the sum of these in the nth period is written as $R(n)$ and the net cash flow in the tth period is written as $R(t)$. Moreover, the *PV* of the entire cash flow stream associated with a durable over n periods is written as:

$$\int_0^n R(t)\,e^{-rt}dt.$$

No single proprietor or firm can expect to last forever. Yet, most expect to outlive several of the durables they purchase. Suppose the firm considers owning m identical durable investments, although it can only own one at a time. Then, *NPV* can be written as:

$$NPV = \int_0^{n_1} R(t)\,e^{-rt}dt + e^{-rn_1}\int_0^{n_2} R(t)\,e^{-rt}dt \qquad (21.7)$$

$$+ \ldots + e^{-r(n_1 + n_2 + \ldots + n_{m-1})}\int_0^{n_m} R(t)\,e^{-rt}dt.$$

The model allows for the possibility that the optimal economic lives of the durables are not equal. We allow for this by designating the economic life of the m durables as n_1, n_2, ..., n_m. To find the values of n_1, ..., n_m that optimize *NPV*, expression (21.7) is differentiated first with respect to n_m:

$$\frac{dNPV}{dn_m} = R(n_m) = 0. \qquad (21.8)$$

This result, of course, is the solution to the model described in Example 21.1, an economic disposal problem. Since no replacement is planned for the mth durable, its solution coincides with the solution of the disposal model. The solution for finding the economic life of the next-to-the-last durable, the $(m-1)^{st}$ durable, is:

$$\frac{dNPV}{dn_{m-1}} = R(n_{m-1}) - r \int_0^{n_m} R(t)e^{-rt}dt = 0. \qquad (21.9)$$

For the $(m-1)^{st}$ durable, the solution differs from the disposal problem because increasing the life of the $(m-1)^{st}$ durable postpones returns from the mth durable.

The solution suggests a principle: an opportunity cost is created when a replacement is postponed by holding the current durable another period. In this case, the opportunity cost is r times the *NPV* attributed to the durable or the amount that could be earned as an annuity from investing the *NPV* of the replacement durable. That annuity value is represented by the term following the minus sign in equation (21.9).

As the number of replacements increases, so does the opportunity cost of increasing the economic life of an existing durable. Consequently, if replacement occurs with identical durables and second-order conditions requiring $R'(t)<0$ are satisfied, then it must follow that $n_{m-1}<n_m$ provided:

$$\int_0^{n_m} R(t)e^{-rt}dt > 0.$$

Finally, with each additional replacement postponed by the use of the current period's durable, the opportunity cost of the durable increases and its economic life is shortened. To illustrate, consider the optimal n_1 value after having solved first for optimal n_m, n_{m-1}, ..., n_2. The first-order conditions are equal to:

$$\frac{dNPV}{dn_1} = R(n_1) - r\left[\int_0^{n_2} R(t)e^{-rt}dt + e^{-rn_2} \int_0^{n_3} R(t)e^{-rt}dt + \ldots \right. \qquad (21.10)$$

$$\left. + e^{-r(n_2+\ldots+n_{m-1})} \int_0^{n_m} R(t)e^{-rt}dt \right] = 0.$$

One can observe that the opportunity cost, the annuity expression following the minus sign in equation (21.10) with m-1 replacements, must be larger than for the annuity in equation (21.9) which represented the opportunity cost when only one replacement was involved.

In this case, the opportunity cost of the first durable is the largest of all the durables. Moreover, net returns at the time of replacement have the pattern $R(n_1) > R(n_2) > ... > R(n_m) = 0$. And again, if $R' < 0$, then $n_1 < n_2 < n_3 < ... < n_m$.

An Infinite Replacement Model

Now suppose the firm considers an infinite stream of replacements. This model is considered by Perrin. For this case, however, because each durable would face an infinite stream of replacements, the opportunity cost as well as the economic life of each durable would be identical.[1]

So, an *NPV* problem is specified in which each durable is held for the same time period n with an infinite number of replacements:

$$NPV = \left(\int_0^n R(t) e^{-rt} dt \right) \left(1 + e^{-rn} + e^{-2rn} + e^{-3rn} + ... \right). \qquad (21.11)$$

The series in the second set of parentheses is geometric. It has the sum S equal to:

$$S = 1 + e^{-rn} + e^{-2rn} + e^{-3rn} + ... = \frac{1}{1 - e^{-rn}}.$$

Now equation (21.11) can be rewritten as:

$$NPV = \left[\frac{1}{1 - e^{-rn}} \right] \int_0^n R(t) e^{-rt} dt,$$

and the first-order condition is:

$$\frac{dNPV}{dn} = \left(\frac{1}{1 - e^{-rn}} \right) R(n) e^{-rn} - \frac{re^{-rn}}{[1 - e^{-rn}]^2} \int_0^n R(t) e^{-rt} dt = 0,$$

and:

$$R(n) = \frac{r}{(1 - e^{-rn})} \int_0^n R(t) e^{-rt} dt. \tag{21.12}$$

The expression $r/(1-e^{-rn})$ is equivalent to the annuity factor $[1/US_0(r,m)]$. It converts $\int_0^n R(t) e^{-rt} dt$ to an annuity A such that:

$$A \int_0^n e^{-rt} dt = \int_0^n R(t) e^{-rt} dt.$$

Another way to describe the solution in equation (21.12) is to note that A or the annuity:

$$A = [r / (1 - e^{-rn})] \int_0^n R(t) e^{-rt} dt,$$

is maximized when A equals $R(n)$. Thus, selecting n that satisfies equation (21.11) maximizes the average return from each and every durable.

Graphically, the replacement period for a stream of infinite replacements can be described as follows. Let the $R(t)$ line in Figure 21.2 represent the marginal (not discounted) return from each durable over its age. Let the solid line, which is equal to the PV of the sum of the durable's service flows over its age, be the PV of $R(t)$. Let the dashed line be associated with the annuity (the annuity conversion factor multiplied by the PV of the durable's services). The time at which the dashed annuity line intersects the marginal return line $R(t)$ identifies the replacement time that maximizes NPV from the stream of durable service flows assuming an infinite number of replacements.

Wherever the line $R(t)$ crosses the horizontal axis, or where $R(t)=0$, shows the value of n corresponding to the economic life of a durable without replacement. In all other cases with m replacements for $1<m<\infty$, the durables will have an optimal economic life between n^* and n.

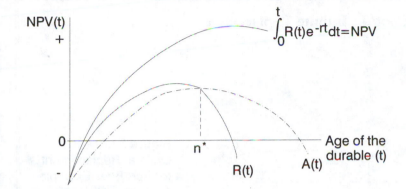

$$\int_0^t R(t)e^{-rt}dt = NPV$$

NPV(t) +

0

n*

R(t)

A(t)

Age of the durable (t)

Figure 21.2
Marginal Return R(t) in the tth Period, and the Annuity A(t) Associated with the NPV(t) at Period t

Example 21.3: Infinite Replacements

Net monthly returns per pen of rare fed beef can be described by the quadratic function:

$$R(t) = -10 + 2t - 0.03\,t^2,$$

which begins negative, turns positive, and then finally at advanced ages of the animals, becomes negative again. The greatest net return for the animals occurs at:

$$R'(t) = 2 - 0.06\,t = 0,$$

where $t=33.3$. If the animals were held until $R(t)=0$, then $t=63$ months.

Assuming infinite replacement, the beef feedlot owner uses equation (21.11) to maximize *NPV* by finding the optimal period to feed each cohort. Letting $r=0.125$, the optimal solution for $t=n$ can then be written as in equation (21.12) and equals:

$$-10 + 2n - 0.03\,n^2 = \frac{0.0125}{(1 - e^{-0.0125n})} \int_0^n (-10 + 2t - 0.03\,t^2)\, e^{-0.0125\,t}\,dt.$$

The solution is found by searching. The solution is found for $n = 51$ months, where $R(51)=13.97$ and the annuity equals 13.87. The graph of this relationship is provided below.

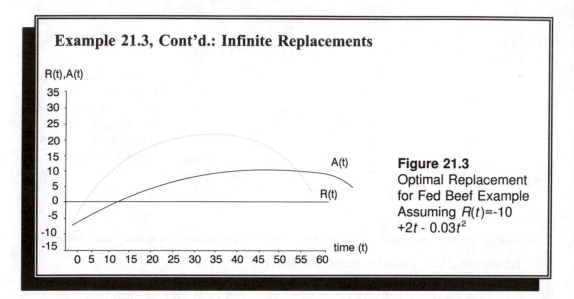

Example 21.3, Cont'd.: Infinite Replacements

R(t),A(t)

A(t)

R(t)

time (t)

Figure 21.3
Optimal Replacement
for Fed Beef Example
Assuming $R(t) = -10 + 2t - 0.03t^2$

Replacement Model Variations

Consider a variation on the above replacement problems by letting the income function be $R^* = \alpha + \beta g(t)$. That is, consider the same replacement models as before only with $R(t)$ linearly transformed to $\alpha + \beta R(t)$. To determine the effect on the optimal economic life of the durables, the finite *NPV* replacement model is written as:

$$NPV = \int_0^{n_1} R^*(t)\,e^{-rt}\,dt + e^{-rn_1} \int_0^{n_2} R^*(t)\,e^{-rt}\,dt + \ldots \qquad (21.13)$$

$$+ e^{-r(n_1 + \ldots + n_{m-1})} \int_0^{n_m} R^*(t)\,e^{-rt}\,dt.$$

The first-order condition for n_m is:

$$R^*(n_m) = \alpha + \beta R(n_m) = 0. \qquad (21.14)$$

Clearly, the n_m that satisfies the above expression for the function $R^*(t)$ will not also satisfy $R(n_m)=0$ in equation (20.8). Moreover, all other economic lives will be affected as well, depending on the size and sign of α and β, because the opportunity cost of postponing replacements changed with the transformation.

Next, consider the first-order condition for the case of infinite replacement. This model is not affected by the linear transformation. For the function $R^*(t)$, the first-order condition is:

$$R^*(n) = \alpha_t + \beta R(n) = \frac{r}{(1-e^{-rn})} \int_0^n R^*(t)e^{-rt}dt = \frac{r}{(1-e^{-rn})} \int_0^n [\alpha + \beta R(t)]\,e^{-rt}dt$$

$$= \frac{r}{(1-e^{-rn})} \left[\alpha \frac{(1-e^{-rn})}{r} + \beta \int_0^n R(t)e^{-rt}dt \right] = \alpha + \beta \left(\frac{r}{1-e^{-rn}} \right) \int_0^n R(t)e^{-rt}dt,$$

which, after canceling, leaves the result:

$$R(n) = \frac{r}{(1-e^{-rn})} \int_0^n R(t)e^{-rt}dt,$$

which is identical to equation (21.12).

The conclusion is that for infinite replacement models, linear transformations of the cash flow stream leave the optimal life of each durable unaffected. This result occurs because changing the income stream with a linear transformation does not change the time period at which the function maximizes its average value.

Technologically Improved Replacements

If the opportunity cost of replacement depends on the number of replacements, then the opportunity cost for each durable should be the same in an infinite horizon model of identical replacement. But, suppose durables are related to one another by a multiplicative factor $(1+h)$. Such changes could be the result of new technology. The effect of technological improvements is to shorten the economic life of the durables being replaced. The following derivations and results will demonstrate this effect.

The *NPV* for this model can be written as:

$$NPV = \int_0^{n_1} R(t)\, e^{-rt} dt + (1+h)\, e_1^{-rn_1} \int_0^{n_2} R(t)\, e^{-rt} dt$$

$$+ (1+h)^2\, e^{-r(n_1+n_2)} R(t)\, e^{-rt} dt + \dots. \tag{21.15}$$

Differentiating with respect to n_1, n_2, ...

$$\frac{\partial NPV}{\partial n_1} = R(n_1)\, e_1^{-rn} - r(1+h)\, e_1^{-rn} \int_0^{n_2} R(t)\, e^{-rt} dt$$

$$- r(1+h)^2\, e^{-r(n_1+n_2)} \int_0^{n_3} R(t)\, e^{-rt} dt \tag{21.16}$$

$$- r(1+h)^3\, e^{-r(n_1+n_2+n_3)} \int_0^{n_4} R(t)\, e^{-rt} dt \dots = 0.$$

$$\frac{\partial NPV}{\partial n_2} = (1+h)\, e^{-rn_1} R(n_2)\, e^{-rn_2} - r(1+h)^2\, e^{-r(n_1+n_2)} \int_0^{n_3} R(t)\, e^{-rt} dt$$

$$- r(1+h)^3\, e^{-r(n_1+n_2+n_3)} \int_0^{n_4} R(t)\, e^{-rt} dt \dots = 0 \tag{21.17}$$

.
.
.

But canceling $(1+h)e^{-rn_1}$ produces the same first-order condition for equation (21.17) as equation (21.16) except that the life of the first durable is n_2 rather than n_1. Thus, n_1 must equal n_2 must equal n_3, and so on. Recognizing the equal lives of all of the durables allows us to write:

$$NPV = \left[1 + (1+h)\, e^{-rn_1} + (1+h)^2\, e^{-r2n_1} + \dots \right] \int_0^{n_1} R(t)\, e^{-rt} dt. \tag{21.18}$$

Because the bracketed expression is a geometric sum, *NPV* in the limit can be written as:

$$\lim_{n \to \infty} NPV = \frac{1}{1 - (1+h)\, e^{-rn_1}} \int_0^{n_1} R(t)\, e^{-rt}\, dt. \tag{21.19}$$

Optimizing with respect to n_1 and canceling results in:

$$R(n_1) = \frac{r(1+h)}{\left[1 - (1+h)\, e^{-rn_1}\right]} \int_0^{n_1} R(t)\, e^{-rt}\, dt. \tag{21.20}$$

The solution without technological improvements ($h=0$) was:

$$R(n_1) = \frac{r}{\left[1 - e^{-rn}\right]} \int_0^{n_1} R(t)\, e^{-rt}\, dt.$$

If $h>0$, then for the concave function $R'(t)>0$ and $R''(t)<0$, that optimal n_1 is reduced or:

$$\frac{dn_1}{dh} < 0.$$

This result again verifies the importance of opportunity costs. As the technological improvements increase the opportunity costs of delayed replacements, the economic life of durables being replaced is shortened.

A Digression on the Average Equals the Marginal Rate of Return Rule

The rule for replacement of identical durables over an infinitely long time period is essentially: equate the return in the last period of use (a marginal return) with the annuity (the weighted average) of the replacement. This digression points out that the solution which equated a marginal return to an average return appears in other settings. Examples are when the choice is to intensify (marginally increase outputs) or to extensify (add new units to the production process).

To demonstrate, let $R(x)$ be the marginal net return on the last unit of input x. Let I be an investment budget that earns r percent, and let y be the units of the durables (such as area of land, or number of identical machines) used in the production process.

The static profit function π can be written as:

$$\underset{x,y}{Max} \ \pi = yR(x) + r(I- yp_x x).$$

Differentiating π with respect to x and y results in:

$$\frac{d\pi}{dx} = R'(x) - rp_x = 0,$$

and:

$$\frac{d\pi}{dy} = R(x) - rp_x x = \frac{R(x)}{x} - rp_x = 0.$$

Either equation produces the optimal solution for x. Equating the two expressions, however, results in the solution for x:

$$R'(x) = \frac{R(x)}{x}.$$

The solution requires x to be allocated such that the marginal return $R'(x)$ from intensifying the use of the variable input x on fixed y equals the average return $[R(x)/x]$ from extensifying by purchasing another unit of y. This solution does not produce a solution for y, or the number of durables. But, then, neither did the identical replacement model.

The analogy between the replacement and production models should be clear. Extending the use of a durable over time is equivalent to intensifying its use. Disinvesting and replacing is like extensifying the use of the durable (adding new ones to production). The solutions to the two problems are similar. Allocate until the marginal return from intensifying the use of a durable equals the average return from extensifying the use of durables.

Point Production Replacement Models

Thus far, the case of continuous cash flows has been considered. Now, we consider the case where the output, such as a harvest, occurs at a point in time. This model is a special case of the earlier result.

This model is written as:

$$NPV = e^{-rn_1} \int_0^{n_1} R(t)\,dt + e^{-r(n_1+n_2)} \int_0^{n_2} R(t)\,dt$$

$$+ \dots + e^{-r(n_1 + \dots + n_m)} \int_0^{n_m} R(t)\,dt. \tag{21.21}$$

The model is explained as follows. The net return from each investment depends on the economic life or the time each output is allowed to mature or grow. This amount is summed using integrals. Since the net cash flows occur at a single point in time, each cash flow is discounted depending on the age n in which the harvest occurs.

Consider the first-order condition for n_m in equation (21.21). It equals:

$$\frac{dNPV}{dn_m} = -re^{-r(n_1 + \dots + n_m)} \int_0^{n_m} R(t)\,dt + e^{-r(n_1 + \dots + n_m)} R(n_m) = 0,$$

or:

$$R(n_m) = r \int_0^{n_m} R(t)\,dt. \tag{21.22}$$

Notice here that the opportunity costs associated with not selling have changed. Because no cash returns are experienced until sale, the disposal occurs earlier than before. (Compare equation (21.22) with equation (21.8).) For the $(m-1)^{st}$ durable, the first-order conditions are:

$$\frac{dNPV}{dn_{m-1}} - re^{-r(n_1 + \dots + n_{m-1})} \int_0^{n_{m-1}} R(t)\,dt + e^{-r(n_1 + \dots + n_{m-1})} R(n_{m-1})$$

$$- re^{-r(n_1 + \dots + n_m)} \int_0^{n_m} R(t)\,dt = 0,$$

and:

$$R(n_{m-1}) = r\left[\int_0^{n_{m-1}} R(t)\,dt + e^{-rn_m}\int_0^{n_m} R(t)\,dt\right]. \tag{21.23}$$

Again, we obtain the result that optimal $n_1 \neq n_2 \neq \dots \neq n_m$. For the optimal n associated with the infinite replacement, we write:

$$NPV = e^{-rn}\int_0^n R(t)\,dt + e^{-2rn}\int_0^n R(t)\,dt + \dots$$

$$= (e^{-rn} + e^{-2rn} + \dots)\int_0^n R(t)\,dt = \frac{1}{e^{rn} - 1}\int_0^n R(t)\,dt,$$

and:

$$\frac{dNPV}{dn} = \frac{-re^{rn}}{(e^{rn}-1)}\int_0^n R(t)\,dt + R(n) = 0,$$

or:

$$R(n) = \frac{r}{1 - e^{-rn}}\int_0^n R(t)\,dt. \tag{21.24}$$

This solution differs from the one with an infinite number of replacements and continuous earning and discounting by the factor e^{-rn}. The difference is attributed to the absence of a discount factor inside the integral to bring earnings back to the present period.

Example 21.4: Optimal Slaughter Age

Pork E. Pig grows pigs for slaughter and wants to know the optimal age to send the porkers to market. To find the age that maximizes the *NPV* for an infinite number of replacement cohorts, Mr. P. solves equation (21.24) where $R(t)$ is the function:

$$R(t) = -0.7 + 0.3\,t - 0.01\,t^2,$$

and r is estimated to be 0.15. The resulting expression is:

$$\int_0^n (-0.7 + 0.3\,t - 0.01\,t^2)\,dt = -0.7\,n + \frac{3\,n^2}{2} - \frac{0.01\,n^3}{3}.$$

The first-order condition, equation (21.24), from which the optimal n is found, is written as:

$$-0.7 + 0.3\,n - 0.01\,n^2 = \left(\frac{0.15}{1 - e^{-0.15\,n}}\right)\left(-0.7\,n + \frac{0.3\,n^2}{2} - \frac{0.01\,n^3}{3}\right).$$

Searching produces the solution $n \approx 0.13$ where n is years.

Rotation Models

Next consider an extension of the replacement/disposal model: the rotation model. The rotation problem replaces one production process with another. The difference between the replacement model just reviewed and the rotation model is that the land or durable on which the rotation occurs is never sold.

Two levels of complexity are involved in rotation problems: dependent and independent rotations. Independent rotations are characterized by loss of productivity over time which can be restored by idleness or by producing a different product. But, the restorative process is not dependent on the length of the alternative productive process.

The dependent rotation problem considers the possibility that both the restoration and the level of restoration depend on the length of the alternative productive process. The simpler of the two models, the independent rotation model, is examined first.

Let the rotation consist of alternatively producing goods A and B. Good A earns a net cash return series described by $R(t)$ and good B earns a net cash return series described by $Q(t)$. An entire rotation of the production of good A followed by good B is n periods, while the shift from the production of good A to good B occurs in the mth (switch) period.

The NPV of the rotation problem following the earlier description is:

$$NPV = -V_0 + \left[\int_0^m R(t) e^{-rt} dt + \int_m^n Q(t-m) e^{-rt} dt \right]$$

$$\left[1 + e^{-rn} + e^{-r2n} + \dots \right] \tag{21.25}$$

$$= -V_0 + \frac{1}{(1-e^{-rn})} \left[\int_0^m R(t) e^{-rt} dt + \int_m^n Q(t-m) e^{-rt} dt \right].$$

Notice the similarity between this sum and the sum of Perrin's infinite replacement problem. This similarity suggests that n can be found in the same way as occurred earlier in equation (21.12). The solution is:

$$Q(n-m) = r(1-e^{-rn})^{-1} \left[\int_0^m R(t) e^{-rt} dt + \int_m^n Q(t-m) e^{-rt} dt \right], \tag{21.26}$$

which is found by maximizing NPV for n. The solution for m, the switch period that maximizes NPV, is found simply as:

$$R(m) = Q(0) + e^{rm} \int_m^n \frac{\partial Q(t-m)}{\partial m} e^{-rt} dt. \tag{21.27}$$

The solution states that the switch should occur when the value of the last year's production of good A equals the value of the first year of production of good B, plus the PV of the change in returns from good B that occurs by reducing the term of good A by one period.

Suppose the production pattern of good B depends on the length of time A is in production. Such dependence characterizes many applied problems including rotation patterns to manage soil diseases and weed seed accumulation whose control depends on how long the land is used to produce an alternative crop.

Net cash return in the tth year of the production cycle, then, is $Q[t\text{-}m, h(m)]$. For such a model, the *NPV* is:

$$NPV = -V_0 + \frac{1}{(1-e^{-rn})} \left[\int_0^m R(t)e^{-rt}dt + \int_m^n Q[t-m,h(m)]e^{-rt}dt \right],$$

and the switch point m depends on:

$$R(m) = Q(0) - e^{rm} \int_m^n \left[\frac{dQ}{dm} - \frac{\partial Q}{\partial h}\frac{\partial h}{\partial m} \right] e^{-rt}dt. \qquad (21.28)$$

Now, the solution adds to the marginal return, $R(m)$, the addition to the output of Q that will occur during the entire production life of B as a result of extending A's production one period.

Applications of the Rotation Model

Case 1: Delayed Service Extraction

A special case of the rotation problem is the delayed service extraction problem. Consider, for example, an investment whose economic life begins at age m and ends in period n. Such might be the case of a growing animal or crop whose useful life is fixed by its age. Also consider that the durable's services over $n\text{-}m$ periods of extraction are altered by the age of the durable when service extraction began. Under some circumstances, it may be in the investor's best interest to delay the time at which service extraction begins (Example 21.5).

To solve this type of investment problem, let the beginning service extraction date be m periods in the future, and let n be the date the economic life of the new investment is terminated. Then, the decision is to find the optimal period in the future in which to begin extracting services from the durable. Using notation established earlier, let $Q(t)$ be net cash flow at age t of the durable. Then, *NPV* can be expressed as:

Example 21.5: Dude Ranch Riders

Sad L. Upp owns a dude ranch that offers riders without horses the opportunity to ride horses on his ranch. Mr. Upp raises his own horses and then rents them out. The age at which the horses begin supplying services is carefully calculated. If they begin too soon, the horses' bones are weakened and the horses fail to develop properly and the horse's useful service life is shortened. Thus, services extracted from the horses too early may reduce their *NPV* because they have a shorter economic life.

$$NPV = -V_0 + \int_m^n Q(t;m)\, e^{-rt} dt. \qquad\qquad (21.29)$$

The first-order conditions can be written as:

$$\frac{dNPV}{dm} = \int_m^n [\partial Q(t;m)/\partial m]\, e^{-rt} dt - Q(m;m)\, e^{-rm} = 0.$$

The first-order conditions prescribe postponing service extraction until the *PV* of the income sacrificed in the mth period equals the *PV* of the additional income earned over the (n-m) periods of production because of delaying the age m at which service extraction begins. Once service extraction has begun, however, it should continue until $Q(n;n)=0$.

Second-order conditions require that the *PV* of income lost in the mth period by delaying production be increasing faster than the *PV* of increased income earned over the (n-m) periods of production.

Case 2: Delayed Investment

Another special case of the rotation problem is the delayed investment problem. In contrast to the delayed production model, consider that delaying the investment does not require the shortening of the economic life of the delayed investment. For example, one might consider the purchase of a new machine whose price or the demand for its services is expected to change in the future. Under some circumstances, it may be in the investor's best interest to delay the investment because of expected declines in the durable's purchase price or increases in the prices paid for the durable's services. If there is a delay in the investment, there is no reason to require that the economic life of the durable be shortened as well. Thus, allow the economic life of the durable to be n periods.

To solve this type of investment problem, let the investment date be m periods in the future, and let $(n+m)$ be the date the economic life of the new investment is terminated. Then, the decision is to find the optimal period in the future in which to make the investment and to begin extracting n periods of service from the durable.

Using the notation established earlier, let $Q(t)$ be net cash flow t periods in the future (not necessarily at durable age t, but at age t of the investment). Also, let $V(m)$ be the durable's purchase price that depends on which period it is purchased. Then, NPV can be expressed as:

$$NPV = -V(m)\,e^{-rm} + \int_{m}^{n+m} Q(t)\,e^{-rt}\,dt. \qquad (21.30)$$

The first-order conditions can be written as:

$$\frac{dNPV}{dm} = -(\partial V(m)/\partial m) + rV(m) + Q(n+m)\,e^{-rn} - Q(m) = 0.$$

The first-order conditions prescribe postponing the investment until the PV of the income sacrificed in the mth period equals the PV of the additional income earned in the $(n+m)^{th}$ period and saved in the purchase. Second-order conditions require that PV of income lost in the mth period be increasing faster than the PV of increased income earned in the $(n+m)^{th}$ period.

Compare equation (21.30) with the rotation model described in equation (21.25). Differences include letting the purchase price depend on the period in which it is purchased and allowing m to increase without shortening the service life or extending the life of an existing investment whose income in the rotation model was described by $R(t)$.

Other examples and extensions of the rotation model could be described. The most obvious would be to allow the second durable to maintain its economic life when m increases. That is, let n be a choice variable. Sufficient for our purposes, however, is to point out the important practical problems that can be addressed by the rotation model.

The Need For More Work

A survey of the disposal and replacement literature suggests the importance of replacement questions. Faris and Chisholm are frequently cited for their contribution to the replacement literature. Perrin's application of Samuelson's work established the rule: replace when net returns in the last period equal the annuity of the replacement.

Burt's study of replacement rules under uncertainty is highly regarded and adds to the understanding of replacement. Kay and Rister (1976) considered the effects of taxes upon the replacement decision; and Bates, Rayner, and Custance analyzed the effect of inflation on machinery replacement. Bradford and Reid observed that much work remains to be done on replacement models, even in the world of certainty.

Differences between buyer and seller expectations and use of the durable being sold need attention. Similarly, the effects of taxation on both buyers and sellers warrant attention in replacement analysis. In this light, the replacement literature is simply a special study in markets—trading a durable between a buyer and a seller. Thus, the focus on cow replacements (Bentley, Waters, and Shumway; Innes and Carman; Trapp; Kay and Rister (1977); Rister and Kay; and Rogers) and machinery replacement (Perrin; Perry and Nixon; Bradford and Reid; Bates, Rayner, and Custance; Weersink and Stauber; McClelland, Wetzstein, and Noles; McNeill) are good representations of the fruitful work that can be done.

Summary

Durables, unlike nondurables, are seldom completely used up in production even at the end of their useful (economic) life. Old buildings, cars, and retired professors are examples of durables that are still around even after withdrawn from active service. Thus, questions of when to dispose, liquidate, or replace durables are important to consider.

Finding the optimal service life of durables involves a continuous-time description of PV models, and thus needs to employ calculus. First-order conditions from the calculus provide the additional equation(s) needed to find the optimal disposal, replacement, or rotation age.

The study of disposal, replacement, and rotation again emphasizes the role of opportunity costs in economic decision models. The optimal service life of the durable was found to depend on what is being sacrificed by retaining the durable for an additional period. In the case of the replacement and rotation models, the opportunity cost is represented by foregone returns from the replacements. Using earlier language, the replacement becomes the challenger and the defender is the durable considered for liquidation.

Endnotes

1. To see this result, observe that after n_1 periods, NPV_{n_1} could be written as:

$$NPV = \int_0^{n_1} R(t)\,e^{-rt}dt + e^{-rn} \int_0^{n_2} R(t)\,e^{-rt}dt + \dots,$$

and:

$$\frac{dNPV}{dn_1} = R(n_1) - r \int_0^{n_2} R(t)\,e^{-rt}dt + \dots.$$

At the beginning of period n_2, *NPV* can be written as:

$$NPV = \int_0^{n_2} R(t)\,e^{-rt}dt + e^{-rn_2} \int_0^{n_3} R(t)\,e^{-rt}dt + \dots,$$

and:

$$\frac{dNPV}{dn_2} = R(n_2) - r \int_0^{n_3} R(t)\,e^{-rt}dt + \dots.$$

Since $\dfrac{dNPV}{dn_1} = \dfrac{dNPV}{dn_2}$, n_1 and n_2 that satisfy the expressions $\dfrac{dNPV}{dn_1} = 0$ and $\dfrac{dNPV}{dn_2} = 0$ must also be equal. Using similar reasoning, $n_1 = n_2 = n_3 = \dots$

Review Questions

1. Explain why replacement models are often solved in a continuous-time framework.

2. Why are replacement models referred to as one of the more complicated *PV* models?

3. Demonstrate for 5, 7, 10, and 12 percent that $ln(1+r)$ is approximately equal to r. What accounts for the small difference? Explain why the difference between r and $ln(1+r)$ increases for higher interest rates. For what value of r would the approximation be exact?

4. Calculate the corresponding $US_0(r/m,mn)$ and $(1-e^{-rn})/r$ values for $r=0.11$, $m=12$, and $n=5$.

5. Explain why underutilized farm (and sometimes abandoned) buildings are found in rural areas. Why do the owners of these buildings postpone dismantling them and using the space for other purposes?

6. Suppose you own a piece of agricultural land. A developer would like to acquire your land to build a golf course. What conditions must be satisfied before the buyer's maximum-bid price would exceed your minimum-sell price?

7. Suppose you own an investment whose net cash return is described by the quadratic formula $R(t)=a+bx+cx^2$. Meanwhile, suppose the value of the investment is described by the function $V(t)=d+ex+fx^2$. If the opportunity cost of capital is r, when should the firm dispose of this durable?

8. Describe some conditions under which durable owners with identical expectations and information would benefit from trading durables.

9. What is the essential difference between disposal and replacement models? Compare the opportunity cost associated with disposing of a durable and replacing a durable.

10. Suppose that a new technology increases net cash return in each period for a particular durable and all of its replacements. How will this change affect the optimal time to replace the durable?

11. Relate the assumptions of the Perrin model to the cash flows generated by the buyer and current owner of a durable.

Application Questions

1. Suppose you are considering replacing an existing durable with one whose purchase price is less than the purchase price of the durable being

replaced. If this decision is made, is size consistency as discussed in Chapter 4 still required? Even in the case of identical replacements, when replacing a used durable with a new durable, how is consistency maintained?

2. For a durable whose net cash flow is continuously declining, $[R(t)' < 0]$, what is the optimal replacement age for this durable with no replacements? With an infinite number of identical replacements?

3. Some economists claim that one requirement for an investment to be fixed in its current use is that its salvage value be less than its current value in use. Do you agree? Of what relevance is this definition of investment fixity to the disposal model?

4. Calculate the average or annuity return for an investment producing the following cash flows. Assume a constant opportunity cost of capital equal to 16 percent:

   $R(0) = -2,500,$
   $R(1) = 1,200,$
   $R(2) = 2,500,$
   $R(3) = 3,000,$
   $R(4) = 2,800,$
   $R(5) = 1,500,$
   $R(6) = 1,000,$
   $R(7), R(8),... = 0.$

   Moreover, assume that whenever the investment is sold, the salvage value is zero. If this is a repeatable investment, what is its optimal life?

5. Compare the decision rules for solving the identical replacement model problem and the point production model with infinite number of harvests.

6. Assume you have leased facilities for raising chickens for N periods. The chickens are to be used for chicken burgers. Thus, no revenue will be earned until the chickens are sold. You expect to raise two different flocks of chickens during the lease period N. The returns on each flock at age t are represented by the function $R'(t)$ such that $R''(t) < 0$. Find and compare the ages of the two flocks: n_1 and n_2. Comment on how the restriction $n_1 + n_2 = N$ alters the opportunity cost of replacement. (Assume this a point production problem.)

References ──

Bates, J.M., A.J. Rayner, and P.R. Custance. "Inflation and Farm Tractor Replacement in the U.S.: A Simulation Model." *American Journal of Agricultural Economics* 61(1979):331-34.

Bentley, E., J.R. Waters, and C.R. Shumway. "Determining Optimal Replacement Age of Beef Cows in the Presence of Stochastic Elements." *Southern Journal of Agricultural Economics* 8(1976):13-18.

Bradford, G.L. and D.W. Reid. "Theoretical and Empirical Problems in Modeling Optimal Replacement of Farm Machines." *Southern Journal of Agricultural Economics* 14(1982):109-16.

Burt, O.R. "Optimal Replacement Under Risk." *Journal of Farm Economics* 47(1965):324-45.

Chisholm, A.H. "Criteria for Determining the Optimum Replacement Pattern." *American Journal of Agricultural Economics* 48(1966):107-12.

Faris, J.E. "Analytic Techniques Used in Determining the Optimum Replacement Pattern." *Journal of Farm Economics* 42(1960):755-66.

Innes, R. and H. Carman. "Tax Reform and Beef Cow Replacement Strategy." *Western Journal of Agricultural Economics* 13(1988):254-66.

Kay, R.D. and M.E. Rister. "Effects of Tax Depreciation Policy and Investment Incentives on Optimal Equipment Replacement Decisions: Comment." *American Journal of Agricultural Economics* 58(1976):355-58.

_____. "Income Tax Effects on Beef Cow Replacement Strategy." *Southern Journal of Agricultural Economics* 9(1977):169-72.

McClelland, J.W., M.E. Wetzstein, and R.K. Noles. "Optimal Replacement Policies for Rejuvenated Assets." *American Journal of Agricultural Economics* 71(1989):147-57.

McNeill, R.C. "Depreciation of Farm Tractors in British Columbia." *Canadian Journal of Agricultural Economics* 27(1979):53-58.

Perrin, R.K. "Asset Replacement Principles." *American Journal of Agricultural Economics* 54(1972):60-67.

Perry, G.M. and C.J. Nixon. "Optimal Tractor Replacement: What Matters?" *Review of Agricultural Economics* 13(1991):119-28.

Rister, M.E. and R.D. Kay. "The Effect of Capital Gains Income on Beef Cattle Replacement Policy and Profit." *Journal of American Society of Farm Managers and Rural Appraisers* 41(1977):62-67.

Rogers, L.F. *Replacement Decisions for Commercial Beef Herds.* Washington State University Agricultural Experiment Station, Bulletin No. 726, 1971.

Samuelson, P.A. "Economics of Forestry in an Evolving Society." *Economic Inquiry* 14(1976):466-92.

Trapp, J.N. "Investment and Disinvestment Principles with Nonconstant Prices and Varying Firm Size Applied to Beef–Breeding Herds." *American Journal of Agricultural Economics* 68(1986):691-703.

Weersink, A. and S. Stauber. "Optimal Replacement Interval and Depreciation Method for a Grain Combine." *Western Journal of Agricultural Economics* 13(1988):18-28.

Chapter 22

Design and Selection of Depreciable Assets

Key words: age, design parameters, durable design, efficiency, flexibility, periodic service capacity, rated capacity, services extracted

Introduction

The most frequent application of present value (*PV*) models is to rank a discrete number of investment alternatives and/or select those with positive net present values *(NPVs)*. Most *PV* applications can be approached in this manner because the number of investment alternatives is few. However, in some cases the investment analysis is more complex.

Suppose, for example, that a firm must construct a new building for storage and manufacturing. The firm intends to design its own building and is faced with an almost infinite number of choices. The building site, dimensions, type of building materials, pitch of the roof, and type of heating and cooling systems are a few of the choices.

Under such conditions, it is not feasible to describe and rank all possible building designs. On the other hand, by not considering all of the alternatives, a preferred design may be overlooked. Then, the question is: How can we approach design problems to find an acceptable solution?

This chapter provides guidelines for modeling a firm's investment decision when the choice alternatives comprise a continuously divisible (and infinite) set. The approach is simplified by basing the investment decision on a common set of characteristics for any design under consideration. Finding an acceptable solution requires an understanding of the tradeoffs among alternative designs for a given budget. The design characteristics important to investment analysis are rated capacity, efficiency, and flexibility. These concepts will be described next, and then applied in some practical design problems.

The analytical approach is analogous to selecting optimal quantities of a variable input in static production analysis. In the latter case, the profit function π equals $pf(x) - p_x x$ where $f(x)$ is a concave-down, twice-differentiable function that allows us to employ calculus to find the level of x that maximizes function π.

In a similar approach, we will assume that the service capacity of the durable is a concave twice-differentiated function of rated capacity, flexibility, and efficiency which are themselves functions of design parameters. Then, the maximizing techniques of calculus can be employed to select the set of design parameters that maximizes the firm's *NPV*, subject to a constraint on the firm's investment budget.

Rated Capacity

The remaining service capacity of a durable at age t, Ca_t, can be written as:

$$Ca_t = Ca\left(\alpha, \sum_{i=1}^{t-1} s_i, t\right), \tag{22.1}$$

where α represents a vector of design parameters, $\sum_{i=1}^{t-1} s_i$ represents services already extracted from the durable, and t is the age of the durable. Moreover, the change in the durable's remaining capacity, Ca_t during the tth period can be found by differentiating equation (22.1) with respect to s_t and t:

$$-\frac{dCa_t}{dt} = -\left(\frac{\partial Ca}{\partial s_t} + \frac{\partial Ca}{\partial t}\right) = L_t. \tag{22.2}$$

The change in capacity L_t, in equation (22.2) is a function of use and time. The relationship in equation (22.2) is portrayed graphically in Figure 22.1. The vertical axis represents the change in capacity (preceded by a negative sign), while the horizontal axis represents services extracted. Vertical distance OA

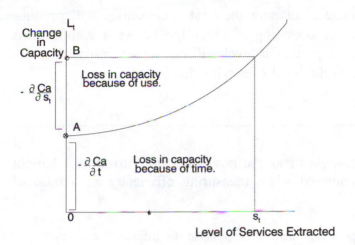

Figure 22.1. The Loss in a Durable's Lifetime Capacity L_t due to Time and Use

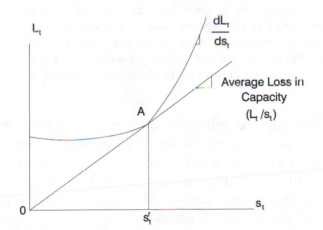

Figure 22.2 Identifying the Rated Capacity at the Point *A* Where the Average Loss in Capacity (L_t/s_t) Equals the Marginal Loss in Capacity (dL_t/ds_t)

represents capacity loss due to the passage of the tth period (the term following the plus sign in equation (22.2)) and distance *AB* represents the additional capacity lost because of the extraction of s_t units of service (the term preceding the plus sign in equation (22.2)).

Consider the average loss in capacity as a result of extracting s_t units of services and the passage of the tth time period. This average is represented graphically in Figure 22.2 as the slope of a ray from the origin to the capacity loss function L_t. The tangency between the ray and the loss function identifies the lowest average loss in capacity per unit of services extracted. Call this point, s_t^r, the durable's rated capacity at time t. This rated capacity, and associated loss in capacity L_t, are represented in Figure 22.2 as point *A*.

An interesting fact associated with s^r is that if all units of services cost $-\partial Ca/\partial s_t^r$, then time costs would be zero.

Mathematically, the rated capacity is found by equating the slope of the loss function, the marginal loss in capacity in response to use (dL_t/ds_t) to the slope of the ray from the origin which equals average loss in capacity (L_t/s_t).

Those durables that operate at or near their rated capacities will produce more usable services than those operating at other levels. As a result, firms with a clearly defined service requirement level will choose or design durables whose rated capacity is close to the level of service demanded.

Efficiency

Efficiency is typically thought of as the ratio of outputs to inputs. Knight described the difficulty encountered when measuring efficiency as a ratio of output to inputs:

> There is a common misconception that it is possible to measure or discuss efficiency in purely physical terms. The first principles of physics or engineering science teach that this is not true, that the term efficiency involves the idea of value, and some measure of value as well. It is perhaps the most important principle of physical science that neither matter nor energy can be created or destroyed, that whatever goes into any process must come out in some form, and hence as a mere matter of physical quantity, the efficiency of all operations would equal one hundred percent. The correct definition of efficiency is the ratio, not between "output" and "input" but between useful output and total output and total output and input. Hence efficiency, even in the simplest energy transformation, is meaningless without a measure of usefulness or value....

Knight's remarks suggest that physical efficiency measures must measure something other than the ratio of outputs to inputs. Instead, physical measures of efficiency must refer to some measure like useful outputs relative to total inputs. For the loss function L_t this efficiency concept is interpreted as the service level divided by the loss in capacity, part of which is attributable to time. Thus, efficiency measured at service level s_t equals:

$$EF(s_t) = \frac{s_t}{L_t}. \tag{22.3}$$

A higher level of efficiency is represented by a greater service level relative to a given loss of capacity, or the same service level for a smaller loss in capacity.

Flexibility

Flexibility refers to the ability to respond or conform to new or changing conditions (*Webster's Ninth New Collegiate Dictionary*, 1987). The durable's design determines the relative costs of extracting services, and hence its flexibility.

At least two kinds of flexibility are important to consider. Use flexibility is associated with how the average cost of extracting services responds to changes in the rate of service extraction (Lev; Rosenhead) and is described next. Adjustment flexibility, or liquidity, reflects differences in acquisition and salvage values of durables, in part attributed to transaction costs. Liquidity was discussed in some detail in Chapter 14.

Use Flexibility

Use flexibility is important because of the long service life associated with durables. Because the optimal service extraction rate may vary over time, the durable capacity must be designed so that it can profitably perform in a variety of economic environments. Thus, the durable's design must allow for its use at several different service levels.

One way to measure durable performance at various service extraction rates is to examine the average loss in capacity function L_t/s_t (Figure 22.3). Average loss in capacity must have an initially downward slope (and may have the usual "U" shape) as long as $\partial L_t/\partial t > 0$. The marginal loss in capacity curve $\partial L_t/\partial s_t$ intersects the average loss curve at its minimum.

Use flexibility involves the change in average losses in capacity as services

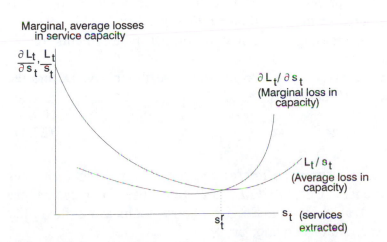

Figure 22.3   Average Loss in Capacity L_t/s_t, and Its Intersection with the Marginal Loss Curve dLt/dst

Average Cost Curves for
Service Extraction

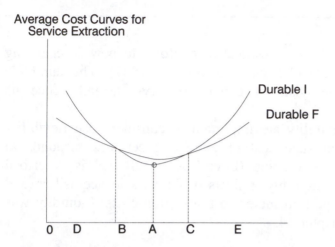

Figure 22.4 Use Flexibility Measure Based on Convexity of Average Cost Curves

are extracted at rates different from the rated capacity (Lev; Robison and Barry; Zeller and Robison). The use flexibility literature began with Stigler's landmark 1939 article. He argued that durable F in Figure 22.4 is more flexible than I because I has a more convex average cost curve. If the durable's flexibility were based on Stigler's convexity definition, the cost curve with the smallest second derivative of the average loss function would be the most flexible.

Of course, more use flexibility measures are available than Stigler's. Lev argued that not only the convexity of the average cost curve, but also the size of rated capacity and the magnitude of the average cost curve at the rated capacity should be included in use flexibility measures.

Regardless of how flexibility is measured, to say that durable F is more use flexible than durable I in Figure 22.4, does not imply F is preferred to I. By inspection, durable I is preferred to F if output is between B and C. If output is less than B or greater than C, durable F is preferred. This example supports the notion that increasing the range of output requirements favors increased use flexibility.

The issue still to be resolved is how to measure use flexibility. Define the average loss function in the tth period as:

$$AL_t = \frac{L_t}{s_t}. \tag{22.4}$$

The expression AL_t''/AL_t' measures the rate at which the average loss changes (the rate at which AL_t bends). But AL_t''/AL_t' cannot be used to measure use flexibility because $AL_t' = 0$ at point OA. So, we choose to measure flexibility $F(s_t)$ as one divided by the rate of bending, or:

$$F(s_t) = \frac{1}{(AL_t''/AL_t')} = \frac{-AL'}{AL''}. \tag{22.5}$$

Example 22.1: Measuring Rated Capacity, Efficiency, and Flexibility

Suppose the loss function L_t is represented by the quadratic function:

$$L_t = \alpha_0 + \alpha_1 s_t^2, \tag{22.6}$$

which depends on design parameters α_0 and α_1, service level s_t, and the passage of the tth time period. The average loss function AL_t equals:

$$AL_t = \frac{\alpha_0}{s_t} + \alpha_1 s_t. \tag{22.7}$$

The rated capacity is found by equating $\dfrac{dL_t}{ds_t} = 2\alpha_1 s_t$ and AL_t. The resulting expression is:

$$2\alpha_1 s_t = \frac{\alpha_0}{s_t} + \alpha_1 s_t.$$

If s_t^r is defined as the rated capacity, it is found by solving the expression above and is equal to:

$$s_t^r = \left(\frac{\alpha_0}{\alpha_1}\right)^{\frac{1}{2}}. \tag{22.8}$$

Suppose, for the function described in equation (22.6), the goal is to measure efficiency at the rated capacity. Then, we can write:

$$EF(s_t^r) = \frac{s_t^r}{\alpha_0 + \alpha_1 (s_t^r)^2},$$

and after substituting the expression in equation (22.8) for s_t^r, we obtain:

$$EF(s_t^r) = \frac{\left(\dfrac{\alpha_0}{\alpha_1}\right)^{\frac{1}{2}}}{\alpha_0 + \alpha_1 \left[\left(\dfrac{\alpha_0}{\alpha_1}\right)^{\frac{1}{2}}\right]^2} = \frac{1}{2(\alpha_0 \alpha_1)^{\frac{1}{2}}}. \tag{22.9}$$

Example 22.1, Cont'd.: Measuring Rated Capacity, Efficiency, and Flexibility

Finally, to find the flexibility measure, the AL_t is twice differentiated:

$$\frac{dAL(s_t)}{ds_t} = -\frac{\alpha_0}{s_t^2} + \alpha_1, \tag{22.10a}$$

$$\frac{d^2AL(s_t)}{ds_t^2} = \frac{2\alpha_0}{s_t^3} > 0. \tag{22.10b}$$

Then, dividing $AL'(s_t)$ by $AL''(s_t)$, we find:

$$F(s_t) = \frac{\alpha_0 s_t - \alpha_1 s_t^3}{2\alpha_0}, \tag{22.10c}$$

$$F(s_t^r) = 0,$$

where $s_t^r = \left(\frac{\alpha_0}{\alpha_1}\right)^{\frac{1}{2}}$. As s_t increases beyond s_t^r, $F(s_t)$
and:
declines. For $\alpha_0 = 300$ and $\alpha_1 = 3$, the graph of flexibility $F(s_t)$ is drawn in Figure 22.5.

Flexibility Measure

$F(s_t) = (s_t/2) - (1/200)\, s_t^3$

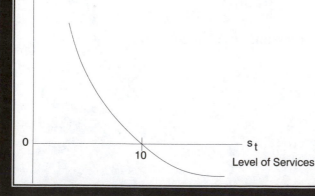

Figure 22.5
A Graph of Flexibility Measures for a Durable with Design Parameters $\alpha_0 = 300$ and $\alpha_1 = 3$

0

10

s_t

Level of Services

For positive changes in the rate of bending to the right of point OA, $F(s_t)<0$. To the left of point OA, for negative rates of bending, $F(s_t)>0$. Thus, for higher use flexibility values, increases in service extraction reduce average costs, allowing firms to reduce average costs as output increases.

The use flexibility measure is intended to indicate how the average loss responds to changes in the rate of service extraction. If the bending rate is very high, then the average cost function is changing rapidly, and the cost of altering output is very sensitive to changes. This situation implies low use flexibility.

Similarly, if the rate of bending is very small (e.g., a nearly linear function), the slope of the AL_t function is close to zero. In this case, output levels may vary considerably without significant changes in the average loss in lifetime capacity.

Three concepts—rated capacity, efficiency, and flexibility—have been introduced. They describe important characteristics about durables that must be considered when designing durables. In Example 22.1, for a durable with a given loss in lifetime capacity function L_t, rated capacity, efficiency, and flexibility are found.

In Example 22.1, rated capacity, efficiency, and flexibility were shown to depend on the durable's design parameters, α_0, α_1, and service level s_t. However, to choose the parameters of the preferred durable design, the decision maker must know the cost of acquiring durables of different designs.

Accountants may supply some of the needed cost data. But if the durable is mechanical, engineers will likely supply much of the needed cost data. If the durables are minerals, geologists might estimate the extraction costs. Finally, cost data on plant and animal durables may require the help of animal and plant scientists. Durable selection is rarely made by economists working alone, but in cooperation with other scientists.

Example 22.2 illustrates a cost function that depends on design parameters choices.

Rated Capacity, Efficiency, Flexibility, and Durable Design

Three durable service capacity measures (i.e., rated capacity, efficiency, and flexibility) describe the durable's change in capacity due to the passage of time and extraction of its services. Each measure answers different questions and applies under different operating conditions. For example, designing the

Example 22.2: Tradeoff in Choosing Between Design Parameters

Suppose the price of the durable described in Example 22.1 is given by $V_0 = \dfrac{\theta}{\alpha_0 \alpha_1}$ where α_0 and α_1 are design parameters selected by the decision maker. Furthermore, let θ be an exogenous parameter determined by market forces external to the firm. Then, the combinations of α_0 and α_1 that can be purchased for the same expenditure V_0 equal:

$$\frac{\theta}{\alpha_0 \alpha_1} = V_0,$$

and:

$$\alpha_0 = \frac{\theta}{\alpha_1 V_0}. \tag{22.11}$$

The tradeoff between the two design parameters α_0 and α_1, holding constant the purchase price of the durable, is:

$$\frac{d\alpha_0}{d\alpha_1} = -\frac{\theta}{\alpha_1^2 V_0}.$$

durable so that its rated capacity matches the rate of service extraction is critical for firms that operate at known, constant service extraction rates. On the other hand, use flexibility is more important for a durable that must perform at many different service levels over its economic life. In both cases, efficiency is critical.

The loss of lifetime capacity function L_t depends on all three durable service capacity measures. Therefore, the firm maximizes its *NPV* function over the design parameters to select those rated capacities, efficiency, and flexibility values that best serve its particular investment needs. The measures of rated capacity, efficiency, and flexibility are greatly simplified if the durable's capacity is unaffected by one or more of these factors.

Durable Classes with Variable Designs ————————————

Just as we have described characteristics of durables and how they depend on design parameters, we next describe four different classes of durables. The four classes of durables permit different design choices and result in different rated capacities, efficiencies, and use flexibilities. Each of four classes of durables is described next. Each is examined with a particular *PV* model application. For notational convenience, s^c will represent maximum periodic service capacity of the durable.

Class 1. $Ca=Ca(\alpha)$ and $s^c=s(\alpha)$: Durables unaffected by time or use

This class assumes that the durable's capacity depends only on its design. The firm can select the most preferred durable, or it can design the durable to obtain the desired capacity.

Durables employed in agricultural production are generally affected by time and/or use. But many other durables do not have their capacities substantially affected by time or use. Some examples include: paintings, musical scores, rings, and wood carvings. The decision maker can control the design of these durables.

Class 2. $Ca_t=Ca(t,\alpha)$ and $s^c=s(\alpha)$: Durables whose decay is time dependent

When remaining service capacity depends on the age and design of the durable, the marginal cost of the durable associated with use is zero. This is because the durable's remaining capacity is not diminished by use. Thus, as long as units of service have a positive value, this class of durable will have services extracted from it at its maximum capacity s^c. Thus, the choice of the durable's maximum service capacity s^c and the economic life over which services are extracted are the two fundamental design choices.

When considering the economic life of Class 2 durables, three considerations are relevant. These are: (1) How long will the services of this durable be demanded? (2) What is the likelihood that new durables will make the current durable obsolete? and (3) What is the likelihood that a new use for this durable will require its adoption, increasing the value of its services?

A building closely fits the description of Class 2. The services demanded from a particular building change over time, its marginal use cost is low, and the length of time over which its services are required is a relevant question for

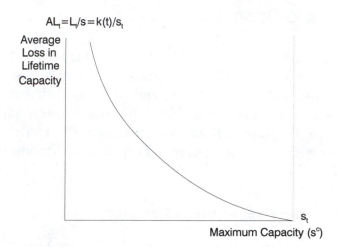

$AL_t = L_t/s = k(t)/s_t$

Average Loss in Lifetime Capacity

s_t

Maximum Capacity (s^c)

Figure 22.6   The Average Loss in Lifetime Capacity when Capacity Loss is a Function of Only Time

most buildings. The application that follows exemplifies the solution to a building design problem.

It is also important to note that the L_t function per period for Class 2 durables is:

$$\frac{\partial Ca_t}{\partial t} = k(t) < 0,$$

a function of the age of the durable. In addition, the average cost of services extracted is continually decreasing because capacity is not affected by use, a relationship described in Figure 22.6. This relationship resembles the *L*-shaped average cost curve observed in agriculture.

If the AL_t function is continually declining, it follows naturally that the rated capacity of Class 2 durables is the maximum periodic service capacity s^c. Moreover, efficiency is maximized at $s_t = s^c$ and use flexibility is:

$$F(s_t) = \frac{-AL'(s_t)}{AL''(s_t)} = \frac{k(t)/s_t^2}{k(t)2/s_t^3} = \frac{s_t}{2},$$

suggesting that flexibility is continually increasing with higher levels of services extracted.

An Application: Selecting a Class 2 Durable

Blu Silo, a grain farmer, expects grain storage requirements on his farm to equal a constant S_0. Blu expects to construct a round silo (blue in color) with a storage capacity of $\pi r_a^2 h$ where $\pi = 22/7$, r_a is the radius of the silo, and h is the silo's height. (The blue paint is included free along with Blu's name printed at the top.) The cost of the base of the silo is a function of the area of the base πr_a^2, while the cost of the sides of the silo structure is a function of the areas contained in the surface of the silo $\pi 2 r_a h$, where $\pi 2 r_a$ is the circumference of the silo and h is the height (or $\pi 2r_a$ is the width and h is the length). Finally, the cost of the roof on the structure is also a function of its area, equal to πr_a^2.

The acquisition cost of a cylinder storage structure with storage capacity $S_0 = \pi r_a^2 h$ is V_0 where:

$$V_0 = (p_r + p_b)(\pi r_a^2) + p_h(\pi 2r_a h), \tag{22.12}$$

and p_r, p_b, and p_h are price parameters describing the per unit cost of materials used in the silo's roof, base, and sides, respectively. The structure is designed to last for n periods and will cost $p_d \pi r_a^2 h$ dollars for disposal where p_d is a per unit capacity disposal cost.

To minimize the acquisition and disposal cost of the silo and still provide the needed grain storage requirements, the net present cost (*NPC*) equation is minimized by finding the optimal values for r_a and h subject to the storage capacity requirement. The *NPC* equation is written as:

$$\underset{r_a, h}{\text{Min }} NPC = (p_r + p_b)(\pi r_a^2) + p_h(\pi 2r_a h) + \frac{p_d \pi r_a^2 h}{(1+r)^n}, \tag{22.13}$$

$$\text{s.t.} \quad S_0 = r_a^2 \pi h.$$

One of the unknowns in the problem can be eliminated by solving for h in the constraint and replacing it in the *NPC* equation. Solving for h from the constraint yields:

$$h = S_0 / r_a^2 \pi. \tag{22.14}$$

We next substitute the result into the *NPC* equation for h. The variable r_a does not appear in the disposal cost portion of the *NPC* equation because it was considered a function of storage requirements S_0, which in this problem, were assumed fixed. The resulting *NPC* equation equals:

$$\underset{r_a}{\text{Min }} NPC = (p_r + p_b)(\pi r_a^2) + \frac{p_h 2 S_0}{r_a} + \frac{p_d S_0}{(1+r)^n}. \tag{22.15a}$$

The optimal radius of the silo is found by differentiating equation (22.15a) with respect to r_a:

$$\frac{dNPC}{dr_a} = 2(p_r + p_b)(\pi r_a) - \frac{2p_h S_0}{r_a^2} = 0, \tag{22.15b}$$

and:

$$\frac{d^2 NPC}{dr_a^2} > 0,$$

satisfying second-order conditions. Finally, the optimal radius r_a is solved for using equation (22.15b):

$$r_a = \left[\frac{2 p_h S_0}{2(p_r + p_b) \pi} \right]^{1/3}. \tag{22.16}$$

Notice that if the cost of building the structure is increased, the radius of the structure also increases:

$$\frac{dr_a}{dp_h} > 0.$$

In addition, if the cost of constructing the base p_d or the roof p_r increases, the optimal radius decreases (and height h increases):

$$\frac{dr_a}{dp_b} < 0,$$

and:

$$\frac{dr_a}{dp_r} < 0.$$

Class 3. $Ca = Ca_t \left(\alpha, \sum\limits_{i=1}^{t-1} s_i \right)$: Durables Whose Decay Depends on Use

Class 3 durables characterize much of what is studied in static production economics. The static neoclassical production function describes a transformation process in which a variable input is completely and instantaneously converted into an output without leaving a residual. Thus, the only important issue is to determine the optimal amount of the variable input to use.

If there are no economies in the purchase of the variable input, then the firm has no incentive to purchase more of the variable input than is used up in

Example 22.3: What Size Should It Be?

Blu, after determining the relationship in equation (22.16), consults the agricultural engineering department for specific cost parameters. They supply Blu with the following:

$$p_h = \$10, \quad p_r = \$15,$$

and:

$$p_b = \$25.$$

Blu has already determined that S_0 equals 10,000 units. Substituting these values into equation (22.16), Blu finds:

$$r_a = \left[\frac{(2)(10)(10,000)}{2(15+25)\left(\frac{22}{7}\right)} \right]^{\frac{1}{3}} = 9.27.$$

Suppose that before Blu purchases the silo, p_b increases to $50. This result has Blu resolving equation (22.16) to find a new optimal radius (a design parameter) equal to:

$$r_a = \left[\frac{(2)(10)(10,000)}{2(15+50)\left(\frac{22}{7}\right)} \right]^{\frac{1}{3}} = 7.88.$$

As a result of the increased cost per unit of the silo's base, Blu builds the silo higher with a smaller radius (and a smaller base).

Having solved for the optimal radius of his silo, Blu calculates the *NPC* of the silo, assuming $p_b=\$25$. This includes the disposal cost after n periods. To find *NPC* Blu substitutes into equation (22.13) $p_r=\$15$, $p_b=\$25$, $r_a=9.27$, $S_0=10,000$, $\pi=22/7$, $p_h=\$10$, $p_d=\$.25$, $r=0.10$, and $n=25$. The first step in finding *NPC* is to solve for h using equation (22.14):

$$h = S_0/r_a^2 \pi = 10,000 / (9.27)^2 (22/7) = 37.03.$$

Then:

$$NPC = (\$15+\$25)(22/7)(9.27)^2 + (\$10)(22/7)(2)(9.27)(37.03)$$

$$+ \frac{\$25(10,000)}{(1.10)^{25}} = \$55,453.$$

each period. This is convenient because the static neoclassical production model is analyzed in a static (timeless) world.

It is not hard to imagine inputs that have some of the characteristics described by the Class 3 durables, namely inputs whose decay occurs only through use. Fuels, chemical compounds used for cleaning and other purposes, feedstuffs, fertilizers, and seeds are examples.

What makes this class of models a *PV* problem is the selection of the design parameter. To allow the model to depend on a vector of design parameters suggests that a particular output, say corn, may be produced by different variable inputs. When this is the case, the problem extends beyond finding the optimal amount of the variable input; it includes selection of which input to use. This input selection problem takes on many of the characteristics of the *NPV* problems that compare average rates of return to total returns.

In Chapter 16, another version of the Class 3 model analyzes an exhaustible natural resource such as reserves of fossil fuels, coal, ground water, etc. Clearly, the capacity of an exhaustible resource depends on the supply of the resource that is diminished by use. The rate of extraction per period is strongly influenced by expected resource prices in the future. The measures of rated capacity, efficiency, and use flexibility for Class 3 durables are easily computed. The AL_t function is s_t / s_t. Thus, the durable has no unique rated capacity. The optimal extraction rate will depend solely on the cost of extraction—not on the loss in remaining capacity of the durable. The efficiency measure also equals one. If extraction costs are ignored and the rate of bending is zero, the use flexibility measure (one over the rate of bending) is not defined. To solve for Class 3 durables, let the net cash returns per period from a durable be $R(s_t)$, let the acquisition price be $V_0[Ca(0,\alpha)]$, and let the salvage price at period n be $V_n \left[Ca(\sum_{i=1}^{n} s_i, \alpha) \right]$ where design parameters α are assumed variable, allowing the problem to be considered in the *PV* framework.

Let the *NPV* model be:

$$\underset{s_1,\ldots,s_n,\alpha}{\text{Max}} \quad NPV = -V_0(0,\alpha) + \frac{R(s_1,\alpha)}{(1+r)} + \ldots + \frac{R(s_n,\alpha)}{(1+r)^n} + \frac{V_n(\sum_{i=1}^{n} s_i, \alpha)}{(1+r)^n}.$$

The first-order conditions are:

$$\frac{dNPV}{ds_1} = \frac{\partial R(s_1;\alpha)}{\partial s_1} - \frac{\partial V_n/\partial s_1}{(1+r)^{n-1}} = 0$$

$$\vdots$$

$$\frac{dNPV}{ds_n} = \frac{\partial R(s_n;\alpha)}{\partial s_n} - \partial V_n/\partial s_n = 0,$$

and:

$$\frac{dNPV}{d\alpha} = -\frac{\partial V_0}{\partial \alpha} + \frac{\partial R_1/\partial \alpha_1}{(1+r)} + \ldots + \frac{\partial R_n/\partial \alpha_n}{(1+r)^n} + \frac{\partial V_n/\partial \alpha}{(1+r)^n} = 0.$$

If $\partial V_n/\partial s_t < 0$ and $\partial R_t/\partial s_t > 0$, the first-order conditions indicate that durable service extraction rates will be greater when the durable is new and that the service extraction rate will decrease over time. The sooner services are extracted, the lower the capacity time cost of holding the service potential and not earning a return.

An Application: Solving for Class 3 Durable Design

Suppose we solve for a Class 3 durable whose capacity is depreciated only by use. Furthermore, assume that the durable's original capacity depends on a design parameter α. In addition, assume that:

$$R_t = p_t s_t \quad \text{for } t = 1, \ldots, n,$$

$$V_0 = \frac{\theta}{\alpha},$$

and:

$$V_n = \frac{\theta}{\alpha} - p_d \sum_{i=1}^{n} (\alpha s_i)^2.$$

NPV for this durable can be written as:

$$\underset{s_1,\ldots,s_n,\alpha}{\text{Max } NPV} = -\frac{\theta}{\alpha} + \frac{p_s s_1}{(1+r)} + \ldots + \frac{p_s s_n}{(1+r)^n} + \frac{\frac{\theta}{\alpha} - p_d \sum_{i=1}^{n} (\alpha s_i)^2}{(1+r)^n}.$$

The first-order condition for s_1 is:

$$\frac{dNPV}{ds_1} = p_s - \frac{p_d 2\alpha^2 \theta_t}{(1+r)^{n-1}} = 0,$$

and:

$$s_1 = \frac{p_s(1+r)^{n-1}}{(2\alpha^2 p_d)}.$$

If the design parameter α is assumed given, then in each period s_t can be solved independent of service levels or prices in other periods. But if α is a choice variable, then first-order conditions for α are written as:

$$\frac{dNPV}{d\alpha} = \frac{\theta}{\alpha^2}\left[1 - \frac{1}{(1+r)^n}\right] - \frac{2p_d \sum\limits_{i=1}^{n} \alpha s_i^2}{(1+r)^n} = 0.$$

The variable α depends on service extraction level $s_t (t=1,...,n)$ and equals:

$$\alpha = \left(\frac{\theta[(1+r)^n - 1]}{p_d \sum\limits_{i=1}^{n} s_i^2}\right)^{1/3}.$$

The design parameter α is a choice parameter only at the time of purchase. At that point, the choice parameter and service extraction levels are interdependent. Example 22.4 illustrates the solution for a Class 3 durable.

Class 4. $Ca_t = Ca\left(\sum\limits_{i=1}^{t} s_i, t, \alpha\right)$: Durables Whose Decay Depends on Time and Use

Class 4 durables represent the natural extension of Classes 2 and 3. The capacity of Class 4 durables depends on the services extracted, the age, and the design of the durable. The design of Class 4 durables must be planned to account for depreciation as a function of both time and use.

The most common examples of Class 4 durables are machines such as cars, tractors, combines, etc. whose remaining capacity depends on both time

Example 22.4: Choosing Service Extraction Levels and Design for a Class 3 Durable

Assume $n=2$, $\theta=\$100$, $p_1=p_2=\$5$, $p_d=\$0.02$, and $r=0.1$. Then, *NPV* can be written as:

$$NPV = \frac{-\$100}{\alpha} + \frac{\$5s_1}{(1.1)} + \frac{\$5s_2}{(1.1)^2} + \frac{\dfrac{\$100}{\alpha} - \$0.02\alpha^2(s_1^2+s_2^2)}{(1.1)^2}.$$

First-order conditions are:

$$s_1 = \frac{5(1.1)}{(0.04)\alpha^2} = \frac{137.5}{\alpha^2},$$

$$s_2 = \frac{5}{(0.04)\alpha^2} = \frac{125}{\alpha^2},$$

and:

$$\alpha = \left(\frac{\theta[(1+r)^n - 1]}{2p_d(s_1^2+s_2^2)}\right)^{\frac{1}{3}} = \left(\frac{(100)[(1.1)^2-1]}{137.5+125}\right) = 0.08.$$

This example illustrates how potential earnings in the future help determine the optimal design of the durable.

and use. The optimal use rates of these durables vary over time with the actual decay. An example of this type of durable is demonstrated next.

An Application: Selecting a Class 4 Durable

The durable's capacity is now recognized as a function of its design parameters, services extracted, and the age of the durable. To show how to find the optimal design of Class 4 durables, we use parts of earlier examples, namely that:

$$V_0 = \frac{\theta}{\alpha_0\alpha_1},$$

and:

$$L_t = \alpha_0 + \alpha_1 s_t^2.$$

Assume that units of service capacity are valued at a per unit price of p_d. If the durable is to last for n periods, its salvage value is:

$$V_n = \frac{\theta}{\alpha_0 \alpha_1} - p_d \sum_{i=1}^{n} (\alpha_0 + \alpha_1 s_i^2).$$

The *NPV* equation for the durable is now expressed as:

$$\operatorname*{Max}_{\alpha_0, \alpha_1, s_1, \ldots, s_n} NPV = -\frac{\theta}{\alpha_0 \alpha_1} + \frac{ps_1}{(1+r)} + \ldots$$

$$+ \frac{ps_n}{(1+r)^n} + \frac{\dfrac{\theta}{\alpha_0 \alpha_1} - p_d \displaystyle\sum_{i=1}^{n} (\alpha_0 + \alpha_1 s_i^2)}{(1+r)^n}. \tag{22.17}$$

The rated capacity, flexibility, and efficiency for this durable have already been found. Solutions are now needed for the optimal value of the design parameters α_0 and α_1. The solutions for α_0 and α_1 describe the durable that maximizes the *NPV* for the firm. First-order conditions for α_0 and α_1 are:

$$\frac{dNPV}{d\alpha_0} = \frac{\theta}{\alpha_0^2 \alpha_1} \left[1 - \frac{1}{(1+r)^n}\right] - \frac{np_d}{(1+r)^n} = 0, \tag{22.18}$$

and:

$$\frac{dNPV}{d\alpha_1} = \frac{\theta}{\alpha_0, \alpha_1^2} \left[1 - \frac{1}{(1+r)^n}\right] - \frac{p_d \displaystyle\sum_{i=1}^{n} s_i^2}{(1+r)^n} = 0. \tag{22.19}$$

Dividing equation (22.18) by (22.19) equals:

$$\alpha_1 = \frac{n\alpha_0}{\displaystyle\sum_{i=1}^{n} s_i^2}, \tag{22.20}$$

and substituting for α_1 in equation (22.17), we solve for α_0. It equals:

$$\alpha_0 = \left[\frac{\theta[(1+r)^n - 1]}{p_d n^2} \sum_{i=1}^{n} s_i^2 \right]^{\frac{1}{3}}. \tag{22.21}$$

The optimal service extraction rates are found by differentiating *NPV* with respect to $s_1, \ldots, s_n$ and equal:

$$\frac{dNPV}{ds_1} = p - \frac{p_d 2\alpha_1 s_1}{(1+r)^{n-1}} = 0$$

$$\frac{dNPV}{ds_2} = p - \frac{p_d 2\alpha_1 s_2}{(1+r)^{n-2}} = 0$$

$$\vdots$$

$$\frac{dNPV}{ds_n} = p - \frac{p_d 2\alpha_1 s_n}{(1+r)} = 0.$$

The graph of s_t for $t = 1, \ldots, n$ is described by the function:

$$s_t = \frac{p(1+r)^{n-t}}{p_d 2\alpha_1},$$

and is described in Figure 22.7.

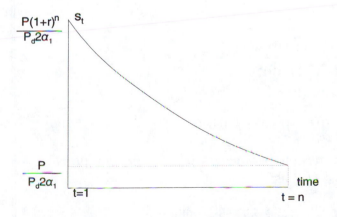

Figure 22.7
The Optimal Level of Service Extraction Over Time for a Durable Whose Service Capacity is a Function of Services Extracted and Age

Example 22.5: Design Choices for a Class 4 Durable

Petoski Power and Plight (*PPP*) supplies electric services to Petoski and surrounding communities. It calculates the demand over the next 10 years (the economic life of its equipment) to be $s_t = 8$. The value of plant and equipment when new is:

$$V_0 = \frac{\$150 \text{ million}}{\alpha_0 \alpha_1},$$

and after n periods of use is:

$$V_n = \frac{\$150 \text{ million}}{\alpha_0 \alpha_1} - \$(0.1)(10)(\alpha_0 + \alpha_1 64)$$

$$= \frac{\$150 \text{ million}}{\alpha_0 \alpha_1} - \$(\alpha_0 + \alpha_1 64).$$

PPP chooses its equipment design using equations (22.20) and (22.21):

$$\alpha_1 = \frac{10\alpha_0}{(10)(64)} = 0.016\alpha_0,$$

and:

$$\alpha_0 = \left[\frac{150[(1.1)^{10} - 1]}{(0.1)(10)^2} \right]^{\frac{1}{3}} = 2.88,$$

and:

$$\alpha_1 = (0.016)(2.88) = 0.046.$$

Having calculated the design parameters of its new equipment, *PPP* calculates the new cost (V_0) as:

$$V_0 = \frac{\$150 \text{ million}}{(0.016)(2.88)} = \$3,255.2 \text{ million}.$$

Example 22.5, Cont'd.: Design Choices for a Class 4 Durable

PPP is regulated by the Petoski Regulatory Commission which determines the price *PPP* can charge its customers. This rate is such that *NPV* for *PPP* is zero. To find *PPP*'s break-even price *p*, the necessary substitutions are made in equation (22.17) using a discount rate of 10 percent:

$$NPV = -\$3255.2 + p \sum_{i=1}^{10} \frac{\$8}{(1.1)^i} + \frac{\$[3255.2 - (28.81) + (0.46)(64)]}{(1.1)^{10}} = 0,$$

and:

$$p = \frac{\$3,255.20 - \left\{ \dfrac{\$3,255.20[2.88 + (0.046)(64)]}{(1.1)^{10}} \right\}}{\displaystyle\sum_{i=1}^{10} \frac{8}{(1.1)^i}} = \$40.70.$$

Summary

This chapter has introduced the problems of variable service extraction rates and optimal design. Static production analysis fixes the design of the durable and sometimes treats its costs as fixed as well. However, design and cost may vary in an *NPV* model.

The problem of durable design has only been introduced in this chapter. Matters can become quickly complicated without employing simplifying assumptions. To solve the economic problems of design and service extraction levels requires knowledge about the design alternatives and their costs. These information requirements suggest a natural alliance between economists and other scientists who study physical and biological constraints.

In discussing durables, four classes were identified. The durable classes were distinguished by the time and/or use pattern of depreciation. Class 1 durables do not lose service capacity. Class 2 durables experience change in service capacity as a result of the passage of time. Class 3 durables change capacity through use. Finally, Class 4 durables change capacity through use and time.

Differences in how durables lose capacity were shown to affect their use flexibility, efficiency, and rated capacity. The importance of use flexibility, efficiency, and rated capacity depends in part on the type of durable being designed and the unique economic environment in which it is expected to operate. All the design issues lead economists from the static model world in which durable designs were considered fixed into a new modelling world in which one of the most important questions is: What is the optimal design?

Review Questions

1. Compare the process of finding the optimal design of a durable in an *NPV* model with the process of determining the optimal units of variable input in a static neoclassical production function.

2. Define in your own words a durable's rated capacity, efficiency, and use flexibility.

3. Under what conditions should the decision maker give more weight to a durable's rated capacity than to its flexibility? When would a durable's use flexibility be more important than its rated capacity loss?

4. For the function: $L_t = \alpha_0 + \alpha_1 s_t$ where α_0 and α_1 are design parameters and s_t is the level of services extracted per period, find the durable's rated capacity, efficiency, and flexibility.

5. Four durable classes were identified in this chapter. All the durable classes allowed the design to vary. The distinction between the durable classes depended on how the lifetime capacity of the durable changed. List two durables for each class that have the described properties.

6. Durables tend to have services extracted at their maximum potential when capacity loss does not depend on use. Suppose a durable's lifetime capacity increased with use and did not depend on time at all. At what capacity would you expect services to be extracted? Explain why.

7. Suppose a durable's lifetime capacity increased with age up to age *j* and then declined. Describe the likely pattern of service extraction rates. Defend your answer.

8. Suppose you are to recommend a preferred design for a cucumber harvester. Who would you likely consult in order to construct a model that would make an informed recommendation? Why would economists working in isolation be unlikely to solve design problems?

9. For a typical farm implement, say a combine, tractor, or corn planter, discuss how the durable's age, level of services already extracted from the durable, and the design (including quality of materials) affect its remaining service capacity.

Application Questions

1. Describe the relationship between the durable's price and its capacity Ca_t. Are there circumstances where changes in the durable's price appear unrelated to changes in its capacity?

2. Consider a durable whose capacity Ca_t is unrelated to the level of services extracted from it (for example, land or buildings) but whose service extraction rates are endogenously determined. Assume that policy makers believe that the level of services extracted from this durable is excessive and needs to be reduced. To accomplish this goal, they reduce the net return on the durable by charging a tax on the units of services produced. (Assume that producing the services is still profitable.) How successful will the policy makers be in their attempt to reduce service levels through taxing service levels?

3. Find a loss in capacity curve L_t whose average value is: (a) "U" shaped; (b) a constant; and (c) increasing linearly.

4. Suppose you are designing a plant to produce gogets. (Gogets are really gadgets modified to be environmentally friendly.) The cost of the plant increases with rated capacity, efficiency, and flexibility. Discuss what factors you might consider in determining the optimum trade-offs between these factors.

5. Explain why all efficiency measures, including physical ones, must involve the assessment of values. (Hint: How does one decide between useful and not useful outputs?)

6. For which durables, those whose capacity changes depend on time or those whose capacity depends on use, will flexibility be more important? Will flexibility be more or less important for durables whose capacity decline is by endogenously determined use?

7. Following procedures used to design the silo in Example 22.3, design a structure rectangular in shape (allow the roof to be flat). Assume $S_0 = 8,000$, $n=10$, $r=0.1$, per unit cost of the wall is p_w=\$0.5, per unit cost of the roof is p_r=\$5, per unit cost of the base is p_b=\$3, and the per unit disposal cost p_d=\$0.25. Solve for the optimal length l, width w, and height h

of the structure subject to the requirement it has a storage capacity of 8,000 units. Also calculate the net present cost of providing storage.

References

Epstein, L.G. "Decision Making and the Temporal Resolution of Uncertainty." *International Economic Review* 21(1980):269-83.

Hartman, R. "Factor Demand With Output Price Uncertainty." *American Economic Review* 66(1976):675-81.

Johnson, G.L. "Theoretical Considerations." *The Overproduction Trap in U.S. Agriculture*, eds. G.L. Johnson and C.L. Quance. Baltimore, MD: Johns Hopkins University Press, 1972.

Jones, R.A. and J.M. Ostroy. "Flexibility and Uncertainty." *Review of Economic Studies* 51(1984):13-32.

Knight, F.H. *The Economic Organization*. New York, NY: 1951. August M. Kelley, Inc., pp. 9-10 (original 1933).

Lev, L. *The Role of Flexibility in the Design, Acquisition, and Use of Durable Inputs*. Unpublished Ph.D. thesis, Michigan State University, 1984.

Marshak, T. and R. Nelson. "Flexibility, Uncertainty and Economic Theory." *Metroeconomica* 14(1962):42-58.

Pindyck, R. "Adjustment Costs, Uncertainty, and the Behavior of the Firm." *American Economic Review* 7(1982):415-27.

Quance, C.L. "Capital." *The Overproduction Trap in U.S. Agriculture*, eds. G.L. Johnson and C.L. Quance. Baltimore, MD: Johns Hopkins University Press, 1972.

Robison, L.J. and M.H. Abkin, eds. *Theoretical and Practical Models for Investment and Disinvestment Decision Making Under Uncertainty in the Energy Supply Industry*. Agricultural Economics Report No. 390, Michigan State University, March 1981.

Robison, L.J. and P.J. Barry. *The Competitive Firm's Response to Risk*. New York and London: Macmillan, 1986.

Rosenhead, J. "An Education in Robustness." *Journal of the Operational Society* 29(1978):105-11.

Sandmo, A. "On the Theory of the Competitive Firm Under Price Uncertainty." *American Economic Review* 61(1971):65-73.

Shalit, H., A. Schmitz, and D. Zilberman. "Uncertainty, Instability and the Competitive Firm." California Agricultural Experiment Station Working Paper No. 234, 1982.

Stigler, J. "Production and Distribution in the Short-Run." *Journal of Political Economy* 47(1939):305-27.

Tisdell, C.A. *The Theory of Price Uncertainty, Production and Profit.* Princeton, NJ: Princeton University Press, 1968.

Tobin, J. "Liquidity Preference as Behavior Towards Risk." *Review of Economic Studies* 25(1958):65-86.

Turnovsky, S.J. "Production Flexibility, Price Uncertainty and the Behavior of the Competitive Firm." *International Economic Review* 14(1973):395-412.

Webster's Ninth New Collegiate Dictionary. Springfield, MA: Merriam-Webster, Inc., 1987.

Williamson, O.E. "Transaction Cost Economics: The Governance of Contractual Relations." *Journal of Law and Economics* 22(1979):231-38.

Zeller, M. and L.J. Robison. "Flexibility and Risk in the Firm." *European Review of Agricultural Economics* 19(1992):473-84.

Zylberberg, A. "Flexibilite, Incertain et Theorie de la Demande de Travail." *Annales De L'Insee* 42(1981):31-51.

Chapter 23

Advanced Risk and Present Value Analysis

by Robert J. Myers and Steven D. Hanson[1]

Key words: arbitrage pricing theory, asset pricing models, capital asset pricing model, risk premia

Introduction

Chapter 11 introduced risk into present value (PV) models and discussed different risk adjustment methods. In this chapter, we examine how different economic theories of investor behavior lead to equilibrium asset pricing equations which take the form of a PV model. For example, suppose we are interested in how farmland prices are determined. This chapter shows that many different theories of investor behavior all suggest that current farmland prices can be expressed as an expected sum of discounted future rents to owning farmland, with the nature of the discount factor depending on which particular theory of investor behavior is being applied. The form of these alternative discount factors depends primarily on how the asset's risk premium is modeled. Risk, therefore, has an important influence over the appropriate discount factor to use in PV models of equilibrium asset prices.

We begin by examining preference-based theories relying on the assumption of expected utility maximization by a representative investor.

---

[1]Robert J. Myers and Steven D. Hanson are Associate Professors of Agricultural Economics at Michigan State University.

Within this framework, different specifications of the risk premium lead to a rich set of alternative forms of the *PV* model for equilibrium asset price determination. One of these specifications leads to the well-known capital asset pricing model (*CAPM*) first developed by Sharpe. Next, we relax some of the more restrictive assumptions underlying the preference-based approach by examining Ross's arbitrage pricing theory (*APT*). The advantage of the *APT* is that it does not rely on particular preference structures or distributional assumptions, and so is considered to be more general than the preference-based expected utility maximization framework. We show that the *APT* model also leads to an asset pricing equation which is a *PV* model, but again the nature of the discount factor is determined by the risk premium inherent in the *APT*. Thus, both preference-based theories and the *APT* lead to asset pricing equations which are essentially *PV* models, differing only by how the discount factor is specified.

General Model

We begin by setting out a general framework for preference-based models of asset price determination. Consider a representative investor with initial wealth w_{t-1}. Under certain conditions (see Ingersoll, pp. 217-219) the preferences and wealth of the representative investor can represent the aggregate effect of many separate investors operating in a market. Thus, representative investor models can be used to characterize market equilibrium prices. The investor allocates wealth between n risky assets and a risk-free bond. Realized wealth at the end of the next period can be defined as:

$$w_t = \sum_{i=1}^{n} r_t^i x_{t-1}^i + r_t^0 \left(w_{t-1} - \sum_{i=1}^{n} x_{t-1}^i \right), \tag{23.1}$$

where r_t^i represents *gross* return on risky asset i held from time t-1 to t (uncertain at t-1);[1] x_{t-1}^i represents investments in risky asset i at t-1; and r_t^0 represents the *gross* return on the risk-free bond, which is known at t-1.

The first (summation) term in the wealth constraint represents the total realized wealth from investing in the n risky assets, which will be uncertain at the time investment decisions are made. The second term represents the realized wealth from investing in the risk-free bond (any initial wealth not invested in the risky assets is invested in the risk-free bond at a known rate of return), which is known at the time investment decisions are made.

The investor is assumed to buy and sell assets so as to maximize the expected utility of next period's wealth, given the wealth constraint discussed above. More formally, the objective function can be expressed as:

$$\max E_{t-1} u(w_t) \quad \text{s.t.} \quad (23.1), \tag{23.2}$$

where E_{t-1} is the expectation operator conditional on information available at t-1 and u is any increasing and strictly concave von Neumann-Morgenstern utility function. The first-order condition (*FOC*) for choosing the optimal investment level for one of the risky assets, say x_{t-1}^f which might be farmland, is found by differentiating the objective function (23.2) and using the constraint (23.1) to get:

$$\frac{\partial E_{t-1} u(w_t)}{\partial x_{t-1}^f} = E_{t-1} \left[\frac{\partial u(w_t)}{\partial w_t} \frac{\partial w_t}{\partial x_{t-1}^f} \right]$$

$$= E_{t-1} \left[u'(w_t)(r_t^f - r_t^0) \right] = 0, \tag{23.3}$$

where $u'(w_t) = \partial u(w_t)/\partial w_t$ is the marginal utility of wealth and r_t^f is the return on asset x_{t-1}^f. The second-order condition for optimality is satisfied by concavity of the utility function.

The difference between the return on the risky asset and on the risk-free bond is called the *excess return*, which should be positive on average because we expect a positive payback for shouldering additional risk. For particular realizations, however, the excess return may be positive or negative reflecting the risky nature of some of the investment alternatives. To help simplify notation, we define the excess return to investment x_{t-1}^f as:

$$y_t^f = r_t^f - r_t^0. \tag{23.4}$$

Substituting this definition of the excess return into equation (23.3) then gives:

$$E_{t-1}[u'(w_t) y_t^f] = 0. \tag{23.5}$$

It is difficult to say much more about the implications of this theory for asset pricing without imposing additional restrictions on the utility function and/or the distributional properties of the risky excess returns. One way to proceed is to assume that the joint density function of w_t and y_t^f, conditional on information available at t-1, can be approximated by a bivariate normal density. As shown in Appendix A, a property of bivariate normal distributions known as Stein's Lemma then allows the *FOC* to be rewritten as:

$$E_{t-1}[u'(w_t)]E_{t-1}(y_t^f) + E_{t-1}[u''(w_t)]cov_{t-1}(w_t, y_t^f) = 0, \qquad (23.6)$$

where cov_{t-1} is covariance conditional on information available at t-1. Rearranging (23.6) yields an important expression for the expected excess return:

$$\overset{\bullet}{E}_{t-1}(y_t^f) = \frac{-E_{t-1}[u''(w_t)]}{E_{t-1}[u'(w_t)]} cov_{t-1}(w_t, y_t^f). \qquad (23.7)$$

Equation (23.7) is an example of what has been called a "fundamental equation for asset valuation" (Constantinides). The fundamental valuation equation is generic in the sense that it leads to different asset pricing theories depending on what additional structure is placed on the right-hand side of the equation. The right-hand side of the fundamental asset valuation equation is called the *risk premium* because it represents the difference between the expected return to the risky asset and the return on the risk-free bond. Placing additional structure on equation (23.7) amounts to imposing alternative theories of the risk premium.

A Constant Risk Premium Model

Suppose we specialize the fundamental valuation equation (23.7) by assuming a *constant risk premium*. That is, the right-hand side of equation (23.7) is assumed to equal some constant δ which does not change over time. While obviously very restrictive, this assumption underlies much of the empirical research on estimating and testing asset pricing theories. Under the constant risk premium assumption, then, equation (23.7) becomes:

Example 23.1: Asset Pricing with Zero Covariance

In a small pacific island nation, there is little arable land and most of the wealth is held in the form of fishing boats and risk-free government bonds. Thus, returns to farmland and total wealth in the community fluctuate independently (zero covariance). In this situation, equation (23.7) implies that:

$$E_{t-1}(y_t^f) = 0,$$

or:

$$E_{t-1}(r_t^f) = r_t^0,$$

where r_t^f is the return to farmland and r_t^0 is the return on the risk-free bonds. Thus, an asset whose return fluctuates independently of total wealth has no risk premium (expected return equal to the risk-free rate) in equilibrium because holding such an asset does not increase (or decrease) the inherent risk in the investor's overall wealth level.

$$E_{t-1}(y_t^f) = \delta. \tag{23.8}$$

In order to solve for an equilibrium pricing equation, we need to note that the gross return on an asset can be defined as:

$$r_t^f = \frac{P_t^f + D_t^f}{P_{t-1}^f}, \tag{23.9}$$

where P_t^f is the price of the asset at time t and D_t^f is the net cash flow (dividend or rent) produced by the asset and received at t. Substituting equation (23.9) into equation (23.8) gives:

$$E_{t-1}\left(\frac{P_t^f + D_t^f}{P_{t-1}^f} - r_t^0\right) = \delta, \tag{23.10}$$

Example 23.2: Farmland Pricing with a Constant Risk Premium

A farmer wants to sell his farm and is trying to determine what price he should get. He knows land rents have been growing at an average rate of 5 percent per year and he expects this to continue indefinitely. Thus:

$$E_t(D_{t+j}) = 1.05^j D_t \quad \text{for } j=1,2,\ldots.$$

Furthermore, interest rates are constant at 9 percent and research has indicated that there is a constant 1 percent risk premium in the market for farmland. Thus, $r^0+\delta=1.09+0.01=1.1$. Substituting these values into the constant interest rate/constant risk premium asset pricing model equation (23.13) gives:

$$P_t = \sum_{j=1}^{\infty} \left(\frac{1.05}{1.10}\right)^j D_t = D_t \sum_{j=1}^{\infty} 0.95455^j$$

$$= 0.95455\, D_t [1 + 0.95455 + 0.95455^2 + \ldots]$$

$$= 0.95455\, D_t [1/(1 - 0.95455)] = 21.00\, D_t.$$

Thus, the equilibrium market price can be determined by multiplying the current rental rate by a factor of 21. For example, if the current rental price is $100 per acre, then the equilibrium price is $2,100 per acre.

or, equivalently:

$$E_{t-1}(P_t^f) + E_{t-1}(D_t^f) = P_{t-1}^f(r_t^0+\delta), \tag{23.11}$$

which is a first-order expectational difference equation in the asset price P_t^f.

It is shown in Appendix B, using repeated substitution and the law of iterated expectations, that equation (23.11) can be solved sequentially to give an expression for the current asset price as an expected sum of discounted future dividends or rents:[2]

$$P_t^f = E_t\left[\frac{D_{t+1}^f}{(r_{t+1}^0+\delta)}\right] + E_t\left[\frac{D_{t+2}^f}{(r_{t+1}^0+\delta)(r_{t+2}^0+\delta)}\right] + \ldots = E_t \sum_{j=1}^{\infty} \frac{D_{t+j}^f}{\prod_{k=1}^{j}(r_{t+k}^0+\delta)}. \tag{23.12}$$

Notice that this asset pricing equation takes the form of a *PV* model with a discount factor that depends on the constant risk premium, as well as on expectations about future risk-free rates of return. This model can be further restricted by assuming the risk-free rate is also a constant $r_t^0 = r^0$. Then, the equilibrium asset price is given by the standard *PV* model:

$$P_t = \frac{E_t(D_{t+1})}{(r^0+\delta)} + \frac{E_t(D_{t+2})}{(r^0+\delta)^2} + \ldots = E_t \sum_{j=1}^{\infty} \frac{D_{t+j}^f}{(r^0+\delta)^j}. \tag{23.13}$$

Expected future dividends or rents are discounted by a constant factor that is the sum of the constant risk premium and the constant risk-free rate of return. Thus, the standard *PV* model of asset price determination can be derived from a preference-based expected utility framework with the special assumptions of a constant risk premium and a constant risk-free rate of return.

A Time-Varying Risk Premium Model

There are a number of ways in which the constant risk premium assumption could be relaxed. Here we concentrate on one simple approach by supposing the representative investor holds just two assets: a risky asset x_{t-1}^f, which might be farmland, and the risk-free bond. In this case, the wealth constraint equation (23.1) implies that the covariance between wealth and the excess return to x_{t-1}^f is proportional to the variance of the excess return, with the proportionality factor being the dollar amount invested in the risky asset. That is:

$$cov_{t-1}(w_t, y_t^f) = x_{t-1}^f var_{t-1}(y_t^f). \tag{23.14}$$

Substituting equation (23.14) into the fundamental valuation equation (23.7) then gives:

$$E_{t-1}(y_t^f) = \lambda_t V_t, \tag{23.15}$$

where $V_t = Var_{t-1}(y_t^f)$ is the variance of the excess return, conditional on information available at t-1, and $\lambda_t = -x_{t-1}^f E_{t-1}[u''(w_t)]/E_{t-1}[u'(w_t)]$ is a measure of the representative investor's degree of risk aversion. Notice that λ_t is a form of relative risk aversion with risk measured relative to investment in the risky asset rather than total wealth (Newbery and Stiglitz).

Example 23.3: Farmland Pricing with a Time-Varying Risk Premium

The farmer from Example 23.2 is still trying to sell his farm. However, new research has shown that the risk premium is not a constant 1 percent as he had previously thought. Instead, it has been found that the risk premium is proportional to the conditional variance of returns to farmland (bigger variance means farming is more risky and so the risk premium increases), so that equation (23.18) is the appropriate farmland pricing formula. Farmland rents are still growing at 5 percent per year and the interest rate is still constant at 9 percent. Furthermore, the risk premium at the current date t is known to be 1 percent (remember it was previously thought to be constant at 1 percent for all time periods). Now, however, the risk premium increases over time as increases in rents lead to a higher variance in farmland returns (and hence more risk). This growth in the risk premium is characterized by a 2 percent growth rate in the discount factor used in the *PV* model:

$$\prod_{k=1}^{j} (r^0 + \lambda V_{t+k}) = (r^0 + \lambda V_{t+1})^j (1.02)^{j-1} \qquad j = 1, 2, \ldots$$

$$= \frac{(1.09 + 0.01)^j (1.02)^j}{1.02}.$$

This adds a 2 percent growth factor to the discount rate compared to the previous example where the risk premium was constant over time. Substituting the expression for the discount rate into equation (23.18) gives:

$$P_t = \sum_{j=1}^{\infty} \frac{(1.05)^j D_t}{[(1.10)^j (1.02)^j / 1.02]} = \sum_{j=1}^{\infty} \frac{(1.02)(1.05)^j D_t}{(1.122)^j}$$

$$= 0.955 \, D_t [1 + 0.936 + 0.936^2 + \ldots]$$

$$= 0.955 \, D_t [1 / (1 - 0.936)] = 14.92 \, D_t.$$

If the current rental rate is again $100, then the value of the farm drops to $1,492 per acre. Thus, a relatively small 2 percent growth in the discount factor, caused by increases in risk over time, is enough to reduce the price of farmland from $2,100 per acre to $1,492 per acre, a reduction of 30 percent.

A common assumption based on theoretical arguments and some empirical evidence is that of constant relative risk aversion (*CRRA*). Assuming *CRRA* (i.e., $\lambda_t = \lambda$ at each time period), then equation (23.15) becomes:

$$E_{t-1}(y_t^f) = \lambda V_t. \tag{23.16}$$

Now, substituting in the definitions of y_t^f and r_t^f gives another expectational difference equation in the prices of the risky investment:

$$E_{t-1}(P_t^f) + E_{t-1}(D_t^f) = P_{t-1}^f(r_t^0 + \lambda V_t). \tag{23.17}$$

And again, using repeated substitution and the law of iterated expectations (see Appendix B), equation (23.17) can be solved to give an expression for the current price of the risky asset as an expected sum of discounted future rents or dividends:

$$P_t^f = E_t\left[\frac{D_{t+1}^f}{(r_{t+1}^0 + \lambda V_{t+1})}\right] + E_t\left[\frac{D_{t+2}^f}{(r_{t+1}^0 + \lambda V_{t+1})(r_{t+2}^0 + \lambda V_{t+2})}\right] + \ldots$$

$$= E_t \sum_{j=1}^{\infty} \frac{D_{t+j}^f}{\displaystyle\prod_{k=1}^{j}(r_{t+k}^0 + \lambda V_{t+k})}. \tag{23.18}$$

This is a version of the *PV* model where the discount factor each period is adjusted by a time-varying risk premium. The value of the time-varying risk premium each period depends on the investor's risk preferences, as represented by the *CRRA* parameter λ, and the degree of risk associated with holding the risky asset, as measured by the variance of the asset's return. In this version of the model, the discount rate becomes higher as the level of risk associated with investing in the risky asset increases.

The Capital Asset Pricing Model

The assumption that investors hold just two assets in their portfolio is clearly quite restrictive in many situations. To relax this assumption, suppose the investor holds a broadly diversified portfolio of risky assets known as the *market portfolio*. Because the market portfolio is broadly diversified, the risk from holding it is systematic in the sense that it cannot be reduced further by following additional diversification strategies. Furthermore, since the representative investor holds the market portfolio, and the return on the market portfolio is the only source of risk to the investor's wealth level, the return on the market portfolio is perfectly correlated with wealth.

To derive the *CAPM*, we start with the fundamental asset valuation equation for the market portfolio:

$$E_{t-1}(y_t^\mu) = \frac{-E_{t-1}[u''(w_t)]}{E_{t-1}[u'(w_t)]} \, cov_{t-1}(w_t, y_t^\mu),$$ (23.19)

where $y_t^\mu = r_t^\mu - r_t^0$ is the excess return of the market portfolio. Rearranging equation (23.19) and substituting it into the fundamental valuation equation (23.7) for a particular asset x_{t-1}^f gives:

$$E_{t-1}(y_t^f) = E_{t-1}(y_t^\mu) \, \frac{cov_{t-1}(w_t, y_t^f)}{cov_{t-1}(w_t, y_t^\mu)}.$$ (23.20)

Now remember that the excess return to the market portfolio is perfectly correlated with wealth. Therefore, the ratio of covariance terms in equation (23.20) can be written as a ratio of the covariance between the return on the market portfolio and the return on the individual asset, to the variance of the return on the market portfolio:

$$E_{t-1}(y_t^f) = E_{t-1}(y_t^\mu) \, \frac{cov_{t-1}(y_t^\mu, y_t^f)}{var_{t-1}(y_t^\mu)}.$$ (23.21)

Finally, the definition of an excess return can be used to rewrite equation (23.21) as:

$$E_{t-1}(r_t^f) = r_t^0 + E_{t-1}(r_t^\mu - r_t^0)\beta_t^f,$$ (23.22)

where $\beta_t^f = cov_{t-1}(y_t^\mu, y_t^f)/var_{t-1}(y_t^\mu)$.

Equation (23.22) is a time-varying version of the static *CAPM* commonly used in finance (Copeland and Weston). The *CAPM* indicates that the expected return to holding a particular asset equals the risk-free rate plus a risk premium; where the risk premium equals the expected excess return to the market portfolio times a measure of the riskiness of investing in x^f_{t-1}. It is important to note that the riskiness of investing in a particular asset (often referred to as the asset's beta) is the residual risk that cannot be diversified away by holding the asset in the market portfolio. This residual risk is measured in terms of the relative impact on the variance of the market portfolio, rather than solely by the variance of the return on the particular risky asset.

Does the *CAPM* also lead to an equilibrium asset pricing equation which takes the form of a *PV* model? Suppose we let the risk premium in the *CAPM* be defined $\gamma^f_t = E_{t-1}(r^\mu_t - r^0_t)\beta^f_t$. Then equation (23.22) can be rewritten as:

$$E(r^f_t) = r^0_t + \gamma^f_t. \tag{23.23}$$

Now substitute in the definition of a return to the risky asset in terms of the asset price and its dividend or rent and we have an expectational difference equation in the asset price. Following the same procedure as before for solving expectational difference equations, we then get:

$$P^f_t = E_t\left[\frac{D^f_{t+1}}{(r^0_{t+1} + \gamma^f_{t+1})}\right] + E_t\left[\frac{D^f_{t+2}}{(r^0_{t+1} + \gamma^f_{t+1})(r^0_{t+2} + \gamma^f_{t+2})}\right] + \dots$$

$$= E_t \sum_{j=1}^{\infty} \frac{D^f_{t+j}}{\prod_{k=1}^{j} (r_{t+k} + \gamma^f_{t+k})}, \tag{23.24}$$

which is a *PV* model with a time-varying discount factor. Notice that the discount factor depends on the risk-free rate of return and a time-varying risk premium as measured by the asset's beta and the expected excess return of the market portfolio. Thus, the *CAPM* is also consistent with a *PV* model for equilibrium asset prices, where each period's discount rate consists of the risk-free rate plus the nondiversifiable risk premium associated with the asset under consideration. In some applications, the model is further restricted by assuming that the risk premium, and sometimes the risk-free rate, are constants. Assuming a constant risk premium $\gamma^f_t = \gamma^f$ and a constant risk-free rate of return, $r^0_t = r^0$, equation (23.24) becomes:

$$P^f_t = \frac{E_t(D^f_{t+1})}{(r^0 + \gamma^f)} + \frac{E_t(D^f_{t+2})}{(r^0 + \gamma^f)^2} + \dots = E_t \sum_{j=1}^{\infty} \frac{D_{t+j}}{(r^0 + \gamma^f)^j}, \tag{23.25}$$

which is similar to the simple standard *PV* model in equation (23.13) except the risk premium represents the nondiversifiable risk associated with the asset.

Example 23.4: Equity Valuation Using the *CAPM*

An investor is trying to value shares in a company, Forest Products, Inc. The shares will be held in a diversified portfolio and so he decides to use the *CAPM*. The risk premium in the *CAPM* is defined as:

$$\gamma_t^f = E_{t-1}\left(r_t^\mu - r_t^0\right)\beta_t^f,$$

where r_t^μ is the return on the market portfolio and β_t^f is Forest Products, Inc.'s beta. Suppose the expected excess return of the market portfolio over the risk-free rate is a constant 4 percent and the beta is constant at $\beta_t^f = 0.5$. Then, the risk premium is a constant at:

$$\gamma^f = (0.04)(0.5) = 0.02.$$

With a risk-free interest rate of 10 percent and a dividend growth rate of 4 percent, the *CAPM* would value shares of Forest Products, Inc. at:

$$P_t^f = \sum_{j=1}^{\infty} \frac{(1.04)^j D_t}{(1.1 + 0.02)^j}$$

$$= 0.92857\, D_t[1 + 0.92857 + 0.92857^2 + \ldots]$$

$$= 0.92857\, D_t[1 / (1 - 0.92857)] = 13\, D_t.$$

Thus, if current dividends were \$5 per share, the current share price valuation would be \$65 per share.

The Arbitrage Pricing Model

The *CAPM* implies that the expected return from any asset is linearly related to a single common market factor, the rate of return on the market portfolio. Conceptually, this implies all investors hold assets in the same proportion in their portfolio. In the real world, this assumption is clearly violated because investors hold a wide variety of different portfolios. Furthermore, even if investors did hold the market portfolio, it would be impossible to observe it because it contains both marketable and nonmarketable assets. In practice, the return on the market portfolio is often proxied by a broad-based market index of stocks such as the Standard and Poor's 500. Even though all investors do not hold identical portfolios, many investors do hold highly diversified portfolios by investing in various mutual funds, and so a broad-based market index may be a good proxy for the portfolios held by many investors.

However, it turns out that the expected rate of return from most assets is systematically related to other market factors besides the return on the market portfolio. Thus, a model which is flexible enough to account for the effects of a variety of marketwide and industrywide factors has the potential to predict expected returns more accurately than the *CAPM*. Along these lines, a more general approach is to assume the rate of return on any asset is linearly related to returns from a set of common factors plus a component specific to the asset under consideration. Formally, this "linear factor" assumption can be written as:

$$r_t^f = E_{t-1}(r_t^f) + \sum_{k=1}^{K} \alpha_{tk}^f F_{tk} + \epsilon_t^f, \tag{23.26}$$

where F_{tk} is the zero mean stochastic return from $t\text{-}1$ to t for factor k which is common to all assets under consideration, α_{tk}^f is the sensitivity of asset f's return to changes in the return of common factor k, ϵ_t^f is the zero mean return from $t\text{-}1$ to t which is specific to asset f, and $E_{t-1}(\epsilon_t^f \epsilon_t^i) = 0$ for $f \neq i$. Writing the factor returns and asset-specific return in zero mean form implies that their average effect is captured by the mean value of the asset's return, $E_{t-1}(r_t^f)$.

The factors are not explicitly identified by the theory but can be thought of as state variables that characterize economic events in the macroeconomy or industry, and which tend to impact asset returns in a systematic fashion across the economy or industry. Examples of such factors might include the risk-free interest rate, unexpected inflation, the return on a broad-based market portfolio, and/or a measure reflecting the term structure of interest rates.

The remaining "nonsystematic" determinants of asset f's return are captured in the term ϵ_t^f. These asset-specific factors do not impact asset prices in a general systematic fashion and so if the number of assets held by an investor is large, this part of the randomness associated with the asset's return is eliminated through diversification. This does not require investors to hold the market portfolio, only a large enough number of assets to reduce the nonsystematic risk to an insignificant level.

After eliminating the asset-specific risk associated with ϵ_t^f through diversification, investors are still faced with the risk associated with changes in the random systematic factors in the economy. It turns out that we can also eliminate this systematic risk by correctly choosing the amount of each asset to hold in the portfolio. This powerful result leaves us holding a portfolio that is risk-free and which, to avoid arbitrage opportunities, must earn a return equal to the risk-free rate of return. This result leads directly to the Arbitrage Pricing Theory (*APT*) equation which can be written as:

$$E_{t-1}(r_t^f) = r_t^0 + \sum_{k=1}^{K} \phi_{tk}\, \alpha_{tk}^f, \tag{23.27}$$

where ϕ_{tk} is price of risk, or standardized risk premium, for the kth factor from t-1 to t (Ross). It is important to note that the *APT* is based strictly on arbitrage arguments and requires no restrictions on risk preferences or distributional assumptions.

To get a better feel for the intuition underlying the *APT*, consider a simple two-asset portfolio in a one-factor economy where the asset-specific risk for each factor has been diversified away. The relevant single factor models generating each asset's return are thus:

$$r_t^f = E_{t-1}(r_t^f) + \alpha_{t1}^f F_{t1}, \tag{23.28a}$$

$$r_t^g = E_{t-1}(r_t^g) + \alpha_{t1}^g F_{t1}. \tag{23.28b}$$

Even though the asset-specific risk associated with each asset has been diversified away, each is still risky because its return is impacted by the stochastic factor F_{t1}. However, suppose we hold the two assets in a portfolio whose return can be written as:

$$r_t^p = q r_t^f + (1-q) r_t^g, \tag{23.29}$$

where r_t^p is the return on the portfolio from t-1 to t and q is the proportion of wealth invested in asset f. Substituting equation (23.28) into equation (23.29), we can write the portfolio return as:

$$r_t^p = [E_{t-1}(r_t^g) + q(E_{t-1}(r_t^f) - E_{t-1}(r_t^g))]$$
$$+ [\alpha_{t1}^g F_{t1} + q(\alpha_{t1}^f - \alpha_{t1}^g)F_{t1}].$$

(23.30)

Now choose q in such a way that the systematic risk associated with F_{t1} is eliminated. Setting $q = -\alpha_{t1}^g / (\alpha_{t1}^f - \alpha_{t1}^g)$ accomplishes this task reducing the portfolio return to:

$$r_t^p = E_{t-1}(r_t^g) + [-\alpha_{t1}^g / (\alpha_{t1}^f - \alpha_{t1}^g)][E_{t-1}(r_t^f) - E_{t-1}(r_t^g)],$$

(23.31)

which is nonstochastic. Our portfolio choice has eliminated the systematic risk associated with F_{t1} and left us holding a portfolio that is risk-free. In order to avoid arbitrage opportunities, the assets in this portfolio must be priced so that the nonstochastic return from the portfolio equals the risk-free rate of return. Setting the portfolio return in equation (23.31) equal to the risk-free rate, r_t^0, and rearranging yields:

$$[\alpha_{t1}^f - \alpha_{t1}^g][E_{t1}(r_t^g) - r_t^0] = \alpha_{t1}^g[E_{t-1}(r_t^f) - E_{t-1}(r_t^g)].$$

(23.32)

Add and subtract the risk-free rate to the right-hand side of equation (23.32) and rearrange to get:

$$\frac{[E_{t-1}(r_t^g) - r_t^0]}{\alpha_{t1}^g} = \frac{[E_{t-1}(r_t^f) - r_t^0]}{\alpha_{t1}^f}.$$

(23.33)

We can define the left-hand side as the standardized risk premium for asset g and the right-hand side as the standardized risk premium for asset f. Thus, the *APT* implies that these standardized risk premia must be equal. Defining this common standardized risk premium for time t as ϕ_t, then equation (23.33) can be written:

$$\frac{E_{t-1}(r_t^f) - r_t^0}{\alpha_{t1}^f} = \phi_t,$$

(23.34a)

$$\frac{E_{t-1}(r_t^g) - r_t^0}{\alpha_{t1}^f} = \phi_t.$$

(23.34b)

Rearranging equation (23.34) allows us to write the expected return from each asset as:

$$E_{t-1}(r_t^f) = r_t^0 + \phi_t \alpha_{t1}^f, \tag{23.35a}$$

$$E_{t-1}(r_t^g) = r_t^0 + \phi_t \alpha_{t1}^g. \tag{23.35b}$$

These are the risk-adjusted rates of return each asset must earn in equilibrium to avoid arbitrage.

This two-asset example illustrates the underlying concepts behind the more general result presented in equation (23.27). It is useful to note that if the sensitivity term is $\alpha_{t1}^f = cov_{t-1}(y_t^\mu, y_t^f)/var_t(y_t^\mu)$ and the standardized risk premium is $\phi_t = E_{t-1}(r_t^\mu - r_t^0)$ in the single-factor model, then *APT* reduces to the *CAPM*. Thus, the *CAPM* is a special case of the more general *APT*.

Does the *APT* also lead to an equilibrium pricing model that can be written as a *PV* model? Let the risk adjusted risk premiums associated with each factor in the general *APT* be represented by $\psi_t^f = \sum_{k=1}^{K} \phi_{tk} \alpha_{tk}^f$. Then, equation (23.27) can be written as:

$$E_{t-1}(r_t^f) = r_t^0 + \psi_t^f. \tag{23.36}$$

Substituting in the definition of a return to the risky asset in terms of the asset price and its cash flow once again gives an expectational difference equation in the asset price. Solving this difference equation using the same procedures used previously gives:

$$P_t^f = E_t \left[\frac{D_{t+1}^f}{(r_{t+1}^0 + \psi_{t+1}^f)} \right] + E_t \left[\frac{D_{t+2}^f}{(r_{t+1}^0 + \psi_{t+1}^f)(r_{t+2}^0 + \psi_{t+2}^f)} \right] + \dots$$

$$= E_t \sum_{j=1}^{\infty} \frac{D_{t+j}^f}{\prod_{k=1}^{j} (r_{t+k}^0 + \psi_{t+k}^f)}, \tag{23.37}$$

which is a *PV* model with a time-varying discount rate. Like the previous models considered, the *APT* can be written as a *PV* model; only now the discount rate consists of the risk-free rate plus the risk premium associated with the nondiversifiable common factors that influence the asset's return. As in the earlier cases, the model can be further simplified by assuming a constant risk-free rate of return and/or a constant risk premium.

Example 23.5: Equity Valuation Using the *APT*

The investor from Example 23.4 is still trying to value the equity Forest Products, Inc. After further research, the investor has determined that the rate of growth in housing starts and the returns from a broad-based market portfolio both impact Forest Products, Inc.'s returns. As a result, the investor decides to use the *APT* to estimate the value of the company's equity. The risk premium, ψ_t^f, for Forest Products, Inc. is defined as:

$$\psi_t^f = \phi_{tm}\,\alpha_{tm}^f + \phi_{th}\,\alpha_{th}^f,$$

where ϕ_{tm} and ϕ_{th} are the risk premiums for the broad-based market portfolio and the growth rate of housing starts, respectively; and α_{tm}^f and α_{th}^f are the nondiversifiable risk associated with the market portfolio and the growth rate of housing starts. Suppose that the risk premiums and nondiversifiable risk are constant over time at the following values:

$$\phi_{tm} = 0.04,$$

$$\phi_{th} = 0.02,$$

$$\alpha_{tm}^f = 0.5,$$

$$\alpha_{th}^f = 1.1.$$

Then, the risk premium is a constant at:

$$\psi^f = (0.04)(0.5) + (0.02)(1.1) = 0.042.$$

If the risk-free interest rate is constant at 10 percent and the dividend growth rate is 4 percent, the *APT* would value shares of Forest Products, Inc. at:

$$P_t^f = \sum_{j=1}^{\infty} \frac{(1.04)^j D_t}{(1.1 + 0.042)^j}$$

$$= 0.91068\, D_t\, [1 + 0.91068 + (0.91068)^2 + \ldots]$$

$$= 0.91068\, D_t\, [1/(1 - 0.91068)] = 10.196\, D_t.$$

If the current dividends were $5 per share, the current share price valuation would be $50.98 per share.

Summary ──

    Asset valuation models in financial economics can generally be characterized as preference-based models or arbitrage-based models. In this chapter, we have seen that the leading economic models of investor behavior under risk within these two paradigms all lead to models that suggest the price of an asset is determined by discounting the future cash flows expected to be generated by the asset. In other words, each of the different economic theories leads to a form of *PV* model for the determination of the equilibrium price of the asset. The different economic theories impact the value of an asset through alternative specifications of the discount rate. The primary differences in the implied discount rates depend on the characterization of the risk premium for the underlying asset.

Endnotes ──

1. The *gross* return is 1 plus the net rate of return. For example, if the asset earns a net return of 5 percent during the period, the gross return for that asset is (1+0.05).

2. The solution to the difference equation is subject to the transversality condition $\lim\limits_{T\to\infty} E_t\{P_{t+T}^f / \prod\limits_{k=1}^{T} (r_{t+k}^0 + \delta)\} = 0$ which ensures the absence of speculative bubbles in the determination of the asset price.

Review Questions ──

1. Discuss the assumptions used to develop the fundamental asset valuation equation.

2. The fundamental asset valuation equation can lead to a variety of asset pricing theories depending on the restrictions that are placed on the equation. Discuss the implications of placing restrictions on the fundamental valuation equation and how these restrictions impact asset prices.

3. Assume that the risk premium is a constant value δ and that the risk-free rate of interest can change over time taking on a value r_t^0. Use the fundamental valuation equation to derive the *PV* model that will determine an asset's price. Discuss what determines the discount rate in the model and how it differs from the standard *PV* model.

4. Suppose that investors hold a single risky asset, farmland, along with a risk-free bond. In this chapter, it was shown that the fundamental asset valuation equation can be used to derive a *PV* model to determine the value of the risky asset. Explain how this *PV* model differs from the one you derived in question (3).

5. If investors hold broadly diversified portfolios, the fundamental valuation equation can again be used to price assets. In this case, asset prices are determined by what is known as the Capital Asset Pricing Model (*CAPM*). Discuss how an asset's rate of return is determined according to the *CAPM*.

6. The *CAPM* also leads to a *PV* model of asset prices. Discuss how this *PV* model differs from those you considered in questions (3) and (4).

7. Explain the primary differences in the assumptions underlying the *PV* models derived from the fundamental valuation equation and the *PV* models derived from the Arbitrage Pricing Theory (*APT*).

8. Discuss the primary differences between the *PV* model derived from the *APT* and the *PV* model derived from the *CAPM*.

Application Questions

1. Suppose that investors hold three assets: a risk-free bond, farmland, and livestock facilities. Use the fundamental valuation equation to derive the *PV* model that determines the value of farmland. For simplicity, assume that $-E_{t-1}\left[u''(w_t)\right]/E_{t-1}\left[u'(w_t)\right]$ is a constant and measures investors' degrees of risk aversion.

2. The after-tax cash flow for an acre of farmland in Michigan was $80 last year and is expected to grow at 5 percent indefinitely. Investors in farmland tend to hold diversified portfolios. The current risk premium for the market is 8.08 percent and farmland's beta is constant and equal to 0.4. The risk-free rate of interest was 3 percent last year, but both it and the market's risk premium are expected to grow at a rate of 1 percent in the foreseeable future. What should farmland sell for in Michigan?

3. Bill is considering the purchase of shares of common stock in a new company that makes a new kind of mouse trap. The projected dividends are $2.00 per share next year and are expected to increase at a rate of 8 percent per year. The risk-free rate of interest is constant at 5 percent. However, because the company is new, the risk premium is 12 percent initially and is then expected to decline by 1 percent each year for four

years, at which time it will level off at 8 percent. What is the most that Bill should pay for the stock?

4.   AgriTrac, Inc. is considering expanding into a new line of tractors. Cash flows are expected to be $750,000 the first year and increase at a rate of 6 percent each year thereafter. The risk-free interest rate is constant at 4 percent. In addition, the systematic risk to cash flows is impacted by two other factors: the market return and the rate of growth in grain exports. The risk premium for the market portfolio is a constant 8 percent and the price of risk for the rate of growth in grain exports is a constant 6 percent. The sensitivity of the returns to the new line of tractors is constant and equal to 0.7 for the market return and 1.3 for the rate of growth in grain exports. Should AgriTrac, Inc. expand if the cost of expansion is expected to be $7,500,000?

5.   Suppose that the following historical information has been collected on returns:

Year	Asset A	Risk-Free Return
1983	12%	7%
1984	11%	7%
1985	14%	8%
1986	5%	7%
1987	9%	6%
1988	7%	6%
1989	12%	6%
1990	8%	5%
1991	9%	5%
1992	11%	5%

a.   What is the average risk premium for asset *A*?

b.   If the average risk premium remains at your answer to (a) and the risk-free rate of interest is expected to be 5 percent next year, 6 percent the following year, and 7 percent thereafter, what discount rates should be used to evaluate an investment in asset A?

References ───────────────────────────────────────

Constantinides, G.M. "Theory of Valuation: Overview and Recent Developments." In *Theory of Valuation*, S. Bhattacharya and G.M. Constantinides (eds.). Totowa, NJ: Roman and Littlefield, 1989.

Copeland, T.E. and F.J. Weston. *Financial Theory and Corporate Policy*, 2nd edition. Reading, MA: Addison-Wesley, 1983.

Ingersoll, J.E., Jr. *Theory of Financial Decision Making*. Savage: Rowman and Littlefield, 1987.

Newbery, D.M.G. and J.E. Stiglitz. *The Theory of Commodity Price Stabilization*. Oxford: Oxford University Press, 1981.

Ross, S.A. "The Arbitrage Theory of Capital Asset Pricing." *Journal of Economic Theory* 13(1976):341-60.

Rubinstein, M. "The Valuation of Uncertain Income Streams and the Pricing of Options." *Bell Journal of Economics and Management Science* 7(1976):407-25.

Sharpe, W.F. "Capital Asset Prices: A Theory of Market Equilibrium Under Conditions of Risk." *Journal of Finance* 19(1964):425-42.

Stein, C. "Estimation of the Mean of a Multivariate Normal Distribution." *Proceeding of the Prague Symposium on Asymptotic Statistics*, 1973.

Appendix A

Stein's Lemma

Bivariate normal distributions have a useful property, known as Stein's Lemma, which can be stated as follows.

If x and y are bivariate normal and g(y) is an at least once differentiable function of y, then subject to mild regularity conditions:

$$cov[x, g(y)] = E[g'(y)]cov(x, y). \tag{A.1}$$

Proof: See Rubinstein or Stein.

Because the covariance between any two variables can be written as:

$$cov(x, y) = E(xy) - E(x)E(y), \tag{A.2}$$

then:

$$E(xy) = E(x)E(y) + cov(x, y). \tag{A.3}$$

Thus, letting $x = u'(w_t)$ and $y = y_t'$, then equation (A.3) can be used to rewrite the *FOC* equation (23.5) in the text as:

$$E_{t-1}[u'(w_t)] E_{t-1}(y_t^f) + cov_{t-1}[u'(w_t), y_t^f] = 0. \tag{A.4}$$

Now, let $x = y_t^f$ and $g(y) = u'(w_t)$ and apply Stein's Lemma (A.1) to the covariance term in (A.4). This leads to the *FOC*:

$$E_{t-1}[u'(w_t)] E_{t-1}(y_t^f) + E_{t-1}[u''(w_t)] cov_{t-1}(w_t, y_t^f) = 0, \tag{A.5}$$

which is the *FOC* equation (23.6) in the text.

Appendix B

Solving Expectational Difference Equations

Equation (23.11) from the text can be rewritten as:

$$P_{t-1}^f = \frac{1}{(r_t^0 + \delta)} [E_{t-1}(D_t^f) + E_{t-1}(P_t^f)]. \tag{B.1}$$

And moving forward one period gives:

$$P_t^f = \frac{1}{(r_{t+1}^0 + \delta)} [E_t(D_{t+1}^f) + E_t(P_{t+1}^f)]. \tag{B.2}$$

Using equation (B.2) to substitute forward for P_t^f in equation (B.1), we get:

$$P_{t-1}^f = \frac{1}{(r_t^0 + \delta)} \left\{ E_{t-1}(D_t^f) + E_{t-1} \left[\frac{1}{(r_{t+1}^0 + \delta)} [E_t(D_{t+1}^f) + E_t(P_{t+1}^f)] \right] \right\}. \tag{B.3}$$

By repeatedly substituting forward for P_{t+j}^f and using the law of iterated expectations, which says that $E_{t-1}[E_{t+j}(D_{t+j+1})] = E_{t-1}(D_{t+j+1})$ for $j = 0, 1, \ldots$, we can write P_{t-1}^f as:

$$P_{t-1}^f = E_{t-1} \left[\frac{D_t^f}{r_t^0 + \delta} \right] + E_{t-1} \left[\frac{D_{t+1}^f}{(r_t^0 + \delta)(r_{t+1}^0 + \delta)} \right] + \cdots, \tag{B.4}$$

or moving forward one period and using summation and product notation gives:

$$P_t^f = E_t \sum_{j=1}^{\infty} \frac{D_{t+j}^f}{\prod\limits_{k=1}^{j} (r_{t+k}^0 + \delta)}, \tag{B.5}$$

subject to the transversality condition in endnote 2. Equation (B.5) is the *PV* model presented in equation (23.12).

Chapter 24

Dynamic Optimization
by Robert J. Myers and Lindon J. Robison[1]

Key words: Bellman's equation, control variables, dynamic programming, maximum principle, policy function, recursive dynamic optimization models, return function, state variables, transition equation, value function

Introduction

Many net present value (*NPV*) models assume service extraction rates have already been selected in a manner that maximized *NPV* for a particular investment. Even in the models in which service extraction rates were found using standard optimization techniques, these models were necessarily limited and made restrictive assumptions to ensure that standard optimization techniques were appropriate. This chapter introduces solution procedures for a broader class of "more complicated *NPV* models" known as recursive dynamic optimization models.

Recursive dynamic optimization models allow for different performance criteria than just discounted cash flows and are well suited to investment problems that have a wide range of continuous choice variables. We begin by outlining the features of recursive dynamic models and discussing generalized solution techniques. The remainder of the chapter then focuses on special recursive models that can be solved with the series summation tools developed

[1]Robert J. Myers is an Associate Professor of Agricultural Economics at Michigan State University. Lindon J. Robison is a Professor of Agricultural Economics at Michigan State University.

earlier in this book. These special models are quite restrictive, in a sense that will be made clear below, but lend themselves to simple solution procedures. The intent of this chapter is to provide an introduction to readers interested in the study of general recursive dynamic optimization problems.

Examples are designed to highlight the basic solution approach, rather than numerical methods, and so abstract from reality in a variety of important ways. Nevertheless, the solution methods outlined in this chapter have been applied to a broad range of practical problems in the areas of agricultural production, marketing, optimal stockpiling of grain, and natural resource management (e.g., Chavas and Klemme; Kennedy; Hsu and Chang; Karp; Gardner; Burt). Those interested in more comprehensive treatments of the theory of recursive dynamic optimization might consult Sargent; Bertsekas; Whittle; and Stokey and Lucas.

Recursive Dynamic Optimization Models ─────────────

Consider a dynamic decision problem where, at the beginning of each time period $t = 0, 1, \ldots, n$, the environment facing the decision maker can be described completely by a vector of *state* variables x_t. In other words, x_t contains all of the information available at t which is relevant to the decision problem. After observing the current state vector, the decision maker chooses a vector of *control* variables u_t to maximize an objective that depends on outcomes over the entire time horizon $t = 0, 1, \ldots, n$.

The state vector evolves according to a set of *transition equations* that define next period's state as a function of the current state and the current control:

$$x_{t+1} = g_t(x_t, u_t). \tag{24.1}$$

Current decisions u_t influence the state that the decision maker will face in the future. Thus, current rewards may have to be traded off against future rewards in order to obtain an overall optimum path for the decision variables u_t.

At each time period, the decision maker receives an immediate reward defined by a *return function*, $f_t(x_t, u_t)$, which depends on the current state and the current control. The immediate reward is high for favorable state and control realizations, but low for unfavorable realizations. The overall objective of the decision maker is to maximize the *NPV* of the return functions over the problem horizon, subject to the constraint that the state vector evolves according to the transition equations:

$$\max_{u_t} \sum_{t=0}^{n} \frac{1}{(1+r)^t} f_t(x_t, u_t) + \frac{1}{(1+r)^{n+1}} V_{n+1}(x_{n+1}), \qquad (24.2)$$

subject to:

$$x_{t+1} = g_t(x_t, u_t) \quad \text{for } t = 0, 1, \ldots n,$$

$$\qquad (24.3)$$

$$x_0 \text{ given,}$$

where r is the discount rate and $V_{n+1}(x_{n+1})$ represents the value to the decision maker of experiencing the terminal state vector x_{n+1}. Under a set of regularity conditions on the f_t, g_t and V_{n+1} functions, this problem can be solved using techniques that are discussed below.

This dynamic optimization problem generalizes the standard *NPV* model in which control variable solutions are already assumed. First, rewards in each t are now represented by the return function $f_t(x_t, u_t)$. This function may represent cash flow from an investment, but could also be the utility generated by the cash flow, the utility generated by consumption goods that the cash flow will purchase, etc. Second, there is a control vector u_t which is chosen at each t. This choice allows for continual adjustments to not only the scale of investment but also to output decisions, marketing decisions, consumption decisions, etc. Thus, while recursive dynamic optimization models have some features in common with standard *NPV* models such as *NPV*, maximum (minimum) bid (sell), and *IRR* models, they also allow for a much more general reward and choice structure.

Dynamic optimization problems that can be characterized in terms of state and control vectors, transition equations, and objectives that are additive in a set of return functions for each period, are considered *recursive*. The advantage of a recursive formulation is that large dynamic optimization problems can be separated into n smaller problems and solved recursively starting at the terminal date n and working backwards to the current date (Sargent). This approach allows the use of some easy to apply, yet powerful solution techniques that exploit the recursive structure of the problem.

Example 24.1: Consumption and Inventory

A subsistence farmer, Bearly Makingit, grows and consumes a single crop. Production, y_t, depends on how much seed is available at the beginning of the season, k_t, according to the production function:

$$y_t = q(k_t).$$

The amount of seed available next season equals current production minus current consumption c_t:

$$k_{t+1} = q(k_t) - c_t.$$

Each period, Bearly receives utility that depends upon the amount of the crop consumed, $U(c_t)$. Bearly's objective is to maximize a discounted sum of utilities over a finite time horizon, subject to the constraint that $k_t \geq 0$ for all t.

The optimization problem can be expressed:

$$\max \sum_{t=0}^{n} \frac{1}{(1+r)^t} U(c_t),$$

subject to:

$$k_{t+1} = q(k_t) - c_t, \quad k_t \geq 0, \quad k_0 \text{ given}.$$

The following definitions apply to this problem:

$$x_t = k_t, \quad u_t = c_t, \quad g_t(x_t, u_t) = q(k_t) - c_t,$$

$$f_t(x_t, u_t) = U(c_t), \quad V_{n+1}(x_{n+1}) = 0.$$

Thus, this problem fits the dynamic optimization framework outlined above.

Solution Techniques

The three main solution techniques for recursive dynamic optimization problems are the calculus of variations, the maximum principle, and dynamic programming. The calculus of variations was developed first. It is the least complex of the three approaches, but is also the most restrictive because it can only be applied to a subset of the general class of recursive models defined above. In particular, the calculus of variations requires that the transition equations take the special form:

$$x_{t+1} = g_t(u_t), \tag{24.4}$$

so that they depend only on the current control, not the current state.

The maximum principle is analogous to finding the stationary points (local maxima, local minima, or saddle point) of a function in static optimization problems. It is the most intuitive of the three methods for those who are familiar with static optimization techniques. The perspective of the maximum principle is that u_t and x_t are chosen *jointly* at each t to maximize the objective functional, subject to the constraint that the optimal paths for u_t and x_t must satisfy the transition equations. The constraints (transition equations) are taken into account using Lagrange multipliers, sometimes called *costate variables* in dynamic problems. Because a chosen value of u_t affects the state of the system at all future dates, and because the states and controls of the system must satisfy the transition equations, this perspective on the problem is intuitively appealing.

Applying the maximum principle to the general recursive problem involves setting up the Lagrangian:

$$L = \sum_{t=0}^{n} \frac{1}{(1+r)^t} \{f_t(x_t,u_t) + \lambda_t [g_t(x_t,u_t) - x_{t+1}]\}$$

$$+ \frac{1}{(1+r)^{n+1}} V_{n+1}(x_{n+1}), \tag{24.5}$$

and differentiating with respect to each u_t, x_t, and λ_t to get the first-order conditions:

$$\frac{\partial f_t(x_t, u_t)}{\partial u_t} + \frac{\partial g_t(x_t, u_t)}{\partial u_t} \lambda_t = 0 \quad (t = 0, 1, \dots n), \tag{24.6a}$$

$$\frac{\partial f_t(x_t, u_t)}{\partial x_t} + \frac{\partial g_t(x_t, u_t)}{\partial x_t} \lambda_t - (1+r)\lambda_{t-1} = 0 \tag{24.6b}$$

$$(t = 1, 2, \dots n),$$

$$-(1+r)\lambda_n + \frac{\partial V_{n+1}(x_{n+1})}{\partial x_{n+1}} = 0, \tag{24.6c}$$

$$g_t(x_t, u_t) - x_{t+1} = 0 \quad (t = 0, 1, \dots n), \tag{24.6d}$$

subject to x_0 given. The recursive structure of the problem now can be exploited to solve these first-order conditions backwards in time starting from the terminal date n.

From equation (24.6c), λ_n can be solved as a function of x_{n+1}. Then, this result, along with equations (24.6a) and (24.6d) can be used to express u_n as a function of x_n. This function, $u_n = h_n(x_n)$, is called a *policy function* and gives the optimal value of the control at n as a function of the state at that period. Finally, the policy function and the transition equation are substituted into equation (24.6b) so that λ_{n-1} can be expressed as a function of x_n. The process then continues recursively backwards in time until $t=0$ is reached. Given an initial state x_0, and the transition equation and policy function for each t, the optimal dynamic paths of u_t and x_t are completely defined.

Example 24.2: Production and Carryover

Kary Over is a farmer who expects to be operating a farm until period n when she retires. Each period, Kary allocates fertilizer u_t to the production of a cash crop. However, there is fertilizer carryover in the soil and the amount of fertilizer carried over from the previous period is denoted x_t. Crop production, y_t, depends on total available fertilizer, $x_t + u_t$, according to the production function:

$$y_t = q(x_t + u_t).$$

A proportion, γ, of the fertilizer available at t is carried over to $t+1$:

$$x_{t+1} = \gamma(x_t + u_t).$$

Example 24.2, Cont'd.: Production and Carryover

Kary maximizes a discounted sum of profits subject to these constraints:

$$\max \sum_{t=0}^{n} \frac{1}{(1+r)^t} [pq(x_t+u_t) - wu_t],$$

subject to:

$$x_{t+1} = \gamma(x_t+u_t),$$

where r is the interest rate; p is the (fixed) output price; and w is the (fixed) fertilizer price.

Setting up the Lagrangian and differentiating leads to the first-order conditions:

$$pq'(x_t+u_t) - w + \gamma\lambda_t = 0 \quad (t=0,1,\dots n), \tag{24.7a}$$

$$pq'(x_t+u_t) + \gamma\lambda_t - (1+r)\lambda_{t-1} = 0 \quad (t=1,2,\dots n), \tag{24.7b}$$

$$-\lambda_n = 0, \tag{24.7c}$$

$$\gamma(x_t+u_t) - x_{t+1} = 0 \quad (t=0,1,\dots n), \tag{24.7d}$$

where $q'(\cdot)$ indicates partial differentiation. Notice from equation (24.7c) that $\lambda_n = 0$ because fertilizer carryover into the next period after Kary has retired is not valuable (to her).

Substituting equation (24.7a) into equation (24.7b) gives:

$$(1+r)\lambda_{t-1} = w \quad (t=1, 2,\dots n).$$

Using this and $\lambda_n = 0$, the first-order conditions then reduce to:

Example 24.2, Cont'd.: Production and Carryover

$$pq'(x_n + u_n) - w = 0, \qquad (24.8a)$$

$$pq'(x_t + u_t) - w + \frac{\gamma w}{1+r} = 0 \quad (t=0,1,\ldots n-1). \qquad (24.8b)$$

Given an explicit form for the production function q, these equations could be solved to get the policy functions $u_t = h_t(x_t)$ for $t = 0, 1, \ldots n$.

Equations (24.8a) and (24.8b) have an intuitive economic interpretation. In the last period, Kary does not care about carryover so she just sets the marginal cost of fertilizer equal to the marginal revenue it generates. But in earlier periods, carryover is important and Kary takes account of the fact that current fertilizer allocations reduce the need to allocate additional amounts next period because of carryover. Of course, the effect has to be adjusted by the proportion of fertilizer carried over, γ, and discounted to account for the opportunity cost of capital.

The final solution technique to be discussed is dynamic programming. The perspective of dynamic programming is that the dynamic optimization problem equations (24.2) and (24.3) is broken down into n stages, one for each time period, and solved recursively backwards in time starting from the terminal date.

First, consider the problem of finding the optimal control in the terminal period n given some realized state vector x_n :

$$V_n(x_n) = \max_{u_n} \{f_n(x_n, u_n) + \frac{1}{(1+r)} V_{n+1}(x_{n+1})\}, \qquad (24.9)$$

subject to:

$$x_{n+1} = g_n(x_n, u_n). \qquad (24.10)$$

Notice that the value assigned to the terminal state vector next period $V_{n+1}(x_{n+1})$ is discounted back to the current period n and added to the current immediate reward $f_n(x_n, u_n)$. The decision maker must also take into account the transition equation (24.10).

First-order conditions for this terminal period problem are:

$$\frac{\partial f_n(x_n, u_n)}{\partial u_n} + \frac{1}{(1+r)} \frac{\partial V_{n+1}(x_{n+1})}{\partial x_{n+1}} \cdot \frac{\partial g_n(x_n, u_n)}{\partial u_n} = 0, \tag{24.11a}$$

subject to:

$$x_{n+1} - g_n(x_n, u_n) = 0. \tag{24.11b}$$

Solving these equations for u_n as a function of x_n gives the period n policy function or decision rule $u_n = h_n(x_n)$. Substituting this result back into the objective function gives the period n *value function*, $V_n(x_n)$.

Moving to the period n-1 problem leads to the objective:

$$V_{n-1}(x_{n-1}) = \max_{u_{n-1}} \{ f_{n-1}(x_{n-1}, u_{n-1}) + \frac{1}{(1+r)} V_n(x_n) \}, \tag{24.12}$$

subject to:

$$x_n = g_{n-1}(x_{n-1}, u_{n-1}). \tag{24.13}$$

In this case, the rewards from making an optimal decision at period n are embodied in the return function $V_n(x_n)$ defined earlier in equation (24.9). Thus, the optimal current decision, assuming that optimal decisions will be made in the future, can be found by solving equation (24.12) subject to equation (24.13). As before, next period's value function must be discounted back to the current period before it is added to the current immediate reward $f_{n-1}(x_{n-1}, u_{n-1})$.

First-order conditions for the problem are:

$$\frac{\partial f_{n-1}(x_{n-1}, u_{n-1})}{\partial u_{n-1}} + \frac{1}{(1+r)} \frac{\partial V_n(x_n)}{\partial x_n} \cdot \frac{\partial g_{n-1}(x_{n-1}, u_{n-1})}{\partial u_{n-1}} = 0, \tag{24.14a}$$

$$x_n - g_{n-1}(x_{n-1}, u_{n-1}) = 0. \tag{24.14b}$$

Once again, these equations can be solved for the optimal policy rule $u_{n-1} = h_{n-1}(x_{n-1})$. And substituting the solution back into the objective function gives the period n-1 value function $V_{n-1}(x_{n-1})$.

The pattern for the recursion is now set. Continuing backwards in time we are iterating on the functional equation:

$$V_t(x_t) = \max_{u_t} \{f_t(x_t, u_t) + \frac{1}{1+r} V_{t+1}(x_{t+1})\},$$ (24.15)

subject to:

$$x_{t+1} = g_t(x_t, u_t).$$ (24.16)

This functional equation is known as *Bellman's equation*. Solving the complete sequence of such problems backwards from the terminal date generates optimal paths for the control and state vectors via a set of policy functions or decision rules $u_t = h_t(x_t)$. It can be shown that there is an equivalence between the solution obtained to recursive dynamic optimization problems using dynamic programming and those obtained using maximum principle methods (see Sargent).

A Linear Adjustment Cost Model

We now turn to some special recursive models that can be solved using the geometric series summation tools developed earlier in this book. A linear adjustment cost model is examined first. Specifying linear adjustment costs is quite restrictive because they imply that a decrease in production leads to negative adjustment costs (i.e., an adjustment revenue). Nevertheless, the linear adjustment cost model is simple to work with and helps demonstrate the link between dynamic optimization methods and some of the techniques developed earlier in this book.

Suppose you are asked to schedule workers for a firm over a time horizon $t = 0, 1, \ldots, n$. Workers, however, are frequently paid differential costs depending on whether or not they work overtime. If production demands were constant, full-time workers would be hired to meet work demands and normal hourly salaries would be paid. Let these normal salary costs and other incidental costs be defined as a function of output produced, y_t. If in period t, y_t is produced, the normal cost incurred by the firm would be $c(y_t)$ where $c'(y_t) > 0$ and $c''(y_t) > 0$.

When, however, production demands vary, and they frequently do, firms incur additional costs (savings). One interpretation is that the additional costs

Example 24.3: Bellman's Equation

We now reconsider Example 24.2, the problem of optimal fertilizer allocation, but this time apply dynamic programming techniques. Bellman's equation for this problem is:

$$V_t(x_t) = \max_{u_t} \{pq(x_t + u_t) - wu_t + \frac{1}{1+r} V_{t+1}(x_{t+1})\},$$

subject to:

$$x_{t+1} = \gamma(x_t + u_t),$$

where $V_{n+1}(x_{n+1}) = 0$. Differentiating Bellman's equation at the terminal period n leads to the static optimizing rule:

$$pq'(x_n + u_n) - w = 0.$$

In earlier periods, the first-order conditional for Bellman's equation is:

$$pq'(x_t + u_t) - w + \frac{1}{1+r} \frac{\partial V_{t+1}(x_{t+1})}{\partial x_{t+1}} \gamma = 0. \qquad (24.17)$$

However, the derivative of the (optimized) value function with respect to the current state is clearly:

$$\frac{\partial V_t(x_t)}{\partial x_t} = pq'(x_t + u_t) + \frac{1}{1+r} \frac{\partial V_{t+1}(x_{t+1})}{\partial x_{t+1}} \gamma.$$

Using equation (24.17), however, this equation reduces to:

$$\frac{\partial V_t(x_t)}{\partial x_t} = w. \qquad (24.18)$$

Leading equation (24.18) one period and substituting into equation (24.17) gives the first-order condition:

$$pq'(x_t + u_t) - w + \frac{\gamma w}{1+r} = 0 \quad (t = 0, 1, \dots n-1). \qquad (24.19)$$

This is precisely the same marginal condition for this problem found earlier using the maximum principle.

are overtime pay if the hours worked are rapidly expanded. This overtime pay is related to the difference in quantity produced between periods.

The profit function π_t in the tth period can now be expressed as:

$$\pi_t = p_t y_t - c(y_t) - \alpha(y_t - y_{t-1}), \tag{24.20}$$

where p_t is the price paid to the firm in period t per unit of y, $c(y_t)$ is the normal cost of producing y_t, and α is an adjustment cost parameter characterizing additional costs (savings) whenever production levels are changed from the previous period. Letting r denote the interest rate, the *NPV* of the firm's profit over the time horizon of interest can be expressed:

$$\sum_{t=0}^{n} \frac{1}{(1+r)^t} [p_t y_t - c(y_t) - \alpha(y_t - y_{t-1})]. \tag{24.21}$$

The objective is to choose a y_t path that maximizes the *NPV* of profits. Define the control for this problem as current output y_t and the state as the previous period's output y_{t-1}. Then, the transition equation just says that next period's state is equal to the current control. Thus, the derivative of the transition equation with respect to the current state is always zero and the first-order conditions from the maximum principle in this case reduce to:

$$p_t - c'(y_t) - \alpha + \lambda_t = 0 \quad (t=0,1,...n), \tag{24.22a}$$

$$\alpha - (1+r) \lambda_{t-1} = 0 \quad (t=0,1,...n), \tag{24.22b}$$

$$\lambda_n = 0. \tag{24.22c}$$

Again, $\lambda_n = 0$ because production left over at the end of the time horizon is assumed to have no value.

Noting that $\lambda_n = 0$ and substituting equation (24.22b) into equation (24.22a) gives the first-order conditions:

$$p_t - c'(y_t) - \alpha + \frac{\alpha}{1+r} = 0 \quad (t=0,1,\ldots n-1),$$

$$p_n - c'(y_n) - \alpha = 0.$$

At each time period except the last, the usual first-order conditions for static optimization are modified as a result of the influence of current output choices on future profits via adjustment costs.

Several alternative formulations of adjustment costs could be used. For example, suppose adjustment costs persist, but their importance declines geometrically over time. This relationship might be represented by a profit function:

$$\pi_t = p_t y_t - c(y_t) - \alpha \sum_{i=0}^{t} \alpha^i (y_{t-i} - y_{t-i-1}),$$

where $0 < \alpha < 1$. *NPV* of profits is then defined:

$$\sum_{t=0}^{n} \frac{1}{(1+r)^t} \left[p_t y_t - c(y_t) - \alpha \sum_{i=0}^{t} \alpha^i (y_{t-i} - y_{t-i-1}) \right]. \tag{24.23}$$

In this case, y_t is the control and the current state vector equals all previous production levels. First-order conditions can then be derived in the usual way using the maximum principle. However, it is instructive to derive the first-order conditions in a slightly different way. *NPV* for an infinite horizon problem can be expressed:

$$NPV = p_0 y_0 - c(y_0) - \alpha(y_0 - y_{-1}) +$$

$$\frac{1}{(1+r)} \left[p_1 y_1 - c(y_1) - \alpha(y_1 - y_0) - \alpha^2 (y_0 - y_{-1}) \right] +$$

$$\frac{1}{(1+r)^2} \left[p_2 y_2 - c(y_2) - \alpha(y_2 - y_1) - \alpha^2 (y_1 - y_0) - \alpha^3 (y_0 - y_{-1}) \right]$$

$$+ \ \dots \tag{24.24}$$

Differentiating with respect to a particular y_t gives:

$$p_t - c'(y_t) - \alpha + \frac{\alpha - \alpha^2}{1+r} + \frac{\alpha^2 - \alpha^3}{(1+r)^2} + \dots = 0 \quad \text{for } t = 0, 1, \dots,$$

Example 24.4: Adjustment Costs

Green-Boiled Tomatoes is a firm that produces tomato sauce. It has a cost function $c_t = 100 + 0.05y_t^2$ where y_t is boxes of tomatoes produced in year t. The firm's management wants to know the optimal quantity to produce in year 3 if the expected price for that year is $400 per box of tomatoes. They recognize that changes in production levels are costly.

The opportunity cost for the investment is equal to 14 percent, and the firm has an adjustment cost parameter of $\alpha = 0.35$.

Using equation (24.26):

$$c_t = 100 + 0.05y_t^2,$$

$$c_t'(y_t) = 0.10y_t,$$

$$400 - 0.10y_3 - \frac{(0.14)\ (0.35)}{(1 + 0.14 - 0.35)} = 0,$$

$$400 - 0.10y_3 - \frac{0.0490}{0.79} = 0,$$

$$y_3 = 3,999 \text{ boxes.}$$

or:

$$p_t - c'(y_t) - \alpha + \frac{\alpha(1-\alpha)}{1+r}\left[1 + \frac{\alpha}{1+r} + \frac{\alpha^2}{(1+r)^2} + \ldots\right] = 0 \qquad (24.25)$$

$$\text{for } t = 0,1,\ldots.$$

The term in square brackets is a geometric series that converges to $(1+r)/(1+r-\alpha)$ if $\alpha < (1+r)$. Thus, equation (24.25) can be expressed as:

$$p_t - c'(y_t) - \alpha + \frac{\alpha(1-\alpha)}{(1+r-\alpha)} = 0,$$

or:

$$p_t - c'(y_t) - \frac{r\alpha}{1+r-\alpha} = 0. \tag{24.26}$$

Equation (24.26) characterizes the optimal production path as a function of r, α, marginal costs, and the path of prices p_t.

Build-Up Models

The next problem to consider involves investment timing. Suppose you own a firm producing an output that must be available by a specific date $t=n$. Consequently, production must be scheduled to meet the deadline. But there are other considerations as well. Production completed before time t wears out at rate d and incurs an opportunity cost of r percent. Let x_t be the stock of output available at the beginning of the period and y_t be production at period t. Then, because output wears out at the rate d, we have the transition equation:

$$x_{t+1} = (1-d)x_t + y_t.$$

The stock of output available at the end of period n is constrained to some fixed amount, $x_{n+1} = B$, and the initial output stock is zero, $x_0 = 0$.

Production costs depend on the rate of production so that higher levels of output are produced at higher marginal costs. A cost function meeting this specification is:

$$c(y_t) = \frac{\gamma}{2} y_t^2; \quad y_t \geq 0.$$

The firm's goal is to minimize the net present cost of having B available at the end of period n:

$$\min \sum_{t=0}^{n} \frac{1}{(1+r)^t} \frac{\gamma}{2} y_t^2, \tag{24.27}$$

subject to the transition equation and the constraint $x_{n+1} = B$.

The Lagrangian for this problem is:

$$L = \sum_{t=0}^{n} \frac{1}{(1+r)^t} \{ \frac{\gamma}{2} y_t^2 - \lambda_t [(1-d)x_t + y_t - x_{t+1}] - \mu(x_{n+1} - B) \},$$

where μ is a Lagrange multiplier for the constraint that final stocks equal B. Using the maximum principle, first-order conditions are:

$$\gamma\, y_t \, - \, \lambda_t \, = \, 0 \quad (t=0,1,\dots n), \qquad\qquad (24.28a)$$

$$-\lambda_t(1-d) \, + \, (1+r)\,\lambda_{t-1} \, = \, 0 \quad (t=1,2,\dots n), \qquad\qquad (24.28b)$$

$$\lambda_n \, - \, \mu \, = \, 0, \qquad\qquad (24.28c)$$

$$(1-d)\,x_t \, + \, y_t \, - \, x_{t+1} \, = \, 0 \quad (t=0,1,\dots n), \qquad\qquad (24.28d)$$

$$x_{n+1} \, = \, B, \qquad\qquad (24.28e)$$

from equation (24.28b), we have:

$$\frac{\lambda_t}{\lambda_{t-1}} \, = \, \frac{(1+r)}{(1-d)},$$

or using equation (24.28a):

$$\frac{y_t}{y_{t-1}} \, = \, \frac{(1+r)}{(1-d)}. \qquad\qquad (24.29)$$

Because both $r>0$ and $d>0$, this result implies that $y_t > y_{t-1}$, and the optimal production levels grow over the time horizon at the rate $(r+d)/(1-d)$. Of course, if $r=d=0$, then production is the same in each period.

While equation (24.29) characterizes an important feature of the optimal production path, it does not provide a complete rule for setting the production level in each period. To solve this problem, the optimal production level in a particular time period must be determined; then the remainder of the production path can be computed using equation (24.29). The easiest production level to

Example 24.5: Optimal Inventory Accumulation

Justn Tyme Corporation signed a contract to deliver 150 tons of building compounds in six years time. They want to know how much they should produce each year in order to fulfill the contract. The product wears out at a rate of 15 percent per year for which the company (the Justn Tyme Corporation) is not reimbursed. The company needs to receive a minimum return for its investments of 12 percent. First compute:

$$\alpha = (1-d)^2/(1+r) = (1-0.15)^2/(1+0.12) = 0.645,$$

and note that $n=5$ because there are six production periods beginning at time zero. The terminal output stock must be 150 tons so equation (24.32) implies:

$$y_n = \frac{(1-\alpha)x_{n+1}}{(1-\alpha^{n+1})} = \frac{(1-0.645)\,150}{0.928} = 57.39.$$

Furthermore, we know from equation (24.29) that:

$$y_{t-1} = \frac{(1-d)}{(1+r)}\,y_t = \frac{(1-0.15)}{(1+0.12)}\,y_t = 0.759\,y_t.$$

Thus, the optimal production path is: $y_5=57.39$, $y_4=43.56$, $y_3=33.06$, $y_2=25.09$, $y_1=19.04$, and $y_0=14.45$. The total output produced in all six years is 192.6 tons, which is greater than 150 tons. However, computing the stock of output at the beginning of each period using the transition equation (24.28d) gives: $x_0=0$, $x_1=14.45$, $x_2=31.32$, $x_3=51.71$, $x_4=77.02$, $x_5=109.02$, and $x_6=150$. Thus, the required stock of output is available at the end of six years.

solve for is the terminal level y_n. Then negative growth rates can be computed back recursively to find $y_{n-1}, y_{n-2}, \ldots y_0$.

To obtain a complete solution, consider the transition equation:

$$x_{t+1} = (1-d)x_t + y_t.$$

Using repeated substitution, this equation can be expressed as:

$$x_{n+1} = y_n + (1-d)y_{n-1} + (1-d)^2 y_{n-2} + \ldots + (1-d)^n y_0. \tag{24.30}$$

But equation (24.29) implies that:

$$y_{n-i} = \frac{(1-d)^i}{(1+r)^i} y_n. \tag{24.31}$$

Now substitute equation (24.31) into equation (24.30) to get:

$$x_{n+1} = y_n + \frac{(1-d)^2}{(1+r)} y_n + \frac{(1-d)^4}{(1+r)^2} y_n + \ldots \frac{(1-d)^{2n}}{(1+r)^n} y_n.$$

Letting $\alpha = (1-d)^2/(1+r)$ and noting that $0 < \alpha < 1$, this equation can be expressed using standard geometric series summation tools as:

$$x_{n+1} = \frac{1}{1-\alpha} (1-\alpha^{n+1}) y_n. \tag{24.32}$$

Thus, knowing $x_{n+1} = B$, we can use equation (24.32) and the definition of α to compute the optimal terminal period production level y_n. Earlier production levels can be derived by applying the negative growth rate implied by equation (24.29).

Carryover Models

Another class of dynamic models involves inputs that affect production in both present and future periods. Fertilizer, pesticides, herbicides, and insecticides are examples of such inputs. Fertilizers, for example, generally influence production levels in future periods as well as the current period because of carryover in the soil. However, the rate of service provision is a function of time, not use. We have already seen examples of carryover models when discussing solution techniques for dynamic optimization problems above. These problems are now considered in more detail using a slightly different formulation.

Let x_t denote the total amount of an input currently available to the production process and let output, y_t, depend on input availability according to the production function:

$$y_t = q(x_t),$$

where $q'(\cdot) > 0$ and $q''(\cdot) < 0$. The current input availability depends on past and current applications according to the transition equation:

$$x_t = (1-d)\,x_{t-1} + u_t,$$

where d is the rate at which the stock of the input decays and u_t is current applications. Notice that current applications are immediately available to the production process.

The objective is to maximize the present value (*PV*) of cash flows from the production process over a finite time horizon subject to the transition equation for the input:

$$\max \sum_{t=0}^{n} \frac{1}{(1+r)^t}\,[pq(x_t) - wu_t],$$

subject to:

$$x_t = (1-d)\,x_{t-1} + u_t \quad (t = 0,1,\ldots,n),$$

where p is the fixed output price, w is the fixed input price, and x_{-1} is given. Any input left over at the end of the time horizon, $(1-d)x_n$, is not valuable to the decision maker.

Define the state for this problem as x_{t-1} and the control as u_t. The first-order conditions from the maximum principle then are:

$$pq'(x_t) - w + \lambda_t = 0 \quad (t=0,1,\ldots,n), \tag{24.33a}$$

$$p(1-d)q'(x_t) + \lambda_t(1-d) - \lambda_{t-1}(1+r) = 0$$
$$(t = 1,2,\ldots,n), \tag{24.33b}$$

$$\lambda_n = 0, \tag{24.33c}$$

$$(1-d)x_{t-1} + u_t - x_t = 0 \quad (t=0,1,\dots,n). \tag{24.33d}$$

Dividing equation (24.33b) by $(1-d)$ and equating terms with equation (24.33a) gives:

$$(1+r)\lambda_{t-1} = (1-d)w \quad (t=1,2,\dots,n).$$

Thus, using this equation and equation (24.33a, c), the first-order conditions reduce to:

$$pq'(x_n) - w = 0, \tag{24.34a}$$

$$pq'(x_t) - w + \frac{(1-d)w}{(1+r)} = 0 \quad (t=0,1,\dots,n-1), \tag{24.34b}$$

$$x_t = (1-d)x_{t-1} + u_t \quad (t=0,1,\dots,n). \tag{24.34c}$$

To interpret these results, consider the case with no carryover, $d=1$. Then, the first-order conditions reduce to the static optimal allocation rule of setting marginal revenue $pq'(x_t)$ equal to the marginal cost w in every period. As the rate of decay gets smaller (carryover increases), however, the optimal allocation pattern changes dramatically. If the initial stock of the input available is zero ($x_{-1} = 0$), the first period allocation will be greater than the static allocation. To see this, differentiate equation (24.34b) with respect to d setting $x_{t-1} = 0$ to get:

$$pq''(u_t)\frac{\partial u_t}{\partial d} - \frac{w}{1+r} = 0,$$

or:

$$\frac{\partial u_t}{\partial d} = \frac{w}{(1+r)pq''(u_t)} < 0.$$

Because $q''(\cdot) < 0$ then $\dfrac{\partial u_t}{\partial d} < 0$, and any decrease in d below the total decay level of $d=1$ will lead to a higher allocation when the stock of input available from the last period is zero.

Example 24.6: Optimal Stock of Fertilizer

A. Spud Farmer is a potato producer with a production function:

$$y_t = 100 + 20x_t - 5x_t^2,$$

where x_t is the stock of fertilizer available at period t. The stock of fertilizer evolves according to the transition equation:

$$x_t = (1 - 0.3)\, x_{t-1} + u_t.$$

Thirty percent of the fertilizer stock last period decays leaving 70 percent available for current production. Spud pays an average of $170 per ton for fertilizer and receives $120 per ton for potatoes.

Taking the opportunity cost of capital at 12 percent, Spud wants to know how much fertilizer he should purchase in order to optimize his operation. If he were a static optimizer (no fertilizer carryover), the optimal solution would be (see equation 24.34a):

$$p(20 - 10u_t) = w,$$

or:

$$u_t = \left(\frac{170}{120} - 20\right)/10 = 1.86.$$

In the dynamic case with carryover, however, we use the first-order condition:

$$p[20 - 10(0.7x_{t-1} + u_t) - w + \frac{0.7w}{1.12} = 0,$$

or:

$$20 - 10(0.7x_{t-1} + u_t) = \frac{170 \times 0.375}{120},$$

or:

$$10(0.7x_{t-1} + u_t) = 19.47,$$

or:

Example 24.6, Cont'd.: Optimal Stock of Fertilizer

$$u_t = 1.95 - 0.7x_{t-1}.$$

The higher the stock of fertilizer available last period, the less fertilizer is allocated today.

Assuming the initial stock of fertilizer is zero, the initial optimal allocation is $u_0 = 1.95$ which exceeds the static optimal allocation of 1.86. In period 1, however, we have:

$$u_1 = 1.95 - 0.7 \times 1.95 \qquad\qquad x_1 = 0.7 \times 1.95 + 0.585$$

$$= 0.585, \qquad\qquad\qquad = 1.95.$$

Similarly, in period 2:

$$u_2 = 1.95 - 0.7 \times 1.95 \qquad\qquad x_2 = 0.7 \times 1.95 + 0.585$$

$$= 0.585, \qquad\qquad\qquad = 1.95,$$

and so on for future periods. Thus, the optimal solution is to maintain the fertilizer stock at $x_t = 1.95$ and the optimal fertilizer allocation at $u_t = 0.585$. This combination will continue until the terminal period when the optimal static allocation rule is used.

In subsequent periods, allocations will fall because of the carryover. Normally, input allocations will fall quickly below the static optimization level because the stock of the input persists for many periods without fully decaying.

Dynamic Response to Price Support Policies

In this section, we consider a problem where knowledge of a support price policy to be introduced in the future alters current production decisions. Suppose a price support policy will be introduced $n+1$ periods into the future. From then on, output prices for this product will be supported at some price p_s above the current market price p. To obtain the support price, however, the producer must limit production (a quota scheme). In particular, producers will only receive the support price if they restrict production to their average output level over the $n+1$ periods prior to the introduction of the scheme. It turns out that the producer will then generally produce at a point where marginal cost exceeds marginal revenue (an excess of economically-desirable production) during all periods before the support price policy is introduced.

To illustrate the result, we examine a firm facing a fixed current price p and a cost function $c(y_t)$ that depends on the level of output produced. Before the price support scheme is introduced, the firm's profit in each period is:

$$\pi_t = p y_t - c(y_t).$$

Assuming that the quota is binding (the entire quota amount is produced), then profit after the price support is introduced will be:

$$\pi_t^s = p_s \frac{x_{n+1}}{n+1} - c\left(\frac{x_{n+1}}{n+1}\right),$$

where x_{n+1} is the aggregate production over periods 0 through n. The aggregate production level evolves according to the transition equation:

$$x_{t+1} = x_t + y_t.$$

The firm's problem is to choose an optimal output path for y_t that solves:

$$\max \sum_{t=0}^{n} \frac{1}{(1+r)^t} [py_t - c(y_t)] + \frac{1}{(1+r)^{n+1}} V_{n+1}(x_{n+1}),$$

subject to:

$$x_{t+1} = x_t + y_t,$$

and $x_0 = 0$. Aggregate production after n periods, x_{n+1}, is now valuable to the firm because it defines the quota level that will be allocated to it. In particular, define:

$$V_{n+1} = \sum_{i=0}^{\infty} \frac{1}{(1+r)^i} \left[p_s \frac{x_{n+1}}{n+1} - c\left(\frac{x_{n+1}}{n+1}\right) \right] = \frac{1+r}{r} \left[p_s \frac{x_{n+1}}{n+1} - c\left(\frac{x_{n+1}}{n+1}\right) \right].$$

Thus, $V_{n+1}(x_{t+1})$ is the (infinite) sum of profits under the price support scheme after it has been introduced, discounted back to time $n+1$. We assume that:

$$V'_{n+1}(x_{n+1}) = \frac{1+r}{r(n+1)}\left[p_S - c'\left(\frac{x_{n+1}}{n+1}\right)\right] > 0, \qquad (24.35)$$

which is equivalent to saying that the quota is binding (the firm would like to produce more than their quota amount at prices p_S and w).

Using the maximum principle, the Lagrangian for this problem is:

$$L = \sum_{t=0}^{n} \frac{1}{(1+r)^t}\{[py_t - c(y_t)] + \lambda_t[x_t + y_t - x_{t+1}]\} + \frac{1}{(1+r)^{n+1}} V_{n+1}(x_{n+1}),$$

and the resulting first-order conditions are:

$$p - c'(y_t) + \lambda_t = 0 \quad (t = 0,1,\dots n), \qquad (24.36a)$$

$$\lambda_t - (1+r)\lambda_{t-1} = 0 \quad (t = 1,2,\dots n), \qquad (24.36b)$$

$$-(1+r)\lambda_n + V'_{n+1}(x_{n+1}) = 0, \qquad (24.36c)$$

$$x_t + y_t - x_{t+1} = 0 \quad (t = 0,1,\dots n). \qquad (24.36d)$$

Using repeated substitution on equation (24.36b) leads to the result that:

$$\lambda_t = \frac{\lambda_n}{(1+r)^{n-t}}.$$

Substituting this equation into equation (24.36a) then gives:

$$p - c'(y_t) + \frac{\lambda_n}{(1+r)^{n-t}} = 0. \qquad (24.37)$$

We know from equation (24.35) that if the quota is binding, then $V'_{n+1}(x_{n+1}) > 0$. And from equation (24.36c), this condition implies $\lambda_n > 0$.

Example 24.7: Production Responses to Price Supports

Prices R. Wright has information that a price support program will be introduced in four years ($n+1=4$), increasing prices from the current $p=7$ to $p^s=10$. This support price will only be available, however, if Wright restricts production to her average production over the prior four years. Suppose Wright has a cost function:

$$c(y_t) = 0.5y_t^2,$$

and the discount rate is 12 percent. Then, profit after the support payment will be:

$$\pi^s = 10\left(\frac{x_4}{4}\right) - 0.5\left(\frac{x_4}{4}\right)^2,$$

every period so that the *PV* in period *n* of all future profits is:

$$V_{n+1}(x_{n+1}) = (1+r)\pi^s/r.$$

Applying equation (24.37), then the optimal production path satisfies:

$$y_t = 7 + \frac{\lambda_4}{(1+r)^{4-t}} \quad (t=0,1,2,3).$$

Without anticipating a price support, then $\lambda_4=0$ and $y_t=7$. This is the profit maximizing level of output without any price support. However, with the price support, then $\lambda_4>0$ and the optimal production level increases beyond the point where marginal cost equals price. How far beyond $y_t=7$ output gets depends on the values of λ_4 and r.

Thus, from equation (24.37), marginal revenue *p* is less than marginal cost $c'(y_t)$ in every period prior to the introduction of the price support scheme. This result causes production to exceed the economically desirable output level in every one of these periods. The reason is that the firm is attempting to build up quota allotments that can then be exploited over the infinite horizon after the support price scheme has been introduced.

The excess production is smallest in earlier periods, when $(1+r)^{n-t}$ is large, and biggest in later periods, when $(1+r)^{n-t}$ is small. Because of the effects of discounting, the firm prefers to bear a larger amount of the costs of excess production closer to the time the support price scheme is to be introduced, rather than bearing them immediately.

Production Decay Models

Continuous production of many agricultural commodities in monoculture results in productivity decay over time. For example, continuous production of potatoes causes increased pest damage reducing average productivity over time. The build-up of weeds has a similar result in crop production. Another similar problem is the decrease in efficiency of pounds gained by animals as they increase in weight. That is, conversion of feed to pounds of animal weight gain diminishes over time as the animal's weight increases. In many ways, these production decay problems are just the opposite of the fertilizer carryover problem discussed earlier.

To formulate this problem, consider a production process with production function:

$$y_t = q(u_t) - s(x_t + u_t),$$

where y_t is output; u_t is the current input allocation, and x_t is the total amount of input that has been allocated in past periods $t-1, t-2, \ldots$ We assume $q'(\cdot) > 0$; $s'(\cdot) > 0$; $q''(\cdot) < 0$; and $s''(\cdot) > 0$. Thus, the first term in the production function $q(u_t)$ represents the usual positive output effect from increasing the current input allocation and the second term $s(x_t + u_t)$ represents the negative output effect from having high cumulative output levels in the past. The transition equation for cumulative output has the simple form:

$$x_{t+1} = x_t + u_t.$$

Suppose the producer aims to maximize discounted profits from this operation over a given time horizon. The producer's problem is stated as:

$$\max \sum_{t=0}^{n} \frac{1}{(1+r)^t} \{p[q(u_t) - s(x_t + u_t)] - wu_t\},$$

subject to:

$$x_{t+1} = x_t + u_t,$$

where p is output price; w is input price; r is the opportunity cost of capital; and x_0 is given. The Lagrangian for this problem is:

$$L = \sum_{t=0}^{n} \frac{1}{(1+r)^t} \{p[q(u_t) - s(x_t + u_t)] - wu_t + \lambda_t[x_t + u_t - x_{t+1}]\},$$

and the first-order conditions from the maximum principle become:

$$pq'(u_t) - ps'(x_t + u_t) - w + \lambda_t = 0 \tag{24.38a}$$

$$(t = 0, 1, \dots n),$$

$$-ps'(x_t + u_t) + \lambda_t - (1+r)\lambda_{t-1} = 0 \quad (t = 1, 2, \dots n), \tag{24.38b}$$

$$\lambda_n = 0, \tag{24.38c}$$

$$x_t + u_t - x_{t+1} = 0 \quad (t = 0, 1, \dots n). \tag{24.38d}$$

These first-order conditions can be characterized as follows. Substitute equation (24.38b) into equation (24.38a) to get:

$$pq'(u_t) - w + (1+r)\lambda_{t-1} = 0 \quad (t = 1, 2, \dots n). \tag{24.39}$$

Now notice from equation (24.38b) that if $\lambda_n = 0$, then $\lambda_{n-1} < 0$ (remember that $s'(\cdot) > 0$). Furthermore, equation (24.38b) also implies that if $\lambda_t < 0$, then $\lambda_{t-1} < 0$ for every t. Thus, because $\lambda_{n-1} < 0$, every λ_t $(t = 0, 1, \dots n-1)$ is negative except for the terminal period costate variable which is zero, $\lambda_n = 0$. From equation (24.39), this shows that:

$$pq'(u_t) > w \quad (t = 0, 1, \dots n).$$

If there were no production decay effects, $s(x_t + u_t) = 0$, the firm would set marginal revenue $pq'(u_t)$ equal to marginal cost w in every period. Thus, the production decay effect causes output to fall below its normal (no production decay) level in every period (marginal revenue is greater than marginal cost, excluding the cost of production decay).

The model is specialized by letting:

$$s(x_t + u_t) = \gamma(x_t + u_t),$$

so that:

$$s'(x_t + u_t) = \gamma,$$

where $\gamma > 0$ is a fixed constant. For this case, equation (24.38b) becomes:

$$-p\gamma + \lambda_t - (1+r)\lambda_{t-1} = 0.$$

Noting that $\lambda_n = 0$ and substituting backwards in time to get the remaining λ_t ($t = n-1, n-2, \ldots 0$) terms gives:

$$\lambda_t = -p\gamma \sum_{i=1}^{n-t} \frac{1}{(1+r)^i}.$$

But, we know that:

$$\sum_{i=1}^{n-t} \frac{1}{(1+r)^i} = \frac{1}{(1+r)} \left[\sum_{i=0}^{\infty} \frac{1}{(1+r)^i} - \frac{1}{(1+r)^{n-t}} \sum_{i=0}^{\infty} \frac{1}{(1+r)^i} \right]$$

$$= \frac{1}{r} \left[1 - \frac{1}{(1+r)^{n-t}} \right].$$

Thus, we have:

$$\lambda_t = \frac{-p\gamma}{r} \left[1 - \frac{1}{(1+r)^{n-t}} \right],$$

or:

$$(1+r)\lambda_{t-1} = \frac{-p\gamma}{r} \left[1 + r - \frac{1}{(1+r)^{n-t}} \right].$$

Example 24.8: Production Decay

Consider Spudtwo Farmer, the son of the potato producer from an earlier example. Spudtwo inherited Spud's farm but now realizes it has production decay as a result of pest build up from cultivating potatoes in monoculture. His production function is:

$$y_t = q(u_t) - s(x_t + u_t),$$

where:

$$q(u_t) = 100 + 20u_t - 5u_t^2,$$

$$s(x_t + u_t) = 2(x_t + u_t).$$

Note that:

$$q'(u_t) = 20 - 10u_t,$$

$$s'(x_t + u_t) = 2.$$

Assuming an output price $p=120$, an input price $w=170$, and a discount factor $r=0.12$, equation (24.40) for this example becomes:

$$120(20 - 10u_t) - 170 - \frac{120 \times 2}{0.12} \left[1.12 - \frac{1}{(1.12)^{n-t}} \right] = 0,$$

or:

$$20 - 10u_t - \frac{170}{120} - 16.67 \left[1.12 - \frac{1}{(1.12)^{n-t}} \right] = 0,$$

or:

$$u_t = 1.85 - 1.67 \left(1.12 - \frac{1}{(1.12)^{n-t}} \right).$$

> ### Example 24.8, Cont'd.: Production Decay
>
> Thus, over a six-year time horizon ($n=5$) the optimal production plan is:
>
> $$u_0 = 1.85 - 1.67 \times 0.55 = 0.93,$$
>
> $$u_1 = 1.85 - 1.67 \times 0.48 = 1.04,$$
>
> $$u_2 = 1.85 - 1.67 \times 0.41 = 1.17,$$
>
> $$u_3 = 1.85 - 1.67 \times 0.32 = 1.31,$$
>
> $$u_4 = 1.85 - 1.67 \times 0.23 = 1.47,$$
>
> $$u_5 = 1.85 - 1.67 \times 0.12 = 1.65.$$
>
> As expected, production increases over time but is less than the static optimizing level of 1.85 in every period.

Substituting this result into equation (24.39) leads to:

$$pq'(u_t) - w - \frac{p\lambda}{r}\left[1 + r - \frac{1}{(1+r)^{n-t}}\right] = 0. \tag{24.40}$$

Because $1/(1+r)^{n-t}$ lies between zero and one for $t=0, 1,\dots n$, then $pq'(u_t) > w$ as before. In this case, however, λ_t starts out as a "big" negative number ($1/(1+r)^{n-t}$ is small) and declines in absolute value over time as $1/(1+r)^{n-t}$ gets closer and closer to one. Thus, at the start of the time horizon, optimal output is reduced more as the producer strives to avoid having negative productivity consequences felt over a longer period of time. Then, production grows as time evolves.

Summary

This chapter introduced recursive dynamic optimization methods and showed how they can be applied to a range of decision problems. The methods allow solutions to more complicated *NPV* models by allowing for different performance criteria than just discounted cash flow, and by encompassing a wide range of choice variables that can be adjusted continually as time evolves.

The recursive methods were applied to finding an optimal production plan under linear adjustment costs, choosing an optimal stock build-up plan when stocks decay over time and a fixed terminal stock level is required, finding an optimal input allocation plan when inputs carry over to affect future production, choosing an optimal production plan when a price support-quota scheme will be introduced at a future date, and choosing an optimal input allocation path under production decay when cumulative production reduces current productivity. In each case, we examined special models that can be solved with the geometric series summation tools developed earlier in this book. More general problems require more powerful solution techniques, including the solution of difference equations.

A theme of this chapter is that optimal dynamic decisions that take a long-run perspective may be inconsistent with optimal static decisions that only focus on the short run. In all of the models in this chapter, it is found that optimal static decisions are only identical to optimal dynamic ones under special and restrictive circumstances. Generally, a long-run perspective causes behavior to diverge from what would be optimal in a static world. The techniques outlined in this chapter are designed to find optimal dynamic decisions after accounting for these long-run consequences.

Endnotes

1. Another solution approach is to note that equation (3.26b) is a first-order difference equation in λ_t that might be solved subject to the terminal condition equation (24.6c). Then equations (24.6a) and (24.6d) together with the initial conditional x_0 could be used to compute the optimal u_t and x_t paths. However, solving difference equations is beyond the scope of this book and is not discussed here.

Review Questions

1. Define the three main components of a recursive dynamic optimization problem.

2. What is the essential difference between the usual *NPV* problem in which service extraction rates are given or solved for, and a general recursive dynamic optimization model? Identify in your discussion if both models are

PV models, if they serve the same general purpose, and why more sophisticated solution techniques may be required to solve truly dynamic models.

3. Distinguish between the three solution techniques for solving recursive models: calculus of variations, the maximum principle, and dynamic programming.

4. Explain how linear transition equations simplify the solution to many recursive dynamic problems and allow the use of geometric summation tools.

5. Explain how production plans might respond to an announcement that $n+1$ years in the future, a price support program would be introduced for firms restricting output to the average level of output for years $1, \ldots, n$.

Application Questions

1. Describe a simple recursive *PV* problem (such as the one described in Example 24.1) that contains a control variable, a return function, a transition equation, a state variable, and a terminal value function.

2. Explain intuitively why the first-order conditions obtained using the maximum principle in Example 24.2 were also obtained from the dynamic programming approach using Bellman's equation.

3. Reconsider Example 24.4 on the Green-Boiled Tomato firm. Suppose that interest rates are expected to fall from 14 to 10 percent. Recalculate the optimal production level of tomato sauce and explain why it increased or decreased.

4. Recompute the solution to Example 24.5 assuming that *d*, the wear out rate, increased to 20 percent. Compare your solution to the earlier one and explain the increases or decreases.

5. Suppose the rate of carryover increased in Example 24.6 (*d* decreased). Explain how optimal fertilizer application would respond.

References

Bertsekas, D.P. *Dynamic Programming and Stochastic Control.* New York: Academic Press, 1976.

Burt, O.R. "Farm Level Economics of Soil Conservation in the Palouse Area of the Northwest." *American Journal of Agricultural Economics* 63(1981):83-92.

Chapman, D. "Computation Techniques for Intertemporal Allocation of Natural Resources." *American Journal of Agricultural Economics* 69(1987):134-42.

Chavas, J.P. and R.M. Klemme. "Aggregate Milk Supply Response and Investment Behavior on U.S. Dairy Farms." *American Journal of Agricultural Economics* 68(1986):55-66.

Gardner, B.L. *Optimal Stockpiling of Grain.* Lexington, KY: Lexington Books, 1979.

Hsu, S.H. and C.C. Chang. "An Adjustment-Cost Rationalization of Asset Fixity Theory." *American Journal of Agricultural Economics* 72(1990):298-308.

Karp, L.S. "Methods for Selecting the Optimal Dynamic Hedge When Production Is Stochastic." *American Journal of Agricultural Economics* 69(1987):647-57.

Kennedy, J.S. *Dynamic Programming: Application to Agriculture and Natural Resources.* New York: Ebenier, 1986.

Lucas, R.E., Jr. "Adjustment Costs and the Theory of Supply." *Journal of Political Economy* 75(1967):321-34.

Rothschild, M. "On the Cost of Adjustment." *Quarterly Journal of Economics* 86(1971):605-22.

Sargent, T.J. *Dynamic Macroeconomics.* Cambridge, MA: Harvard University Press, 1987.

Stokey, N.L. and R.E. Lucas, Jr. *Recursive Methods in Economic Dynamics.* Cambridge, MA: Harvard University Press, 1989.

Whittle, P. *Optimization Over Time: Dynamic Programming and Stochastic Control*, vols. I and II. New York: John Wiley and Sons, 1982.

Yotopoulos, P.A. "From Stock to Flow Capital Inputs for Agricultural Production Functions: A Microanalytic Approach." *Journal of Farm Economics* 49(1967):491-95.

Appendix A-1

US_0 $(r/m,\ mn)$ Tables

Appendix Table A-1. Present Value of a Uniform Series $\quad V_0 = \$1\left[\dfrac{1-(1+r)^{-n}}{r}\right] = US_0(r,n)$

n	0.5%	0.75%	1%	1.5%	2%	3%	4%	5%	6%	7%
1	0.9950	0.9926	0.9901	0.9852	0.9804	0.9709	0.9615	0.9524	0.9434	0.9346
2	1.9851	1.9777	1.9704	1.9559	1.9416	1.9135	1.8861	1.8594	1.8334	1.8080
3	2.9702	2.9556	2.9410	2.9122	2.8839	2.8286	2.7751	2.7232	2.6730	2.6243
4	3.9505	3.9261	3.9020	3.8544	3.8077	3.7171	3.6299	3.5460	3.4651	3.3872
5	4.9259	4.8894	4.8534	4.7826	4.7135	4.5797	4.4518	4.3295	4.2124	4.1002
6	5.8964	5.8456	5.7955	5.6972	5.6014	5.4172	5.2421	5.0757	4.9173	4.7665
7	6.8621	6.7946	6.7282	6.5982	6.4720	6.2303	6.0021	5.7864	5.5824	5.3893
8	7.8230	7.7366	7.6517	7.4859	7.3255	7.0197	6.7327	6.4632	6.2098	5.9713
9	8.7791	8.6716	8.5660	8.3605	8.1622	7.7861	7.4353	7.1078	6.8017	6.5152
10	9.7304	9.5996	9.4713	9.2222	8.8926	8.5302	8.1109	7.7217	7.3601	7.0236
11	10.6770	10.5207	10.3676	10.0711	9.7868	9.2526	8.7605	8.3064	7.8869	7.4987
12	11.6189	11.4349	11.2551	10.9075	10.5753	9.9540	9.3851	8.8633	8.3838	7.9427
13	12.5562	12.3423	12.1337	11.7315	11.3484	10.6350	9.9856	9.3936	8.8527	8.3577
14	13.4887	13.2430	13.0037	12.5434	12.1062	11.2961	10.5631	9.8986	9.2950	8.7455
15	14.4166	14.1370	13.8651	13.3432	12.8493	11.9379	11.1184	10.3797	9.7122	9.1079
16	15.3399	15.0243	14.7179	14.1313	13.5777	12.5611	11.6523	10.8378	10.1059	9.4466
17	16.2586	15.9050	15.5623	14.9076	14.2919	13.1661	12.1657	11.2741	10.4773	9.7632
18	17.1728	16.7792	16.3983	15.6726	14.9920	13.7535	12.6593	11.6896	10.8276	10.0591
19	18.0824	17.6468	17.2260	16.4262	15.6785	14.3238	13.1339	12.0853	11.1581	10.3356
20	18.9874	18.5080	18.0456	17.1686	16.3514	14.8775	13.5903	12.4622	11.4699	10.5940
24	22.5629	21.8891	21.2434	20.0304	18.9139	16.9355	15.2470	13.7986	12.5504	11.4693
25	23.3456	22.7188	22.0232	20.7196	19.5235	17.4131	15.6221	14.0939	12.7834	11.6536
30	27.7941	26.7751	25.8077	24.0158	22.3965	19.6004	17.2920	15.3725	13.7648	12.4090
36	32.8710	31.4468	30.1075	27.6607	25.4888	21.8323	18.9083	16.5469	14.6210	13.0352
40	36.1722	34.4469	32.8347	29.9158	27.3555	23.1148	19.7928	17.1591	15.0463	13.3317
48	42.5803	40.1848	37.9740	34.0426	30.6731	25.2667	21.1951	18.0772	15.6500	13.7305
50	44.1428	41.5664	39.1961	35.9997	31.4236	25.7298	21.4822	18.2559	15.7619	13.8007
60	51.7256	48.1734	44.9550	39.3803	34.7609	27.6756	22.6235	18.9293	16.1614	14.0392

(continued)

Appendix Table A-1. (continued)

n	8%	9%	10%	11%	12%	13%	14%	15%	16%
1	0.9259	0.9174	0.9091	0.9009	0.8929	0.8850	0.8772	0.8696	0.8621
2	1.7833	1.7591	1.7355	1.7125	1.6901	1.6681	1.6467	1.6257	1.6052
3	2.5771	2.5313	2.4869	2.4437	2.4018	2.3612	2.3216	2.2832	2.2459
4	3.3121	3.2397	3.1699	3.1024	3.0373	2.9745	2.9137	2.8550	2.7982
5	3.9927	3.8897	3.7908	3.6959	3.6048	3.5172	3.4331	3.3522	3.2743
6	4.6229	4.4859	4.3553	4.2305	4.1140	3.9975	3.8889	3.7845	3.6847
7	5.2064	5.0330	4.8684	4.7122	4.5638	4.4226	4.2883	4.1604	4.0386
8	5.7466	5.5348	5.3349	5.1461	4.9676	4.7988	4.6389	4.4873	4.3436
9	6.2469	5.9952	5.7590	5.5370	5.3282	5.1317	4.9464	4.7716	4.6065
10	6.7101	6.4177	6.1446	5.8892	5.6502	5.4262	5.2161	5.0188	4.8332
11	7.1390	6.8052	6.4951	6.2065	5.9377	5.6868	5.4527	5.2337	5.0286
12	7.5361	7.1607	6.8137	6.4924	6.1944	5.9176	5.6603	5.4206	5.1971
13	7.9038	7.4869	7.1034	6.7499	6.4235	6.1218	5.8424	5.5831	5.3423
14	8.2442	7.7862	7.3667	6.9819	6.6282	6.3025	6.0021	5.7245	5.4675
15	8.5595	8.0607	7.6061	7.1909	6.8109	6.4624	6.1422	5.8474	5.5755
16	8.8514	8.3126	7.8237	7.3792	6.9740	6.6039	6.2651	5.9542	5.6685
17	9.1216	8.5436	8.0216	7.5488	7.1196	6.7291	6.3729	6.0472	5.7487
18	9.3719	8.7556	8.2014	7.7016	7.2497	6.8399	6.4674	6.1280	5.8178
19	9.6036	8.9501	8.3649	7.8393	7.3658	6.9380	6.5504	6.1982	5.8775
20	9.8181	9.1285	8.5136	7.9633	7.4694	7.0248	6.6231	6.2593	5.9288
24	10.5288	9.7066	8.9847	8.3481	7.7843	7.2829	6.8351	6.4338	6.0726
25	10.6748	9.8226	9.0770	8.4217	7.8431	7.3300	6.8729	6.4641	6.0971
30	11.2578	10.2737	9.4269	8.6938	8.0552	7.4959	7.0027	6.5660	6.1772
36	11.7172	10.6118	9.6765	8.8786	8.1924	7.5979	7.0790	6.6231	6.2201
40	11.9246	10.7574	9.7791	8.9511	8.2438	7.6344	7.1050	6.6418	6.2335
48	12.1891	10.9336	9.8969	9.0302	8.2972	7.6705	7.1296	6.6585	6.2450
50	12.2335	10.9617	9.9148	9.0417	8.3045	7.6752	7.1327	6.6605	6.2463
60	12.3766	11.0480	9.9672	9.0736	8.3240	7.6873	7.1401	6.6651	6.2492

(continued)

Appendix Table A-1. (continued)

n	17%	18%	19%	20%	21%	22%	23%	24%	25%
1	0.8547	0.8475	0.8402	0.8333	0.8264	0.8197	0.8130	0.8065	0.8000
2	1.5852	1.5656	1.5465	1.5278	1.5095	1.4915	1.4740	1.4568	1.4400
3	2.2096	2.1743	2.1399	2.1065	2.0739	2.0422	2.0114	1.9813	1.9520
4	2.7432	2.6901	2.6386	2.5887	2.5404	2.4936	2.4483	2.4043	2.3616
5	3.1993	3.1272	3.0576	2.9906	2.9260	2.8636	2.8035	2.7454	2.6893
6	3.5892	3.4976	3.4098	3.3255	3.2446	3.1669	3.0923	3.0205	2.9514
7	3.9224	3.8115	3.7057	3.6046	3.5079	3.4155	3.3270	3.2423	3.1611
8	4.2072	4.0776	3.9544	3.8372	3.7256	3.6193	3.5179	3.4212	3.3289
9	4.4506	4.3030	4.1633	4.0310	3.9054	3.7863	3.6731	3.5655	3.4631
10	4.6586	4.4941	4.3389	4.1925	4.0541	3.9232	3.7993	3.6819	3.5705
11	4.8364	4.6560	4.4865	4.3271	4.1769	4.0354	3.9018	3.7757	3.6564
12	4.9884	4.7932	4.6105	4.4392	4.2784	4.1274	3.9852	3.8514	3.7251
13	5.1183	4.9095	4.7147	4.5327	4.3624	4.2028	4.0530	3.9124	3.7801
14	5.2293	5.0081	4.8023	4.6106	4.4317	4.2646	4.1082	3.9616	3.8241
15	5.3242	5.0916	4.8759	4.6755	4.4890	4.3152	4.1530	4.0013	3.8593
16	5.4053	5.1624	4.9377	4.7296	4.5364	4.3567	4.1894	4.0333	3.8874
17	5.4746	5.2223	4.9897	4.7746	4.5755	4.3908	4.2190	4.0591	3.9099
18	5.5339	5.2732	5.0333	4.8122	4.6079	4.4187	4.2431	4.0799	3.9279
19	5.5845	5.3162	5.0700	4.8435	4.6346	4.4415	4.2627	4.0967	3.9424
20	5.6278	5.3527	5.1009	4.8696	4.6567	4.4603	4.2786	4.1103	3.9539
24	5.7465	5.4509	5.1822	4.9371	4.7128	4.5070	4.3176	4.1428	3.9811
25	5.7662	5.4669	5.1951	4.9476	4.7213	4.5139	4.3232	4.1474	3.9849
30	5.8294	5.5168	5.2347	4.9789	4.7463	4.5338	4.3391	4.1601	3.9950
36	5.8617	5.5412	5.2531	4.9929	4.7569	4.5419	4.3453	4.1649	3.9987
40	5.8713	5.5482	5.2582	4.9966	4.7596	4.5439	4.3467	4.1659	3.9995
48	5.8792	5.5536	5.2619	4.9992	4.7614	4.5451	4.3476	4.1665	3.9999
50	5.8801	5.5541	5.2623	4.9995	4.7616	4.5452	4.3477	4.1666	3.9999
60	5.8819	5.5553	5.2630	4.9999	4.7619	4.5454	4.3478	4.1667	4.0000

Appendix A-2

Definitions of Frequently-Used Variables

Definitions

Variable	Definition
t	Time subscript corresponding to the age of a durable Thus, when t is subscripted to r, r^*, i, or V, it implies that variable's value when the durable is at age t. In discrete time, a variable subscripted by t signifies the variable's value at the end of period t-1 or the beginning of the tth period.
r	Nominal discount rate; also the internal rate of return (*IRR*) of an investment.
r^r	Reinvestment rate.
r^f	Interest rate charged on a loan; also the annual percentage rate (*APR*).
r_t	Discount rate in period t.
r^d	Stated interest rate on disguised interest cost loans.
r^b	Blended interest rate.
r^c	Coupon rate of interest.
i	Inflation rate.
r^*	Real discount rate: $$r* = \frac{(1+r)}{(1+i)} - 1.$$
r^e	The effective (annual) interest rate.
e^r	Continuous time discount where $e^r = \lim_{m \to \infty} \left(1 + \frac{r}{m}\right)^m$.
r^a	Accounting rate of return measure.

V_0	Present value of an investment.
V_t^a	Accounting or book value in the tth period.
$V_t^b\left(V_t^s\right)$	Maximum-bid price (minimum-sell price) at age t of the durable.
n	Number of service periods remaining for a durable or number of years to loan maturity.
m	Number of compounding periods within a year; switch period in an n period rotation model; number of replacements.
L_0	Present value of a loan.
L_0^*	Present value of a concessionary interest rate loan with an outstanding loan balance of L_0.
A	A constant payment or annuity.
R_t	A durable's realized net cash flow in the tth period.
$R(t)$	Realized net cash flow defined as a function of time t.
N	Number of agricultural firms participating in a particular agricultural land market.
M	Number of nonagricultural firms participating in a particular agricultural land market.
g	Nominal growth rate.
g^*	Real growth rate: $$g^* = \frac{(1+g)}{(1+i)} - 1.$$
d	Nominal decay rate.

d^*	Real decay rate: $$d^* = \frac{1-d}{1+i} - 1.$$
b	Geometric factor in the equation: $$S = Rb + Rb^2 + \ldots + Rb^n,$$ where R is a constant.
T	A constant marginal income tax rate.
θ_t	A tax adjustment coefficient.
$US_0\left(\dfrac{r}{m}, mn\right)$	The present value of a \$1 annuity received for mn periods discounted at rate r/m: $$= \frac{1}{\left(1 + \dfrac{r}{m}\right)} + \frac{1}{\left(1 + \dfrac{r}{m}\right)^2} + \ldots + \frac{1}{\left(1 + \dfrac{r}{m}\right)^{mn}},$$ $$= \frac{1}{(r/m)}\left[1 - \frac{1}{\left(1 + \dfrac{r}{m}\right)^{mn}}\right].$$
T_g	Capital gains tax rate.
T_p	Property tax rate.
$E_{V_0, 1+r}$	Elasticity of V_0 with respect to $(1+r)$ defined as: $$\frac{dV_0}{d(1+r)} \frac{(1+r)}{V_0}.$$
D	Duration measure.
A_t	The tth payment on a constant principal payment loan.
p	The percentage of a loan charged (points) to close a loan.

p_x	The price of an input x.
π	Instantaneous profit.
$f(x,s)$	Timeless production function that relates expendable inputs x and durables services s to output $f(x,s)$.
F	Fixed cost incurred as a result of the passage of time.
NPV	Net present value equal to the discounted sum of time dated cash flows associated with an investment, enterprise, or project.
IRR	Internal rate of return or the geometric mean (minus 1) of a cash flow series whose $NPV=0$.

Index of Names

Index of Topics